W9-ATB-446

1. Lemnos (island)
2. Mytilene, on Lesbos (island)

Bosporus

CRIMEA

BLACK SEA

CASPIAN SEA

Tomis

Odessus

Amastris

Trapezus

Byzantium/
stantinople

BITHYNIA

PONTUS

ARMENIA

Nicomedia

Amaseia

GALATIA

CAPPADOCIA

Ancyra

Pergamum

Caesarea (Mazaca)

Smyrna

ASIA

Edessa

MESOPOTAMIA

Tigris

Aphrodisias

CILICIA

Carrhae

hesus

Tarsus

OSROENE

Halicarnassus

Antioch

RHODES

SYRIA

Euphrates

P

Hierapytna

CYPRUS

Raphaneae

Palmyra

A

Ctesiphon

Paphos

Emesa

R

Seleucia

MARE

Tyre

Damascus

T

Naqsh-I-Rustam

Caesarea

Bostra

H

Persepolis

Qumran

Jerusalem

Dead Sea

I

A

Canopus

Petra

Alexandria

AEGYPTUS

ARABIA

Nile

PERSIAN GULF

RED SEA

Dendera

Coptos

Ancient World Mapping Center 2003

F   G   H   J

THE ROMANS

From Village to Empire

THE ROMANS

From Village to Empire

Mary T. Boatwright
Daniel J. Gargola
Richard J. A. Talbert

NEW YORK   OXFORD
OXFORD UNIVERSITY PRESS
2004

Oxford University Press

Oxford   New York
Auckland Bangkok Buenos Aires Cape Town Chennai
Dar es Salaam Delhi Hong Kong Istanbul Karachi Kolkata
Kuala Lumpur Madrid Melbourne Mexico City Mumbai Nairobi
São Paulo Shanghai Taipei Tokyo Toronto

Published by Oxford University Press, Inc.
198 Madison Avenue, New York, New York, 10016
www.oup.com

Oxford is a registered trademark of Oxford University Press

Library of Congress Cataloging-in-Publication Data

Boatwright, Mary Taliaferro.
   The Romans: From Village to Empire / Mary T. Boatwright, Daniel J. Gargola and
Richard J. A. Talbert.
        p. cm.
   Includes bibliographical references and index.
   ISBN 0-19-511875-8 (cloth : alk. paper) — ISBN 0-19-511876-6 (pbk. : alk. paper)
   1. Rome—History. I. Gargola, Daniel J. II. Talbert, Richard J. A., 1947– III. Title.

DG 209.B58 2004
937—dc22   2003053670

Frontispiece: *Head from Italica.* The magnificent marble head (2 ft/60 cm in height) which features throughout the book was found in a public area of Italica in southern Spain, one of the earliest Roman communities established outside Italy (see Chapter Four). Today the head is in Seville's Archaeological Museum. The diadem and high tower signify that the figure is the city's goddess of Fortune, a vital protective deity. The style of the head—deeply carved hair and lips contrasting with smoothly finished cheeks and brow—is characteristic of sculpture dating to the first half of the second century A.D. This was when Italica, as the prosperous ancestral home of the emperors Trajan and Hadrian, proudly embarked upon an ambitious expansion program requiring large public buildings and much new statuary. Thus this serene female image symbolizes the city, and by extension Roman civilization, at the peak of its glory.

Page vi: Part of the Roman Forum today, viewed from the Tabularium on the lower slope of the Capitoline hill. The extensive structure barely preserved above ground level is the Basilica Julia, begun by Julius Caesar, completed by Augustus, and much used for lawcourt hearings. The trees in the background are up on the Palatine hill.

Printing number: 9 8 7 6 5

Printed in the United States of America
on acid-free paper

We dedicate this book to members of a younger generation,
in the hope that they, too, will share our
fascination for the Romans and their history

Joseph and Sammy

James

Francesca and Ludovica

CONTENTS

Maps xv–xvi
Figures xvii–xix
Preface xxi–xxiii
Acknowledgments xxv
Notes to the Reader xxvii

 1 Early Italy

Italy and the Mediterranean World 1
The Evidence 4
Italy Before the City 6
The Iron Age in Etruria, Latium, and Campania 7
    Greeks and Phoenicians in the Central Mediterranean 9
The Rise of Cities 10
    Beginning of Writing 12
    Appearance of an Elite 12
    Cities and Monumental Architecture 16
    Warfare in the Orientalizing and Archaic Periods 20
    Social and Economic Organization 23
Greeks and Etruscans 25
    Greek Cities of Southern Italy and Sicily 26
    Etruscans 28

Rome's First Centuries

Emergence of an Urban Community 32
The Romans and Their Early History 37
      Table 2.1 Dates of Rome's Kings According to Varro 38
      Box 2.1 Plutarch, *Romulus* 11 39
Rome Under the Kings 40
Rome and the Latins 45
The Early Republic 48
    Beginning of the Republic 48
    Rome and Its Neighbors in the Fifth Century 51
    Struggle of the Orders 53

Rome and Italy in the Fourth Century

Fall of Veii and the Sack of Rome 58
The City and Its Institutions in the Fourth Century 59
    Officials 60
    Senate 63
    Assemblies of Citizens 67
      Box 3.1 Servius Tullius' Creation of the
        Census (Livy) 69
      Table 3.1 Roman Assemblies 71
    The City, Its Gods, and Its Priests 71
      Box 3.2 The Roman Games (Dionysius of
        Halicarnassus) 73
Rome and Central Italy 75
    Warfare and the Civic Order 75
    Rome in Latium and Campania 77
    Samnite Wars 84
Expansion of Roman Hegemony in Italy 86
    Wars in Central and Northern Italy 87
    Conquest of the South 88
War and the Roman State 94

4 **The Beginnings of a Mediterranean Empire**

Sources 97

The Nobility and the City of Rome 98

    Box 4.1 Triumph of Scipio Africanus (Appian) 101

Wars with Carthage 104

  First Punic War (264–241) 105

  Second Punic War (218–201) 111

    Box 4.2 Romans' Vow of 217 (Livy) 116

A Mediterranean Empire 119

  Governors, Provinces, and Empire 120

  Spain 123

  Greece and Asia Minor 127

    Box 4.3 Slave Trade on Delos (Strabo) 133

  North Africa 134

 5 **Italy and Empire**

Senators, Officials, and Citizen Assemblies 136

Italy and the Consequences of Empire 140

  Changing Relations Between Rome, Its *Municipia*,
    and Allies 141

  Roman and Italian Elites 144

    Box 5.1 Scipio Africanus' Army Loots Carthago
      Nova (Polybius and Livy) 146

  Demographic and Economic Changes 149

Roman Politics from the Mid-Second Century 153

  Scipio Aemilianus 154

  Tiberius Gracchus 156

    Box 5.2 The Background to Tiberius Gracchus'
      Land Proposal (Appian) 158

  Gaius Gracchus 160

6 Italy Threatened, Enfranchised, Divided

War with Jugurtha (112–105) 166
Italy Threatened from the North (113–101) 170
Changes in the Roman Army 171
Marius' Career in Roman Politics 171
    Box 6.1 Marius' Bid for the Consulship (Sallust) 172
Sixth Consulship of Marius and Second Tribunate of
    Saturninus (100) 173
Administration of the Provinces 176
Tribunate of Livius Drusus (91) 179
Social War (91–87) 180
Tribunate of Sulpicius Rufus (88) 183
Sulla's First March on Rome (88) 185
Cinna's Rule (87–84) 187
Sulla's Second March on Rome (83–82) 189

7 The Domination of Sulla and Its Legacy

Sulla's Proscriptions (82–81) 193
Sulla the Dictator and His Program (82–81) 194
    Senate 194
    Tribunate 197
    Equites, Courts 197
    Citizens 197
    Governors 199
Verdicts on Sulla's Program 200
    Box 7.1 Cicero's Defense of Sextus Roscius 201
Lepidus' Rising and Its Aftermath (78–77) 204
Challenge from Sertorius in Spain (80–73) 205
    Box 7.2 Pompey's Letter from Spain (Sallust) 206
Spartacus' Slave Revolt (73–71) 207
Consulship of Crassus and Pompey (70) 208
Roman Women 209
Pompey Frees the Mediterranean of Pirates (67) 211

Threat from King Mithridates VI of Pontus 213
Sulla's Campaign Against Mithridates (87–85) 215
Lucullus' Struggle with Mithridates (74–67) 216
Pompey's Defeat of Mithridates (66–63) 218
Roles of Crassus and Cicero in Rome (65–63) 219
Catiline's Rising (63–62) 221

8 End of the Republic: Caesar's Dictatorship

Sources 225
Pompey's Return from the East (62) 225
Pompey and Political Stalemate in Rome 227
Partnership of Pompey, Crassus, and Caesar 233
Caesar's First Consulship (59) 234
Clodius' Tribunate (58) 236
Cicero's Recall and the Renewal of the
     Triumvirate (57–56) 238
Caesar's Campaigns in Gaul (58–51) 239
Death of Clodius and Pompey's Sole Consulship (52) 242
Prospect of Civil War (51–49) 244
Causes and Consequences of Caesar Crossing the
     Rubicon (January 49) 246
Cicero's Governorship of Cilicia (51–50) 248
Civil War Campaigns (49–45) 251
Caesar's Activity as Dictator (49–44) 254
Caesar's Impact upon the City of Rome 258
Political Prospects for Rome, and for Caesar 261

9 Augustus and the Transformation of the Roman World

Reactions to the Assassination of Caesar (44–43) 267
Emergence of a Second Triumvirate (43) 271
Battle of Philippi (42) 273
     Box 9.1 Laudatio Turiae 274
Perusine War (41–40) 277
Elimination of Sextus Pompey and Lepidus (39-36) 278

Antony in the East (42 onwards) 279
Clash Between Antony and Octavian (36–30) 284
Octavian as Sole Ruler (30 Onwards) 288
"The Republic Restored" 291
Second Settlement (23) 292
Latin Literature in the Late Republic and Augustan Age 293
Succession 295
        Table 9.1 The Julio-Claudian Family 296
Senate and *Equites* 299
Army 301
The Empire and Its Expansion 304
        Box 9.2 Oath of Loyalty 304
City of Rome 309
Attitudes Outside Rome 312
Res Gestae of Augustus 313
Augustus: Final Assessment 315

10 The Early Principate (A.D. 14–69): The Julio-Claudians, the Civil War of 68–69, and Life in the Early Empire

Sources 317
The Julio-Claudian Emperors: Civil Government and
        Military Concerns 318
Tiberius (14–37) 320
        Box 10.1 Senatorial Decree Concerning the
        Elder Gnaeus Piso 323
Gaius (Caligula) (37–41) 324
Claudius (41–54) 328
        Box 10.2 Claudius' Speech on the Admission of
        Gauls to the Senate 329
Nero (54–68) 332
Civil War in 68–69 335
Economic and Social Change 337
Army 338
Economy 339
Intellectual Life 340
"Beneficial Ideology" 341

Cities and Provinces 342
Diversity: Women, Local Languages, and Culture 345
Religious Practices and Principles 347
Imperial Cult 350

11 Institutionalization of the Principate: Military Expansion and Its Limits, the Empire and the Provinces (69–138)

Sources 353
Institutionalization of the Principate 354
Vespasian (69–79) 357
Titus (79–81) 362
Domitian (81–96) 362
A New, Better Era? 364
Nerva (96–98) 365
Trajan (98–117) 367
Hadrian (117–138) 373
    Table 11.1 The Antonine Family 375
    Box 11.1 Hadrian Inspects Troops at Lambaesis,
       Numidia 378
Roman Cities and the Empire's Peoples 379
Theaters and Processions 381
Circuses and Chariot Racing 383
The Amphitheater, and Gladiatorial Games 386
Other Urban Amenities 388
Education 390
State Religion and Imperial Cult 391

12 Italy and the Provinces: Civil and Military Affairs (138–235)

Sources 393
Antoninus Pius (138–161) 394
Marcus Aurelius (161–180) and Lucius Verus (161–169) 395
    Box 12.1 A Greek Provincial Praises Roman
       Citizenship 396
    Box 12.2 Morbidity and Mortality in the
       Roman Empire 399

Commodus (176–192, Sole Augustus after 180) 405
Septimius Severus (193-211) 406
    Table 12.1 The Severan Family 407
    Box 12.3 Deification Ceremonies for Pertinax in
      Septimius Severus' Rome 409
Caracalla (198–217, Sole Augustus after 211) 413
Macrinus (217–218) 414
Elagabalus (218–222) 414
Severus Alexander (222–235) 415
Roman Law 416
Roman Citizenship 421
    Box 12.4 Grant of Roman Citizenship (*Tabula
      Banasitana*) 422
Rome and Christianity 425
    Box 12.5 Pliny, Trajan, and Christians 427

13 The Third Century, the Dominate, and Constantine

Sources 431
Mid-Third Century 432
Aurelian (270–275) 437
Diocletian, the Tetrarchy, and the Dominate (284–305) 438
    Box 13.1 The Tetrarchs Introduce their Edict on
      Maximum Prices 445
Dissolution of the Tetrarchy (305–313), and the Rise of
    Constantine (306–324) 447
    Box 13.2 Galerius' Edict of Toleration (Lactantius) 450
Constantine and the Empire 454

Timeline 459
Glossary 479
Principal Ancient Authors 491
Art Credits 499
Index 501
Gazetteer 513

MAPS

Endpaper, front   Roman Italy

1.1   Italy and Sicily   3

1.2   Southern Italy and Sicily   27

1.3   Etruria and the Po Valley   29

2.1   Rome and Environs   33

2.2   The Forum Area   36

2.3   Latium and Southern Etruria   46

3.1   Latium and Campania   78

3.2   Samnium   85

3.3   Southern Italy   89

4.1   Western Mediterranean in the Mid-Third Century   106

4.2   Southern Italy and Sicily   107

4.3   Northern Italy   113

4.4   Iberian Peninsula   117

4.5   Greece, the Aegean, and Western Asia Minor   129

6.1   Rome's Foreign Wars, 113–82   168–169

6.2   Social War   181

7.1   Sulla's Veteran Settlements in Italy   196

7.2   Rome's Wars in Italy and Abroad, 78–63   202–203

8.1   Rome's Empire in 60 B.C.   226

8.2   Campaigns of Caesar, Crassus, and Pompey, 58–45   240–241

8.3   Settlement of Veterans in Italy by Julius Caesar and Augustus   257

8.4   Rome in the Late Republic   259

9.1   Roman Campaigns, 44–30   268–269

9.2   Expansion of the Empire in the Age of Augustus   306–307

9.3   Rome at the Death of Augustus   310

10.1   Roman Empire in A.D. 69   326–327

11.1   Rome's Northern Provinces Around A.D. 100   363

11.2   Eastern Expansion of the Empire in the Early Second Century   368

11.3   Rome Around A.D. 100   384

12.1   Campaigns of Marcus Aurelius and the Severan Emperors   400–401

13.1   The Empire's North and West in the "Age of Crisis"   433

13.2   Roman Empire of Diocletian and Constantine   440–441

13.3   Rome in the Age of Constantine   448–449

Endpaper, back   Roman Italy

FIGURES

Page vi The Roman Forum and the Palatine Hill vi

1.1 Etruscan chariot-body panel 14

1.2 Banquet scene, Murlo 15

1.3 Plan of the Palace at Murlo 17

1.4 Reconstruction of the Portonaccio Temple, Veii 19

1.5 Umbrian warrior figure 22

1.6 Processional frieze, Acquarossa 22

2.1 Statue of Apollo, Portonaccio Temple, Veii 37

2.2 Statue of Minerva, Lavinium 47

2.3 "Tomb of the Augurs" fresco, Tarquinii 55

3.1 Ficoroni Cista 65

3.2 Relief of games, Clusium 74

3.3 Warrior plaque, Praeneste 80

3.4 Plan of Cosa 83

4.1 Bronze ingot 111

4.2 Early Roman *denarius* 118

4.3 Plan of the encirclement of Numantia 126

5.1 Temple of Dionysus model, Vulci 142

5.2 "House of the Faun" plan, Pompeii 147

5.3 Etruscan funerary urn, Perugia 148

6.1 Italian coin issues during the Social War 182

6.2 Reconstruction of the sanctuary of Fortuna Primigenia, Praeneste 191

7.1a,b Amphitheater, Pompeii 199

7.2 Bust, possibly Sulla 200

7.3 Coin of Mithridates issued in Asia 214

7.4 Bust of Cicero 222

8.1 Bust of Pompey 227

8.2 Plan of the Settefinestre villa 228

8.3a,b,c Fishpond near Circeo 230–231

8.4 Bust of Julius Caesar 254

8.5 Coin bearing the image of Julius Caesar 255

8.6 Forum Romanum and the new Fora of Caesar and Augustus 260

8.7a,b,c Curia Julia, exterior and interior 262–263

9.1 Coin of Brutus 273

9.2 Bust of Mark Antony 276

9.3a,b,c Images of Cleopatra 280–281

9.4a,b,c,d Images of Octavian/Augustus 282–283

9.5 Coins of Antony and Cleopatra 285

9.6a,b,c Augustan victory monuments at Actium and La Turbie 286–287

9.7 Gold coin of Octavian, 28 B.C. 289

9.8a,b,c,d,e,f Busts of Sulla (possibly), Cicero, Pompey, Julius Caesar, Mark Antony, Livia 290

9.9 Bust of Livia 297

9.10 Centurion's tomb monument 303

9.11a,b,c Finds from the Teutoburg Forest massacre 308

9.12 South frieze of the Ara Pacis Augustae 311

10.1 "Sword of Tiberius" relief 319

10.2 Relief of Claudius subduing Britain, Aphrodisias 331

10.3 Gold coin of Nero and Agrippina, A.D. 54 332

10.4 Freedman's funerary monument, Mainz 344

10.5 Statue of Eumachia, Pompeii 345

10.6 Bilingual funerary inscription, Varna 346

10.7 Relief dedicated to the Nutrices, Ptuj 348

11.1 Section from the "Cancellaria reliefs", Rome 355

11.2   Panels from the Arch of Titus, Rome 359

11.3   View of Trajan's colony at Timgad 369

11.4   Two bands of the relief on Trajan's Column, Rome 372

11.5   Statue of Hadrian, Hierapytna 379

11.6   Roman theater, Mérida 382

11.7   Roman charioteer's funerary monument 385

11.8   Mosaic amphitheater scenes, Zliten 387

11.9   Pont du Gard, near Nîmes 389

12.1   Bronze coin of Antoninus Pius 395

12.2   Relief of Claudius' harbor, north of Ostia 397

12.3   Relief of Marcus Aurelius conducting a religious ceremony, Rome 403

12.4   Bust of Commodus as Hercules 405

12.5   Painting of Septimius Severus and his family 412

12.6   Family tombstone, near Székesfehérvár 423

12.7   View of Lepcis Magna 424

13.1   Rock carving of Valerian's submission to Shapur, Naqsh-i Rustam 435

13.2   Group portrait of the Tetrarchs, Venice 442

13.3   South side of the Arch of Constantine, Rome 452

13.4   Colossal bronze head of Constantine 454

PREFACE

The descendants of the first settlers on the hills overlooking a ford across the Tiber River eventually controlled most of Europe, the Near East, and North Africa for centuries. Still today, a millennium and a half later, the legacy of this extraordinary achievement by the Romans exerts a powerful influence in a rich variety of spheres worldwide—not least among them, architecture, art, language, literature, law, and religion. Although the writings and material remains that survive are inevitably no more than a tiny, random sample of what once existed, there is still quite enough to impress and engage us, and to permit a fair degree of insight into many dimensions of the nature and development of Roman civilization. Of course there are aspects—related to politics or strategy or social practices, to name only three areas—which we can never hope to understand fully. Even so, that does not deter a large body of interested inquirers from continuing to formulate questions and discuss answers as part of an ongoing dialogue. This activity has proved especially fruitful since the mid-nineteenth century: From then onwards, at an increasing pace, advances in scholarship, technology, and exploration have hugely improved the control and appreciation of the material at our disposal. These advances have also led to many exciting new discoveries, as well as stimulating ventures into fresh areas of inquiry over a broader range than ever. The expanding pursuit of inquiry, discovery, and (re)evaluation is sure to continue. Current knowledge, interests, and opinions are by no means fixed or exhausted; each generation chooses its own mix of elements in Roman history.

The distinctiveness of this book lies in its synthesis of the Roman state's changing character and expansion from earliest beginnings to the fourth century A.D. It is a book aimed primarily at average college-educated readers who lack prior engagement with ancient Rome, but who are eager to gain something more than a superficial introduction to its history. Our editor, Robert Miller, invited us to plan and write the book as a partner for Oxford's successful *Ancient Greece* by S. B. Pomeroy, S. M. Burstein, W. Donlan, and J. T. Roberts. What clinched our acceptance of his invitation was a shared awareness (as Roman history instructors) of the patent need for such a treatment; nothing for quite this central purpose has been published in recent decades.

Our scope, we determined, would be the evolving nature of the Roman community, its state institutions, and forms of rule, together with its expansion and some of the consequences. Next to no background knowledge would be expected, nor any acquaintance with languages (ancient or modern) other than English. For Rome's history to unfold most meaningfully for newcomers to it, we concluded that the presentation needed to be mainly, though by no means invariably, narrative. Yet since we are covering a truly vast canvas in terms of time, space, and human interaction, many topics and trends can only be touched on here, despite the fact that it would in principle be possible to discuss them at length in their own right. In these instances, our book consciously limits itself to providing no more than the foundation and context essential for proceeding further.

An important feature that distinguishes our treatment from others now available is that its focus on Rome's political and institutional history is coupled with an awareness of how such a narrative is inseparable from social, cultural, economic, art historical, and other types of history. We have sought to offer at least glimpses of many different aspects of Roman life, particularly through quotations from ancient writings, maps, line drawings, and illustrations with substantial captions. Although ours does not set out to be a book about "Roman civilization" as such, we hope that it will lay the foundation for a sound appreciation of Roman culture—in plenty of its manifestations—as well as of Roman history in a more strictly defined sense.

We returned time and again to the issue of where to close. Discussion and experiment convinced us that a book of this length could hardly find space for the major fourth-century developments following the emperor Constantine's attainment of sole control (A.D. 324) without seriously impairing the coverage up to that date. We acknowledge that this endpoint makes our book less appealing to readers whose interests postdate the Roman Republic and fix instead on the period when Rome was a world-class power ruled by emperors—say, from the time of Julius Caesar or Augustus into the fifth or sixth century. A focus on this later period, however, calls for a different book altogether from one beginning with early Italy a millennium before.

Our variation of the amount of narrative at each stage, and of its pace overall, is also deliberate. Often indeed, our choices are limited by immense variations in the quantity, quality, and range of surviving source material from period to period; repeatedly, the means to answer a key question or to probe some significant shift just does not exist. In the opening chapters, a complex array of Roman institutions and practices has to be introduced, and for the early centuries of the Republic only a sketchy impression at best can be offered of Rome's external affairs; so the narrative here covers long periods briefly, and proceeds thematically. From the mid-second century B.C., by contrast, our knowledge improves, and a succession of developments occurs, both at home and abroad, which have to be grasped in more depth not only for their individual importance but also for their cumulative impact. The ensuing end of the Republic, and the emergence from it of a stable regime that halted a ruinous cycle of civil wars, are such fundamental, well documented changes that they justify closer attention. Thereafter, once the Roman Empire is enlarged and stabilized from around the beginning of the Christian era, we have tried to balance narrating affairs of state with introducing more topics thematically, since both these approaches are invited by a relative abundance of literary, documentary, and archeological evidence. Throughout, we have had to make hard choices about which dates, events, ideas, names, topics to mention (and at what length), and which to omit. We have deliberately sought to reflect only opinions that—while often perforce remaining controversial—at least enjoy some measure of acceptance among current experts. We recognize that any introductory book, no matter how thorough or absorbing, can only open the way to learning more. We hope that our efforts will encourage teachers and students alike to supplement, question, and explore further all the material offered here.

With these aims in mind, at the start of each chapter we briefly survey the main sources that form the basis of knowledge for the period it covers, and at intervals we insert "boxes" that reproduce a variety of ancient writings to give a vivid sense of their character and historical value. Each chapter closes with a short listing of books recommended for further reading. In addition, at the end of the book, we offer a timeline, a glossary, and a listing of the principal ancient authors mentioned.

Our book's aims, and its presentation, are carefully matched, therefore. At the same time, we adhere to practical stipulations about length, format, illustrations, and the like, set by our publisher. As coauthors, we determined that, broadly speaking, each of us should take responsibility for three successive stages—Gargola far into the second century B.C., Talbert to the end of the Republic and establishment of the Principate, Boatwright thereafter. At every stage each partner would (and did) review drafts by the other two, as well as consider comments made correspondingly. Our goal was to ensure that the treatments should integrate into a coherent whole, although, naturally enough, three individual voices are still detectable. That seems fitting enough: It was the achievement of the Romans themselves, after all, to forge from many different peoples a distinctive and compelling history.

Mary T. Boatwright, Durham, North Carolina
Daniel J. Gargola, Lexington, Kentucky
Richard J.A. Talbert, Chapel Hill, North Carolina

ACKNOWLEDGMENTS

Preparation of this book proved a sterner, lengthier challenge than any of its co-authors had ever anticipated. We are all the more grateful, therefore, for the generous assistance of many colleagues and students over several years. In particular, Professors Tom McGinn and Nathan Rosenstein stand out for their exceptional kindness and concern in prompting us to rethink draft materials. For mapmaking, the contribution of Tom Elliott, Director of the Ancient World Mapping Center, has been substantial and quite invaluable. The creation of tables and maps was further assisted by Molly Maddox (Duke), and by Rachel Barckhaus, Alexandra Dunk, and Nora Harris (UNC, Chapel Hill). To all those named, and others, we offer our warmest thanks.

NOTES TO THE READER

To assist further investigation of the themes introduced by this book, suggested readings are listed at the end of each chapter. In addition, for reference, the revised third edition of the *Oxford Classical Dictionary* (*OCD*) edited by Simon Hornblower and Antony Spawforth is highly recommended (Oxford: Oxford University Press, 2003). Rigorous coverage of Rome's entire history is offered by the ongoing second edition of the *Cambridge Ancient History* (Cambridge: Cambridge University Press), beginning at Volume VII Part 2 (1984); the presentation of this extensive work, however, is at a very advanced scholarly level.

A timeline, a glossary, and a listing of the principal ancient authors mentioned are to be found at the end.

The Ancient World Mapping Center at the University of North Carolina, Chapel Hill, offers free digital copies of each map that it produced for this book: visit http://www.unc.edu/awmc/downloads

Some "boxes" translate Latin texts to be found in the periodical *L' Année Epigraphique* (*AE*) and in Hermann Dessau (ed.), *Inscriptiones Latinae Selectae* (Berlin: Weidmann, 1892–1916) (*ILS*).

1

EARLY ITALY

For centuries before the formation of cities, Italy was a land of villages and the outside world impinged on life only fitfully. Urban life appeared here long after it had emerged in other parts of the Mediterranean basin. Over time, some settlements slowly became larger and more complex socially, economically, and politically, and the leaders of these more highly structured towns and villages gloried in their connections with the wider Mediterranean world. In the seventh and sixth centuries B.C., some communities achieved the status of cities, with elaborate social systems, monumental buildings and temples, and formal public spaces; others would follow in later centuries. These urban centers would long remain the chief centers of power in Italy.

ITALY AND THE MEDITERRANEAN WORLD

Italy (Italia in Latin) is a long peninsula, encompassing slightly less than 100,000 square miles (260,000 sq km), that juts out from the northern or European coast of the Mediterranean Sea. In the far north, the Alps (Latin, Alpes) divide Italy from the rest of Europe. To their south, the valley of the Po (Latin, Padus)—Italy's largest river—contains land with great agricultural potential. Except for the plains along the eastern coast, the Apennine mountains separate the Po Valley from the rest of Italy. Peninsular Italy begins south of the Po Valley. The peninsula is about 650 miles in length (1,040 km), and it never is more than 125 miles wide (200 km); the sea is always fairly close. The Apennines dominate the peninsula. From their northwestern end, where they meet the western Alps and the sea, these mountains run almost due east in a narrow and virtually unbroken line that nearly reaches the Adriatic Sea; this portion of the chain separates the Po Valley from Etruria, an early center of urban life. As they approach the eastern coast, the mountains turn sharply to the south, running in a series of parallel ridges that in places reach almost 10,000 feet in height (3,000 m). In its northern half, the main chain lies much nearer to the Adriatic than it does to the Tyrrhenian Sea on the western side of the peninsula. South of Rome, however, the mountain chain gradually leaves the eastern coast and approaches the western, ending in the southwestern promontory of Bruttium. The mountains on the island of Sicily (Latin, Sicilia), separated from the mainland only by a narrow strait, are a continuation of this chain, which ultimately reappears in the mountains of Tunisia, Algeria, and Morocco in North Africa.

The first great centers of population and civilization arose in the coastal regions. The Adriatic coast, with few harbors and little space for large-scale settlement, was for a long time backward. For much of their length, the Apennines leave no more than a narrow coastal plain. Only in the south, where the mountains approach the Tyrrhenian coast more closely than they do the Adriatic, are there broad plains. Much of the plateau of Apulia, however, is semi-arid; only a few river valleys here were sufficiently fertile and well-watered to support substantial populations. The peninsula's southern (Ionian) shore also has narrow plains or semi-arid ones. The mountains of Bruttium closely confined some coastal communities. Even so, in some more favored areas, sufficient land and water could be found for large settlements. Towns appeared early here, and some became wealthy and important.

The west coast was the most favored. Here, well-watered and fertile lands proved capable of supporting large populations, many harbors gave access to the sea, and four rivers—the Arnus (modern, Arno), Tiberis (modern English, Tiber), Liris, and Volturnus—all navigable in small boats, barges, and rafts for some distance, gave easy passage to the interior. Three of the regions facing the Tyrrhenian Sea had especially prominent places in the history of ancient Italy. Etruria, the land of the ancient Etruscans, is the northernmost; this region of fertile hills, forests, and lakes, roughly bounded by the Arno and Tiber rivers, saw some of the earliest centers of urban life. Two important plains occupy the coast to its south. First comes Latium. East to west, the Latin plain ran from the sea to the foothills of the Apennines. North to south, it covered the stretch of coast between the lower Tiber River and the northern limits of Campania. Rome itself (Latin, Roma) would rise here on the banks of the Tiber, just across the river from the southernmost Etruscan centers. Centering on the Bay of Naples and its hinterland, the Campanian plain is the southernmost of the three regions.

The surrounding mountains and seas did not isolate the peninsula. Although the Alps seem quite formidable from the Italian side, large-scale movement across them has always been possible, and the inhabitants of the Po Valley have often had closer cultural links and firmer and friendlier relations with groups across the northern

Map 1.1 *Italy and Sicily*

mountains than they did with peoples to their south. From an early period, ships have traveled from Italy across the Mediterranean, moving goods, people, ideas, and institutions. Much of this traffic was only local, but at times long-distance commerce developed and flourished. Before Rome succeeded in dominating the peninsula, seaborne connections flourished only fitfully along the Adriatic, although the mouth of the Po River on occasion received much trade. The peninsula's southern and western shores were more open. Good harbors could be found along the coasts of the Ionian and Tyrrhenian seas, and the richer and more extensive plains provided valuable hinterlands.

Italy occupies a strategic point in the Mediterranean world. The island of Sicily, off the southwest tip of the peninsula, divides the Mediterranean Sea in two, and maritime traffic between east and west necessarily passes by the island. Ships seeking to enter the Tyrrhenian Sea from the Ionian and Sicilian seas had to pass through the narrow Straits of Messina before they could proceed north along the Italian coast or west along the north shore of Sicily. This passage could be dangerous: Greek writers would place there the whirlpool Charybdis and the monster Scylla, who fed on ships' crews. Other important routes passed to the south of the island, eventually funneling through the passage between western Sicily and Cape Bon in modern Tunisia, about 100 miles away (160 km). The island could also serve as a virtual bridge between Italy and North Africa, facilitating north-south traffic across the central Mediterranean. In later periods maritime powers often fought for control of the island, and the state that ultimately would dominate it could expand east and west with some ease.

THE EVIDENCE

Archeological investigations provide the evidence for the history of Italy before the appearance of cities and organized states, because writing develops only as urban life was emerging. The material remains of ancient cultures can provide insights into important aspects of societies: how people organized and arranged their houses and their settlements; the ways they earned their living; the objects they made and how they used them; the commercial and cultural contacts they established with neighbors and with more distant peoples. At first glance, moreover, the recovery of the physical traces of the lives of earlier inhabitants seems to avoid many of the problems associated with the interpretation of often biased and value-laden texts (see Chapter Two).

But archeological evidence also has its own limitations. Only a few activities leave clear physical traces, and the remains are often very difficult to date and to interpret. Archeologists, moreover, often restrict their investigations to a limited range of sites. Thus, tombs and monumental public buildings for long received more attention than ordinary houses or settlements. Archeologists now often focus more on settlements and houses, and they regularly employ surface surveys—

involving the systematic examination of traces on the surface left by centuries of human use—to learn more about settlement patterns. At the same time, in order to shed light on the environment and the economy, excavators have sought to recover plant and animal remains and to subject them to increasingly sophisticated analysis. Yet there are limits to these approaches. Much of life remains inaccessible. Excavations and surveys usually reveal more about a society's technology, settlement patterns, and economy than they do about the events that shaped the inhabitants of a community, about the political and social institutions and practices that organized their lives, and about the system of beliefs that guided relationships with neighbors, family members, rulers, and ruled.

This necessary emphasis on the material, technical, and economic aspects of communities has a further, and important, consequence. Archeologists often identify "cultures" on the basis of a number of shared traits, practices, and forms in funerary rites, in technology, in material goods, and in economic life; but these archeological cultures should not be confused with cultures defined through other means. After all, groups that differ in many ways can construct similar buildings, they can make virtually identical tools and ornaments, and they can earn their livings in many of the same ways. Artifacts and techniques, in other words, can cross ethnic, linguistic, and political borders. Archeological cultures, then, are collections of traits in material goods, in technology, in funerary practices, in settlement forms, and in economic life. They are not political or linguistic units, nor need they have a single ethnic identity, either in their own eyes or in the opinions of their neighbors.

Finally, the broader significance of finds is not always apparent, and major problems in interpretation can arise. Many of the most significant of the recovered objects have been found in tombs. The burial rites of many ancient communities required that grave goods be interred with the deceased, but the extent to which tombs and grave goods reflect the organization of society is controversial. Some burials, for example, are richer than others in the same cemetery, and the usual inference is that the deceased, in life, stood out in wealth and in status. In other cemeteries, burials may have been very similar in layout and in their contents. Here, scholars often suggest that the associated settlements had a more egalitarian social structure. Neither of these inferences is certain: burials are the remains of a burial rite, and fashion or belief may well have had more influence on deposits than other factors. At the same time, it is far from certain that all members of settlements received formal burials of the kind that have left detectable and datable traces in the archeological record. What survives, then, may be evidence for the practices of only a portion of the inhabitants of the towns and villages associated with a particular cemetery. Votive deposits, another important category of evidence, provide similar problems in interpretation. In Italy and in much of the Mediterranean world, worshippers deposited objects in sacred places to fulfill a vow or to thank the presiding deity for favors. When these sanctuaries, shrines, caves, or groves became crowded with gifts, those in charge would make room by burying the offerings. Again, the finds primarily illuminate the range of objects deemed suitable as a gift to a god, although they may also reveal something about the kinds of objects available in the community and the techniques involved in their manufacture.

ITALY BEFORE THE CITY

The basic pattern of social and economic life in peninsular Italy was established early. For centuries after the first appearance of agriculture around 4000 B.C., Italy was a land of villages with simple forms of economic and social organization. Settlements were very small, usually with no more than a few huts and outbuildings and less than one hundred inhabitants. Villagers planted barley and several types of wheat, and they raised sheep, goats, cattle, and pigs. Their technology was simple, and signs of occupational specialization are few. For millennia, Italian communities produced pottery in a range of styles and forms. At other times and places, the production of pottery could be a highly skilled craft, and devices were in use which require a high degree of expertise, such as the potter's wheel, for example, which allows for more regular shapes, and high-temperature kilns, which provide harder and finer surfaces. In Italy, neither the potter's wheel nor high-temperature kilns were used before the appearance of cities. In earlier centuries, too, specialized potters were almost certainly not involved in the craft; the manufacture of ceramics, in other words, was primarily a household activity. Tools necessary in everyday life were generally made of wood, bone, or stone.

The social and political organization of these villages was relatively simple and egalitarian. There are no signs of marked distinctions in wealth, nor are there indications that adults made their living in markedly different ways. Elsewhere and at other times, kinship, age, and gender often served as the chief means of internal regulation in communities of this scale. The existence of larger "tribal" entities is uncertain; links between neighboring settlements could easily be managed within structures of kinship and intermarriage.

The use of metals provides the only clear example of more sophisticated techniques and some craft specialization. Around 2000, copper tools and ornaments appear in the material remains. In the succeeding Early (c. 1800–1600) and Middle (c. 1600–1300) Bronze Ages, a limited range of tools, weapons, and ornaments were made of bronze, an alloy of copper and tin. Metalworking was a task for specialists, since it requires both expertise and organization: materials must be acquired, often from great distances, and the processes of refining the ore and casting the metal require knowledge and skill. In the Middle Bronze Age, throughout peninsular Italy artifacts of copper and bronze exhibit much standardization in form and techniques of manufacture; this may indicate that experts moved from village to village in search of markets for their skills.

Italian metallurgy also shows marked influences from outside the peninsula. To the east of Italy, in the Balkans and beyond, complex and highly organized societies, ruled by kings with the assistance of bureaucratic and military elites, were firmly established in the second millennium B.C. The Mycenaean civilization of Greece exercised considerable influence on some of the cultures of central Europe and the central and western Mediterranean, motivated, at least in part, by the need to acquire metals. Mycenaean pottery appears in Sardinia, where copper was mined, as early as the fourteenth century, and there are clear signs of contact, probably through intermediaries, with the metal-producing regions of central Europe and Britain. At this time, metallurgical techniques and styles came to exhibit a high degree of standardization over great distances and across many societies, since the Mycenaeans' search for metals seems to have encouraged a movement of craftsmen and of manufactured objects between the metal-producing and metalworking regions of central Europe, Spain, Italy, and Greece. Most Italian communities, smaller and simpler economically, socially, and politically than their eastern contemporaries, probably participated in this world only peripherally. Exchanges fell off sharply when Mycenaean power began to fade in the twelfth and eleventh centuries.

Outside influences did not affect all areas of Italy equally. Mycenaean merchants and settlers were active along some of the coasts of Italy and Sicily: Scattered finds of pottery have been found along the southern half of the Adriatic shore, as well as along the south coast of Italy and its west coast as far north as the Bay of Naples, along the east coast of Sicily, and on the Lipari islands. In southern Italy and eastern Sicily, where relations were most intense, settlers from the east may actually have founded settlements. Here, local communities may also have imitated some aspects of Mycenaean social organization: A ruling warrior elite seems to have emerged in some communities, and in a few places larger and more elaborate dwellings may indicate the presence of native rulers. Central Italy did not develop as rapidly or in quite the same way. During the Recent Bronze Age (roughly the thirteenth and early twelfth centuries), settlements here grew in size and in number, an indication that the population was increasing; a typical village may now have had a population in excess of one hundred. The inhabitants of many settlements placed their dwellings on hilltops, presumably for reasons of defense, and occasionally they strengthened their position further with ditches and dikes, a practice that was less frequent earlier.

THE IRON AGE IN ETRURIA, LATIUM, AND CAMPANIA

Beginning in the ninth century, there occurred a series of developments in Italy leading, by the seventh century, to the appearance of the cities that would turn out to dominate Italian history. Archeologists refer to the years between the start of the ninth century and the last third of the eighth as the Iron Age. The extraction of metal from the ore and the working of the iron require complex and sophisticated techniques, and the making of steel is an even more elaborate process. Iron has important advantages over bronze. Iron ore is relatively common, so that the acquisition of this metal is a much simpler and cheaper process; when used in the form of steel, tools and weapons can be made harder and better able to retain an edge. Eventually, the use of iron would lead to cheaper products, which can be employed for a wider range of functions and by a larger portion of the population. For centuries after the introduction of iron, however, a wide range of objects, utilitarian and otherwise, continued to be made of bronze, wood, bone, and stone.

In the ninth and eighth centuries, Etruria, Latium, and Campania saw the rise of an inter-related group of cultures that would eventually develop into major centers of power and wealth. In Etruria, the Iron Age culture of these centuries is known as "Villanovan" from the estate near modern Bologna where archeologists first found traces of its material culture. Beyond Etruria, Villanovan settlements also appear in some areas just across the Apennines—such as around modern Bologna especially—and in Campania, where Capua and other centers show close connections with southern Etruria by sea or by the land route up the valleys of the Liris, Anio, and Tiber rivers. One of Villanovan culture's most significant traits was the greatly increased size of its settlements. Beginning around 900, certain ones began to grow larger, sometimes through the abandonment of earlier villages and the concentration of population at a few centers. For the most part, these central places were on easily defended plateaus, where the natural features of the site, occasionally reinforced by ditches and banks, formed the primary defense. In southern Etruria, which has been more fully researched, settlements at the future sites of Caere, Tarquinii, and Veii may each have had over one thousand inhabitants. To judge by the distance between them, the chief centers may have controlled territories as large as 350–750 square miles (900–1,940 sq km). At first, land away from the core may have only been sparsely inhabited, but by the eighth century some large settlements seem to have established smaller secondary ones near the limits of their territory, perhaps as a way of securing control over their borders, or because the main center was now too densely inhabited to accommodate further population growth.

In their internal organization, these new and larger settlements still remained relatively simple, consisting of clusters of huts separated by small open spaces. Each of the smaller clusters that together made up the whole may have represented a kinship group or the inhabitants of an earlier, now abandoned village. Settlements often had several cemeteries, each used by a single cluster of huts or by a few neighboring groups, a sign that they perceived some common identity. Farming and the raising of pigs, cattle, sheep, and goats remained the primary economic activities. The absence of the potter's wheel probably shows that the manufacture of pottery had yet to develop as an occupational specialty. Metalwork, on the other hand, plainly was a matter for specialists who performed their functions beyond their own and neighboring villages. Since these settlements show no sign of elaborate social systems or clearly identifiable distinctions in wealth, let alone of formal layouts and public buildings (all marks of the cities that would emerge in the eighth and seventh centuries), they are best characterized as "proto-urban," rather than as "urban".

Placed between Villanovan Etruria and Campania, Latium developed its own regional culture around 1000. This "Latial culture" was once seen as a variant of Proto-Villanovan and Villanovan, and it shares many features with them. For the most part, Latin settlements were located on hills or on spurs that projected from the Apennines into the plain. Iron Age settlements in Latium generally were smaller than their counterparts in Etruria. The cluster of villages occupying the future site of the Latin city of Gabii offers the most detailed picture of a Latin settlement of the ninth and early eighth centuries. Gabii was on a narrow isthmus separating two small lakes. Before the formation of the city, a cluster of small settlements filled the isthmus and part of the rim of the northern lake; cemeteries were located at each end of the settled zone. In all likelihood, no village in Latium ever had more than one hundred inhabitants at any point during the ninth century. After about 800, however, a number of settlements there, like their Villanovan neighbors, began to grow larger because of internal growth and the abandonment of outlying villages.

For the ninth and early eighth centuries, the burials at Gabii provide some evidence for the social order of a Latin settlement. Graves in its two cemeteries were arranged by rite and by the age and gender of the occupant. Adult men lie at the center; here cremation was the exclusive rite in one cemetery and the dominant practice in the other. Around the center were situated the graves of women and of young men; here, inhumation was the dominant practice. Young women interred on the periphery were often buried with bronze objects and ornaments of glass paste and of amber. These cemeteries seem to have been family burial grounds, and the different practices show that certain status distinctions were determined by age and by gender. Yet there are signs that some men possessed a distinctive position in the community: In the male cremation burials miniaturized weapons, such as swords and spears, are common—they are not found in male inhumation graves—and the occupants may have claimed some special status related to warfare. Toward the end of the ninth century, these cremation burials end, but the status groups associated with them may well have persisted, expressing their social position in new ways (see next section).

Greeks and Phoenicians in the Central Mediterranean

Outside contacts markedly affected both the pace and the nature of change in the centers of the Villanovan and Latial cultures. In the late ninth century, as well as in the eighth, maritime contact with the eastern Mediterranean again became a prominent factor in the development of central Italian societies. The Phoenicians led the way. The coastal regions of the modern states of Syria and Lebanon on the eastern shore of the Mediterranean were their homeland, and the first traces of their civilization appear there around the beginning of the second millenium B.C. The Phoenicians' world centered on a number of cities, each with its own king, priests, palace, and temples, and each ruling the surrounding countryside. Long-distance trade by land and by sea was important in the social and political order of a Phoenician city-state: Kings and temple priesthoods participated, as did associations of rich and powerful merchants. Around 1000, the leaders of some of these cities, especially Tyre and Sidon, the most powerful of the Phoenician states, began to send out settlers and trading expeditions, first to the nearby coast of Cyprus, but soon as far away as Spain. Eventually, Phoenician settlers would establish a series of new cities along the coasts of western Sicily, Sardinia, northern Africa, and southern Spain. Carthage (Latin, Carthago), probably founded around 800 in the territory of modern Tunisia, would become the most powerful of these new settlements—and Rome's great rival.

Greeks followed shortly afterward. After the collapse of Mycenaean civilization during the twelfth century, contacts between Italy and the Greek world had declined rapidly. Trade and population revived during the ninth century, and, at the same time, larger, richer, and more complex communities started to form again, which over generations would develop into city-states. Around 800, contacts between Greece and Italy began to increase. By 775, some Greeks established a settlement on the island of Pithecusa in the Bay of Naples, and a few Phoenicians may also have settled there. In this new community, and in others that would be founded later, trade and access to metals played an important role—Pithecusa shows signs of ironworking on a large scale—but the search for farmland was vital, too, and before long would become the most important factor.

Greek settlements on the mainland soon followed. Cumae, founded around 750, was the first, and others would follow in the seventh, sixth, fifth, and fourth centuries. Eventually the eastern, southeastern, and northern coasts of Sicily would be dotted with Greek city-states, as would the south and west coasts of Italy as far north as Campania. Later, Romans would call these mainland areas of Greek settlement "Great Greece" (Latin, *Magna Graecia*). In the seventh and sixth centuries, the Greek colonies here, like other communities in Greece and in the coastal regions of central Italy, would follow more or less parallel paths that led to the formation of city-states.

THE RISE OF CITIES

Beginning in the middle of the eighth century and continuing over the next three centuries, Etruria, Latium, and Campania witnessed a series of political, social, and cultural innovations that would result in the formation of the first central Italian city-states. The appearance of this new form of social and political life was a broad phenomenon that characterized many regions and ethnic groups. In Italy, city-states became the dominant form of organization in Etruria, Latium, Campania, and the Greek regions of Sicily and southern Italy. Outside the peninsula, city-states would cover Greece and the western and southwestern coasts of Asia Minor and many of the areas in which Phoenicians settled. Broad similarities in form, however, should not mask the great diversity in detail and the many local variations that could be found in important aspects of urban life. Cities, in other words, could share many of the ways they organized government, war, and religion without really being very much alike.

A city-state was both a kind of settlement and a form of political, military, and social organization. Fully developed city-states usually possessed a clearly defined urban core, with special areas designated for elite and for communal ends, and cemeteries encircling it. Beyond, its surrounding territory contained scattered shrines, hamlets, and farmsteads, along with a few settlements, smaller than the central city and without a fully developed communal life. The scale of these city-states varied greatly. In the contemporary Greek world, a "typical" one may have had approximately one thousand inhabitants and perhaps a territory of around forty square miles (100 sq km); its army would have numbered no more than a few hundred men. In central Italy, many of the emerging city-states would have been somewhat larger—many certainly controlled more territory than was the case in Greece—and, by the end of the sixth century, some had populations of several tens of thousands.

Some formal political organization was essential. In a typical city-state, elite residences, political life, and communal religious activity were all concentrated in and about the center. Here, members of elite families displayed their status, competed with their peers, and exercised leadership over their own followers, even, on occasion, over the city as a whole. At first, aristocratic families and their retainers dominated most emerging city-states. In the seventh and sixth centuries, kings reigned in some. By the early fifth century certain cities possessed formal offices and priesthoods, filled by a process of election, and held for terms of one year. Arrangements such as these would eventually become standard in communities with a city-state form of organization.

City-states emerged through a number of interrelated processes. First, an aristocracy, with its own distinctive way of life, developed. This process almost certainly began before it becomes visible in the archeological remains. Over time, aristocratic families concentrated in the larger settlements, making them centers of wealth and power. The leaders of these more powerful communities began to construct larger and more elaborate buildings, and to set aside formal spaces where the population of the settlement and its surrounding countryside would gather for occasions deemed important to the city. Eventually, institutions regulating the community as a whole appeared and began to overshadow individual families and their leaders.

In central Italy, scholars divide the formative age of the city-state into two broad phases: the Orientalizing Period (c. 725–580) and the Archaic Period (c. 580–480). In its origins, this division has much to do with artistic styles and with clear, direct foreign influences: The Orientalizing Period earned its name because of the appearance in tombs and votive deposits of luxury goods imported from the "Orient"—Greece, Syria, and Egypt—or of locally made imitations of these imports. These two periods also mark, if only roughly, other developmental stages. In the earlier period, monumental architecture commissioned by the elite becomes conspicuous, as does literacy. From around 600, the basic communal institutions of the city-state come into view, the governing elite broadens in some ways, and large-scale warfare between cities begins. The course of these developments probably varied considerably from city to city, and the evidence rarely allows a full picture of the process to be reconstructed for any one place. The history of Rome in this period, however, is the best documented of all (see Chapter Two).

Beginning of Writing

During the eighth century, writing came to Italy, and written texts now supplement the archeological evidence. Around 740, someone in the Greek settlement of Pithecusa scratched into the surface of a jug a short text in Aramaic, a script and language of Syria. At about the same time, mourners placed in a grave a cup inscribed in Greek, one of the earliest examples of the Greek alphabet found anywhere in the Mediterranean world. The Greek language and script were to have a long life in Italy and would exert great influence there. By 700, texts in one or another of the languages of Italy itself appear, written in scripts derived from the Greek. The earliest known Etruscan documents date from the very beginning of the seventh century; known texts of the seventh and sixth centuries now number in the many hundreds. Early documents in Latin are less common: Only a very few can be placed in the seventh century, and less than one hundred in the sixth and fifth centuries.

The surviving texts of the eighth through the fifth centuries are generally short, difficult to interpret, hard to date, and not very informative. Inscribed on stone, bronze, or pottery, their contents generally are brief and formulaic, and the languages in which they are written are often not well understood today. Some identify the occupants of tombs. Others proclaim the owner or maker of an object. Still others record the dedication of gifts placed in temples and shrines. A few are longer, but these are only preserved in fragments for the most part, and their contents are obscure. No evidence survives of a bureaucratic use for writing, such as one finds in some other Mediterranean societies. Despite the absence of a bureaucratic purpose, however, writing in Italy was closely associated with the elites of its cities, and the earliest written texts accompany their activities.

Appearance of an Elite

Toward the end of the eighth century, some families in the coastal regions of Etruria, Latium, and Campania began to demonstrate that they possessed wealth, status, and power on a scale far greater than others in their communities had attained. These emerging elite families, like many others in the Mediterranean world at the time, sought to distinguish themselves from others in their communities through a distinctive way of life with the appropriate personal ornaments, weapons, and other marks of status. Many of the objects, and the imagery of wealth and power associated with them, had their origins in Greece and the Near East, where they were used in a similar fashion by leading social groups.

Tombs provide the earliest signs of these families and their pretensions. In the eighth century, tombs with rich deposits of grave goods become more common: At Gabii, some tombs of the mid-eighth century are markedly richer than others, and a few exceptionally rich tombs contain chariots. By the end of the century, powerful families proclaimed their position in their town or village in the so-called "princely" burials. These new princely burials emphasize families and their place in their communities. The builders of many of the new tombs constructed them so that they could receive multiple burials over the years, a sign that each was intended to be the burial site of a family or a lineage. Grave goods reveal a broad concern among the elite for conspicuous displays of wealth and status—and the willingness to expend much wealth in pursuit of these ends. Tombs and burials, after all, are arranged by the survivors, and in them the kin of the deceased can make clear statements about the social position they think that the dead occupied in life—not to mention the position which the survivors themselves wish to be seen as maintaining. Families often placed their tombs along the main roads into the settlement, where they could be seen and admired by others. Tombs and their contents, then, would have proclaimed to passersby the wealth and status of those interred within, and of their families as well.

Tombs in the new manner were much more elaborate and required a larger commitment of resources than was the case earlier. At Etruscan Caere in the seventh century, one family constructed a tomb, known today as the Regolini-Galassi Tomb, with a corridor over 120 feet long (36 m) and six feet (1.8 m) wide and a burial chamber on either side of this aisle. Its builders cut the lowest part of the wall into the underlying rock, and built the upper portion with large stone blocks that formed a vault over the aisle. Finally, they covered the entire structure with a large earth mound or *tumulus* about 150 feet (45 m) in diameter, and set up a low stone wall surrounding its base.

The contents of the tombs also served to distinguish the new burials from their predecessors and from those of their less fortunate contemporaries. Elite tombs often contain large quantities of metal objects and fine pottery, imported or of local manufacture. At Castel di Decima in Latium, mourners in the late eighth century buried a young man with personal ornaments of silver and bronze, iron weapons, a chariot, bronze tripods, other bronze vessels, and a range of Greek and Phoenician pottery. In another, later burial in the same cemetery, a young women was interred with over ninety bronzes and imported ceramics, while her body was covered with gold, silver, and amber jewelry. Most finds of Greek and

Phoenician pottery, jewelry, and other metal work—and of locally produced imitations too—have been made in tombs of this kind.

The new aristocratic tombs were not a single artistic or social phenomenon, nor were they restricted to only one ethnic or linguistic group. Instead, they attest to the formation of a broad central Italian elite culture. Burials on this pattern can be found along the west coast of Italy from the north of Etruria to the south of Campania, and later they can be found well inland too. The practice certainly crossed linguistic divides. It is present in areas whose inhabitants spoke Etruscan, and in others where Latin was the dominant language. Under this broad diffusion, there could be much local variation in funerary rites and practices, as well as in the layout and construction of tombs. Some were larger than the Regolini-Galassi, while many others were smaller. Some had many burial chambers, while others had only one. Funeral rites, whether cremation or inhumation, varied from place to place (and sometimes from tomb to tomb), as did the wooden or stone coffins or sarcophagi in which bodies were buried, and the funerary urns in which ashes were placed. What these burials have in common are the prestige objects deposited in graves and many of the decorative themes on walls and on sarcophagi. Over time, much of this original unity would break down, as local elites each followed their own course of development.

Figure 1.1 *Chariots occupied a prominent place in public displays of status, and they were often highly decorated for that purpose. This bronze panel covered the front of a chariot-body interred in a grave high in the Apennines around 550. The two sides of the chariot were similarly decorated. The relief depicts what is probably an arming scene, where the woman on the left hands the man on the right his shield and helmet. The birds flying over their heads may represent good omens. The side panels, not shown here, depict two warriors fighting over the body of a third, and a warrior driving a chariot pulled by winged horses. The chariot was probably produced in an Etruscan workshop.*

Associated with these ways of death was an aristocratic way of life. In the emerging cities members of the leading families also came to adopt and display a distinctive lifestyle, which marked them off from the mass of the population and often united them more or less closely with the leading families in other communities. Again, evidence from tombs is central, since mourners deposited in the tombs objects that played a prominent role in an aristocratic self-image, and especially objects used in the ceremonies that defined and proclaimed this image. Thus, horses, chariots, rich armor and weapons, personal ornaments, and the equipment for feasting and drinking were all particularly important in this connection.

In Italy, much of this new lifestyle remains obscure, but a comparison with the Greek world, which influenced Italy greatly, may help to clarify some of its features. Greek aristocrats proclaimed their position in the community through elaborate displays of family, wealth, and virtue. Skill and leadership in war also played a prominent place in this self-image. Male members saw themselves as heroes, which explains in part the popularity of epics such as Homer's *Iliad*. Warlike display was certainly important among central Italian elites too. Their burials regularly contained arms and armor, often in large quantities, and the representations of combat to be found on a range of objects may well reflect claims to fighting skills and leadership in war. Weapons were not even limited to male tombs, and their presence in women's tombs could indicate that skill in war was seen as a family attribute rather than just an individual one. Certain finds, such as the large bronze shields often embossed with elaborate designs, are too light and fragile for use in battle, although they are highly suitable for display on ceremonial occasions.

Ceremonial drinking and feasting occupied a prominent place in the aristocratic lifestyle in many parts of the Mediterranean world. In Greece, male aristocrats held ceremonial drinking bouts or *symposia* (singular, *symposium*), in which poetry, song, displays of wit and invective, and conversation all had an important place.

Figure 1.2 *Banquet scenes were common in the art of archaic Italy. This drawing reproduces such a scene on a terracotta frieze from the palace at Murlo. The artist shows the guests reclining on couches, as was customary in the Greek world too. A mixing bowl of the kind often found in aristocratic tombs rests on a stand between the two couches. One of the guests plays a lyre.*

In these gatherings, elite males in a community and their guests from elsewhere created links among themselves and proclaimed their distinction from others. Essential implements in such gatherings—bowls for mixing wine, cups, and tripods—were often expensive, and they served as symbols of a special, and highly desirable, way of life. The bulk of the bronze vessels and tripods included in Italian elite graves, along with most of the imported ceramics and their local imitations, were designed and made specifically for these occasions, which suggests that formal feasting and drinking occupied a similar position in the self-definition of the Italian elite. In Greece, guests at symposia were virtually all male; in the Italian world, artistic representations show that wives participated too.

Extravagance was a prominent feature of elite burials of the eighth and seventh centuries, but their sixth- and fifth-century successors were on a much-reduced level. The "princely" burials of the eighth and seventh centuries are relatively rare; clearly, they held the remains of only a tiny portion of the population. The elite tombs of the following centuries exhibit a wider range of sizes, and grave goods generally are fewer, less costly, and less exotic. Despite the reduced scale, these burials were still the prerogative of a select group, and their builders shared some values with their seventh-century predecessors. Construction required a commitment and display of resources on a scale that most contemporaries could not match. Burial chambers often replicated rooms in the houses that the deceased would have occupied when alive. The walls of many such chambers, moreover, were covered with elaborate frescoes, certainly a task calling for skilled artisans; scenes of feasting were common, illustrating some continuity with earlier ideals. More families may have interred their members in a relatively expensive manner than was the case earlier: At Etruscan Volsinii, for example, inscriptions deposited between 550 and 500 reveal the presence of at least ninety families rich enough to build tombs. Placing a tomb was no longer solely the choice of the family: At some major centers, formal cemeteries or *necropoleis* (singular, *necropolis*), located on the margins of the settlement, contained the burials, while grids of streets determined the placing of tombs. In later periods, communal institutions overshadowed any single elite family, and the broadening of the elite from the sixth century may well reveal an early stage in this process.

Cities and Monumental Architecture

In the ninth and eighth centuries, settlements in Etruria, Latium, and Campania consisted of collections of huts with no traces of planning, formal organization, or public buildings, let alone private dwellings on a significantly larger scale than their neighbors. From the beginning of the seventh century, however, members of elite families began to construct larger, more elaborate, and more expensive structures in the main centers of population. They also began to lay out and ornament the public spaces that would define communal life for centuries, all signs of their ability to muster resources and labor on an increasingly lavish scale.

Residences of the elite form the earliest among these new kinds of edifices that are visible in the archeological record. From the beginning of the seventh century, the wealthy and powerful started to construct larger houses made of brick or stone and roofed with terracotta tiles. Some possessed elaborate and colorful exterior ornamentation. These new structures, built with techniques that had reached Italy from the eastern Mediterranean, required more capital and more labor than did earlier dwellings; surrounded by lesser structures, they would have proclaimed their owners' status much more clearly. Later, intermediate groups in the towns, not as wealthy or as powerful but still well-off, would copy these structures, although on a smaller scale.

A few buildings display wealth and status more appropriate to rulers than to aristocrats, perhaps the residences of the kings that legends and histories later associated with this time. The large structure constructed around 575 at Murlo in the countryside near modern Siena provides the clearest example. This so-called "palace" consisted of four blocks of rooms around a central courtyard. The courtyard itself was surrounded on three sides by a colonnade, while the fourth side probably held a shrine, and it may also have had a place for a throne. Builders covered the rooms with over 30,000 square feet (2,800 sq m) of terracotta rooftiles, which would have required a formidable outlay of resources in fuel, kilns, and labor. The palace at Murlo had an earlier, less well-known seventh-century prede-

cessor, which was destroyed by fire. Acquarossa, near modern Viterbo, saw the construction of a similar house during the sixth century. At Rome, another palace, known as the Regia, was built according to the same general plan toward the end of the seventh century.

The elaborate decorations of the palace at Murlo reveal some of its functions and much of the same ethos already seen in tombs and in grave goods. The builders of the palace adorned walls and rooflines with elaborate terracotta sculptures and friezes, some depicting human and divine figures and real or mythical animals, and others representing banquets, processions, horse races, and groups of warriors marching behind leaders in chariots— all prominent forms of elite behavior and display. Certain scenes show standing and seated human figures apparently engaged in some ceremony or

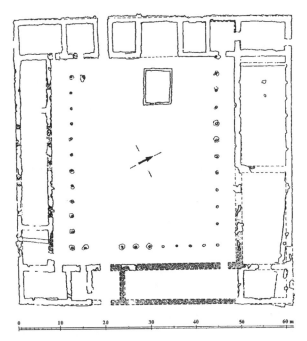

Figure 1.3 *Plan of the Palace at Murlo*

public business, and one carries a special curved staff or *lituus* that would serve in Etruria and Latium as a symbol of office for nearly a thousand years.

The ways in which the palace at Murlo was used are not entirely clear. It may have served as a residence for a ruler or for the leading family in the town. Certainly, some of the ceremonial activities depicted in the friezes must have taken place within its courtyard. Fragments of fine pottery attest to banquets and symposia. The presence of a shrine indicates that religious rites were performed in the palace too; the Regia at Rome also possessed shrines to several gods. Possibly the ruler held court there in the presence of his followers and the leaders of other prominent lineages. Thus, it may have been the regular site of feasts, religious ceremonies, and small-scale political meetings.

Slightly later, the ruling families in many of the emerging cities began to establish larger and more elaborate meeting places for the residents of their cities. Structures like Murlo could have accommodated relatively few participants and observers. In later periods, the leaders of cities regularly gathered the citizens in public assemblies to announce political decisions and to mobilize popular support for them. Leaders also staged elaborate public and ceremonial displays of their status and of their public roles. In these ceremonies, religious rituals addressed to the gods of the city often played a prominent part, for the performance of such rites also emphasized the leading role of the elite families that dominated civic life. Large-scale gatherings of the residents of a community, and the rituals that often accompanied them, served as a visual sign of the increasing unity of the city-state. In this connection, the governing elites of many emerging city-states established well-defined public spaces—together with temples and shrines surrounding them—to serve as the stage for their activities and the center of such limited government as these communities possessed.

As part of this development, the ruling elites of central Italy made the cult places of their communities grander and grander. From around 600, the inhabitants of some cities and towns began to build large, elaborate temples to their gods. These edifices, which shared many features with the earlier palaces, especially in their decorations, were often located on the central square of a settlement or on a hill overlooking it, where they would dominate the city's physical appearance. Although there could be considerable variation in ornament and in details, temples in central Italy generally were built upon a high platform or *podium*, fronted by a porch with columns; crowning the structure were a peaked roof of terracotta tiles and such terracotta decorations as statues, friezes, and antefixes. In later periods, these structures had an important place in communal identity, and they served functions beyond the strictly religious: In Rome, for example, officials performed many of their duties here, and speakers addressed their audience from a temple podium, where they would be highly visible.

These new cult places in some ways were an elaboration and a monumentalization of earlier practices. Organized cults did not begin with the seventh century. Excavations at the sites of some sixth- and fifth-century temples have unearthed

Figure 1.4 *This reconstruction of the so-called Portonaccio Temple at Veii (built c. 500) illustrates some of the typical features of a central Italian temple. It was built upon a high platform or podium. In front was a deep colonnaded porch, and behind was the chamber or* cella *where the cult statue of the god and some of the most precious offerings were stored. Along the ridge and edges of the roof, terracotta sculptures were placed (termed "acroterial" statues after the bases or* acroteria *on which they stood). The altar would have been somewhere in front of the temple; most ceremonies here would have been outside (not inside) and public.*

votive deposits that contained objects much older than the temples. In the Latin city of Satricum, the area later occupied by a temple contained a simple hut of ninth-century date (with a hearth) that may have served as a cult place. Around the middle of the seventh century, this hut was replaced by a rectangular stone building with terracotta roof decorations; a votive model of this structure clearly shows it to have been a temple. Comparable development from hut to temple may also be seen at Velitrae, Lanuvium, and Gabii. At other places, sacred groves or open-air altars first occupied the sites of later temples.

Temples and open-air shrines formed the stage for many of a city's most important religious rites, and they also provided the site for other elaborate displays of wealth and power by the governing elite. Votive offerings were prominent in central Italian cult places. These objects, offered to thank a god for answering a prayer or for giving some other sign of divine favor, could vary greatly in kind, in expense, and in quality. Individuals occupying a wide range of statuses made dedications, but those made by members of elite families would have stood out. Some of these more prestigious gifts bore inscriptions identifying the person who had made the dedication—one of the earliest uses of writing in Italy—and in the process, they would have marked this individual, in the eye of the viewer, as one favored by the god.

As wealth came to concentrate in cities and towns, many communities began to expend resources on their defense. For centuries, villages were often located on easily defensible hills or plateaus, which the inhabitants might strengthen with ditches, dikes, and palisades. From the eighth century, some communities began to construct more elaborate and expensive defensive systems. Many fortified themselves by first digging a deep, broad ditch (*fossa*), and then using the excavated earth to construct a thick, high mound (*agger*) inside it. Fossa and agger defenses do not necessarily surround an entire city; in general, only the most vulnerable areas were strengthened in this manner. A few cities built still more elaborate fortifications. At the beginning of the sixth century, the Etruscan city of Rusellae built itself a wall of large mud bricks mounted on a stone base, and in the sixth and fifth centuries, the Etruscan centers of Caere, Tarquinii, Vulci, and Veii built walls with stone blocks. Again, these fortifications seldom extended completely around the settlement.

Warfare in the Orientalizing and Archaic Periods

The eighth, seventh, and sixth centuries saw major changes in the frequency of warfare, as well as in its scale, and degree of organization. The new ways of making war affected not only relations between the emerging cities, but also the role and power of aristocracies, the political and social organization of the communities themselves, and their physical layouts. In the fourth century and later, when our evidence is much better, it is clear that some cities made war in a very formal and highly organized manner. They fielded large armies led by the political leaders of the city as a whole, and these armies fought formal battles in which soldiers were massed in large and regular formations (see Chapter Two). Before this date, however, simpler and less structured forms of warfare prevailed: There were few or no set battles; quick raids for cattle and other loot predominated; warriors served not as members of the community, but rather as followers of an aristocratic leader who had organized the enterprise. While the nature of the transition from one mode of warfare to another is clear enough, the stages and the timing of the shift are very obscure: It was probably a long process with much local and regional variation. From 600, however, the evidence shows traces of an ever-intensifying warfare between cities, while later literary sources even provide the names of prominent leaders in war.

Some aspects of the shift stand out more than others. The increasing scale and sophistication of the fortifications that came to surround many communities plainly illustrate both the greater intensity of warfare and the higher levels of organization in war making. By contrast, shifts in military organization and tactics, and changes in the political and social structures that may have accompanied them, are far more obscure. In the Greek world, which was the source of important innovations, the new way of war making centered on hoplite infantry, who were protected by body armor or corselets (made either of metal or of leather reinforced with metal), bronze greaves (leg armor), and bronze helmets. These hoplites carried a large circular shield or *hoplon*, and were armed with both a spear and a sword or dagger.

This new equipment, the hoplite panoply, made the warrior less vulnerable to the weapons of others, and so favored close combat over fighting at a distance with weapons that were thrown. At the same time the panoply made combatants less mobile in the field, so that hoplites fought in a dense formation, or phalanx, where warriors were protected and reinforced by those on either side. So long as each soldier kept his place, the phalanx had considerable offensive and defensive power. The new tactic emphasized formal battles over a more fluid warfare of raid and counter-raid. Moreover warfare between phalanxes generally favored the larger formation over the smaller, so that communities had a positive incentive to increase the number of men serving in their armies. The development of the hoplite phalanx was a long process: The new equipment appeared first (perhaps as early as the last decades of the eighth century), but the phalanx itself developed only slowly, and some communities did not make the full transition to it until the sixth or fifth centuries.

The cities of central Italy may have followed a broadly similar course of development. After around 700, weapons and body armor became more expensive, more complex, and perhaps more widely diffused over the adult male population of some communities. In the eighth and seventh centuries, deposits of weapons and armor (or models of them) are common in the wealthier graves. In seventh-century graves in Etruria, elements of the hoplite panoply begin to replace equipment of an earlier pattern. By the end of the century, hoplite equipment can be found in aristocratic graves in the coastal regions of Etruria, Latium, and Campania. Around 600, representations of helmeted warriors carrying round shields and moving in dense formations begin to appear on vases and friezes. Finally, in the sixth century, figurines of warriors wearing the hoplite panoply appear in votive deposits, especially in Etruria.

The presence of the equipment, however, does not necessarily imply the existence of large armies fighting in regular formations. First, the range of forms for shields, helmets, weapons, and body armor seems too wide and too variable for the degree of standardization often associated with the hoplite phalanx. Moreover, grave goods, votive deposits, and new artistic representations provide very uncertain evidence for changes in tactics. Objects deposited in graves or in sanctuaries are the relics of rites whose relationship to other aspects of communal life must remain somewhat problematic. Proclamations of status were integral to aristocratic funerals, and for a long time warfare of one kind or another held an important place in the self-image and self-representation of Italian elites. Some shields, helmets, and corselets seem too ornate and too fragile ever to have been used in combat; objects such as these probably had more to do with ceremonial

displays than with the actual conduct of war. Even the presence of serviceable equipment on the hoplite pattern need not imply that the original owner fought in a phalanx, because the prominent exhibition of foreign, and especially Greek, objects (or local copies of these items) was a notable feature of aristocratic self-presentation. The significance of the dense groups of marching warriors represented on vases or friezes may also be disputed: Some experts view them as depictions of phalanxes marching into battle, while to others they are processions and armed ritual dances. Nevertheless, it is certain that some cities did slowly adopt more regular and larger-scale ways of making war.

Perhaps the most obscure aspect of these changes is the matter of leadership and recruitment. Early in the history of the Greek city-state, aristocratic families and factions dominated the life and the decision making of their communities. Fighting forces consisted of members of the elite and their retinues and dependents, while military leadership was largely a function of the ability to raise and lead a personal armed following. Among the developed Greek city-states of the fifth century, communal institutions such as citizen assemblies and election of officeholders had superseded the earlier aristocratic leadership in many areas of civic life, and communal norms and institutions had come to be central to warfare. To a large degree, equipment was standardized across the army, and military service had become a function of citizenship and wealth rather than merely the result of birth or dependence on a leading family. In the larger cities, at least, adult males were ranked according to wealth in a way that determined eligibility for

Figure 1.5 This Umbrian bronze votive figure of a warrior wears some of the equipment of a hoplite, including a helmet with a high, very prominent crest. It probably dates from the fifth century.

Figure 1.6 This mid-sixth century terracotta frieze from the palace at Acquarossa depicts two warriors equipped as hoplites on the far left, following in procession behind a man with a bull and a chariot with two riders. The winged horses signify that the procession belongs in the realm of myth. The man with the bull may be identified as the Greek hero Heracles, the Latin Hercules.

military service along with a range of other political rights and duties. While serving, hoplites belonged to clearly distinguishable subunits of the phalanx that were organized on the basis of residence; the adult male citizens of the city came to elect their own military leaders, and formally voted on matters of war and peace.

In central Italy, certain cities slowly made a similar transition, although some of them may never have taken it very far. In these emerging urban communities, the leading families dominated in war; just as in the Greek world, the ability to raise a personal military following was a prominent aspect of leadership and an important prop to the power of the rising aristocratic families. Really outstanding individuals, moreover, were able to attract followers from distant places—often younger members of aristocratic families elsewhere—who were looking for adventure, fame, and wealth. In some cities—Rome is the best-known—communal institutions would also come to overshadow individual families in making war. Yet it is possible for armed followings based on a powerful individual or a leading family to coexist for considerable periods of time with other modes of recruitment based on citizenship or residence (see Chapter Two). Indeed, it is possible that Rome's preeminence, and that of a few other towns, may have been due, to some degree, to its reorganizing while neighbors did not.

Social and Economic Organization

Elite families dominated the social and economic life of their cities just as they did their political, religious, and military organization. The wealth and power of the upper classes rested upon their control over their followers and other dependents as well as over land. Prominent individuals mobilized groups of men for war, led them in battle, and, if successful, distributed the fruits of victory: land, cattle, captives, and the movable goods of the defeated. In peacetime, leading families also assembled dependents to farm their land, guard their herds and flocks, and attend to household tasks. Agriculture was becoming more complex, more capital-intensive, and perhaps more profitable. Beginning in the eighth century, the cultivation of grape vines, so essential to a culture with ceremonial drinking, spread to central Italy, along with the planting of olive trees. Powerful families probably played an important role in this process and in the accumulation of wealth that would have accompanied it. In the late seventh and sixth centuries, potters in Etruscan coastal centers made pottery vessels, *amphorae*, for the storage of olive oil and wine; some of these wine amphorae have been found along the coasts of southern France and northeast Spain.

Long-term ties of dependency bound many of the inhabitants of the new cities to aristocratic leaders. Links between members of the elite and their followers could be defined in terms of "patrons" and "clients." Ideally, the patron granted protection to his clients, who followed this protector in war and in politics and served him in other ways when appropriate. In some cases, a powerful family may have controlled entire villages or clusters of dwellings in a larger settlement.

The communities of central Italy possessed what has been called a "gentile" organization. Romans, for example, belonged to a clan or *gens* (plural, *gentes*). At first, a gens consisted of an aristocratic lineage or group of lineages and some of their lesser followers and dependents. A special system of nomenclature characterized groups formed in this fashion: Members were identified by a name or *nomen* (plural, *nomina*) that identified their gens, and they also had a first or personal name, the *praenomen*. Names in this style appear on inscriptions from the seventh century, although it is unclear whether that is a recent development or just the first appearance in writing of an already established practice. All of a city's residents need not have been either aristocrats or dependents of some aristocratic family. In some cities, independent elements of the population could certainly be found. Eventually, they too came to be organized into gentes, so that every member of a community would belong to a gens.

For many, dependence on the rich and powerful was unavoidable. So long as communal organizations were relatively weak, only powerful families, with their many armed retainers, could offer protection from war and other forms of violence. Debt formed another route to dependency. In many societies of the ancient Mediterranean world, debt established—and was intended to establish—a long-term relationship between borrower and lender. Farmers who possessed only a small plot of land were highly vulnerable to crop failure, and they had great difficulty in assembling a surplus that would see them through bad years. In the semiarid environment of much of the Mediterranean basin, crop failures or low yields because of drought were fairly frequent, a circumstance that regular warfare could only aggravate. Many men were forced to turn to their wealthier neighbors for assistance, borrowing to feed their families or to plant their next crop. Debt incurred in this fashion, it should be noted, would probably never be repaid; debtors would never gain enough wealth to repay in full, and they would continue to need further assistance in lean years. Instead, debt created a permanent relationship in which debtors lost control of their land and their labor, while creditors gained followers and a permanent workforce. In many early city-states of Greece and Italy, debt formed one of the chief sources of social conflict.

The production of luxury goods, and trade in them too, probably focused on elite households. In the Mediterranean world of the time, the specialists who made the prestigious products desired by the rich and powerful were for the most part itinerant. Such specialists made their living, in other words, by moving from place to place, offering their services to the wealthy in each. While employed, they would be supported by their customers, who would maintain them in their households. In the seventh and sixth centuries, some producers of ceramics and metalwork certainly came to Italy from abroad, usually Greece, but on occasion from Phoenician areas too.

The leaders of some cities took a clear role in sponsoring and protecting long-distance trade, and the presence of foreign prestige items in sanctuaries and elite tombs confirms that local elites were eager to benefit from such trade. In the sixth century, Caere and Tarquinii set up secure locations in which foreign merchants could operate, and they also made treaties with other cities to protect shipping. The Greek city of Sybaris, moreover, founded dependent colonies at Laus, Scidrus, and Poseidonia on the west coast of the peninsula, so that merchants could travel from Sybaris to Campania and farther north by land, thus evading the tolls imposed by Rhegium on ships using the narrow straits between Sicily and Italy.

One should not imagine, however, that the ruling elites of such cities participated personally in long-distance trade. A desire to own goods from distant places need not imply a personal interest in arranging their acquisition and transport. Indeed, the exchange of goods could be a very complex phenomenon. Members of the Greek upper classes, for example, professed contempt for trade and traders, but they still engaged in exchange with outsiders. In the eighth, seventh, and sixth centuries, much of this exchange took the form of gift giving and of hospitality, which established mutual obligations. Individuals of equivalent social standing in different communities sometimes exchanged gifts (usually items of prestige) and, in the process, recognized each other's social position. Inferiors also gave gifts to their superiors in return for protection and good favor; foreign traders are known to have given gifts to members of the local elites for just this purpose. Like Greek aristocrats, Roman elites at a later date (see Chapter Five) also professed scorn for commerce and traders, and there are Etruscan inscriptions showing the existence of a similar culture of gift giving. Leading individuals could benefit from trade without entering into a commercial relationship, and perhaps without even coming into much contact with traders. Italian aristocrats, in other words, were not merchants.

GREEKS AND ETRUSCANS

The seventh, sixth, and fifth centuries were the great age of the Etruscan and Greek cities of Italy and Sicily. In addition to the evidence provided by archeology and by inscriptions (which often prove to be obscure and uninformative), the histories of these societies are illuminated by a few literary texts. Some of them are even contemporary with the last stages of the Archaic Period; they identify major figures and events, and shed light on social and political organization. All these texts, however, were composed at a considerable distance from the communities themselves. In Greece, the writing of histories began in the fifth century. In the last third of that century, two of the greatest Greek historians wrote—if only tangentially for the most part—about events in the West. First, while elaborating upon the background to the celebrated clashes between the Persian Empire—the leading power in the eastern Mediterranean at the time—and the Greek city-states, Herodotus (died before 420) described in varying detail the history of several Greek cities of Sicily and southern Italy, and especially of the powerful "tyrants" who were often their rulers. Second, Thucydides (c. 460–c. 400) outlined the foundation of the Greek colonies in Sicily (two to three centuries before he wrote), and commented briefly on their subsequent history as part of his account of the Athenian expedition against Syracuse (the largest Greek city on the island) during the Peloponnesian War between Athens and Sparta (431–404). Centuries later, other Greek writers, such as Diodorus Siculus (died after 21 B.C.), a Sicilian Greek himself, and the biographer Plutarch (died after A.D. 120), also dealt with events at this early period, using and adapting previous historical works that do not survive today.

Unlike the Greeks, the Etruscans are largely silent. Some Etruscans probably did write histories and chronicles of their own cities, but only a few, slight traces of these works remain. The cities of coastal Etruria sometimes appear in the writings of Greek and Roman historians. In the Greek texts, the Etruscans appear as enemies, competitors, and pirates, cruel and faithless. The Roman writers were less hostile, but no less ethnocentric (see Chapter Two).

Greek Cities of Southern Italy and Sicily

By the end of the eighth century, some of the Greek colonies of Sicily and southern Italy began to take on the forms of city-states (Greek, *polis*). Several became notably powerful, dominating extensive hinterlands and large populations. Only a fraction of the inhabitants, however, would have been citizens of the ruling polis, for these Greek cities made sharp distinctions between citizens and noncitizens, and even between the descendants of the first Greek settlers and the offspring of later arrivals. At sixth-century Selinus, for example, the original walled enclosure of the seventh-century colony (covering under 24 acres/10 hectares) contained temples and a residential district for the elite. Poorer residents, by contrast, lived in a large cluster of crowded dwellings outside the walls, or in scattered houses and villages in the countryside. At the same time, Syracuse had come to dominate a large territory. This comprised the city itself and the lands cultivated directly by its citizens; a number of military strongholds with permanent garrisons; the semiautonomous Greek colony of Camarina with its own citizens and territory; a number of villages inhabited by native Sicels who had been reduced to the status of serfs working the lands of the governing elite; and finally a few areas where Sicels maintained a semiautonomous status. Elsewhere the Greek cities of Gela and Acragas (both on the south coast of Sicily) maintained similar arrangements, as did the south Italian cities of Taras (Latin, Tarentum), Sybaris, and Croton.

The Greek cities of Sicily and Magna Graecia suffered from sharp internal divisions. Narrow oligarchies, composed of the descendants of the first settlers, for a long time controlled the best land and the public offices. At Syracuse, they were called the *gamoroi*, those who shared the land; in other cities, the governing groups were called the *hippeis* or horsemen. In addition to these wealthy families, Greeks of a less exalted status formed the citizen body or *demos*, and their military service

Map 1.2 *Southern Italy and Sicily*

Shrines in the territories of some cities promoted relations both between communities in Italy and with the outside world. In the Orientalizing Period, aristocratic households may have mediated much long-distance trade, but in the sixth century a broader institutional involvement developed in some places. At Graviscae and Pyrgi, the ports of Tarquinii and Caere respectively, elaborate temple complexes received dedications from local notables as well as from Greek, Phoenician, Latin, and Etruscan merchants. In some cases, local gods were identified with foreign ones: At Graviscae, the local Turan was equated with the Greek Aphrodite, while at Pyrgi the Caeretan deity Uni was linked with the Phoenician Astarte. Around 500, in a long inscription in Etruscan and Phoenician, the ruler of Caere recorded a dedication he had made; his choice of languages illustrates the importance of Phoenicians here (coming from Carthage perhaps, or from another western colony). Thus cult places such as these served as centers of interaction between peoples of different origin under the patronage of the host community. Elsewhere in the Mediterranean at this time sanctuary sites are known to have filled the same function.

Traces of Etruscans are not limited to Etruria. In some places, Etruscan settlements followed Villanovan predecessors, just as they did in Etruria itself: Capua and Nola in Campania, as well as Felsina (modern Bologna), across the Apennines, are good examples. New Etruscan centers appeared elsewhere in the Po Valley in the course of the sixth and fifth centuries. Small groups of Etruscans also inhabited places that remained essentially non-Etruscan, because inscriptions in the Etruscan language have been found in many places in Latium (including Rome itself), Campania, and Umbria.

In the Archaic Period, Etruscan elites were among the most active in Italy, but the nature of their interaction with non-Etruscan communities is not always clear. Some scholars suggest that Etruscan practices spread with the movement of elites and their followers, who would come to dominate a preexisting community. Some of the Etruscan centers in the north may have begun in just this way: Hatria, from which the Adriatic Sea received its name, and Spina, a major trading center from the closing decades of the sixth century, may originally have been Greek cities. Roman writers of a later date thought that two of Rome's last three kings were of Etruscan descent, and they believed that some of Rome's core institutions and practices were of Etruscan origin. Even so, it is by no means clear how far the emergence of cities in regions such as Latium is to be credited to Etruscans. In the seventh and sixth centuries, the chief Etruscan communities were among Italy's richest and most powerful urban centers; as such, they would plainly have had marked influence, either imposed directly through the power they exerted over their neighbors, or indirectly through the models they provided for others. The similarity in material culture that many scholars regard as signifying the undoubted presence of an Etruscan elite may rather be due to the formation of an international elite style—one that crossed ethnic boundaries, and was shared by numerous local elites imitating each other to increase their own prestige. By the same token, the presence of Etruscan speakers may indicate only that the newly forming city-states in many regions were for a time open to outsiders. The Romans, it should be noted, thought that Lucius Tarquinius Priscus—the first Etruscan king of Rome, and father of the second—came to Rome from Tarquinii as an immigrant, not as a conqueror.

SUGGESTED READINGS:

Aubet, Maria Eugenia. 2001 (second edition). *The Phoenicians and the West: Politics, Colonies and Trade*. Cambridge: Cambridge University Press.

Banti, Luisa. 1973. *Etruscan Cities and Their Culture*. Berkeley, Los Angeles, London: University of California Press.

Cornell, Timothy J. 1995. *The Beginnings of Rome: Italy and Rome from the Bronze Age to the Punic Wars (c. 1000–264 B.C.)*. London and New York: Routledge. An intensive survey of Rome's early centuries based on archeological and literary evidence. Since the ancient historical writers who treated this period all wrote several centuries later, the value of their testimony continues to be hotly debated by modern scholars. Professor Cornell's view of the accuracy of Roman traditions is a more favorable one than that reflected in the first two chapters of the present book.

Spivey, Nigel. 1997. *Etruscan Art*. London: Thames and Hudson. This work is broader than its title indicates, covering art throughout central Italy and placing it in its social context.

river, a small plain gave access to the Tiber ford; this plain would become the *Forum Boarium*, the chief market and harbor of urban Rome.

The hills and valleys here were inhabited long before Rome became a city. Archeologists have found scattered fragments of pottery datable back to the Middle Bronze Age, but the site may not have been permanently settled until much later. The earliest known burials—hence undoubted traces of settlement—date to around 1000; with similar interments at other Latin sites, they mark the beginning of the first phase of the "Latial culture." During the three millennia since, Rome has for long been densely settled, so that little in the way of surface surveys or systematic large-scale excavations is possible today. However, finds do show that several small clusters of huts occupied the hills, and perhaps also the valleys between them and the plain by the river. Some of these hamlets shared cemeteries, but it would seem that no sense of common identity linked all the hamlets on the hills. In this respect, early Rome was little different from other Latin centers, although it may have been more populous than most.

After c. 800, signs appear that a larger and more highly organized community was emerging. Burials begin to concentrate at a few large cemeteries on the margins of the settled area; meanwhile the scattered cemeteries, each shared by a few hamlets, begin to fall into disuse. The first graves in the Esquiline *necropolis*—in the seventh and sixth centuries Rome's chief cemetery—date to this period. At the same time, finds of Greek pottery on the site of the Forum Boarium may show not only that the inhabitants of Rome were in contact with distant places, but also that the plain along the Tiber River had already taken up its later role as market and port. Later too, this area would be the site of the *Ara Maxima*, an altar dedicated to the Greek hero Heracles (Latin, Hercules) and associated with commerce; his cult may have been established here as early as the eighth century.

Perhaps the most striking indications that a more highly organized community now occupied the site of Rome have emerged along the northeast slopes of the Palatine hill. Here, recent excavations have uncovered a mid-eighth-century wall, built of clay and timber on a stone foundation, running along the bottom of the hill. The wall's function is uncertain: Some scholars believe it to be a fortification, while others suggest that it marked some sacred boundary. Between 675 and 550, three successive stone walls followed the line of the early clay-and-timber wall; but by around 530 the usefulness of all these walls had ended, for builders now covered them with a large earth platform supporting a number of private dwellings. Even though the construction of the first wall naturally required much organization and effort, the identity of the workforce remains obscure. Residents of the villages on the Palatine may have been responsible, although it is possible that people from other hills also participated, making the wall an early sign of an increasingly united community.

From the middle of the seventh century, the Romans began to transform the valley separating the hills into the civic and religious center of the city, the Forum Romanum. Earlier, this valley—much of which was marshy and liable to flooding—

held no more than a few clusters of huts and some cemeteries. The first phase of construction, which began around 650, turned part of the valley into a place where Romans could gather for communal events; for this purpose, the huts were cleared, the valley's lowest areas were drained and filled, and a rough surface of beaten earth was laid. A quarter of a century later, this pavement was refurbished and extended by filling in more wetlands. Henceforth the Forum would serve as the chief place for large public assemblies and ceremonies in the city.

As the political center of the city, the Forum also became Rome's most prominent building site. Near the end of the seventh century, the *Regia* (see Rome Under the Kings) was erected along its edge. At the end of that century, builders laid out another public space, later known as the *Comitium*, and along its edges they constructed a large stone building that is probably to be identified with the later *Curia Hostilia*. The original uses of the Comitium and the Curia Hostilia are obscure. In later periods at least (and possibly from the outset too), they were crucial to the functioning of the Roman state: The Comitium was a sacred space where officials would summon citizens to vote, to hear legal cases, and to make (or be informed about) important public decisions; the Curia Hostilia served as one of the meeting places for the council of elders known as the *senate*.

During the sixth century, a sanctuary dedicated to the god Vulcan was laid out not far from the Comitium. Around the middle of the same century, at the opposite end of the Forum, the first building on the site of the later Temple of Vesta (which contained the sacred hearth of the city) was constructed near the Regia. By the last third of the century, the *Sacra Via*, the chief processional route of the city, had been paved and graded as it entered the southeast corner of the Forum. Around the beginning of the fifth century, temples to Saturn and Castor were constructed on the south side.

In addition to the Forum Romanum, two other major centers of Rome's civic and religious life, the Capitol and the Forum Boarium, also began to be adorned with larger, more elaborate structures. At the end of the seventh century, builders cleared the huts from part of the plain along the banks of the Tiber and established a sacred space, which in all likelihood contained an altar. The first temple here, probably dedicated to Fortuna, was built in the second quarter of the sixth century; it was rebuilt a generation later, and decorated with terracotta friezes and statues of the Greek hero Heracles and the Greek goddess Athena. On the Capitoline hill, the Romans began to construct the temple of Jupiter Best and Greatest (Jupiter Optimus Maximus) around the beginning of the sixth century; when completed toward the end of the century, this structure was one of the largest temples in Italy. Last but not least (although the matter is controversial), the Romans of the sixth century may have protected parts of their city by excavating a *fossa* that was fifty-five feet (16.5 m) wide in places, and by constructing an *agger* to a height of forty feet (12 m).

A wealthy and powerful elite lived in the city. Goods deposited in seventh-century tombs reveal the presence of aristocratic families able to expend resources in

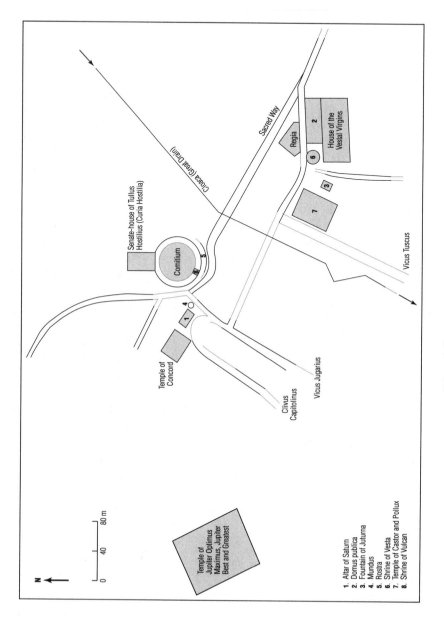

Map 2.2 *The Forum Area*

N

0   40   80 m

Temple of
Jupiter Optimus
Maximus, Jupiter
Best and Greatest

1. Altar of Saturn
2. Domus publica
3. Fountain of Juturna
4. Mundus
5. Rostra
6. Shrine of Vesta
7. Temple of Castor and Pollux
8. Shrine of Vulcan

Temple of
Concord

Clivus
Capitolinus

Vicus Jugarius

Senate-house of Tullus
Hostilius (Curia Hostilia)

Comitium

Cloaca (Great Drain)

Sacred Way

Regia

House of the
Vestal Virgins

Vicus Tuscus

large-scale displays of their status. Wealthy Romans also constructed buildings for their personal use. By 625, houses built of stone and roofed with tiles had replaced some of the huts on the Velia. More such houses would soon follow on the Palatine and other hills. Around 530, the walls that had marked the northeast corner of the Palatine were covered by a large earth platform. On it at least four substantial private dwellings were constructed, with large reception rooms or *atria* (singular, *atrium*) and other rooms grouped around enclosed gardens—features that would mark Roman aristocratic houses for centuries. By the end of the sixth century, dwellings spread over most of the hills, making Rome one of the largest cities in Italy.

THE ROMANS AND THEIR EARLY HISTORY

At Rome, an active tradition of history writing supplements the evidence of archeology and the brief and fragmentary texts of archaic inscriptions. Rome's own historians, writing centuries later, gave detailed accounts of the early history of their city. Seven kings supposedly ruled in Rome. Romulus founded the city, along with some of its most important political institutions. Numa Pompilius set the pattern for Rome's religious life. Their successors built temples, founded institutions, and, like their predecessors, waged war on Rome's neighbors. Servius Tullius, the sixth king, was virtually a second founder of the city. Accounts of the reign of Tarquinius Superbus, Rome's last king, justify his fall and the end of the monarchy. The dates that Roman scholars gave to Romulus' foundation of the city vary widely, although most fall in the eighth century. Marcus Terentius Varro (116–27 B.C.), one of Rome's greatest scholars, thought that Romulus founded Rome in 753, a date that came to be generally adopted.

The reliability of these histories is far from certain. Their authors wrote centuries after the events they recounted; they filled their works with anachronisms

Figure 2.1 *This terracotta statue of the Greek god Apollo decorated the roof of the Portonaccio Temple at Veii, which was probably dedicated to the goddess Minerva (see Fig. 1.4). Other acroterial statues attached to the temple represent Heracles and possibly Hermes; the figure of a woman with a child eludes identification, however. A sculptor from Veii named Vulca is said to have made the cult statue of Jupiter Best and Greatest on the Capitol, which was dedicated in 509—about the same time, in other words, as the Portonaccio shrine.*

Table 2.1 Dates of Rome's Kings According to Varro

Romulus, 753–715;

Numa Pompilius, 715–673;

Tullus Hostilius, 673–642;

Ancus Marcius, 642–617;

Lucius Tarquinius Priscus
    (The Elder Tarquin), 616–579;

Servius Tullius, 578–535;

Lucius Tarquinius Superbus
    (Tarquin the Proud), 534–510.

and patriotic mythmaking; they regarded the city as unchanging in many important ways; they presented its history in a fashion that often ignored or minimized the influence of neighbors and allies. Romulus certainly is a figure of myth: His name merely means "the Roman," and he serves to explain both the existence of the city and its name. The remaining monarchs may actually have lived and ruled—their family names were all in use at some time in Rome—but the deeds attributed to them are full of myths, moralizing tales, fabrications, and the political propaganda of later ages.

The Greeks taught the Romans to write histories. Greek and Roman historians came to develop clear ideas about how one should write history and why. Historians, it was thought, should either compose accounts of a single, significant event, such as a war; or they should record a city's history from its foundation to the author's own day; or they should describe in general the history of the civilized world. The first two of these choices would prove popular among Roman authors. Moreover, proper histories should glorify one's city, and entertain or instruct one's readers. In order to entertain, historians offered quantities of vivid and dramatic stories adorned with colorful details. To instruct, they focused on leading individuals, the situations that these faced, and the effects of their actions on their city. Such accounts, it was hoped, would provide memorable examples of actions that good citizens should either imitate or avoid.

The first Greek histories were written in the fifth century, but the earliest Roman ones did not appear until over two centuries later. Quintus Fabius Pictor, the first Roman historian, offered an account—written in Greek, not Latin—of Rome's history from its foundation to his own day (c. 200). Others soon followed. Half a century later, Marcus Porcius Cato the Elder wrote the first prose history in Latin; its title, *Origins*, indicates one of its major themes. These early works do not survive, although their influence persisted. In fact both Greek and Roman historians composed their works in ways that nowadays we would more or less equate with plagiarism, since they often incorporated segments of the works of others into their own. Today, our knowledge of this historiographical tradition of early Rome derives from two Roman writers in particular—Marcus Tullius Cicero (106–43), and Livy (Titus Livius, 59 B.C. to A.D. 17)—as well as from such Greek authors as Diodorus Siculus (mid to late first century B.C.), Dionysius of Halicarnassus (late first century B.C.), Plutarch (before A.D. 50–after 120), and Cassius Dio (late second and early third centuries A.D.).

Roman historians only rarely undertook what a modern historian might recognize as research. Undoubtedly, Romans of a later age had access to information regarding earlier centuries that was, in modern terms, reliable. Some documents did survive, although later Romans found them difficult to decipher and interpret. Monuments often carried very brief inscriptions identifying their builders and perhaps the occasion for their construction. One group of priests, the pontiffs, maintained a year-by-year account of significant events, the so-called pontifical annals. These annals, which began no later than the fifth century, identified the chief elected officials who held office each year, noted victories and perhaps defeats, recorded the foundation of temples, and set out a wide range of unusual or dramatic events that were thought to reveal the will of the gods in some way: Such events included famine, earthquakes, freak storms, and lightning strikes sustained by prominent buildings or monuments.

However, few Roman historians seem to have consulted the old texts directly. Instead, they largely relied on interpretations of them (not always accurate) encountered in the works of earlier writers. They also resorted to other sources that modern historians might find less dependable. For example, popular or priestly aetiologies—stories told to explain or justify a religious rite by setting out an account of its first appearance—often found their way into histories. Historians made use of family traditions too. In fourth-century Rome, as well as later (see Chapter Three), a relatively small circle of prominent families held most of the high offices and commanded most of the armies. These leading families asserted their greatness by proclaiming the offices and deeds of their ancestors; in the process, it was often suspected, they also exercised their powers of imagination.

BOX 2.1: *When recounting Rome's early history, both Roman and (later) Greek historians often imagined the city's first leaders as initiating and performing practices that later would be typical of its officials. Here Plutarch presents Romulus as founding Rome with just the same rites that the founders of Rome's own colonies used in the fourth century and later (see Chapter Three).* Plutarch, *Romulus* 11: Romulus buried Remus in the Remonia, together with the servants who had reared him. He then began to build his city, after summoning experts in sacred customs and writings from Etruria, who taught him everything as if in a religious rite. A trench was dug around what is now the *Comitium*, and in it were deposited first fruits of whatever was considered good by custom and necessary by nature. And finally, each man brought a small portion of their native soil and threw it in, where it mixed together. They call this trench the *mundus*, as they do the heavens. Then, they marked out the city in a circle around this center. And the founder, after placing a bronze ploughshare on the plough and yoking to it a bull and a cow, ploughed a deep furrow around the boundary lines, while those who followed behind turned the clods thrown up by the plough inwards toward the city, leaving none to face outward. With this line, they mark out the course of the wall, and it is called by contraction the *pomerium*, in other words 'behind the wall' (*post murum*). And where they intended to place a gate, they lifted the plough and left an empty space. And this is why they regard the entire wall as sacred except for the gates.

Finally, Roman historians, like their Greek models, felt free to invent parts of their narratives. In principle, historians were bound by the facts: They should describe only wars that had actually taken place, and they should accurately identify the victors and the vanquished. But they could also embellish their narratives when they had little factual guidance. Thus they added minor actions, claims about motives, and even specific words and deeds when they thought their accounts required them. To be sure, there were a few agreed guidelines: Attributions should be plausible; they should be both true to character and illustrative of it; and they should not contradict known events. Inevitably, however, a common consequence of such additions was to project back into the past the attitudes and practices of the author's own day. Roman historians tended to think that their city, in its essentials, was unchanging from an early date. Thus, they had no difficulty in believing that Romans of earlier centuries had the same attitudes and values as did their descendants, and that in the distant past the city had functioned socially and politically in much the same way as it would later.

Separating fact from fancy is always a difficult task, and modern scholars have long disagreed over the degree to which Roman tradition can be considered reliable. In this regard, today's scholars are often better disposed to the Romans than their predecessors were. Roman histories do contain an uneasy mixture of fact, supposition, and outright invention. Much is doubtless true. From the sixth century on, the main outline of wars, conquests, and the dedication of new temples is in all likelihood substantially correct. The prominent individuals we read of may not only actually have lived, but they may also have done things that resemble, if only remotely, the deeds attributed to them. This said, there are also unquestionably elements that were shaped by their dramatic possibilities, or by their usefulness as a means of praising virtue and condemning vice. There is no shortage of lurid stories and moralizing tales in which heroic men and women do great deeds or suffer tragic fates, and no dearth of villains either, some of whom suffer for their misconduct.

As a result, the Roman historical tradition, when coupled with the evidence from archeological excavations and from inscriptions, does permit the broad outlines of the city's early history to be known with some confidence—for the sixth and fifth centuries especially. On some specific points, moreover, this picture of the city and its institutions in the Orientalizing and Archaic periods can be supplemented by using evidence from later practices that are known to have had their origins in this early period. The earliest forms of these institutions may well have varied considerably from later and better-known versions, but in certain cases we can be sure that they were present in one form or other.

ROME UNDER THE KINGS

Kings certainly once ruled in Rome. *Rex*, the Latin word for king, appears in two fragmentary sixth-century texts, one a long inscription from the shrine of Vulcan, and the other a potsherd found in the Regia. And kingship persisted in Rome in the form of a priestly office, the *rex sacrorum*, that continued the king's religious functions long after the political and military powers had been lost. Rome was not the only Italian city with a king, but it is far from clear how common monarchy was. As we saw in Chapter One, tyrants, who seized power forcefully and often ruled in the same way, governed many of the Greek cities of southern Italy and Sicily during the sixth and fifth centuries. Kings led a number of Etruscan cities too, from the seventh century into the opening years of the fourth. With the exception of Gabii, which supposedly had a king imposed on it by the last king of Rome, no other Latin city is known to have had kings of its own. Apart from the Greek colony of Cumae, which was ruled by tyrants for a time, the internal arrangements of Campanian cities are almost completely unknown. Generally speaking, some cities may never have had kings, or had them only intermittently. Roman historians did believe that their monarchy had not been hereditary, so that each king had to establish his right to rule. In the traditional list of seven kings, it should be noted, there is only one instance where a father and his son both held the throne, although even here the reign of another intervened.

Romans of a later date associated their kings with leadership in war, the construction of temples and other public buildings, the performance of religious rites, and the granting of judgments in legal disputes. These early rulers, we are told, defeated many of the surrounding towns and villages, forcing some of their inhabitants to move to Rome, while others were permitted to remain in what would become no more than small rural centers without much civic life. Archeologists have found the remains of towns near Rome, some of which were wealthy and powerful in the seventh century, but no more than fortified villages in the sixth. In later periods, the Romans regularly celebrated rites that marked the boundaries of their territory centuries earlier. Certain rituals preserved the memory of a time when Roman territory encompassed only about seventy-five square miles (190 sq km), and Rome's frontiers were no more than five miles (8 km) from the city in any direction. By the end of the sixth century, however, Rome had become a much larger place: Its territory probably covered almost 300 square miles (780 sq km), while the population may have been as high as 35,000.

The area around the Forum Romanum contained a number of places linked to rites and activities that Roman historians later associated with kingship. Around 625, the Regia was constructed along the same general pattern as the "palaces" at Murlo and Acquarossa, with small chambers surrounding a central courtyard. The building had a clear religious function. In it, shrines to Mars and Ops Consiva, the gods of war and of wealth, served as the focus of a range of sacred tasks performed by the kings and their priestly successors. In the sixth century, the Regia probably formed part of a larger complex that included the temple of Vesta, containing the sacred hearth of the city, and the *domus publica*, later the house of the leader of an important college of priests and quite possibly the sixth-century dwelling of the kings. Not too far away, in the area sacred to the god Vulcan, was found a long sixth-century law, today very fragmentary, which seems to record regulations of a ritual nature that in some way involved the king.

The aristocracy, too, had its own political, religious, and military roles in the city. Roman historians later held that the leaders of the city's aristocratic families met in a council of elders known as the senate, which chose the kings, helped them make policy, and on occasion resisted their initiatives as they saw fit. Aristocratic councils were common in the world of the city-state: They can be found in many Greek cities and are known, at a later date, in many Italian ones, including Rome itself. Some kind of council—at this date certainly aristocratic in character—probably did function in the Rome of the kings. For long, this senate met in the building known as the Curia Hostilia, supposedly first built by Tullus Hostilius; as noted earlier, excavations have shown that a large stone building was constructed on the site around 600. Like kings, prominent members of the Roman elite also had their own religious roles. Later Romans believed that certain aristocratic families enjoyed especially close relations with the gods; in time, too, prominent families certainly did come to monopolize the most important priestly offices.

Like other cities of central Italy, Rome seems to have witnessed a certain mobility of elite families during the seventh, sixth, and early fifth centuries. Some aristocrats and their followers moved from city to city, taking up in the new place the position they had abandoned in the old. The Elder Tarquin was thought to have moved to Rome from the Etruscan city of Tarquinii. Around 500, the aristocratic family of the Claudii, which centuries later would provide emperors for Rome, first came to the city with a great body of clients, having left its native Sabine country to the northeast after suffering political setbacks there. A few leaders of private armies gained an especially prominent place in the history of central Italy during the sixth and early fifth centuries. Some of them dominated their own cities, while others sought wealth and power away from home. Romans of a later age liked to believe that their kings had ruled with the consent of the leading families and the people. In practice, however, the entry of powerful individuals and their followers into a new city may have been tantamount to conquest. At the Etruscan city of Vulci, for example, a tradition survived that a prominent war leader from there once seized and ruled Rome. As late as 460, Appius Herdonius, a Sabine, seized the Capitoline hill with armed clients and tried without success to dominate the city.

One of the chief characteristics of a fully formed city-state was a citizenry organized communally to fulfill its roles in politics, religion, and war. In Rome, the mass of adult male citizens was known as the *populus Romanus*. At some indeterminate point, this populus gained the right to give assent to officeholders and their policies, a practice that would eventually become formalized as a vote. The bulk of Rome's population was integrated into the city's institutions through intermediary groups based on kinship, real or imagined. In Rome, as in some other cities, several clans or *gentes* formed a larger unit known as a *curia* (plural, *curiae*). The Roman curiae, supposedly thirty in number, came together to form three tribes, the Tities, Ramnes, and Luceres.

Like other elements of Rome's social and political order, these curiae had important religious functions. In later, better-documented times, curiae met for communal meals during major festivals and for the performance of their own religious rites. Their only known officials, *curiones*, *libones*, and *flamines*, either were priests or at least possessed many priestly attributes. Rome's oldest aristocratic families dominated these positions, and they would maintain this control long after they had lost their monopoly of other priestly offices at the end of the fourth century (see Chapter Three).

The tribes had an essential role in Rome's political and military organization. When the city made war, its army—the followers of the king and of powerful members of the elite, along with some sort of general levy—was organized by tribes, with each one providing its own unit of cavalry and of infantry. Aristocratic families probably dominated their tribal contingents just as they did the curiae.

During the sixth century, a reform superseded this organization of tribes and curiae, but did not eliminate it. The sixth king, Servius Tullius, supposedly created new forms of classifying and organizing the population—the beginnings of the Roman *census*, in other words, which in later periods would be one of the central institutions of the city (see Chapter Three). The core of the new arrangement was the regular compilation of a list of adult male Romans, in which they were classified by wealth and by residence, rather than by kinship. In the world of the city-state, citizens provided their own arms and armor when serving in the city's army. Aristocrats clearly possessed the resources to equip themselves in this manner—they certainly could afford to deposit military equipment in their tombs—and they may have supplied weapons and armor to their followers too. Tullius' census divided Romans into those who could afford to equip themselves for service on foot (known as the *classis*, "those summoned"), and those who could not (*infra classem*, "below those summoned").

Citizens who belonged to the classis—probably along with those who could serve in the cavalry, and just possibly those who were judged to be infra classem also—were further subdivided into units known as centuries (*centuriae*; singular, *centuria*). In the strictest sense, the term centuria should denote a group of exactly one hundred men; however, in later periods at least, the size of a centuria could be quite different from this supposed norm.

Units likewise termed centuriae also occupied a primary position in the organization of Rome's armies in the field, and in fact the use of the term in this military context almost certainly preceded its adoption for the census. Roman commanders raised armies by summoning citizens to gatherings where they chose their soldiers from those eligible to serve. The force raised in this way was called a legion (*legio*; plural, *legiones*), which signified that it stemmed from a selection process—the verb *legere* meaning either "to collect" or "to pick". Under the kings, the legion selected each year was the army of the city. In later centuries, the term came to denote a unit of several thousand men serving under one of the commanders who held office for the year (see Chapter Three). From the earliest period for which we have information, a legion was always subdivided into sixty centuries. The centuries of the census, however, were not the same as the centuries of the legion. Later, for certain, the former came to comprise voting units in one type of citizen assembly (see Chapter Three), and this function may even have been original, so that from the outset this "assembly of centuries" represented the citizenry under arms.

Although it may not have been part of the original census, citizens soon came to be assigned to tribes that received their members from defined territories. Servius Tullius supposedly divided the city itself into four "urban" tribes for its residents, and this number was never increased. At the same time or shortly after, "rural" tribes were added for the inhabitants of the countryside, and their number was to grow as Roman territory expanded. These territorial tribes served as the mustering units of the Roman army. Residents of the city assembled for military service in their four tribes. Members of the rural tribes probably gathered in a tribal mustering center, which would have been a prominent, and no doubt fortified, place in its territory.

Tullius' creation of these tribes did not require the elimination of the three original ones, which continued to perform some of their old functions. Consequently, Roman citizens now belonged to two tribes in two different tribal systems. Over time, however, the new tribes came to be considerably more important than the old, and membership in one became a mark of citizenship. By the first century B.C., there were even some Romans who did not know their own curia, but all would have been able to name their territorial tribe.

Accounts of Servius Tullius' life and reign are full of dramatic events, turns of fortune, and tales of divine intervention, and many of the incidents recorded about his life may be more a matter of myth than of history. Descriptions of his reforms, moreover, contain elements that only became standard at a later date. Nonetheless, the key features were probably in place by the early fifth century at the latest. The oldest territorial tribes, those closest to the city, bear the names of families who were prominent in the first decades of the Republic, but less prominent later. Later Roman historians thought that Tullius ruled without the consent of the senate, and that he was sometimes hostile to it. In some contemporary Greek cities, where institutions like the Roman census can also be found, the creation of a list of citizens and the reassignment of the population to new subunits certainly did have the effect of lessening aristocratic control; newly created means of organization acted to decrease the importance of older ones in which members of the elite had possessed hereditary rights of leadership. The reforms credited to Tullius may well have had similar goals—an early stage in the long process whereby political power based on a personal armed following would give way to power gained and exercised through more formal, communal, and regulated means. But it is possible that practical considerations also played a role. In the sixth century, Rome's territory now greatly exceeded its size in the seventh, so that smaller territorial tribes, and more of them, would make the mustering of the army a quicker, more convenient operation.

ROME AND THE LATINS

A shared identity linked the cities of Latium. Much later, Roman writers would maintain that the ancestor of all Latins was Aeneas, a noble Trojan who escaped from Troy as it fell to the besieging Greeks. After many adventures, Aeneas landed in Latium near the future city of Lavinium, where he formed a new people from his own followers and from the aboriginal inhabitants of the area. His son would found Alba Longa, the seat of kings who would rule Latium and found the other Latin cities. This tale certainly does not depict historical events: Latins were not Trojans, and Alba Longa probably never existed as a city and as the seat of a powerful dynasty of kings. But the myth does serve a distinct purpose: It expresses an unmistakable sense of a perceived relationship between the cities of Latium, and it also connects them to one of the most important "events" in Greek myth, celebrated in the epic poems, the *Iliad* and the *Odyssey*, that were so central to Greek culture. Moreover, the inhabitants of Latium did have much in common. They shared the name of Latin (*nomen Latinum*), and they used variants of the Latin language. From the beginnings of the "Latial culture" around 1000, they also possessed a common material culture.

The belief in an identity that transcended the separate communities of Latium received clear expression in religious ritual. At certain festivals, Latin settlements came together for the performance of communal rites. The Latin Festival, or *Latiar*, held in honor of Jupiter Latiaris (Jupiter of the great feast of the Latins), was the most prominent. Each spring, towns and villages possessing the right to take part—the Romans later knew of thirty—shared common sacrifices and banquets on the Alban Mount, the supposed site of Alba Longa. The Latin festival survived the end of the political independence of the Latin communities in the fourth century (see Chapter Three), because Roman officials continued to supervise its performance for centuries thereafter. The Latins also possessed common cults at other sites. At Lavinium, a group of Latin cities, probably thirteen in number, sacrificed at a shrine to the Penates, or household gods; centuries later, when Rome had taken over the shrine, Roman officials still performed rites there to the Penates of the Roman People. Another cluster of cities, towns, and villages shared worship in the grove of the goddess Diana at Aricia, and there may have been further groups that made common use of sacred groves near Tusculum and Ardea. The Roman king, Servius Tullius, allegedly established another shrine to Diana on the Aventine hill, just outside the limits of the city of Rome, for all the Latins to use.

These sanctuaries and the rites that took place in them are certainly old, although the date of their first appearance is unknown. At two of the sites, prominent cult

Map 2.3 *Latium and Southern Etruria*

structures appeared in the sixth century, at just the time when cities were also first building temples to their own gods. At Lavinium, archeologists have found the sanctuary of the Penates just outside the city's fortifications. In it, beginning in the sixth century, were built thirteen monumental altars, each of which probably belonged to one of the cities that sacrificed there. Later representations of the cult statue of Diana on the Aventine, which would have been housed in her temple there, show it to have been of a sixth-century type. Temples built within cities during the sixth and fifth centuries often occupied the sites of open-air sanctuaries at which cult activity would date much further back. The same may well be true of the interurban sanctuaries at Rome, Lavinium, and other places.

Latins' sense of a shared identity also found expression in other ways. In the Greek world, the ideal city-state or *polis* was a closed community: Few outsiders became citizens, intermarriage with noncitizens was sometimes discouraged, and the right to own land was restricted to citizens. Latin cities were less exclusive—at least with other Latins. Later, all Latins possessed the right of *conubium*, permitting them to make a lawful marriage with a resident of any other Latin city (children of the marriage gained the citizenship status of the father; children born outside marriage received their mother's status). Equally, the right of *commercium* allowed Latins to own land in any of the Latin cities and to make legally enforceable contracts with their citizens. In addition, all Latins had the right (*ius migrationis*) to take up citizenship in any other Latin city merely by establishing residence there. These rights achieved formal expression no later than the fourth century, although it is likely that they were, in some form, much older. Such shared rights—and the common religious rites too—may be relics of the time before the appearance of cities divided the people of Latium into clearly separated communities.

Despite all this sharing, the Latins were not politically unified. The proliferation of rites and cult centers, shared by cities in various combinations, plainly demonstrates the absence of any single overarching organization, religious or political, during the seventh and sixth centuries. Latin communities certainly waged war against one other, and the largest and most powerful of them competed among themselves for primacy, often at the expense of the weaker communities. In these circumstances, cities grew by war, and the political institutions that would later unite the Latin communities

Figure 2.2 *Just outside the walls of the city of Lavinium, not far from the thirteen altars of the Latin cities, a temple of the goddess Minerva was built around 500. In the third century, the temple was apparently cleaned and remodeled, and over one hundred terracotta statues were placed in a votive deposit. The statue shown is of Minerva, probably the temple's original cult statue.*

remains obscure. Perhaps having a larger number of officeholders was occasionally more important than having fewer, but more powerful, magistrates.

In times of emergency, the Romans resorted to an office with extraordinary powers. In the fourth and third centuries, Roman magistrates appointed one man to serve as dictator in emergencies, or in a major war when a unified command seemed desirable. Dictators were not elected. Instead, a consul designated a single man for the post in a ceremony that took place in the dead of night. The new dictator then appointed a "master of cavalry" (*magister equitum*) as second-in-command to assist him. Dictators were thought to possess the undivided power of the old kings of the city, and they surrounded themselves with symbols of royal power; perhaps for this reason, they were bound by a series of ritual prohibitions limiting their conduct. A dictator remained in office for six months or for the duration of the emergency, whichever was shorter; meantime the consuls remained in office, but served under the dictator's command. The roots of this office certainly lie in the wars and civic disturbances of the fifth century.

Annual magistracies require a process of selection. In later periods, Roman citizens, meeting in assemblies, elected individuals to fill the offices (see Chapter Three). Such assemblies certainly functioned during the fifth century, and they may even have functioned under the kings, but little is known of their powers and mode of operation then. In the first century B.C., an assembly of curiae (*comitia curiata*) met to ratify the choice of officials made by others, to witness the inauguration of priests, and to approve certain adoptions and wills. By that date, when this "curiate" assembly met, each of the thirty curiae was represented by a single citizen, who cast its vote. In early Rome, its meetings must have been better attended, but its functions may not have been different: Registering assent or witnessing the actions of leaders may have been all that ever was expected of it. Assemblies organized by tribes or by centuries also operated during the first century of the Republic's existence. In later periods, the "Centuriate" assembly chose the highest officials and rendered judgments in important cases. It is uncertain when it gained these functions, but the mid-fifth-century law code of the Twelve Tables does mention a "greatest assembly" that gave judicial rulings in the same kinds of cases later judged by the centuries. The adjective "greatest" itself demonstrates that this was not the only citizen assembly at the time.

Some fifth-century laws give a glimpse of contemporary Roman society. According to Rome's historians much later, popular agitation to limit the consuls' power and to make the laws public by writing them down for the first time led to the creation in 450 of a special commission of ten men or "decemvirs" (*decemviri*). They were to hold supreme power for one year, superseding the consuls, and by the end of this year they were to produce a body of laws to regulate the Republic. In some accounts, a second such commission was chosen for the following year to complete the task. The final result was the "Laws of the Twelve Tables," which served for centuries as the fundamental text in Roman law. Accounts of both commissions are filled with the kind of elaboration typical of our sources. The second group of decemvirs was painted in especially tyrannical colors: One of them, Appius Claudius, lusted after Verginia, whose father killed her in order to prevent her from being seized by the would-be tyrant. This tale bears obvious similarities to the story of Lucretia and, like it, serves to justify attacks on the holders of legitimate offices. Claudius' actions supposedly resulted in the fall of the decemvirs and in the moderation of some of their measures. The laws, however, did exist, and some of their provisions survive.

That said, these Laws of the Twelve Tables were not a code in the modern sense. They attempted no systematic treatment of all of the law. Instead, they were a collection of specific, detailed, and narrowly focused provisions. They best fit a society where the family and the household are the fundamental units of social life, and agriculture and animal rearing the primary economic activities. The authors of the laws addressed aspects of marriage and divorce, inheritance, and the rights of a father over members of his household. They attempted to regulate disputes over the ownership of land and its boundaries, farm buildings and fences, livestock, fruit-bearing trees, and slaves, as well as conflicts that arose over injuries to persons or property. Procedural matters loom large. Rome possessed neither a police force nor a bureaucracy, so that plaintiffs themselves were responsible for notifying the other parties, for ensuring their attendance in person for trial in the Forum or Comitium, and for collecting any judgments awarded. When defendants did not appear for trial, the Twelve Tables authorized plaintiffs, after summoning witnesses, to seize defendants by force and bring them to court. (If the defendant was old or ill, however, the plaintiff had to provide a cart; cushions were optional.)

Debt and its consequences were among the lawmakers' central concerns. At Rome, as in other cities of the ancient Mediterranean world, debt could force small-scale farmers into a state of permanent dependency (see Chapter One). The Twelve Tables prescribed that creditors must assure the debtor's appearance in court, and must carry out all judgments. Debtors had thirty days to pay a debt in default or to satisfy a judgment against them. In the event that a debtor did not pay in time, the creditor could seize and hold him, unless some other person pledged to pay the debt if the debtor ran away. The creditor next brought the debtor to the Forum on three successive market days; if the debt still remained unpaid, he could then sell him into slavery "abroad, across the Tiber." Etruria lies across the Tiber from Rome and the rest of Latium, so these words "abroad, across the Tiber" may indicate that Romans could not legally be held as slaves in Rome itself or in Latium. Although the Twelve Tables mention it only in passing, one other way that a debtor might satisfy a creditor was by entering into a relationship of debt-bondage, or *nexum*; such individuals (*nexi*) served their creditor as long as the debt remained unpaid.

Rome and Its Neighbors in the Fifth Century

The circumstances in which the Romans found themselves changed dramatically around 500. In consequence, the fifth century seems to have been a difficult time for the inhabitants of Latium, Campania, and the Greek cities of the south. The settled coastal plains of the west and south were disturbed by the movements of peoples and bands of warriors beyond their margins. The inhabitants of the valleys and plateaus of the central Italian highlands did not live in an urbanized social environment. Villages were the chief settlements here, and in their economies the herding of animals seems to have been more important than agriculture. Raiding may well have been ubiquitous; some villages shared fortified hilltop places of refuge where they and their herds could take shelter when attacked. By the beginning of the fifth century, ruling elites had begun to merge and form federations. Although these combinations did not result in cities and the more highly organized life associated with them, they were capable of collective action on a larger scale than before, especially when it came to raiding, warfare, and self-defense.

One further aspect of life in the highlands added to the problems of the cities on the coastal plains. In response to famine, scarcity of land, or other misfortune, the highlanders of central Italy had developed the custom of dedicating some of their children to the gods, and then expelling them when they reached adulthood so that they would be forced to find homes and land elsewhere. This widespread practice, known as a "Sacred Spring," may well have been long established (considerable uniformity of language among these highlanders reinforces the likelihood that they had a common ancestry).

By the beginning of the fifth century, the highlanders—either as raiders seeking plunder, or young men looking for new homes—had begun to press on the coastal plains. In 473, the Greek cities of Tarentum and Rhegium attempted to prevent the Messapii of Apulia from sending out new settlements, and in consequence they suffered what Herodotus (7.170) calls the most severe defeat ever experienced by Greeks. The cities of the west coast—Greeks, Latins, and the Etruscans of Campania—also came under attack. In Campania, a warband from the highlands of Samnium captured Etruscan Capua in 423 and Greek Cumae around 420. Much later, the historian Diodorus Siculus (12.76.4) would report that these Samnites defeated the Cumaeans in battle, besieged and captured their city, enslaved the surviving men, and took for themselves the town and its women. Farther south, Lucanians attacked Thurii (a newly founded city on the site of Sybaris) in 433, and captured Poseidonia in 410. By the end of the century, Velia and Neapolis (modern Naples) were the only Greek cities remaining on the Tyrrhenian coast. Along the southern (or Ionian) coast, the major Greek centers survived, although by now their prosperity and power were largely eclipsed.

Latium suffered too, and very severely in the case of some cities. Sabines, Volsci, and Aequi emerged from the hills that bordered Latium in an arc from northeast to southeast; archeologists have found some of their fortified hilltop refuges. Rome itself suffered from their depredations, and some Latin cities fell. Roman authors would later report battles quite close to the city, and they would claim that Rome led the other Latins in the common defense. It may well be the Romans took this kind of lead, but we still remain ignorant of how it compared to the role played by some of the greater Latin centers, such as Tibur and Praeneste. In any event, by the end of the century Rome and its Latin allies had the upper hand. Steadily, Volsci, Aequi, and Sabines were first repelled, and then pushed back. In the process, Latin cities that had fallen or been abandoned were reoccupied as colonies (*coloniae*, singular, *colonia*). Here the victors established new settlers to serve as garrisons, gave them land around the town that had been freed by the victory, and organized it as a city-state with officials of its own. Last but not least, the new foundation was assigned a recognized place as an ally of Rome and the other Latin cities.

Roman tradition associated model figures with these wars. Gnaeus Marcius Coriolanus, who earned his third name or *cognomen* from his leadership of the army that captured the Volscian town of Corioli (its exact location is no longer known), left Rome because of his unpopularity there and took refuge with the Volsci he had previously defeated. Becoming a leader of the Volsci, Coriolanus led their armies against the Romans with great success, and (we are told) failed to capture Rome only because he heeded the pleas of his mother Veturia and his wife Volumnia, models of the virtuous Roman matron. Lucius Quinctius Cincinnatus provides a more positive example. In 458, Cincinnatus was summoned from his fields to serve as dictator after the Aequi had trapped a Roman army in the mountains. Within sixteen days, he had gathered an army, defeated the Aequi, rescued the beleaguered Roman army, resigned his dictatorship, and returned to his farm. There could be no better model of the modest and dutiful citizen. Although there is much embellishment in these stories, which undoubtedly grew in the telling, real people and situations may lie behind them.

Struggle of the Orders

In the fifth and early fourth centuries, Rome also faced severe internal conflicts that accompanied its foreign wars. Roman historians later included in their histories frequent reports of famine, and of strife over land and debt. Food shortages and quarrels over fields and their produce are common occurrences in small-scale agricultural societies, and the warfare of the fifth century, with its disruption of social arrangements and the devastation of fields, must have aggravated the situation. Competition between members of the Roman elite for leadership in the city may often have led to violence and disorder. This strife, however, was aggravated by deeper conflicts, reflecting aspects of the basic organization of the Republic and of Roman society in general. Modern scholars call this conflict the "Struggle of the Orders."

Certain kinds of conflict were endemic in the archaic city-states of both Italy and the Greek world. One concerned access to magistracies because, after the expulsion of a king, leading families often tried to monopolize the new offices in their communities. A second area of conflict concerned the ability of officials to punish at will. A third and final one involved the roles of magistrates and citizen assemblies, in particular the ability of such assemblies to choose officeholders freely and to make laws requiring or forbidding certain actions by magistrates. Each of these sources of strife was present in Rome during the fifth and fourth centuries, although all need not have been matters of controversy simultaneously.

Roman historians of a later date believed that a long conflict between two opposing groups, *patricians* and *plebeians*, characterized the first centuries of the Republic. To be a patrician, a Roman had to belong to one of a very few families. The origins of the patriciate are unknown: From the eighth century, in Rome and elsewhere, wealthy, powerful families assumed leading roles in their communities, and some, or most, of those that made up the Roman patriciate may have had their origins here. At any rate, Roman patricians claimed privileges that ensured their leadership of the city. Later, Rome's historians thought that patricians enjoyed the exclusive right to hold high office under the Republic. This belief can only be accepted with modifications, however. In the lists of those who served as consuls or military tribunes with consular powers during the fifth and early fourth centuries, the overwhelming majority of names do indeed belong to gentes that were either patrician or are known to have included patricians. But some entries, most of them concentrated in the first half of the fifth century, bear names that were plebeian at a later date. In a few instances, an official with a seemingly plebeian name may have belonged to a patrician branch of his family that subsequently died out without leaving a trace, but as a general explanation, this probably will not do. So in all likelihood, with the foundation of the Republic, certain families were able to establish a monopoly over the new offices, although it was perhaps neither as secure nor as absolute as Roman authors later believed.

Patricians also claimed to have exclusive rights over the religious life of Rome, a central aspect of communal life. It is true that priestly offices long remained the prerogative of the patriciate, and claims to secular offices also rested on a religious foundation. Roman kings and the magistrates who succeeded them possessed as a mark of their office the right to take the auspices (*auspicium*), rites by which an officeholder sought the approval of the gods to take up his office for the first time and, while serving, divine consent for all of his official actions. Patricians regarded the auspices as their own possession. In later centuries, in the rare instances when both consuls died in office, the auspices were thought in some way to return to the patricians. A patrician senator was then chosen as *interrex* for five days, followed by others in turn until one was able to arrange the election of new consuls. Roman historians believed that the interrex was a regal institution, with *interreges* serving between the death of one king and the installation of his successor. The name itself—"between kings"—would seem to confirm this belief.

The plebeians are much more shadowy than the patricians. Plebeians certainly far outnumbered patricians, but they need not have encompassed all of the inhabitants of Rome outside the patrician group: It remains possible, for example, that the clients of the great families counted as neither patricians nor plebeians. The Roman plebs was not a very homogenous group, since it contained individ-

Figure 2.3 *In this fresco of around 500 B.C. from the "Tomb of the Augurs" at Tarquinii, two men wrestle over three metal cauldrons which are probably the prizes of their contest. The cloaked figure to the left carries a curved staff or* lituus, *which was a sign of kingship and, at Rome, a mark of the priests known as augurs, who had charge of the "auspices." One of the chief ways to take the auspices was by defining a field of vision with a* lituus, *and then observing within it the behavior of birds. Here, the cloaked figure seems to be supervising the contest, while the lituus and the birds flying over the combatants may indicate that he was seeking to foretell the result.*

uals with a range of statuses and roles in the city. Some were not even poor, although most probably were. In the fifth and early fourth centuries, plebeians were able to supply leaders from their own ranks, so that some plebeians clearly had standing in the community. As a result, the mass of plebeians may not have been very unified in its concerns. Matters of land distribution and of debt would probably have concerned the poor more than the well-to-do, while access to office may have interested the leaders of the plebeians more than the bulk of their followers. In these circumstances, the plebeian leadership may have been more capable of mustering followers at times when debt, high food prices, and poverty were proving especially burdensome. Roman historians later believed that the plebeians' main weapon was the "secession," a kind of strike in time of war, and that their major successes derived from this. In a secession, plebeian members of an army would withdraw to a hill outside of Rome, choose their own leaders, and refuse to cooperate with the magistrates of the city until their grievances had been addressed.

Successes by the plebeians created a dual organization in the city. Consuls and military tribunes were seen as leaders of the Roman people as a whole, the populus Romanus, and they were expected to provide political, military, and religious leadership in matters of general concern. Meantime, the plebeians created a parallel organization of officials and cults that addressed only matters specific to the plebs and, at least in theory, did not affect the rest of the populus Romanus. The plebeians' first major gain was the right to choose their own leaders, the tribunes of the plebs (*tribuni plebis*); their title may have been intended to provide a clear contrast with the military tribunes (*tribuni militum*, literally "tribunes of the soldiers") who were, in many of these years, the Republic's chief officials. At the same time, plebeian tribunes, and the plebeian *aediles* who assisted them, established their own cult site at the temple of Ceres, the goddess of grain, on the Aventine hill; the close relationship between the chief officials of the city itself and the temple of Jupiter Optimus Maximus on the Capitol may have served as a model. In later periods, the Roman plebs met in tribes to elect tribunes, and this may well have been the case in the fifth century too.

Much of the early history of the tribunate is obscure. Roman historians later believed that the powers of the office all began with the elections of the first tribunes, but this almost certainly would not have been the case. By the second century, the tribunes of the plebs held a wide range of functions—protecting individuals, blocking official actions they considered improper, convening the senate, proposing legislation—but they did not acquire them all at once. At first, their responsibilities may have been limited to providing leadership, and to protecting individuals threatened with severe treatment by magistrates. Roman historians later agreed that a key complaint by plebeians concerned their vulnerability to arbitrary actions by magistrates. There are numerous tales of consuls executing or punishing individuals because of personal enmity, political differences, or the desire to seize their possessions. Many of the details may well be inventions, but the basic claim is probably accurate. *Auxilium*, the giving of aid, was central to the tribunes' office. They even had the right to intervene physically between an official and the targets of his wrath, freeing the victims or preventing the official and his attendants from seizing them. The authority of their physical presence was reinforced by their "sacrosanctity." Plebeians took an oath to regard anyone who laid hands on a tribune as an outlaw liable to be killed without penalty; the phrase used to indicate the nature of the penalty—"let him be accursed" (*sacer esto*)—shows that the culprit was in some way regarded as condemned to pay a penalty to the gods.

At the end of the fifth century, then, some of the characteristic political and religious institutions of republican Rome were already in place, although they would be greatly modified and expanded in succeeding centuries. At the same time, because of the constant warfare during the fifth century, the Romans preserved much of their leading role in northern Latium. Here, too, this base for their power would be much expanded in the following centuries.

SUGGESTED READINGS:

Beard, Mary, John North, and Simon Price. 1998. *Religions of Rome*, Vol. 1, *A History*; Vol. 2, *A Sourcebook*. Cambridge: Cambridge University Press.

Cornell, Timothy J. 1995. *The Beginnings of Rome: Italy and Rome from the Bronze Age to the Punic Wars (c. 1000–264 B.C.)*. London and New York: Routledge.

Gabba, Emilio. 1991. *Dionysius and the History of Archaic Rome*. Berkeley, Los Angeles, London: University of California Press. A study of how the Greek historian Dionysius of Halicarnassus put together his account of the history of early Rome.

Grandazzi, Alexandre. 1997. *The Foundations of Rome: Myth & History*. Ithaca and London: Cornell University Press.

Miles, Gary B. 1995. *Livy: Reconstructing Early Rome*. Ithaca and London: Cornell University Press.

3

ROME AND ITALY
IN THE FOURTH CENTURY

The fourth and early third centuries marked an important turning point in the Romans' history. From the middle of the fourth century, they clearly began to develop and elaborate the political system of the classical Roman Republic, which would govern the city and eventually much of the Mediterranean world for centuries. It was the same period, too, which saw Rome's domination of Italy firmly established, as well as the formation of those institutions and practices that would ensure its leadership not only there, but also in due course likewise across the Mediterranean.

FALL OF VEII AND THE SACK OF ROME

Early in the fourth century, a Roman victory made the city preeminent in its region. Around 396, the Romans succeeded in capturing the Etruscan city of Veii after a siege. Veii, about ten miles (16 km) from Rome, was a wealthy and powerful city-state, which, like Rome, dominated some of its smaller neighbors. In the fifth century, Rome and Veii had fought over land and over the leadership of smaller cities, without either gaining a distinct advantage. The Romans marked their victory by eliminating Veii as an autonomous city-state. Veii's land became Roman territory, and some of its citizens became Roman citizens. Rome also enslaved or expelled the remainder of the population, and Roman officials settled some Roman citizens on parts of Veii's territory that were made vacant as a result. Although the site of the city itself remained inhabited, it no longer possessed a full range of civic institutions, and functioned instead as a center for Romans dwelling nearby.

Rome's victory was matched by a defeat. Around 387, a large army of Gauls that had been plundering in the upper Tiber Valley moved down the river toward Rome, defeated a Roman army, and entered the city. In the opening decades of the fourth century, Gauls dominated the valley of the Po River and the northern portion of the plains along the eastern coast of the Italian peninsula. Their origins lie across the Alps in central Europe, and their advance into northern Italy formed part of a larger movement that would carry Gallic tribes to the margins of the Greek world, and even (in the third century) into Asia Minor. By the end of the fifth century, the Etruscan cities north of the Apennines were hard-pressed by Gauls, and some may already have been wiped out.

The Gauls did not have an urban culture and the social and political organization that went with it. Instead, their political life centered on aristocratic families and their armed retainers. Prominent leaders could assemble large forces, and they faced relatively few communal restraints on their actions. Gallic warbands, some apparently fairly large, would raid across the Apennines for centuries. Cities of northeast Etruria and the upper Tiber Valley were especially vulnerable to them, but their southern neighbors were not immune either. Such Gallic raids would persist, with decreasing frequency, well into the third century. Greeks and Romans would long continue to regard Gauls as uncivilized, warlike, predatory, and expansionistic. The Gallic sack of Rome did not have as long-lasting effects as the Roman capture of Veii, but it did leave its mark, and reports of Gallic invasions could lead to panic in Rome for centuries thereafter.

Roman historians would later make Marcus Furius Camillus the hero both of the final war against Veii and of the recovery after the sack of Rome. As dictator, he commanded the Roman army that captured Veii. After the Gauls had entered Rome, Camillus was supposedly once again made dictator, defeated the Gallic army, and recovered the treasure that the Gauls had taken from the city. As dictator yet again, he was reported to have had a central role in opening the highest offices to plebeians in 367, a crucial event in the Struggle of the Orders (see next section). In all, Rome's historians thought that he had been military tribune with consular powers six times and dictator five times. Camillus is perhaps as much a figure of myth as of history: Details of his life seem to have been continually embellished from the fourth century to the first century B.C. By the latter date, he had become, in history and in legend, virtually a second founder of the city. As a result, to tease out his actual accomplishments from the myth may well be impossible. Without doubt, however, he must have been one of the leading figures in Rome during the opening decades of the fourth century.

THE CITY AND ITS INSTITUTIONS IN THE FOURTH CENTURY

The political order that would govern Rome in later, better-documented centuries emerged in a series of reforms and reorganizations that began during the

the sacred boundary of the city of Rome, however, consuls and praetors possessed only a more limited kind of imperium, qualified by the term *domi* ("at home"); here, they had no authority to command troops, or to ignore or brush aside all lesser officials. More generally, imperium was associated with certain symbols thought to derive from the kings, such as lictors bearing fasces, the special toga (toga praetexta), and the curule chair. To symbolize their superiority, consuls had twelve lictors, while (in the third century at least) their inferiors the praetors had only two. On the other hand, dictators—greater than the consuls— had twenty-four lictors, supposedly the number possessed by the kings. Within the pomerium, the fasces were carried with the axes removed, so as to symbolize the officeholder's more limited right of punishment here.

In addition to consuls and praetors, the Romans also filled a number of lesser positions. From 366, they elected two *curule aediles* annually, an office created as the counterpart to the two plebeian aediles. Between them, the four aediles maintained temples and the city's streets, and they also supervised its markets, where they judged disputes arising from business there. *Quaestors*—an office that apparently dated back to the mid-fifth century—took care of public money. In particular, this responsibility required them to supervise the treasury (later, at least, located in the temple of Saturn), as well as to oversee the funds that generals took on campaign.

The ten tribunes of the plebs were the most important of the lesser officeholders. Like consuls and praetors, they possessed the right to summon citizens to vote. However, many of their most important powers were essentially negative, because it was they who—through their ability to block public actions that they considered unlawful or inappropriate—guaranteed the rights of citizens against ill-treatment by other magistrates (see Chapter Two). Tribunes were very much officials of the city, and, in later periods at least, they were prohibited from spending much time outside of it. Beyond the first milestone outside the pomerium, tribunes no longer possessed the ability to prevent consuls and praetors from acting as they wished, so that they could not interfere with a general on campaign.

Later, in the third and second centuries, tribunes of the plebs secured the passage of nearly all laws, but the early history of Roman legislation remains controversial. Roman laws or *leges* (singular, *lex*) were usually limited in scope, instructing or permitting officials to take certain actions, or setting up rules to regulate officeholders. A law was generally known by the name of the one or more officials who placed it before the citizens for a vote. Thus, a law proposed by Gaius Licinius and Lucius Sextius would be a *lex Licinia-Sextia*. During the last secession of the plebs, which took place sometime around 287, the dictator Quintus Hortensius sponsored a law, the *lex Hortensia*, that supposedly gave to citizen assemblies meeting under the presidency of a tribune of the plebs the right to enact laws binding on the entire community, rather than just on the plebs. However, later Roman historians thought that tribunes had begun to sponsor legislation right from the time when their office was first established in the early fifth century; thus many notices of such laws, and brief summaries of their contents, are preserved. At a very early date, patricians had possessed the right to approve all leg-islation before it was presented to the people, but the senate subsequently claimed this as its exclusive prerogative. Later, only tribunes and the Plebeian assembly were exempted from having to seek senatorial approval. It is possible that any leg-islation proposed by tribunes had once required the senate's consent if it was to be binding on all Roman citizens, and that what the lex Hortensia did was to free tri-bunes and the Plebeian assembly from this restriction hereafter.

The two *censors* held the only office that was not annual. From 443, these cen-sors replaced the consuls as supervisors of the *census* (see Chapter Two); usually elections would be held every five years, and the successful candidates would hold office for around eighteen months. The census only counted Roman citizens. However, it was much more than a mere enumeration of them; rather, in time it developed into an elaborate operation that assigned them to their proper places in the city. Censors were important figures, therefore, and this importance only increased after they began to choose the senate from the last decades of the fourth century (see Senate section). Their decisions could cause conflict. For example, critics of Appius Claudius Caecus, censor in 312, claimed that he passed over bet-ter qualified men for inclusion in the senate, and that he enrolled some residents of Rome itself (probably poorer citizens and freed slaves) in rural tribes rather than in the four urban tribes, which were considered to be less prestigious. Sim-ilar conflicts would recur in the following centuries.

This collection of officials did not form a government on the modern pattern. There was no central direction of policies, and there need be little coordination among officeholders. Higher magistrates did not possess the power to command or instruct lesser magistrates, although in specific instances they could forbid them to take any action at all. Either consul could block the actions of his col-league, who held the same office and possessed identical powers; there was no requirement that the two consuls (let alone any other group of officeholders) agree or coordinate their efforts. In particular, the ten tribunes of the plebs, who had the greatest powers of obstruction, were under no obligation to reach agree-ment among themselves about the value of laws or the propriety of official actions before any of them acted. Indeed, even a single tribune was entitled to proceed with a proposal or other action without regard for the opinions of his col-leagues. Any exercise of powers of obstruction, it should be noted, required the obstructing official to confront directly and personally the official taking the action to be blocked: "Intercession" (*intercessio*), the technical term for this step, derives from a verb meaning "to step between".

Senate

Their rights aside, Roman officials were expected to consult others before acting. In Rome itself, the senate filled this advisory role. Away from the city, officehold-ers sought advice from a smaller group, although it might include some senators

Later, if Festus is accurate, the impact of Ovinius' law would have been to transform the senate from a temporary collection of individuals, poorly placed to assert themselves as a group against magistrates, into a long-serving body independent of the annual magistrates and much better fitted to exert its collective weight in Roman public life.

At the same time, the Roman elite seems to have asserted itself against its more powerful and popular members. In the fourth century, a very small number of individuals dominated officeholding in Rome. Consequently, in the years between 366 and 291 fourteen men between them held fifty-four consulships, over one-third of the total, and eight of these fourteen held the office as many as thirty-eight times. These same men also held other offices, some more than once. The patrician Lucius Papirius Cursor was consul five times, served once as dictator, and once as magister equitum. Another patrician, Marcus Valerius Corvus, was consul six times and dictator twice; he is known to have held office twenty times. The plebeian Quintus Publilius Philo served as consul four times, and he also was chosen dictator, magister equitum, and censor. These repeated electoral victories are clear signs that such successful individuals possessed enduring prestige and popularity in the citizen assemblies, and it may well be that especially prominent officeholders would have faced few checks on their actions beyond the need to maintain popularity among the voters. By contrast, less fortunate members of the elite would have faced all the greater difficulty in reaching high office and in asserting themselves against their more powerful competitors.

Such concentration of power in a very few hands did meet resistance. In 342, Lucius Genucius, a tribune of the plebs, had a law passed that prohibited the holding of more than one office at the same time, or of the same office more than once in any ten-year period, a practice known as "iteration." For two decades or so, this law proved effective, with few men holding the consulship more than once; but in the 320s, when Rome was under pressure from war, some again held further consulships within ten years. The goal of restricting iteration would ultimately be attained, showing that opposition to the practice was strong, at least among the Roman elite. After 290, Romans who achieved success in their political careers were rarely consul more than once, only a few gained the office twice, and no more than a handful more than twice.

This limitation on multiple officeholding had important consequences. First, it spread the available offices over a slightly larger group, enabling some individuals to rise higher now than they had previously been able. Then, it meant that virtually every holder of an office was now inexperienced in it, and thus in need of advice. Finally, it lessened, although it did not eliminate, the importance of popularity; for anyone to court popularity in the hope of staying in office over an extended period was now pointless. As a result, in the course of their career politically active individuals were more likely to focus their attention on the senate; its importance rose as a result, and senators were more prone than ever to be very supportive of its claims to privilege.

Assemblies of Citizens

Underpinning offices and senate were assemblies of citizens who chose new office-holders and authorized important public actions. Roman assemblies, however, were not representative bodies of the kind found in modern states. Instead, adult male Roman citizens listened to debates personally, and voted directly and openly not only to elect new leaders every year, but also to approve (or reject) proposed laws. Elections, the enactment of laws, decisions on war and peace, trials for public crimes, and discussions of other state business all took place in large public meetings where citizens, by their votes, chose officeholders, accepted (or rejected) policies and laws, and issued verdicts in trials. These gatherings were open to any citizen who wished to come, so that attendance could vary markedly from one occasion to another, and the composition of no two assembly meetings would ever have been exactly the same. Assemblies were also a focus for competition and conflict. In later, better-documented periods, we find ambitious members of the city's elite seeking popularity among the citizens and alliances with individuals who could influence votes. In addition, assemblies, and the preparations for them, served as opportunities for citizens as a body to voice their discontents.

In public meetings, the officials of the city kept a firm control over the agenda. Only holders of certain offices—consuls, praetors, and tribunes of the plebs—possessed the power to summon citizens to meetings to elect new officeholders, to discuss matters of importance, and to decide on laws and policies. *Contiones* (singular, *contio*) were occasions just for discussion and debate. The official who had called the meeting addressed the crowd himself, and also brought forward others whose opinions he wished citizens to hear. *Comitia* and *concilia* were assemblies where they actually voted. These assemblies met only at Rome—so that any citizen resident elsewhere who wished to vote had to come to the city to do so—and the voting had to be completed within a single day. Once again, the official who called the meeting controlled the agenda, and the assembled voters could do no more than accept or reject the candidates or the proposals put before them. When assemblies gathered for a discussion or a vote, the senate met at the same time in a nearby temple or other sacred building to provide advice. At any assembly, therefore, ordinary citizens had little freedom of speech or initiative. There was no opportunity for any of them to address the meeting; they could not put forward any proposal or any candidate for election; nor could they seek to amend a proposal presented by the presiding official. All they could do was to vote for or against. In practice, however, despite this official control of both the agenda and the speakers, citizens could still register dissatisfaction with the proceedings informally, through demonstrations, heckling, and occasionally even by destroying an official's insignia of office, such as his fasces or his official chair.

The fact that Roman citizens did not cast their votes in a mass made the census one of the city's vital political institutions. By the fourth century, it had become highly complex, and had come to serve a larger range of functions than when it was first instituted in the sixth or early fifth century (see Chapter Two). Property, reputation, and place of residence remained fundamental to the operation of the developed census. Once new censors were chosen, all citizens made declarations to them, in which they identified themselves and their places of residence, and listed their property and their dependents. From these declarations, and on their assessment of each citizen's character, the censors assigned men to centuries and tribes and also made distinctions of age. Censors assigned the wealthiest to the centuries of the cavalry, while they placed those who were too poor to serve in the army in the single century of the *proletarii*. All those considered eligible for service in the infantry were placed in a further group of centuries, ones that were now arranged in a series of classes, each signifying minute gradations of wealth and status. Throughout this entire process, it should be remembered, censors maintained the right to examine any citizen's physical condition and way of life. They could express their disapproval of a citizen in various ways—by rebuking him publicly, by registering a cause for complaint in a "note" (*nota*) attached to his name in the roster of citizens, or by imposing penalties.

By the fourth century the census had shifted from being primarily an aspect of military organization. Membership in a century set voting rights as well as military duties, and it also determined eligibility for payments of *tributum*, assessments of money for emergencies that fell most heavily on the members of the wealthiest centuriae. Centuries, moreover, no longer strictly corresponded to forms of military service. For example, the *equites*, the cavalry in wartime, were now not recruited exclusively from the so-called equestrian centuries, and some of the men placed in the leading centuries of the infantry must have served on horseback in fact. At the same time, in all probability the complex hierarchy of the infantry centuries no longer corresponded closely to any distinctions in the military service that their members actually performed.

The categories established at regular intervals in the census were the basis of all assemblies. The Centuriate assembly (*comitia centuriata*), which only an official with imperium could summon, was organized like the army with the presiding official acting as a commander and the voters as soldiers. For this reason, it met only outside the sacred limits or pomerium of the city, since commanders could not issue binding orders to their soldiers within Rome. Voting was oral, and each citizen, when summoned to vote, signified his acceptance or rejection of any candidate or proposal by word of mouth. This voting was organized and tallied by centuries, which voted in turn. Each century possessed one vote, which was itself determined by the votes of a majority of the century's members who were present. Victory in a straight majority of centuries determined the outcome. In general, the Centuriate assembly elected new consuls, praetors, and censors, and voted on matters of war and peace.

Procedures in this assembly favored any presiding official, and also the wealthiest citizens. In elections, the former was entitled to accept or reject the names of would-be candidates, although it is unclear how freely this right was exercised in

BOX 3.1: *When recounting the alleged activities of Servius Tullius, sixth king of Rome, the historian Livy (1.42.4–43.9) described in detail his creation of the census. Together with a similar passage in Dionysius of Halicarnassus'* Roman Antiquities *(4.16.1–18.3), this is the most complete surviving account of the classes that made up the census. There remain problems with both accounts—in particular, elements of speculative reconstruction are detectible— and the link between a census class and its members' military equipment was almost certainly not as rigid as portrayed here. In any event, Livy's census certainly fits third-century conditions better than those of the sixth, where both he and Dionysius place their descriptions. Note that* juniores *were male citizens between seventeen and forty-five years of age, while* seniores *were older. Later, during the second century, the distribution of centuriae may have been changed in a way that reduced the influence of the first class.*

Servius Tullius then began by far the greatest work of peace. Just as Numa was the author of religious laws, so Servius shone among posterity as the founder of all distinctions within the city and of the orders that mark out the grades of fortune and dignity. For he began the census, a most useful measure for so great a future empire, since it distributed the burdens of war and peace, not individually as before, but according to level of wealth. From the census, for use in war or peace, he then defined classes and centuries and the following gradations.

From those who had a census of 100,000 *asses* [a monetary unit] or more, he formed eighty centuriae, forty each of seniores and juniores; all were called the first class. The seniores were to be ready to guard the city, the juniores to wage war abroad. For armor, they were to provide helmet, round shield, greaves, and breastplate, all of bronze, as protection for their bodies; as weapons, they were to have a spear and a sword. Two centuriae of carpenters and smiths, who served without weapons, were added to these; they had the duty of making siege machines in war. The second class was instituted from those who had a census of between 75,000 and 100,000 asses; from these, both seniores and juniores, twenty centuriae were enrolled. They were to use a long rectangular shield instead of a round one; except for the breastplate, their remaining arms were the same as for the first class. Servius Tullius wished the census of the third class to be 50,000 asses. Here, he made the same number of centuriae as in the second class, with the same distinctions of age. There was no difference in their equipment, except that the greaves were omitted. In the fourth class, the census was 25,000 asses. The same number of centuriae were formed, but their equipment was different, because they had to provide only a spear and a javelin. The fifth class was larger, and thirty centuriae were formed for it; these men carried slings and stones for missiles. With them were hornblowers and trumpeters divided into two centuriae. The census of this fifth class was 11,000 asses. Those whose census was less than this, the remainder of the population, formed a single centuria and were exempt from military service.

When the equipment and distribution of the infantry had been arranged, he enrolled twelve centuriae of cavalry from the leading men of the city. He also formed a further six centuriae of cavalry—three had been instituted by Romulus—under the names by which they had been inaugurated.

practice. The votes of the rich carried far more weight than those of the poor, since the rich occupied a large number of small centuries. The eighteen equestrian centuries voted first, and, as each finished voting in turn, the results were publicly proclaimed to guide the vote of the remaining citizens. Next, the richest centuries of the infantry voted, followed in turn by those who were progressively poorer.* As the vote went down the scale, moreover, the number of centuries diminished, so that many more voters were crammed into fewer voting units. The *proletarii*, too poor to be eligible for military service, all occupied the single century which was slated to vote last. In any case, voting always ceased as soon as a sufficient number of centuries had voted to settle the outcome for or against. Frequently, therefore, the lower centuries, which contained the great mass of citizens, would never have been called upon to vote at all, in particular whenever the rich showed themselves to be in broad agreement.

Assemblies of tribes were neither as complex nor so blatantly weighted toward the rich as was the Centuriate assembly, although poorer citizens, especially if they lived far from the city, may have found it hard to attend these assemblies, too. As we saw in Chapter Two, every Roman citizen belonged to a tribe determined by place of residence. Those who lived in Rome itself filled four "urban" tribes, while those resident elsewhere belonged to one of the "rural" tribes whose number was slowly increased as Rome's power expanded; by 241 that number had reached thirty-one, where it remained. Potentially, therefore, the votes of members of "rural" tribes could carry more weight in these assemblies, if those members could afford to be present.

Tribunes of the plebs summoned citizens by tribes to elect their successors as tribunes or to accept or reject proposed laws; whenever a tribune did this, the assembly was known as the Plebeian assembly or *concilium plebis*. On other occasions, consuls or praetors summoned the tribes to fill certain minor offices; they probably did not preside over assemblies to vote on legislation until much later. Again, in all these instances citizens cast their votes one tribe after another; the voting order was determined on every occasion by lot, with each tribe in turn accepting or rejecting the candidates or the proposals under consideration. The first candidates acceptable to a majority of the tribes filled the offices. A law, too, passed (or was rejected) as soon as the bare majority of tribes for or against was attained; voting ceased at that point. In these assemblies, therefore, many of the citizens present could not know until well into the day itself whether or not they would in fact be called upon to vote.

---

*Eventually, a slight modification was introduced whereby a single century chosen each time by random lot from among the wealthiest juniores centuries of the infantry voted before the cavalry.

Table 3.1 Roman Assemblies

	Centuriate assembly	Tribal assembly	Plebeian assembly
Composition	All citizens	All citizens	Only plebeians
Voting Units	193 centuries	35 tribes (after 241 B.C., 31 rural and 4 urban)	35 tribes
Presiding Officials	Consul or praetor	Consul or praetor	Tribune of the plebs
Elections	Elects consuls, praetors, and censors	Elects curule aediles, and quaestors	Elects tribunes of the plebs, and plebeian aediles
Legislative Powers	Normally votes only on issues of war and peace	Votes on proposals made by a consul or praetor	Votes on proposals made by a tribune of the plebs
Judicial Powers	Hears citizens' appeals on capital charges	Issues verdicts in trials	Issues verdicts in trials

The City, Its Gods, and Its Priests

Religion formed an important part of Rome's organization, and the prominent remains of cult places show that this was true from the beginning of the city. Roman religion cannot be separated from the city and its public institutions or from the social groups, neighborhoods, towns, and villages that made up the Republic of the Roman people; in all these, there was hardly any body with a sense of common identity and interests that lacked its own divinities, which it worshipped in its own ways. Thus, Rome itself had its protecting divinities, and the city's officials and priests took the lead in cultivating them. Households contained shrines to the *lares*, ancestral spirits, and the *penates*, the protective divinities of the house, while old aristocratic families maintained their own special relations with major gods. Away from Rome, the towns and villages inhabited by Roman citizens had their own special temples, shrines, and cult activities. In the countryside, some forms of religious activity concentrated around crossroads.

Other practices centered on individuals and their concerns, and they were not as bounded by family, neighborhood, or even citizenship as were the cults of the Roman people. When confronted with difficult choices or stressful situations, many people made vows to favored deities, to be fulfilled if and when the desired outcome should be achieved. Those about to undertake journeys or projects could try to determine the attitude of the gods towards their plans through rites of divination. Some especially prominent shrines, even outside of Roman territory, drew such pilgrims from considerable distances. The temple of Fortuna Primigenia in the allied city of Praeneste, for example, drew many seeking good fortune in their activities (see Chapter Six). In the fourth century and later, healing shrines dotted much of rural central Italy: At many, archeologists have found terracotta feet, hands, limbs, eyes, and other anatomical models left by worshippers as tokens of their vows.

Figure 3.2 *In this fifth-century relief from Clusium, officials on the left observe contestants in* ludi. *The farthest left of the participants in these games is probably an armed dancer, while a female dancer and a flute player are immediately to his right. The figures on the platform are clearly officials, since the one in the middle carries a curved staff or* lituus. *The seated figure to his right is a scribe, writing the results of the games (or of the judges' decisions) on a tablet.*

The "augurs" were at least as important. Like the pontiffs, they possessed their own areas of expertise, central to the political organization of the city. The first of these were the auspices, essential to an official's power. Before taking office or before beginning any public action, an official was expected to consult Jupiter, the god of the auspices. This could be done by watching the flight of birds or by observing the feeding of chickens kept for the purpose. Although magistrates performed the rite, it was the augurs who were thought to be the experts in its proper forms and in the interpretation of the results. Augurs also possessed knowledge of the rituals necessary to "inaugurate" certain places. Consequently, magistrates and pontiffs could dedicate sacred sites, such as temples and shrines, only after the augurs had prepared the location. Augural responsibilities for rendering sites sacred had political implications: Places where magistrates performed many of their essential functions had to be inaugurated, as did locations where the senate met and the people voted. At first, there were only three augurs, but by the end of the fourth century their number had been increased to nine; at this time, plebeians were permitted to serve, filling about half of the positions. Like the pontiffs, the augurs too were increased to fifteen in the first century B.C.

Women possessed a more prominent place in the religious life of the city than they did in politics. The six Vestal virgins performed the rites of Vesta, the Roman goddess of the hearth, from her shrine near the Regia in the Forum Romanum.

Among their tasks was to tend the sacred flame; its extinction would endanger the city itself. The wives of the pontifex maximus and of the *flamen* or priest of Jupiter (the *flamen Dialis*) shared in some of their husbands' ritual responsibilities. Women of elite families, moreover, were thought to have dedicated the temple of the Fortune of Women (*Fortuna Muliebris*) early in the Republic, and this temple long served as a center for their religious activities. Women and girls had defined places in processions and in other celebrations. Some of the larger conflicts of Roman society had repercussions in this sphere too. In 295, patrician women prevented the participation of Verginia, a patrician woman who had married a plebeian, in rites at the temple of Patrician Chastity (*Pudicitia Patricia*); she then founded on her own a new shrine of Plebeian Chastity (*Pudicitia Plebeia*).

ROME AND CENTRAL ITALY

During the fourth century and the opening decades of the third, Rome became the dominant city in Italy. Wars, battles, victories, and defeats—all illustrated by acts of Roman heroism and the perfidy of Rome's enemies—fill Roman accounts of this century. Despite this wealth of detail, however, a clear narrative of the wars is not possible. There is the usual problem of exaggerated victory claims, not to mention a desire to blame Rome's enemies for all conflicts. Furthermore, the changing alliances of the period confused later authors, and Roman opportunism among these shifts may have embarrassed some. In addition, Roman families descended from the commanders in these wars occasionally made claims for their ancestors that were unjustified. Indeed, in some instances, Roman historians were unable to decide who had commanded in a battle or a campaign because several families claimed that their ancestors had been in charge.

No single continuous narrative is preserved for much of the early third century. The surviving books of Livy's monumental history break off in 290, and they only resume with a full account of the century's last two decades. The third-century portions of Dionysius of Halicarnassus' history, which originally reached to 264, survive only in fragments. From the biographer Plutarch we possess a life of Rome's enemy Pyrrhus. In other sources, records of the foundation of colonies are almost certainly near complete and their dates dependable; they serve as a good indicator of the spread of Roman power and the fates of nearby communities. By contrast, the details of wars and battles, accounts of diplomacy, and the assignment of credit for victory and blame for defeat, are all probably much less reliable.

Warfare and the Civic Order

War occupied a central place in the civic and religious structure of many city-states, but this was especially true of Rome. By the fourth century, Rome had evolved a pattern of warfare that centered on campaigns undertaken almost

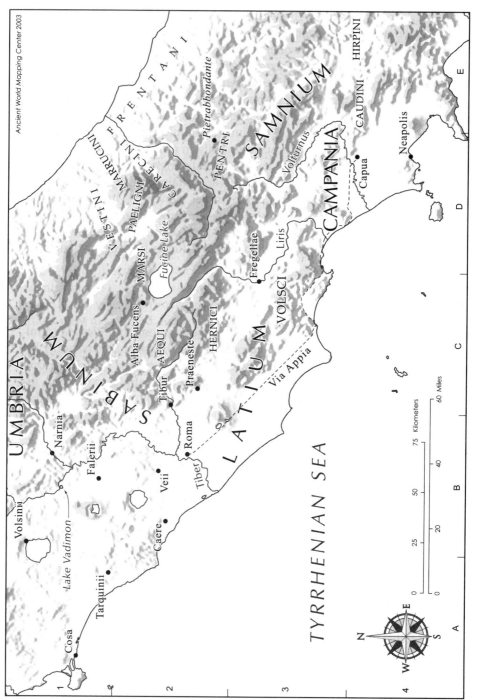

Ancient World Mapping Center 2003

UMBRIA

SABINUM

Volsinii

Lake Vadimon

Narnia

Falerii

Caere

Veii

Tiber

Roma

Tibur

Praeneste

AEQUI

Alba Fucens

MARSI

Fucine Lake

PAELIGNI

VESTINI

MARRUCINI

CAECINI

F R E N T A N I

FRENTANI

Pietrabbondante

PENTRI

SAMNIUM

HIRPINI

CAUDINI

Volturnus

Capua

Neapolis

CAMPANIA

Liris

Fregellae

HERNICI

VOLSCI

LATIUM

Via Appia

Cosa

Tarquinii

TYRRHENIAN SEA

N E S W

25   50   75   Kilometers

0   20   40   60 Miles

A   B   C   D   E

1

2

3

4

Map 3.1 *Latium and Campania*

In the third quarter of the fourth century, Roman commanders proceeded to wage wars and make alliances with states that were more powerful than their nearest Latin or Etruscan neighbors; in the process, they succeeded in extending Roman power over all of Latium and northern Campania. In Campania, the invasions of the fifth century had not eliminated city life. Instead, victorious groups of warriors from the highlands had largely adopted the urban lifestyle of those they had defeated, creating in the process a culture with marked Greek, Etruscan, and Italic elements. In the fourth century, the cities of northern Campania had rallied around the leadership of the largest city, Capua. These *Campani* fought against the cities of southern Campania, against Neapolis (modern Naples) and other cities of the coast, and against the Samnites to their east.

During the fourth century, the Samnites were the strongest group in the central highlands. In the valleys of Samnium, archeological evidence reveals a dense pattern of rural settlement with the inhabitants living in scattered villages, where they raised crops, vines, and livestock. City-states had not taken root here, but a powerful military confederacy of tribes had emerged. The district, or *pagus*, governed by its own magistrate and assembly, was the basic political unit. Each pagus comprised a few neighboring villages, a shared fortified hilltop refuge that was often small and inaccessible, and rural sanctuaries that served as cult centers for the scattered population. Groups of *pagi* in turn formed larger units or tribes—Hirpini, Caudini, Carecini, Pentri—each with its own officials and assemblies. Together, the four tribes named made up a larger Samnite confederacy, with its own leaders and cult sites, such as the large rural sanctuary at modern Pietrabbondante. Both the tribes and the Samnite confederacy itself, it should be noted, really only functioned as groups in time of war. The Samnites were very aggressive, and they possessed a formidable military reputation.

In the late 340s and early 330s, Roman armies fought Latins, Volsci, Campanians, and possibly Samnites, while Campanians and Samnites also conducted wars of their own. The details of all these conflicts are obscure, marked by shifting alliances that would greatly confuse later Roman writers. Capua and its allies appealed to Rome for help against the Samnites, who were pressing against communities in the lower Volturnus River valley, one of the chief routes from the Samnite highlands to the coastal plains of southern Latium and Campania. The result was what later authors would call the First Samnite War (343–341), although it is far from clear how much fighting between Romans and Samnites actually took place.

At about the same time, the Latin War (341–338) marked the end of any autonomy for the Latin cities. Fearing Roman encroachment, some of these cities joined to oppose Rome, an event that Roman authors later would portray as a revolt. The Latins received some assistance from Volscian and Campanian communities; the Samnites, on the other hand, because they had ambitions in the valley of the Liris River, took Rome's side in this war. In 340, the Romans won a major victory in northern Campania. The actions of one of the consuls in command went into legend. Titus Manlius Torquatus, this consul's son, killed an enemy soldier in single

Seeking to hold new territory or allies by founding colonies was an old Roman and Latin practice (see Chapter Two), but now the process became considerably more formalized and under Rome's exclusive control. Colonies were to be fully functioning city-states with their own fighting forces and capable of their own defense. In some colonies, the settlers remained Roman citizens and were enrolled in a tribe. Such citizen colonies were small—300 adult men—and they were generally situated along the coast, at harbors, or at the mouths of rivers. Most colonies were larger, however, with 2,500, 4,000, or 6,000 adult male settlers; colonists in these new communities lost Roman citizenship, but they received instead the privileges enjoyed by the citizens of towns with Latin status. From the late fourth to the early second century, the Romans established at least fifty-three colonies in Italy at locations open to enemy attack, in recently subjugated regions liable to revolt, at strategic river crossings and road junctions, and on vulnerable sections of coastline.

To create a colony, the Romans chose three men (*triumviri coloniae deducendae*), generally high-ranking former magistrates, to lead out the colonists to a site, and there give them land and establish the necessary institutions of self-government. Each colony was to have as its center a fortified settlement, which was the residence of most of the colonists and the site of its government and public cults. In some cases, the founders located the new settlement in a town or fortification from which the original inhabitants had been expelled; in others, they began the process of building a completely new town. Alba Fucens, founded in 303 on land taken from the Aequi, and Cosa, established in 273 on land that Etruscan Caere lost, are the best-known Latin colonies of the period. Both were founded on high, inaccessible hills. Excavations have shown that the founders fixed the line of the urban fortifications, and marked out the streets and the sites for the local forum, comitium, and temples. In the process, triumvirs and settlers sometimes appropriated sacred sites of the displaced population; on other occasions, they created new sites, patterned on Rome's. One Roman writer later would describe colonies like these as "small images of the Roman people" (Gellius, *Attic Nights* 16.13.9). In Latin colonies, a few colonists received larger allotments so that they might serve as the governing elite of the new city.

To found colonies and make viritane assignments, Roman magistrates had to survey and subdivide extensive tracts of land. With relatively simple instruments that enabled them to lay out right angles and measure straight lines, Roman surveyors constructed networks of boundary paths in order to divide tracts of land into large rectangles or squares; they then subdivided these into the plots that individual settlers would receive. Traces of such divisions, detected through aerial photography or careful mapping on the ground, have been found at a number of fourth, third, and second century colonies and viritane assignments.

In the wars of conquest and the political accommodations that followed them, Roman officials developed the military alliances and the institutions that would enable them to dominate Italy and, later, much of the Mediterranean world.

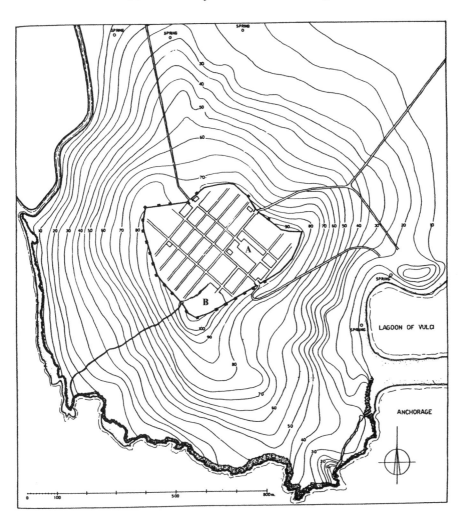

Figure 3.4 *The Latin colony of Cosa, founded in 273, occupied a high and easily defensible hill along the coast overlooking a nearby Etruscan town. This plan of the site shows the line of the walls and the sites of the town's (A) forum and (B) arx (the equivalent of the Capitol), necessary for a civic life on the model of Rome.*

Rome, like other city-states, did not possess a bureaucracy or an elaborate political and administrative establishment. It would be an impossibility for Roman officials to continue expanding their state indefinitely if they intended to govern new territories and their inhabitants directly, or if they wished to exploit subordinate communities to the full. Rather, in their efforts to bind communities, the Romans instead created a hierarchy of settlements defined by relationship to themselves. Thus some were deemed to be fully a part of the Roman political order; others shared partially in Roman rights; still others remained ostensibly

subsequent construction of another aqueduct in 272, *Anio Vetus*, by the censor Manius Curius Dentatus, confirms that the growth of the urban population continued throughout the period of Italian expansion.) The second project was a long road from Rome to Capua in Campania that would become known as *via Appia*. This road, primarily military in purpose, was intended to give armies a faster, easier march from Rome, where they first were mustered, into the region around Capua. Its construction is a clear sign of how intense operations were in Rome's wars with the Samnites, and probably also an indication that Roman leaders expected these wars to be long-lasting. Later, other censors would arrange for the construction of further roads to speed armies into regions of intense campaigning.

From 312, the Romans also sent commanders and armies against other cities and confederations, a proof of the state's extensive resources. In 311, Roman armies advanced up the Tiber Valley against the Etruscan cities of Perusia, Cortona, and Arretium, and three years later, they would campaign against another Etruscan city, Volsinii. These wars generally ended in truces, either for a single year or sometimes for as long as fifty years. In 299, however, the Romans did found a Latin colony at Narnia, less than fifty miles (80 km) up the Tiber from the city. Between 306 and 304, Roman armies overcame the Hernici and the Aequi, in the hills to the southeast of Rome. These campaigns were said to have been especially harsh, with many of the hill towns of the Aequi destroyed and their populations massacred. Their neighbors—Marsi, Paeligni, Marrucini, Frentani, and Vestini—made peace with Rome, presumably on Roman terms, between 304 and 302. Again, the Romans founded several new colonies on confiscated lands.

The Third Samnite War (298–290) secured Rome's leadership. Hostilities seem to have begun over Roman activities in Lucania. By the end of 297, a coalition of Samnites, Etruscans, Umbrians, and Gauls formed, although its actions were not well-coordinated. In 295, the two consuls of the year decisively defeated a force of Samnites, Umbrians, and Gauls in a great battle at Sentinum in Umbria. In 291, another Roman consul defeated the Samnites at Aquilonia; soon afterwards, the Romans would establish the colony of Venusia nearby. After this defeat, the Samnites again made peace.

In many of these wars, the Romans created allies, rather than new citizens. Allied communities, too, contributed to the growing military strength of Rome. Greek Neapolis, for example, provided ships to supplement Rome's small navy. Others provided soldiers for the Roman army. Allied communities were expected to raise their own forces, but in war they served under Roman officers appointed by the commander of the Roman army to which they were assigned.

EXPANSION OF ROMAN HEGEMONY IN ITALY

In the century between the fall of Veii and the end of the Third Samnite War, therefore, the Romans had united Latium, parts of northern Campania, Veii and some of its smaller neighbors, and the former territories of the Aequi and Hernici as far as the Fucine Lake (Latin, Lacus Fucinus). In the wars of the fourth century, Rome had also emerged as the most powerful state in Italy. Away from this core, however, Roman power rested only on a few isolated colonies, dependent upon Rome for their safety, together with a number of often unwilling allies who were forced by circumstances to accept such a relationship for a time. Many of these communities were restive, some were hostile, and virtually all wished to pursue interests of their own. So here Roman ambitions and claims to leadership had to be continually asserted and reasserted; even so, the ample reserves of men of military age provided by the network of colonies and municipia gave Rome an advantage that would become more marked through the third century.

Wars in Central and Northern Italy

The pattern of annual campaigns in central and northern Italy that had characterized the last decade of the fourth century continued well into the third. In 290, just after the Roman victory in the Third Samnite War, Manius Curius Dentatus, consul in that year, ravaged the land of the Sabines, who lived in scattered villages, and then reached the Adriatic Sea. As a result of this campaign, the Romans established a Latin colony at Hatria, and made the Sabines Roman citizens without the right to vote. Roman armies also conducted regular campaigns into Etruria and Umbria, especially along the valley of the Tiber. These wars were complicated, with shifting alliances between states, and they often involved Gauls. In 284, the Gallic Senones defeated a Roman army at Arretium in northern Etruria. In the following year, by contrast, another Roman army defeated the Gallic Boii and some of their Etruscan allies at Lake Vadimon, about fifty miles (80 km) north of Rome. By 283, the Romans had expelled the Senones from a portion of their territory, which would become known as the *ager Gallicus*. There, the Romans would establish colonies at Sena Gallica (in 283) and Ariminum (in 268; modern Rimini).

In the 280s and 270s, Roman armies forced most of the cities of Etruria and Umbria into a dependent status. By 280, the Romans had made alliances with the Etruscan cities of Vulci, Volsinii, Rusellae, Vetulonia, Populonia, Volaterrae, and Tarquinii. Caere was treated more severely: Upon its defeat in 273, it became a municipium (without the vote) and some of its land was confiscated. By the 260s, few, if any, communities in Etruria, Umbria, and Picenum possessed any real independence. Attempts to reassert it were severely punished. The Picentes revolted in 269. When defeated, they lost territory—a Roman colonial commission established the colony of Firmum there—and they were made citizens without the vote; some Picentes were also deported to the southern margins of Campania. In Etruria, the revolt of Falerii in 241 was the last. A Roman army captured and destroyed the city, and then forced its inhabitants to settle at a nearby location more open to attack. Falerii's chief deity, the goddess Minerva, was moved to Rome as *Minerva Capta* (Captured Minerva).

Sharp internal conflicts characterized many Etruscan cities. The majority of their populations had only a restricted role in community government, and this limitation may have contributed to the persistent Etruscan defeats. In 265, the wealthiest and most powerful families of Volsinii lost control of their city and sought Roman intervention. Marcus Fulvius Flaccus, consul in 264, captured the city, which he destroyed, although in this instance, too, some of the survivors were then permitted to settle at a less defensible site nearby. When civic disturbances occurred in allied cities, Roman officials and the Roman senate usually supported the leading families, a policy which in many instances may well have encouraged these families to submit to Roman leadership.

Conquest of the South

At the end of the Third Samnite War in 290, Rome's hold over the Samnites and Lucanians was precarious, and its power over more distant communities was virtually nonexistent. In the first half of the third century, the Romans also campaigned regularly in the southern regions of the Italian peninsula, but these wars would involve a different kind of enemy, leading to changes in Roman methods of making war.

Roman officials quickly involved themselves in the affairs of the Greek cities of southern Italy. In 285, Thurii appealed to Rome for protection from the Lucanians and Bruttii. Gaius Fabricius Luscinus then forced the Lucanians to abandon their siege of Thurii, and he left a Roman garrison there for its protection. Shortly afterwards, other cities—Locri, Rhegium, and Croton—also successfully sought Roman protection. This growing Roman presence now alarmed the citizens of Tarentum, the largest Greek city in the region and often ambitious to lead the others. In 282, the Tarentines attacked and sank some Roman warships that had appeared outside their harbor, apparently in violation of an agreement between the two cities. The Tarentines then marched on Thurii, expelled its Roman garrison, and replaced the ruling oligarchy with a more democratic regime. Tarentum took these actions, it should be noted, while Rome was heavily involved in wars against Etruscans, Umbrians, and Gauls.

In the far south of Italy, the Romans were entering a region in turmoil. Tensions between oligarchic and democratic factions were common in the Greek cities there and in Sicily. Generally speaking, the more democratic leaders wished to give increased power and freedom of action to voting assemblies of citizens; they sought to enable these assemblies to instruct and restrain elected officials; and they wanted to open elected offices to a wider circle. Supporters of a more oligarchic order, on the other hand, sought to limit magistracies to the very wealthy, or perhaps even to the members of a few families; they wished to restrict the powers of citizen assemblies and their freedom of action; and they tried to elevate advisory councils of leading citizens, the local equivalents of the Roman senate, into the chief organ of government. Strife between such factions could lead to violence,

Map 3.3 *Southern Italy*

providing one of the chief reasons for other states to be called upon for help. Roman leaders earned a well-deserved reputation for favoring oligarchic groups over democratic.

At the same time, the Greek cities along the south coast of Italy were often under fierce pressure from the Samnites, Lucanians, and Bruttii. When threatened in this way, the cities would appeal to other cities and rulers in the Greek world for help. In the decades before Rome's intervention, the Tarentines and their neighbors had sought the aid of a number of strong military leaders who possessed more powerful armies than did most city-states. Agathocles was the most recent of them to respond. By the end of the fourth century, he had made himself ruler of the Sicilian city of Syracuse, and had begun to build up a military state—based on large numbers of mercenary soldiers—that encompassed much of the island and several cities in southern Italy. Agathocles died in 289 and his empire fell apart, but the Greek cities of southern Italy continued to turn to other powers from outside the peninsula. So in 281, when a Roman consul and his army entered Tarentum's territory in reaction to its earlier attacks on Roman ships and garrisons, the Tarentines sought assistance from Pyrrhus, king of the Molossians in Epirus across the Adriatic. Pyrrhus' intervention would differ from earlier interventions in its scale and in its consequences.

Dramatic changes had occurred in the political and cultural life of the Greek world during the decades before and after 300. In the fifth century, city-states had dominated Greek political, social, and cultural life, and monarchy and tyranny had largely disappeared. Kingship, as well as forms of community organization that were not centered on the city, survived only among some societies on the margins of the Greek world, where Greeks viewed the inhabitants as barbarous. In the fourth century, however, monarchy became a central political institution again, and kings would now overshadow the city-states of Greece. Changes in warfare fuelled this transition. City-states had made war with citizen armies fighting limited campaigns. In the fourth century, by contrast, military operations grew larger in scale and were less bound by traditional limits. Mercenary soldiers joined levies of citizens or subjects, and novel, more expensive techniques for besieging cities and fighting battles were developed. Individual city-states possessed neither the population nor the wealth to engage in warfare on this scale for long. It was the kings on the margins of the Greek world who did.

The rise of the kings of Macedon was central to this shift in political and military organization. Macedon was a land of villages and towns, ruled by kings who were strongly influenced by Greek culture. In the fifth century, Macedon had been relatively weak, open to foreign invasions and divided by feuds between members of the royal family and their followers. Greek cities to its south had intervened in its wars, plundered and exploited its territory, and founded colonies along its margins. Then in the fourth century, Macedonian kings began to gain a firmer hold over their kingdom, and started to turn it into a formidable military power. Philip II (reigned, 359–336) in fact became the dominant power in Greece.

His army comprised Macedonians performing their traditional military service for the king, troops contributed by allies, and mercenaries serving the king personally for pay and plunder. After his victory over an alliance of cities in 338, Philip succeeded in uniting most of the cities of Greece into an alliance known as the League of Corinth, and gaining for himself the permanent post of *hegemon* or commander. As hegemon, he had the right to call on the allies to contribute soldiers and money for common military expeditions under his command.

Philip's son, Alexander III (Alexander the Great), vastly extended the territory under his control. With the forces under his command, he invaded the Persian empire, the largest, richest, and most powerful empire of its day, stretching from the Greek world to its west as far as India to its east, and from central Asia in the north to the southern frontiers of Egypt in the south. In campaigns that lasted until his death in 323 at the age of thirty-three, Alexander defeated Persian forces in a series of major battles, led his armies through the principal regions of the empire, and even eliminated its king and the monarchy itself. Before his early death, Alexander began to establish his own rule instead. The phenomenal nature of his accomplishments made him a towering figure to most of his contemporaries and successors, and many considered him to be a god. In later generations, plenty of kings and generals—Romans among them—would seek to imitate him and to be hailed his equal.

Alexander's empire did not long survive him, however. Rather, for decades following his death, his generals engaged in lengthy struggles for power, wealth, and dominance. By the end of the fourth century, the more successful leaders, now calling themselves kings, had begun to build rich and powerful states with elaborate military establishments. These new monarchies were often unstable and liable to rapid shifts in their frontiers and territory. Wars, conspiracies, and assassinations were common occurrences. Although Greek cities were able to preserve a certain civic existence within these new states or even, if especially fortunate, to maintain a precarious independence, they still lost much of the control over their own affairs that had long been so integral to Greek political ideals. Now cities had to fear such royal intrusiveness, the imposition of taxes if they were too weak and vulnerable to avoid them, and occasionally the establishment of a garrison in the city itself or in its territory.

Some of the new kingdoms would survive over the following three centuries, and together they would create a distinctive political culture—now known as Hellenistic—that was to exercise a marked influence even in lands that no Greek or Macedonian king ever succeeded in ruling. Hellenistic kingship was personal rather than ethnic or territorial. Kings ruled because they were wealthy, powerful, and able to rule, not because they were governing long-established states according to traditional procedures. In these circumstances, kings and their supporters placed special emphasis on the material bases of their power—great wealth and large armies. They also advertised the personal qualities of the ruler, exaggerating or inventing deeds and characteristics that would show him to be

Tarentum became a Roman ally. Wars with the Samnites and the Lucanians continued into the 260s. The foundation of Latin colonies at Paestum in 273, Beneventum in 268, and Aesernia in 263 mark their defeat. By this time, the Romans had reduced to the status of allies, voluntarily or otherwise, around 150 once-independent communities. Another important consequence of Rome's war with Pyrrhus and the associated involvement in the affairs of the Greek cities of the south was an altogether closer engagement with the Greek world and its culture. Although there would be no direct Roman participation in the wars of the Hellenistic states until the last decades of the third century, well before that Rome was no longer just an Italian power. Hellenistic monarchies and leagues of Greek cities now had to factor Rome into their plans, and their wars affected Rome.

WAR AND THE ROMAN STATE

In over a century of virtually continuous warfare, Roman officials and armies established their city as the most powerful in Italy, and they erected around it a network of alliances that made Rome a key participant in the larger politics of the Mediterranean world. This pattern of regular warfare merits explanation, although no single element or cause can serve as the key to all of Rome's wars.

Several features of Roman society and politics encouraged acceptance of, and perhaps the active search for, frequent wars. Possession of the military virtues was central to the self-image of the Roman elite, to the ways they competed among themselves for offices and honors, and to their claims to leadership in their city and over the elites and inhabitants of other communities (see Chapter Four). Regular warfare provided ambitious Romans with the opportunity to display their bravery and skill, and to accomplish deeds that would spread their fame among the citizens—vital achievements for those who wished to reach high office. Indeed, the office of consul, the highest in Rome and the focus of elite competition, was itself substantially military in nature, and its occupants would have expected, and probably desired, to command armies in the field. Military command, moreover, had given successful members of the Roman elite a leading role both in their own city and in the surrounding ones of allies and dependents. To maintain this position, they felt obliged to punish cities that challenged Rome or refused to remain subordinate, and equally to protect dependent communities or groups within them who proved loyal.

Decisions over war and peace were not just for the most prominent members of Rome's elite to take. The Roman practice of campaigning virtually every year required consensus among the populace and between the voters and the members of the ruling elite. Citizens voting in assemblies regularly chose the men who would lead them in war, and it was citizens again who served in the forces that fought the wars. Successful warfare brought tangible benefits to many Roman citizens. For example, victorious armies plundered, and even common soldiers could expect to share in the loot. Land, too, was a prize. The captured land distributed in the colonies and viritane assignments of the period would have enabled many poorer Romans to receive a plot that was sufficient to support themselves and their families. Demands from the poor for land redistribution were not the cause of turmoil at Rome, therefore, that they often were elsewhere; wealthy Romans had comparatively little cause to fear that their property was in danger. In the last decades of the fourth century, moreover, our sources preserve regular accounts of mass enslavements of defeated enemies. Some of the newly enslaved probably were sold outside of Italy. Others were put to work on the lands and in the households of Roman citizens, beginning a gradual shift away from the labor systems of archaic Rome, which had been based on dependent clients and debt-slaves. It may be no accident that a law passed near the end of the fourth century prohibited the old practice of *nexum*, which condemned Roman citizens to bondage if they failed to repay their debts (see Chapter Two).

Altogether, the acquisition of wealth through regular campaigns no doubt reduced the level of internal conflicts in the city. Accounts of the fifth and much of the fourth century record recurrent strife between the elite and segments of the populace over land, debt, and access to offices. Such conflicts seem to have lessened in the late fourth and early third centuries, and this shift—which included an end to the Struggle of the Orders—may itself have been a consequence of the wars. The demands of the poor for land and freedom from debt, and the desires of the rich for a dependent labor force for their estates, could all now be met at the expense of Rome's neighbors.

Internal factors are not the whole picture, however. Roman historians later regarded these wars as essentially defensive in nature, aimed at restraining aggression by others or at punishing disloyalty by cities which had supposedly accepted Roman leadership. From this perspective, therefore, Roman expansion was a successful response to the aggressive actions of others. Such a viewpoint may indeed plausibly explain some campaigns against some enemies, but it is unlikely to apply universally. Even so, it is important to recognize that other states, whether friend or foe of Rome, had their own agendas, ambitions, and military traditions. Some of these communities were themselves aggressive and expansionist, and they may, on occasion, have forced the Romans to respond to their initiatives. Unfortunately, the surviving evidence, which focuses so strongly on Rome itself, does not permit the full recovery of these other, less successful histories.

SUGGESTED READINGS:

Beard, Mary, John North, and Simon Price. 1998. *Religions of Rome*, Vol. 1, *A History*; Vol. 2, *A Sourcebook*. Cambridge: Cambridge University Press.

Cornell, Timothy J. 1995. *The Beginnings of Rome: Italy and Rome from the Bronze Age to the Punic Wars (c. 1000–264 B.C.)*. London and New York: Routledge.

Hanson, Victor Davis. 1998. *Warfare and Agriculture in Classical Greece*. Berkeley, Los Angeles, London: University of California Press. Although Greek cities of the fifth and fourth centuries form the focus, the book's conclusions are equally applicable to war between the city-states of Italy.

Harris, William V. 1979. *War and Imperialism in Republican Rome, 327–70 B.C.* Oxford: Oxford University Press. A controversial examination of Roman attitudes toward war and the ways that they shaped Roman actions.

Salmon, E. Togo. 1967. *Samnium and the Samnites*. Cambridge: Cambridge University Press.

4

THE BEGINNINGS OF A
MEDITERRANEAN EMPIRE

In the 130 years following the end of the war with Pyrrhus, the Roman Republic became the dominant state in the Mediterranean. In the city itself, moreover, a new elite group, the nobility, emerged to take the lead in Rome's political structure; at the same time its foremost members became some of the wealthiest and most powerful individuals in the Mediterranean world. Participation in wars over a far wider geographical span, together with the consequent expansion of Roman power beyond the Italian peninsula, would now put major strains on the Republic's traditional structure and on its customary ways of making war and forging alliances.

SOURCES

No single continuous narrative survives for the entire period, but from the last two decades of the third century through the first third of the second century, the evidence is reasonably full and some of it is contemporary. The surviving books of Livy's history of Rome break off in 290 and resume with a full account only in 218; from this point, they run without interruption until 167, when the surviving text comes to an end. The biographer Plutarch wrote lives of five Roman commanders of the period: Quintus Fabius Maximus, Marcus Claudius Marcellus, Titus Quinctius Flamininus, Marcus Porcius Cato the Elder, and Lucius Aemilius Paullus. Finally, the Greek author Polybius (c. 200–after 118) wrote a "universal history," in which the theme of Rome's expansion from the middle of the third century to his own day was central; extensive portions of this work survive. As a young man, Polybius was active in Greek political and military matters, but after

167 he lived mostly in Rome, where he became closely acquainted with important members of the Roman elite. At the same time, inscriptions (Greek as well as Latin) offer us insights and information about a range of Roman practices both in Italy and elsewhere in the Mediterranean.

THE NOBILITY AND THE CITY OF ROME

The opening of offices and priesthoods to plebeians that occurred during the fourth and third centuries resulted in the formation of a new governing elite in Rome with a distinctive way of life. This elite, collectively known as the "nobles" or *nobiles*, would govern Rome and its empire throughout the period of expansion in the third, second, and first centuries. Archaic Rome had been governed by relatively few individuals from a small group of families. However, the city's new leadership, also a group of limited size, would differ from the old in significant ways. The patriciate was always an aristocracy of birth: Membership in certain families itself sufficed to grant patricians their place in the city and the associated privileges. In addition, especially prominent leaders of the archaic period possessed personal military followings that gave them a political importance irrespective of whether or not they held any formal political office. Although some patrician families would achieve prominent places in the new elite too, this elite was not an aristocracy of birth, nor did its leading members possess significant military forces of their own. Instead, individuals and families had to establish and maintain their place in the city within a framework of elective offices, priesthoods, and formal religious and political institutions.

Officeholding was central. The new nobility rested on its members' ability to win offices and gain priesthoods. In this context, it was above all the magistracies that a man held which marked out his own position in the city as well as that of his family. Indeed, the Latin word *nobilis*, in its most restricted sense, designates an individual with an ancestor who had been chosen consul. By its very nature, this new order was a highly competitive one. More contestants, patricians as well as plebeians, now sought a limited number of positions. In Rome, as in other city-states, offices were in practice open only to the rich, and, more particularly, only to those rich who maintained a respectable way of life—whose wealth, in other words, derived primarily from landholding, and not from trade or from the practice of a "sordid" profession, such as auctioneer or scribe or buying and selling in the market. The position of the new elite families, however, was less secure than that of the patriciate of the past. In each generation, these officeholding families had to provide new and successful seekers of offices; families that failed to do so could otherwise drop out of the governing elite. Meanwhile, a few men from families that had never held office did succeed in gaining at least lower magistracies; these individuals were termed "new men" (*novi homines*). If their descendants maintained and improved upon this success, they could become new members of the nobility.

The rise of the nobility accompanied, and reinforced, other developments in Roman public life. The emphasis on offices—and especially the office of consul—would result in the gradual creation of a hierarchy of positions, each of which conferred on its holders a successively higher status. In its developed form, these offices, from lowest to highest, would be quaestor, tribune of the plebs, aedile, praetor, and consul. The prohibition against holding the consulship more than once or twice became firmly established in the third century, and enabled two men to hold this office each year who had never done so before. The other offices tended to be held earlier, and since there was a greater number of openings for them, more families were able to compete successfully at this level. Some families in fact filled out the lower offices for generations without ever achieving a consulship. The tribunate of the plebs now came to serve not only as an office of value in its own right, but also as a desirable early stage in the career of members of prominent plebeian families. As a result, the tribunate lost much of its radical nature—although it retained the powers for this to return later—and tribunes became part of the established order, as did the Plebeian assembly over which they presided.

It was during the third and second centuries that the senate took on its leading role in the city, and these centuries in many ways marked its high point. This was the period when its "influence" or *auctoritas* peaked, in other words when its direction of affairs won highest respect. The censors began to enroll primarily former officeholders, who in practice would serve for life. At some point in these centuries, tribunes of the plebs gained the right to summon meetings of the senate; they also came to be enrolled in it after holding office. These two developments (which cannot be dated precisely) mark the integration of plebeian officials into the official order of the city. As a gathering of former officeholders, the senate came to be organized internally in the same hierarchical fashion as were the magistracies. Former consuls tended to lead in the senate because they had held the highest office, and those individual senators who were considered to have the most prestige dominated the meetings. Thus, the senate came to be seen as a store of virtues, prestige, and experience.

In this competitive and hierarchical environment, prominent individuals could be very protective and assertive of their claims to status. Members of Rome's elite liked to think that the pursuit of praise or fame (*laus*) and glory (*gloria*) was integral to their way of life. The Roman public virtues were primarily military—indeed, the primary meaning of the Latin noun *virtus* is manly courage—and they were closely linked to the holding of offices. It was above all military success that led to laus and gloria. In the first century B.C. the historian Sallust would even claim (*Catilinarian War* 7. 3–6) that competition for gloria was one of the key factors in Roman expansion. The primary source of fame was officeholding, and the higher offices earned a man greater esteem or *dignitas* than the lower. In the late second and first centuries, other forms of elite activity, such as skill in public speaking or in the law, also came to be seen as praiseworthy, but never to the same extent as holding magistracies. Officeholders wished their term of office to stand out in some way. Leading Romans missed no opportunity to proclaim their merits and accomplishments, and often asserted their superiority over the achievements of their competitors. Failure to recognize someone's accomplishments to the degree he expected—to be disrespectful to his dignitas, therefore—could provide a cause for lasting enmity.

Two examples may serve to illustrate the drive. First, in 221 Quintus Caecilius Metellus, who would be consul in 206, gave the funeral oration (*laudatio*) for his father; a summary of it is recorded by Pliny the Elder in the first century A.D. (*Natural History* 7.139–40):

> Quintus Metellus—in the oration in which he gave the highest praise to his father Lucius Metellus, who was *pontifex*, twice consul, dictator, *magister equitum*, member of a board of fifteen men to distribute land, and the one who first led elephants in a triumph during the First Punic War—wrote that his father had accomplished the ten greatest and best feats which wise men seek in their lifetime: He had wished to be the top warrior, the best orator, the bravest commander, to have personally directed the greatest affairs, to have the highest honor, to be the most wise, to be esteemed the most distinguished senator, to acquire immense wealth in a good way, to leave many children, and to be the most celebrated figure in the city. It fell to him to achieve all this, and no one else since Rome's foundation had been his match.

Second, the earliest of the epitaphs in the third-century tomb of the Scipios records that: "this man Lucius Scipio [consul in 259], as most agree, was quite the best of all good men at Rome." Both this epitaph and Metellus' funeral laudatio stress that the deceased had accomplishments that were greatest and best; perhaps even more significantly, both insist that the two men were widely seen as having had them.

The great pressure to assert a man's claims changed not just public life, but also Rome's physical appearance. The third and second centuries saw increasing elaboration of the city's ceremonial and religious life in ways that emphasized the power and glory of the official who staged the rites. Displays of wealth, luxury, and military power were at first limited to officeholders, but other members of wealthy and powerful families would eventually mount them too so as to add to the collective glory of their family. In the second century, according to Polybius (31.26), Aemilia, the wife of Publius Cornelius Scipio Africanus (see Box 4.1), wore rich clothes, rode in a smart carriage, and was accompanied by a large retinue of servants when she participated in religious observances with other women; in the rites themselves, too, she used ritual vessels made of gold and silver. After her death, her grandson by adoption, Scipio Aemilianus, gave these objects to his mother Papiria, who had remained at home during such functions, since she was too poor to make the appropriate display.

Since war was the chief arena in which members of the elite could exhibit their virtue and gain fame and glory, leading citizens craved public recognition of their military accomplishments. The chief celebration of victory was the triumph, a formal procession of a victorious general and his army through the city. The triumph was in fact an old ceremony in Rome. At first, the triumphal procession, which may have originated among the Etruscans, was primarily a rite intended to purify an army returning from battle or to thank the gods for a victory. In the late fourth and third centuries, however, under the influence of the elaborate ceremonies of the Hellenistic kingdoms to the east, the Roman triumph became less a celebration by the community and the army than a glorification of the virtues and achievements of the officeholder who had commanded the army in its victory. In the triumph, the victorious general or *triumphator*, accompanied by senators and other elected officials, led his army through the city together with prisoners, displays of captured property, and tableaux and paintings depicting key episodes in his victory. The figure of the triumphator stood out clearly, because he wore the gold and purple costume of the old kings, he painted his face to resemble the cult statue of Jupiter Best and Greatest in the temple on the Capitoline Hill, and he rode a four-horse chariot, just as did representations of the god.

BOX 4.1: *The triumph of Scipio Africanus at the end of the third century as described by the historian Appian* (Punic Wars 66). *Note that mocking rituals formed a part of the triumph, just as they did of the processions that marked the Roman Games (see Box 3.2).*

Everyone in the procession wore crowns. Trumpeters led the advance, and wagons laden with spoils. Towers were borne along representing the captured cities, and pictures illustrating the campaigns; then gold and silver coin and bullion, and similar captured materials; then came the crowns presented to the general as a reward for his bravery by cities, by allies, or by the army itself. White oxen came next, and after them elephants and the captive Carthaginian and Numidian leaders. Lictors wearing purple tunics preceded the general; also a chorus of harpists and pipers—in imitation of an Etruscan procession—wearing belts and golden crowns, and marching in regular order, keeping step with song and dance. One member of the chorus, in the middle of the procession, wearing a body-length purple cloak as well as gold bracelets and necklace, caused laughter by making various gesticulations, as though he were dancing in triumph over the enemy. Next came a number of incense-bearers, and after them the general himself in a richly decorated chariot.

He wore a crown of gold and precious stones, and was dressed, in traditional fashion, in a purple toga woven with golden stars. He carried a scepter of ivory, and a laurel branch, which is invariably the Roman symbol of victory. Riding in the same chariot with him were boys and girls, and—on the trace-horses either side of him—young men, his own relatives. Then followed the men who had served him on campaign as secretaries, aides, and armor-bearers. After these came the army itself marshalled in squadrons and cohorts, all of them crowned and carrying laurel branches, the bravest of them bearing their military prizes. The men praised some of their officers, and ridiculed or criticized others; during a triumph there are no restrictions, and everybody can say whatever they like. When Scipio arrived at the Capitol the procession came to an end, and he hosted the traditional banquet for his friends in the temple.

The triumph was the single most important ceremony that any Roman in public life could hope to perform. Eventually a list of triumph-winners, the *fasti triumphales*, would be put on prominent display in the city to mark out their accomplishments for all time. The decision over whether or not a victory warranted a triumph was too important to be left to the commander alone. At some point, the senate asserted its control. In consequence, victorious commanders and their armies waited outside the *pomerium* while the senate debated their accomplishments. Because a triumph was so prestigious, conflicts were common. When the senate denied one to Gaius Papirius Maso, consul in 231, for his efforts on the island of Corsica, he proceeded to stage his own at the Alban Mount, the old cult center of the Latins, without senatorial approval. Other disappointed commanders, too, would come to celebrate triumphs here on their own authority, and although these ones offered less prestige than those which ended at the Capitol in Rome, they likewise were recorded and remembered.

Lesser magistrates also had opportunities for public display. From an early date, the great religious festivals of the Roman state had included games or *ludi*. At first, these comprised a procession, followed by chariot-racing in one of the open spaces, the Circus Maximus or the Circus Flaminius, just outside the pomerium. In the mid-fourth century, occasions for dramatic performances (*ludi scaenici*) were added to these circus games. During the third, second, and first centuries, such festivals would become more and more spectacular, as an increasing number of contests and plays in the Greek style were added to the traditional events. By the second century, if not earlier, the senate budgeted funds to finance the spectacle, but the presiding official was expected to add more of his own, to increase the display and his own fame. Indeed, the opportunities for self-advertisement were so attractive that more festivals and more festival days were steadily added to the public calendar. In addition, prominent Romans could stage games of their own on days not designated for any in the city's official religious calendar. Dedicators of temples, for example, did this to mark their dedications, and from the end of the third century generals also began to do so in order to thank the gods for bringing them victory.

A public figure was particularly concerned to preserve the memory of his accomplishments. By their very nature, victories were ephemeral: Memories of rites would fade, too, and new victors and new victories would always be occurring to obscure the old. Hence, from the last decades of the fourth century, leading Romans sought to enshrine the memory of their accomplishments in prominent monuments; the Latin word *monumenta* (singular, *monumentum*) is actually related to the verb meaning "to remind" or "to instruct". Often, initiatives of this type involved the official religion of the city, which in turn was so closely connected to its political life and to its leading families. When beginning a campaign or preparing for battle, for example, Roman commanders made vows in which they promised new temples, adornments for existing shrines, and elaborate rites to favored deities should they prove successful. As a result, generals would come to build dozens of temples in prominent places both inside the city and immediately outside its walls. In addition to statues of the gods and altars for their worship, temples often housed statues of the victor and prominent inscriptions recording his name and the names of the peoples he had defeated. Perhaps to highlight their prowess further, some commanders even introduced new gods especially associated with victory: Bellona Victrix in 296, Jupiter Victor in 295, and Victoria in 294. These novel deities reflect not only Roman preoccupations, but also the similar cult of Victory developing in the Greek world at the same period, around Hellenistic kings especially. By the end of the third century, monuments to past leaders surrounded the places where magistrates performed their tasks, where the senate held its meetings, and where assemblies of citizens gathered to hear debates and to vote.

Advancement of a family's claims to status came to involve remembering and celebrating the specific offices held by its members in earlier generations and their notable achievements in those capacities. Certain types of display were designed simply to encourage family members to imitate or outclass their ancestors. Other types were more public, because the deeds of famous ancestors helped advance the claims to office made by their descendants, who supposedly had inherited their virtues. This desire to proclaim the glory of one's ancestors led some aristocrats to stress an additional name, the *cognomen*, which, when added to their *praenomen* and *nomen*, announced their descent from a particular member of their *gens*; thus, the Cornelii Scipiones used the cognomen Scipio to identify themselves as lineal descendants of a common ancestor within the larger gens Cornelia. It seems that some families were not entirely honest in their claims: the historian Livy (8.40.4–5) would later complain that families claimed magistracies and victories for themselves falsely, and, in the process, compounded the difficulties of determining the history of the late fourth and early third centuries.

Portrait masks of wax, or *imagines* (singular, *imago*), offered another means of proclaiming the greatness of a family's ancestors. Prominent Romans kept masks of those ancestors who had held high offices or performed famous deeds in the *atria* or reception halls of their houses, where they would be visible to visitors and passersby. Funerals provided an especially important occasion for such families to display the imagines of officeholders in their past, and to proclaim their versions of the family history. The more public stages of the funeral began at the house of the deceased, where the body had lain in state. From the house—decked with signs of mourning—a funeral procession with relatives, friends, musicians, dancers, and professional mourners, made its way to the Forum. There, a prominent male member of the family, a son if one was available, delivered a funeral speech or *laudatio* to the assembled citizens, describing the offices that the dead noble had held and the memorable feats he had accomplished. According to Polybius (6.53.1–54.5), who witnessed these funerals in the middle of the second century, actors riding in chariots actually wore the family's imagines in the procession, with each carrying the symbols of the offices held by the man whose imago he wore. In the Forum, the actors sat on the ivory chairs of officeholders placed around the speaker's platform. Then, after the speaker had finished praising the deceased, he would proceed to list the offices and praise the accomplishments of each of the men whose imagines were displayed around him.

Like other public ceremonies, these funerals became more elaborate over time. From the middle of the third century, combats between pairs of gladiators also formed part of the proceedings. The first known gladiatorial games were staged during the funeral of Decimus Junius Brutus in 264; by the end of the third century, the sons of Marcus Aemilius Lepidus would put on combats with twenty-two pairs of gladiators. In addition, leading families sought to expand the number of public funerals they could stage. At first, such funerals were restricted to officeholders, but families eventually began to stage them for male members who had held no office and for women of the family; both would provide occasions for the display of ancestral virtues. It also became the practice for wives to bring the imagines of *their* ancestors to their husbands' houses, adding to the display.

WARS WITH CARTHAGE

Wars with Carthage—called Punic from the Latin adjective *punicus* or Phoenician—dominate Roman history in the middle and late third century. Carthage was the most powerful of the cities that had emerged from the Phoenician colonization of the ninth through sixth centuries (see Chapter One). Carthage came to control, directly or indirectly, a considerable territory. In North Africa, the Carthaginians and other Punic cities nearby held the richest parts of modern Tunisia. By one means or another, the city of Carthage and members of its elite also exploited subordinate communities of their territory's original population. By the end of the fourth century, the Carthaginians controlled an area almost equivalent to Latium and Campania combined, although they restricted their citizenship much more than did the Romans. Still farther away, Carthage exercised some leadership, if only intermittently, over rulers of various tribes and confederacies; the Numidians, in modern Algeria, were the most important.

Carthage also expanded its power and influence by sea. From the end of the seventh century, the Phoenician settlements of western Sicily, Sardinia, and the Balearic Islands were subordinate to Carthage in some way. By the end of the sixth century, the Carthaginians controlled the coasts of Sardinia, where they established colonies of their own and controlled mines in the interior. In the sixth, fifth, and fourth centuries, Carthaginian armies fought, with varying degrees of success, against the Greek cities of Sicily. Carthage also had contacts, if sometimes distant and indirect, with cities in Italy. As part of their struggles with the Sicilian Greeks and to protect their trade, the Carthaginians concluded treaties with some central Italian communities, including Rome. The first of these Roman-Carthaginian agreements was probably made as early as c. 500, and others followed, although the precise number made thereafter is uncertain.

First Punic War (264–241)

War broke out between the Romans and the Carthaginians as a result of a three-way struggle between Carthage, Rome, and Syracuse over the strategic city of Messana (modern Messina), which controlled the straits between Italy and Sicily. During the chaos that set in following the death of Agathocles of Syracuse in 289 (see Chapter Three), a band of Mamertines, Campanian mercenaries of the deceased king, had seized Messana for themselves and began to plunder the surrounding countryside. Early in the 260s, Hiero, the commander of Syracuse's army, defeated these Mamertines in battle and advanced on their city; his victory in fact gave him the opportunity to proclaim himself king. Meanwhile a Carthaginian admiral came to the Mamertines' aid, installing a garrison in Messana. As a result, Hiero abandoned the siege he had begun.

Roman armies soon became involved. The presence of a Carthaginian force within their city provoked dissension among the Mamertines. Some apparently hoped for a treaty with Carthage that would give them greater freedom of action, but others preferred to seek Roman assistance and protection. The Roman senate was divided on the issue, but one of the consuls of 264 (in all likelihood Appius Claudius Caudex) successfully proposed to a citizen assembly that the Mamertines be given Roman protection. Claudius was certainly the consul who then set off for Sicily with his army. Meantime the Mamertines—perhaps with the assistance of no more than a Roman advance guard—expelled the Carthaginian garrison from Messana; for this failure, the garrison commander was supposedly crucified later. Claudius then arrived and entered the city. Both King Hiero and the Carthaginians responded: A Carthaginian fleet blockaded Messana, while Carthaginian and Syracusan armies each set up camp outside it.

More intensive warfare broke out in 263, when Rome sent out both consuls, with a large force of Romans and allies. The consuls advanced into Hiero's territory, seized some towns there, and received the surrender of others. Hiero then made peace, and became an ally of Rome. The consuls of the next year advanced into western Sicily and besieged the Greek city of Agrigentum (modern Agrigento), where the Carthaginians had concentrated their forces. They tried to force the Roman commanders to abandon the siege. However, after a battle in which both sides appear to have lost heavily, the Carthaginian generals managed to evacuate their forces from the city without further loss. The citizens of Agrigentum suffered much more severely. On the next day, the Roman army entered the city, plundered it, and sold thousands of the citizens into slavery. Meanwhile the Carthaginians replaced their unsuccessful commander with Hamilcar Barca, who would continue to command the Carthaginian forces on the island for the remainder of this long war.

After the sack of Agrigentum in 262, the Romans and Carthaginians entered a period of stalemate. Some cities that had previously defected to the Romans now resumed their alliance with Carthage, while others joined Rome for the first time.

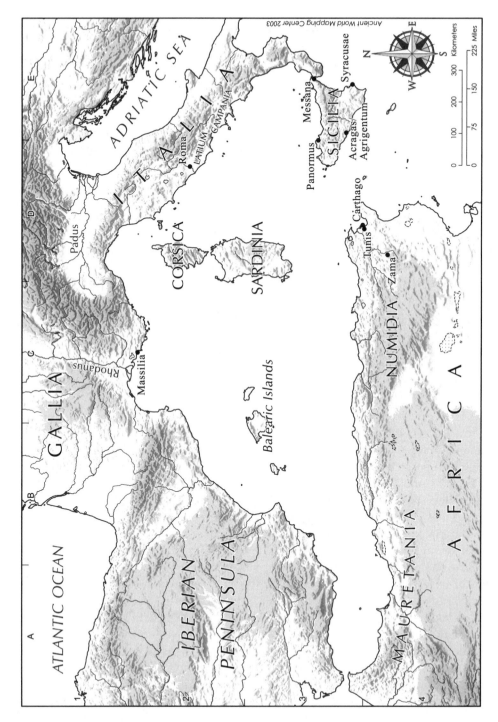

Map 4.1 *Western Mediterranean in the Mid-Third Century*

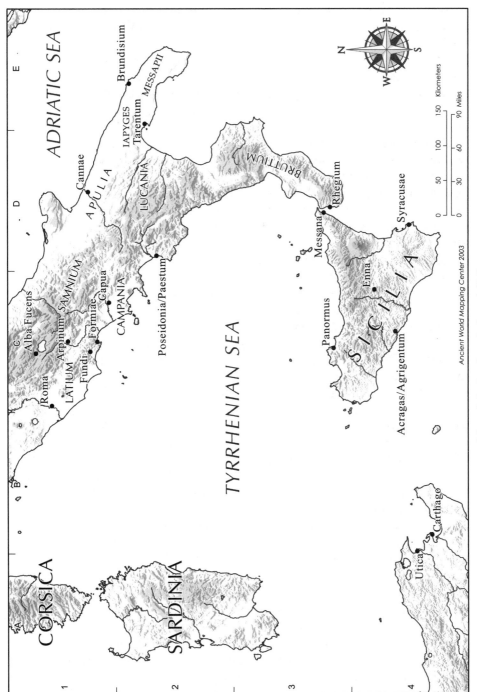

Map 4.2 *Southern Italy and Sicily*

Ancient World Mapping Center 2003

Both sides faced extraordinary difficulties. Carthage possessed one of the most powerful war fleets in the Mediterranean, but it depended upon mercenaries to fill out its armies. Because of this strength at sea, Carthaginian forces were able to hold towns on the coast, where reinforcements could easily be landed. Rome, on the other hand, had a large army, though only a small fleet, with its Greek allies providing many of the ships and crews. Roman commanders were able to bring armies across the narrow straits between Sicily and Italy, but the strength of the Carthaginian fleet made it impossible for them to expel Carthaginian forces from Sicily.

The Romans responded by building warships to challenge Carthage at sea. This was not an easy task. Shipbuilding was complex and expensive. Commanding ships and fleets, moreover, was a skilled operation that differed greatly from the leadership of an army, and warships by definition required large numbers of skilled oarsmen to propel them and maneuver them in battle. Here, the Carthaginians, with their long naval tradition and large fleet, had a great advantage, but the Romans were able to adapt remarkably quickly. Copying Carthaginian methods of construction, the Romans began by building about one hundred large warships, and over the course of the war, they would build many more. For sailors and oarsmen, they turned to their allies and also recruited Roman citizens too poor to serve in the army. Roman fleets soon began to win battles at sea, although they also lost many ships, failures which Roman authors (and Greek ones friendly to Rome) often attributed to inclement weather. Gaius Duilius, consul in 260 and commander in one of the earliest of Rome's naval victories, celebrated the first triumph gained at sea; as a striking monument to his victory, he set up a column in the Forum decorated with the bronze rams of captured ships.

For a time, Rome and Carthage both won victories and suffered defeats, and neither side could gain a decisive advantage. In 256, both consuls took the further initiative of crossing to North Africa with an army and a fleet, so as to attack Carthage itself in the hope of bringing the war to a quick conclusion. One of these consuls, Marcus Atilius Regulus, duly defeated the Carthaginians in battle, captured the city of Tunis (near Carthage), and provoked a rebellion among some of Carthage's Numidian allies. Early in 255, however, Xanthippus, a Greek mercenary commander in Carthaginian service, defeated and captured Regulus.

Roman writers would later turn this humiliation, so offensive to Roman sensibilities, into a patriotic myth that contrasted the supposed virtues of the consul and the vices of his captors. Later, according to the tale, the Carthaginians allowed Regulus to return to Rome in order to negotiate either a peace or an exchange of prisoners, making him promise to return if his efforts were to prove unsuccessful. When the senate refused to negotiate, Regulus returned to Carthage where he died, exhibiting in the process the good faith (*fides*) that members of Rome's elite thought to be a defining characteristic of their class and their city. Some versions, moreover, would maintain that the Carthaginians tortured Regulus to death—Roman authors thought cruelty to be one of the chief traits of Carthaginians—but this may well have been an attempt to counter reports that Regulus' wife tortured Carthaginian prisoners.

After the failed invasion of North Africa, warfare continued on land and sea for fifteen years. In Sicily, Roman commanders slowly gained the advantage, since the Carthaginians lacked sufficient resources to fight simultaneously against the Romans and against their former Numidian allies in North Africa. In the process, much of Sicily was devastated. In 254, for example, the Romans captured Panormus (modern Palermo), the most important city on the north coast of Sicily; many of its citizens paid a ransom, but those who could not afford the payment set by Rome were enslaved. In 241, the Carthaginians gave Hamilcar, their commander in Sicily, authority to negotiate a peace. The result was that they agreed to leave Sicily and pay Rome a large indemnity.

Hostilities did not end here, however. At the end of the war, the Carthaginians had insufficient funds to pay their mercenaries, who were owed for many years of service. So the large mercenary army assembled in North Africa mounted a revolt, which soon spread to some of Carthage's Libyan and Numidian allies. The whole conflict here led to atrocities by both sides, until 237, when the Carthaginian army finally succeeded in gaining the upper hand. Meantime elsewhere, mercenaries serving Carthage in Sardinia joined the revolt and killed their general. When Carthage dispatched more mercenaries to the island, these too revolted, killing their general and massacring Carthaginians indiscriminately. Eventually, after victory had been achieved in North Africa, the Carthaginians planned to send another army to Sardinia, but before they could, the mercenary commanders there begged Rome for assistance. Disregarding earlier agreements with Carthage, Roman officials now chose to intervene, threatening war and insisting that Carthage abandon the island and pay a further substantial indemnity. The Carthaginians, exhausted by interminable warfare, agreed.

Although Roman magistrates and senators may not have realized it at this point, it was in fact victory in the First Punic War that led to the creation of Rome's first permanent commitments outside Italy. In the decade following the assertion of Roman claims to Sardinia, nine consuls and at least one praetor campaigned against the inhabitants of the island, as well as against those of the neighboring island, Corsica. Campaigns in the interior of both islands would continue intermittently for a further century. While fighting Carthaginian forces in Sicily, Roman commanders had already granted protection to communities there, and had probably even made arrangements of a more permanent nature with some. Previously, when the Romans had forged alliances and granted protection to communities in Italy, they had made few commitments that required the permanent presence of Roman officials and Roman forces. Now, the senate may at first have intended that friendly cities in Sicily should enjoy the same sort of undemanding relationship. By 227, however, the decision had been made to station a commander and troops permanently in Sicily, Sardinia, and Corsica. In that year, the Centuriate assembly elected four praetors for the first time, with the intention that one of them should regularly be sent to Sicily and another to Sardinia-Corsica. Thus these islands became the first of Rome's "provinces" outside the Italian peninsula (see A Mediterranean Empire).

The First Punic War, and to a lesser degree the war with Pyrrhus that preceded it, marked an important stage in Rome's imperial development. In Rome's traditional pattern of warfare, consuls and praetors raised armies each spring and discharged them in the fall after the end of the campaigning season. Consequently, Roman soldiers could be self-supporting, since they always returned home in time to plant their crops and provide for themselves and their families in the following year. In some of the wars of the third century, however, this long-established practice no longer met Roman needs. Although they did still raise armies and fleets for less than a year's service during the Pyrrhic War and the First Punic War, they also kept some armies in the field over the winter and maintained garrisons in distant towns and forts. In part, this modification to traditional practice may have been a response to the greater distances that Roman armies now had to travel in order to reach their enemies. But Rome had also begun to compete with cities and kings who raised their forces in a different way: In particular, the mercenary armies of Pyrrhus and the Carthaginians typically remained in the area of operations over the winter, and were quite capable of seizing towns and forts during the Romans' absence.

In response to the new forms of warfare, Roman practices underwent some adjustment. Fleets required money for the construction and supply of ships; their crews could not live off the land as an invading army could. Soldiers kept through the winter in garrisons or camps distant from their farms also needed some means of support. Traditionally, Roman commanders had for the most part sought to supply their armies either by living off the land, or by demanding the necessary funds and provisions from allies and subjects in the vicinity. Rome's administrative organization, like that of most city-states, was rudimentary, and its ability to direct a range of activities correspondingly limited. Elected officials arranged and performed the major rites and ceremonies of the city, they raised and led its armies, and they heard complaints and granted judgments in legal cases. These core functions apart, the Roman state possessed little in the way of a permanent apparatus. To be sure, from time to time the state needed supplies and labor for religious rituals, for public building projects, and for the army. In these circumstances, however, Roman officials would typically turn to private contractors or *publicani* (singular, *publicanus*) to fulfill needs that a more bureaucratized society would accomplish with state officials. Some publicani were undoubtedly involved in equipping and supplying Roman fleets and armies.

By the middle of the third century, there are clear signs that the Romans were expending public funds on a larger scale than they had in the past. Roman citizens were not subject to regular taxation, but when some exceptional, urgent need arose, a citizen assembly could authorize magistrates to collect a special payment or *tributum*, assessed on the basis of the *census*. It was when ancient communities

Figure 4.1 *In addition to silver coins—which at first appear to have circulated primarily in southern Italy, where the use of money was long established—the Romans began to cast bronze in the form of ingots or coins; there is little doubt that these circulated more locally, and may have been intended for distribution to soldiers. This bronze ingot, dating between 275 and 242, bears an elephant on one side and a sow on the other; the elephant is probably a reference to the war with Pyrrhus.*

faced the necessity of making regular payments on a large scale—either for war or for other public projects—that they usually began to mint coins in silver. When the Romans first made use of such high-value coins, late in the fourth century, they relied on ones produced at irregular intervals by Campanian mints. During the Pyrrhic War, however, they began to mint their own, using Greek weights and designs. Eventually, in the last two decades of the third century, they introduced a complete range of denominations with Roman weights and designs. Rome's traditional style of warfare had not called for substantial sums of money. Now, however, Roman officials and the senate would face a steady need for cash, especially in the largest wars.

Second Punic War (218–201)

The Second Punic War broke out over Spain. Leadership of the Phoenician cities of the Iberian peninsula, together with influence in the interior there, had long been a major prop of Carthaginian power. The Carthaginians used Iberian mercenaries to fight in their wars; Iberian gold, silver, and other metals to pay and equip their soldiers and sailors; and Iberian timber to build their ships. After the end of the First Punic War, they attempted to extend their power in the peninsula and increase their access to its rich resources. In 237, Hamilcar Barca, previously Carthage's general in Sicily, landed in Spain; from then on, he regularly conducted military operations and extended Carthaginian power there until his death in 229. At that point he was succeeded by Hasdrubal, his son-in-law, who governed and campaigned until he too died in 221. After Hasdrubal's death, Hannibal Barca, Hamilcar's own son born in 247, became the chief Carthaginian commander in Spain.

This increase in Carthage's power provided the occasion for a new war with Rome. The diplomatic activity lying behind its outbreak is very obscure, mainly because our sources are pro-Roman and anti-Carthaginian and seek to put Hasdrubal, and especially Hannibal, in the wrong. In 226, the Roman senate—for reasons unclear to us—dispatched an embassy to Hasdrubal, and pressed him to agree to limit Carthaginian power in Spain. The result was a treaty in which the Carthaginians undertook not to send any military force across the Ebro River. A few years later, however, Hannibal attacked the city of Saguntum, south of the Ebro, and the Saguntines appealed to Rome. The senate apparently claimed that Saguntum—despite its location—was in some way dependent upon Rome or had a right to Roman protection; but again there is no knowing when or how this supposed relationship with Rome had developed. In any event, Rome sent no relief force, and Saguntum fell to Hannibal in 219. In the following year, and apparently after some debate, the senate sent an ultimatum to the Carthaginians, demanding that they hand over Hannibal. The Carthaginians refused, and the Roman envoys then declared war.

The senate evidently expected to be able to predict where the war would be fought. It instructed one of the consuls of 218, Publius Cornelius Scipio, to lead his army and fleet to Spain, while the other, Tiberius Sempronius Longus, was to go first to Sicily in order to prepare an invasion of North Africa from there. Hannibal, however, did not wait in Spain for the arrival of Roman forces. Instead, in the spring of 218, he left his headquarters in Spain and surprised Rome by daring to attempt the long march to Italy. Scipio failed in an attempt to stop Hannibal's army from crossing the Rhone River in what is now southern France. After this failure, Scipio sent most of his own men on to Spain under the command of his brother, Gnaeus Cornelius Scipio, while he himself returned to Italy. Later in the year, despite difficulties and much loss of life, Hannibal successfully crossed the Alps into Italy. Here, at the Trebia River, he defeated Tiberius Sempronius Longus (who had rushed north), and virtually destroyed his army in December 218.

Despite these remarkable achievements by Hannibal, however, the Romans still possessed most of the advantages. Rome's fleet far outclassed that of Carthage. For this reason, Rome's leaders had apparently expected to be able to fight the war in Africa and Spain, both of which they could reach by sea. At the same time, Rome's control of the sea meant that Hannibal could only receive limited reinforcements by ship while in Italy. Here, the Romans possessed great reserves of manpower, although they could not mobilize all their potential soldiers at one time. According to Polybius (2.23), several years before the war, the Romans had ordered their allies to compile lists of men eligible for military service. According to these lists, 250,000 Romans and Campanians could be summoned to serve in the infantry and 23,000 in the cavalry, along with 80,000 Latins who could serve on foot and 5,000 potential cavalrymen. Altogether, Samnites and Lucanians, along with Messapians and Iapygians from Apulia, could provide up to 150,000 infantry and 26,000 cavalry, while several small groups in the mountains of central Italy could muster another 20,000 infantry and 4,000 cavalry.

Map 4.3 *Northern Italy*

The record as transmitted by Polybius is plainly incomplete—there are no Etruscans, Umbrians, Bruttii, or Greeks here, for example—and it is unclear whether those actually serving in Rome's armies at the time were included in the totals given. Even so, there can be no question that Hannibal had far fewer soldiers. Polybius (3.56) saw a bronze tablet that Hannibal later erected in the south of Italy; his claim here was that he had 12,000 African and 8,000 Iberian infantry, and no more than 6,000 cavalry, when he entered Italy. He may have hoped to win victories that would be sufficiently impressive to encourage the Romans to make peace, or Rome's allies to revolt. If so, he would be only partially successful in achieving such aims.

When Hannibal crossed the Alps, he entered a region disturbed by warfare between Romans and Gauls. In 232, a tribune of the plebs, Gaius Flaminius had proposed and carried a law instructing officials to assign land taken from the Gauls here in small parcels to citizens. One consequence was that the two largest tribes, the Boii and Insubres, became more openly hostile. In 225, they crossed the Apennines into Etruria with a large force of infantry, cavalry, and chariots, and defeated a Roman force. Later in the same year, the two consuls—one of them hurriedly recalled with his army from Sardinia—trapped the Gauls between their own pair of armies at Telamon, less than one hundred miles (160 km) from Rome, and won a major victory. Over the next few years, Roman armies regularly invaded and devastated the territories of the Boii and Insubres, and, in 219, Roman commissioners founded colonies at Placentia and Cremona. In the next year, however, the Gauls succeeded in capturing Placentia. When Hannibal arrived, they made common cause with him, and some would join his army.

Hannibal's successes continued in 217. When he crossed the Apennines and invaded Etruria, Gaius Flaminius marched to block him, but Hannibal succeeded in ambushing and destroying this consul's army at Lake Trasimene. At this starkly critical juncture for Rome, Quintus Fabius Maximus, already twice a consul, was appointed dictator. He adopted a firm strategy of avoiding battle with the Carthaginians unless there were conditions especially favorable for the Romans. Instead, he harassed Hannibal's army on the march, attacked detachments foraging for supplies, and looked for any opportunity to exploit some advantage. For this reason, he was mockingly dubbed "the Delayer" (*Cunctator*). Fabius' strategy was most unpopular, and incurred sharp criticism not least from his own magister equitum, Marcus Minucius Rufus, who persuaded a citizen assembly to make him co-dictator, an unprecedented post. According to accounts that favor Fabius, Rufus then deployed his army rashly, and his more cautious colleague had to rescue him from the Carthaginians.

The consuls of 216, Gaius Terentius Varro and Lucius Aemilius Paullus, did not follow Fabius' strategy either. Instead, they marched against Hannibal with a combined army of Romans and allies that may have numbered as many as 80,000 soldiers. The battle they fought at Cannae in Apulia was a further Roman disaster: Paullus lost his life, and only a small fraction of the army escaped. Afterwards, some of Rome's allies began to change sides. The cities of Sabinum, Etruria, and

Umbria largely remained Roman allies. In the south, however, many Samnites, Lucanians, and Bruttii either served as soldiers in Hannibal's army, or provided supplies for it, or fought against the Romans on their own. Capua in Campania, one of the largest cities in Italy and a Roman *municipium* for the past century, also joined Hannibal's alliance; Roman writers would claim that it was the mass of citizens who decided to reassert Capua's autonomy in this damaging way, against the wishes of the local elite. In Sicily, some Syracusans also persuaded their fellow citizens to support Carthage. In 212, Hannibal captured Tarentum, although a Roman garrison held out in a fort on the harbor, preventing the use of the only major port he would gain.

After the defeat at Cannae, Roman commanders reverted to avoiding battle with Hannibal's army, while harassing it and limiting its freedom of movement. At the same time, other Roman armies attacked disloyal cities and allies, too many in number for Hannibal to protect. In Sicily, Marcus Claudius Marcellus captured Syracuse in 213. Two years later, Capua fell, and the Roman commander then ordered the executions of the city's leading citizens and sold much of the population into slavery. In 209, the Romans recaptured Tarentum too, sacked it, and enslaved its inhabitants. After this date, Hannibal and his depleted army were more or less confined to Bruttium in the extreme south of Italy.

In the midst of the war in Italy, Roman magistrates and the senate searched for signs of divine disfavor and for ways to bring better fortune to Rome. Livy's history of these years is full of reports of freak storms and uncanny events in which the gods revealed their displeasure with Rome. In response, the Romans took great care to perform the traditional rites flawlessly, while increasing their scale and grandeur. Should this approach fail to appease the gods, they also made elaborate vows which promised unprecedented sacrifices in the event of Roman victory. In addition, officials and the senate sought to introduce new gods to the city and gain their protection. In 205, after a series of distressing portents, the senate consulted Roman priests and the Greek oracle at Delphi. Both recommended bringing the Great Mother (*Magna Mater*) from her sanctuary in Asia Minor to Rome. So, in the following year, the goddess' cult image—a black meteorite—and some of her priests arrived in the city. However, the senate seems not to have realized what her worship entailed. The cult of the Magna Mater centered on self-castrated priests, ecstatic rites, and wild singing and dancing. After its introduction, shocked Roman officials would act to isolate these priests from Roman citizens, and would enact laws preventing citizens from participating in the more disturbing forms of the cult.

The war in Spain proved decisive. The Carthaginians had never gained a firm grip on most of Spain. Their power rested on the Phoenician and Punic colonies along the coasts and in the valley of the Baetis River (modern Guadalquivir), a region of towns and villages where they and their Phoenician predecessors had long been active. In the years before the outbreak of the war, Carthaginian commanders had expanded their influence northward along the narrow plain between the coast and the eastern edge of the great central plateau that makes up much of

BOX 4.2: *In 217, the Roman senate and citizen assembly ordered that an extraordinary vow be made to preserve the Republic from disaster. The vow was eventually carried out over two decades later, in 195. Note the solemn, almost legalistic form of the vow as a promise that the Roman people will perform certain actions, if the gods do their part first.*

Livy 22.10: After the senate had passed these resolutions, the praetor consulted the college of *pontifices*, and Lucius Cornelius Lentulus, the *pontifex maximus*, gave his opinion that first of all the people should vote on the question of a "sacred spring," since this could not be vowed against the wishes of the people. The question was put to them thus: "Do you wish and instruct that this action be carried out as follows? If the Roman Republic and its people are preserved for the next five years (as I would wish it to be) in these wars—that is, the Roman people's war with the Carthaginian people, and the wars with the Gauls on this side of the Alps—let the Roman people offer as a sacrifice to Jupiter what the spring produces from the flocks of pigs, sheep, goats, cattle, whatever is not already consecrated, starting from the day determined by the senate and people. Let him who will perform the sacrifice perform it at whatever time, by whatever form of ritual he wishes; however it is done, let it be deemed to have been done correctly. If an animal that ought to be sacrificed dies, let it count as outside the vow and let no guilt attach to the sacrificer; if anyone harms or kills an animal unawares, let it not be a crime; if anyone steals an animal, let no guilt attach to the people nor to him from whom it was stolen; if he sacrifices on a day of bad omen unawares, let it be deemed to have been done correctly; whether by night or day, whether a slave or free man performs the sacrifice, let it be deemed to have been done correctly; if it is performed earlier than the senate and people have ordered, let the people thereby be absolved and free of obligation."

Spain. This too was a region of towns and villages, but it also held a few coastal cities, Greek or Phoenician in origin, and some Spanish communities, which were in the process of becoming cities. Hasdrubal's foundation of New Carthage (Latin, Carthago Nova; modern Cartagena), where he built a strongly fortified city on a fine harbor, and Hannibal's capture of Saguntum mark two important stages in this advance. Within the region, Carthaginian power rested on some of the coastal cities, garrisons in important places, a large and well-trained field army, and a constantly shifting network of alliances. On the central plateau itself, Carthaginian power was even more limited. Here, communities generally were small, with economies based primarily on herding and only secondarily on the limited cultivation of crops. Settlements possessed no more than rudimentary forms of political organization, and unstable leadership. On this plateau the Carthaginians found mercenaries as well as allies, although typically not dependable ones; at the same time, other communities here were hostile.

In 218, Gnaeus Scipio landed at Emporiae (modern Empúries), a coastal settlement on the far northeast coast of Spain; his brother, Publius Scipio, joined him in

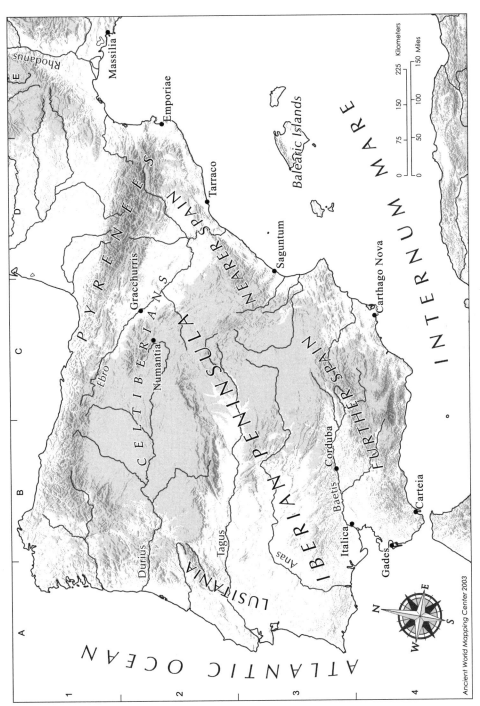

Map 4.4 *Iberian Peninsula*

Ancient World Mapping Center 2003

the following year. Before the beginning of the second war with Carthage, the Greek city of Massilia (modern Marseille, in France) established friendly diplomatic relations with Rome. The Massiliots had founded a series of colonies and trading posts along the coasts; Emporiae was one of the most successful. At the outset, then, Roman armies intervened as enemies of the Carthaginians, but also perhaps as allies and protectors of some small cities in the region. In the first years of the war, Rome's commanders duly secured the safety of Greek communities under their protection, expelled small Carthaginian garrisons from towns near the mouth of the Ebro River, and established control over the lower Ebro Valley and along the coast, perhaps as far south as Saguntum. Amid these campaigns, they made Tarraco (modern Tarragona) their main base of operations; it would become one of the chief centers of Roman power and influence in the peninsula.

The effort to support armies and fleets in Spain soon strained the capacity of the Roman state. In 215, the Scipios reported that they were unable to secure sufficient supplies from Spain itself, and they requested that food, clothing, and provisions for their navies be sent from Italy. Because of the many demands elsewhere, the senate concluded that it was incapable of meeting this request. Instead, it instructed a praetor to seek bids for contracts to supply the Roman commanders in Spain on condition, however, that the contractors would receive payment only when the necessary funds became available. Nineteen such contractors (*publicani*), organized into three companies, made successful bids, although they stipulated that they should be exempted from military service and that the state should insure their ships and cargoes on the way to Spain.

Figure 4.2 *From around 211, the Roman state began to mint silver coins known as* denarii *with its own original designs and with Latin inscriptions. The* denarius *would long remain the most common silver coin. This early example bears a helmeted image of the goddess Roma on the obverse, and the Dioscuri (Castor and Pollux, twin sons of Jupiter) on the reverse. These designs, too, would long remain standard.*

Gnaeus and Publius Scipio remained as commanders in Spain until their deaths in battle in 211. As early as the following year, Roman voters assigned the Spanish command to another Publius Cornelius Scipio, in fact the son of Publius and the nephew of Gnaeus. His post was atypical, one of the deviations from proper procedure that the pressure of the war permitted: He held no formal magistracy but was sent out instead as a private citizen with the right to command, a *privatus cum imperio.* In 209, he captured Carthago Nova, one of the chief centers of Carthaginian power. In the next year, he succeeded in crossing the mountains between the coast south of Saguntum and the headwaters of the Baetis River. In the latter area—a valley of vital importance to the Carthaginians—the remaining major battles of the war in Spain were fought. However, even though Hasdrubal, Hannibal's brother, was defeated by

Scipio, he was then able to follow his brother's route into Italy and attempt to join their two armies. But in 207, at the Metaurus River along the Adriatic coast of Italy, his army was stopped and beaten, and he lost his own life, thus extinguishing any hope that significant reinforcements might reach Hannibal. By the end of 206, the Romans had overcome virtually all Carthaginian forces in Spain.

As consul in 205, Scipio's task was to prepare for the invasion of North Africa. In the following year he and his army landed outside the city of Utica not far north of Carthage, and with the help of the Numidian ruler Masinissa defeated the Carthaginians in battle. The Carthaginian leaders then summoned Hannibal back to Africa, and he obeyed even though he had to leave his army behind in Italy. The decisive encounter between the Roman and Carthaginian forces occurred in 202 at Zama, where Scipio won another victory. He then returned to Rome for a lavish triumph, and added Africanus to his other names, immortalizing his victory for his descendants. Later, stories circulated claiming that Jupiter Optimus Maximus, chief god of the city, held him in special favor.

Peace was concluded in 201. The terms of the treaty severely restricted Carthaginian power and blocked any prospect of its revival. The Carthaginians surrendered their fleet, were burdened with crippling indemnity payments, lost all their territory outside of the core around Carthage and the other Punic cities in northern Tunisia, and were prohibited from waging war outside this territory without Roman permission. Meantime, Masinissa emerged as a staunch Roman ally with control of an enlarged Numidian kingdom.

Altogether, this prolonged war had imposed grave strains upon the Roman authorities, its citizens, and the citizens of allied states. Much of Italy was devastated by the continuous campaigning there. For the entire duration, the Romans had to maintain armies in Spain, Sardinia, and Sicily, as well as in Italy. The consequent need for numerous commands disrupted traditional political arrangements, while the many armies and the high casualty rates required an unusually large percentage of the male population to be drafted. To fill the ranks, Rome even drafted criminals and slaves, and some of the allies proved incapable of providing more soldiers. At Cannae, around eighty senators were said to have been killed, in addition to the many thousands of ordinary soldiers who lost their lives there; this depletion of the senate was so substantial that men who had never held office were chosen to make up its numbers. Nonetheless, despite all the setbacks, Rome remained undaunted throughout, and emerged from the war with a dominant position in the central and western Mediterranean that its leaders would exploit in the following decades.

A MEDITERRANEAN EMPIRE

After the Second Punic War, Roman power soon spread through much of the Mediterranean world. At the start of his work the Greek historian Polybius, who witnessed this development personally, described the fifty-three years following the end of the second war with Carthage as a period that was unique in history, since within this short span the Romans succeeded in subjecting "nearly the entire civilized world" to their rule. Once again, no single cause explains all of Rome's wars at this date. In region after region, the governing elite seems to have had no clear plan for expanding Rome's power or for establishing its authority. Instead, they just seem to have made arrangements piecemeal as they responded to the unfolding of events. Moreover, despite the Roman state's need for funds, there appears to have been no desire at first to promote the systematic exploitation of conquered communities' economic resources, although awareness of this type of potential would slowly gain ground.

Governors, Provinces, and Empire

During the Second Punic War and in the decades that followed, Roman armies were stationed in many places, often distant from Rome. Since Roman political and military leadership was closely tied to the tenure of a limited number of annual offices, these far-flung campaigns put great burdens on offices and officeholders. First, the number of armies often exceeded the number of consuls and praetors, Rome's traditional military commanders. Then, some assigned areas of operations were so far from Rome that the time needed for commanders and armies to travel there reduced the amount of actual campaigning which could be undertaken during the magistrate's year in office. Last but not least, generals operating in ever more distant theaters of operation gained greater freedom of action, because they were increasingly far away from observation by other magistrates and by the senate.

Some of these difficulties were met by increasing the number of high officials. During the closing stages of the First Punic War, Roman assemblies elected not only two consuls but also two praetors annually. After the end of that war, the Romans expelled the Carthaginians from Sicily, Sardinia, and Corsica. Accordingly in 227, Roman voters began to choose two additional praetors to serve as commanders in Sicily and Sardinia respectively, an apparent recognition of the regular need for officials to watch over Roman interests there. After the Second Punic War, the number of praetors was again increased by two to provide leaders for Roman forces in Spain. Within a few years, this arrangement too was modified, and it became the practice to elect four praetors one year, then six the next, alternately. In fact this number of consuls and praetors still did not suffice to provide commanders for all Rome's armies, but nevertheless expansion of the number of officeholders ceased until the first century B.C. Tenure in these offices, after all, was the primary route to fame and glory, and to continue increasing the number of occupants meant diluting their prestige markedly.

To meet the increased demand for commanders, the Romans also resorted to extending the terms of some officials, a procedure known as "prorogation." In the late fourth century and during the First Punic War, a few officials with a limited task to complete had occasionally continued in office for a short time after their magistracies had expired. In their additional period of service, such officeholders were known as *proconsul* or *propraetor*, because each served in place of a consul or a praetor. During the Second Punic War, when the need for commanders was high, the practice became more common, and commands were sometimes extended for a year or more. After the war, prorogation became a regular practice. Prorogued officials had a different legal status from those actually in their year of office, and they had no authority in Rome itself, where they held no magisterial rank. Commands were extended in one of two ways. Sometimes, voting assemblies extended the commands of serving officials, or even assigned provinces to private citizens, where they were to serve as promagistrates; on other occasions, the senate did likewise on its own authority. During and after the Second Punic War, it was most common for the senate to act.

More generally in the late third and second centuries, the senate took the lead in the conduct of wars and diplomacy. It received ambassadors from other states and listened to their statements. From time to time, it chose some of its own members to serve as legates (*legati*; singular, *legatus*) to go on embassies outside of Italy, or to advise a governor who was winding up a major campaign. The senate also took the primary responsibility for assigning duties to officials. Each year, senators decided the tasks that would be divided among the new consuls and praetors. After the election, the new consuls cast lots to determine the consular assignment each would have, while the new praetors shared out their tasks in the same fashion. Alternatively, the members of each group also had the right to determine assignments by mutual agreement before lots were cast, a process known as *comparatio*. Romans believed the casting of lots to reflect the will of the gods; this method also avoided contentious debates in the senate as rival magistrates sought to convince their fellow senators to give them the most attractive assignments.

Roman officials abroad often had considerable freedom of action to wage war, make alliances, and set the terms of peace—perhaps greater freedom than many senators found desirable. In practice, most sanctions took the form of judgments on a magistrate's actions after he had returned to Rome and left office. Even so, the senate sometimes refused to accept treaties that a commander had negotiated, leaving his successor to establish new arrangements. On several occasions, senatorial decrees sought to force officials to free defeated enemies who had been improperly enslaved, but efforts to remedy such injustices were seldom wholly successful. The most persistent problem, however, concerned charges of extortion and corruption. In the late third and second centuries, prosecutions for official misconduct, such as cowardice, incompetence, and corruption, served as the primary means of controlling an official's behavior in office (see Chapter Five). This said, such prosecutions could only take place after an official had returned to Rome and laid down his office.

Engagement beyond Italy grew steadily during the second century, but still this extension of Roman power and influence developed very unevenly and with much variation, as officials and senate responded to events. The creation of "provinces" was the main vehicle for Roman expansion. In modern English, a province usually denotes a subdivision of a larger state or country with well-defined borders and a capital of its own; today, a state's creation of a province often involves the formal subordination of the territory and its reorganization according to a definite plan. In time, the Latin term *provincia* would gain this meaning too, but for long it did not denote anything so fixed or definite. In the late third and early second centuries, and probably earlier, the term merely denoted the sphere of operations given to a Roman official, defined by task and location. In theory, colleagues in office all possessed the same powers and functions, but in practice they were usually expected to exercise them separately. Some served at the same place, but had different *provinciae*: Of the two praetors who usually remained in Rome, one, known as the "urban" praetor, was assigned the supervision of lawsuits between citizens, while the other, called the "peregrine" praetor, handled disputes involving noncitizens. Consuls and praetors who were assigned the command of armies as their provincia typically campaigned in different regions, although in large-scale conflicts more than one could be assigned the same region and they then had to share authority somehow.

Provinciae could be short-lived and ill-defined, although their number at any one time could never exceed the total of available consuls, praetors, and promagistrates. In some cases, officials were assigned provinciae that remained in existence only for a single project, campaign, or war. In others, provinciae remained in existence for some time, receiving new officials as soon as the previous ones left office. A consul's or praetor's provincia was primarily military in character. Equally, a governor's actions were largely shaped by his need to command his and his allies' army against Rome's enemies, to protect friendly cities from attack, and to obtain the money and supplies needed to support his forces. Gradually, in the longer-lasting provinces, governors took on other tasks, such as arbitrating disputes between cities, hearing legal cases, and supervising financial arrangements.

The Roman elite did not believe its leadership to be restricted to the regions—more or less well-defined—where Rome happened to be maintaining provinciae. Whenever a community surrendered or put itself under Rome's protection, magistrates and senate thought that it thereby became part of the *imperium* of the Roman people (*imperium populi Romani*). Although this word is the root of the English "empire," the Latin term does not denote a clearly delimited territory, nor does it imply any administrative responsibilities by the victors or prescribed duties by the defeated. As was the case with the imperium of magistrates, the Roman leadership considered that it had the right to command the defeated and to be respected by them, even though it did not necessarily make such demands very often.

At the beginning of the second century, the Roman state lacked the institutions or the administrative apparatus needed to exploit thoroughly the regions that were in some way its dependencies. Outside of Italy, the Romans slowly adopted different practices as they began to develop more financial sophistication in government. To gain necessary supplies and funds, governors would now impose payments of tribute on some communities and individuals, and require the contribution of supplies by others; any funds or items demanded had to be gathered together by the communities themselves. Meantime, certain especially favored cities and persons would be freed from all but the most extraordinary demands.

In addition, state contractors or *publicani* were active outside of Italy, although the extent of their operations is unclear. As we saw above, during the Second Punic War publicani in Rome contracted to supply the forces in Spain with food, clothing, and equipment; almost half a century later, others would contract to provide clothing and horses to Roman forces in Greece. Arrangements such as these may not have been the norm, however. On other occasions, the senate instructed governors of provinces such as Sicily to purchase grain locally and arrange for its shipment to the combat zone. Yet there were areas in which the use of publicani did expand, although it remains uncertain whether these individuals were Romans, citizens of other Italian communities, or residents of the provinces. From at least the 170s, Roman magistrates, acting on decrees of the senate, leased the exploitation of certain lands and resources. Toward the end of the second century, officials in Rome would also arrange contracts for the collection of taxes and rents from entire provinces and cities; this was to become the most prominent and controversial function of publicani in the first century.

Spain

To judge from its actions, the senate seems to have had no well-defined notion of how to proceed in Spain following the end of the Second Punic War. Some senators may have wished to disengage, but Rome had become too entangled in the affairs of the peninsula to leave easily. Other senators were evidently eager to punish communities that they thought had betrayed Rome or had proven to be especially bitter enemies; Roman commanders did in fact take such punitive action over several years. Roman officials also had allies and interests to protect, and these allies often attempted to persuade Rome to intervene in struggles with their neighbors. Toward the end of his time in Spain, Scipio Africanus had settled some of his wounded veterans at Italica—not far from modern Seville in the lower valley of the Baetis River—probably to protect his forces against any return by the Carthaginians. This town would become a major center of Roman power. From the start, it was a mixed settlement with firm local roots: The Roman and Italian veterans who formed the core of its population would have sought wives locally. The decision in 198 to choose two more praetors each year may well amount to an acknowledgment by the senate that Rome's involvement in the peninsula was to be long-lasting.

The nature of a command in Spain during the early second century can be appreciated from the campaigns of 195 and 194, one of the few instances at this date when Nearer Spain received a consul as governor. Accounts are especially detailed, and they probably derive in large part from the writings of the commander himself, Marcus Porcius Cato the Elder, who was lavish with self-praise. Once arrived in Spain, he first assisted the citizens of Greek Emporiae (Rome's main port of entry into the peninsula), who were so frightened of their Iberian neighbors that they refused to leave the town at night except in large groups, and forbade Iberians to come inside their city walls. At the same time, Cato sought to supply his troops as well as train them by seizing crops and plundering the countryside, thereby in all likelihood only worsening much of the tension around Emporiae. Later in his term of office, Cato campaigned in the lower Ebro Valley and farther south along the coast. In the course of these wars, he plundered freely, ignored arrangements made by earlier commanders, and claimed to have firmly settled the affairs of his province. The amount of captured treasure he displayed in his subsequent triumph and the size of the "donatives"—a commander's distributions of money to his soldiers at the end of a campaign—together testify to his success in plundering, but later events confirm that Nearer Spain was far from settled; succeeding governors would continue campaigning in the same areas for several decades.

For almost forty years, Spain received praetors as commanders. The senate usually assigned two *provinciae*: Nearer Spain (*Hispania Citerior*), centered on Tarraco, the Massiliote colonies, and the lower Ebro Valley; and Further Spain (*Hispania Ulterior*), the valley of the Baetis River. Both governors conducted small-scale campaigns with relatively limited forces, at first near the centers of their power and later at some distance, fighting against groups and confederations on the peninsula's central plateau.

Away from the coast and the Baetis Valley, Roman commanders found it difficult to establish control over the population, or to form any lasting ties of alliance and subordination. The inhabitants here lived in dispersed settlements, and often they were highly mobile, abandoning their towns and villages at the approach of an army only to return after it had departed; their dependence upon herding for a livelihood merely enhanced their freedom of movement. Sometimes communities were organized in larger tribes and confederacies, but for the most part they united only when a prominent leader arose. The authority of any such leader was typically no more than fleeting, however. He would retain followers for as long as he remained successful; but once he failed, the armies and alliances he had built could dissolve with great rapidity. Some Roman commanders attempted to install displaced Iberians in more settled communities, which might prove easier to control. Thus Tiberius Sempronius Gracchus, governor of Nearer Spain in 180 and 179, created a number of new towns, one of which he named Gracchurris after himself.

From the middle of the 150s, warfare became more serious and larger in scale, and the senate often assigned *provinciae* to consuls. These wars centered on two groups, the Lusitanians and the Celtiberians; later, the historian Florus (1.33) would claim that these two were so troublesome because they were the only ones with competent leaders. The Lusitanians inhabited the region to the northwest of the Baetis Valley and to the southwest of the central plateau crossed by the Tagus and Anas rivers (modern Tejo and Guadiana). According to Roman historians, Lusitanian raiders ravaged the fields of Rome's subjects, and in 155 they even defeated the armies of two praetors. In 150, Servius Sulpicius Galba, commanding in Further Spain, invaded Lusitania and persuaded some Lusitanians to surrender, but he then massacred thousands and sold the survivors as slaves. This Roman treachery helped Viriathus (who had escaped the massacre) to emerge as a powerful leader and to assemble a following among both his fellow Lusitanians and other disaffected groups in Spain. He waged war with marked success, defeating several Roman armies. Eventually in 139, Quintus Servilius Caepio, having failed to defeat him in battle, arranged for his assassination. As a result, Decimus Junius Brutus, consul in 138, was able to make peace, giving Viriathus' surviving followers land to cultivate. Brutus then began to campaign even further toward the northwest of the peninsula.

At about the same time, the Romans also entered into a lengthy series of wars with the Celtiberians. Their settlement at Numantia occupied a strong position on a high ridge in the upper reaches of the valley of the Durius River (modern Douro). In the 150s, 140s, and 130s, no less than five Roman consuls commanding in Nearer Spain made unsuccessful attacks on it, and two of them—Quintus Pompeius in 141 and Gaius Hostilius Mancinus in 137—had to negotiate peace terms, which the senate later rejected, in order to secure the safe withdrawal of their armies. Publius Cornelius Scipio Aemilianus, the victor over Carthage in the Third Punic War (see North Africa section) and chosen consul for the second time for 134, finally put an end to this war. After an eight-month siege, the Numantines—reported as numbering 4,000—surrendered to Scipio in 133. Traces still survive of the wall he constructed to surround the town, and of the seven camps he built for his soldiers; the remains of six other camps testify to earlier, failed attempts on the town.

Through all these wars, Roman arrangements in Spain were becoming more settled and more profitable to the Roman state. Parts of Spain became the home of Romans and Italians, not to mention others who claimed Roman or Italian ancestry. In 171, the senate ordered a Roman commander to settle the children of Roman soldiers and Spanish women—under Roman law, the children of such marriages would not have been Roman citizens—at Carteia on the south coast, where they were to form a new community with the same rights that Latin colonies possessed in Italy. Either early in the 160s or in 152 (he served in Spain twice), Marcus Claudius Marcellus founded Corduba (modern Córdoba), another mixed settlement like Italica, further down the Baetis River. There can be no question that during the same period some Roman citizens and Italian allies migrated to Spain privately in search of opportunities and profit, although few traces of such individuals happen to survive in our sources.

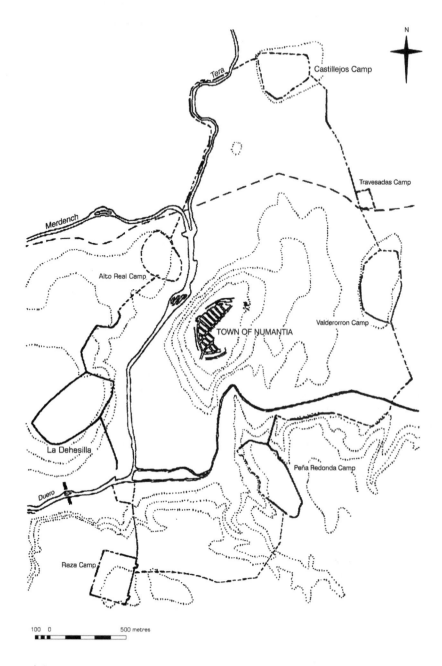

Figure 4.3 *According to the historian Appian (Iberian Wars 90–91), Scipio Aemilianus encircled Numantia with seven forts. He linked them by a ditch and a palisade more than forty-eight stades (6 miles/9.6 km) long; behind these works he constructed a stone wall with towers every 100 feet (30 m). Last but not least, he blocked the river with tree trunks. By these means, he closely surrounded the city and cut it off from its countryside. Substantial traces of the forts on their hilltops and of the wall are still visible. Scipio's own headquarters was probably at the northernmost fort, known as Castillejos.*

In the decades immediately following the end of the Second Punic War, Roman financial arrangements in Spain were for the most part simple. Commanders raised money to pay their troops, and food to feed them, through plunder and forced contributions. Each commander, moreover, seems to have made his own arrangements, disregarding any pattern established by his predecessors whenever a change was felt to be convenient or necessary. However, the command of Tiberius Sempronius Gracchus in Nearer Spain in 180 and 179 marks a turning point. During his time in the province, he tried to specify more clearly the obligations of some of the allied communities under his authority, and to regularize their financial contributions. By midcentury, some communities in both provinces provided 5 percent of their grain each year, while others paid a fixed sum of money. Even so, there was no single system that regulated all of Rome's Spanish subjects.

Over time, the Romans also began to exploit Spain's mineral resources more systematically. In 195, Cato the Elder in some way arranged for the operators of certain mines north of the Ebro River to make regular contributions of iron and silver. The deposits of ore here were limited in fact, and the collection of this tax in metals need not have been very complicated, let alone notably profitable. Later operations were on a larger scale, however. Mines on the fringes of the Baetis Valley and in the hills behind New Carthage certainly proved more lucrative. Polybius (34.9.8) described the latter mines as extending over an area of about one hundred square miles (260 sq km), where 40,000 miners working in the pits recovered enough silver each day to provide the Roman state with as much as 10,800 pounds (4,900 kg) of ore annually. Diodorus Siculus (5.36–38) claimed that Italians exploited these mines, using a vast workforce of slaves who toiled day and night under horrific conditions and frequently died from exhaustion.

Greece and Asia Minor

After the end of the Second Punic War, the Romans also began to intervene more regularly in the politics and diplomacy of the Balkans and Asia Minor. Polybius (1.3.6) maintained that, after their defeat of Carthage in 201, the Romans reached out to grab Greece and Asia. But the truth was undoubtedly far more complex than a simple scheme of Roman aggression.

The eastern Mediterranean was a bewildering mix of kingdoms, tribal states, city-states, and leagues of city-states, all with shifting alliances and enmities. Three kingdoms tended to dominate. First, the kings of Macedon had long sought to extend their power over the Greek cities of the south, the islands of the Aegean, and neighboring kingdoms in the Balkans. Second, the Seleucids of Syria had once ruled an extensive state that reached from the Mediterranean to the frontiers of India, but by now much of it had fallen away from their rule. Third, the Ptolemies of Egypt fought Syria for control over Palestine; with their powerful fleet, they also dominated and protected some of the islands in the Aegean, and they often intervened in the affairs of cities on the Greek mainland. Around these three great monarchies, there were many lesser states, sometimes allied with larger ones and commonly on the lookout to pursue their own advantage. Unlike in Spain, the Romans would employ elaborate diplomatic and administrative protocol to confront these well-established and powerful states to the east; consequently this gave Roman intervention here a very different character.

Roman forces first crossed the Adriatic Sea before the Second Punic War. In 229, both consuls campaigned against an Illyrian ruler whose ships had attacked vessels belonging to Italian merchants who were citizens of communities under Roman protection. In this brief war, the consuls helped the Greek cities of Corcyra, Apollonia, and Epidamnus to expel their Illyrian garrisons, and they then placed these communities under Roman protection. Almost a decade later, the consuls of 219 received as their shared *provincia* a war against another Illyrian ruler seeking to expand his power southwards.

Roman actions in Illyria and Epirus came to involve another, more powerful ruler. The First Macedonian War (215–205) grew out of the Second Punic War. After Rome's defeat at Cannae in 216, Philip V, the Macedonian king, probably suspicious of Roman interventions across the Adriatic, began to negotiate with Hannibal. Discovery of their alliance led to war between Rome and Macedon. The senate sent a praetor with ships and soldiers, and, after several years of campaigning, he began to assemble a coalition of cities, leagues, and kings that felt threatened by Macedon. The two most important were the Aetolian League—communities in western Greece that elected leaders, made war as a group, and were feared as pillagers—and Pergamum in western Asia Minor, a long-time enemy and rival of Macedon, ruled by King Attalus I. This coalition of allies did not make war according to a common strategy, nor did the Romans, with so many commitments elsewhere, pursue the war vigorously. Attalus disengaged in 208, and the Aetolians made peace with Philip in 206. In the next year, Philip and the Romans made peace, the so-called Peace of Phoenice, in which both sides essentially kept what they held.

The Second Macedonian War (200–196) marked the beginning of the next stage of Roman intervention. Immediately after the end of the war with Carthage, Rome's former ally Attalus of Pergamum, together with some Greek cities, successfully urged intervention in Greece, a plea that must have gained strength from resentment among the Roman elite over Philip's earlier alliance with Hannibal. The first Roman commanders campaigned in the west, shielding allies and trying to force the passes over the mountains into Macedon itself. Titus Quinctius Flamininus, consul in 198 and proconsul for several years after, did then penetrate this far, and—with the assistance of his Greek allies—was able to defeat Philip's army at Cynoscephalae in 197. In the peace that followed, Philip agreed to withdraw his garrisons from Greek cities, surrender most of his fleet, and pay Rome a large indemnity. Shortly afterwards, therefore, the senate ceased assigning *provinciae* in this area.

Rome's actions here stand in stark contrast to its behavior in Spain. To judge by actions alone, the Roman senate could be thought to have had no desire for a per-

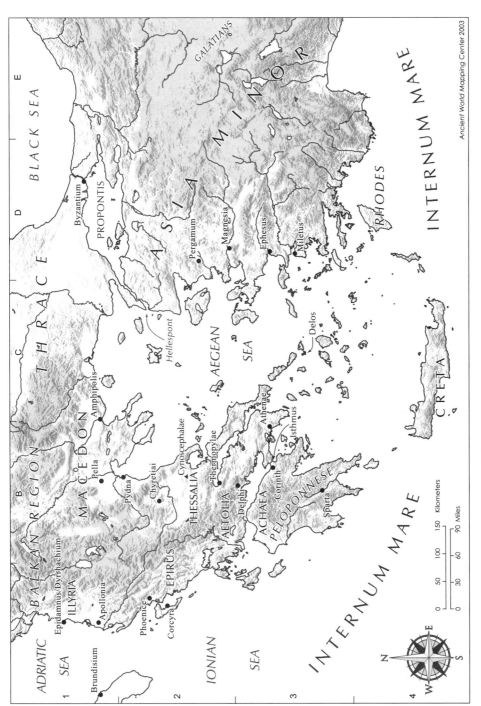

Map 4.5 *Greece, the Aegean, and Western Asia Minor*

manent military presence in the region. It would be mistaken, however, to infer that consequently Rome's leaders did not regard themselves as preeminent here. After his victory, Flamininus proclaimed the freedom of a number of Greek cities at the Isthmian Games, where thousands had gathered for the festival. Proclamations of freedom had a long and honored place in Hellenistic diplomacy, and Flamininus' decree shows how Romans adapted themselves to local practices while maintaining their own leadership. Kings typically issued proclamations of freedom to win over allies, and to weaken rivals by encouraging their subject-cities to defect. Such "freedom" usually meant no foreign garrisons, no tribute, and no change to existing laws; however, it did not mean that the newly freed city could also omit to acknowledge the leadership of a larger and more powerful state.

Subsequent events would reveal how seriously the senate took its claims to leadership. The first major military intervention following the Second Macedonian War came shortly after the withdrawal of Roman armies. Antiochus III, king of Syria, had restored much of the grandeur and power of the Seleucid dynasty, and, after a seven-year campaign into eastern Iran, he was regarded by some as a second Alexander. While Rome was engaged with Philip V, Antiochus had extended his power in Asia Minor, largely surrounding the small kingdom of Pergamum; he had even recovered part of Thrace, which had once belonged to his predecessors. Before the beginning of the Syrian War (192–189), he had frequent exchanges of embassies with the Romans, as well as with a number of Greek cities and rulers; there were also such exchanges among the Greek cities and leagues themselves. In all this diplomacy, Antiochus achieved some success, most notably an alliance with the Aetolians, former allies of Rome, who felt they had not been sufficiently rewarded for their participation in the Second Macedonian War.

Hostilities began in 192, when Antiochus sent a small force across the Aegean Sea to Greece, where it joined with the armies of some allied states. Early in 191, the consul Manius Acilius Glabrio crossed with his army from Brundisium to Apollonia, marched across the mountains into Thessaly, and defeated Antiochus and his allies at Thermopylae. In the next year, the senate sent a commander with an army and a fleet across the Aegean, where they joined forces with Eumenes, who had succeeded Attalus as king of Pergamum. Finally in 189, Lucius Cornelius Scipio, the brother of Africanus, defeated Antiochus' army at Magnesia. Antiochus had to abandon all his claims to Asia Minor, refrain from making alliances in Greece and around the Aegean, surrender most of his ships and his war elephants, and pay an exceptionally large indemnity. In Asia Minor, Roman officials and legates then divided Antiochus' territory among Eumenes and other allies.

Gnaeus Manlius Vulso followed this victory with a campaign against the Galatians, Gallic migrants who had entered Asia Minor in the previous century and had for decades posed a threat to the kings of Pergamum as well as to settled communities throughout the region. Vulso's campaign was highly successful, devastating many of the communities of the Galatians and forcing them to accept peace on Roman terms. Within a few years, the senate again assigned no more provinciae in Greece, the Balkans, and Asia Minor for some time.

A primary goal in these wars was stability in Greece together with preservation of Rome's position in the Greek world. Roman forces returned to Greece because Antiochus III appeared to be challenging Rome's leadership there, and because some of Rome's allies seemed to be willing to join him. Such a desire to lead, but not necessarily to rule or to exploit systematically, evidently lay behind other Roman actions in the area. At first, it would seem, the senate attempted to assert Roman preeminence largely through diplomatic means. The Greek world possessed a complicated political and diplomatic culture. Here, rulers and cities both formed and broke alliances as needs and opportunities arose, the weaker sought protection from the stronger, and the parties to a dispute (be it domestic or foreign) sought arbitration by outside powers. For the powerful, alliances, calls for protection, and requests for arbitration were signs of their strength and their benevolence. For the less powerful, they were means to gain benefits that were otherwise unattainable, in exchange for giving public thanks and acknowledging dependent status.

Rome's elite adapted to these practices. The senate itself received foreign embassies and, when possible, granted their requests. Senatorial legates arbitrated boundary disputes, decided which cities should be free and self-governing and which should be subject to another, forced kings to give up garrisons, and sometimes merely observed. We have evidence of some Greek cities thanking prominent Romans for their benefactions in the proper way. Chyretiai, for example, honored Flamininus for returning property that the Romans had seized during the war against Philip V by erecting a monument on which his letter granting the city's requests was inscribed. In the letter, Flamininus used appropriate language for a benefactor, claiming that he wished the citizens to "learn of our nobility of character," and announcing that the Romans did not wish "to be avaricious, but instead thought good will and a good reputation to be of the highest importance." In their interventions, the senate and its legates tended to act most willingly and firmly against those who resisted giving due recognition to their leadership, or who seemed likely to disrupt it, or even to contemplate supplanting it.

The Third Macedonian War (171–168) ended the Macedonian monarchy. For years, prominent Romans had distrusted Philip's son and successor, Perseus, and were willing to listen to complaints against him. Perseus' marriage to a daughter of Seleucus IV, Antiochus' successor as king of Syria, no doubt increased their suspicions. In 172, Eumenes of Pergamum came to Rome with a long list of complaints against Perseus, and, with these as pretexts, the senate decided on war. The result was that in 168 Lucius Aemilius Paullus defeated Perseus at Pydna, where he had concentrated his army. The terms of the peace were severe. Perseus was transported to Rome, where he was paraded in Paullus' triumph; later, he was imprisoned in the Latin colony of Alba Fucens. Macedon was divided into

to some cities under its control. When the Achaeans refused to comply, war began. In 146, Lucius Mummius defeated the League's army and captured Corinth, one of the richest and most famous cities in Greece. As a dire warning to other Greeks, he then plundered and destroyed it, and sold many of its citizens into slavery.

North Africa

To the west, Roman armies and fleets were waging war against Carthage at the same time. The Third Punic War (149–146) began as a result of longstanding quarrels between the Carthaginians and Masinissa, king of the Numidians (as noted earlier in the chapter). For years, Masinissa had been making provocative demands of the Carthaginians, and in the resulting arbitrations, Roman ambassadors had generally supported the Numidian king. For equally long, too, some leading Romans had not hesitated to voice the enmity and suspicion they felt towards Carthage. In particular, according to one tradition, for several years before Rome finally declared war, Cato the Elder ended every speech he made in the senate with the demand that Carthage must be destroyed. Eventually, the exasperated Carthaginians used force to resist Numidian claims, and the senate made this step the cause for war. When a Roman army and fleet arrived in 149, however, the Carthaginians immediately surrendered in the apparent hope that they would receive acceptable terms. At first, the Roman commander demanded hostages, and then, when the Carthaginians complied, the surrender of all Carthaginian arms. When these too were handed over, the Carthaginians were next told to abandon their city and live elsewhere. At this point, they finally acknowledged that there was no viable option but to resist.

For over two years, Roman forces besieged the city. It was not until early in 146 that, under the leadership of Scipio Aemilianus (grandson through adoption of Scipio Africanus), they were able to force their way inside. In days of street fighting, they killed thousands of Carthaginians, enslaved many thousands more, and completely destroyed the city. Afterwards, Scipio and his senatorial advisors imposed heavy penalties on the Punic cities that had remained loyal to Carthage, while rewarding those that had changed sides. From now onwards too, the senate regularly assigned Carthage's former territory here as a provincia called "Africa." This destruction of Corinth and Carthage during the same year marked the end of an era in Roman expansion; Roman historians later would believe that both events also signaled the beginning of Rome's moral decline.

SUGGESTED READINGS:

Beard, Mary, John North, and Simon Price. 1998. *Religions of Rome*. Vol. 1, *A History*; Vol. 2, *A Sourcebook*, Cambridge: Cambridge University Press.
Goldsworthy, Adrian K. 2000. *The Punic Wars*. London: Cassell.

Gruen, Erich S. 1984. *The Hellenistic World and the Coming of Rome.* Berkeley, Los Angeles, London: University of California Press.

Gruen, Erich S. 1992. *Culture and National Identity in Republican Rome.* Ithaca, New York: Cornell University Press.

Harris, William V. 1979. *War and Imperialism in Republican Rome, 327–70 B.C.* Oxford: Oxford University Press.

Richardson, J. S. 1986. *Hispaniae: Spain and the Development of Roman Imperialism, 218–82 B.C.* Cambridge: Cambridge University Press.

5

ITALY AND EMPIRE

After the Second Punic War, Roman power spread throughout much of the Mediterranean world. This expansion was accompanied by major changes in the social, political, and cultural life of Rome and many other Italian communities as a result of the burdens of military service, the great wealth acquired through conquest, the consequent movements of people, and the deeper exposure to foreign ideas and practices. The first half of the second century marked the high point of the domination of the state by the senate and the nobility. Thereafter, in the third quarter of the century, a steady accumulation of political tensions and divisions would lead to the emergence of new forms of political activity that would undermine the senate's leadership.

SENATORS, OFFICIALS, AND CITIZEN ASSEMBLIES

During this heyday of power and prestige for the senate and nobility, it was the norm for members of a relatively few families to hold the offices of consul and censor. At the same time, the consensus of senators, expressed in the form of decrees, exercised a strong influence over policy making. In the second century, the 300 senators were chosen from former officeholders, and each senator, once chosen, served for life unless he was convicted in court, or unless a subsequent pair of censors dropped him from the senatorial roll for some moral failing. When an officeholder consulted the senate, senators registered their opinion in the form of an advisory decree or *senatus consultum*, rather than an order, since the formal role of the senate was to advise. Senatorial decrees were not determined by a strict majority vote. Instead, leading senators or *principes* (singular, *princeps*)—the members who generally had held the highest offices, belonged to the leading families, and had acquired the greatest fame and glory—sought to create a broad consensus for or against policies and individuals.

Since the late fourth century, the senate had taken for itself a wide range of rights and privileges that enabled its members to exercise considerable influence over public affairs. In the years following the Second Punic War, the senate determined the tasks that magistrates would perform, fixed the funds that governors would receive to finance their operations, selected the magistrates whose terms in office would be extended, and ruled on the acceptability of treaties that generals in the field had negotiated. On occasion, the senate chose some of its members to serve as "legates" (*legati*; singular *legatus*) to go on embassies or to assist a governor in his province. At some point, the senate also acquired the power to determine the validity of rulings issued by priestly colleges on matters of sacred law and ritual procedure. Altogether, the senate's place in the Roman political order rested on its great prestige and authority, and on the acquiescence of elected officials who themselves were senators. At the same time, however, the fact is that the senate lacked any specific power to command, to punish, to enact laws, or to implement policies.

In law and by custom, Rome's "government" corresponded to the officeholders who were elected to fill specific posts for limited periods of time. Only they could call meetings of the senate and of citizen assemblies, hear legal cases and issue judgments, command armies, and perform public rites and ceremonies. In the city, their ability to act could be obstructed by certain other officials and priests. Higher magistrates did not command or instruct lesser magistrates in Rome, although they could forbid them to act at all in specific cases. Consuls and praetors could each block the actions of colleagues who held the same office and possessed identical powers, but they could only do this when present personally on the spot. Within the city, tribunes of the plebs could likewise block any magistrate's action, but once again personal intervention was a requirement.

In the city, too, state religion forced many magistrates to adhere closely to established procedures; on occasion, religion could equally serve to check their activities. In particular, when consuls and praetors were in Rome, a wide range of mandatory rituals surrounded their public actions. Moreover, omissions or flaws in the performance of rites could have serious consequences. If colleges of priests found fault, and if the senate concurred, the official's act would be declared invalid. On other occasions, even a single augur could order the postponement of a public meeting, for example, if he announced that he had seen signs that the gods desired such a delay. This right of priests and senate to nullify magisterial actions in the city did not extend to the tribunes of the plebs, although some senators would advocate making them, too, subject to the same checks.

Elected officials, and through them the senate, also controlled the voting assemblies of Roman citizens, which alone could enact legislation and fill offices through elections. Only certain officials—consuls, praetors, and tribunes of the plebs—could call citizens together for a vote. In addition, at any legislative assembly, the presiding official alone chose the speakers to address the assembled citizens, and he alone fixed the text of each proposal, which could only be accepted or rejected without amendment. Votes had to take place within a single day, and voters had to be present in person. So any citizen who did not live in the city, but wished to vote, had to make the journey from near or far to attend; in all likelihood, only the wealthiest normally had the time or inclination to come from any notable distance, unless the proposal to be voted on was of exceptional interest or importance. It is likely in any case that all eligible citizens could not have been accommodated if an assembly turned out to attract an exceptional crowd: In the middle of the second century, for example, there were around 400,000 adult male citizens, but the Campus Martius—the place where elections of consuls and praetors were usually held—could only accommodate about 70,000 at most.

In the third and early second centuries, moreover, the tribunes of the plebs, who had once mobilized citizens against the governing elite during the Struggle of the Orders (see Chapter Two), had become more a part of the established order. Few tribunes now used the powers of their office to put forward laws that most senators opposed, or to obstruct official actions with broad senatorial support. In the first decades of the century, tribunes generally put forward proposals that had already met with senatorial approval, or blocked actions by magistrates in the city that were known to displease many senators. In consequence, with no candidates outside the elite to support for election or tribunes to put forward proposals, the mass of Roman citizens could make their opinions known only through demonstrations and heckling.

Few officials defied a senatorial consensus for long. To be sure, the senate's decrees were only advisory and it could not formally compel obedience, yet still the great majority of officials largely followed its wishes. Officeholders had an interest in preserving the power and position of a body to which they themselves belonged. In addition, the senate collectively, and leading senators individually, could obstruct the political advancement of senators who had isolated themselves too much from the majority of members. Only the senate could grant triumphs, for example—essential distinctions to maintain a commander's fame and glory (see Chapter Four). Candidates for office, moreover, required allies in the senate at election time, and the more prestigious these allies were, the better. Last but not least, the senate's assumption of the power to assign tasks to each group of officials annually allowed it to exercise great influence.

Meantime it should not be forgotten that some of the governing elite were concerned to prevent prominent and popular senators from overshadowing their peers by too wide a margin. Senators after all, especially the most prominent among them, were participants in a constant competition for fame and glory, and certain very ambitious individuals within this circle may occasionally have desired to achieve an unduly preeminent place in the city. From the beginning of the senate's rise in the late fourth and early third centuries, officials made attempts therefore—probably with the support of most senators—to limit an individual's ability to stand out too far above his peers (see Chapter Three). Limits on the number of times that anyone could hold high office were clearly a key restriction in this respect. The great fame achieved by commanders both in the Second Punic War and in the numerous subsequent wars may well have induced many senators to favor restricting their most ambitious colleagues still further, although such legislation was not always successful.

However, during the decades following the Second Punic War a series of laws did now attempt to force senators' careers into a more regular, obligatory pattern. It became a formal requirement that anyone who stood for election as quaestor (the lowest senatorial office) had to have already completed ten years of military service. Moreover the offices were formed into a fixed hierarchy, within which individuals had to advance step by step from lesser offices to higher. In the fourth century and earlier, by contrast, it could happen that a more powerful office would sometimes be held before a lesser one; even in the early third century, some men were consul before they became praetor. However, a law enacted after the Second Macedonian War made it mandatory that from now onwards anyone seeking election as consul must have already served as praetor. In 180, a tribune Lucius Villius successfully proposed the first law fixing the minimum age at which the offices of praetor and consul could be held, and requiring that at least ten years should always elapse before a holder of either of these offices should be able to hold the same one again. Later, after this interval had not been observed when Marcus Claudius Marcellus gained the consulship for the third time in 152, further legislation prohibited holding the office of consul more than once.

Altogether, the eventual result was the development of a standard *cursus honorum* or hierarchy of senatorial offices within which contemporaries competed against one another to move up from quaestor to praetor to consul, and even censor. At each stage, of course, more competitors would fail to advance, because successively fewer positions were available. In addition, the offices of tribune of the plebs and aedile were optional—no patrician could even seek the tribunate unless he irrevocably renounced his status and became a plebeian—but most senators tried to gain one of these two offices in between serving as quaestor and seeking election as praetor.

Threats of prosecution were the sole check on the actions of officials when away from the city of Rome. In practice, only a limited number of perceived offenses against public order were investigated. In most such instances—especially when ordinary citizens were the suspects—Roman officeholders personally conducted investigations (*quaestiones*) commissioned by the senate or by a law passed in a citizen assembly. With the advice of assessors whom they chose themselves (usually fellow senators), presiding officials received accusations, sought out evidence against those suspected of crimes, listened to arguments in defense, proclaimed their verdicts and ordered punishments, and rewarded informants. The punishment usually followed soon after the verdict.

When senators or former magistrates were themselves the subject of the investigation, a different procedure was followed. In the late third and second centuries, prosecutions for official misconduct—charges such as cowardice, incompetence, and corruption—generally took place before assemblies of citizens, who would vote on the fate of the defendants. From the second century onwards, prosecutions of former officials in fact became a common feature of the Roman political order. Trial hearings offered a natural opportunity for a prominent citizen's rivals to try and damage his prestige, and many leading senators faced multiple prosecutions in the course of their careers. Even Scipio Africanus eventually withdrew from public life to avoid further such harassment.

From 149, a series of laws began to create permanent courts—so-called *quaestiones perpetuae*—to try certain specific offenses by magistrates and senators. In that year, a tribune Lucius Calpurnius Piso carried a law establishing such a court to hear charges of extortion in the provinces (see Chapter Six). According to this Calpurnian law, accusers presented their cases to juries chosen from members of the senate, who would then issue verdicts that could not be appealed. Later, similar permanent courts for other offenses would be established, in some of which it was permissible to prosecute nonsenators too. In time, as we shall see below, the question of who should comprise the juries of all the permanent courts would become a contentious political issue.

ITALY AND THE CONSEQUENCES OF EMPIRE

Italy had long been a land with marked regional differences in language, economic and social organization, and political and religious life. By the end of the Second Punic War, communities with Roman citizenship were concentrated in Latium, Campania, southernmost Etruria, Sabinum, and a few adjacent areas along the Adriatic coast; those cities possessing full citizenship were mostly nearer to Rome than those with only partial citizen rights. Both levels of citizen community still also maintained much of their original culture, although they did adapt themselves to some Roman forms and procedures. The citizen communities aside, substantial regions of Italy—for example, Etruria, Umbria, Lucania, Samnium, Bruttium, and the Greek cities of the south—all remained as allies with their own customs and practices, and no Roman citizen rights.

During the second century, however, much of Italy experienced profound changes that disrupted long-established political and social practices. Some of the changes stemmed from wartime devastation and from the harsh peace that Rome forced on disloyal allies. Others derived from the movements of people within the peninsula made possible by the greater integration of Italian communities. Still others were consequences of the vast influx of wealth derived from Rome's wars outside of Italy. At the same time, as the result of warfare, diplomacy, and business dealings, members of the elite throughout Italy gained a closer familiarity with Greece and Asia Minor; the societies they encountered here were older, wealthier, and more complex, and offered attractive models to emulate in many respects.

Changing Relations Between Rome, Its *Municipia*, and Allies

The Second Punic War and its aftermath imposed severe strain on Rome's network of alliances and cities with shared citizenship. Some remained loyal, but at great cost in lost lives, devastated farms and fields, and increased internal political tensions. Others abandoned their relationship with Rome, and sought greater freedom of action in an alliance with Hannibal and Carthage. When Rome recaptured the cities of former allies, its commanders unflinchingly ordered the executions of leading citizens and the enslavement of many others. In the course of the arrangements made after the end of the war, moreover, many communities in southern Italy suffered massive confiscations of land, which badly hurt their citizens and their economies. In the second century, too, Roman officials came to involve themselves more deeply in the internal affairs of cities, and to distinguish more sharply between Roman citizens and their Italian allies. By the end of the century, relations between Rome and some of its allies had worsened considerably.

In the Po Valley and in peninsular Italy, Roman officials conducted large-scale settlement projects. Immediately after the Second Punic War, commissioners settled veterans of campaigns in Spain, Sicily, and North Africa on some of the land confiscated from rebellious allies. Over the next two decades, the senate and assemblies ordered the establishment of a dozen new colonies, and the reinforcement of five existing ones in the territories of allies they presumably considered to be untrustworthy. During the 180s and 170s, Roman officials established eight more colonies in connection with campaigns in northern Italy, and in 173 they distributed small plots of land taken from the Gauls to Romans and Latins in more scattered settlements, without the formation of any new urban center to serve as the focus of self-government. Altogether, these various projects may have settled as many as 50,000 men and their families in colonies, together with an unknown number of other recipients in the veteran assignments of 200 and in the land distributions of 173. In 180, moreover, Roman officials moved up to perhaps 50,000 Ligures from their homes in northern Italy, and settled them on confiscated land in the south.

During the war with Hannibal and for two decades after its end, the senate had regularly instructed magistrates and promagistrates to search out signs of disloyalty in some allied cities and to punish those suspected of it. This task was by definition intrusive, and, on occasion, such magistrates' actions may well have been harsh. Attempts to search out perceived threats to good order wherever they might be found were not limited to charges of assisting Rome's enemies. Three times between 184 and 179, the senate assigned to praetors the task of investigating the many poisonings said to be taking place. For the Romans, the crime of poisoning (*veneficium*) included not only doing harm through drugs or potions, but also causing injuries through magic and the casting of spells; it was, thus, a category of offense readily open to rumor and panic.

Another series of investigations may have been even more intrusive and extensive. In 186, Roman officials and senators became disturbed by the practices and wide diffusion of the cult of the god Bacchus, the Greek Dionysus. This Bacchic cult was deeply entrenched in the cities of Campania and the south, but its devotees could also be found in Rome and other cities: In Etruscan Volsinii, for instance, a grotto was dedicated to Bacchus in a public space in the city during the third century. His worship often involved groups with no official sanction, outside of a city's normal religious and political framework. Moreover, in these rites there could be shouting, frenzied dancing, the use of cymbals and drums, drinking, and some sexual license. In Rome itself, the cult may have become more active in recent years, mixing men and women, some from prominent families, and performing nocturnal rites in secret.

Figure 5.1 *Late in the second century, a number of objects associated with the worship of Dionysus were placed in a votive deposit just outside the north gate of the Etruscan city of Vulci. Among them were a terracotta statue of a seated Dionysus and a small terracotta model of a temple. The two reclining figures in the pediment of the temple represent Dionysus and Ariadne (Etruscan, Fufluns and Ariatha) in a sacred union.*

According to the historian Livy (39.8–19), Spurius Postumius Albinus, one of the consuls of 186, began the investigation after receiving reports that worshippers included ritual murders and poisonings in their nocturnal rites. The senate then issued a decree ordering a search for Bacchic priests in both Rome and the rest of Italy, forbidding initiates to gather for rites, and instructing investigators to seek out criminals and performers of immoral acts. Lesser officials were to guard against nocturnal meetings and fire, always a danger in a crowded city such as Rome. Other provisions of this senatorial decree—which is known from an inscription found in Samnium—ordered the dismantling of shrines, prohibited the mixing of men and women on ritual occasions, forbade men to be priests, and banned secret rites and the swearing of oaths. The deliberate destruction of the Bacchic grotto at Volsinii early in the second century may have been prompted by the decree. The consul Postumius in fact spent his entire year implementing it, and Livy believed that his investigations resulted in many executions. Two years later in 184, the senate assigned Apulia to a praetor as his province and ordered him to look into the cult, end its troublemaking there, and prevent the worship from spreading. In the next year, another praetor received the same assignment.

An expansion of full Roman citizenship and a hardening of the distinctions between Romans and non-Romans accompanied greater Roman surveillance over local affairs in Italy. Among Romans, the chief division had been between residents of municipia with the right to vote in Roman elections, and residents of communities without this right. Over much of the third and second centuries, the full citizenship with voting rights was gradually extended to more cities that had not previously possessed it. The Sabines received this privilege in 268, while Arpinum, Formiae, and Fundi became municipia with it in 188. Because of the patchiness of our surviving evidence, the stages and rapidity of the process remain unclear. By the end of the second century, however, in all probability only a few citizen communities would still not have gained the right to vote. All these extensions of the right to vote, it should be remembered, required assigning each community concerned to a Roman tribe; this was now done, not by creating new tribes, but by assigning new communities to existing ones.

At the same time, the distinctions between Romans and Latins became more pronounced. In the first decades of the second century, the right of Latins to take up Roman citizenship by moving to Rome was progressively restricted. Acting on the complaints of Latin communities that feared losing their citizens, the senate first agreed to require all Latins who wished to move to Rome (and thereby acquire Roman citizenship) to leave behind in their community a son who could fill their place. In the 180s and 170s, the senate also assigned magistrates the task of expelling Latins from Rome, and removing from the rolls of Roman citizens those who had improperly acquired the status.

One incident can illustrate changed perceptions of the relationship between Rome and its Italian allies. In 173, the consul Lucius Postumius Albinus, while traveling to Campania on official business, sent a message ahead to Praeneste (an allied city in Latium) instructing its officials to come out to meet him (a mark of special honor), to prepare to accommodate and entertain him at their own expense, and to provide pack animals for his baggage. The historian Livy (42.1.7–12), who reports the incident, claims that it was unprecedented. The senate customarily supplied Roman officials with mules and tents so that they might not be a burden to the allies. Prominent Romans, when journeying away from the city, normally stayed with other wealthy individuals with whom they shared hospitality, housing their hosts when they came to Rome. Only ambassadors, forced to make a sudden journey from Rome, could require more, and they were limited by law to one pack animal from each city through which they passed. Postumius' demands proved successful, however, and Livy reports that such behavior became more common. Outside of Italy, it is true, for some time past Roman officials had provided for their own maintenance in this arrogant fashion; now, some were treating Italian allies—who had borne many of the burdens of Rome's wars—just as they did Roman subjects elsewhere.

At the same time, the Romans seem to have gradually shifted more of the burdens and fewer of the benefits of waging war to the Latins and other Italian allies. Here, the evidence is too uncertain to do more than outline a general trend. At any rate, during the second century the numbers of Roman citizens probably increased more rapidly than did the populations of Latin and allied cities. Many of the latter, after all, had suffered badly in the Second Punic War, and some had lost land that would later be distributed to Roman citizens. No doubt the Romans had always apportioned the burdens and benefits of warfare unequally, but there are signs now that allied communities were carrying more of the burdens for a smaller share of the profits. During the second century, the ratio of Roman citizens to Latins and other allies in Rome's armies varied between rough equality to two allies for each Roman. By the end of the century, however, allied contingents seem to have regularly outnumbered Roman ones. In addition, in 167 the senate suspended the collection of *tributum* from citizens, since the treasury was full with the profits of expansion (the Third Macedonian War had proved especially lucrative: see Chapter Four). By contrast, Latin and allied cities in all likelihood still had to tax themselves to maintain their own soldiers.

This movement toward increased differentiation between Rome and its Italian allies was accompanied by a greater imitation of Roman institutions and practices. Latin colonies, founded by Roman officials, had long been organized in a Roman manner. Now, some allied communities began to imitate Rome more closely. Especially in the south of Italy, more communities began to use Latin in official inscriptions, and there are signs of an increased use of Roman law, even in communities that were not formally bound by it. Moreover, some allied communities began to give to their officials Latin titles, such as aedile or quaestor, or to call their own advisory council a senate.

Roman and Italian Elites

The political and social orders of Rome and its municipia and allies each rested on small groups of wealthy, prominent families, who held magistracies and priesthoods, and who filled out the ranks of the senate or its equivalent in the many smaller cities of Italy. In the second century, these ruling elites of Rome and of many other Italian cities grew richer through the profits of empire. They began to beautify their cities, and to proclaim their position in them through public building projects on an ever-larger scale. They also came to adopt an increasingly similar way of life, strongly influenced by Hellenistic Greece.

The social orders of Italian towns and cities were complicated and hierarchical. All forms of wealth were not considered equally honorable or desirable. The holders of magistracies based their wealth on land, on government, and on the profits of war; by contrast, direct participation in trade, even on a fairly large scale, could threaten their status. Successful merchants sometimes sought to improve their own position and that of their descendants by abandoning trade and becoming landowners themselves. In Rome, moreover, senators were specifically debarred from participating in trade and in holding public contracts as *publicani*. Even so, ways could be found around the limits imposed by law and custom. Finance, for example, was honorable if undertaken on a sufficiently large scale, and if the lending of money was divorced from any direct participation in the activities funded.

Status certainly affected the ways in which individuals could profit from Roman expansion. Roman magistrates and senators had the greatest opportunities and the greatest benefits. In Italy, transfers of wealth had long accompanied Roman warfare. Victorious Roman armies plundered the cities and camps of the defeated, and Roman conquest often resulted in mass enslavements and the confiscation of land. The wars outside of Italy, in Greece and Asia Minor especially, resulted in seizures of property and enslavements on a scale that the Romans had never experienced before. Immense wealth certainly changed hands amidst combat and the disorder that followed. Soldiers of the victorious armies plundered houses, temples, and camps. Prominent Romans also arranged for the transfer home of art treasures, furniture, and other valuables in addition to objects of gold, silver, and precious metals. Through plunder, the seizure of royal and sacred treasuries, and the imposition of tribute, Roman commanders themselves came to control large amounts of wealth. Some they probably apportioned to allies, but they brought the bulk of their gains back to Italy, where they displayed it in their triumphs. Afterwards, they distributed some formally to their soldiers according to rank, turned over another part to Rome's treasury, and retained a portion for their own use.

Plunder was not the only reward of victory. Roman commanders who were assigned *provinciae*, together with their assistants, as well as legates either on embassies or on missions to observe and help settle affairs, all had regular opportunities for personal gain. Members of the Roman elite in the provinces routinely demanded that the local inhabitants feed and house them, often at great expense, and provide them with transport. The biographer Plutarch (*Cato the Elder* 6) claims that the general practice of governors of Sardinia was to make the Roman treasury pay for their personal upkeep and transport, while requiring Sardinians to bear the cost of maintaining their servants and friends in luxury. When he was governor, however, Cato the Elder, famed for his frugality, required the Sardinians to contribute remarkably little to his own support and that of his entourage. Plutarch's account may well be exaggerated, but there is no question that governors and legates did arrange support by these means, and some even demanded gifts as an inducement to reduce requisitions or to grant exemptions from them altogether. In addition, governors and their closest advisors received or extorted gifts from people who wished to ingratiate themselves or to receive favors.

The acquisition of new wealth on a large scale was not limited to magistrates, senators, and members of their entourages. *Negotiatores* were certainly present in Greece in some number, and they could probably be found in Spain too (see

BOX 5.1: *Plunder was a major source of wealth for commanders and soldiers alike, and the Romans developed highly formalized ways of acquiring it and distributing it. In the first passage, Polybius describes the manner in which the army of Scipio Africanus looted Carthago Nova in 209. Some of the wealth gained in this fashion was displayed in the commander's triumph, and, after he had left office, he often distributed a portion to his soldiers as a "donative," as Livy's account of the triumph of Gnaeus Manlius Vulso in 187 illustrates.*

(Polybius 10.15.4–16.9) When Scipio thought that a sufficient number of soldiers had entered the city, he sent most of them—as is the Roman custom—in pursuit of the inhabitants, with orders to kill everyone they encountered, sparing nobody, and not to start pillaging until the order was given. They do this, I think, to inspire terror, so that when cities are taken by the Romans, one may see not only the bodies of human beings, but also dogs, cut in half and the dismembered limbs of other animals. On this occasion, these scenes were many, because of the number of people in the city. . . . After this, once the signal was given, the massacre stopped and they began to plunder. At nightfall, those Romans who had received orders to remain in the camp did so, while Scipio with his thousand men camped in the citadel. Through the military tribunes he ordered the rest of the troops to leave the houses, and then instructed them to collect their plunder in the forum, maniple by maniple, and to guard it by sleeping there. . . . On the next day, the plunder collected in the forum was divided among the legions in the usual way. After capturing a city, the Romans deal with this matter as follows: Depending on the city's size, on some occasions a certain part of each maniple and, on others, whole maniples are assigned to collect plunder, but never more than half of the army does this, the rest remaining under arms either inside the city or outside, ready for any trouble. . . . All the men who are ordered to plunder bring back what they have taken, each to his own legion, and, after this has been done, the military tribunes distribute the loot equally among everyone, including not only those in the protecting force, but also those guarding the camp, the sick, and anyone absent on a special assignment.

Livy (39.7.1–5): In his triumph, Gnaeus Manlius carried 212 gold crowns, 220,000 pounds of silver, 2,100 pounds of gold, 120,000 Attic *tetradrachmai* [a silver coin], 250,000 *cistophori* [another type of coin], and 16,320 gold *Philippei* [yet another coin]. There were also many Gallic arms and spoils carried in carts, and 250 enemy leaders were led before his chariot. To his soldiers, he gave forty-two *denarii* [the standard Roman silver coin], and to centurions twice this; in addition, he gave infantrymen double pay, and cavalrymen triple.

Chapter Four). State contractors or publicani also profited from the desire of Roman commanders to erect monuments to their achievements. There were increased opportunities for publicani outside of Italy as well, although the extent of their operations is unclear initially.

The vast influx of wealth into Italy changed the appearance of many cities and the ways of life of their leading families. Wealthy Romans now built elaborate

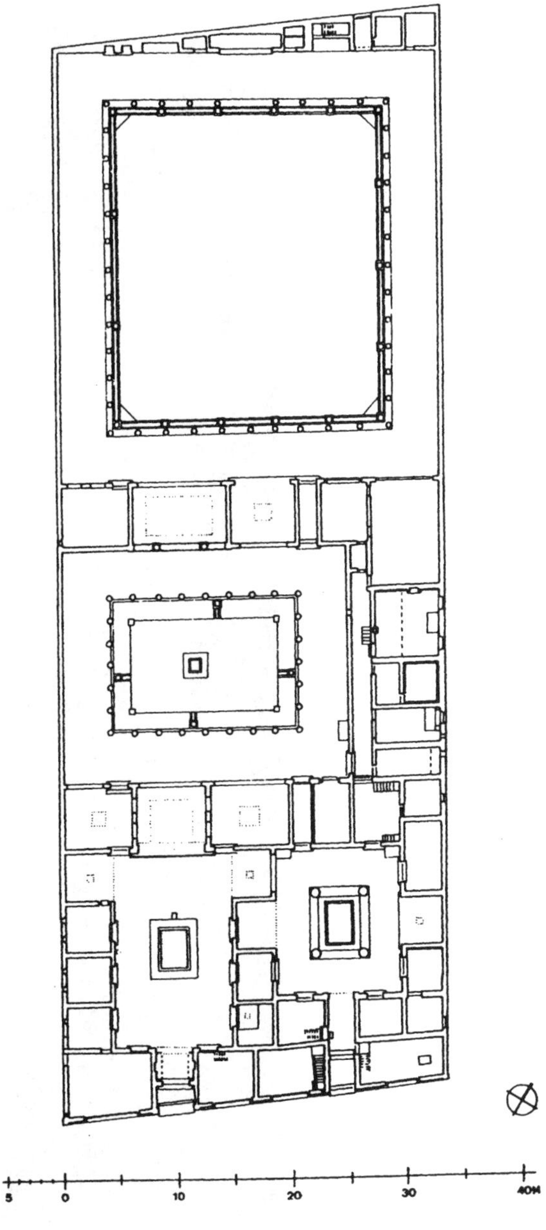

Figure 5.2 *The "House of the Faun" at Pompeii in Campania is one of the most elaborate second-century houses known in Italy. Later extended, it covers about 31,000 square feet (2,800 sq m). The only known residences of comparable size at this date are royal ones, such as at Pella in Macedon. The lower part of the plan shows the house's two reception halls or* atria; *above them are its two peristyle courtyards. In all, this house, which probably belonged to a member of the local elite, is more reminiscent of Greek palaces and public buildings than of the earlier dwellings of central Italian aristocrats.*

private houses and financed the construction of temples, public buildings, and monuments in prominent locales. Many members of the local elites that dominated the other cities (both citizen and allied) of the peninsula behaved in a similar manner, building houses—some of which rivaled royal palaces in size—and adorning their cities with temples, baths, theaters, and monuments to their own accomplishments. Cities in Latium and Campania—the core of Roman power, and home of the richest local elites—led the way. The wealthiest and most powerful of the Samnites followed, turning their sanctuary sites into elaborate complexes. The Etruscans, farther away from the main commercial centers, also participated, but to a lesser degree. For many of these projects, architects and builders imitated a Hellenistic style of building in both private houses and public structures.

Imitation of the Greek world was not limited to styles of building. In the third and early second centuries, magistrates staging festivals had come to favor playwrights— such as Livius Andronicus, Gnaeus Naevius (died in 201), Plautus (died c. 184), and Terence (died c. 159)—who imitated Greek styles. Later, participation in a Hellenizing literary and philosophical culture came to be a mark of elite status that linked individuals across communities. By the end of the Second Punic War, some members of Rome's elite were writing histories, at first in Greek and later in Latin too (see Chapter One). During the second century, members of the leading families

the Roman elite often freed some of their slaves, and, under Roman law, these freedmen and freedwomen received the status of Roman citizens, if their former owners were citizens. Despite this prospect of advancement for some, much of Rome's population was still ill-housed and led only a marginal existence. Tensions between rich and poor seem to have become more pronounced.

Changes in the countryside accompanied the growth of cities and fueled it. The constant wars outside the peninsula added to the mobility of the population of Italy. Some sought opportunities in Spain or the east, while many served in Rome's armies there. Wars in distant places made military service more burdensome for some Romans and allies. In the first half of the second century, the total free population of Italy probably numbered around three million. The Romans kept a substantial proportion of the adult males from citizen and allied communities under arms: perhaps 120,000 men in a typical year, and, on occasion, even more. Soldiers who served outside of Italy could be away from their homes for years: Absences of four to six years probably were common, with some men serving for over a decade. Military service on this scale and of this duration disrupted communal life and the organization of labor. Most of the soldiers in Rome's armies were small-scale farmers, and prolonged absences must have weakened their ability to maintain themselves and their families on their lands. Indeed, the pressures of military service may well have encouraged some to abandon the land and move to the cities. Some Roman authors also believed that the demands of military service led wealthy landowners to shift away from hiring free laborers to employing slaves, who were not subject to conscription, to work their lands.

Warfare outside the peninsula also disrupted long established patterns of agriculture. The traditional economies of Italian city-states were based on farming and herding. In most districts, the arable land would be divided among the relatively few estates of the rich and a far larger number of smallholdings, cultivated by the owner and his family with perhaps the assistance of a few slaves. The ownership of land was closely tied to citizenship. The chief landowners of a city were its ruling elite, and its small-scale farmers formed the mass of its military levy. Under Roman law, only Romans and Latins could own land around Rome, in colonies, and in municipia. The Roman elite, although far wealthier than the elites of municipia and allied cities, probably concentrated the bulk of its holdings relatively close to the city. At the beginning of the second century, senators primarily owned lands in Latium, southern Etruria, Campania, and those portions of Sabinum that were closest to the city.

Land was the chief prop of the fortunes of the powerful, but landowning on any scale is always dependent on the availability of labor to farm it. In the fourth and early third centuries, Rome's elite increasingly turned to slaves, either born and raised in the household, or taken in large numbers in Roman wars, or purchased from abroad, the victims of piracy and other people's wars. In addition, from the beginning of the second century, if not earlier, Roman landowners employed tenant farmers, sharecroppers, and occasional free laborers. In the second century, slavery in Italy became larger in scale and importance as Roman armies forced larger numbers into slavery, and as more slaves became available as a result of warfare and piracy elsewhere in the Mediterranean world.

Slavery in Italy was a complex phenomenon. Some slaves worked in the fields, or guarded the herds and flocks of their owners. Others were servants in the households of the wealthy. Still others served as managers, accountants, and teachers. Masters typically employed skilled slave craftsmen to make products for domestic use and for sale in the market. For some, slavery was a temporary condition. Slaveowners in Italy often permitted slaves to acquire personal property, and some could purchase their freedom by this means. For other slaves, freedom could come as a reward for services. In either case, freedmen and freedwomen were expected to continue to provide services and owe deference and loyalty to their former masters; they frequently served as managers and business agents.

The influx of wealth and slaves from foreign wars, and the vulnerability to military service of tenant farmers, sharecroppers, and hired laborers, presented members of the landholding elites of Italy with a range of options. In the middle of the second century, Cato the Elder wrote a handbook On Agriculture (*De Agricultura*) that illustrates some ideal features of one type of holding. Cato's estate of around 100 acres or 40 hectares (one of several its imagined owner would possess) was operated by either a slave or a freeman as manager; he supervised no more than a few dozen slaves—the most that could be kept fully employed throughout the year—and also hired seasonal free laborers to help with planting and the harvest. This holding specialized in a single crop, grapes for wine or olives for oil, which was to be sold for the owner's profit. Such intensive cultivation of a single crop depends on the proximity of a market sufficiently large to absorb its produce and the produce of other similar estates in the region. Perhaps for this reason, Cato placed his estate in southern Latium or northern Campania, near to Rome and the Campanian cities. Both Cato's handbook and others thought to have been written about the same time give the impression that specialized holdings of this type were a relatively recent phenomenon, perhaps a response to Rome's growth.

The raising of animals was another option for those with capital, land, and slaves. The second century witnessed an expansion in the practice of transhumance. Owners assembled large herds of cattle and flocks of sheep and goats, which they turned over to slaves to guard and to lead. These slave shepherds took their charges on long journeys each year while seeking out sufficient pasturage to feed them. During winter, the shepherds concentrated their animals in meadows in the warmer lowland, then during summer they led them to highland pastures. The migrations from highlands to lowlands and back again crossed many civic boundaries, and, if care was not taken, they could badly damage fields and crops. Transhumance requires a great deal of land (not necessarily of very high quality), and it was most common in the south of Italy where the population was less dense. Herding on this scale also requires the existence of a market in large cities where the owners or their agents could convert meat, leather, or wool into cash.

During the second century, there are signs that the Roman elite, and perhaps also certain leading families of cities elsewhere in Italy, came to control more land than they had in the past and in more distant locations. Some they gained through purchase or through marriage, or by taking for themselves land that the Romans had confiscated from their former enemies, but had not yet assigned to any public purpose. On other occasions, these wealthy families expropriated the holdings of small-scale farmers who had moved to the city or were absent for long periods on campaign. Roman historians, moreover, were convinced that the wealthy forcefully expelled some of the poor from their lands.

The result was an agricultural economy with marked regional variations in crops, land tenure, and labor systems. In some areas, estates such as Cato's imaginary ideal one were common or even predominant. Here, access to secure markets may have been the chief determinant, and the fertile plains of Latium, Campania, and parts of southern Etruria the most common locations, along with similar places near harbors and sizable communities. Elsewhere, the cultivation of grain or other crops through tenants and sharecroppers was more frequent. In yet further locations—especially in regions that were hilly or distant from markets—smallholdings and subsistence farming persisted, and perhaps even expanded. Exceptionally, in parts of Etruria, landowners may have continued to exploit clients and dependents in the archaic manner into the first century (see Chapter One).

The use of slaves on a large scale presented dangers for the Roman political system. In 185, Lucius Postumius Tempsanus was assigned to suppress an uprising in Apulia, where groups of slave shepherds were robbing people in the countryside; he is said to have condemned around 7,000 men to death, although Livy (39.29.8–9) reports that many escaped execution. In the Roman world, pastoral slavery often was associated with brigandage. Slave shepherds, whose occupation made them difficult to supervise, were generally armed to protect their charges from carnivorous animals and thieves, and sometimes it was only by resorting to force that they could assert their right to use pastures and springs.

The most alarming instance of the danger created by extensive use of slaves occurred in Sicily, in full view of the Roman elite. The island's economy, like that of Italy, was complicated and diverse. In some regions, estates produced grain on a large scale; in fact, the island was one of the primary sources for food for the city of Rome. In other regions, pastoral slavery was common. The First Slave War began around the city of Enna in the middle of the island. Eunus, its leader, a slave from Apamea-on-the-Orontes in Syria and a wonderworker who claimed the patronage of the Syrian goddess Atargatis, recruited a number of slave-shepherds, armed and free to roam the countryside. One night in 136, he gathered them outside the city, encouraged them to break into the slave barracks on the estates that surrounded it, and to free the field slaves housed there, who were usually kept shackled. With this force of several hundred, he then broke into Enna, and began a massacre in which some slaves resident in the city joined. The next day, he declared himself to be king. A month later, another rebellion began around the city of Agrigentum, where more massacres took place. Eventually, the rebellion spread to include about half of the island. Its suppression proved a long, hard task. At first, the Roman praetors who held Sicily as their *provincia* attempted without success to defeat the rebels, suffering several defeats in the process. In 134, the senate decided to make Sicily a consular province, an indication of the seriousness in which they held the war. The third of these consular commanders finally ended the war in 132.

ROMAN POLITICS FROM THE MID-SECOND CENTURY

In the third quarter of the second century a few members of Rome's governing elite began to base their position in the city more on their ability to court popularity and to mobilize crowds than on their standing with their fellow senators. Some of these men were charismatic military figures, eager to reach new offices and fresh heights of glory; others were more confrontational tribunes. In many ways, the shift they initiated represents a return to an older style of leadership, before the reforms of the late fourth and early third centuries began to elevate the senate above any individual officeholder. Both the growth of the city of Rome and the changes in the Italian countryside may have fueled the new development. The population of the city was now disturbed by starker contrasts between rich and poor, as well as by the presence of many people who had been forced through changes in the countryside to migrate to the city. As a result, crowds in Rome would have been larger, and their emotions more easily stirred.

In many ways, the institutional basis of the senate's position was weak. Because of the nature of the Roman political order, the senate's leadership depended on its high prestige and on the willingness of officeholders and candidates to acquiesce in important matters to senatorial consensus. At the same time, by law officeholders possessed considerable powers of self-assertion, and, if they sought popular support, there was little to restrain them. Tribunes, moreover, possessed formidable powers to act, as well as to block the actions of others, should they wish to exercise this authority. From the late 150s, a few tribunes become notably more active. In 151, for example, following popular resistance to a consular levy of soldiers for Spain, tribunes imprisoned the consul when he ignored their vetoes. In 145, another tribune, Gaius Licinius Crassus, attempted unsuccessfully to enact a law removing the right to choose new priests from the priestly colleges and transferring it to citizen assemblies instead. In 139, the tribune Aulus Gabinius enacted the first law requiring secret ballots, rather than having citizens declare their votes in full view of the city's leaders. Two years later, another tribune's proposal instituted the use of secret ballot for trial verdicts.

During this period, figures such as Scipio Aemilianus and Tiberius and Gaius Gracchus would develop new styles of popular leadership, ones that would be much imitated in succeeding generations. There is no continuous narrative history of the years from 167 to 121 and beyond, however. The career of Scipio Aemilianus may be pieced together out of Appian's accounts of the Third Punic War and the Numantine War, and from Plutarch's biography of Scipio's father, Lucius Aemilius Paullus. The tribunates of the two Gracchi are better documented. Plutarch wrote biographies of both brothers, while Appian opened his account of Rome's civil wars with their activities. Tiberius and Gaius Gracchus, moreover, were famous orators, and later authors preserved extracts or summaries of some of their speeches. Further, more occasional, references can be found in works by a range of authors. Yet problems remain. The brothers' actions and characters became the focus of much bitter controversy, and the propriety of their conduct and the responses of their opponents were vigorously disputed. As a result, the political positions of our sources have strongly influenced the representations of both brothers.

Scipio Aemilianus

Scipio Aemilianus was born in 185 or 184. His father was Lucius Aemilius Paullus, the victor over Perseus at Pydna, and his grandfather was one of the consuls defeated at Cannae in 216. He was adopted by Publius Cornelius Scipio, the son of Scipio Africanus, who had defeated Hannibal. Scipio Aemilianus first served as consul in 147. In the previous year, he had initially sought election as aedile. However, popular discontent over the failure of Rome's generals to win a quick victory in the Third Punic War created an opportunity that he exploited, and he switched his candidacy to the consular election, where he was successful. His success was extraordinary. He was considerably below the minimum age for consul, and he had yet to hold the office of praetor; he was, in other words, just the kind of candidate that the laws sought to bar.

With the backing of the senate, the consul who presided over the elections duly sought to bar Scipio's candidacy. According to Appian (*Punic Wars* 112), widespread protests were then voiced in the assembly, and some in the crowd asserted that the people possessed the right to elect whomever they wished. When one of the tribunes announced his intention to prevent any vote unless the consul permitted Scipio to stand for office, the senate gave way, instructing the tribunes to put forward a law permitting this, on the understanding that the regular requirements would once again be upheld the following year. After the election, Gaius Livius Drusus, who was chosen to fill the other consular position, requested that lots be cast to determine their *provinciae*, the normal procedure. Again, a tribune intervened, proposing that a citizen vote determine the assignment of provinces. Accordingly, in this exceptional way Scipio was assigned the war against Carthage. There, he would prove very successful, destroying the city in 146 and earning the cognomen of Africanus, as had his grandfather through adoption.

This election reveals some of the potential weaknesses of the senate's rule. Restrictions on eligibility for office—a vital means by which senators sought to protect themselves against their more popular peers—had force only so long as no one mobilized mass outrage against them, and no tribune asserted the citizens' right to vote as they wished; in that event, angry crowds and obstinate tribunes could force magistrates and senate to yield. Scipio's reputation for bravery and military skill, gained in Macedon, Spain, and North Africa, may have been the source of much of his popularity, but popular support, to be effective, must be organized and directed. Suspicion that a candidate had sought office improperly or too eagerly could lead to threats of prosecution. When a less prominent candidate defeated an opponent who was higher in the nobility, complaints that the winner was guilty of *ambitus*, the excessive pursuit of offices and popularity, were sometimes made. On at least two occasions in the first half of the second century, laws regulating ambitus were passed. In addition, other laws of this period limited large-scale, elaborate entertainments, which were often mounted by candidates to attract popular support. Clearly, Scipio and his chief supporters were somehow able to find the means of mobilizing the support required in 148.

Scipio showed the same willingness to rely on popular support later in his career. In 142, he sought election as censor, an office that was both prestigious and powerful, usually held by former consuls. His rival, Appius Claudius Pulcher, is said to have been backed by the majority of the senate, while Scipio had more support from the city populace. A central element in campaigning involved *ambitiones* (singular, *ambitio*), formal walks through the Forum, where the candidate, accompanied by prominent supporters, greeted citizens and requested their support. To have prominent supporters was thought to reflect well upon a candidate, and thus candidates for office liked to be surrounded by especially prominent men as they made their ambitiones. According to Plutarch (*Aemilius Paullus* 38), Scipio went to the Forum with men of low birth, some of them freedmen, who were able to gather a crowd and force issues by shouting and stirring up passions. He won the office of censor too.

In 135, Scipio again sought election as consul. When he first stood for this office, Roman armies had proven unsuccessful against Carthage. Now, a series of Roman commanders had failed against Numantia in Spain. Once again, his tremendous military prestige helped him gain office. As in his first campaign for the consulship, he also had to overcome a legal prohibition on his candidacy. After Marcus Claudius Marcellus had been consul for the third time in 152, a new law prohibited holding the office more than once. Scipio eventually found a way around the prohibition (although just how he did so remains unclear), and he was chosen consul for 134. The majority of senators then showed their dissatisfaction by refusing to vote him funds for the campaign in Spain, and by prohibiting him from drafting new soldiers. Scipio's spirited reaction was evidently to raise 4,000 men through voluntary contributions of troops by allied cities and by foreign kings who wished to gain or hold his favor; at the same time wealthy friends offered him funds. His campaign against Numantia was successful, increasing his prestige and glory still further.

BOX 5.2: *Appian opened his account of the civil wars that would destroy the Roman Republic with an account of Tiberius Gracchus' reform, including an introductory short description of the history of Roman "public" lands. He is probably drawing upon Gracchan sources, and he makes no distinctions between the lands of Roman citizens and noncitizens; he also gives allies more prominence that Roman politicians probably would.*

(*Civil Wars* 1.1.7–10): As they subdued one part of Italy after another in war, the Romans took part of the land and founded cities; alternatively, instead of establishing garrisons, they chose colonists from their own people to go to cities that already existed. In each instance, they immediately divided the cultivated part of the captured land among settlers, or sold or leased it. But they lacked the time to allocate the large quantity of land that was uncultivated because of hostilities, and so they proclaimed that anyone wishing to use it could do so on payment of a tenth of the produce from arable land or a fifth of orchard produce. They also established a tax on those who grazed animals, both larger and smaller ones. And they did all this to increase the number of Italians—whom no other people matched for hardiness in their opinion—and to have allies close by them.

But quite the opposite occurred. The rich gained possession of most of the undistributed land, and in time grew confident that they would not be deprived of it. They used persuasion or force to purchase or seize land adjoining their own or any other smallholdings belonging to poor men, and they came to operate vast tracts instead of single farms. They employed slaves as farmers and herdsmen, because free men could be drafted from farming into military service; at the same time, they profited from their investment because the slaves had many children and no liability to military service, and their numbers increased freely. For these reasons, the powerful became extremely rich, and the country's slave population escalated. Meanwhile the Italians suffered from depopulation and manpower shortage, and were worn down by poverty, taxes, and military service. Moreover if they had any respite from these misfortunes, they found themselves unemployed, because the land was in the hands of the rich who used slaves as farmers rather than free men. In consequence, the Roman people became concerned that they might no longer have plenty of allies from Italy, and that their control might be jeopardized by such a mass of slaves.

They did not consider reform, because it seemed neither easy nor altogether fair to deprive so many individuals of so much land that for such a long time they had personally cultivated and built upon and equipped. Eventually, however, at the tribunes' instigation, with reluctance they decided that nobody might hold more than 500 iugera of this land, nor graze more than 100 larger and 500 smaller animals on it. They also required a specific number of free men to be employed, who were to observe and report what was going on. They embodied these decisions in a law, which they swore to observe, and they prescribed penalties, thinking that the excess landholdings would immediately be sold to the poor in small parcels. But in fact no one paid attention to either law or oath. Instead, some gave an impression of observing them by making bogus transfers of land to their relatives illegally, while the majority just ignored the law completely.

Eventually the point came when Tiberius Sempronius Gracchus, a man of noble birth, outstanding ambition, and formidable oratorical powers—and on all these counts very well known to everyone—became tribune and made a powerful speech about the people of Italy, declaring that they were excellent fighters and related to the Romans by blood, but were declining slowly into poverty and depopulation and had not even the hope of a remedy. . . . After saying this, he proposed to renew the law that no individual should hold more than 500 iugera, but modified its previous provisions by adding that children of occupiers could have half this amount. The rest of the land was to be distributed to the poor by three elected men who were to rotate annually. It was this provision which especially disturbed the rich, since the three men would prevent them from ignoring the law as before, and they would be unable to buy up the land of those who received allotments, because Gracchus had foreseen this prospect and was proposing to ban such sales.

In the past, tribunes had generally used their vetoes against consuls and praetors. A tribune's interference with the actions of another tribune was relatively rare, and the tribune who sought to veto a proposal of a colleague usually gave way if the colleague was able to muster popular or senatorial support against the obstruction. In dramatic confrontations in public meetings, Tiberius sought unsuccessfully to persuade or to pressure Octavius to withdraw his veto. He even attempted to increase the pressure on his opponent by blocking other public business himself and by locking the public treasury. Finally, he sought to remove his intransigent colleague from office—a step that was also unprecedented—seeking to justify the action by the assertion that a tribune who attempted to obstruct the people's ability to vote had failed in his duty to protect their rights. Here, he was successful, and the Plebeian assembly did remove Octavius from office, and then replaced him with another tribune. Soon after, the assembly enacted the agrarian law. In a later assembly, voters chose Tiberius himself, his brother Gaius, and his father-in-law, Appius Claudius Pulcher, to be agrarian commissioners.

Tiberius' efforts to enact his law and the attempts of his opponents to block it had escalated through a series of unprecedented actions, which must have increased tensions between the participants and among the citizen body as a whole. This escalation and the rancor that accompanied it did not end with the law's passage. The senate had long had the right to determine the amount of public funds that magistrates would receive to perform their duties. Now, senators voted the Gracchan triumvirs only a trivial sum. At this time, by coincidence, word reached Rome of the death of Attalus III, king of Pergamum, who had no heirs and had left his kingdom to the Romans in his will. In consequence, Tiberius acted in a way that undercut the senate's claims to manage Rome's foreign affairs and its finances. He successfully introduced to the Plebeian assembly a new proposal turning over Attalus' treasure to the triumvirs, so that they could finance their operations and give benefits to those poor for whom there was insufficient land.

Tiberius then announced that he would run for reelection as tribune, another act without apparent precedent. His motive, we are told, was fear that his enemies would seek to prosecute him when he left office, and that they would attempt in some way to nullify his agrarian law. In the electoral assembly, after the first two tribes had voted for Tiberius, his opponents began to assert that it was illegal for him to seek reelection, and, amid arguments, the assembly was adjourned. As the day for the new vote approached, crowds began to gather around the Capitol where the vote would be held, while the senate met in the nearby Temple of Fides. Here, Tiberius' opponents apparently argued that he was seeking to make himself tyrant, and they sought unsuccessfully to persuade the presiding consul Scaevola to authorize the use of force against him. Then, Scipio Nasica, the *pontifex maximus*, with a number of other senators and their retainers, left the meeting of the senate and attacked Tiberius and his supporters with wooden cudgels, according to one account killing two to three hundred. One of Tiberius' colleagues as tribune beat him to death with the leg of a stool. This may well have been the first political murder of a Roman officeholder for a very long time; the only possible precedents lie as far back as the fifth century. When Scipio Aemilianus at Numantia heard of Tiberius Gracchus' death, he quoted a verse from Homer's *Odyssey*: "So may perish all others who venture on such wickedness." After his return to Rome, when he made clear his disapproval of Gracchus' law, Scipio lost the popularity he had held for so long.

In the following year, 132, the senate assigned both consuls the task of conducting a formal investigation into the conduct of Tiberius' supporters. Their investigation was harsh, and they are reported to have ordered executions, although no other senators seem to have suffered. Alarming portents convinced the senate and the members of the priestly college charged with their interpretation that the goddess Ceres, patron deity of the tribunate, was angered by the murder of the sacrosanct tribune, and expiatory sacrifices were made.

Tiberius Gracchus' murder did not result in the clear triumph of his opponents. The land commission, in particular, continued to operate. Crassus replaced Tiberius Gracchus on the triumvirate, and when he and Claudius died, Marcus Fulvius Flaccus and Gaius Papirius Carbo were chosen to replace them; Flaccus and Carbo would both reach the office of consul. A few inscribed boundary markers document the commission's impact in Campania, Picenum, Samnium, Lucania, and Apulia, areas where large tracts of land had been confiscated at the end of the Second Punic War. The Gracchan commissioners seem to have encountered much resistance, and some disorder may have accompanied their judgments and settlements. In 129, however, Scipio Aemilianus succeeded in blocking further action, by claiming (on grounds that are now obscure) that the commission was interfering with the rights of allied communities.

Gaius Gracchus

When Gaius Gracchus sought the tribunate for 123, his candidacy was much anticipated by opponents and supporters alike. In the years after his brother's death, lines of conflict had hardened; many hoped for a revival of reform, while others feared it. As quaestor in 126, Gaius had been assigned to accompany the consul Lucius Aurelius Orestes to Sardinia. The senate prorogued Orestes' governorship three times, perhaps to keep Gaius away from Rome. In 124, however, Gaius returned to Rome without waiting for an end to the consul's promagistracy. He apparently received a hero's welcome in the city, where many expected him to be the new advocate for the citizenry. Huge and enthusiastic crowds came to Rome for the election. Despite attempts to undermine his popularity, Gaius' candidacy was successful. In 123, he even gained reelection as tribune, an action that had led to his brother's death. His associate Marcus Fulvius Flaccus also sought and won election as tribune for 122, an unprecedented act for a former consul.

In our sources, Gaius Gracchus appears as a more complex and more confrontational figure than his brother. Tiberius' reform had limited goals at first; he became more controversial as opposition grew. Gaius introduced a large number of laws, covering a wide range of matters, which suggests that he had a clear legislative agenda. His laws are the only direct evidence for his plans, and their provisions and chronology are often unclear. Analysis of this legislation, moreover, can support different views of his goals. In an unfriendly account, Diodorus Siculus (34/35.25) claimed that Gaius Gracchus sought to bring down the senate, and for this reason tried to stir up others against it. More probably, Gaius merely wished to curb some of the excesses of the senate's rule, rather than eliminating it altogether.

As tribune, Gaius began a long, fast-moving series of actions that must have greatly encouraged his supporters, while arousing the fears of his opponents. He is reported to have been an electrifying speaker, perhaps the best of his day, capable of moving crowds with tremendous displays of enthusiasm and emotion. Our sources often depict him as surrounded by crowds of associates and well-wishers. The frequent meetings of the citizen body necessary to enact his many laws would have created a constant feeling of excitement among supporters and opponents alike. Like his brother, he probably did not bring any of his proposals to the senate for discussion. Even so, he too had supporters among his fellow senators, although they seem a more shadowy group and on the whole less senior than Tiberius' had been. Perhaps the most prominent was Marcus Fulvius Flaccus, a member of the agrarian commission alongside Gaius himself, and consul in 125. On occasion, others cooperated too, although the depth of their commitment is far from certain.

In his two terms as tribune of the plebs, Gaius Gracchus introduced a wide range of laws, although our knowledge of their sequence and contents is far from complete. Among his earliest measures were laws aimed against the investigations that had led to the execution of so many of his brother's supporters. In the past, the senate had authorized most investigations, and, by extension, the punishments that had resulted from them. Laws passed by citizen assemblies authorized other prosecutions: The juries of senators that judged cases of extortion, for example, were authorized by a law proposed by a tribune in 149. One of Gaius' laws now imposed a capital sentence on any magistrate who had imposed a capital sentence as a result of a *quaestio* or investigation that had not been authorized by the vote of a citizen assembly. After the passage of this law, Publius Popillius Laenas, who as consul in 132 had presided over the executions of Tiberius' supporters, went into exile, probably to avoid prosecution. Another law, probably connected in some way with the first, imposed the death penalty on anyone serving as a judge in some quaestio, who accepted a bribe to declare an innocent defendant guilty.

Gaius also introduced a range of laws that he probably expected to be popular among the bulk of the city's population. He renewed his brother's land law, but with some modifications: His commissioners no longer had the power to determine which lands were "public" and which were private, an apparent recognition of the controversy that these powers had caused and the resistance they had inspired. Later, he would secure the passage of laws authorizing the foundation of several colonies in Italy and one—to be named Junonia—in North Africa on the site of Carthage. Another early measure would also have contributed to his popularity in Rome. In all likelihood the city's poorer residents often faced difficulty in obtaining sufficient grain at a price they could afford. The aediles had long supervised the city's markets—where they sought to ensure, for example, that merchants used the proper weights and measures, that they did not mix any gravel with grain, and did not hoard grain in the hopes that prices would rise. More recently, some officials had sought to increase the amount of grain available in the city. Gaius Gracchus took this initiative one step farther. His law now guaranteed citizens the right to purchase in Rome a set amount of grain each month at a fixed price. Thus the state now had to arrange for a regular supply of grain, and to make up the difference whenever the fixed price for citizens turned out to be lower than the market price; it also had to construct granaries and improve harbor facilities.

Certain measures may have been crafted to define and limit some of the senate's most important prerogatives, although it is possible that they were merely aimed against prominent abuses. One law required that senators decide before elections the provinces that would be allocated between the new consuls. Gaius may have intended this law—which remained in effect after his death—to free the process of determining provinces from the intrigues of new consuls, their friends, and their opponents. Another law prescribed that taxes in the new province of Asia (formed out of the old kingdom of Pergamum) should be collected by Roman publicani bidding for contracts at Rome—the first known instance when these state contractors collected the revenues from an entire province. Some have seen this measure as sign that Gaius wished to mobilize the publicani against the senate, but it may have been aimed simply against official corruption in the province.

Perhaps the most important limitation of the senate's role concerned membership on the juries of the standing courts. In 149, a tribunician law had determined that juries made up of senators would judge cases involving corruption in the provinces. Here, accusers petitioned the urban praetor to put together a jury comprising selected senators. These jurors heard testimony and then rendered their verdict, which could not be appealed. Since only former officeholders and senators could be defendants in these cases—only they were in a position to extort money from provincials—the result of the measure was that in these matters senators would judge other senators. Gaius Gracchus' jury law now created a new list of jurors that probably excluded senators altogether, perhaps a response to the way in which senatorial jurors had handled prominent trials. Instead, lists of potential jurors were in future to be chosen from the class of citizens called *equites*. Clauses that survive on a bronze tablet may be part of this law. If the identification is correct, Gaius plainly went to great lengths to exclude any senator or any juror closely related to one.

The equites formed an important part of the Roman elite, and, in the late second century, they seem to become more clearly distinguished from the membership of the senate. In Rome, an *eques* (plural, *equites*) literally meant a cavalryman. Originally, officials conducting the *census* had enrolled those eligible to serve in Rome's cavalry in the equestrian centuries. Later, probably during the fourth century, others who possessed sufficient wealth to supply their own horses were also expected to serve in the cavalry, although censors did not enroll them in the equestrian centuries; they too came to be called equites, even though they did not possess the voting privileges held by those who were actually enrolled in the designated centuries. Publicani who undertook major contracts would certainly have been included in their numbers. A few years before Gaius' tribunate, there appears to have been an attempt to bar senators from membership in these centuries, perhaps in an effort to create an equestrian order distinct from the senatorial, or merely an attempt to create more spaces for nonsenators. Much later, the historian Appian (*Civil Wars* 1.3.22) would claim, with some exaggeration, that Gaius had made the equites "rulers over the senate and the senators virtually their subjects."

Probably in Gaius's second term, he and Marcus Fulvius Flaccus proposed to extend Roman citizenship. During the second century, as we have already observed, Rome's allies came to bear more of the burdens of empire while receiving a declining share of the benefits, and Roman officials began to treat their Italian allies in many of the same harsh ways that they treated their subjects outside of Italy. Tiberius Gracchus' land reform may have aggravated the problem, since most of the activity of the commissioners seems to have taken place in the lands of allies. In 126, a tribune Marcus Junius Pennus carried a law ordering the expulsion of all non-Romans from Rome. Flaccus, when consul in 125, had proposed extending Roman citizenship more widely, and giving those who did not want citizenship the right of appeal against harsh actions by Roman magistrates; the matter had to drop, however, when he left for his province. Now in 122, Gaius Gracchus unsuccessfully proposed a law which would give Roman citizenship to all Latins, and the privileges of Latins to all the Italian allies. This measure, which is unlikely to have been popular among the citizens of Rome, may have begun the decline in Gaius' popularity that would result in his death.

Gaius' opponents did not confront him in the same manner that their predecessors had opposed his brother Tiberius. No tribune seems to have dared to block his laws, as Octavius had done a decade earlier. Instead, some of his enemies attempted to win away his followers through programs of their own. In 123, Quintus Fabius Maximus, a governor in Spain, shipped grain from his province to Rome in an apparent attempt to undermine Gaius' popularity among the beneficiaries of his grain law. Gaius' most successful opponent was Marcus Livius Drusus the Elder, tribune of the plebs in 122. Like Gaius, Drusus was an effective speaker, and was often surrounded by crowds of enthusiastic supporters. In an apparent effort to undermine the popularity that Gaius had gained by reenacting his brother's agrarian law and by his own colonial laws, Drusus proposed to found a series of colonies in which land would be given to more people. While Drusus campaigned for his measure, Gaius Gracchus and Flaccus left Rome to direct the foundation of the colony at Carthage. When they returned, the political situation had changed drastically, and their popular following was not as large or as secure as it had once been. In ways that are obscure to us, Gaius also lost ground among the equites.

After his return, Gaius sought a third term as tribune for 121. This time, he was unsuccessful. The details of his defeat are unclear, but his supporters apparently alleged that the vote had been manipulated in some way. In 121, when Gaius was now out of office, the consul Lucius Opimius and several of the tribunes began to try to revoke some of his laws. Plutarch (*Gaius Gracchus* 13.1) claims that they also tried to provoke Gaius and Flaccus into some action that could be branded illegal. An attempt to repeal the law authorizing the foundation of the colony at Carthage began the final confrontation. Gaius and Flaccus, with a large following, attended the meeting where one of the tribunes was seeking to marshal support for the proposed repeal. At this assembly, in a confrontation between the supporters of both sides, a herald of the consul Opimius was killed. Opimius treated the death as a direct and deliberate attack against the state, and he summoned Gaius and Flaccus to the senate to defend themselves. When the two failed to appear, Opimius called on wealthy citizens to gather with their servants to defend the state. Gaius, Flaccus, and their supporters then withdrew to the Aventine hill, so long associated with the Roman plebs. Opimius offered no concessions, and even imprisoned a son of Flaccus, who had come to him as an envoy. Opimius then ordered an attack, in which some archers from the island of Crete whom he had stationed nearby joined—a possible indication that he had planned for just this outcome. Flaccus was killed in the fighting, and Gaius Gracchus committed suicide. Three thousand of their supporters are reported to have died in the fighting and in the prosecutions that followed.

Opimius based his actions on what came to be called the "Final Decree of the Senate" (*senatus consultum ultimum*), where senators instructed the consul "to take care that the state suffered no harm"—that is, to do what he considered necessary to preserve the political and social order without regard for the normal protections and rights due to citizens. These events leading up to Gaius' death were the first occasion on which the senate passed such a decree, and its legality would long be contested. In this "ultimate decree" (the SCU), senators asserted their ability to authorize investigations and punishments just as they had done after the death of Tiberius Gracchus, and in just the way that Gaius Gracchus had tried to prevent in his own laws.

The tribunates of Tiberius and Gaius Gracchus were to begin a tumultuous period in Rome's domestic politics, and their careers and their fates illustrate both the strengths and the weaknesses of their office. As long as a popular leader could muster a large following as they did, he could exercise considerable power in the city. This popularity had to be constantly reinforced, however. Some of the laws and issues of these years—land and grain distributions, control of the courts, and extensions of citizenship—would long remain prominent in the programs of ambitious tribunes. At the same time, opponents had little ability to block popular tribunes through normal means, so that resorting to violence would also remain an option.

In the following decades, a sharp division in political styles would develop among members of the Roman governing elite. Some would follow the traditional methods of competition within the senatorial order, making the traditional alliances and building coalitions of senators to back their plans and their ambitions. Those who furthered their careers in this manner came to be known as *optimates*, a label that marks their self-identification as the best people in the city. Others sought wider popularity among the citizen body as a way to advance careers and agendas, and the term *popularis* (plural, *populares*) identified them. In some cases, it should be noted, ambitious Romans could behave as optimates or as populares at different times in their careers.

SUGGESTED READINGS:

Astin, Alan E. 1967. *Scipio Aemilianus*. Oxford: Oxford University Press.

Beard, Mary, John North, and Simon Price. 1998. *Religions of Rome*, Vol. 1, *A History*; Vol. 2, *A Sourcebook*. Cambridge: Cambridge University Press.

Bradley, Keith R. 1989. *Slavery and Rebellion in the Roman World, 140 B.C.–70 B.C.* Bloomington: Indiana University Press.

Rickman, Geoffrey. 1980. *The Corn Supply of Ancient Rome*. Oxford: Oxford University Press.

Shatzman, Israel. 1975. *Senatorial Wealth and Roman Politics*. Brussels: Latomus.

Stockton, David. 1979. *The Gracchi*. Oxford: Oxford University Press.

ITALY THREATENED, ENFRANCHISED, DIVIDED

Any Romans who had hoped that the brutal elimination of Gaius Gracchus and his associates in 121 might mark an end to violence and turmoil were to be sadly disappointed by the outcome of events during the following twenty years or so. Unfortunately, the surviving ancient accounts of this period (and well beyond) are for the most part too sketchy for us to monitor the unfolding of events in depth, let alone offer satisfactory explanations for many of them. A senator of the mid-first century, Sallust (Gaius Sallustius Crispus), made the war with Jugurtha the subject of a moralizing, rhetorical monograph. For a broader perspective, however, we must rely above all on the biographer Plutarch, whose *Lives* of Marius and Sulla survive, and the narrative of Rome's civil wars composed by the historian Appian.

WAR WITH JUGURTHA (112–105)

Despite our uneven understanding, two developments in the years after Gaius Gracchus' death emerge clearly enough as special challenges for the state and the source of lasting change. Both were external, and both took Rome by surprise. At the center of the first was a Numidian named Jugurtha, who had been adopted by King Micipsa, the son and (since 148) successor to Rome's longstanding ally Masinissa; Jugurtha's own father was a brother of Micipsa who died prematurely. Micipsa, however, also had two sons of his own, both younger than Jugurtha. So on Micipsa's death, around 118, the kingdom was left jointly to all three. But any hopes of a working partnership were soon dashed, especially after Micipsa's sons had complained of how Jugurtha was placed above them. Consequently, Jugurtha had one (Hiempsal) murdered, and the other (Adherbal) driven out of Numidia altogether. Adherbal then begged help from Rome, so in 116 the senate dispatched a commission of inquiry headed by Lucius Opimius, the brutal consul of 121; it divided the kingdom, assigning the west to Jugurtha and the more developed east to Adherbal. Jugurtha's acceptance of this settlement is notable, as is the senate's willingness to intervene so deeply in what were, after all, the affairs of a foreign state. To be sure, Numidia was an old ally of Rome, it now had a long common border with the Roman province of Africa, and Rome naturally wanted a stable neighbor there. Perhaps the senate's hope was that this degree of intervention would suffice to ensure long-term stability.

If so, Jugurtha soon demonstrated otherwise by invading Adherbal's territory; by 112 he had him trapped in his capital Cirta (modern Qacentina/Constantine, in eastern Algeria). The senate's protests left Jugurtha unmoved. Eventually Adherbal surrendered, and Jugurtha executed him along with some Italian businessmen in Cirta who had been Adherbal's supporters. Romans' sharp reaction to these outrages now impelled the senate to send forces to discipline Jugurtha, though their campaigns had limited success at best. Diplomacy was tried again, too, but proved futile, especially in 111 when Jugurtha even came to Rome, only to be required by a tribune's veto not to speak there at all. In 110, the senate rejected a treaty made by a Roman commander in the field, and general dissatisfaction with its whole handling of the Numidian problem came to a head. Understandably, Jugurtha was suspected of having bought the silence or support of various senators; after all, he had had close personal links with upper-class Romans from an early age, when he had served at Numantia under Scipio Aemilianus.

The effectiveness of the Roman forces in Numidia improved under Quintus Caecilius Metellus in 109–108, and likewise from 107 onwards under the commander who displaced him (in circumstances treated below), Gaius Marius. Only in 105, however, was the war at last brought to an end when Marius' quaestor, Lucius Cornelius Sulla (another figure we shall return to), successfully persuaded Jugurtha's ally King Bocchus of Mauretania to betray him to the Romans. Jugurtha was then executed after being paraded in Marius' triumph the following year. Meantime Bocchus was granted part of Numidia to add to his own kingdom, while a brother of Jugurtha was made ruler of the rest. Roman honor was thereby restored, and an unreliable neighbor to the province of Africa removed. Otherwise, however, it is striking how minimally the settlement of 105/4 differs from what Opimius' commission had determined just over a decade earlier. Rome exacted no direct permanent gain from this costly, prolonged series of embarrassments; there was no wish to annex Numidia. The fundamental shortcoming—just as on several occasions earlier in the second century—was the senate's lack of capacity for determining the extent and the timing of any Roman intervention in the affairs of a foreign state.

Map 6.1 *Rome's Foreign Wars, 113–82*

E   F   G

BLACK SEA

PONTUS

Danube

BITHYNIA   PAPHLAGONIA

Byzantium

CAPPADOCIA

MACEDONIA

Dardanus

lisium

*AEGEAN
SEA*

A S I A

Pergamum

CILICIA

Orchomenus

Chaeronea

Ephesus

Antioch

Athenae

S Y R I A

INTERNUM MARE

Cyrene

Alexandria

A E G Y P T U S

Nile

Ancient World Mapping Center 2003

ITALY THREATENED FROM
THE NORTH (113–101)

The second development that surprised and challenged the Roman state towards the end of the second century was a migration south by groups of German peoples, principally the Cimbri and Teutones. Why they left their homeland in north Jutland is not certain; possibly they were suffering from a combination of population growth and the loss of low-lying land to encroachment by the sea. By 113 they had drifted as far as the eastern Alps, where they defeated a Roman consul and his army who had been sent to observe them. Next, by entering the Rhone river valley (Latin, Rhodanus), they naturally posed a threat to Rome's province of Transalpine Gaul (formed in 121), in particular after they had defeated another consul and his army in 109. Further Roman defeats followed in 107, and again most seriously of all at Arausio (modern Orange) in 105, where the catastrophic losses stemmed in part from the refusal of Quintus Servilius Caepio (a noble who had been consul in 106) to cooperate with his superior, the *novus homo* consul Gnaeus Mallius Maximus.

The tribes' next move was evidently northwards, rather than south towards Italy; but in Rome, understandably, feelings of panic prevailed. News of the disaster at Arausio came not long after confirmation of Jugurtha's capture. So at the elections for the consulship of 104, with the war in Numidia now known to be over, Marius was elected in his absence and assigned the command in Gaul. For this purpose, the law of the late 150s permitting no more than a single tenure of the consulship had also to be somehow set aside; we do not know who took the initiative in doing this, or the means adopted. Even more remarkable is Marius' subsequent reelection as consul every year through 100, by which date he had held the office for five years consecutively and six in total. These reelections are a puzzle insofar as he might just as well have been continued in his command as proconsul. In all likelihood, however, there was an overwhelming desire on the part of voters to guard against any repetition of the standoff between Caepio and Mallius at Arausio; Marius was to remain in command without question.

In the event, the tribes' movement north in 105 gave Marius the precious breathing space he needed to restore the Roman army's strength with recruitment, training, and new equipment. By the time that the tribes did eventually turn south, he was able to defeat the Teutones at Aquae Sextiae (modern Aix-en-Provence in southern France) in 102, and the Cimbri at Vercellae in northern Italy the following year. With the threat from the tribes thus removed, Marius was appropriately hailed as Rome's savior and offered two triumphs (he took only one); his election as consul for 100 reflected popular gratitude.

CHANGES IN THE ROMAN ARMY

Without question, the end of the second century saw changes not only to the recruitment of the Roman army (see next section), but also to its equipment, training, and battle formation (for training, see further Figure 7.1). More problematic, however, is just how extensive and sudden these changes were, as well as how far they were initiated by Marius himself (as our sources maintain). It may have been he who made the eagle a legion's principal standard, and who had javelins (*pila*; singular, *pilum*) produced with a weak rivet; once thrown, the shaft would buckle on landing and become useless to the enemy. It was evidently Marius, too, who required soldiers to carry more of their gear themselves than had been regular practice; hence the quip that they had become "Marius' mules" (*muli Mariani*). Less clear is the degree to which Marius reformed the army's battle formation. What we hear of battle formation from Julius Caesar's extensive descriptions in the mid-first century shows marked differences from Polybius' account in the mid-second. In particular, by Caesar's time there are no longer three distinct ranks of infantry identifiable by age and equipment, nor do Romans serve as cavalry or light-armed troops at this date. Instead, the two latter roles are now filled by allied auxiliaries, while the heavy infantry has become a uniform body of Romans grouped in larger formations (cohorts of four to five hundred men) than had been the norm a century earlier. Given Marius' urgent need to recruit widely and provide inexperienced men with fast, effective training to meet the threatened invasion of Italy from the north, it is tempting to speculate that he played some part in advancing these important changes, even if their introduction began earlier. What the army lost by them in flexibility, it gained in cohesive fighting power, and this was a vital boost after its series of demoralizing recent defeats.

MARIUS' CAREER IN ROMAN POLITICS

In the competitive atmosphere of Roman politics, multiple triumphs and consulships represented enviable distinction even for a noble of impeccably distinguished background. For a novus homo like Marius, they were honors beyond his wildest dreams. Now is the point, therefore, to review Marius' political career, with particular reference to appreciating its relationship to his military success and the resulting impact on the Roman state. Marius was born about 157 near Arpinum, a town sixty miles (96 km) southeast of Rome. His family had equestrian status, but was otherwise only prominent locally; even so, he was somehow able to serve under Scipio Aemilianus at Numantia, and he distinguished himself there. Not until after further military service, however, did he attempt to stand for office at Rome, and then only with the backing of a leading noble family, the Metelli. With this help he gained the quaestorship sometime in the late 120s, followed by the tribunate in 119. Thereafter he failed in his attempt to become aedile, and only just secured election as praetor in 115. His prospects for further political advancement were bleak; to build up the necessary wealth and influential support was a hard struggle. He did proceed to benefit financially, however, from a governorship in Further Spain, and was then able to make an advantageous marriage to Julia, whose family—the Julii Caesares—was an ancient patrician one, though not notably distinguished in the recent past (the famous Julius Caesar, born in 100, was to be her nephew).

In Spain, Marius had revealed a talent for guerilla warfare. This, and the family's previous relationship, prompted Quintus Metellus to make him his second-in-command when he set out against Jugurtha in 109. The two of them quarreled the following year, however, when Metellus denied Marius leave to go to Rome and stand for the consulship of 107. Allegedly, with a noble's condescension towards a novus homo, Metellus recommended the fifty-year-old Marius to wait until his own twenty-year-old son was ready to be a candidate too. Marius returned to Rome and ran for the office regardless, tapping his links with the equites (see Chapter Five), and stressing the need for a change from so much corrupt, ineffectual leadership by nobles. Scipio Aemilianus had successfully exploited such sentiments in

---

BOX 6.1: *This sketch by Sallust of how Marius advanced himself to the point where he eventually dared to stand for the consulship may be uncritical, not to say exaggerated and inaccurate in certain respects. However, its tone is still instructive, as are the aspects selected for attention:*

Even prior to this stage [in 108], Marius had been obsessed by a powerful longing for the consulship, an office which he was amply qualified in every way to fill, except that he did not come from an old family. He was a hard worker, a man of integrity, and a highly capable soldier. He devoted his energies to warfare. His private life was unremarkable, and he was no slave to passion or riches; all he craved was glory. His birthplace was Arpinum, where he had spent all his boyhood. As soon as he reached the age to enlist, he had gone on active service, training himself in this way rather than by any course of Greek rhetoric or city polish. With this fine education his sound character soon matured. So on the first occasion that he stood for election as military tribune, even though many citizens did not know him by sight, they were sufficiently aware of his record that all the tribes voted for him. Thereafter he won one office after another, invariably shouldering his responsibilities in such a way that he was thought to merit the next higher one. Even so, despite the worth he had demonstrated thus far, he never—and I say this of a man who later would be ruined by overambition—dared to aspire to the consulship. This was still a time when plebeians might win other offices, but the consulship was handed down by the nobles from one of their own number to the next. For this distinction, a "new man" (novus homo)—no matter how famous he might be, or how outstanding his record—was considered unworthy, and even tainted. (*Jugurthine War* 63)

earlier times of crisis, and Marius was now able to do the same. When the senate tried to thwart him by reappointing Metellus as commander in Numidia, the Plebeian assembly overruled it and appointed Marius (much as it had appointed Scipio to the command against Carthage).

Although authorized to draft men for his campaign in 107, Marius was wary of the difficulties he was likely to encounter if he attempted this. Instead, therefore, he limited himself to calling for volunteers, promising them rewards. He was even willing to take men of the lowest census rating, who would normally not be recruited because of their lack of property and, by extension, their presumed lack of commitment to the state's welfare. With hindsight, this step has been seen as the source of lasting harm, and Marius has been criticized for not anticipating the difficulties of rewarding his volunteers, as well as for not grasping the degree to which they might prove willing to advance the political ambitions of their commander. Even so, to expect such foresight of Marius or anyone else in 107 is hardly realistic. At that date neither he personally, nor the state generally, could afford to wait and rethink methods of army recruitment. The need for forces to defeat Jugurtha was too urgent, and the manpower available through the regular draft no longer adequate.

In the event, despite opposition, generous plots of land in Africa were readily assigned to the surviving volunteers as a reward in 103. The magistrate whom Marius had to thank for arranging this legislation was an ambitious tribune, Lucius Appuleius Saturninus; he was at odds with the senatorial establishment, and clearly drew inspiration from the example of the Gracchi. At the same time he was even less afraid of confrontation than they, and he cultivated Marius as a potentially valuable patron who would be able to provide military backing in a crisis, if required. It is likely, but not certain, that during 103 Saturninus also introduced a proposal that made Gaius Gracchus' grain distribution scheme more attractive in some way (and more costly for the treasury); if so, this may have helped gain voters' support for the assignment of land to Marius' veterans.

SIXTH CONSULSHIP OF MARIUS AND SECOND TRIBUNATE OF SATURNINUS (100)

In 100, Marius again needed help in rewarding veterans—this time those who had defeated the Cimbri and Teutones—and he was again willing for Saturninus to act on his behalf. Saturninus was no less a controversial figure than before. He had also developed a working partnership with Gaius Servilius Glaucia. As censor in 102, Quintus Metellus (Marius' old commander) had proposed removing both men from the senate, but his colleague in office would not agree. Now, in 100, Saturninus was tribune again, and Glaucia praetor. Saturninus' legislative proposals were exceptionally wide-ranging, and it was quite predictable that they would provoke opposition. It was not just Marius' veterans that he wanted to settle (on land in

Transalpine Gaul). He also proposed the foundation of colonies and allocation of land in Greece and Sicily for veterans of campaigns which had recently ended there, as well as allocation of land in Cisalpine Gaul for Roman civilians. Such sweeping initiatives, if approved, were sure to make him a highly influential figure.

If this were not provocation enough, his opponents were offended by a clause which required all senators to take an oath to respect the law within five days of its passage; otherwise they would face a crippling fine and expulsion from the senate. The opposition also found fault with the right that Marius was granted to confer Roman citizenship on a small number of the settlers in each of the new colonies. This confirmed that not just Roman citizens, but also allies, were to benefit from the program, and it offered the chance to insinuate that Marius, in his sympathy for improving the allies' status, would next want to extend citizenship far more widely. Popular hostility to the extension of citizenship was again stirred up, just as it had been against Gaius Gracchus. Saturninus might conceivably have deflected it by including among his proposals something of special benefit to voters who lived in Rome itself or close by, in the way that he seems to have done in 103 by manipulating the grain distribution; but, for whatever reason, this time he took no such precaution.

The opposition did everything possible to prevent a vote on the proposals: Tribunes imposed vetoes, and calls were made to disband the assembly on religious grounds because thunder had been heard. Saturninus brushed all these obstacles aside. Once it was clear from the mood of the assembly that the proposals were likely to be rejected, Marius' veterans were deployed to keep hostile voters away by force, and they in turn reacted violently. In the event the veterans won the confrontation, but it took this ugly use of force to ram the proposals through. The immediate need for senators to take the oath embarrassed Marius and raised the tension still further; only Quintus Metellus refused, and he left Rome as soon as Saturninus proposed his exile.

Next Saturninus achieved his own reelection as tribune for 99, but he then overstretched himself in working to have Glaucia made consul. On election day, Marius as the presiding magistrate rejected Glaucia's candidacy since it did not meet the legal requirements. Saturninus then proceeded to have his followers beat a rival candidate to death, and tried to have a law passed permitting Glaucia's candidacy; but even with further resort to violence this attempt failed. The senate was now thoroughly alarmed by such disorder, and for the second time passed its "ultimate decree" (the SCU) instructing the consuls to secure the safety of the state. That step forced Marius to decide whether or not to remain loyal to his associates. He chose to take the lead in pursuing them, and their group soon surrendered to him after receiving an assurance that they would not be summarily executed. When Marius did no more than confine them in the senate house, however, a lynch mob quickly formed to take revenge for their violent treatment of fellow citizens. Men from the mob then climbed to the roof, tore off the tiles, and battered Saturninus, Glaucia, and the others to a gruesome death.

Subsequently, it would seem that the land assignments enacted by Saturninus were respected, but most of his colonies were never founded. The degree to which he was a responsible Popularis politician as opposed to just a manipulative self-seeker is hard to judge. Understandably enough, all the surviving accounts of his activity are hostile. None, on the other hand, mentions a law which may well be his initiative, preserved only in two inscriptions; it is among the first we know of that seeks to ensure conscientious, honest administration on the part of provincial governors (see Administration of the Provinces, below). Despite such apparent good intentions abroad, there can be no question that Saturninus' impact on political life at Rome was a damaging one. He had proved even more domineering a tribune than Gaius Gracchus, not least because he had grasped how effectively Marius' veterans could be deployed in political struggles, thereby introducing a new and disturbing level of violence to Rome's public affairs. The danger of recruiting the poorest men as volunteers, and offering them rewards which their commander was not in a position to bestow himself, was all too starkly confirmed. The men themselves had everything to gain, and nothing to lose, simply by supporting their commander. The legality or morality of his ambitions were not their concern, and in any case they would seldom feel capable of evaluating such issues with confidence. As Sallust reflects (*Jugurthine War* 86.3): "If a man is ambitious for power, he can have no better supporters than the poor: They are not worried about their own possessions, since they have none, and whatever will put something into their pockets is right and proper in their eyes."

To be sure, Saturninus appreciated the special value of having veterans to call upon in the event of force being used against him by the senate—as it had been eventually against Gaius Gracchus, who lacked any such support of his own and was thus soon eliminated. But where Saturninus perhaps proved naive was in expecting Marius' continued support as alarm mounted within the senate. With hindsight, the argument could be made that Marius should have seized the opportunity to use his associates and his veterans to establish himself as supreme ruler and reformer of the state. To argue thus, however, would be to misunderstand Marius. He had no plans for reform. Rather, even as a novus homo of unprecedented distinction, what he craved most deeply was confirmation that the senatorial establishment now respected him as one of themselves rather than as still the outsider whom Quintus Metellus had so crushingly rebuffed in 108. Once Marius had at last woken to the realization that Saturninus was only intent on pursuing his own advantage in a more and more reckless way, the choice of whether or not to take his side became straightforward. Marius' overriding concern was to maintain the senate's esteem.

Its gratitude to him for decisive implementation of the SCU proved to be short-lived, however. He steadfastly opposed calls to restore Quintus Metellus from exile, and when such a proposal passed in 99 he left Rome for a year or two, claiming that he had a religious vow to fulfil in the East. On his return from there, he was politically active again, but never prominent until an extraordinary turn of events early in the 80s.

ADMINISTRATION OF THE PROVINCES

As explained above in Chapter Four, Rome's annexation of territories beyond Italy—which eventually comprised an "empire" of "provinces"—was a gradual, haphazard process. It is equally important to appreciate that the individual circumstances of an annexation, or the established character of particular communities and their administration, could lead to striking, permanent variations in their treatment. If existing arrangements for administration or taxation were acceptable to Rome, and functioning satisfactorily, there was no wish to overturn them for the sake of achieving uniformity.

Despite all the continuing variation, by the late second century norms for the administration of the provinces had taken shape, and can be outlined with some confidence. The underlying concerns were similar to those for Italy at an earlier stage in Rome's growth. Consequently, each provincial community or people was to continue locally autonomous, staying free from internal strife as well as from warfare with others. Tax (often agricultural produce rather than money) was normally payable to Rome, but there was no regular obligation to furnish manpower for the army. The fundamental components of a province and its organization were encapsulated in a "law of the province" (*lex provinciae*), which defined each community's form of constitution, its boundaries, its relationship with Rome, and its tax obligations. This law could be amended, but only by the senate and people in Rome. Naturally, it was every governor's ultimate work of reference; he was also obliged to adhere to all other relevant Roman legislation. To address matters of current concern, he issued his own edict (often merely repeating what one or other of his predecessors had prescribed).

Each governor had a quaestor assigned to him by the senate, whose special responsibility was to oversee Rome's financial interests in the province. The senate also assigned scribes, lictors, and other orderlies. It was for the governor himself to choose a handful of "legates" (*legati*), who were then officially recognized by the senate. Such men would be upper-class associates, or even relatives, of the governor (normally, but not necessarily, fellow senators), on whom he conferred authority as his deputies. Because their assistance could be of the greatest value, they were often chosen for some special skill or experience—in warfare, for instance. In addition, a governor would usually invite other friends (*amici*) or relatives to join his entourage (*cohors*). They would not have the legates' official status, although they might be included whenever the governor formed a *consilium* in the traditional way to seek advice on cases or issues calling for his decision. Last but not least, governors and their staffs were recommended (though not required) to leave their wives behind. At best, wives were reckoned not to have sufficient stamina for all the traveling required; at worst, their interference in official business was always to be feared.

A governor was supreme in his province. Everyone—civilian or soldier, Roman citizen or alien—was bound to obey his orders. In principle, Roman citizens had some right of appeal; in practice, however, this might prove difficult to exercise. The governor alone had the right of execution, so that cases liable to require a capital sentence had to be referred to him, along with certain other types of major charges. In addition, he could order instant execution, especially if he suspected a serious threat to Rome's main concern, the peace and security of the province.

Unless deterred by bad weather, or diverted by the need to go on campaign, a governor's customary routine would be to move from one major community to the next, checking on the welfare of each, and adjudicating the cases, petitions, and other matters brought to him. Inevitably, his checks could seldom be more than superficial; lack of time hampered him, as well as shortage of staff and limited expertise.

For even the most conscientious of governors, this tour was a daunting challenge—encountering regions and cultures with which in all likelihood he had little or no prior acquaintance, and engaging with populations who were by no means necessarily well disposed to Rome. Because most provincials understood neither Latin nor Greek, and Roman interest in learning other languages was minimal, reliance upon interpreters was frequently essential. Appropriate behavior within societies where the giving and receiving of gifts was standard practice (as in the Greek East especially) posed a particular dilemma for fair-minded governors; to accept all gifts (or bribes) was clearly criminal, but to refuse everything might only cause offense.

Less responsible governors felt no such anxiety, and instead—with varying degrees of greed—exploited the opportunities which their situation offered. While the temptations were infinite, the term of office in which to indulge them was unlikely to exceed a single year. Many a governor had heavy debts to pay off, often ones incurred on the latest occasion that he had competed for office in Rome. Although the senate allocated an ample lump sum for a governor's expenses, he received no salary. His orders and verdicts were not to be questioned, Rome was far away (from a distant province, messages could take weeks in summer, longer in winter), and for the most part provincial news attracted little attention there, so long as Roman interests were not under threat. It was not even necessary to be a notably venal judge. Instead, for example, how ungracious to refuse a gift spontaneously offered by a city requesting that troops be billeted elsewhere after the campaigning season. How easy, no less, to multiply the legal allowance for buying food when traveling. To claim this fixed cash amount from one community daily was permitted; yet if the claim were made in *each* community traversed during the day, which could refuse?

Some of the most painful dilemmas for fair-minded governors were likely to be created not by provincial subjects, but by the syndicates (*societates*) of private contractors, or *publicani*, who collected taxes on Rome's behalf. Whenever the tax contract for a major province was auctioned (Asia's five-year contract was the largest), a huge capital outlay was required to secure the winning bid. To operate effectively, a large tax-collecting syndicate had to maintain ships and branch offices, employ hundreds of staff (predominantly slaves or freedmen), and in many respects function as a bank. In addition, because it existed to deliver a profit to the partners who provided the capital, it could hardly afford to be patient or indulgent in its dealings with taxpayers. A governor too ready to lend a sympathetic ear to their complaints was by definition most unwelcome to a syndicate, and it would not hesitate to pressure him into rethinking his attitude by exerting its influence—often formidable—both in the province and at Rome. Accordingly, governors who persisted in strictness towards tax-collecting syndicates were exceptional, and they suffered for it. Otherwise provincials had little recourse against these syndicates' rapacity, and they deeply resented this helplessness. Worst of all was their plight in those instances where a governor unashamedly collaborated with a syndicate in fleecing taxpayers.

The senate, for its part, was acutely aware of Rome's dependence upon the tax-collecting syndicates for providing revenue; in consequence, efforts to discipline their operations too strictly would only prove self-defeating. This said, we should recognize that from the mid-second century there was an influential body of opinion in the senate eager to see members on a provincial assignment held to a high standard of conduct. As noted in Chapter Five, in 149 the novel step was taken of instituting a special jury court (*quaestio de repetundis*) to hear complaints lodged against such senators. Subsequently, Gaius Gracchus as tribune in 123–22, Saturninus as tribune in 100, Sulla as dictator in 82–81, and Julius Caesar in his first consulship (59) were all responsible for legislation which sought to discipline governors and make them more accountable. Even so, adequate means of enforcement could not be found, while general principles which seemed admirable when advocated in Rome might well turn out more awkward to uphold under specific conditions in a province. Cicero, as governor in Cilicia (also see Chapter Eight), would find himself faced with such dilemmas. Caesar likewise, both earlier in Spain and later in Gaul, blatantly ignored principles which his own legislation upheld. The convictions that Rome as a responsible ruler had obligations to the provinces, and that leading provincials who supported Roman rule should be treated as partners rather than mere subjects, were still not widely shared among senators at the end of the Republican period.

It is hard to determine how effectively the quaestio de repetundis acted to reduce misconduct by governors. The plain fact that no more than a limited number of the cases heard there led to conviction must have been heartening to those governors willing to risk prosecution. There was much else to give a defendant hope. A governor could only be charged after his term of office had ended. The court only sat in Rome, and its proceedings were all in Latin. Its jury comprised upper-class Romans exclusively (at different periods, senators or equites, or both), who would readily sympathize with a fellow Roman, and might also prove corruptible. Meantime, the provincials laying charges had to bear all the difficulty, risk, and expense of engaging advocates, assembling evidence, and producing witnesses. Even should they secure a conviction, there would be further uncertainty over whether they could successfully reclaim the cash or stolen items awarded to them; for example, it was easy enough for a convicted defendant to remove himself into comfortable, self-imposed exile beyond the reach of Roman jurisdiction.

We can surely conclude, then, that the prospect of a trial in the quaestio de repetundis was little or no deterrent to those governors willing to risk prosecution. Less easily quantifiable, by definition, is the proportion of governors averse to incurring the personal strain and exposure of a trial, no matter how favorable the prospects for evading conviction. Even so, it would be wrong to imagine that such men all governed honestly in consequence. For those who shrank from tangling with deep-rooted local disputes and rivalries, and sought a means of ensuring that they would not become the target of a prosecution, one practical safeguard was to identify the most powerful interest groups and then simply follow their guidance. In gaining protection of this sort, such a governor might well have to abandon any higher sense of responsibility to the province as a whole. But in all likelihood he had only been assigned there randomly by the lot, lacked any sense of commitment to the area, and saw no value in jeopardizing his own future prospects during a mere year's tenure.

TRIBUNATE OF LIVIUS DRUSUS (91)

Surviving accounts of the 90s are too fragmentary to give us adequate insight into the unfolding of political developments during that decade. At least it is plain that the existing tensions remained high. Moreover we know that the consuls of 95 went out of their way to provoke the allies by establishing a commission to investigate dubious claims to Roman citizenship, especially those accepted by the censors who had held office in 96. In 91, however, there emerged a tribune, Marcus Livius Drusus, with a wide-ranging program designed to overcome several of the principal difficulties. He was the son of the Livius Drusus who had opposed Gaius Gracchus, and like his father he acted in the interests of the Optimates. This may seem surprising at first sight, given that some of his measures were more characteristic of Populares. But the younger Drusus evidently acknowledged the pressing need to effect some major changes soon if serious conflict was to be avoided, and in these circumstances he wanted the initiative (and the credit) to belong to the Optimates.

So, in order to resolve the issue of whether the members of the jury courts should be senators or equites, Drusus proposed that they all be senators, but that 300 equites be made senators. He further proposed the foundation of colonies and the distribution of "public" land to poor citizens, and finally a grant of Roman citizenship to all Latins and Italians. Although some of these proposals seem to have been passed by the Plebeian assembly, each of the groups most affected by Drusus' program soon began to question whether their prospective gains would outweigh the losses. Some Optimate senators were not sure that they wanted the

Figure 6.1 *By the late third century, production of Roman coinage each year was normally made the responsibility of young men embarking on a career in public life. Within a further century it had become accepted that, in choosing types, these "moneyers" might take the opportunity to commemorate their place of origin or some special achievement by an ancestor. It was not yet typical Roman practice, however, to refer to contemporary events, as the rebels did during the Social War. Note their personification of "Italia," as well as the vignettes of eight warriors swearing an oath in front of a standard, and the (Italian) bull trampling and goring the (Roman) wolf; the language used on the second of these two coins is Oscan, which was widely spoken in southern Italy.*

was just unrealistic. It would seem that only a minority of the rebels were so extreme in their thinking, notably the Samnites and Lucanians; the majority were fighting mainly for higher status within the Roman alliance.

To Rome, on the other hand, the rebels' effectiveness during 90 demonstrated that they had to be granted the advancement they had long sought. This realization made the tragedy of the war all the more poignant, because it was exposed as an entirely avoidable conflict provoked by the Romans' persistent inability to overcome their own shortsightedness. Years later Cicero recorded a telling piece of personal reminiscence from his late teens:

> The consul Gnaeus Pompeius [Strabo], son of Sextus, conferred with the Marsian commander, Publius Vettius Scato, between their two camps. I was

there, serving as a recruit in Pompeius' army. . . . After Scato had greeted him, Pompeius asked, "How shall I address you?" "As a friend at heart," said Scato, "but by necessity an enemy." Everything about their discussion was calm, with no fear, no mistrust, not even notable hatred. For the allies were aiming, not to rob us of our state, but to be received as members of it. (*Philippics* 12.27)

During fall 90 Rome did in fact offer citizenship to all communities of allies which had remained loyal, as well as to those which had joined the rebels, but either had already abandoned hostilities or would do so by a specified date. This offer was not enough to prevent continued hard fighting during 89. Corfinium fell to the Romans, however, and eventually (in November) the rebels' last major stronghold at Asculum. The unashamedly pro-Roman historian Florus (2.6) later summed up this grim climax to the war: "Pompeius Strabo [cos. 89] made a universal waste by fire and sword, and set no end to the slaughter until by the destruction of Asculum he avenged the spirits of so many armies, consuls, and plundered towns." In addition to Cicero, among the very young men gaining their first military experience under Pompeius Strabo were his own son Pompey, and also Catiline (For their subsequent prominence, see later sections). Poppaedius died in battle. After 89 only a few rebel communities continued to hold out, including Nola in Campania. Meantime a second law was passed at Rome, which seems to have extended the offer of citizenship to those allies who were ineligible at the time of the previous grant in 90. Also in 89, communities directly north of the Padus River (in the "Transpadane" region, part of Rome's newly formed province of Cisalpine Gaul) were awarded Latin status.

It would be hard to overstate the importance of the Social War as a turning point with consequences stretching over the next several decades. It was Italy's first, sudden exposure to the traumas of full-scale civil conflict, a prelude (as it turned out) to successive, more prolonged bouts of similar horror over the next sixty years. It changed the administrative, political, and cultural complexion of Italy from the Padus River southwards. Communities which had run their affairs in accordance with a wide variety of constitutions of their own making now gradually abandoned these in order to become Roman municipia. Urbanization was encouraged for this purpose. At the same time, members of all allied communities gained the right to vote, and to run for office, in Rome itself. Last but not least, these changes fostered the spread of Latin and the disappearance of regional languages such as Etruscan, Oscan, Umbrian, and Messapic.

TRIBUNATE OF SULPICIUS RUFUS (88)

As we have seen, when Rome finally offered citizenship to the allies, this was done only under duress. There was a further respect in which the award can be regarded as either grudging or cautious, and in consequence the cause of violent reactions for several years to come. This was the restriction of the new citizens to

to be adamantly opposed to such a crime. Sulla himself realized the risk he ran in even broaching the possibility to his men. But he also had a sound appreciation of where their priorities lay, pointing out that if he simply accepted his removal from the command, then in all likelihood his replacement Marius would recruit other forces to take to Asia Minor, and these would become the ones to enjoy the rewards of easy victories there rather than themselves. This was an argument the men readily grasped, whereas the rights and wrongs of the constitutional and moral issues were far tougher for them to determine. In particular, poor citizens who had volunteered or been drafted when Rome suddenly needed recruits to fight the Social War had little incentive to consider those issues. A lucrative eastern campaign under Sulla was their brightest—indeed their only—prospect, and they would support him to secure it. So when officers sent by Marius arrived to take over command of the army, the men stoned them to death. All of Sulla's own officers, on the other hand, except one, deserted him. In contrast to the men, they were sufficiently conscious of the illegality of a march on Rome not to want any part in it.

Sulla's anticipation of the reaction that his fateful step would provoke was largely accurate. There was never much doubt that he would gain control of Rome, because Sulpicius, Marius, and the senate were taken completely by surprise. It had never even occurred to them that Sulla would attempt this kind of coup (he would hardly have been allowed to leave for Campania otherwise), and they had no organized body of troops on hand. At the same time Sulla himself was not fully prepared for the desperate, even if makeshift, resistance that his army encountered from everyone in the city as it entered Rome, and he had to rally his men when their nerve came close to breaking.

Once in control of the city, Sulla immediately prevailed on the senate to declare a group of twelve—Sulpicius, Marius, his son of the same name aged about twenty-two, and nine others—enemies of the state because of their violent, seditious behavior. This maneuver created the impression that by contrast Sulla's own no less violent, seditious reaction was legitimate. It also—very disturbingly—made instant outlaws of Roman citizens without any trial, and let them be hunted down and killed. Next, Sulla cancelled all the measures passed by Sulpicius after the imposition of the iustitium. This meant that Sulla himself was now restored to the Mithridatic command, and Pompeius Rufus to his consulship; it also meant, however, that the new citizens were not to be redistributed among the thirty-five tribes. All this Sulla quickly achieved with his army still present in the city. To try to reduce the universal resentment felt towards him, he now sent it back to Campania. But its departure meant that, at the elections which followed, voters could take the opportunity to articulate their hostility. Neither of the candidates elected to the consulship for 87 was supported by Sulla, although afterwards he did successfully persuade both to swear that they would leave his measures intact. That done, he rejoined his army and proceeded to the East with it. Meantime, of the group outlawed by him, only Sulpicius had met his death as he fled. After some narrow escapes, Marius and his son had managed to reach Africa, where many of his veterans were settled.

CINNA'S RULE (87–84)

With Sulpicius now dead and Sulla departed to the East, there was some hope that 87 might turn out a less traumatic year than 88 had been. In fact it was not, because one of the consuls, Lucius Cornelius Cinna, was somehow persuaded to take up the cause of redistributing the new citizens among the thirty-five tribes. Evidently during the course of his election the previous year he had not declared any such concern, but he now became an implacable advocate of the cause. His fellow consul Gnaeus Octavius remained opposed to it, the tribunes were divided (some vetoed the proposal), and rioting ensued. Cinna then left Rome and traveled through Italy rallying support—behavior for which the senate removed him from office and declared him an enemy or *hostis*. Marius seized the opportunity to return from Africa and offer Cinna his assistance, which was accepted. Both sides took desperate measures to raise troops; slaves were offered their freedom in return for serving; and the Samnites (who were still stubbornly at war, having rejected Rome's concessions to the allies) in the end agreed to support Cinna. Eventually, late in the year, after a siege, Rome fell to Cinna and Marius. The consul Octavius refused to flee, and so was killed on the spot. Cinna and Marius then embarked on a bloody purge of their opponents and enemies, most of whom were dispatched without even the most perfunctory trial. Sulla was outlawed in his absence. Looting and killing by the freed slaves who had helped to capture Rome was at first tolerated, but when they would not stop they were rounded up and massacred.

By some irregular means Cinna and Marius had themselves made consuls for 86, and duly entered office on January 1. Amid the widespread carnage and destruction Marius now felt a measure of gloating satisfaction. Finally he had overcome his enemies, as well as fulfilling a bizarre prophecy made to him as a young man that he would live to become consul seven times. He could also begin preparations to lead an army against Mithridates. By mid-January, however, he was dead, perhaps of pneumonia. It was a tragic end for a man who had both saved the Republic and then in old age done much to undermine it. When Sulla had asked the senate to outlaw him in late 88, the courageous response of the *pontifex maximus* Quintus Mucius Scaevola was that a man with Marius' record could never be called an enemy of Rome (Valerius Maximus 3.8.5). Despite the political ineptitude that Marius had shown during his sixth consulship in 100, Scaevola's claim held up to 89. But it is quite impossible to justify the way in which Marius exploited the opportunity offered to him by Sulpicius the following year. To be sure, he was not solely to blame for the damage done to the Republic then, just as earlier in 107 he cannot reasonably be expected to have foreseen the disruptive political potential that his recruitment of poor volunteers would unlock. The fact is, however, that from 88 Marius discarded all sense of responsibility towards the state in favor of vengeful self-seeking at any cost. In consequence, his own reputation and the entire state both suffered irreparable harm.

Marius was replaced as consul by Lucius Valerius Flaccus, but leadership of the state remained with Cinna. In the short term, no major figure set out to oppose him. Everyone, after all, was bruised and exhausted by the recent conflicts, and preferred to wait and see how his plans might develop, as well as how Sulla might fare against Mithridates. In fact, the extent to which Cinna formulated plans for the longer term is unclear. All he could manage immediately was to tackle pressing crises, among which he did *not* include redistribution of the new citizens throughout the thirty-five tribes; they were still kept waiting. A financial crisis did receive attention, however. We only know the outcome, which was a law allowing debtors to pay back no more than one quarter of what they owed at that date—a devastating blow, in other words, to creditors, whose loan capital was drastically diminished. At least the law underlines for us the disruption and massive loss of confidence that affected everyone financially and economically.

Cinna's other immediate problem was to determine the attitude he now would take towards Sulla, whom he had made an outlaw. Formally, his decision was to treat Sulla as such; in consequence, his fellow consul Flaccus was dispatched to Asia Minor with two legions to take Sulla's place in the fight against Mithridates (this campaign is treated more fully in Chapter Seven). At the same time there is reason to think that Flaccus was authorized to explore quietly whether Sulla would be open to reaching some kind of accommodation with Cinna. Sulla of course was not; he placed no trust in Cinna or Flaccus. At least he did not proceed against Flaccus, any more than Flaccus contemplated trying to ally with Mithridates against him—a prospect truly frightening to Sulla. In fact, during the following year (85) Flaccus was killed in a mutiny fomented by his own subordinate Gaius Flavius Fimbria, previously Marius' associate and quaestor, and known for his ruthlessness. Fimbria then proceeded to corner Mithridates and evidently might even have captured him, had Lucius Licinius Lucullus, the quaestor in command of Sulla's fleet, responded to his pleas for assistance.

Sulla, however, felt no inclination to authorize help for Fimbria. Instead, it suited his purpose better to let Mithridates escape for the time being and to make peace with him; then Sulla attacked Fimbria and drove him to suicide. It is true that Mithridates was still a formidable foe, but had he been captured there was no one on his side of comparable stature to replace him. Really, we have to see Sulla's preference for missing this opportunity, and instead terminating hostilities in 85, as the product of his own selfish ambition to return to Rome with a minimum of delay. Granted, he did proceed to spend the next eighteen months reestablishing Roman control in the province of Asia, with many rich pickings, incidentally, to placate his soldiers, who had wanted to pursue Mithridates; but this was also a time to prepare for the fighting he was sure to encounter in Italy. At any rate, as we shall see in Chapter Seven, Sulla's decision to give priority to his return, leaving Roman interests in the East open to renewed threat from Mithridates, was to have far-reaching consequences in the longer term. Meantime, it is true, Sulla's only viable prospect for his own future safety was first to emerge unscathed from this eastern campaign, and then to reestablish himself at Rome—a daunting double challenge, which in the end he only just surmounted.

Once news of Sulla's preparations for return reached Rome, Cinna and his handpicked colleague for the consulship of 85, Gnaeus Papirius Carbo, began rallying troops and resources against him. Both had themselves reelected consuls for 84. Their plan was to face Sulla in Greece, and they had already dispatched some advance contingents when Cinna was killed in the course of a mutiny at the port of Ancona on the Adriatic. There is no knowing how differently events might have unfolded if he had lived longer, or how a clash between him and Sulla would have turned out. It looks as if Cinna's reelection as consul through 86–84 had been simply an attempt to maintain control in a time of crisis, not any reflection of a rethinking of how the state should be ruled in the longer term. Our ability to assess Cinna suffers from the fact that the meager surviving information on him is uniformly hostile, but there is little reason to think of him as a potential savior of the state prematurely cut down.

After Cinna's death in 84, Carbo recalled the contingents dispatched from Italy, and decided that any stand against Sulla should be made there, not abroad. It was probably he, too, who at this critical juncture finally had a law passed providing for the redistribution of the new citizens in the thirty-five tribes. He may in addition have supported a decree of the senate that called for the disbandment of all armies.

SULLA'S SECOND MARCH ON ROME (83–82)

If this decree was intended to embarrass or deter Sulla, it did neither. As soon as he landed at Brundisium with his five legions in spring 83, he was joined by two men who both had reason to keep out of Cinna's way, Marcus Licinius Crassus, aged thirty-two and son of the consul of 97, and Gnaeus Pompeius ("Pompey") aged twenty-three, son of the consul of 89 who had captured Asculum in the Social War. Pompey had coolly raised three legions from his father's former supporters and veterans in Picenum, and now placed this private army at Sulla's disposal. In general, Rome and most of Italy were initially hostile to Sulla. The memory of his first march on the city in 88 remained a bitter one, and the new citizens could see little hope of redistribution throughout the thirty-five tribes if he were to gain control. In the event, however, the resistance to him suffered from divisiveness. Some commanders fought Sulla's forces, but others attempted negotiation, and there were many desertions to his side by troops for whom a prolonged struggle had no appeal. Moreover Sulla now offered an assurance that he would respect the redistribution of all the new citizens among the thirty-five tribes—except for the Samnites, on whom he refused to bestow any recognition at all. That naturally strengthened their opposition to him.

In Rome, too, there developed more deeply committed resistance in 82 with the election of Carbo as consul again (he had not been consul in 83), alongside Gaius

Marius, the son of Rome's savior. Even the potency of Marius' name, however, could not prevent the city itself falling into Sulla's hands. "Young" Marius escaped to make a stand at Praeneste, twenty-three miles to the east (modern Palestrina). Gradually, the fighting that raged all over northern and central Italy during 82 came to center on this stronghold, from which "Young" Marius could be neither relieved nor dislodged. Eventually, fellow commanders of his, together with a Samnite force led by Pontius Telesinus, sought to relax Sulla's grip on the siege by making a diversionary attack on Rome from the north. On November 1, 82 they took up a position one mile outside the Colline Gate. Sulla dashed from Praeneste to confront them. When the battle began in the late afternoon, the left wing under his own command collapsed, but the right under Crassus broke the enemy. Very gradually, after a period of despair, the two men's forces at last gained the upper hand after nightfall. Telesinus was killed. If we can credit the account of the historian Velleius Paterculus, this "gallant man deeply imbued with hatred of the Roman name," knew full well how critical the battle was to the Samnite cause:

> Telesinus was everywhere among his men repeatedly saying that Rome's last day had come, and shouting that they must pull down and destroy the city: "The wolves who prey on Italian freedom will never disappear unless we wipe out the wood which is their lair." (2.27)

With Sulla's narrowly won victory at the Colline Gate, effective resistance to him in Italy came to an end. Praeneste soon surrendered, and "Young" Marius was killed. Elsewhere, Sicily and Africa were still in the hands of Sulla's opponents, but Pompey was sent to each of these provinces in turn, winning them back with a devastating efficiency that gained him the nickname "Young Butcher." One of his victims was Carbo, who had fled to Sicily after Sulla's victory at the Colline Gate. After these successful campaigns Sulla, who had already given his step-daughter in marriage to Pompey, now instructed him to discharge almost all his forces. Pompey wanted the further reward of a triumph, however, and so returned to Italy with his men for the purpose rather than disbanding them. Sulla tried to refuse on the technical grounds that Pompey was not a senator. But when reminded by Pompey that "more men worship the rising sun than the setting one" (Plutarch *Pompey* 14), Sulla gave way, and even addressed him by the name conferred by the troops in Africa, Magnus or "The Great." So as the climax to the first phase of his astounding career, Pompey, an eques not yet twenty-five, duly celebrated a triumph in March 81 with disregard for both the spirit and the letter of the law.

Meantime from November 82 Rome and Italy were at Sulla's mercy, resigned to whatever fate he had in store for them. Thanks to all the bloodshed, their conqueror in this latest bout of civil war now enjoyed a far tighter grip than Cinna or Marius had ever achieved. In addition, unlike his predecessors, he possessed a clear vision of the reforms required in his opinion to return the state to its old stability, as well as a steely determination to put them into effect. Even so, we may note at once that he did keep his promise to uphold the redistribution of the new citizens throughout the thirty-five tribes. Their repeated readiness to fight for

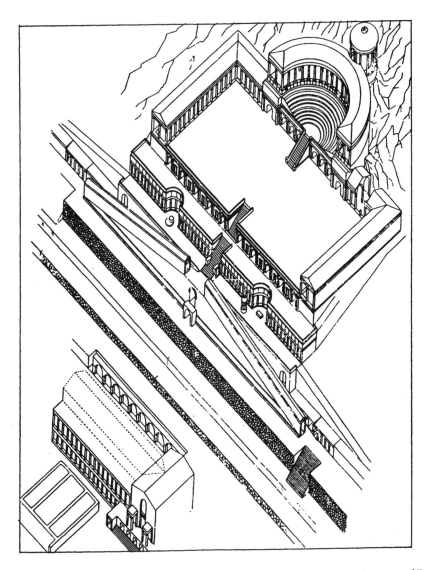

Figure 6.2 *Praeneste (modern Palestrina), situated on a spur of the Apennines east of Rome, was always appreciated as a cool refuge from summer heat in the city, and many wealthy Roman families had villas in its vicinity. It was also the site of an important sanctuary, the largest in Italy, dedicated to Fortuna Primigenia ("Firstborn Fortune"). The massive surviving remains reflect construction of the late second century B.C., with an amazing series of barrel-vaulted terraces ascending a steep hillside on which the modern town is also built; ramps link the terraces. As the reconstruction shown here clearly demonstrates, architectural inspiration came from famous sanctuaries of the Greek world, such as those at Pergamum and Rhodes. The cult of the goddess drew not only men from Rome, Italy, and farther afield—especially those seeking success in politics or warfare—but also women eager for children. An additional attraction at Praeneste was an oracle associated with the cult; the responses made to those who consulted it took the form of inscribed wooden* sortes *(literally "lots").*

unclear because the figures given in different sources vary considerably; 500 seems the minimum figure, and it could have been two, or even three, times that. More important than the number, however, is the clear fact that Sulla's supporters cynically exploited the opportunity to instigate an indiscriminate witch hunt throughout Italy, to pay off old personal scores, to enrich themselves, and to acquire property at auction for a fraction of its true value. Names were improperly added to the proscription lists, and misidentified victims were killed "in error."

Sulla, insofar as he was even aware of these abuses, seemed not to care. He was sufficiently vengeful himself to order that Marius' bones be exhumed and scattered. We do not know what answer, if any, he gave to his loyal associate, the senator Quintus Lutatius Catulus, who had the courage to ask him whether anyone was to be left alive; at least the question highlights the helpless fear felt even by his own supporters (Catulus himself did in fact survive). Roman society had an ingrained respect for the law and for due legal process. Not surprisingly, therefore, of all the forms of violence that Sulla unleashed against his fellow citizens in the course of his career, it was the proscriptions which were remembered with the most lasting horror and revulsion. Moreover, by targeting men of wealth and initiative, as well as excluding their sons and grandsons from public office, the proscriptions caused severe social and economic disruption, and for too long deprived the state of talent that it could ill afford to lose. Not until 49, as it turned out, would the debarment from public office be lifted.

SULLA THE DICTATOR AND HIS PROGRAM (82–81)

Also in November 82, the senate recognized as legal all Sulla's past actions as both consul and proconsul. It officially conferred on him an additional name, Felix or "fortunate"; Sulla had always believed in his personal luck. Most important of all, the senate initiated the procedure which led to Sulla's immediate appointment as dictator charged with bringing order back to the state and formulating laws. The name and style of the office purposely recalled the traditional office of dictator, which remained familiar to Romans, although in fact no appointment had been made to it now since the end of the Second Punic War over a century earlier. In vital respects, however, Sulla's dictatorship departed from the traditional model. His appointment to it specifically validated all his actions in advance; thus he could execute anyone without trial, and was not required to submit any legislative proposal to a citizen assembly. In addition, there was no time limit to his tenure of this office.

Senate

The absence of such a limit, however, should not be taken as a sign that Sulla envisaged remaining dictator indefinitely. Far from it. Instead, he was committed to restoring the state to the stable condition which, in his view, it had enjoyed under the guidance of the senate a half-century and more ago, until Tiberius Gracchus and a succession of other ambitious leaders proceeded to upset its balance with increasingly damaging consequences. The senate's persistent weakness, as Sulla saw it, was that its predominance could readily be challenged. Moreover, most recently its numbers had been badly depleted in all the civil strife; perhaps no more than about 150 members still survived out of the normal total of around 300. Sulla therefore wasted no time in both making up this total and also introducing around 450 further members, so that altogether the senate now became double its traditional size, and its meeting place (the *curia*) on the north side of the Forum Romanum was enlarged. By definition, the new members came from the equestrian class, because this was the group of wealthiest Roman citizens outside the senate. Many equites had opposed Sulla, and had been proscribed. On the other hand, the most loyal of those who had supported him now gained this reward, at the same time further weakening equestrian identity and influence in the process. Even so, that was hardly a matter of regret to Sulla, since it diminished one potential source of challenge to the senate.

To help maintain a total of around 600 senators, Sulla raised the number of quaestors (the lowest senatorial magistracy) to twenty. Just how steep an increase this figure represented in the number being elected annually we happen not to know, but in all likelihood it was substantial, perhaps even a doubling. In addition, Sulla enacted that quaestors should become members of the senate immediately after their year of office, instead of having to wait until they could be enrolled at the next census (taken every five years).

At the same time, junior senators' advancement through the cursus honorum inevitably became a more competitive struggle, because Sulla only increased the number of praetorships annually from six to eight, and he left the number of consuls at two. Orderly competition for office seemed essential to him, and to this end he revived certain old restrictions which had been either ignored or set aside in recent decades. These were, first, that only ex-quaestors were eligible for the praetorship, and likewise only ex-praetors for the consulship; and second, that these successive offices could not be held before the ages of thirty, thirty-nine, and forty-two respectively. Third, and very important, there must be a ten-year interval between holding any particular office again. In practice, this restriction would apply most often to the consulship, and make it impossible to repeat the electoral successes of Marius and Cinna above all.

Sulla evidently soon gained the chance to demonstrate his personal commitment to this set of rules. In 81, Quintus Lucretius Afella, who had finally dislodged "Young" Marius from Praeneste the previous winter and then sent his head to Sulla, as a reward demanded the privilege of standing for the consulship, although he was blatantly unqualified. The account given by the Greek historian Appian (*Civil Wars* 1.100–101) may be inaccurate in some of its details, but the general point is unmistakable:

a

b

It was no accident that much of the settlement occurred within easy marching distance of Rome itself. Similarly, in remote areas, Sulla permitted his supporters to acquire large landholdings. He was severest of all in Samnium, as the geographer Strabo explains (5.4.11):

> Sulla's proscriptions did not end until he had destroyed or driven from Italy all who bore the Samnite name. When asked the reason for this terrible anger, he explained that experience had taught him that no Roman would ever know peace as long as they had the Samnites to deal with. So the towns of Samnium have become villages, and some have even vanished altogether.

Governors

Outside Italy, in Sulla's view, the state had most to fear from the commander who could persuade his troops to join him in attacking Rome, just as Sulla himself had done twice. The shorter a commander's term, the less time he would gain to cultivate his troops. Accordingly, Sulla's hope was that at the end of their original term of office as many consuls and praetors as possible would accept one-year provincial governorships, with their *imperium* extended as proconsul or propraetor. There was no law requiring such acceptance, however.

Sulla revived, and perhaps added to, the existing restrictions on a governor's activity within his province, which, like so much else, had been ignored in the recent past. These restrictions were that only with prior authorization from Rome could a governor make war or leave his province, either alone or at the head of his troops. In addition, he must leave the province within thirty days of his successor's arrival there.

Facing page

Figure 7.1a,b *Pompeii, famous as one of the Campanian cities overwhelmed by the volcanic eruption of Mt. Vesuvius in A.D. 79, preserves an amphitheater seating perhaps 20,000 spectators in thirty-five rows, surrounding an arena measuring 220 × 115 feet (67 × 35 m). An inscription dates the dedication of the structure to about 70 B.C., thus making it one of the earliest known amphitheaters to be erected in permanent stone form, and a marked advance on the temporary wooden structures which continued to be used in the forum at Rome and elsewhere. In addition, the dedication specifically identifies Pompeii's amphitheater as a structure commissioned for their own benefit by the veteran colonists who were settled there by Sulla within the previous decade, and who (as Cicero confirms) were for long resented by the established members of the community. Evidently the new, tougher, military training associated with Marius at the end of the second century incorporated gladiators' fighting techniques. In the likely event that the veterans at Pompeii had been among the recruits trained in this way, they might well have been eager to maintain an interest in gladiatorial combat. Moreover, the innovative erection of a permanent amphitheater in stone for the purpose acted as a stark warning to any hostile, ousted citizen that its builders' appreciation of effective fighting methods remained keen, and that they were here to stay.*

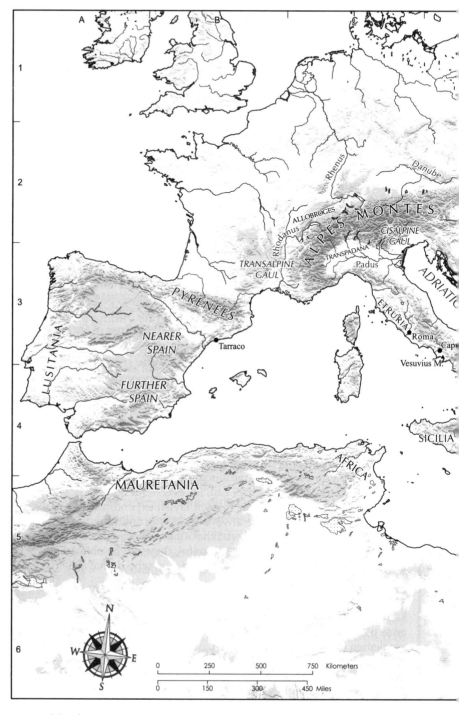

Map 7.2 *Rome's Wars in Italy and Abroad, 78–63*

E   F   G

Bosporus

CRIMEA

BLACK SEA

Danube

PROPONTIS   PONTUS   ARMENIA

Zela

BITHYNIA   PAPHLAGONIA   Tigranocerta

MACEDONIA   Cyzicus   CAPPADOCIA   PARTHIA

AEGEAN   Pergamum   A   S   I   A
SEA   CILICIA   Antioch   Euphrates

Athenae   S   Y   R   I   A

Rhodes

CRETA   I   U   D   A   E   A

INTERNUM MARE   Jerusalem

Cyrene   Alexandria

A   E   G   Y   P   T   U   S

Nile

BOX 7.2: *Excerpt from Pompey's letter sent to the senate from Spain in 74, as it appears in a fragment of Sallust's* Histories *written in the 30s. In accordance with the conventions of ancient historiography, this version with its readily identifiable rhetorical elements is likely to be Sallust's rather than Pompey's own; but it no doubt retains the drift of what the latter originally wrote.*

(fragment 2.98) If it were against you [the senate] and my country and household gods that I had undertaken all the toil and dangers which have accompanied the many occasions since my early manhood when under my leadership the most dangerous enemies have been routed and your safety secured, you could have decreed no sterner steps against me—absent as I am—than you have been doing up to now. In defiance of the normal age limits, I have been thrust out to take part in a savage war against an enemy of proven quality [Sertorius]; and yet, so far as you are able, you have destroyed me by famine, the most miserable of all deaths. Was it in anticipation of this that the Roman people sent their sons to war? Are these the rewards for wounds and blood so often shed for the state? Weary of writing and sending deputations, I have used up all my private wealth and expectations, and you meanwhile over a space of three years have barely granted me the expenses of one. In heaven's name, do you think I am a substitute for the treasury, or that an army can be maintained without pay and provisions? . . .

   Thus my army and the enemy's are in the same position: For neither of them gets paid, and both of them, if they win, can come to Italy. I call your attention to this, and ask you to take notice of it, and not to compel me to find a way out of my difficulties by abandoning the interests of the state for my own. Nearer Spain, insofar as it is not occupied by the enemy, has been devastated either by ourselves or by Sertorius with terrible carnage, except for the coastal cities; moreover these are a drain on our resources and money. Last year Gaul provided Metellus' army with pay and provisions; now, because of a bad harvest, it is hardly able to support itself. I have used up not only my property, but my credit as well. You are my last resort: If you do not help, my army—against my wishes and as I have predicted—will cross to Italy and bring with it the entire Spanish war.

Perperna and his fellow officers had expected to gain by their disloyalty to Sertorius remains a puzzle; just possibly they imagined that Pompey would reward them.

   Even harder to fathom is Sertorius' vision for the future. There is no question of his success in brilliantly inspiring and manipulating the native peoples upon whom he chiefly relied for support. They were impressed by the divine inspiration that he claimed to gain through a white doe, as well as by his military leadership, which included ingenious exploitation of guerilla tactics. At the same time he established a Roman school for aristocrats' sons, and acted like a Roman magistrate, even eventually forming his own senate. What larger end he had in view, however, remains elusive. He surely cannot have championed the expulsion of the Romans from the entire peninsula. On the other hand, it is difficult to believe that native peoples remained his loyal following for so long merely in order to insist that opponents of Sulla, rather than supporters, continue to be their rulers. To what degree, therefore, Sertorius deliberately misrepresented himself to the native peoples, or at what stage they finally acknowledged their aims to be irreconcilable with his, are issues that remain a puzzle.

SPARTACUS' SLAVE REVOLT (73–71)

With the elimination of Sertorius and Perperna in 73, the senate was relieved of one crisis at least. It was fortunate, therefore, that another developed only now. This occurred in Italy itself, when a group of seventy-four slaves led by a Thracian, Spartacus, and a Gaul, Crixus, escaped from a gladiatorial training school at Capua. In no time, the stronghold they established on Mt. Vesuvius attracted not only runaway slaves, but also free workers on rural estates, eventually 70,000 men and more in all. At first, the Roman forces hurriedly sent against them were defeated. Spartacus urged his followers to head north out of Italy, and to disperse back to their different lands of origin before Rome could prepare a major assault. Crixus countered by proposing that they loot southern Italy first, and this they proceeded to do until he and the force with him were wiped out by a Roman army in 72. Spartacus meantime did head north; but for some unknown reason he turned back after he had won a victory in Cisalpine Gaul, made for Rome itself but then thought better of it, and finally seized Thurii in the south.

At this stage, after further Roman defeats, the senate decided to put Crassus—who had won the battle at the Colline Gate for Sulla in November 82, and had been praetor in 73—in sole charge of the offensive against Spartacus; he took over the consuls' four legions, and raised six more. Since the senate was still short of funds, he may have been chosen partly for his wealth: "Rich" in his view was a description applicable only to someone with the means to maintain a legion out of his own pocket. With the forces he raised, Crassus drove Spartacus' force still farther south through Bruttium to the sea. Spartacus' hopes of crossing to Sicily were dashed when the pirates who had promised ships failed to provide them. His force was then literally hemmed in by Crassus, and it only managed to break out in 71 at the third attempt. Meantime Spartacus had tried in vain to negotiate with Crassus, and the senate in its continuing alarm had summoned Pompey back from Spain (where he was still helping communities recover), as well as the proconsul of Macedonia back across the Adriatic. Crassus naturally hoped that he could finish off the war alone, and he almost did so, winning a battle in Lucania in which Spartacus was killed, and then lining the Via Appia from Capua to Rome with 6,000 crucified captives. However, 5,000 slaves who managed to escape and flee northwards were caught and slaughtered by Pompey, who was therefore able to claim to the senate that *he* was responsible for finally ending the war.

and by extension an influential figure in a community's affairs, albeit out of the public eye for the most part.

Within the household, too, a wife could gain lasting influence through motherhood. How far she was likely to have the ability to control her childbearing remains unclear. Without question, Roman women shared—mainly just by word of mouth—a rich store of information about both contraception and abortion, but its effectiveness is far harder to determine; to judge by surviving texts, some of it was downright dangerous. In any event, few women eager to rear children to adulthood would quickly limit their family's size. So many children were likely to die either at birth or as infants that as many as three out of five might never reach adulthood. Even then, life expectancy was low. A bride in her late teens would be lucky if she had even one grandparent still alive to attend the wedding; the chance that her mother would still be living was no better than 60 percent, and her father 50 percent. As a mother, it was normal for a Roman woman to be closely involved with the upbringing of her children, imparting values and assisting the advancement of sons in particular. Naturally, a wife who was skilled in running the household, acted as a gracious hostess, and behaved with unfailing dignity and discretion in public, could prove a powerful influence on her children and a priceless asset to her husband, especially if his position required him to be away from home for long periods (see further in this connection the "Laudatio Turiae," Box 9.1, in Chapter Nine).

It is true that respectable society held a wife to a higher standard of personal behavior than her husband. His involvements with other women could largely be tolerated so long as they were not blatant, and not with married women of supposedly respectable background. A wife, by contrast, who became involved with any other man, especially one of lower social status, could not expect the same tolerance. Divorce, however, could be initiated by either partner to a marriage. In Roman law, marriage itself was a purely private act, which required no formal ceremony—although a celebration was often held—nor any certification by the state. Rather, a relationship where both partners were eligible (neither could be a slave, for example), and behaved towards one another as husband and wife, constituted a legally valid marriage. By the same token, either marriage partner could formally mark the termination of the relationship with a divorce by simply informing the other, even through a third party, without necessarily stating a reason. Divorce was a purely private matter, therefore. As already mentioned, a husband contemplating this step would need to consider his obligation to return some or all of the dowry, depending upon the circumstances; he could be sued if he did not. The wife, for her part, if she had produced children, would have to weigh the likelihood that after a divorce they would remain with their father, since they were regarded as belonging to his family, not hers. Typically, little stigma attached to divorce or remarriage. To some wives, however, the ideal was to be *univira*, never to have more than one husband, even if they were widowed and were in a position to remarry.

Although it means looking ahead to the end of the first century B.C., it is appropriate to mention here the opinion of Augustus (Rome's ruler at this date) that by then the upper classes in particular were no longer showing sufficient respect for marriage, nor for its vital role in rearing children to maintain families and indeed the community as a whole. In Augustus' view, too many respectable Roman men were choosing to remain bachelors; some men who did marry made unsuitable matches, or condoned adulterous behavior by their wives; and married couples capable of producing children were deliberately remaining childless. It is all but impossible to be sure how accurate these perceptions really were. Even so, there is no doubt about the strength of Augustus' lasting concern to remedy what struck him as a crisis. He promoted some complex legislation for this purpose in 18–17 B.C., and had it revised as late as A.D. 9.

In one law, first, penalties were introduced for both men and women who remained unmarried, or who married but for whatever reason failed to have children, between the ages of twenty-five and sixty for men, and twenty and fifty for women. Second, members of the senatorial class that he instituted were debarred from marrying any ex-slave or anyone not regarded as respectable, such as an entertainer, for example. And third, all validly married couples who did have children were rewarded on a sliding scale: the more children, the more benefits.

In another law, a husband who became aware of adultery by his wife now had to divorce her and then prosecute her (the same did not apply in the case of an adulterous husband, but his wife could still divorce him). Even if the husband, or his father-in-law, caught the wife in the act of adultery, he could not treat her violently, although under certain conditions the male partner could be killed on the spot. For the husband not to prosecute his divorced wife within two months was itself an offense, and a third party could then prosecute instead; it would have to be a private individual who took this step, since Rome never had public prosecutors. On conviction for adultery, a woman stood to lose half her dowry and one-third of her other property; she also faced exile to an island, and could never remarry. Her male partner, if still alive, could likewise be prosecuted and punished.

The striking feature about all these measures is the way in which they regulate by law for the first time a wide variety of spheres which Romans had always regarded as entirely private. In many respects, the measures represent blunt, disruptive interference. Moreover, despite Augustus' strong commitment to the values underlying them, there is no sign that they were particularly successful in altering society's behavior or attitudes. The main reaction that they provoked was one of resentment.

POMPEY FREES THE MEDITERRANEAN OF PIRATES (67)

At the end of 70, Crassus and Pompey staged a public reconciliation, but both ignored Sulla's hope that as senior magistrates they would agree to take up a

once Rome began to play a role in the affairs of Asia Minor from the early second century. This role was certain to become larger and more permanent following Roman annexation of the kingdom of Pergamum as the province of Asia in 129.

Mithridates, the older of two sons, was only eleven when his father was assassinated in 120. His mother Laodice then ruled as regent, favoring her younger son, until around 113 Mithridates (aged about eighteen) managed to oust them both and assert sole, personal control. His next concern was to raise both his personal standing, and that of his kingdom, which he did dramatically over the next few years by bringing the Crimea and the northern shores of the Black Sea under his control; these areas gave him immense material resources and manpower. He also pressed further and more aggressively than any of his predecessors into Paphlagonia and Cappadocia, eventually (about 101) even making his eight-year old son nominal king of Cappadocia. He tried to gain Roman recognition of these conquests, but can hardly have been surprised by growing Roman coolness towards him. When he and Marius (traveling in Asia Minor) met in 98, Marius is said to have advised him sternly "either to be greater than the Romans or to obey them" (Plutarch, *Marius* 31). Later, after a Cappadocian rebellion in the mid-90s, the senate ordered him to abandon that kingdom, and sent a governor (Sulla, in fact) to install a new ruler. Mithridates acquiesced in this instance, preferring to postpone the clash with Rome that seemed increasingly unavoidable. Around the same time (mid-90s), as it happened, he gained the notable advantage of an alliance with the major kingdom of Armenia to the southeast of his own; his daughter married its new king, Tigranes I. Then in 90, when Rome was preoccupied with the Social War in Italy, Mithridates caused the king of Cappadocia to flee, and expelled the young king Nicomedes from Bithynia, west of Paphlagonia. But, surprisingly, when a force of five Roman legions arrived, he agreed to withdraw.

At that point, however, the Roman commanders fatally miscalculated. They urged the newly restored kings of Cappadocia and Bithynia to take revenge, and to recoup their financial losses, by invading Pontus. Nicomedes did so, thus finally provoking Mithridates to action which he began to take in 89. That year and into the following summer of 88, Mithridates' westward sweep proved invincible. His cavalry alone were sufficient to destroy Nicomedes' army when it entered western Pontus; the king himself was taken prisoner, and Mithridates' infantry never even struck

Figure 7.3 Once King Mithridates VI of Pontus had occupied the Roman province of Asia in 89, he showed no hesitation in issuing coins there with his image (modeled on Alexander the Great) on one side, and his name, title, and associated symbols on the other. The language used is Greek, and this example carries the date "Year 2" of a new era.

a blow in this encounter. As he advanced west, three Roman commanders in succession were defeated next, none with difficulty. With resistance to him generally decreasing therefore, Mithridates soon had all of western Asia Minor under his control. In what had been the Roman province of Asia for the previous forty years, he was for the most part welcomed as a liberator.

He sought both to allow expression of hatred for Roman rule, and to reinforce his own position there, by secretly arranging for a massacre of all resident Romans or Italians along with their families and Italian freedmen. This horrific "Asian Vespers" took place on a day in spring or early summer 88; the death toll was said to have been in the region of 80,000.

SULLA'S CAMPAIGN AGAINST MITHRIDATES (87–85)

By now Rome was less preoccupied than before by crises in Italy. The Social War was largely won, and so war was declared against Mithridates, to be waged by Sulla with five legions. As we have seen, however, he had unusual difficulties to overcome in claiming this command and then arranging for his departure from Rome. This prolonged delay left Mithridates free to consider advancing still farther west, which he decided to do in 88 when invited to occupy Athens by opponents of Rome there. Once Sulla and his army finally set out in 87, therefore, it was Greece they made for. They did successfully take Athens and its port the Piraeus by siege, but Mithridates meantime dispatched to central Greece an army commanded by his general Archelaus that was perhaps three times larger than Sulla's. So it was here that the two decisive battles were fought in summer 86, at Chaeronea and Orchomenus. Both were overwhelming victories for Sulla, and as a result almost all Archelaus' forces were wiped out. Sulla then offered terms: Mithridates should relinquish all his conquests since 90, and become an ally of Rome; at the same time he should give Rome eighty ships from his fleet, as well as 3,000 talents in compensation (equivalent to 72 million sesterces).

At this point, despite all the setbacks in Greece, Mithridates was disinclined to accept such terms, and it was hard for Sulla to pursue him further without a fleet, which he was only now beginning to assemble. Meantime control of the Aegean Sea remained with Mithridates. In Asia Minor, however, he had to deal with growing unrest, as well as with the unexpected menace posed by the two Roman legions of Gaius Flavius Fimbria. As we saw in Chapter Six, this was the force under Lucius Valerius Flaccus dispatched by Cinna in 86 to take over from Sulla in view of the latter's outlaw status. It had marched directly along the north shore of the Aegean and then into western Asia Minor, without diverting south to Greece. So it did not encounter Sulla, but under the ruthless command of Fimbria—an officer who took the lead after a mutiny against Flaccus—it successfully closed in on Mithridates during 85. On one occasion in fact, he might actually have been surrounded and captured, if Lucius Licinius Lucullus, the quaestor in charge of Sulla's fleet, had agreed to cooperate.

In fall 85, therefore, as the threats to his control escalated, Mithridates finally agreed to accept the terms that Sulla had offered a year before. The two men met and reached agreement at Dardanus, on the Asian shore of the Hellespont. Both had much to gain by abandoning the struggle at this point. For his part, Mithridates had to acknowledge his inability to maintain the impact of the stunning blows he had delivered to Roman power in Asia Minor and Greece. On the other hand, the compensation he was called upon to pay for this havoc was light, and the whole area of his rule before 90—Pontus and the Black Sea—remained unscathed, and as productive as ever. The opportunity to fight another day might well return. He could be soundly prepared then, and there seemed every likelihood of the chance to exploit some future crisis facing Rome. It was precisely because of the current atmosphere of crisis there that Sulla, for his part, wanted to make peace and return home as soon as possible. It was not at all in his immediate interests to pursue Mithridates further, with or without Fimbria's help. All he was concerned to do first was to reestablish the Roman province of Asia. This he did with unwavering harshness, imposing among other burdens a demand for 20,000 talents in indemnity and tax arrears from the cities there; Mithridates by contrast had been asked for only 3,000. After doing terrible harm, Sulla and his army eventually left Asia in 84, spent the winter in Athens, and sailed to Italy in spring 83.

His decision not to pursue Mithridates further met with no favor among his men, and their view was shared by Lucius Licinius Murena, who was left as governor of Asia on Sulla's departure. Over the next two years Murena in fact acted independently in mounting three successive raids on Mithridates' territory. It was only the third of these that Mithridates dared resist, and once he had defeated and expelled Murena's force, an envoy from Sulla called an end to this fighting. Murena's action at least warned Mithridates that some Romans had no intention of leaving him in peace, but saw him as a threat to be eliminated at the first possible opportunity. Such Romans certainly supported the decision made around this time to station a commander regularly in southern Asia Minor. Officially his province was called Cilicia, because the initial priority was to suppress the pirate strongholds there, though in practice the first governors focused their attention on regions farther west. They could also keep watch on Mithridates to the north, as could the Roman governor of Asia from the west.

LUCULLUS' STRUGGLE WITH MITHRIDATES (74–67)

The sense of being hemmed in by Rome was only increased for Mithridates in 75, when Nicomedes of Bithynia died and bequeathed his kingdom to Rome. Rome's decision was both to accept the bequest and to resume the fight against Mithridates, regardless of the agreement reached at Dardanus. Lucullus, consul in 74, was made governor of Asia and Cilicia jointly, with five legions at his disposal. Before he advanced the following spring, however, Mithridates struck first by moving west from Pontus, through Paphlagonia, into Bithynia, where he laid siege to the key port city of Cyzicus on the Propontis. Surprisingly, the city held out, reinforced by Lucullus' land and naval forces, even though Mithridates had a larger army and navy. With the onset of winter he was no longer able to supply his forces, and so had to withdraw them back to Pontus. His mistake had been to concentrate so single-mindedly on the siege.

Lucullus, on the other hand, had achieved victory in 73 without risking a major battle. The following year he was bold enough to advance into Pontus, and penetrated more deeply there in 71. When Mithridates' cavalry attacked, the Romans repulsed it with heavy losses. Subsequently, when the king decided upon a withdrawal to the mountainous kingdom of Armenia, his infantry no longer had the cavalry's protection, and so incurred severe casualties from Roman pursuers. Tigranes, king of Armenia, respected his long-standing alliance with Mithridates to the extent of giving him refuge, but otherwise disappointed him by refusing to be drawn into the conflict between Pontus and Rome. Lucullus meantime, in his determination to overcome Mithridates, resolved to cross the Euphrates River and invade Armenia. This was a momentous and unauthorized step, since he had no instructions for extending his campaign in this way, and Armenia was a state which had previously lain quite outside Rome's orbit.

The further risk that an invasion of Armenia might in turn provoke its more powerful neighbor to the east, the Parthian empire, hardly seems to have struck Lucullus. In the event, he invaded Armenia in 69, and after a great battle captured and razed its southern capital Tigranocerta. Parthia—a huge kingdom extending beyond the Caspian Sea, but often unstable—declined to intervene. Tigranes and Mithridates both eluded capture, however, and the failure of Lucullus' energetic operations to pursue them finally provoked his troops to mutiny by late 68. The men were exhausted, in particular the two legions which had come to Asia Minor under Flaccus and Fimbria in 86, and had served there ever since. By chance just at the time of the mutiny, Mithridates managed to make his way back to Pontus with a small force. He stirred up revolt, and wiped out the main body of Roman troops stationed there at a battle near Zela in summer 67. Lucullus had already withdrawn from Armenia by then, but did not reach Pontus in time to prevent this unraveling of what he had achieved there; equally, he was unable to campaign further because of his men's refusal to cooperate. Dissatisfaction with him at Rome was only fueled by *publicani*. They resented his measures as governor of Asia to assist its communities in paying off the crippling debts incurred after Rome's repossession of the province.

POMPEY'S DEFEAT OF
MITHRIDATES (66–63)

During the summer of 67, two new commanders arrived from Rome to take over Lucullus' huge sphere of command between them, but they had never expected to be faced by such a crisis, and it soon became clear that they were not equal to retrieving Rome's position. All Lucullus' success seemed to be reversed: Mithridates had recovered Pontus, and Tigranes had invaded Cappadocia. When this disastrous news reached Rome, it is no surprise that dismay and frustration led to pressure for more decisive action. One of the tribunes for 66, Gaius Manilius, consequently proposed that all the Roman forces in Asia Minor and the entire conduct of the war be handed to Pompey. Given his swift and total success against the pirates the previous year, this solution seemed unarguable, and there was none of the fierce opposition that had resisted Gabinius' proposal the previous year. Yet again, therefore, Pompey was invited to take an extraordinary command to retrieve a situation where others had failed. This outcome left Lucullus embittered, because he had come so close to eliminating Mithridates. Lucullus was to resent Pompey as a successor who had deprived him of the victory that was largely his; no wonder that he is said to have compared Pompey to a "parasitical bird," whose habit was to settle on corpses killed by others (Plutarch, *Pompey* 31). Looking further back, we may reflect that this particular opportunity for Pompey, and the difficulties associated with it, need never have arisen in the first place had Sulla set himself different priorities in the mid 80s.

In 66, Pompey moved fast, as usual, to restore the Roman position. He now persuaded the king of Parthia not to help Mithridates or Tigranes, but instead to attack Armenia, a key development which forced Tigranes to abandon his invasion of Cappadocia. Pompey himself drove Mithridates to the far east of Pontus, and defeated him there. In consequence, Mithridates finally abandoned Pontus, and made his way overland round the Black Sea to the Crimean Bosporus, the last secure part of his realm. He reached here by summer 65. Pompey chose not to pursue him, but instead to secure the submission of Tigranes, which he did without difficulty by late 66. Tigranes was allowed to retain the core of his kingdom, but all the other territories he had acquired were now forfeited to Rome. Pompey then took the year 65 to suppress resistance in this distant region altogether, marching almost as far as the Caspian Sea, and demonstrating Roman power; the region was mostly divided among dependent rulers, however, rather than being annexed. In 64 Pompey was preoccupied with reorganizing part of Pontus as a Roman province, but late in the year marched south to annex Syria and then proceeded on to Judaea, where he captured Jerusalem after a three months' siege in 63. His justification for all this further invasion and annexation was that effective, reliable rulers in the Roman interest were simply lacking here. In addition, although Parthia was not yet the obvious threat that it would later become, Pompey may have welcomed the chance to block the possible growth of its influence.

Predictably, Pompey was criticized at Rome for taking these other initiatives while Mithridates was still free. If Pompey had merely assumed that the king would be a spent force once he fled from Pontus, that may have been a mistake, because in fact Mithridates did set about vigorously building up power in the Crimean Bosporus once he reached there in 65. His troops, however, no longer shared his zeal, and it was a revolt on their part that led to his death in 63, either by suicide or possibly assassination; his son Pharnaces succeeded him. So finally died a king whose relentless struggle against Rome over a period of about thirty years forms an episode of exceptional importance for Rome's development. In this struggle he delivered stunning blows, gave hope to other enemies of Rome, and left a deep mark on Roman politics and outlook both during his lifetime and long after.

ROLES OF CRASSUS AND CICERO IN ROME (65–63)

Pompey's unbroken success and luck in the East aroused envy at home, as well as concern for how he might act on his return: In particular, would he seek sole power like Sulla, bringing further bloodshed and terror? No one brooded over these issues with greater jealousy and apprehension than Crassus. After his consulship in 70, we know next to nothing of his activities until he became censor in 65, but from then onwards we can detect him searching desperately to secure some kind of influence or authority with which to stand up to his former colleague. As censor, he proposed extending Roman citizenship to the Transpadana, the region of Cisalpine Gaul north of the Padus river; whoever carried out such a measure would automatically gain prestige and influence. Likewise he proposed accepting as genuine the dubious will of Ptolemy Alexander (who had died at least fifteen years previously), in which he bequeathed his kingdom of Egypt to Rome; again, whoever was sent to organize the annexation—and at this point it could hardly be Pompey—had much to gain. Crassus' colleague in the censorship, however, objected to both proposals, and the pair of them resigned their office with the census left unfinished.

The elections conducted in 64 for the two consuls who would hold office during the calendar year 63 were to have a particularly significant outcome. We know that seven candidates stood, but three dominated the race. Two were "nobles"— Gaius Antonius Hybrida, whose father had been consul in 99, and the patrician Lucius Sergius Catilina, better known today as Catiline. Both were suspect figures who had served under Sulla, and in very dubious circumstances had escaped conviction for major offenses; both were also in the typical senator's predicament of having seriously overspent in their competition for political office. At least they settled on the logical economy of cooperating against their main rival, the exceptional figure of Marcus Tullius Cicero. It was potentially to his disadvantage that he was a *novus homo*; thus no member of his family had previously been a sena-

been risking bankruptcy in order to distribute more lavish bribes than ever. He owed his failure in part to Cicero, who demonstrated his personal distrust by having a bodyguard escort him to preside on election day in September, and wearing a breastplate visible under his toga. Catiline had already roused widespread alarm by championing the cause of those who were poor, in debt, or dispossessed, and calling for cancellation of debts and redistribution of land. Although he did attract a large following in this way, with several senators among them, these were altogether not the class of voter that carried most weight in the Centuriate assembly where consuls were elected; so it was understandable enough that the wealthier, more conservative voters should prefer less controversial candidates.

In despair at proceeding by legal means, Catiline and his associates now began to gather forces for an armed revolution and other outrages such as arson and murder. However, since not everyone distrusted Catiline as completely as he did, Cicero had to proceed against him with care, and above all secure condemnatory evidence that was unassailable. Once it was confirmed in late November that Catiline, taunted by Cicero and hounded by creditors he could not pay, had left Rome to take command of forces gathered in Etruria, the senate did declare war on him. Finally, at the beginning of December, the evidence that Cicero sought came into his hands from envoys sent to Rome by a Gallic people, the Allobroges. They had been invited to join Catiline and his associates—including a few senators, one of them currently praetor—in planning to set fire to Rome later in the month. At a meeting of the senate on December 3 Cicero was able to confront the associates with the letters bearing their own seals, obtain their confessions of guilt, and arrest five of them. This swung public opinion firmly behind him. Two days later, when he asked the senate what was to be done with the five, the decision after a tense debate was execution, a sentence which Cicero carried out at once.

Public opinion was soon sharply divided over this action, however. To his admirers, Cicero was now *Parens Patriae*, Father of his Country, a new founder of Rome.

Opponents, by contrast, saw this summary execution of citizens without trial as illegal and unjustified. Even with the declaration of war against Catiline, there was some force to that argument, and later Cicero would be forced to confront it. For the moment, he was extravagantly proud of what he had done, and would in fact never waver from the view that he had taken the right course of action in the crisis. The executions aside, we may agree that his energy and resourcefulness did avert what promised to be a catastrophe for Rome. Meantime,

Figure 7.4 *Bust of Cicero*

however, he and others ensured that the deeper causes of so much discontent were not remedied. In the end, because he believed that it was now more important for him to remain in Rome, he did not take up the provincial governorship he had intended to.

The debate in the senate on December 5 gave further prominence to Caesar, who took the lead in opposing the execution of Catiline's associates, as well as to Marcus Porcius Cato, who successfully urged this extreme step. Cato was the great-grandson of Cato the Censor, who had been such a towering figure in Roman politics and culture during the first half of the second century. Born in 95, "Young" Cato was still a junior senator—about to become tribune for 62—but was already championing an inflexible devotion to conservative, Optimate principles in the tradition of his great ancestor.

It remains unfortunate that the only accounts we have of Catiline's attempt at revolution are uncompromisingly hostile. These are mostly speeches by Cicero, and a study by the historian Sallust written about twenty years later. Nothing survives from Catiline's side to bring some balance into the picture. At this point, however, with his leading associates in Rome dead, his cause must have seemed hopeless. Early in 62, he and his forces in northern Etruria were trapped between two armies dispatched by the senate, and defeated. The casualties in this clash were high; Catiline's followers included many Sullan veterans as well as peasants, and all of them preferred to fight to the finish along with their leader.

Not long after Catiline's death and the brutal suppression of his attempt at revolution, news arrived from Pompey that his work in the East was completed, and that he and his army were returning home. Suspense over the vital issue of what he would then do was about to reach its climax. Was Rome now about to acquire by violence, or alternative means, another strong leader and reformer on the model of Sulla? Would there be further civil war? Or was the state to remain divided and adrift, as it seemed to have been ever since Sulla's retirement? In this predicament, major threats abroad could only be tackled by resort to extraordinary commands, most conspicuously those created for Pompey himself. Meantime at home, the state was vulnerable to corruption, conspiracy, and rebellion, while little or nothing was done to relieve the miserable plight of the poor both in the city of Rome and throughout Italy.

SUGGESTED READINGS:

Badian, Ernst. 1968 (second edition). *Roman Imperialism in the Late Republic*. Ithaca, New York: Cornell University Press.

Beard, Mary, and Michael Crawford. 1999 (second edition). *Rome in the Late Republic: Problems and Interpretations*. London: Duckworth. Accessible discussion of major cultural, political, and social aspects, designed for readers who already have a grasp of the main framework of events and their geographical setting.

Keaveney, Arthur. 1982. *Sulla: The Last Republican*. London and Sydney: Croom Helm.

Kleiner, Diana E.E., and Susan B. Matheson. 1996. *I Claudia: Women in Ancient Rome*. New Haven: Yale University Art Gallery. An exhibition catalog, offering not only ample illustration and discussion of each object, but also concise essays on many key aspects of women's lives.

Lacey, Walter K., and Brian W.J.G. Wilson. 1970. *Respublica: Roman Society and Politics According to Cicero*. Oxford: Oxford University Press. An extensive collection of extracts from Cicero's speeches and writings, with introduction and comments.

Nippel, Wilfried. 1995. *Public Order in Ancient Rome*. Cambridge: Cambridge University Press.

Rawson, Elizabeth. 1983 (revised edition). *Cicero: A Portrait*. Ithaca, New York: Cornell University Press.

Seager, Robin. 2002 (revised edition). *Pompey the Great*. Oxford: Blackwell.

Treggiari, Susan. 2002. *Roman Social History*. London and New York: Routledge.

END OF THE REPUBLIC:
Caesar's Dictatorship

SOURCES

From the late 60s onwards, for a period of twenty years, the richness of our source material improves immeasurably because we have not only speeches and philosophical writings by Cicero, but also quantities of private letters that he wrote to friends and others, in particular the prominent *eques* Titus Pomponius Atticus, whom he had known from boyhood. Most of this correspondence was always intended to remain confidential, so that its commentary on current events and personalities is splendidly frank and indiscreet. Contemporary material of a very different type comes from Julius Caesar, who published narratives of his wars in Gaul and his civil war campaigns; in these, Caesar always strives to present himself in a favorable light. Among later works of importance, there are again many *Lives* by Plutarch (Pompey, Crassus, Caesar, Cicero, Lucullus, "Young" Cato, Brutus), and a very readable biography of Julius Caesar by Suetonius (Gaius Suetonius Tranquillus). He and Plutarch were contemporaries in the late first and early second centuries A.D. The significant growth and diversity of nonhistorical literature during the Late Republic is outlined in Chapter Nine.

POMPEY'S RETURN FROM THE EAST (62)

The dazzling wealth and glory with which Pompey returned from the East in 62 outclassed all previous Romans' conquests. There was truth in his own public

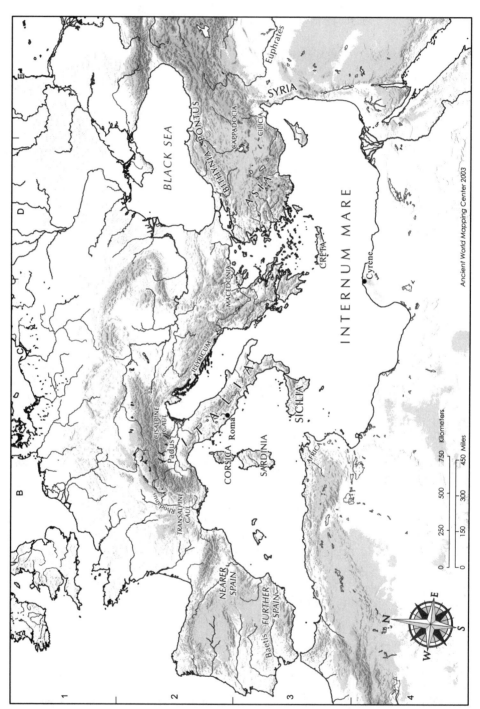

Map 8.1 *Rome's Empire in 60 B.C.*

Ancient World Mapping Center 2003

boast that he had found Asia a frontier province, and left it at the heart of the empire (Pliny, *Natural History* 7.99). He had been courted by kings and princes, and offered god-like honors. He founded cities such as Nicopolis, "victory city," near the site of his final defeat of Mithridates in eastern Pontus. He took possession of Syria and made it a province. He enlarged the province of Cilicia, and reorganized Bithynia and part of Pontus into a single, combined province. Otherwise he entrusted eastern Asia Minor— most notably Cappadocia and Armenia—to rulers sworn to uphold Roman interests; some even paid taxes to Rome. Only with Parthia does no pact seem to have been made, but he left strong Roman garrisons in both Cilicia and Syria to guard against any Parthian incursion there.

Figure 8.1 *Bust of Pompey*

The wealth that Pompey brought back from Mithridates' treasure stores and elsewhere was quite simply staggering; inevitably it set rich and poor still further apart. Pompey delivered to the treasury 20,000 talents in gold and silver (equal to 480 million sesterces). To each of his soldiers he gave a minimum of 6,000 sesterces (a year's basic pay was 450). Officers were far more lavishly rewarded, and his own personal wealth now dwarfed that of Crassus. For the longer term, his conquests and annexations in the East were reckoned to have raised Rome's annual revenues from 200 million to 340 million sesterces. His achievement there was to be epitomized in the theater complex begun in the Campus Martius after his magnificent triumph in 61, and dedicated six years later in 55 (see Map 8.4). Rome had never seen anything like it. The theater itself was built in stone; linked with it was a vast portico containing a heroic, nude statue of Pompey himself holding a globe, the symbol of a world conqueror, and surrounded by personifications of the fourteen "nations" he had subdued.

POMPEY AND POLITICAL STALEMATE IN ROME

When Pompey finally reached Brundisium in late 62, he surprised everyone who feared and envied him by simply disbanding his army. It emerged that he had no intention of retaining it to march on Rome and seize power. Such restraint need come as no special surprise. After all, his political involvement had never been deep, he felt no particular attachment to any political group or set of ideas, and he had been away for the past five years or so. He might hardly be expected to match Sulla's passion for imposing a fresh political or social blueprint on Rome.

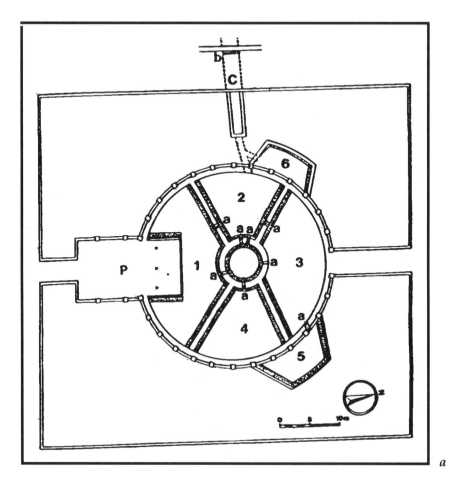

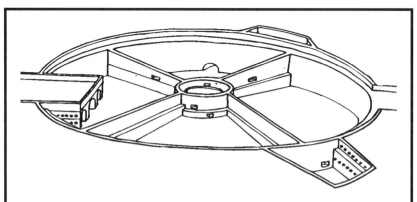

c

Figure 8.3a,b,c *A fashionable form of conspicuous consumption on the part of those made super-rich by Rome's imperial expansion during the second and first centuries* B.C. *was the construction of luxurious villas. Among the most envied features of such an establishment was an artificial fishpond, so much so that Cicero (in a private letter to Atticus) could term the rich Optimates who so frustrated him as "fishponders"* (piscinarii), *while gossips spread tales of aristocrats who wept for the death of their favorite eel. Numerous such ponds are known from Italy in particular, although in many instances their design and development can be difficult to reconstruct in detail when those on or near the shore (using saltwater) have suffered sea damage, or when—as in the instance illustrated here—the pond underwent successive modifications and remained in use into the twentieth century. Even so, this pond north of Circeii (modern Circeo, about 60 miles/96 km south of Rome) offers excellent illustration of many typical features. Set within a rectangular terrace, it is a circle about 110 ft. (33 m) in diameter and 7 ft. (2 m) deep, with one central tank and four others (1–4) fanning outwards from it separated by walkways; two trapezoidal tanks (5–6), added later, extend beyond the circle. Openings (marked "a") interconnect the tanks. The pond was supplied by a link ("c") to a sea channel, as well as by a freshwater spring which bubbled up in tank 2; the sluice gate "b" made it possible to regulate the salinity of the pool water. A platform surrounded by a low parapet wall extends out over tank 1. It is carried on three parallel vaults, in which are set many amphora jars on their sides (the same feature occurs in tanks 5 and 6; see drawing); all of this is designed to provide shade and hiding places, especially suitable for eels. From the platform, the owner and guests could view the pond, and even dine there. There is unfortunately no evidence to uphold the tradition which makes the celebrated general Lucius Licinius Lucullus the owner of this pond, even though he was wealthy and a noted piscinarius. Such ponds were not necessarily mere decoration and self-indulgence. They were likely to produce more than a single establishment could consume, so fish could either be presented as gifts or sold; saltwater fish were valued over freshwater.*

massive bribery of the jury determined the verdict, and he was narrowly acquitted. So Cicero's devotion to truth and principle here only served to create a dangerous, implacable enemy for himself. Otherwise among leading Romans any such devotion was largely subordinated to personal and political rivalry, to the lasting detriment of the senate in particular.

As it turned out, Pompey had to face the frustration of seeing his requests stalled not just in 61, but also in 60. Lucullus, Cato, and other Optimates took pride in being consistently obstructive. A tribune's proposal for major redistribution of "public" land (of the type made three years earlier in 63) was thwarted, as before, on suspicion that in practice it would serve to benefit the handful of senators placed in charge rather than Pompey's veterans and the mass of poor citizens in need of land.

By chance, during 60 two other unrelated requests arose which Cato took the lead in blocking. First, the syndicate that had won the major contract for collecting Rome's taxes in the province of Asia when this was last auctioned (possibly by the censors in 65) now found itself in difficulties. The amount of its winning bid—which had to be paid to the treasury in advance—was proving far larger than the syndicate found itself able to recoup through tax collection. Because it was now facing a heavy loss, it asked the senate to consider renegotiating the contract and thus, in effect, refunding part of the bid. The plea was hardly a strong one, given that syndicates entered bids at their own risk, and the state had no obligation to assist them if they miscalculated and overstretched. Even so, Crassus, who had himself been censor in 65, gave his strong support to the plea. Cato with equal vigor succeeded in blocking it, without regard to the fact that other equites with business interests would consequently take offense.

The second request was made by Caesar. He had been praetor in 62, and then took up the governorship of Further Spain. He was lucky to have been able to leave Rome at all, because his creditors went to court to prevent him slipping from their grasp, and they would have succeeded in this insult, had not Crassus agreed to be guarantor for some of his debts. So Caesar blatantly exploited his year as governor to recoup what it had cost him to win election as pontifex maximus and praetor. The unprovoked attacks that he launched on peoples in the far west of the Iberian peninsula yielded sufficient loot for him not only to clear his deep debts, but also to make substantial payments to the treasury. By the time that he returned to Rome mid-year in 60, the senate had voted him a triumph. His personal goal now, however, was to stand for election to the consulship of 59, and he had arrived just in time to register as a candidate. But for this registration he would have to cross the *pomerium* and enter the city. That step would automatically serve to rob him of his triumph, because a returning commander who was voted one could only cross the pomerium into the city on the day of the ceremony itself, and not before.

So Caesar asked the senate for permission to register as a candidate for the consulship without being physically present. By this means, he anticipated, he would both be able to celebrate his triumph, and still compete for the office without having to wait a further year or more. The concession was one that had been extended—in times of dire crisis—to no less than a member by marriage of Caesar's own family, Marius. In the present political climate, however, to request it was provocative; and predictably enough, Cato persuaded the senate to deny it to Caesar. Given that a triumph was generally held to be the highest distinction to which any Roman could aspire, and that the chance to compete for the consulship arose every year, Caesar now surprised his opponents. It was the triumph that he let go; instead, he crossed the pomerium to register as a candidate for the consulship.

The reaction in the senate was one of alarm. Caesar was so popular that he stood an excellent chance of being elected. Nothing could be less welcome than seeing him then exploit the opportunities offered by one of the large or wealthy provinces typically assigned to consuls. So now, when it came to determining those provinces in this instance (prior to the elections, as required by Gaius Gracchus' law; see Chapter Five), the senate deliberately assigned commissions to police the forests and tracks of Italy—significant tasks in their own way, no doubt, but hardly commensurate with consular prestige, and certainly not with the ambition of someone like Caesar. Moreover these assignments seemed all the more inappropriate in view of the serious disturbances now affecting Roman interests in Gaul.

PARTNERSHIP OF POMPEY, CRASSUS, AND CAESAR

For all his popularity, Caesar was well aware that it would take money and support in abundance to secure his election as consul for 59. Many senators were contributing to a fund established to ensure the election of a rival candidate, Marcus Calpurnius Bibulus, Cato's son-in-law; Cato himself thought this cause so vital that he was prepared to overlook the widespread bribery that it entailed. Caesar had no such lavish help to hand, but he happened to be on good terms with both Pompey and Crassus, and he was keenly aware of how they too had been thwarted by Cato and the majority of senators. To date, Pompey and Crassus had been too estranged from each other to work together, but Caesar now arranged a reconciliation. He further arranged that the three of them would join to overcome the opposition and to achieve their goals; after all, their combined resources were formidable. Pompey and Crassus both had money and influence; Pompey could call upon his veterans, not to mention other clients and colonists in most areas of the Roman world; and Caesar could expect to gain a consul's authority. Pompey, the leading partner, stood to gain most at once; Caesar as the junior might hope to gain most in the long term; the potential gains for Crassus in the middle were less predictable.

Before the end of the year the three invited Cicero to join them, but after much anguished soul-searching he declined on grounds of principle. His hopes that all responsible members of society would work in harmony to keep the state stable (as they had rallied briefly against Catiline) were now thoroughly dashed. On a more personal level, he was dismayed, too, that his grandiose vision of a partnership between himself and Pompey—statesman collaborating with general, like Laelius and Scipio Aemilianus in the mid-second century (see Chapter Five)—had aroused no enthusiasm in the hero after his return from the East. This coldness was all the more hurtful to Cicero's vanity after his assiduous efforts to protect Pompey's interests previously. Cicero was well aware of the significance of the newly formed partnership. It is commonly referred to today as the First Triumvirate, but was soon branded more appropriately by hostile contemporaries as the "Three-Headed Monster." It was a secret pact at first, and only ever informal, but it could be expected to make a devastating impact.

At the same time, in growing isolation, Cicero felt as alienated as ever from Cato and the group of snobbish, bickering Optimate aristocrats who were his associates. He grasped that it was their shortsighted, unimaginative obstructiveness which had driven Pompey, Crassus, and Caesar together. Cicero protested in a letter to his friend Atticus around this time: "[Cato] with all his patriotism and integrity is sometimes a political liability. He speaks in the senate as though he were living in Plato's republic* instead of Romulus' cesspool" (21.8SB).

CAESAR'S FIRST CONSULSHIP (59)

On election day, Caesar and Bibulus were chosen as consuls for 59. So the fund to ensure the latter's election had fulfilled its purpose; but there was also point to the cruel joke that it ought to have been a double fund for two candidates, since Caesar had not been kept out. Once in office, he began by striving to be conciliatory, in particular over the proposal for land redistribution which he put forward first. This deliberately incorporated safeguards designed to overcome senators' objections to the previous schemes advanced by tribunes in 63 and 60. Even so, it was soon clear from the debate in the senate that Bibulus, Cato, and their supporters were not to be placated. They now resorted to filibuster tactics, declaring themselves opposed on principle to *any* land redistribution proposal. In his frustration Caesar therefore resolved to ignore the senate, and to bring the proposal directly to the Tribal assembly for a vote. Since both Caesar and his opponents could call upon tribunes for support, Bibulus believed that it would be more effective for him to give notice that on each day when it was lawful for an assembly to meet, he would be watching the sky for omens, which would automatically invalidate any assembly.

Caesar fixed a day for the vote regardless, and on it ugly scenes unfolded. Not only were the fasces of Bibulus' lictors smashed, but a basket of excrement was

---

*A famous utopia conceived by the fourth-century Greek philosopher Plato.

also flung over him. A tribune who tried to veto the proceedings was thrown from the platform, and several people were injured in the riot that erupted. Bibulus fled to safety, and Cato was expelled by force when he tried to make a speech. With this opposition removed, and some semblance of order restored, the proposal was voted through—to the benefit of Pompey's veterans, among many others. The following day, Bibulus failed in an attempt to have it invalidated by the now frightened senate, and as soon as he appeared in public to make a speech, an order for his imprisonment was given by a tribune on Caesar's side, Publius Vatinius. Even though protests by other tribunes ensured that this order was not carried out, it had become very dubious whether Bibulus could ever risk exercising his office in public again. Eventually, the course of action he settled upon was to stay at home, declaring that he was watching the sky for omens. This he intended as a means of invalidating any assembly that met, although controversy continued to surround the legal issue of whether such a declaration issued from his house, rather than at the assembly itself, was valid for the purpose.

To Caesar at least, the issue was immaterial, because from now onwards he just disregarded Bibulus anyway; the quip that the consuls of 59 were not Bibulus and Caesar, but Julius and Caesar, had point to it. His next step was a provocative demand that every senator swear an oath to respect the land distribution measure. This recalled Saturninus' demand during Marius' sixth consulship in 100, and, unlike on that occasion, every senator did eventually swear. Having asserted himself over the senate in this way, Caesar then proceeded to ignore it, and invite no more obstructions, by taking three key proposals direct to the Tribal assembly for voting. All passed. The first refunded to the tax-collecting syndicate for the province of Asia one-third of its overambitious bid; the second formally ratified Pompey's arrangements in the East at last. The third, also of special concern to Pompey, was a comprehensive measure to regulate the conduct of senators who governed provinces, including procedures for hearing charges brought against them and severe penalties for those found guilty. This important law both incorporated and expanded clauses in earlier such measures, including those enacted by Saturninus and Sulla; over the succeeding centuries it would be modified, but never superseded.

In these ways Caesar duly repaid Pompey and Crassus for becoming his partners. Even so, the three of them were still nervous of opposition. Lucullus, for example, had tried to the last to block the ratification of Pompey's arrangements in the East. More significantly for the longer-term, when Cicero was rash enough to complain about the current political situation in a law court speech, Caesar took this as the cue to let Clodius have his remarkable wish—raised before, but rejected—of changing status from patrician to plebeian, and thus becoming eligible to stand for a tribunate. Caesar as pontifex maximus and consul presided at the ceremony, with Pompey's assistance as augur. It was carried out at once, so that Clodius could have the chance of being elected one of the tribunes for 58, which in due course he was, much to Cicero's dismay.

Rome for Macedonia rather than awaiting prosecution. Clodius then had a measure passed officially declaring him an exile. It was in fact at this point, in late March 58, that Caesar finally left Rome to take up his command in Gaul.

Clodius' vindictive treatment of Cicero created widespread outrage which was only sharpened by his next moves, both of which suggest that he was now letting his popularity with the mass of citizens in Rome blind him to all other considerations. He provoked Pompey over aspects of Eastern policy, and when Pompey and Gabinius protested, he had the two of them physically assaulted by his supporters, and the consul's fasces smashed. He also called into question the validity of Caesar's acts as consul the previous year, even though one of these had been his own change of status from patrician to plebeian.

CICERO'S RECALL AND THE RENEWAL OF THE TRIUMVIRATE (57–56)

Pompey became so frightened for his personal safety that for a long period from mid-58 onwards he dared not venture out of his house in Rome. But he did encourage two of the tribunes of 57, Titus Annius Milo and Publius Sestius, to recruit gangs to combat those of Clodius. He also supported the senate's persistent efforts in 58, and again in 57, to arrange for Cicero's recall from exile. This issue became the centerpiece of opposition to Clodius. The recall was finally achieved by a vote of the Centuriate assembly at the beginning of August 57; large numbers of citizens from communities all over Italy answered Pompey's appeal to be present and thus overwhelm the hostility of voters from Rome itself.

Cicero reached the city about a month later to find it in the grip of a severe shortage of grain, and the senate deadlocked over how to resolve the problem. It was his motion for yet another extraordinary command that finally won acceptance—that Pompey be given control of grain supplies throughout the Roman world for five years. However, with the onset of winter, even Pompey could not immediately provide relief. By the following spring (56), therefore, his prestige had suffered, and he was harshly attacked in the senate by Cato, now back in Rome after successfully annexing Cyprus. Pompey suspected Crassus of supporting not only Cato, but also Clodius, whose gang warfare with Milo raged on unchecked. Meantime Cicero felt confident enough to work against the interests of the Triumvirate, and Lucius Domitius Ahenobarbus (who expected to be elected consul for 55) declared that he would press for Caesar's command in Gaul to be terminated.

With their enemies now poised to exploit any rifts emerging between them, the Triumvirs soon resolved to renew their pact with fresh measures for its security. In April 56, Caesar was free to take the lead at a meeting held at Luca (modern Lucca, in Italy), just within the southern border of his province of Cisalpine Gaul. Other senators were invited to attend too, and a strikingly large number of them came. The main item of agreement was that Pompey and Crassus would arrange to have the forthcoming elections postponed until after the campaigning season. They would then both stand for the consulship, and enough of Caesar's soldiers would come to Rome on leave to ensure that Ahenobarbus lost the vote. Thereafter, with the help of supportive tribunes, Pompey and Crassus would arrange major, long-term commands for themselves, and at the same time would extend Caesar's term in Gaul. More immediately, unequivocal loyalty would be demanded of Clodius, and Cicero would be reminded about the pledge of good behavior he had given on return from exile.

A crestfallen Cicero heeded the warning, and the rest of the agreement also took shape according to plan. The elections for the consulship were in fact postponed until January 55, so that an *interrex* was needed to hold them; Pompey and Crassus were the successful candidates. The Spanish provinces and Syria were assigned to them, each for five years, and Caesar was given the same extension in Gaul through 50 or early 49; our sources fail to preserve the exact terminal date. Because of his responsibility for the city's grain supply, Pompey had always intended to remain in Rome, and to administer his province through deputies ("legates"). He was content with Spain, therefore, while Crassus was delighted with Syria. It offered him the prospect of campaigning against Parthia, and thus of finally matching the glory which first Pompey and now Caesar had won by victorious military exploits in unknown lands.

Those hopes were not to be fulfilled, however. When Crassus eventually set off from Syria in 53, first the cavalry force commanded by his younger son pursued the Parthians too recklessly and was surrounded; then the main Roman army was trapped near Carrhae. Roman losses in this catastrophe exceeded 30,000 men, including Crassus himself and his son, along with the legionary standards. It was a final misfortune for a man who after his first consulship in 70 experienced persistent difficulty achieving the further distinction that he craved. He was jealous of Pompey's extraordinary achievements, and despite joining the Triumvirate he never adapted successfully to the changed political atmosphere.

CAESAR'S CAMPAIGNS IN GAUL (58–51)

During the winter following each of his first seven campaigning seasons in Gaul, Caesar wrote an account or "commentary," and then probably made it available for immediate circulation in Rome; his subordinate officer Aulus Hirtius subsequently added an account to cover the years 51 and 50. All eight accounts survive. While their clarity and detail are invaluable, there is equally no escaping their bias in favor of Romans generally and Caesar himself in particular. Nor is there any other account with which to compare these, above all one that offers a more objective view of Caesar's opponents.

On taking up his command at the end of March 58, Caesar's urgent concern was to forestall the Helvetii, a Celtic people settled on the Swiss plateau, from

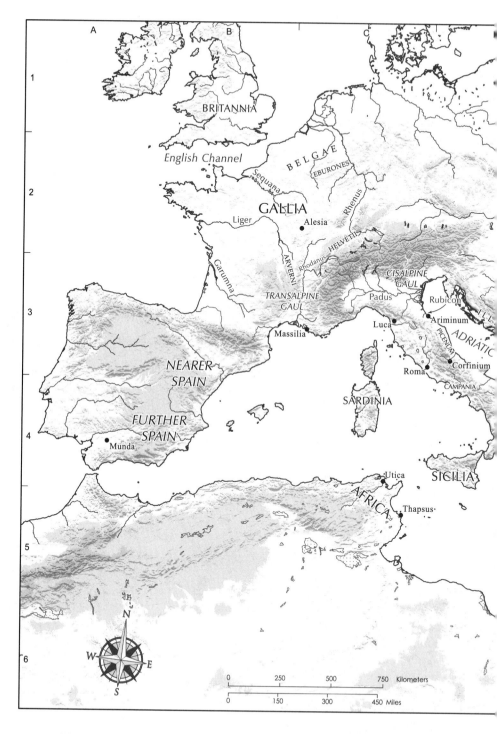

Map 8.2 *Campaigns of Caesar, Crassus, and Pompey, 58–45*

E   F   G

CRIMEA

BLACK SEA

PONTUS
Nicopolis
Zela

nnus/
chium
MACEDONIA
Carrhae

PARTHIA

Pharsalus

A S I A
Amanus Mons
CILICIA
Euphrates

CARIA
SYRIA

Salamis

CYPRUS
JUDAEA

INTERNUM MARE

Cyrene
Alexandria

A E G Y P T U S

Nile

Ancient World Mapping Center 2003

embarking on a disruptive westward migration. This he soon achieved after major clashes, but his success at once drew him into struggles between peoples farther north. Another battle enabled him to break the control which the Germanic Suebi had been exerting within Gaul, and to drive them back across the Rhine River (Latin, Rhenus). By establishing winter quarters for 58–57 in northeast Gaul, Caesar alerted the peoples there to the prospect that he would next try to dominate them. Intertribal tensions led some to seek his friendship, but in 57 others made unsuccessful preemptive strikes, provoking clashes which brought most of today's northern France and Belgium under his control. Only the far northwest remained insecure, and this—together with the Atlantic coast—was subjugated in 56. By stages, therefore, Caesar unexpectedly found himself achieving Roman domination of Gaul's entire vast area. Granted, he had not engaged with the peoples in the center, but they were now surrounded, and at this point gave no cause for concern.

Rather, in 55 Caesar looked elsewhere to enhance his military reputation. He first drove more Germanic peoples out of northern Gaul across the Rhine River, marking it once again as the prospective limit of Roman control. Then he crossed to southern England, officially in order to cut off aid sent from there to his Gallic opponents, but no doubt also to gauge the prospects for a full-scale invasion. Although he did return to England in 54, from the following year onwards he was no longer free to do so. Suppression of risings in northern Gaul, by the Eburones and Belgae especially, preoccupied him during 53. A greater challenge followed in 52, however, when a fearsome coalition of peoples from central Gaul led by a prince of the Arverni, Vercingetorix, began a widespread revolt against Roman rule. Its timing was intended to worsen Caesar's political position, and it achieved that goal by compelling him to postpone the reentry to office in Rome that he had been hoping for. Eventually, however, Caesar's boldness, speed, and inexhaustible energy outwitted Vercingetorix, who was besieged at Alesia (modern Alise–Ste. Reine) and forced to surrender. Such resistance as remained to the imposition of Roman control throughout Gaul was suppressed the following year, 51.

It would be hard to understate the damage shamelessly inflicted upon the entire plundered and devastated region and its peoples. Ancient estimates that one million Gauls were killed in the course of Caesar's campaigns, and another million enslaved, are credible. Caesar meantime developed his taste and talent for supreme command, while his army had no match for experience and fighting quality. There were financial rewards, too; for Caesar himself and his top officers these were so vast that the treasury in Rome received distinctly less than its due.

DEATH OF CLODIUS AND POMPEY'S SOLE CONSULSHIP (52)

Political life at Rome remained violent and disrupted. A climax came in January 52. Once again, magistrates had not been elected for the year ahead of time. Clodius was campaigning to be elected praetor, Milo to be consul. A major clash occurred between their gangs near Bovillae, ten miles (16 km) south of Rome on the Via Appia. Clodius was wounded and captured, and then finished off on Milo's orders. When his corpse was brought to the city, the populace was so distraught, and its mood so hostile to the senate, that they took up the outrageous suggestion of using the senate house itself as a funeral pyre. The whole structure and its furnishings burned too.

The sense that the city was slipping into anarchy now impelled the senate to pass its "ultimate decree" (SCU), to levy troops throughout Italy, and to adopt the novel expedient of making Pompey sole consul; a dictatorship was also discussed, but rejected. Even Cato was alarmed enough to give his support. Pompey quickly introduced measures that would bring to trial those responsible for the worst of the recent instances of bribery and violence—among them Milo, who was condemned and went into exile at the independent Greek city of Massilia (modern Marseille). Pompey also made it the law that, after any consul or praetor's year of office, five years must elapse before he could proceed to a governorship. This interval would allow time for any prosecution of misconduct during office. It would also drastically curtail a senator's opportunity to exploit an immediate governorship as the means of rapid repayment for heavy debts so often incurred during office or while campaigning for it; five years' worth of interest would prove a crushing burden. However, introduction of the new law did not deter Pompey from renewing his own absentee governorship of Spain for five years.

By unfortunate coincidence, it was around this time that Caesar first seems to have become seriously anxious about his future. Hopes he may have nursed previously of returning from Gaul well before serving out his full term there were now dashed by the need to subdue Vercingetorix's formidable rising. Once that was achieved, the terminal date of his command, in 50 or 49, would be coming into sight anyway. Timing aside, he knew that—after the turmoil of his consulship in 59—the normal procedure for a governor's return would be sure to lead to his political ruin. This procedure required him to become a private citizen again on recrossing the pomerium into Rome; and were he to seek further office, it would be with this private status that he would have to register in person as a candidate. Caesar fully expected that, no matter how short the period for which he became a private citizen again, his enemies would use it to bring charges against him. If he were to have any future in Roman public life, he had to gain exemption from the normal procedure, so that there would be no break between his serving as governor (with exemption from prosecution), and his immediately entering a new office (most naturally a consulship) with continued exemption.

To achieve such a seamless transition, however, Pompey's support would be essential, and at this stage his attitude to the issue of exempting Caesar from one or more of the legal requirements seems to have been ambiguous. The personal link between them provided by Julia, Pompey's wife and Caesar's daughter, had been broken prematurely in 54, when she died in childbirth aged about nineteen. Since then, Pompey had declined to pursue any proposal by Caesar for a further

Even so, the search for compromise continued, and Curio's concern for Caesar's interests was maintained by two of the tribunes for 49, Quintus Cassius Longinus (*not* Caesar's future killer) and Marcus Antonius (better known today as Mark Antony). On January 1, 49, Curio, now acting as Caesar's envoy, read the senate a letter in which Caesar proposed that he and Pompey lay down their commands simultaneously and submit to the judgment of the Roman people. This plea was ignored, however. Instead, the consul presiding called for a vote on a proposal that Caesar must disband his army by a specified date, or be automatically considered an enemy of the state; this vote was at once vetoed by the tribunes Cassius and Antony.

A few days later, other compromises were raised: Caesar should be permitted to try to proceed without a break to a second consulship, retaining meantime only Cisalpine Gaul and Illyricum with two legions, or even just Illyricum with a single legion. The degree to which these proposals represented sincere efforts to avoid a clash, rather than mere postures, is impossible to determine. Pompey at least was willing to consider such schemes, but any chance of their adoption was quashed by those senators (like Cato and at least one of the consuls) who were determined to force a confrontation with Caesar. On January 7, it was they who successfully persuaded the senate to pass its "ultimate decree" (SCU) again, instructing all magistrates in this instance "to see to it that the Republic suffers no harm." The tribunes Cassius and Antony were then warned that their safety could no longer be guaranteed if they chose to remain in Rome; so they and Curio fled north to Caesar.

CAUSES AND CONSEQUENCES OF CAESAR CROSSING THE RUBICON (JANUARY 49)

Pompey and his associates were unperturbed by their flight, and because of the winter season they expected no immediate developments. However, this mood of complacency at Rome was soon to be punctured by the shocking news that on or about January 10 Caesar had crossed the Rubicon, north of Ariminum, with one legion. Since this river formed the boundary between his province of Cisalpine Gaul and Italy, and he had absolutely no authority to bring troops across it, the significance of his action was plain. He had committed himself to civil war, and had done so with characteristic speed: "Let the die be cast," he is supposed to have said as he crossed the river (Plutarch, *Caesar* 32). All but one of his officers stayed with him, a striking reversal of Sulla's experience when he marched on Rome for the first time in 88 (see Chapter Six).

In part, Caesar justified his resort to civil war as a defense of the constitution which, he claimed, his opponents had abused by such means as resorting needlessly to the SCU and rejecting the legitimate rights of tribunes. At the same time Caesar did not hide particular concern for his own *dignitas*. In his view, it was disrespectful, petty, and inappropriate for the senate to dictate his future. He maintained that, as a senior senator and outstanding commander in Rome's service, he did not deserve to be faced with political ruin.

Caesar's opponents naturally disputed his view. They claimed to be safe-guarding the constitution against the extreme demands of a rebellious governor. To us at least, if not to many contemporaries, this devotion to constitutional pro-priety must have something of a hollow ring to it when Pompey of all people took a leading role. After all, his long career had time and again shown minimal respect for such lofty principles. On the other hand, it is only right to acknowl-edge that those who objected to Caesar remaining protected from prosecution had a valid point to make. Such a request to remain in effect above the law flout-ed one of the basic principles of the Republic, the more so when it was made by such an ambitious, unscrupulous figure. That said, a case for accommodating Caesar or compromising with him can also be recognized. To this extent, the out-break of civil war in January 49 under such conditions was by no means inevit-able. In view of developments since Sulla's dictatorship, however, compromise now could equally be regarded as just the postponement of an inevitable clash over some comparable challenge to the Republic sooner rather than later.

Cicero concluded that in the event both Pompey and Caesar were prepared to risk civil war because neither wanted to defer to the other; rather, each wanted to be supreme. This was certainly the kind of attitude reflected by many of their associates. Most notably, the Optimates were determined to cut Caesar down to size, and they saw Pompey as acting for *them*, rather than as they for him. Not surprisingly, their relationship with him remained uneasy, and this must be one reason why Pompey never brought the passionate personal commitment to his cause that Caesar was to display to such devastating effect.

Even so, it is important to recognize that at the outset most senators either stood with Pompey and the Optimates against Caesar, or had no wish to become involved. In particular, almost no ex-consuls took Caesar's side, and most of his senatorial associates were either young or disreputable or both. In Cicero's view, Caesar's cause had no moral or constitutional basis. At the same time he felt antagonized and disillusioned by the Optimates and Pompey, and in the end only stayed with them out of personal devotion to Pompey.

How the rest of society throughout Italy would react was hard to predict. In fact the general feeling turned out to be dread of more Sullan-style proscriptions and, in contrast to the 80s, a complete lack of engagement with the issues dividing the senate. Even the wealthy and better educated were indifferent to what they viewed as aristocrats' rivalries of no consequence to themselves. The poor meantime were for Caesar. They were keenly aware of how little the Optimates had ever cared for their plight, and they certainly did not rush to enlist under Pompey.

With hindsight, the formation, continuation, and then breakup of the First Triumvirate inevitably dominate our view of the 50s, and it is all too easy to con-clude that it was the Triumvirate which "led" to the outbreak of civil war a decade later. Such a view calls for further reflection, however. Potentially there were countless ways in which the Triumvirate might, or might not, have evolved, and the issue was never a major preoccupation for most contemporaries. For years, Caesar in Gaul was even more liable than Crassus to meet his death on campaign. Caesar seems not to have been seriously concerned about preparing a suitable return to Rome until as late as 52, and Pompey wavered over how to react to his requests in this connection for considerably longer. Between them, Pompey's eventual stand and Caesar's ultimate defiance did become the trigger for civil war, but this particular outcome was hardly predictable far in advance. The Republic was already beset by a formidable array of interrelated problems and pressures, both external and internal, at every level of society—issues that those in authority were no longer able or willing to tackle on an adequate scale. Willpower aside, they lacked the machinery, resources, and cohesion for the purpose. It is only realistic for us to believe that by now this highly dangerous predicament was liable to lead to breakdown or conflict of some kind. Within the broader, long-term context, it may seem largely fortuitous that the fatal clash arose in 49 over no more than a dispute concerning a single senator's future, one from which even many of his fellow members wished to distance themselves.

CICERO'S GOVERNORSHIP OF CILICIA (51–50)

Numerous letters written by Cicero during his governorship of Cilicia and Cyprus in 51–50 provide uniquely rewarding insight into upper-class Roman attitudes towards provincial administration during the late Republic (on this topic in general, see Chapter Six). Much of what he wrote was addressed to close friends and never intended for wider circulation, so that it preserves a frankness missing from his public statements. With his active involvements as politician and advocate at Rome, Cicero (like many of his fellow senators) had never taken the opportunity to govern a province, and he also declined the invitation to become Caesar's legate in Gaul in 58, even though it would have enabled him to shake off Clodius. However, Pompey's law of 52, requiring a five-year gap between holding office as praetor or consul and proceeding to a governorship, created a temporary shortage of senators eligible for appointment. In these circumstances Cicero was prevailed upon to go to Cilicia.

In view of his own past record, he knew that his performance there would attract special scrutiny. In particular, he had gained fame from publishing his remarkable speeches which in 70 led to conviction of Gaius Verres. Cicero had served as prosecutor in this notorious case brought by the Sicilians whom Verres had robbed and exploited as governor. Verres' gains had been all the more outrageous because in the event his one-year tenure was twice extended to make a total of three years. So, as he liked to say, he would be able to keep the first year's profit for himself, pay his patrons and attorneys with the second year's, and then lavish all the third, most lucrative year's profit on the jury (1 *Verrines* 40). Cicero therefore set out for Cilicia determined not merely to act honestly and responsibly, but to be a paragon among governors for self-control, justice, approachability, and clemency (his own choice of merits, *To Atticus* 114.5SB). He expected the same of his staff too. They can hardly have been pleased when he insisted that they not even claim the regular, permitted allowances, and when he later refused to share out among them, in the customary way, what remained unspent of the senate's allocation for expenses; instead he scrupulously returned this surplus to the state treasury.

The provincials were surprised by Cicero's self-denial, and duly grateful. He found it harder to protect them from his fellow Romans. From summer 51 onwards, for example, his close friend Marcus Caelius Rufus kept pestering him to have some panthers trapped and sent to Rome for the games that he would be giving as aedile the following year. Cicero was willing to oblige, but as late as April 50 reports:

> About the panthers: Skilled hunters are, on my orders, hard at work looking for them, but they are in remarkably short supply and those there are grumble, I am told, because they are the only creatures in my province for whom traps are laid, and so, it is said, they are moving out of my province into Caria. However, the job is being energetically taken in hand. . . . (*To his Friends* 90.2SB)

Meantime Caelius casually asked Cicero to oblige a friend with a favor which is surely not quite as trivial as he represents it:

> I recommend to you Marcus Feridius, a Roman *eques*, the son of a friend of mine, a worthy and hard-working young man, who has come to Cilicia on business: I ask you to treat him as one of your friends. He wants you to grant him the favor of conferring tax-exempt status upon certain lands from which cities derive income—a thing which you may easily and honorably do, and which will put some grateful and sound men under an obligation to you. (*To his Friends* 82.4SB)

Another senator, Marcus Junius Brutus (best known for later conspiring to assassinate Julius Caesar), urged Cicero to help two businessmen friends of his recover a loan made to the city of Salamis in Cyprus. The more that Cicero learned of this matter, the more shocked he became. The interest rate on the loan had illegally been fixed at 48 percent. The businessmen had been allowed to use a squadron of cavalry to harass the city council for repayment; the cavalry had then confined the members in their meeting place, starving five to death. Eventually, Brutus revealed that his "friends" were in fact his own agents, and that the loaned money was his, not theirs. To his credit, Cicero had the cavalry withdrawn at once, and then strove to persuade the businessmen to cut their losses by settling for repayment at the maximum legal interest rate (12 percent), which the Salaminians agreed to. This was not acceptable to Brutus, however, so Cicero could only leave the matter open.

In private correspondence Cicero time and again expressed delight that service as governor might boost his reputation, but declared that otherwise he gained no special satisfaction from the assignment, and longed to be back in Rome. As he wrote to Caelius Rufus near the end of his term,

> The city, the city, my dear Rufus, stay in it and live in its limelight. All foreign travel—as I have reckoned from an early age—is insignificant and degrading for men whose work could shine at Rome. Since I know this very well, I wish I had stood by my opinion. To me, all the profit I make from the province can't compare with one little stroll together and one of our chats. (*To his Friends* 95.2SB)

We later happen to learn that his legal profit from the governorship actually amounted to a cool 2,200,000 sesterces.

The fact that Cilicia's eastern border lay exposed to incursions from the Parthian forces which had already entered Syria alarmed Cicero, but also fulfilled his craving for achieving some military distinction. As it turned out, campaigning was to be his main preoccupation for the first five months (to the end of 51), and the news of his approaching force evidently did contribute to the Parthians' decision to withdraw. He then turned instead to attacking communities in the Amanus mountains, which were nominally part of his province, but had never acknowledged Roman rule. He created enough havoc here to be hailed "Imperator" by his men, and he then begged his friends in the senate to support the vote of a triumph; but in the end he was awarded only the lesser distinction of an "ovation." More seriously, he was alarmed from the outset by the ill-preparedness and low morale of the two legions in Cilicia. Even so, despite his urging and the continuing danger from Parthia, the senate did nothing to strengthen them.

On a more personal level, Cicero suffered from constant anxiety that, with the growing political tension at Rome, the senate would instruct all governors to remain at their posts beyond the expiry of the regular one-year term. For Cicero, such an extension would not only be unbearable in itself; but it would also rob him of the opportunity to contribute to critical debates in the senate for which, he argued to Caelius, he ought rather to be recalled early. In September 51, Caelius responded sympathetically both on this issue and on the risk of having to face the Parthians; at the same time he is too cheerfully cynical to share Cicero's expectation that Caesar's future will be settled at all soon:

> How worried you may be about the prospects for peace in your province and the adjacent areas I don't know, but for my part I am on tenterhooks. If we could so arrange it that the size of the war should be proportionate to the strength of your forces, and could achieve just enough for glory and a triumph while avoiding the really dangerous and serious clash, that would be the most desirable outcome. But I know that as matters stand any move by the Parthians will mean a major conflict; and your army is hardly capable of defending a single pass. Unfortunately nobody allows for this; a man charged with public responsibility is expected to cope with any emergency, as though every item has been put at his disposal in complete preparedness.

> Moreover, I see no prospect of your being relieved because of the controversy about the Gallic provinces. Although I expect you have settled in your own mind what you are going to do in this contingency, I thought that, since I see it coming, I ought to inform you, so that you may take your decision further ahead. You know the routine. There will be a decision about Gaul. Somebody will come along with a veto. Then somebody else will stand up and stop any move about the other provinces, unless the senate is given a free hand to pass decrees on all of them. So we shall have a long, elaborate charade—so long that a couple of years or more may drag by with these maneuvers. (*To his Friends* 83SB)

As events turned out, Cicero was free to leave Cilicia at the end of his year's service in the regular way (thus in July 50); the law may even have forbidden him to stay longer. There seemed no prospect that a successor would arrive at all soon, however. Consequently, Cicero was concerned about who should be left in temporary charge, but the reasons he offers for his eventual choice hardly reveal a lasting preoccupation with the long-term welfare of the province. His younger brother Quintus—a capable soldier, who had manfully served as his senior legate—seemed the natural choice. "But," as Cicero explained to Atticus,

> there are difficulties about my brother: First of all, I don't think I can persuade him to do it, because he can't stand the province, and I agree with him that nothing could be a more unpleasant bore. Then what sort of brotherly behavior would it be on my part, supposing that he didn't like to refuse me? Remember that a big war is thought to be on in Syria, it looks like overflowing into this province, there is no protection here, no extra funds have been voted. Is it an affectionate brother's job to pass this on to Quintus? Is it a thorough governor's job to leave it to a nonentity? (*To Atticus* 117.2SB)

Eventually, affection does prevail over thoroughness, and Cicero passes his authority to the newly arrived quaestor, who (it must be acknowledged) was the proper choice after Quintus. Even so, Cicero is defensive to Atticus: "I have put Coelius in charge of the province. 'But he's only a boy,' you'll say, 'and perhaps stupid, irresponsible, and lacking in self-control.' Quite. But there was no other way" (*To Atticus* 121.3SB).

CIVIL WAR CAMPAIGNS (49–45)

Having crossed the Rubicon River in January 49, Caesar soon dispelled fears that he would be a second Sulla or a vengeful Catiline. As he moved fast down the east coast of Italy, communities went over to him with little or no resistance, including even the entire region of Picenum, Pompey's own home territory. Lucius Domitius Ahenobarbus tried to make a stand with a substantial force at Corfinium (capital of the rebel Italian alliance forty years before), but Caesar quickly gained the advantage, and Ahenobarbus' own men forced him to surrender. The fact that even here Caesar released all captives, executed no one, and declined to

Caesar returned from Spain through southern Gaul and northern Italy, and only reached Rome again in October 45. Altogether, his difficulties in overcoming the Pompeians, and the length of time it took him, are not to be underestimated. He had taken some extraordinary risks, and had repeatedly been on the verge of defeat. Just as in Gaul during the 50s, only an astonishing degree of perseverance and good fortune carried him through. Further campaigning lay ahead too. By fall 45 it had already been settled that he would leave Rome on March 18, 44 to lead a major campaign against the Parthians—who were continuing to threaten Syria—and avenge the disastrous defeat at Carrhae in 53. He clearly expected to be away for a considerable time, because by the time of his departure the holders of the annual magistracies for the next three years had been named.

CAESAR'S ACTIVITY AS DICTATOR (49–44)

At least during late 45 and early 44 Caesar had a breathing space in Rome, in which to address concerns other than military campaigns. As it turned out, this and the similar intervals between earlier campaigns would prove to be his only opportunities to offer an impression of a longer-term vision for the Roman world, and his own place within it, prior to his assassination on March 15, 44. Unfortunately, for these vital matters we lack his personal testimony, the limited insights in Cicero's correspondence are unsatisfactory, and otherwise the fullest source material dates to very much later. By then, all kinds of dubious traditions and misrepresentations had developed, both favorable and unfavorable. Contemporary coins and inscriptions contribute frustratingly little. The result is that many different shades of opinion about Caesar become possible, and the quality of his achievements and intentions remains highly controversial.

In discussing them, we should first be aware of how his official status developed. He held the dictatorship for a few days in fall 49 (on his first return from Spain) in order to preside over elections, in which he himself was made consul for 48; this was his second consulship, after the first in 59. In 48, after the victory at Pharsalus, he was made dictator for a year. It was with this authority that he held elections on his return from the East in fall 47, and was made consul for 46. After the victory at Thapsus that year,

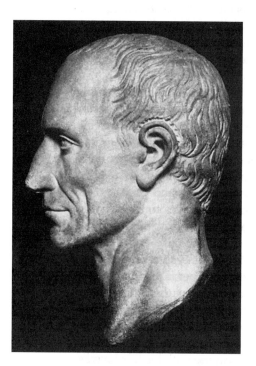

Figure 8.4 *Bust of Julius Caesar*

Figure 8.5 *Julius Caesar as dictator was the first living Roman with the audacity to permit his image to appear on coins. The issue shown here, by the moneyer Lucius (Aemilius) Buca in 44, dates to the final weeks of his life: It portrays him wearing a crown, and describes him pointedly as "perpetual dictator." Among the symbols on the reverse, the clasped hands affirm the trust between Caesar and his army, while the globe represents Roman aspirations to world power.*

the senate voted him annual dictatorships for the next ten years, along with various other lavish and unprecedented honors, including the right to nominate the only candidates for some offices. While remaining dictator, Caesar was also sole consul for much of 45, until he resigned in the fall. In 44 he was consul again (for the fifth time), and from sometime in February he had his dictatorship converted into a perpetual one.

We do not know the official purpose for making him dictator in any instance except the first, very brief one in 49, although it was presumably always to restore the state. As in Sulla's case, there seems to have been no particular concern to adhere to the traditional norms for this emergency office, especially the six-month time limit.

Caesar must surely win praise for his prompt, even-handed attention to pressing social problems. One of the most deep-rooted was that of debt, which had long affected all levels of society, as the widespread support for Catiline's rising demonstrated. An already serious situation was made critical, however, by the outbreak of the civil war. As confidence evaporated, lenders began to demand repayment of their loans, and real estate values collapsed. A serious shortage of coinage for circulation developed, because people hoarded whatever they had; in this society, after all, there was in effect no paper money, not to mention banks as we know them. Desperate borrowers began to agitate for a complete cancellation of debts. Lenders, by contrast, were appalled by the loss they would suffer if such an extreme solution to the crisis were adopted. It would be even more damaging than the measure implemented in the crisis of 86, which had cancelled three-quarters of all borrowers' obligations.

By early 48 at the latest, Caesar grasped the seriousness of the situation and both sides' fears. His approach was the moderate one of trying to offer some relief to each. Consequently, he ordered that property must be accepted for repayment at its prewar value, and he reintroduced an old law which prohibited anyone from holding more than 60,000 sesterces in cash. Coin held in excess of that amount (not huge by upper-class standards) would have to be spent in some way, and should thus find its way back into circulation. Even so, these measures were not enough to placate borrowers, some of whom raised an armed rebellion, which had to be put down by force after the senate had passed its "ultimate decree" (the SCU) for the purpose. Among the rebel leaders was even a praetor, Cicero's old friend, Marcus Caelius Rufus; he was killed in the fighting. Caesar did then act further to help borrowers by canceling interest payments due since early 49, for example, and permitting tenants to pay no rent for a year. Overall, it is true, he came nowhere near to eliminating the problem of debt, but he was responsive and creative enough to alleviate it in a balanced way.

Equally in need of attention was the calendar. The Roman civic year had only 355 days, with provision for an extra month to be inserted from time to time in order to match the solar year. This "intercalation" had been so neglected in the recent past, however, that by the early 40s the Roman year and the solar year were about three months apart. Caesar therefore adapted the Egyptian solar calendar to Roman use. To catch up, the year 46 was lengthened to a unique 445 days, and thereafter each year would have 365 days, with an additional day to be inserted in leap years between 23 and 24 February (as a second 23 February; nothing was added at the end of the month). This "Julian" calendar was only to be modified again after another millennium and a half by Pope Gregory XIII in 1582, when it effectively attained the form still in common use today.

Caesar was naturally concerned to settle his veterans, and at the same time ready to dispel fears that he would proscribe and confiscate for this purpose as Sulla had done. In fact his attitude towards defeated enemies was typically one of forgiveness (*clementia*), and even though there does appear to have been some confiscation of land in Italy, it must have been on a limited scale. Not many veterans were settled there (15,000 perhaps) and, unlike Sulla's men, they were widely dispersed.

Instead, most veterans, along with many of the poor from the city of Rome, were settled overseas—on land that either belonged to the Roman state already, or was confiscated from communities which had joined the fight against Caesar, in Spain, Africa, and the East especially. Caesar's two most ambitious settlement projects were perhaps the new colonies founded on the sites of Carthage and Corinth; both had remained undeveloped since their destruction a century earlier in 146.

Like all Roman colonies, his foundations were certainly intended as centers of Roman strength and culture, but altogether there seems no cause to claim that he had in mind very specific ideas of either garrisoning or romanizing the empire when he selected their sites. Even the number of his colonies is unclear, given that few had developed far by the time of his death; others established later in his name may, or may not, have been among his plans.

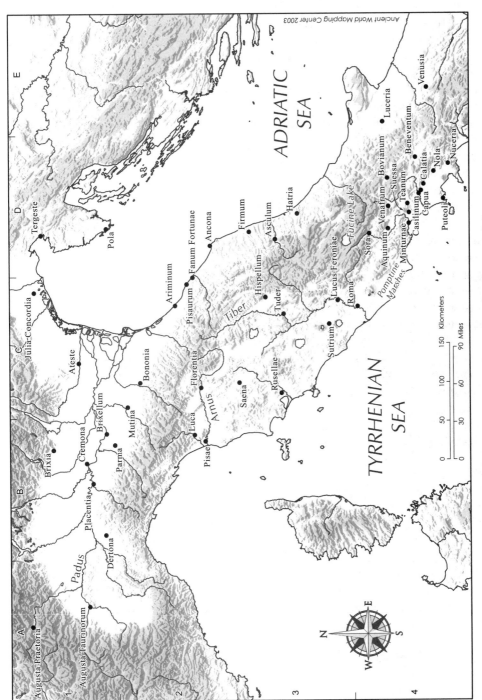

Map 8.3 *Settlement of Veterans in Italy by Julius Caesar and Augustus*

Ancient World Mapping Center 2003

There is the same uncertainty with regard to existing communities whose status Caesar is credited with raising. "Julian" in the name of a community with Latin rights or Roman citizenship could signify an award either by him or by the future emperor Augustus. Even so, in all likelihood there were some communities that he favored in this way, in Spain especially. Again, how far his motive here was to spread romanization, as opposed to express gratitude for support against the Pompeians, is impossible to judge. The grant of Roman citizenship to the Transpadana region by a law of 49—something that Crassus had proposed as censor in 65—certainly has the appearance of a reward for help during his Gallic campaigns. On the other hand, this seems a less likely explanation for his award of Latin status to the entire province of Sicily, all the more exceptional in that the island was predominantly Greek.

Altogether it may be possible to discern in Caesar's measures a new impetus to raise the status of approved provincials and to make them Rome's partners rather than merely subjects. Even so, to see this as a well formulated aim, consistently applied, would be excessive. His attitude to provincial government shows the same ambivalence. In line with his own law of 59 regulating it, he could act considerately. In particular, we know that he abolished the oppressive system whereby a syndicate of *publicani* collected tax in Asia after making the winning bid at an auction in Rome; he now permitted the communities to collect it themselves. On the other hand, there is no sign that he planned any large reform of provincial government, and when he needed men and resources for his civil war campaigns he exacted them from provincials with much the same unfeeling ruthlessness as the Pompeians did, and as he himself had done during the 50s while in Gaul.

CAESAR'S IMPACT UPON THE CITY OF ROME

There was much in the city of Rome to claim Caesar's attention. To reduce unemployment, many of its poor were offered a fresh start in the new colonies overseas. Others who depended on the free grain available monthly to any Roman citizen (as instituted by Clodius in 58) were liable to suffer when Caesar limited these rations to a total of 150,000. Evidently as many as 320,000 citizens had been collecting them at that point. If he had contemplated cutting costs further by simply abolishing the free ration as Sulla had done, he no doubt concluded that the blow to his popularity would be too great. He did arrange for better supervision of the supply of grain to the city, and he is said to have been planning improved access to it generally from overseas, with a new harbor at Ostia and a canal from Tarracina.

Major new projects for public buildings also acted to reduce unemployment in the city. One of these, the Forum Julium (north of the original Forum Romanum), was sufficiently advanced for Caesar to dedicate it in 46; its purpose was to provide more space for lawcourts.

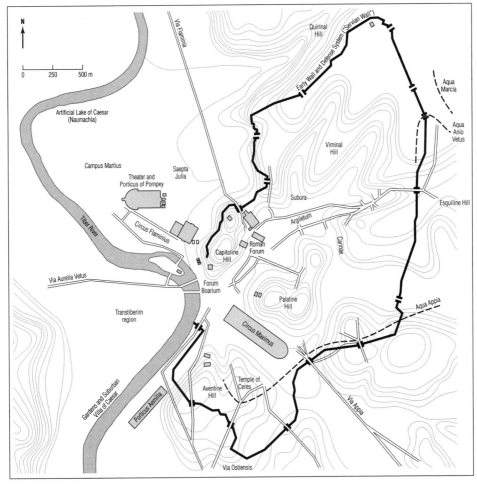

Map 8.4 *Rome in the Late Republic*

Within the map:

N

0   250   500 m

Via Flaminia

Artificial Lake of Caesar
(Naumachia)

Quirinal
Hill

Early Wall and Defense System ("Servian Wall")

Aqua
Marcia

Aqua
Anio
Vetus

Viminal
Hill

Campus Martius

Saepta
Julia

Theater and
Porticus of Pompey

Subura

Esquiline Hill

Tiber River

Circus Flaminius

Argiletum

Carinae

Roman
Forum

Capitoline
Hill

Via Aurelia Vetus

Forum
Boarium

Palatine
Hill

Aqua Appia

Transtiberim
region

Circus Maximus

Gardens and Suburban
Villa of Caesar

Porticus Aemilia

Aventine
Hill

Temple of
Ceres

Via Appia

Via Ostiensis

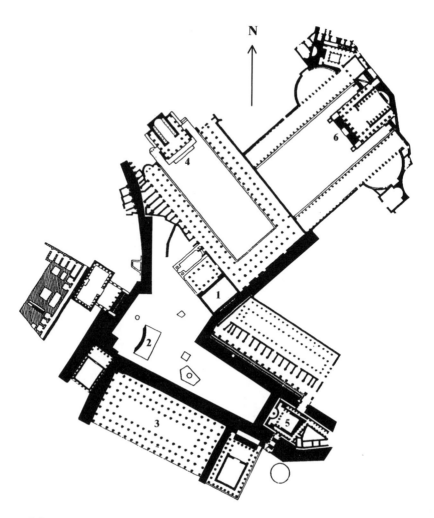

Figure 8.6 *From the mid-50s Caesar used huge sums he had gained in Gaul to fund new construction in the Forum Romanum and to purchase land for a new forum to the north. Once he became dictator, these projects were advanced and expanded. In the Forum Romanum he relocated and rebuilt both the Curia (1) and the Rostra (2), as well as replacing the old structures on the entire south side with a huge, new Basilica Julia (3). The new Curia Julia (see Fig. 8.7) was integrated into his plan for a Forum Julium (or Forum Caesaris), dominated by a temple (4) to his family's divine ancestor Venus. As it turned out, most of what he had begun was still incomplete at the time of his assassination, and was only finished by Augustus. He in turn closed off the eastern end of the Forum Romanum with a new temple to Caesar as Divus Julius (5). In addition, he opened up a further forum (covering about 400 × 275 ft./122 × 84 m) beyond Caesar's; its shape at the northeast end had to remain irregular because the private owners there refused to sell their land to Augustus, and he declined to expropriate it. The focal point of this Forum Augustum was the magnificent temple (6) to Mars the Avenger (Mars Ultor), dedicated in 2 B.C., where Augustus instructed the senate to meet whenever wars or triumphs were on its agenda. Flanking the temple on either side were a colonnade and semicircle; into the rear walls of both were set niches containing statues of Rome's "great men" (summi viri) going back to earliest times. Altogether this forum serves as a potent symbol of Augustus' extraordinary achievements and of his concern to uphold and advance Rome's traditional greatness.*

By contrast, work on another, the Saepta Julia, a huge enclosure for voting situated on the Campus Martius, was only to be completed in 26; the extensive use of marble in its construction was still unusual (see Map 8.4, above). However, after his firsthand experience of Alexandria, the greatest city of the Mediterranean, Caesar was all the more keenly aware of how unimpressive Rome seemed, and how bruised by the turmoil of the recent past. A new senate house was still needed to replace the one that had served as Clodius' funeral pyre in 52, and Caesar was authorized to build it. More generally, flooding by the Tiber in 54 had destroyed much mudbrick-built housing in low-lying areas of the city, and a major fire in 50 had caused further widespread damage.

None of these projects was finished in Caesar's lifetime, but they still demonstrate decisively how he intended both to enhance the city's appearance and to leave his own permanent mark on it. Such buildings, after all, would bear his name prominently, and have statues or other images of him in and around them. Supposedly, too, Caesar planned to add to the area of the city by diverting the Tiber. There were said to be other grandiose schemes for a huge temple of Mars, a theater to rival Pompey's, and a library on the model of Alexandria and other leading Greek cities. Temples to Concord and Clemency, two virtues that Caesar specially favored, were decreed by the senate in his honor.

Although all these latter schemes remain impossible to assess because Caesar never implemented them, it is quite plain that he wanted to make Rome a center of culture and education by attracting there leading intellectuals, doctors, and lawyers throughout the Mediterranean world. A plan to simplify and codify all of Roman law is even attributed to him. In his will he certainly did make a public facility of his villa and gardens across the Tiber, and the art collection there.

From the measures he took, there can be no doubt that Caesar wanted to reward his supporters, and to glorify the city of Rome as well as himself. More broadly, we can see that he wanted to bring stability and prosperity to the entire Roman world. There seems little question that, in the limited intervals of time open to him, he did take encouraging steps in the right direction. Even so, there is no knowing how he would have continued, because he never gained the opportunity.

POLITICAL PROSPECTS FOR ROME, AND FOR CAESAR

Caesar's work was cut short by his own closest associates, the senators. He seems not to have appreciated how badly he needed their continued support and respect. He did considerably increase the senate's size. Under him, the total membership of around 600 set by Sulla was expanded to 900. Inevitably, many of the new members were men he wished to reward, and they came from a somewhat wider variety of communities and social backgrounds than hitherto. Of course, traditionalists found fault, and exaggerated their grumbles. Among the ex-army

a

Figure 8.7a,b,c *This structure is today a prominent feature of the north side of the Forum Romanum. Once Rome's senate house, in the seventh century it became a church. Over time, with successive rebuildings and embellishments, the floor had eventually risen more than 20 feet (6 m) above the ground level in antiquity. Excavation in the forum at the end of the nineteenth century, however, showed that at least part of the ancient floor was still in place, and held out the tantalizing prospect that, if all later accretions were removed, much of the original structure might still be found intact underneath. An ambitious initiative during the 1930s did duly uncover and restore it; [a] shows the removal of additions to the rear and side in progress. The senate house thus revealed [b] had been erected after a fire in A.D. 283; the conspicuous horizontal openings either side of the front doors were for medieval tombs. It reproduced the design of the building commissioned by Julius Caesar as dictator and dedicated by Octavian as the Curia Julia in 29 B.C. (the very ancient senate house which this in turn replaced—enlarged by Sulla, and then torched as Clodius' funeral pyre in 52— had been situated nearby). The interior of the restored structure [c], viewed here from the front doors, is a tall, open chamber measuring 84 × 58 feet (26 × 18 m). Only the floor now offers an impression of the fine marble that originally covered most of the walls too. Along either side are three broad steps where senators sat on benches; at the far end is a dais for the magistrate presiding. When the senate was in session, only members could enter, but the front doors had to remain open, allowing spectators a chance to follow the proceedings from there. So a chamber identical to the one seen here was the setting for memorable occasions which attracted immense (and audible) public interest, like the conclusion of Augustus' "First Settlement" (see Chapter Nine) or the trial of Gnaeus Calpurnius Piso the Elder (see Chapter Ten).*

b

c

officers introduced by Caesar were alleged to be some as low in rank as centuri-on. For certain, the new members must have included men from many Italian communities that had only gained Roman citizenship within the past forty years or so, and were seeing one of their own become a senator for the first time. There is no question, too, that Caesar did introduce a few members from Spain and Gaul as well, but contemporary jokes about their gaucheness—having to discard their pants for togas, and ask directions to the senate house—were simply malicious. Notably, Caesar did not introduce any Greeks.

To maintain the senate's size, and again to reward his supporters, Caesar dou-bled the number of quaestors set by Sulla from twenty to forty annually, and the number of praetors likewise from eight to sixteen. Inevitably, elections lost sig-nificance once Caesar gained, and used, the right to fill offices by nomination. By the same token, his dictatorships freed him from the need to pay attention to other magistrates, or to consult the senate except as a formality. Consequently, he poured scorn on Sulla for resigning the dictatorship, mocked the tribunate whose veto could not obstruct him now, and even dismissed the Republic itself as "nothing, a mere name with neither form nor substance" (Suetonius *Deified Julius* 77). On one notorious occasion, he omitted the basic courtesy of rising from his seat when a senatorial deputation led by the consuls came to see him. His subsequent excuse—that he was too weak from diarrhea to stand up—failed to convince, since he later walked home.

The senate itself—out of fear, or flattery, or even contempt—encouraged his growing arrogance by voting him a stream of ever more extraordinary powers and honors, most of which he accepted. By the beginning of 44 the image of his head was appearing on coinage, a distinction never before accorded to a living Roman. Antony had also been chosen, though not yet instituted, as priest of a temple authorized by the senate for worship of Caesar as a god. Public worship of a living ruler was a Greek practice (see Chapter Ten), but it had no real prece-dent at Rome, and was completely contrary to the very concept of a republic.

Much the same may be said of kingship. Once again, it is unclear how far, if at all, Caesar wanted this distinction. The Greek world had indeed had kings, some of whom impressed Romans. Admittedly, too, elements of Rome's own archaic kingship had been carried over into the Republic. For Caesar to go as far as to take the title of *rex*, however, would be a giant leap, certain to offend almost everyone with any regard for the Republic. Early in 44, when some members of a crowd hailed him as king, he reacted by stating that he was Caesar, not Rex—a play on the fact that Rex is also a Roman surname (*cognomen*). Then, at a festival in mid-February (the Lupercalia), Antony made several attempts to crown him with a dia-dem of laurel as he sat on his golden chair, wearing a purple toga and gold wreath. Caesar rebuffed all the attempts, finally ordering that the diadem be taken to the temple of Jupiter, "who is the Romans' only king," on the Capitol. There is no knowing whether Caesar and Antony were deliberately colluding here to test pop-ular reactions, or whether Antony was acting just on his own initiative (and if so,

did he mean to bestow honor, or discredit?). Whatever interpretation be preferred, Caesar never did actually claim kingship, even though he may have toyed
with the possibility. The fact that Cleopatra and her baby son Caesarion came to
Rome in 46 and remained there can only have fuelled suspicions that Caesar had
it in mind to found a dynasty.

By early 44, there was no further authority that fresh honors could confer on
him. He already had absolute power. As he well knew, he was hated for that, and
for the way he used it. After all, a dangerous consequence of his clementia was
the survival of many of his enemies, plenty of them still in the senate. Even so, to
him the Republic was dead, and he could see no secure alternative means of regulating the state's affairs for the future except through himself. His adoption of
the title "perpetual dictator" during February 44 confirmed this conclusion. In
any event, reform would now have to be put off until his return from the Parthian
campaign to which he had long been committed.

To many senators, this new title and the prospect of Caesar's long absence
marked the end of all hope, the final provocation. Naturally they resented the permanent removal of their own authority; beyond that, Caesar's complete and
seemingly irreversible abandonment of all republican principle now became
insufferable. They had to act before his departure on March 18, and so determined
to kill him publicly in the senate at the last meeting he would attend, on the Ides
(fifteenth) of March—just as Romulus had been killed when he became a tyrant,
according to one tradition. The leaders of the sixty or so members in the plot were
two praetors, Marcus Junius Brutus and his brother-in-law Gaius Cassius
Longinus. Both had taken Pompey's side and been pardoned by Caesar. Both
claimed descent from ancient families with a tradition of championing Rome's
liberty; a celebrated Brutus had led the expulsion of the last king, Tarquinius
Superbus.

Caesar fell at the foot of a statue of Pompey. Assassination by his peers was a
tragic end for a man who had fought so long and hard to become unrivalled first
man in Rome. But along with that insatiable ambition a certain naiveté was
detectible. Somehow Caesar always seemed to imagine that, while he must be
accorded special rights in deference to his dignitas, the rest of the state can, and
will, continue to function around him in the regular, legal way. Eventually it
could not. By early 44, even many of his supporters in the senate found it intoler-
able that they must all remain deprived of their dignitas for the foreseeable
future. Hence they concluded that his personal interest could not continue to be
so privileged above that of everyone else.

SUGGESTED READINGS:

Gruen, Erich S. 1995 (reissue of 1974 original, with new Introduction). *The Last Generation
of the Roman Republic*. Berkeley, Los Angeles, London: University of California Press.

This detailed, controversial account accords greater weight to the continuation of established institutions and practices during the period than to the elements that triggered change. The new Introduction offers an invaluable overview of the different approaches taken to the fall of the Roman Republic during the twenty years following the book's original publication.

Meier, Christian. 1995. *Caesar: A Biography*. London: HarperCollins.

Mouritsen, Henrik. 2001. *Plebs and Politics in the Late Roman Republic*. Cambridge: Cambridge University Press.

Rawson, Elizabeth. 1985. *Intellectual Life in the Late Roman Republic*. Baltimore: Johns Hopkins University Press.

Syme, Ronald. 1939 (and often reprinted). *The Roman Revolution*. Oxford: Clarendon Press. Classic treatment of the changes to state and society from the formation of the First Triumvirate to the death of Augustus (A.D. 14); a difficult, yet powerful, book.

Tatum, W. Jeffrey. 1999. *The Patrician Tribune: Publius Clodius Pulcher*. Chapel Hill and London: University of North Carolina Press.

Treggiari, Susan. 1996 (second edition). *Cicero's Cilician Letters*. London: London Association of Classical Teachers.

Yavetz, Zwi. 1983. *Julius Caesar and His Public Image*. London: Thames and Hudson.

AUGUSTUS AND THE TRANSFORMATION OF THE ROMAN WORLD

The surviving record for the period of not quite sixty years from the assassination of Julius Caesar to the death of Augustus is a notably mixed one. Speeches and letters by Cicero give a full, vivid picture of the turbulent initial phase. Thereafter Appian's civil war narrative is important until it ends with the death of Sextus Pompey in 35. Also essential is Plutarch's *Life* of Antony, though neither it nor any other source presents events from Antony's perspective, which is a serious obstacle to our understanding of the 30s. Cassius Dio's uninspired year-by-year account composed early in the third century becomes vital from the mid-30s, especially for the Principate of Augustus; it is in fact our only such record for that entire formative period. The lively biographies of Augustus and Tiberius by Suetonius are valuable too, although the presentation is thematic and the focus primarily on each subject's background and character. From the time of Augustus onwards, many more documents come to be inscribed on stone or bronze, and there are some remarkable survivals from this varied body of materials. Among them, naturally, his own record of the achievements he wished to be remembered for occupies a very special position (see *Res Gestae* of Augustus, below).

REACTIONS TO THE ASSASSINATION OF CAESAR (44–43)

As soon as they had struck their blows, the senators who had conspired to assassinate Caesar hailed "liberty" and its senatorial embodiment, Cicero. They must have realized, however, that further obstacles to liberty's full return could well

267

emerge. In the immediate confusion and panic, much would obviously depend on the attitude of Antony, Caesar's fellow consul, and of Marcus Aemilius Lepidus, the aristocratic former consul who was his deputy (*magister equitum*) as dictator and commander of the troops in Rome. When Antony summoned the senate two days later on March 17, 44, he gained its support for a compromise whereby no action would be taken against the assassins, but at the same time all Caesar's measures and appointments would remain valid. The intention was to heal divisions and prevent disruption of the state's management, but the effect was also to diminish the aim of the assassination. The compromise certainly failed to anticipate the mood soon shown by the people at Caesar's public funeral and the reading of his will, which left them his extensive property across the Tiber and bequeathed each individual 300 sesterces. There was now a mass outcry against the assassins, which Antony himself encouraged. It remained so intense that by mid-April the leaders Brutus and Cassius had been driven from Rome. Cleopatra returned to Egypt with her son without delay. Lepidus, too, left the city to assume command of troops in southern (Narbonese) Gaul and Nearer Spain, where Sextus Pompey was rebuilding his cause after the defeat at Munda in 45 (see Chapter Eight). Before departing, however, Lepidus—with Antony's support—first contrived to have himself made *pontifex maximus* in Caesar's place.

Meantime, as soon as he heard of the assassination from his mother, Caesar's eighteen-year-old grand-nephew Gaius Octavius left Apollonia (across the Adriatic from Italy, in Illyricum), where he had been studying, and sailed to Brundisium. He was accompanied by Marcus Vipsanius Agrippa, a friend of about the same age, but from an undistinguished family, who was to remain his close, loyal associate. Octavius' mother Atia was the daughter of Caesar's sister, Julia; his father Gaius Octavius was a first-generation senator (*novus homo*) who had been praetor in 61 and died two years later. Their son Gaius Octavius was born in September 63, and had accompanied Caesar on his Spanish campaign in 45 (see Table 9.1, below). Now, when he reached Brundisium, he learned that in a will drawn up the previous year Caesar had adopted him and made him his principal heir. Once in Rome, and against the advice of his stepfather, he formally declared his acceptance of the inheritance, and took the name Gaius Julius Caesar Octavianus, although he always preferred to omit Octavianus for greater effect. However, the modern convention used here is to refer to him as Octavian in order to distinguish him from the dictator Caesar.

In view of Octavian's youth and inexperience, Antony at first did not view him as a threat. But it soon became clear that Octavian was succeeding in his attempt to displace Antony as leader of Caesar's friends and supporters, especially among the city populace and the veterans. When asked by Octavian to release Caesar's money, Antony found various reasons not to, and Octavian then won tremendous popularity by selling off his own property in order to pay the bequest of 300 sesterces to each citizen. Thereafter too, amid the turmoil of the next few months, Antony increasingly lost ground to Octavian, who proved adept at attracting support with offers of money and appeals to Caesar's memory. Meantime in August, Brutus and Cassius decided to take advantage of an official reason to leave Italy altogether, offered by the senate when it made them governors of the minor combined province of Crete and Cyrene. By the end of November, Antony in turn chose to abandon his struggle to deprive Octavian of support in Rome, and instead to leave with an army for the province of Cisalpine Gaul that he had arranged to be assigned. He was to find, however, that the governor already in position, Decimus Junius Brutus Albinus (one of the conspirators, but not to be confused with Brutus the leader), was in Mutina (modern Modena) and refused to leave. Accordingly, Antony proceeded to lay siege to the city.

Cicero now seized the initiative in proposing that the senate at last assert itself by eliminating Antony, whom he persistently represented as a would-be dictator. This removal, after all, was a step which he and many others had long since come to believe ought to have been taken at the same time as the assassination of Caesar. Moreover, urged Cicero, for this purpose the senate could strengthen its own forces—under the command of the two consuls for 43, Aulus Hirtius and Gaius Vibius Pansa Caetronianus—by enlisting the help of Octavian and the large body of troops he had raised privately for himself. Consequently, in January 43 Octavian was offered, and accepted, authority (*imperium*) subordinate to that of the consuls, and membership of the senate with the right to be called on to speak among the ex-consuls. Attempts to reach a negotiated settlement with Antony failed, and when the decisive clashes occurred in April he was defeated and Mutina relieved.

EMERGENCE OF A SECOND TRIUMVIRATE (43)

Unfortunately for Cicero and the senate, however, both consuls were casualties of the fighting. Decimus Brutus and his troops were weak from their long siege, and so quite unable to pursue Antony effectively as he retreated westwards. Decimus Brutus was instructed by the senate to take over the deceased consuls' forces, but he received no support from Octavian, who declined to take orders from him. Octavian appreciated that he, too, had no prospect of eliminating Antony successfully at this stage. So Antony was able to make his way west and join Lepidus, who had so far been assuring the senate of his loyalty, but needed little persuasion by his own men and by Antony to switch allegiance. Meantime Octavian insisted that his immediate priority must be to secure appropriate rewards for his men from the senate; only his election to one of the vacant consulships, he told them, would ensure that these rewards were forthcoming. Predictably, the senate would not hear of permitting a nineteen-year-old to stand for that office, however remarkable he might be. Even so, they were forced to re-think in August when Octavian marched on Rome at the head of eight legions. Later that month he duly became consul with his relative Quintus Pedius, Caesar's nephew, who died later the same year.

BOX 9.1: Laudatio Turiae

This long Latin document, inscribed on stone at Rome, originally had two columns, of which only the second survives, and not all of it. It takes the form of a laudatio *or eulogy to be delivered at a funeral by an upper-class husband for his wife. We know the name of neither, although scholars have customarily (but erroneously) referred to her as Turia, since a literary source happens to preserve a story about a woman of that name which is comparable to part of this record. The wife praised here must have died around the beginning of the Christian era. For these extracts, the original paragraphing is retained, but no indication is given of the many instances where the text is badly damaged and has to be restored. For the wife's legal position and the nature of* manus *marriage, see "Roman Women" in Chapter Seven. Among the many qualities which she exemplifies, note her care for the extended family, and her offer to divorce her husband because their inability to have children threatened the continuation of the family line.*

You were suddenly left orphaned before the day of our marriage when both your parents were murdered in lonely country. It was mainly due to you that the death of your parents did not remain unavenged, because I had already departed to Macedonia, and your sister's husband Gaius Cluvius likewise to the province of Africa.

You put so much effort into performing this sacred duty by insisting upon a prosecution and due punishment that, even had we been available, we should not have been able to do more. Rather, the credit is all yours, in partnership with that most respected of women, your sister.

While you were engaged with this duty, and the perpetrators had been punished, you immediately left your family home to safeguard your virtue, and moved to that of my mother, where you awaited my return.

You were then pressured to declare that your father's will, in which you and I were made heirs, was invalid on the grounds that he had taken his wife into a manus marriage. . . . This would have required you, and all your father's property, to revert to the guardianship of those pressing the point. Your sister stood to inherit nothing, because she had passed from the manus of your father into Cluvius'. Even though I was away, I am aware of how you reacted to these claims, and of the presence of mind with which you held out against them. . . .

Your resolution made them desist and not bring up the issue any further. As a result, you single-handedly accomplished the defense of your reverence for your father, the respect due to your sister, and your loyalty to me.

It is rare for a marriage to last so long, to be ended by death rather than broken by divorce; ours turned out to last forty-one years without upset. I only wish that it could have been my death which ended it, since it would have been fairer for me as the elder to go first.

Why should I mention your personal qualities? You were chaste, obedient, obliging, agreeable, an active wool-worker, pious but not to excess, in dress fashionable but not glamorous, and altogether discreetly elegant. Why should I speak of your affection for your relatives and your devotion to the family? You showed the same concern for my mother as for your parents, and provided the same restful retirement for both, displaying overall the countless qualities found in every matron who seeks to be well thought of. It is your own distinctive merits that I stress. Few men have encountered their like, and been able to make them known and vouch for them; human destiny has kept them rare.

Together we have taken care to preserve the entire inheritance received from your parents. You were not concerned to add to it, since you handed it all over to me. We shared responsibility such that I took care of your property, and you looked after mine. . . .

You demonstrated your generosity with regard to very many relatives, and especially in your devotion to the family as a whole. There are other noble women of whom the same might readily be said, but only one matched you in this respect, your sister. . . . Certain female relatives of yours you brought up in our household, and you equipped them with dowries so that they could attain a status worthy of your family. Gaius Cluvius and I put our heads together about these dowries that you had settled upon. While we approved of them, we did not want you to diminish your own inheritance, so we tapped our resources and used our property to pay them. . . .

You provided the greatest support for my flight [from proscription in 43/42], helping me with your jewelry in particular by handing me all the gold and pearls from your person. . . . You deceived our enemies' guards. . . . Even though your courage kept urging you to try and test the strength of the military, you restrained yourself. The clemency of those for whom you had such plans offered a better approach. Amid all this you had the resolution not to let slip any undignified remark. . . .

Caesar [Octavian] was right when he said that it was you who made it possible for him to restore me to my native land because, but for the arrangements you made for him to save me, even his promises of help would have been in vain. . . .

I will acknowledge, however, that your plight made for the most terrible event of my life. It was when I had been restored to my country—as a useful citizen of it still—by the generous decision of Caesar [Octavian], who remained overseas. His colleague [as Triumvir], Marcus Lepidus, who was in Rome, objected to my reinstatement. When you prostrated yourself on the ground at his feet, he did not just fail to raise you up, but you were caught and dragged along the way slaves are, your body was all bruised. Even so, you reminded him most resolutely about Caesar's edict with its congratulations on my reinstatement. After hearing his response and enduring his abusive, cruel insults, you openly denounced him as the person who should be known as responsible for all my perils. Later he suffered for his behavior. . . .

Once peace returned to the world and the Republic was restored [in the 20s], it was then a time of rest and contentment for us. We did long for the children that already for some time fate had begrudged us. If fortune in its usual caring way had allowed them, what would the two of us have lacked? Advancing age ended our hopes. . . .

Doubting your own fertility and distressed at my childlessness, you talked of divorce so that I—by remaining married to you—should not forfeit the hope of having children and be miserable as a result. You said that you would leave and hand over the household to another, fertile, woman—your sole aim being that, in line with the familiar harmony between us, you should seek out and arrange suitable circumstances for me. You insisted that you would regard these children-to-be as shared and as if your own. You would not make any division of our property, which to date had been shared, but it would continue to be under my control and, with my consent, adminstered by you. You would not regard anything as split or separated, but from then on your relationship to me and the respect you paid me would be that of a sister or mother-in-law.

I must admit to having become furious enough to be out of my mind; I was so aghast at your proposals that I could barely regain self-control. . . .

to abandon hostilities against the Triumvirate. In return, he was to retain control of Corsica, Sardinia, and Sicily, and be given the Peloponnese, all for five years; he was made an augur at once, and was promised a consulship in 33. Octavian had Antony to thank for help in reaching this pact, although of course he had no wish to adhere to its humiliating terms any longer than absolutely necessary. Antony, for his part, was concerned to see that the threat presented by Sextus Pompey did not extend eastwards.

ELIMINATION OF SEXTUS POMPEY AND LEPIDUS (39–36)

The extreme fragility of the agreement reached at Misenum was soon exposed. Sextus Pompey took offense when Octavian divorced Scribonia in fall 39, and again when Antony delayed handing over the Peloponnese to him. Meanwhile Italy continued to suffer from raids by pirates and their harassment of grain ships. These raiders may not have been under Sextus Pompey's control, but even so Octavian blamed him publicly for the distress created. Two major clashes between their fleets followed in spring 38—off Cumae, and in the Straits of Messina—both of which Sextus Pompey won decisively, although he then did not dare to follow up his advantage. His hesitation offered Octavian a respite, in which he begged Antony for help. Once again, Antony may not have been unduly dismayed by Octavian's plight, and may even have been pondering whether he might prefer to see Sextus Pompey emerge as victor. Eventually, however, at a long, tense meeting with Octavian at Tarentum (modern Taranto) in summer 37, the Triumvirate was renewed (probably to the end of 33), and Antony did consent to help him further, under certain conditions. In particular, Octavian was to postpone any new offensive until the following year, probably in order to synchronize with Antony's plans for the East. Octavian was also to send about 20,000 men there in return for being permitted to keep 120 of the warships accompanying Antony.

For Octavian, the advantage of this exchange was that the ships were immediately at his disposal, whereas his own commitment to provide men was only a promise for the future—which in fact he never honored properly. As consul in 37, Agrippa now took the lead in coordinating a supreme effort to deliver Sextus Pompey a knockout blow at last. Twenty thousand slaves were freed and trained as rowers. Lepidus even agreed to bring help from Africa—which he had not done in 38. He proved willing to contribute up to sixteen legions to a three-pronged attack on Sextus Pompey in Sicily during summer 36. It began badly, with many of Octavian's ships wrecked in storms, but thanks to Agrippa's leadership the enemy fleet was eventually annihilated in a series of naval battles which reached their climax off the northeast of the island at Naulochus. Three hundred ships engaged on each side here, and only seventeen of Sextus Pompey's escaped. He himself then managed to reach Asia Minor, where he hoped that

Antony's governors would welcome him. Soon, however, his efforts there to revive his cause seemed too much of a danger and an embarrassment, and he was pursued and executed in 35. The energy with which he had unflinchingly maintained the cause inherited from his father is remarkable, as is the degree of success that he achieved. With a little more boldness, in 38 especially, he might even have displaced Octavian.

Instead, as it turned out, Sextus Pompey's decisive defeat at Naulochus prompted Lepidus to conclude that *his* time to displace Octavian had arrived. He was, after all, very much Octavian's superior in age and family background, and no doubt deeply resented his exclusion from the crucial meetings at Brundisium, Misenum, and Tarentum. On the other hand, he had never matched Octavian's passion for power, let alone his willingness to take risks. So now, when Lepidus demanded that Sextus Pompey's land forces surrender to him, Octavian objected. The fierce argument was only resolved by Octavian brazenly entering Lepidus' camp and inviting all the troops—Lepidus' own and Sextus Pompey's—to recognize *him* as their commander. Not for the first time, his audacious personal appeal succeeded. As a result, Octavian was now able to humiliate Lepidus by removing him from the Triumvirate, taking control of Africa from him, and requiring him to live as an exile at Circeii about sixty miles south of Rome. Nominally, however, he was permitted to retain his membership of the senate and the office of pontifex maximus.

Octavian's victory at Naulochus thus became a doubly significant turning point for him, because it eliminated not only Sextus Pompey at last, but also one of his fellow Triumvirs. In addition, doubts about his military ability were now resolved; strictly speaking, the victory may have been Agrippa's, but the credit still went to Octavian. For the first time, too, undisputed control of Italy was within his grasp, together with the prospect of being able to begin its return to stability and prosperity.

ANTONY IN THE EAST
(42 ONWARDS)

This is the point for us to go back and trace developments in the East following Antony's victory at Philippi in October 42. Here there was much to occupy him over a vast expanse of territory. Funds had to be raised urgently for paying troops and settling veterans; disloyal local rulers had to be replaced; and consideration had also to be given to resuming the offensive against Parthia that Julius Caesar's assassination had forestalled. As part of all this activity, it made sound sense for Antony to establish good relations with the ruler of the richest independent state of the eastern Mediterranean, Cleopatra, Queen of Egypt. The meeting which he requested at Tarsus in Cilicia in 41 was not their first; they should have met previously when Cleopatra took up residence in Rome during Caesar's dictatorship.

a

c

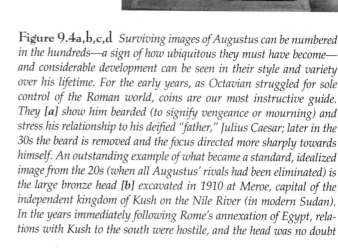

b

Figure 9.4a,b,c,d *Surviving images of Augustus can be numbered in the hundreds—a sign of how ubiquitous they must have become—and considerable development can be seen in their style and variety over his lifetime. For the early years, as Octavian struggled for sole control of the Roman world, coins are our most instructive guide. They [a] show him bearded (to signify vengeance or mourning) and stress his relationship to his deified "father," Julius Caesar; later in the 30s the beard is removed and the focus directed more sharply towards himself. An outstanding example of what became a standard, idealized image from the 20s (when all Augustus' rivals had been eliminated) is the large bronze head [b] excavated in 1910 at Meroe, capital of the independent kingdom of Kush on the Nile River (in modern Sudan). In the years immediately following Rome's annexation of Egypt, relations with Kush to the south were hostile, and the head was no doubt*

d

booty from a Meroitic raid into the new province. Notably, it was then buried below the steps leading up to a royal temple of Victory, so that anyone approaching the shrine would have the satisfaction of treading it underfoot. A full-size statue [c] with a head of similar type and a fold of the toga covering it, found in Rome, presents Augustus as the most pious of citizens. Another [d], from Livia's villa north of the city, renders him as military leader. The central scene on his breastplace depicts the Parthian king's return of Roman standards to a Roman soldier (or possibly the god Mars), in other words the climax of Augustus' successful diplomacy in 20. The wider array of gods above and below confirms that Augustus has achieved the right relationship with them too, and that his sway extends far beyond territory directly controlled by Rome.

Pompey demanded his presence in Italy; the repulse of the Parthians was therefore deputed to Publius Ventidius. He in fact achieved this so effectively over the
next two years (through summer 38) that there was little for Antony to contribute,
even though he did return to the East with his new wife Octavia in fall 39. The
spring and summer of 37 saw him back in Italy with a large fleet, however, with
the need to determine the most advantageous role to adopt in the worsening
struggle between Octavian and Sextus Pompey.

Octavia had accompanied Antony back to Italy, but she was left behind when
he returned to the East in fall 37; she had already had one daughter by him, and
would give birth to another early in 36. In Octavia's absence, Cleopatra now
joined Antony in Syria. At this stage he acknowledged paternity of the twins born
in 40, and in 36 she had another son by him. The nature of their relationship from
now onwards is hard to define. To Egyptians, it was evidently not quite a marriage, although they may have favored it as a sound step by Cleopatra to strength-
en her rule. There is no knowing how much Antony was influenced by a desire to
help her in this way, nor what private vision she may have had for her own future
and that of her kingdom. Maybe Antony had fallen too deeply in love to worry
about the consequences of the relationship, good or bad. Even if this is right, we
still have to wonder at his evident lack of concern for the impression made upon
his own wife Octavia, her brother Octavian, and Roman public opinion in general. Moreover, even should he divorce Octavia, as a Roman citizen he could never
contract a marriage recognized in Roman law with an alien like Cleopatra.

During 37 the Parthian king's decision to abdicate had led to the eruption of
civil war there, and so created the ideal opportunity for a Roman counterinva-
sion. This Antony launched in 36 at the head of sixteen legions and many other
troops. He did penetrate successfully deep into Media, but at a critical point his
ally the King of Armenia panicked and withdrew vital cavalry support. Antony
was then driven back with the devastating loss of as much as one-third of his
great army. Roman opinion naturally contrasted his stunning defeat here with
Octavian's victories over Sextus Pompey in the same year, an extraordinary reversal of both men's military reputations to date.

CLASH BETWEEN ANTONY AND
OCTAVIAN (36–30)

From the fall of 36, the Roman world had just two rulers, Antony in the East and
Octavian in the West. The key issue now, we might imagine, was how long this
divided rule might continue. There need be no doubt that Octavian saw it as only
the prelude to a struggle for sole power. Thus the campaigns he undertook
against tribes in Illyricum between 35 and 33 were intended not only to enhance
his military reputation, but also to keep his forces in training. Meantime he intensified his hostile propaganda against Cleopatra and Antony.

Antony, by contrast, remained preoccupied with the tense situation on the eastern edge of his territory. We simply have no clue to why he took so long to react to the growing threat from Octavian in the West. It was no doubt unwelcome to him, but it was blatant, and he can hardly have thought it safe to ignore. As it was, he concentrated on subduing Armenia, partly to exact vengeance for its king's desertion in 36, partly to establish a strategic bridgehead for a further invasion of Parthia. This he did achieve in 35 and 34, despite being distracted in the first of these years by an acute embarrassment of Octavian's devising. He dispatched Octavia with supplies and troops in token fulfillment at last of the exchange agreed in 37. After hesitation Antony accepted this aid, but he instructed Octavia not to proceed beyond Athens, and spent the winter of 35–34 in Alexandria with Cleopatra. The nature of his marriage with Octavia was now all the more perplexing, although still neither partner exercised their right to divorce the other.

Antony's behavior on returning to Alexandria in 34 seemed even more cavalier. To celebrate the conquest of Armenia, he staged what might be viewed as a pastiche of a Roman triumph, and then in an extravagant ceremony—the so-called "Donations of Alexandria"—he distributed eastern lands (some of them Roman provinces) to Cleopatra, her three children by him, and her son by Julius Caesar, as each sat on a golden throne. To be sure, these actions amounted to little more than empty gestures, no doubt mainly designed to gratify Egyptians, but it is easy to see how a far more sinister construction could be placed upon them in Rome. They flaunted Antony's relationship with Cleopatra, drew attention to his appreciative reliance upon Egypt's resources and support, and left the impression that he meant to establish a powerful Egyptian dynasty.

By the following year, 33, however, Antony at last recognized that he must give priority to preparing for a clash with Octavian. He and Cleopatra moved to the Aegean, and set in motion a massive transfer of troops all the way from the eastern end of the Mediterranean to Greece. Some of his advisers urged that it would improve his image in Rome if she were sent home, but even so he acknowledged the impossibility of demanding that she leave, given all the ships and money she was providing. What could not be put off further, however, was Octavia's divorce. For all the bad impression it would create, Antony finally took this step in 32; to wait for her to take it, at her brother's prompting, would only look worse.

Octavian, for his part, was well aware that Antony still had many highly placed friends and supporters in Rome. No doubt it was deliberately to provoke them that, in 32, he attended the senate with an armed guard. In any event, both of the consuls

Figure 9.5 *Coins of Antony and Cleopatra recall the "Donations of Alexandria," he on one side wearing a tiara and "Armenia Conquered" following his name, she on the other described "Queen of kings and of her sons who are kings."*

TERRA·MAR[IQ]VE·NEPTVNO·E[T]

a

Figure 9.6a,b,c *The custom of leaving a commemorative monument or trophy at the site of a victory was a Greek one which spread to Rome. Two striking examples erected by Augustus are illustrated. The first is a 200 foot-long (61 m) podium wall [a] into which were inserted the prows (rostra) of thirty-four warships captured from Antony at the decisive battle of Actium in 31 (the rostra in the forum at Rome were so called because they were similarly decorated). The wall enlarged the precinct of an old temple of Apollo at the southern entrance to the Ambracian Gulf, where Antony had pitched his camp. From uncovering and measuring the wall sockets for the prows [b], archeologists have been able to deduce the likely size of the ship from which each came; some of the ships were clearly immense. The second monument shown [c] was erected about 7 B.C. at modern La Turbie, a site brilliantly chosen for its visibility high above modern Monaco, where the mountains plunge down to the sea. This monument still stands to a height of 115 feet (35 m), and with its original cone roof (now missing) it may have risen 50 feet (15 m) higher. On it is recorded Augustus' subjugation of "all the Alpine peoples from the Adriatic to the Mediterranean Seas"; the names of forty-five peoples follow. It seems likely that Augustus intended this monument to match one placed by Pompey at the eastern end of the Pyrenees after his Spanish campaigns in the 70s.*

b

c

and a large number of other senators (we lack a reliable figure) duly took offense, and fled to Antony. Even then, Octavian sought further means of justifying his cause. He actually descended to the shameless illegality of seizing Antony's will, which had been deposited with the Vestal virgins, and publicizing its alleged provisions. These supposedly included arrangements for burial in Alexandria, and lavish gifts to Antony's three children by Cleopatra. As a further, more solemn precaution, Octavian took the unusual step of arranging for civilians throughout the West to swear a personal oath of loyalty to him (see Box 9.2, "Oath," below) in the war that was declared against Cleopatra. This declaration was made against her alone, not Antony too; all suggestion of civil conflict was studiously avoided.

Once the two sides' large forces encountered each other, at Actium in western Greece in 31, the ensuing action proved surprisingly undramatic. Throughout the summer each side sought to trap and blockade the other, much as Caesar and Pompey had done at Dyrrhachium in 48. Antony was forced more and more on the defensive. Eventually, at the beginning of September, he ordered a major breakout by his fleet. In the brief clash, both he and Cleopatra did burst through successfully with their squadrons, but for some reason they then sailed on—she back to Alexandria directly, he via Libya first. That left the rest of the fleet, and their entire land forces, at Octavian's mercy. All quickly gave up the fight.

The following year, 30, after elaborate preparation, Octavian mounted a full-scale assault on Alexandria, by land from east and west simultaneously. In the event, however, the city fell at the beginning of August with almost no resistance. Antony's fleet deserted, and he committed suicide, perhaps in reaction to a false report that Cleopatra had done so. In fact she was captured and spared; but then she, too, took her own life nine days later, possibly to avoid the humiliation of being paraded through Rome in Octavian's triumph. Caesarion, her son by Julius Caesar, was executed. Egypt's wealth came into Octavian's hands, and the kingdom was annexed as a Roman province. Octavian at once recognized how valuable an acquisition it could be to anyone aiming to rival him. Consequently, from the outset, the top Roman officials and commanders sent to Egypt were all equites, and no senator could even visit there without permission.

OCTAVIAN AS SOLE RULER (30 ONWARDS)

So, at the age of only thirty-three, Octavian had finally achieved the undisputed control of the Roman world which had been his unwavering ambition through fourteen years of civil war. To this end, he had been responsible for death, destruction, confiscation, and unbroken misery on a scale quite unmatched in all the previous phases of Roman civil conflict over the past century. Time and again he had returned from the brink of disaster, thanks to his skill as a propagandist, his ability to attract able associates, and his willingness to sacrifice any principle to one overriding purpose. Now, after this utterly amazing outcome, it became his concern to maintain the supremacy he had gained. The fact that he was also to do this successfully over a period of forty-four more years is hardly less miraculous than his elimination of all rivals to date.

Among the challenges of every description facing Octavian after his restoration of peace in 31–30, the nature of his own official position for the future was a particularly delicate and pressing issue. There had been no renewal of the Triumvirate after its lapse, probably at the end of 33. In practice, however, he continued to exercise a Triumvir's sweeping powers, even after beginning to hold a consulship annually from 31 onwards. Nobody was in a position to contest such irregularities, especially after the oath of loyalty had been sworn. Even so, Octavian wanted a more secure footing for the long term. The fundamental question was the nature of the regime that should now rule Rome. Two possibilities were surely to be avoided. The first was Caesar's style of autocracy; with its contempt for traditional forms of government, and its leanings towards dynasty and divinity, it had only led to his assassination. A second, related possibility would be to develop some form of sole rule that relied primarily upon the army. Octavian's civil war experience must have warned him against attempting this; he had seen too often how fickle and undisciplined soldiers could be. Rather, he believed that from the traditional republican framework itself could emerge a way forward which would both satisfy the upper classes' desire to reestablish the supremacy of the senate, and at the same time enable him to keep control. However, to restore the Republic without retaining some form of personal control can never have struck him as a serious option. The outcome of such an attempt by Sulla—when he was almost twice Octavian's age—offered no encouragement.

Octavian signaled his choice of approach in 28 by acknowledging for the first time that he and his partner in the consulship, Agrippa, were coequals. Then, at a carefully staged meeting of the senate in January 27, he handed back all his authority to the senate and people. To calm members in their alarm, he at once consented to remain consul, and to take responsibility for Spain, Gaul, Cilicia, Cyprus, Syria, and Egypt for ten years, on the grounds that these areas were in particular danger from invasion or revolt. Wherever it should become safe to do so within ten years, however, he undertook to hand the area back to the senate

Figure 9.7 *The coin shown is a gold piece, from an issue not known until 1992, probably minted in the province of Asia. It dates to Octavian's sixth consulship (28 B.C.), and its reverse shows him wearing a toga, sitting on his magistrate's chair, holding out a scroll, with the words (in Latin) "he restored to the Roman people their laws and rights." This remarkable find underlies the perception that the changes we term the First Settlement were not all made at a single meeting of the senate in January 27, but instead began in 28 as a series of steps.*

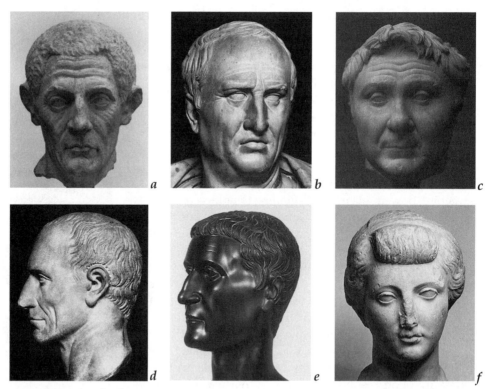

Figure 9.8a,b,c,d,e,f *By the first century B.C., intensified competition in public life made leading Romans more eager to promote themselves. As a result, images of many such individuals were created during their lifetimes in one medium or another, and also copied later. No living Roman appeared on a coin, however, before Julius Caesar in the 40s. At least coin portraits (whether contemporary or posthumous) are usually named. By contrast, that is seldom the case for busts or gems, for example, so that there is almost always some degree of doubt about their identification. In addition, of course, it may be naïve to assume that even a securely identified portrait accurately reproduces its subject's appearance. It would be more typical for it to reflect the way in which whoever commissioned the portrait (the subject personally, or an admirer) wanted the subject to be seen and remembered. This appearance may still be instructive, therefore, but is unlikely to be true-to-life. Despite the stark features, identification of a travertine head [a] as Sulla must remain insecure. Among several busts portraying the same elderly man, one bears the name* CICERO, *and this is regarded as a genuine ancient identification; the example shown seems likely to be a later copy of an original made in his lifetime [b]. A marble bust [c] found in the tomb of the Licinii family near Rome is likewise convincingly identified as Pompey. It, too, is probably a later copy of an original made in his lifetime, and matches posthumous coin portraits as well as descriptions of his appearance (including the "crest" of hair especially associated with Alexander the Great). Moreover, Licinii in the first century A.D. are known to have taken pride in a family connection with Pompey. Because the man portrayed by another marble head bears a close resemblance to Caesar as he appears on coins, this bust [d] has been identified as his. A green basalt bust found near Canopus (close to Alexandria) in Egypt [e] may well be Antony—portrayed with a trim, reflective appearance that (on coins, at least) changes during the 30s to a heavier, less reflective one. The last bust shown [f] can confidently be identified as Livia. Altogether, her surviving portraits suggest that she only ever wished to be portrayed as a young, ideal Roman matron, who never aged. Her hairstyle—also favored by Augustus' sister, Octavia—is a novel one; its elegant simplicity may be a pointed rejection of the more elaborate, sectioned style worn by Cleopatra.*

sooner. Clearly, he could not govern all of them personally, still less command the troops stationed there, so he was granted authority to appoint deputies ("legates") to serve for whatever terms he should fix. The expectation was that he would continue to be reelected consul himself. Governors of all other provinces would now once again be chosen by lot from ex-consuls and ex-praetors to serve for one-year terms in the traditional manner.

Along with this grant, often referred to today as the "First Settlement," the senate bestowed upon Octavian the new name Augustus, and also renamed the month of his birth, Sextilis, in the same way. With the sense of "revered," this name has a semireligious connotation, and was deliberately intended to symbolize Octavian's decisive break with his violent past. The times were now to be normal, with peace and the Republic restored.

"THE REPUBLIC RESTORED"

How genuine is this claim? Certain ancient writers much later, looking back with the advantage of hindsight, represent it as a sham, because they are keenly aware of how authoritarian the rule which dates from this point would become over time. It is vital to appreciate, however, that contemporaries enjoyed no such insight into the future. Their comparison would be to the past. By this measure, there is no question that the First Settlement allowed the Republic's traditional institutions and offices to function with a degree of independence and stability unknown since, say, the formation of the First Triumvirate in 60–59. Augustus wanted a return to the rule of law, and sought a legitimate, regular position within such a framework. Those who had no grasp of constitutional issues might refer to him as *imperator* (hence "emperor"), but he represented himself as no more than *princeps*, a bland, informal term signifying merely "leading figure." Previously there had been many *principes* (Caesar, Cicero, Crassus, Pompey, and others), whereas now there was to be only one. Hence this new phase in Rome's history is termed the Principate. Even this single Princeps might in time relax his hold further. The First Settlement, after all, was made for no more than ten years. To this extent there was cause for hope. There was also now the realization, unlike in 44, that another assassination would not of its own accord serve to make the senate supreme again. Rather, there would be another vicious power struggle, as well as popular outrage even fiercer than the hostility which Caesar's death had aroused; both prospects were unbearable so soon after the horrors of the long Triumviral period.

For his part, Augustus understood, as Caesar had not, how vital the senate's support was to his control of the Roman world. He further realized from Caesar's experience that an ostentatious display of authority—by means of special titles, and dress, and other trappings—was counterproductive; it gave offense without bestowing more power. Instead, Augustus believed that the authority he could

disclaimers of the modern world. Similarly, the special value that has been placed on originality in art and literature ever since the development of cheap copying technologies makes many today suspicious of Roman authors' "borrowings" from Greek literature. But it would be simplistic to deny originality and independence to great writers, a group that includes almost all those Roman authors whose work has been preserved through the centuries.

That said, some literature of the Late Republic was openly political and biased. Beginning in the late second century, Quintus Lutatius Catulus, Sulla, and certain other prominent figures wrote autobiographical works; Sulla's was even in Greek. Julius Caesar's surviving *Commentaries on the Gallic War* and *Commentaries on the Civil War* give us the flavor of this type of autobiography, which presents information in a way overwhelmingly favorable to the author. Powerful men were also the objects and recipients of flattering historical works or biographies: Theophanes of Mytilene, who received Roman citizenship from Pompey in gratitude, wrote about Pompey and his achievements, and particularly played up his likeness to Alexander the Great. Yet authors could equally well refuse to write for their influential friends, as we know happened when Cicero asked the poet Lucius Lucceius to commemorate his exploits during Catiline's conspiracy. Cicero consequently resorted to composing an epic poem himself, *On His Own Consulship*, from which only a few verses survive.

Given the limitations of mass communication, even authors whose work did not have a marked political character were associated with a patron or "circle." One such author is Lucretius (?94–51), whose Epicurean philosophical poem, *On the Nature of Things*, is addressed to the senator Gaius Memmius. Memmius is also linked to a very different type of poet, Catullus (?84–54). Better known because of the striking immediacy of his love poems, he served on Memmius' staff when the latter governed Bithynia in 57–56. Even so, politics are a marginal concern in the poetry of both Lucretius and Catullus. The fact that Catullus became a friend of Caesar, despite having previously attacked him and his companions in some poems, warns us not to attach undue significance to political elements in the literature of the time.

More important for Lucretius, Catullus, and others was the development of Latin literature, particularly the refinement of its formerly unsophisticated language into one capable of philosophical, lyric, and other kinds of expression. Catullus is identified with a movement now called "neoteric," whose adherents embraced Hellenistic culture and poetry in a search for new forms and content. As we noted when discussing the literary sources for early Roman history in Chapter Two, Rome's relative slowness in developing literature, as well as the broad attraction of Greek culture, meant that Latin authors of all types tended to turn consciously to Greece for their models. This trend further advanced once the booty reaching Rome included libraries. For example, when Sulla brought Aristotle's library to Rome as loot from his capture of Athens, he provided a rich stimulus for Latin works on philosophy and natural science. Cicero's vast output included works of both types, and he, Lucretius, and others consciously strove to make the

Latin language more expressive and precise. From the second century, Roman libraries had developed first privately and then publicly with sponsorship from Julius Caesar. By the end of the Republic, Latin authors were also turning back to earlier Latin works for inspiration and material.

Thus, Vergil's epic poem, the *Aeneid*, is a multilayered work. As Vergil (70–19) charts one of the foundation myths of Rome—the establishment of the Roman race in Italy by the Trojan hero Aeneas—he skillfully weaves in references to Homer's *Iliad* and *Odyssey*, as well as to Ennius (one of Rome's first poets), Lucretius, and others. At the same time Vergil constantly alludes to and even mentions Augustus, whom he knew from belonging to the circle of the eques Gaius Maecenas, one of Augustus' close associates. Yet the *Aeneid* is neither a pastiche of earlier writings, nor mere propaganda for Augustus. Vergil makes the material his own, whatever its source, and any biases he may have felt are expressed with sufficient nuance to contribute to the entrancing complexity of the epic.

Two other poets considered classic and representative of the Augustan Age are Horace (65–8) and Ovid (43 B.C.–A.D. 17). Horace, the son of a freedman but also part of Maecenas' circle, has a charming self-deprecatory persona in much of his writing. However, this persona does not obscure his brilliant crafting of different meters and genres, as he fashions new types of Latin poetry on earlier Greek models, in his *Odes* especially. Horace's work, too, is no simple translation of Greek forerunners, and he couples innovations derived from Greek literature with his own sentiments. Nor is Horace Augustus' spokesman, despite his personal connection to him. At times his skepticism is almost painful, as when he searches to discern what is noble and valuable in Rome after the bloody excesses of the civil wars.

Ovid was supported by the leading senator Marcus Valerius Messalla Corvinus. Yet Ovid was ambivalent about the Principate. In A.D. 8 Augustus banished him far from Rome to Tomis (modern Constanta, Romania) on the west coast of the Black Sea. Ovid was never to be recalled, even though he wrote two series of poems from there, which contained both general appeals and ones directed specifically to the Princeps. Altogether, Ovid's extensive output reflects wide interests, from love (such as the didactic *Art of Love* written around 1 B.C.) to myth (*Metamorphoses* or "Transformations," composed in epic hexameters), and even the Roman year (*Fasti* or "Calendar," which charts Roman religious rituals and legends day-by-day). Although he wrote mainly in elegiac couplets, he turned to many kinds of Greek literature for inspiration and material. For all his debt to these models, his poems are strikingly original and dazzling, even disturbing at times.

SUCCESSION

From the First Settlement of 27 onwards, despite his claims to have restored Rome's traditional constitution, Augustus in practice infringed a basic principle of any republic by quietly wielding a quite disproportionate amount of personal

Table 9.1 The Julio-Claudian Family

*This family tree is a deliberately selective one, omitting certain individuals and marriages. The abbreviations b., d., cos. signify respectively born, died, consul (in the year stated). All dates given are certain, or almost certain; dates A.D. are those normally used for the individuals concerned; descriptors in italic (e.g. the younger) offer additional identification. Emperors' names are in CAPITALS. Names **bolded** are in **boldface**. The figure in parentheses immediately before or after the name of an individual who married more than once specifies this marriage's place in the sequence. = signifies a marriage; the figure above = gives the date of the marriage, where known.*

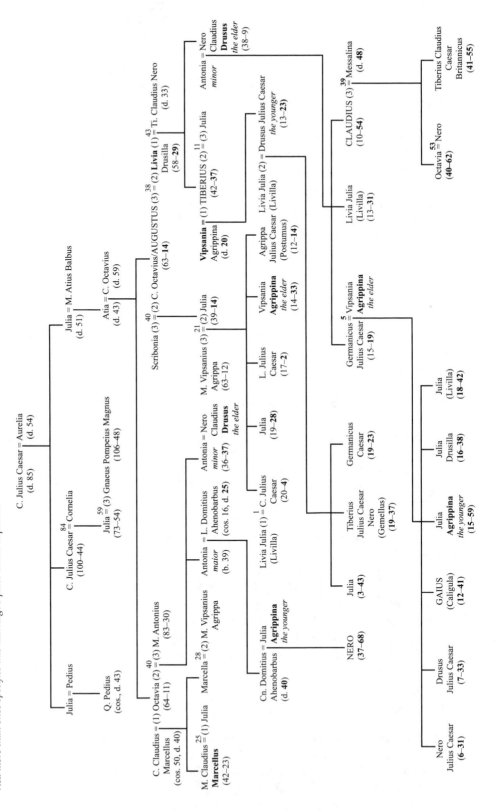

authority. From an early stage too, he developed another highly unrepublican pre-occupation by planning to pass on his position to a capable successor of his own choosing, and if at all possible a blood relative. To uphold both his family's interests and those of the state for the purpose was certain to prove an extraordinary challenge. But most Romans would surely have agreed that a power struggle after Augustus' death was to be avoided at almost any cost. Moreover, given the depth of family pride in Roman society, his passionate desire to install a successor of his own blood must at least have met with some understanding, even on the part of contemporaries opposed to such a plan.

That said, for him to gain the acceptance of any successor was still extraordinarily delicate, not only on grounds of principle, but also because he only ever had one child—a daughter Julia, from his short-lived marriage to Scribonia. His wife thereafter, Livia Drusilla, whom he married in 38, never had children by him, despite having produced two sons by her first husband Tiberius Claudius Nero—Tiberius (born in 42) and Drusus (born in 38).

In view of the fact that work on Augustus' huge mausoleum in Rome's Campus Martius began in the early 20s, he must have been giving his death and its possible consequences some thought even at that date. Only in 25 was anyone singled out who might seem destined as a possible successor, when Julia married Marcus Claudius Marcellus (born in 42), son of Augustus' sister Octavia by her first husband. Julia and Marcellus produced no children, however, and he died prematurely in the fall of 23. Moreover, a few months earlier when Augustus himself had expected to die, it was to his loyal associate and contemporary Agrippa that he gave his signet ring, not to young Marcellus. That desperate gesture demonstrated the embarrassing absence of viable plans for any succession at this stage. Had Augustus died then, it seems very dubious whether Agrippa could have taken over at all smoothly. He held no office (and thus had no legal authority), he was not a family member (and thus would not be one of the principal inheritors of Augustus' wealth), and he was viewed as an upstart by aristocratic senators. Rivalry between them would surely have erupted into civil war.

Fortunately for the stability of the Roman world, Augustus did not die in 23, and in fact his persistently poor health even improved thereafter. But this crisis now stirred him to make adequate arrangements for the succession. Since he had no remaining male blood relatives, he again turned to Agrippa, prevailing upon

Figure 9.9 *Bust of Livia*

him in 21 to divorce Marcella (his second wife, Marcellus' sister) and marry Julia. Agrippa already had imperium bestowed on him for a mission in the East. In 18 this was renewed (perhaps even made *maius*), and *tribunicia potestas* added. Agrippa was the first person with whom Augustus shared this latter power, and it became the mark of a designated successor. Augustus was overjoyed that the marriage of Agrippa and Julia had already produced a son, Gaius, born in 20. A second, Lucius, followed in 17; both were adopted by Augustus as his own sons the same year.

Gaius and Lucius were still only children, however, when Agrippa died unexpectedly in 12, aged about fifty. Augustus now therefore looked to his elder stepson Tiberius for the first time. He in turn was asked to divorce his wife Vipsania Agrippina (Agrippa's daughter by his first wife, Caecilia Attica) and marry his stepsister Julia. He did so with great reluctance, not least since it was only the previous year that Vipsania had given birth to a son, Drusus. The new marriage became a failure, and the son it produced died in infancy. Tiberius was granted imperium and tribunicia potestas for five years in 6, but soon afterwards he evidently felt so alienated by the efforts to advance Gaius—who was now about to enter public life—that he withdrew to become a recluse on the island of Rhodes. His official position was not renewed, and he only returned to Rome in A.D. 2, still out of favor. Julia by contrast had not left Rome, but in 2 B.C. Augustus felt obliged to exile her for scandalous sexual misconduct with several partners, including Iullus Antonius, a son of Antony and Fulvia.

Augustus' dynastic ambitions now brought him greater grief than ever when both adopted sons died young, Lucius in A.D. 2 and Gaius two years later. In 5 and 2 B.C. respectively, Augustus had even occupied the consulship to introduce each to public life, the only times he ever took that office after 23. Gaius became consul himself in A.D. 1; his marriage to Livia Julia (Livilla) the previous year remained childless. Augustus had so fervently desired one or both these young men to succeed him that their deaths were the most cruel blow; he wanted it remembered that "Fortune snatched them from me when they were young" (*Res Gestae* 14.1). By A.D. 4 his only practical option was to turn back without enthusiasm to his elder stepson Tiberius (the younger stepson, Drusus, had died in 9 B.C.). At last, Tiberius was no longer merely a stopgap for others. He was now adopted by Augustus as his son, and had imperium and tribunicia potestas conferred on him for ten years; when those powers were renewed in A.D. 13, his imperium was specifically made equal to that of Augustus.

So against all the odds, when Augustus died the following year 14, there duly occurred the smooth, undisputed transition to a capable new Princeps that he had so long planned for. Fate had by no means permitted him to secure his top choice of successor, let alone a blood relative. Nonetheless Tiberius was reliable, experienced, and faced no obvious rival (by contrast, what if Gaius and Lucius had both lived? or if Tiberius and Julia had had sons?). Beyond that, a sound foundation was laid for Augustus' broader concern to maintain the regime which he had developed for the long-term benefit of the Roman world.

SENATE AND *EQUITES*

In a prayer, Augustus once referred to his regime with studied vagueness as the "best condition," *optimus status*. If we now turn to reviewing some of its most important aspects, it is appropriate to begin with the senate and its members. No other group stood to lose so much by any shift away from the traditional form of the Republic. Caesar had demonstrated this all too starkly. Augustus not only wished to avoid his fate, but he also recognized how much reliance his restored Republic placed upon senatorial support. A strong, active senate, comprising an outstanding elite of wealthy statesmen, was therefore at the center of his vision for the future. So in order to remove unworthy members, he conducted two major reviews himself—acting like a censor for the purpose, although this office was not revived on a regular basis either now or later. The first review, as early as 29, reduced the senate from about 1,000 to 800, with Octavian placed at the head of the roll as *princeps senatus*. The second review, in 18, removed a further 200. This left a body of about 600 members (the size that Sulla had made it), to which the normal means of entry was by election as one of the twenty quaestors annually—again a reversion to Sulla's number, which Caesar had doubled. By the time of the second review, Augustus had further elevated the senate as a new, exclusive social class to which members and their families belonged. He also made 1,000,000 sesterces the minimum level of wealth for any senator; previously, none had been specified beyond the 400,000 required of an eques. It is hard to believe that the new minimum made much practical difference, when senatorial membership had always been known to demand a lavish outlay among other qualifications; but the intention to reinforce exclusivity is clear.

Generally speaking, Sulla's rules regulating a senator's rise through the *cursus honorum* were once again observed. Elections were conducted freely, too, although Augustus did intervene in some key respects. It became his prerogative to fix the number of praetors to be elected each year, and both for this office as well as lower ones he seems to have recommended a certain number of candidates, whose election was thus in effect assured. To what extent, if at all, he acted likewise for the consulship remains obscure. He certainly did introduce an important change for it from 5 B.C. onwards, whereby the pair who entered office on January 1 resigned midyear, thus requiring "suffects" to replace them. Since it was above all the honor of attaining the top magistracy that senators sought—with length of tenure a matter of indifference—this new practice was a brilliant means of satisfying more aristocrats' ambitions, while still maintaining the tradition that only a pair of consuls should be in office at any time.

Even if a senator about whom Augustus had reservations did rise through the cursus honorum, that was little cause for alarm; a senior magistrate's scope for action was now severely limited. Rather, the practical value of a praetorship or consulship was the eligibility it conferred for holding the empire's top military or administrative positions. Most such appointments were for the Princeps to make, and he did little to depart from the tradition that senators alone should be chosen to fill them. Hence in practice ambitious senators needed to cultivate and maintain Augustus' favor, however much he might protest that they were free to do as they pleased. Already in 27, at the time of the First Settlement, most legions were stationed within his provinces, and by his death only one (in Africa) was not. Thus almost all legionary commanders were his legates (ex-praetors, or sometimes less senior senators), as were the governors of the provinces where these forces were stationed (ex-consuls or ex-praetors, corresponding to the significance of the region). Within Rome and Italy, senior senators also came to be given administrative responsibilities in spheres of greater concern to Augustus than they had ever been to the Republican senate. They supervised the distribution of free grain rations in Rome, for example, as well as the upkeep of the city's aqueducts and public buildings, and the main roads of Italy.

It need be no surprise that the morale of the senate as a corporate body seems generally low throughout the reign. Plenty of old families had faded during the civil war period, many members survived only to be removed, and the remainder had to adjust their outlook and expectations. The same applied to new entrants, whom Augustus (himself the son of a novus homo) followed Julius Caesar in cautiously encouraging from Italy and the Latin-speaking West. But for any senator to dream of emulating Gaius Gracchus or Cicero was now unimaginable, naturally. The dilemma, rather, was how best to act in an environment where the Princeps' opinion had always to be respected, and nothing that he requested or supported could be denied. Augustus went out of his way to attend the senate, to consult it respectfully, and to encourage debate; he even formed a committee of members to determine the agenda in advance of meetings. However, this step only sharpened the sense that the senate now met primarily to approve what had already been decided in private elsewhere, especially with regard to such key issues as state finances, foreign affairs, and the disposition of the army. Augustus strove to improve attendance by a variety of means—among them, quorums, fixed dates for meetings, fines for absentees—but these, too, only reinforced the fear or resentment felt by disenchanted members. Others meanwhile resorted to flattery, and almost all hesitated to articulate opinions. Really, it was not until Tiberius' reign that the senate's morale was boosted by the adoption of some important new functions. Even then, inevitably, the basic issue of the relationship between Princeps and senate was to remain tense and unresolved.

In contrast to senators, equites had no cause to feel immediately threatened by Augustus' development of the Principate. Rather, because the Roman Republic had done almost nothing to tap their particular managerial and financial talents in its service, equites were gratified when Augustus took the novel step of seeking out their assistance. He significantly increased the number of officer positions in the army reserved for them, and it became understood that such service was normally expected of any eques hoping to hold a civil post in the Princeps' service. The sphere where Augustus particularly enlisted equites was in managing all the various properties which came under his control by one means or other, and in representing him in the courts in this connection. Soon enough, no doubt, he must have had such equestrian "procurators" in every province of the empire (the Latin noun *procurator* simply means "agent").

Strictly speaking, they were all just his private staff. Even so, procurators within his own provinces gradually came to be entrusted with assignments in the public domain—handling tax payments, for example, commanding troops, and even governing an entire province. In this latter connection, the most outstanding example was Egypt where, from its annexation in 30, all the top Roman officials and commanders were equites exclusively. Security was surely the reason here—equites would not share senators' political ambitions—and it again must have been what prompted Augustus to place his own guardsmen, the Praetorian Guard, under the command of a pair of equestrian prefects from 2 B.C. onwards. Some years later, in A.D. 6, a disastrous fire in Rome prompted him to form a patrol force of "watchmen," or *vigiles*, to combat such outbreaks, under the command of an eques. Then soon afterwards, following a severe grain shortage, he recognized the need for permanent monitoring of its supply to the city, and asked another eques to undertake this responsibility. He certainly could as well have chosen senators in these two last instances, and we can only speculate on why he decided not to. Maybe it was simply that the individual he considered most suitable for appointment in each case just happened to be an eques. At least, the explanation that he was deliberately aiming to develop an "equestrian division" of a "civil service" should be rejected. His employment of equites was extremely limited, and never more than a succession of unstructured responses to pressing needs.

ARMY

Augustus' bitter experience during the long civil war period had demonstrated the importance of the army to his rule, yet also the many dangers that it posed. He had himself encouraged disloyalty on the part of his opponents' troops, while also needing to combat it among his own men. Now he had to secure the entire army's unshakable loyalty, as well as to reform the traditional Republican arrangements for recruitment and discharge. For some decades past, these had been far from satisfactory. In particular, the old model of the army as a militia into which citizens with property were drafted for relatively short periods had long broken down.

After his victory at Actium, Augustus' immediate concern was to discharge at least 140,000 men from both sides, and perhaps more; Egypt's wealth enabled him to buy them land instead of confiscating it, and to give them a little cash (see Map 8.3). This left a standing army of twenty-eight legions (each about 5,000 infantrymen), which must represent the size of force that Augustus regarded as strategically adequate for the long term, and at the same time affordable. Not until 13, however, do we hear of new conditions of service. The changes were radical. In principle, henceforth all legionaries would be volunteer citizens who committed to serving for a fixed number of years, at the end of which—if they stayed loyal and survived to be honorably discharged—they would receive a fixed bounty payment. During their service they could not legally be married; Augustus was no doubt eager to keep his forces mobile, and he perhaps wanted to avoid all claims by dependents. In cash, the bounty equaled about thirteen years' pay (thus sufficient to support most veterans to the end of their lives), although we find some instances where it comprised land with proportionately less cash. Initially, a legionary's term of service was set at fifteen years with a further four as reservist, but various setbacks forced Augustus to raise those figures to twenty and five respectively, and even then it seems that men might be held longer. Finding the necessary funds for such substantial bounties was evidently enough of a struggle that in A.D. 6 Augustus established a special "military" treasury, the *aerarium militare*, administered by ex-praetors, for this sole purpose. He funded it himself initially, and for the future made the proceeds of a sales tax and an inheritance tax payable to it. For citizens, therefore, from 13 onwards military service became a lifetime career choice, and the army a professional force. For the great majority, the end of the draft, not to mention the general atmosphere of peace, were a marked and very welcome change.

Julius Caesar had already doubled soldiers' pay, and—except in the singular case of his own Praetorian Guard—Augustus did not seek to buy their loyalty by raising it further. Nor was he eager to continue the civil war practice of bribing soldiers with "donatives." Only certain contingents had benefited from these special payments, and even they had by no means invariably received all that was promised by rival leaders. As sole leader, Augustus, by contrast, now limited himself to infrequent, modest donatives, paid to the entire army. He did, on the other hand, quite deliberately give a huge boost to the regular pay of centurions (legionary officers), who now received anything from thirteen to over fifty times the basic rate depending upon rank and seniority. Previously, the pay differential between officers and men had been small. So, as Augustus had seen during the civil wars, when mutiny broke out centurions had in some instances sided with the men, and thus provided leadership which would otherwise have been lacking. Now, however, Augustus rewarded centurions so handsomely that they would be much less likely to identify with mutineers.

With increasingly rare exceptions, all top army officers (senators and equites) were Augustus' own legates, appointed by him and serving for whatever period he might determine. For a long time, from fear of rivals, he chose not to entrust large groupings of legions to the command of aristocrats, preferring either members of his own family or "new men" (as his own father had been). More broadly, he ensured that it was now he and his family to whom all soldiers swore their oath of loyalty—not to their officers, who were only his deputies. Just how solemn a regard soldiers would have for this oath is impossible to gauge, but the

Figure 9.10 *This tomb monument was erected by the brother of a centurion, Marcus Caelius—said here to be originally from Bononia (modern Bologna) in northern Italy—who died in what is referred to as "Varus' war," in other words the massacre in the Teutoburg Forest in A.D. 9 (see Fig. 9.11). The inscription specifically gives authority for Caelius' bones to be placed in the monument subsequently—unlikely prospect though that was (compare Fig. 10.6 for the issue of reusing a tomb). Caelius is presented as the model of a successful career officer in Augustus' reshaped professional army. His age (53) and high status as a centurion of the first rank are specified. As part of his uniform, he wears a very distinguished set of decorations for valor—an oak-leaf "civic crown" (corona civica) for saving a fellow citizen's life, torques hanging from his shoulder straps, medallions on his chest, and bracelets on each wrist. In his right hand he grasps the dreaded stick of vine wood (vitis), with which all centurions maintained discipline. The sense of his proud status is enhanced by the inclusion of a freedman either side of him; whether they were with him, their patron, at the time of his death is left unclear.*

deliberate focus of all loyalty on the single figure of the Princeps does seem to have been successful in creating a strong bond. Mutinies and strikes against the established regime remained a very real concern throughout Augustus' rule and far beyond. In general, however, his efforts to maintain the army's loyalty proved remarkably successful over the long term.

THE EMPIRE AND ITS EXPANSION

The army was to be used both to protect Rome's empire and to expand it. Augustus saw no contradiction when he sought praise both for bringing peace and for making conquests even more extensive than those of Pompey or Caesar. In his own words, his peace was one "secured by victories" (*Res Gestae* 13, "parta victoriis pax"). It is hard to define his various goals for the expansion of Roman power. There is no question that in any case these underwent changes over such a long period of rule, and there were plainly major disappointments and failures too. Moreover his geographical grasp was nowhere near as complete or accurate as ours.

BOX 9.2: Oath of Loyalty

It was specifically to Augustus and his family that soldiers came to be required to take a regular oath of loyalty. Despite no more than a random scatter of evidence, it is clear that Augustus also used oath-taking as a means of promoting civilians' loyalty to himself—even if not necessarily on the same regular basis, or with quite the same degree of legal compulsion. In practice, however, it is hard to imagine many individuals declining the "opportunity" to take such an oath when "offered" one, as civilians in the West were as early as 32. There follows the text of a Latin oath sworn by the magistrates, senate, and people of Conobaria, not far north of Gades (modern Cádiz) in southern Spain, probably in connection with the introduction of Gaius Caesar to public life in 5 B.C. Note that Marcus Agrippa (Agrippa Julius Caesar), Agrippa's posthumous son by Julia born in 12, is named here among the members of the imperial family; later, however, in A.D. 6 Augustus removed him from the family, allegedly for some mental disability or character flaw. The text survives on a bronze tablet with holes drilled top and bottom so that it could be posted in public.

In all sincerity I avow my concern for the safety, honor, and victory of imperator Caesar Augustus, son of the Divine Julius [Caesar], pontifex maximus, and of Gaius Caesar, son of Augustus, Leader of Youth [Princeps Juventutis, a purely honorific title], consul designate, pontifex, and of Lucius Caesar, son of Augustus, and of Marcus Agrippa, grandson of Augustus. I shall bear arms, and shall hold as friends and allies the same ones I understand to be theirs. I shall consider as my enemies, too, those whom I observe in opposition to them. And should anyone take action or make plans against them, I shall pursue him to the death by land and by sea. (*AE* 1988. 723)

It is possible that for a long time he had "world conquest" somehow in mind, along the lines claimed by his great Republican predecessors. This could certainly furnish some explanation for expeditions ordered in the 20s south from Egypt and far into the Arabian peninsula, as well as for his determination to subdue the huge area between the Rhine and Elbe rivers. To stretch so far in each of these instances proved a failure in practical terms. The image they fostered was still a glorious and exotic one, however, which diplomatic dealings with rulers as far away as Britain and India only reinforced (but no further expedition was sent to Britain to resume Caesar's initiatives there).

Meantime Augustus was aware after Actium that several areas within the empire were not secure, and that from a strategic viewpoint it was altogether a badly fragmented whole. Its Latin-speaking West and Greek-speaking East were so far apart from one another that for each to split off under its own ruler was quite conceivable. During the mid 30s this is possibly what Antony assumed would happen, and it eventually did from the fourth century. Moreover, with the empire so vulnerable to outside threats throughout the civil war period, it was sheer good fortune that no such invasion occurred then.

Augustus himself devoted considerable time during the 20s to imposing Roman control throughout the Iberian peninsula, especially its rugged northwest, which had never been subjugated previously. At the same time he authorized others to embark upon the immense task of extending Roman control northwards in central and eastern Europe as far as the Danube River. This led to the creation of the provinces of Raetia, Noricum, Dalmatia (an expansion of Illyricum), Pannonia, and Moesia, and meant that there was now Roman territory linking the empire's western and eastern halves. A related initiative, long overdue, was to bring the entire area of the Alps under Roman control. As late as the teens B.C., tribes there could threaten southern Gaul and northern Italy with their raids (see Figure 9.6).

In the East, there was much less campaigning, and in general Antony's administrative reorganization remained in place. Apart from Egypt, the two notable additions to the empire were the large region of Galatia in central Asia Minor in 25, and Judaea in A.D. 6; both were former "client kingdoms." Several other states maintained this status; as such, they were not ruled by Rome, but respected Roman interests. Augustus' major concern in the East was to forge a viable long-term relationship with Parthia, the one state on any of the empire's borders which had demonstrated the potential to be a serious threat. To exact some form of vengeance for the defeats of Crassus and Antony seemed essential. On the other hand, Augustus felt unable to spare substantial forces to guard against Parthian incursions, and he was still less enthusiastic about mounting his own major offensive there. Since he also appreciated that it was the exception rather than the norm for Parthia to act as a well-organized, aggressive military power, he risked relying upon tough diplomacy rather than force. By this means, in 20, he did achieve the return of legionary standards captured from Crassus and Antony, and gained

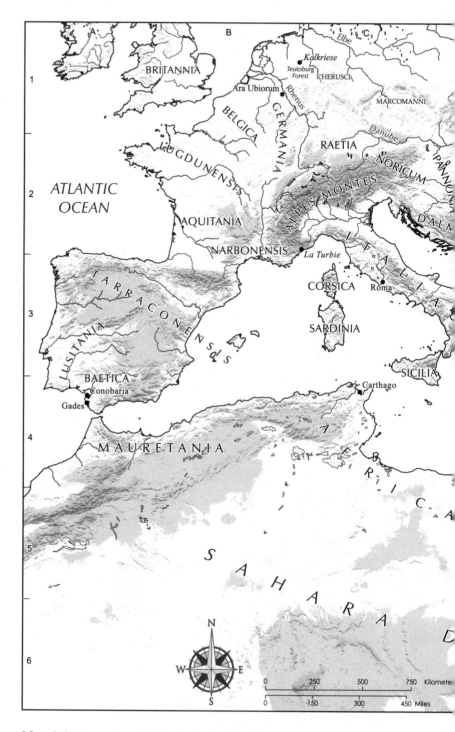

Map 9.2 *Expansion of the Empire in the Age of Augustus*

E

F

G

CASPIAN SEA

BLACK SEA

Tomis

Danube

OESIA

ARMENIA

BITHYNIA-PONTUS

Amaseia

Byzantium

Ancyra

GALATIA

MESOPOTAMIA

EDONIA

CILICIA

Euphrates

A S I A

Antioch

PARTHIA

Ephesus

SYRIA

ACHA A

RHODES

CYPRUS

CRETA

IUDAEA

TERNUM MARE

Alexandria

Cyrene

ARABIA

E G Y P T

RED SEA

Nile

E R T

KUSH

Ancient World Mapping Center 2003

Meroe

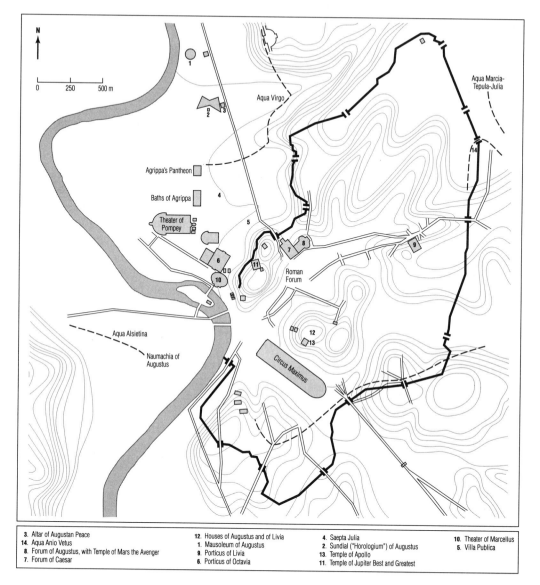

N

0   250   500 m

Aqua Marcia-
Tepula-Julia

Aqua Virgo

Agrippa's Pantheon

Baths of Agrippa

Theater of
Pompey

Roman
Forum

Aqua Alsietina

Naumachia of
Augustus

Circus Maximus

3. Altar of Augustan Peace	12. Houses of Augustus and of Livia	4. Saepta Julia	10. Theater of Marcellus
14. Aqua Anio Vetus	1. Mausoleum of Augustus	2. Sundial ("Horologium") of Augustus	5. Villa Publica
8. Forum of Augustus, with Temple of Mars the Avenger	9. Porticus of Livia	13. Temple of Apollo	
7. Forum of Caesar	6. Porticus of Octavia	11. Temple of Jupiter Best and Greatest	

Map 9.3 *Rome at the Death of Augustus*

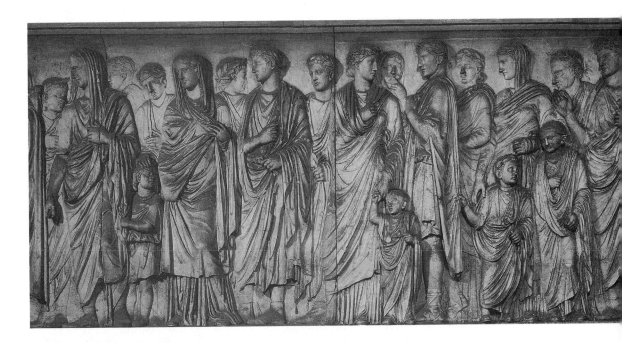

Figure 9.12 *South frieze of the Altar of Augustan Peace (Ara Pacis Augustae), Rome. Augustus himself records (Res Gestae 12.2) that this altar was voted by the senate to mark his return to Rome from Spain and Gaul in 13, and that an annual sacrifice was to be performed there. Surrounding it was a walled precinct (38 × 35 ft./12 × 11 m), with reliefs in marble on the two longer sides depicting a religious procession of the imperial family and many other participants (all about three-quarters life-size). The effect is to convey a lasting impression of Augustus' concern for peace, inclusiveness, and religious devotion. Discoveries of the relief panels have been made ever since the late sixteenth century, although there was no effort to assemble them until the late 1930s, when this was done hastily and without sufficient regard to the restorations which they underwent even in antiquity. For this reason alone, all identifications of individual figures should be made with greatest caution. That said, the tall male figure towards the left of the section shown is often taken to be Agrippa, accompanied by his young son Gaius; equally, the female at the center here, facing back (see detail), may be Antonia minor, with her young son Germanicus. In any event, close examination of her dress has led some scholars to believe that the join immediately to her left is a mistake, and that these two panels should not abut one another.*

Figure 8.6), and extensive development of the Campus Martius. Augustus' mausoleum and the Altar of Augustan Peace are among the monuments constructed in the latter area.

There were multiple benefits to these initiatives. All served to glorify Augustus' rule and to boost his popularity; he himself bragged that "he found Rome a city of brick, and left it one of marble" (Suet. *Augustus* 28). The construction work provided employment for the free poor in huge numbers. Perhaps as many as 1,000,000 inhabitants were now crammed into the city. Improvements to services were tangible daily reminders of a concern for this population that had been absent during the Republic. For example, thanks to Agrippa's efforts in particular, three new aqueducts were built, and a permanent organization established to maintain the entire water supply system. No aqueduct had been built since the 120s, when the city's population had been nowhere near so large. Also, after an alarming grain shortage, Augustus arranged in 22 that the monthly distributions of free grain should be supervised by four senators (ex-praetors). Since these free rations went to no more than about 200,000 recipients, the population as a whole was still heavily reliant upon commercial suppliers (Figure 8.2). So sometime after A.D. 7, in response to more shortages, Augustus took the further step of appointing an eques to oversee the entire import of grain to the city, most of it shipped from Egypt and Africa.

Rome became a safer place with the establishment of three "urban cohorts" (perhaps 1,500 men in total) to maintain law and order; their commander, the City Prefect, was a senior senator. In practice they were reinforced first by the three (out of nine) cohorts of Augustus' own guardsmen, the Praetorian Guard, that were regularly stationed in the city (one such cohort comprised at least 500 men); then also, from A.D. 6, by the force of 3,500 or so "watchmen," or *vigiles*, of freedman status, whom Augustus recruited to try and reduce the devastation caused by fires.

Last but not least, Augustus knew the value of providing the people of Rome with memorable entertainment. It need be no surprise that when recording the achievements he wished to be remembered for, he included the shows he had sponsored—eight gladiatorial games, three athletic games, twenty-six beast hunts, one mock naval battle, the special "Secular Games" of 17 B.C. symbolically inaugurating a new age (*saeculum*), and twenty-eight other shows. These events could involve the participation of thousands of people.

ATTITUDES OUTSIDE ROME

In Italy and the provinces, too, Augustus' rule was widely welcomed. He made little change in the established pattern of provincial administration. It may be that his novel step of slowly taking a census of the entire empire region by region increased the burden of Roman taxation. Even so, this was made bearable by the return of peace and stability, as well as by the sense that now, at last, there was a responsible, approachable ruler in control who was personally concerned to remedy distress and injustice. Moreover he funded construction work all over the empire, especially the building and repair of roads on a massive scale, and the foundation of colonies. The latter—twenty-eight of them in Italy alone, according to Augustus himself (*Res Gestae* 28.2; see Map 8.3)—were primarily, although not exclusively, for the settlement of veterans.

In the East, the sheer extravagance of the devotion shown by Greeks actually became a cause of concern to Augustus at an early stage. Ever since the fourth century, there had been public cults of rulers as benefactors in the Greek world, Alexander the Great especially. Once Rome became involved there from the second century, cults sprang up to *Roma* as well as to individual Roman commanders, including Antony. Augustus welcomed similar devotion to himself with some caution. He stipulated that Roman citizens should only worship "Roma *and* Augustus," thus discouraging any development of a personal cult. This would be sure to offend conservative Roman sentiments, as the experiments during Caesar's dictatorship had confirmed (see Chapter Eight). With the same reasoning Augustus gave no encouragement to any such cult of himself in Rome itself, Italy, or the more romanized of the western provinces. On the other hand, he did promote it at Lugdunum (modern Lyon) in Gaul and at Ara Ubiorum (modern Köln/Cologne) in Germany as a means of fostering loyalty. Its effectiveness in these more recently annexed regions was mixed; Gauls or Germans who resented the imposition of Roman rule were only alienated further by it.

This selective promotion of what we generally refer to as an "imperial cult" is in fact just one means among many by which Augustus exploited religion to strengthen his own position. People of widely differing status and wealth were called upon to participate, across the entire empire. For example, in each town or city, formation of a group of freedmen was encouraged, who would maintain a cult of Augustus' *genius* or "vital spark." These *Augustales* thereby enjoyed a public role which their slave origin otherwise denied them. At a higher social level, delegates from each community in a province had the honor of forming a "council"—*koinon* in the Greek East, *concilium* in the Latin West—to celebrate the imperial cult. In legionary barracks, Augustus' image was placed with the standards, and associated with the cult that these received.

RES GESTAE OF AUGUSTUS

Augustus left a personal record of his "achievements" (*res gestae*), which was read out in the senate after his death. He had evidently begun its composition long before, and had thereafter updated it at least partially from time to time. Its format and style recall the autobiographical inscriptions left by earlier great Romans, although Augustus' record is doubtless more extensive than theirs had been. This said, with no more than thirty-five paragraphs, most of them short, it can hardly be considered a lengthy document. It was to be inscribed on bronze pillars at the entrance to his mausoleum in Rome, and copies must also have been set up for public view throughout the empire. The text happens to be known to us only through three such copies, all by chance from communities in Galatia. By far the most complete of them is still to be seen, with a Greek translation, on the walls of a temple dedicated to "Roma et Augustus" at the provincial capital, Ancyra (modern Ankara, Turkey).

Augustus' primary concern in formulating the document was to make a deep, immediate impact on admiring readers or hearers. Despite the relentlessly monotonous presentation in the first person singular, such an audience could only be impressed by so many incomparable achievements and honors, the solemn devotion to duty documented by a stream of remarkable statistics, the bountiful public expenditures (in Rome itself, especially), and the rapid blur of names for individuals, places, peoples, and regions, plenty of them marvelously exotic and unfamiliar. Fittingly enough, the climax of the work is its final paragraph, commemorating the bestowal of the title Pater Patriae, "Father of his Country," upon Augustus by the senate, *equites*, and people in 2 B.C.

Perhaps inevitably, given its traditional nature and purpose, the work does not stand up well to more critical approaches, rewarding though it can prove to attempt them. It is easy to see that the scope and presentation of material are unashamedly selective, in particular, wherever the long period before Augustus became sole ruler is concerned. Consequently, no rival or enemy in those struggles is ever mentioned by name, whether Roman (Brutus, Cassius, Lepidus, Antony) or foreign (Cleopatra); the clashes with Sextus Pompey are merely said to have been with pirates (25.1). Later, too, the defeats eventually suffered in Germany are ignored, so that no modification is made to the claim: "I brought peace to the Gallic and Spanish provinces as well as to Germany, throughout the area bordering on the Ocean from Gades [modern Cádiz] to the mouth of the Elbe River" (26.2). As vital an element to Augustus' control as his possession of *maius imperium* from 23 is never mentioned either; by contrast, he states unequivocally that no one rivaled him in auctoritas (34.3).

An overriding concern of the work is to illustrate the responsibility and restraint with which Augustus faithfully served the Roman people throughout his life. The honors and recognition that he received in return are duly recorded too, along with explicit reminders that—despite his constant responsiveness to senate and people—he declined anything which might seem excessive or untraditional. Extra triumphs he declined, therefore (4.1), as well as dictatorships (5.1), a perpetual consulship (5.3), and usurpation of the office of pontifex maximus (10.2); in short, "I would not accept any office inconsistent with the custom of our ancestors" (6.1). No less vital to the work's purpose is the sense conveyed that Augustus is a leader who acts honorably, spends his own money for the public's benefit, and is devoted to peace. So if his enemies seek pardon, he spares them whenever possible, even in a civil war (3.1–2); under his rule, the temple of Janus is closed with unprecedented frequency (13; traditionally signifying a time when Rome was waging no war); he duly pays for land on which to settle his veterans (16.1), and gives them and others cash from his own pocket (17–18); his good faith encourages more foreign peoples than ever to make offers of friendship with Rome (32.2). Meantime, as the latter part of the work fully demonstrates without any sense of contradiction, Augustus has spared no effort to recover (27.3), expand, and consolidate Roman territory by force of arms: "I extended the territory of all those provinces of the Roman people on whose borders lay peoples not subject to our rule" (26.1). Altogether the clear intention is to reinforce respect, gratitude, and loyalty not merely to the deceased Augustus for his past achievements, but also by extension to his successor for the future.

AUGUSTUS: FINAL ASSESSMENT

Augustus' goal as Princeps was to involve all sections of society and gain their lasting support. In one form or another his name and image were prominent everywhere, even on coins. There remains the ugly fact that a large measure of his success stemmed from the death and destruction he had previously ordered through fourteen years of civil war. After this ordeal—only the latest of several during the previous half-century—everyone was desperate for peace, stability, and reconciliation. Among the politically active upper classes, many of the most energetic were dead, and there was grudging acknowledgment that some form of monarchy was the only practical safeguard against the recurrence of ruinous personal rivalries which, among much else, blocked large-scale social or economic change. The rest of society was indifferent to the loss of whatever political role it had ever had, since this had become increasingly meaningless. Augustus did irk the upper classes with his novel, and repeated, attempts to regulate by law a range of private moral and social matters such as marriage, childbearing, and adultery (see Chapter Seven). On the other hand, the upper classes were gratified by Augustus' studied respect for them, as well as by his continued exclusive reliance on them for commanding the army and administering the empire along traditional lines. Senators and their families were now marked out more distinctively than ever, and equites were offered a role in administration for the first time.

Both Augustus' transformation of the city of Rome and his largely successful desire to expand Roman power by force of arms brought him much popularity. Peace within the empire was counted the greatest blessing, along with the end of any draft for citizens. A "professional" army with a clear focus of loyalty was a development welcomed universally. Welcome, too, were his manifest concern for everyone's welfare, his basic respect for the rule of law, and his reluctance to flaunt supreme authority, let alone exercise it hastily. There is no question that he learned much from the prior experience of Sulla, Pompey, Caesar, Antony, and other leading figures. Gradually he came to appreciate, as they had not, that it was possible for him to retain control *and* at the same time restore the institutions of the Republic along with much of its outlook. Many changes could thus be linked to the past and tradition, and several were represented as an overdue return to neglected past practice. Altogether, by appealing to conservative sentiments which he shared himself, and at the same time instituting a new, personal style of long-term, responsible leadership, Augustus saved and reshaped the Roman world. As he claimed himself, "By new laws passed on my proposal I brought back into use many exemplary practices of our ancestors which were disappearing in our time, and I personally transmitted exemplary practices to posterity for their imitation" (*Res Gestae* 8.4). For him to succeed in this way, rather than by introducing more visible change—as Antony might conceivably have done in his place—was by no means natural or inevitable; but it worked.

By A.D. 14 it was at least clear that Augustus had used his sole power beneficially, whether or not this could ever become sufficient justification for all the blood spilled to gain it. That aside, in his all but sixty years as a public figure, there had been setbacks, failed experiments, and disappointments of all kinds, which he felt keenly to the end. In extreme old age, the major challenges to Roman control in Dalmatia, Pannonia, and Germany, and the huge losses they brought, were painful blows. A source of more prolonged personal sorrow was the gradual extinction of every hope of passing his position to a blood relative, despite successive bright prospects. Nonetheless, the *optimus status* or "best condition" which he forged for the revival of the Roman world was an astonishing achievement, even if it did ultimately value peace and security above freedom. How far his prayers for its endurance would be answered, only time could tell.

SUGGESTED READINGS:

Barrett, Anthony A. 2002. *Livia: First Lady of Imperial Rome.* New Haven and London: Yale University Press.

Campbell, Brian. 2002. *War and Society in Imperial Rome, 31 B.C.–A.D. 284.* London and New York: Routledge.

Earl, Donald. 1968. *The Age of Augustus.* London: Elek Books. A concise, perceptive overview, incorporating an extensive set of superb illustrations.

Favro, Diane. 1996. *The Urban Image of Augustan Rome.* Cambridge: Cambridge University Press.

Galinsky, Karl. 1996. *Augustan Culture.* Princeton: Princeton University Press.

Morton Braund, Susanna. 2002. *Latin Literature.* London and New York: Routledge.

Walker, Susan and Peter Higgs. 2001. *Cleopatra of Egypt: From History to Myth.* Princeton: Princeton University Press.

Wells, Colin. 1992 (second edition). *The Roman Empire.* Cambridge, MA: Harvard University Press. This wide-ranging survey spans the assassination of Julius Caesar to the early third century.

Zanker, Paul. 1988. *The Power of Images in the Age of Augustus.* Ann Arbor: University of Michigan Press.

THE EARLY PRINCIPATE
(A.D. 14–69)

The Julio-Claudians, the Civil War of 68–69, and Life in the Early Empire

SOURCES

Most literary sources for this chapter center on members of the imperial family, now called the Julio-Claudians because of their relation by blood or adoption either to Augustus, who was adopted into the Julian family by Julius Caesar's will, or to Livia, whose sons had been born into the Claudian family (see Chapter Nine). Reading the lively portrayals of political manipulation and human frailty in the biographies of Suetonius, the *Annals* of Tacitus, and Cassius Dio's *History*, it is easy to forget the rest of the Roman world. Tacitus' *Histories*—which begins at Nero's death, covers the civil war of 68–69, and breaks off in 70 while discussing the Germano-Gallic revolt of Civilis (see Chapter Eleven)—similarly tends to focus on Rome's elite. Plutarch wrote biographies of Galba and Otho, two of the contenders in 68–69, and his information largely corresponds with that preserved by Tacitus and Cassius Dio. The latter's history survives primarily in abbreviated or excerpted form after 46; we cannot identify the presumed common source. Taking its lead from our literary sources, therefore, the first part of this chapter offers a chronological account of civil government and military affairs in the early Principate.

Information about wider social history and matters outside of Rome—the subject of the chapter's second half—comes from nonhistorical literature, such as the poems of Ovid (see Chapter Nine). In addition, papyri, coins, and archeological material—including silverwork, tombstones, and historical reliefs, as well as more mundane pottery and glass—provide vivid details overlooked by the authors. Inscriptions supply valuable insights into laws and procedures in Rome and other communities (see Box 10.1, which gives part of the senatorial decree concerning the elder Gnaeus Piso). *Acts of the Apostles* offers a fascinating glimpse into the incipient Christian religion in Judaea and the eastern Mediterranean; Jewish life is reported in the *Jewish Antiquities* and the *Jewish War*, both by Josephus. Philo, a Jewish philosopher from Alexandria, documents Jewish-Greek tensions there, as well as attempts made from Egypt to engage the attention of the Princeps, in this case Gaius. Between them, the surviving materials illustrate many changes throughout the Roman world, including growing prosperity for the political elite in cities.

THE JULIO-CLAUDIAN EMPERORS: CIVIL GOVERNMENT AND MILITARY CONCERNS

The relations between each emperor and his subjects encompassed dealings with the highest orders, that is, senators and *equites*, and with the masses comprising the populace of Rome itself and Roman subjects elsewhere. Julius Caesar's assassination had revealed how dangerous it was for a Roman ruler to shame or humiliate his supposed peers in any way. Augustus had deliberately opted to portray himself as a princeps who was *primus inter pares*, first among equals, rather than as *rex* or *dictator*, thus emphasizing civil rather than military power.

The personal tone of his relationships with individuals had disguised or mitigated his transformation of Rome's institutions; further, the civil upheavals of the end of the Republic had brought many new men into the upper orders. Through Augustus' genius, charm, and diplomacy, not to mention his deceitfulness and bribery, they had been convinced to work with him for the good of the state. Congeniality and accessibility (*comitas*, *civilitas*) were among the imperial virtues. Augustus' immediate successors came from his extended family so that, although the principle was never enunciated, a single dynasty ran the Roman empire from 14 to 68. Yet Augustus' virtues were not genetic. The political difficulties of his successors usually stemmed from neglecting civil consensus and from alienating Rome's traditional political and military elite.

Equally significant for success or failure was the emperor's relationship to the army and Rome's military traditions. The yearly oaths of allegiance to the Princeps and imperial family were by no means the armed forces' only ties to the imperial house. The feast days of deified emperors and empresses—first Augustus; next, ephemerally, Gaius' sister Drusilla; then Livia and Claudius—were holidays for the camps. The emperor was commander-in-chief of all armed forces by virtue of his *maius imperium*. Restriction of the right of a full triumph to him or a member of his family after 19 B.C. underlines his military preeminence. Men outside the imperial house could and did still receive "triumphal ornaments," which included some of the symbols of a triumph, but not the right to enter the city in a triumphal procession. Alternatively, they could be awarded an "ovation," a procession in which the victorious general entered the city on foot or on horseback rather than in a triumphal chariot. But neither of these accolades was as impressive as the traditional triumph.

The state's military traditions meant more than armed men loyal to Rome. As its history amply confirms, the military and imperial growth were two of Republican Rome's key elements. Social, political, and religious rituals, as well as the economy, sustained Rome's militarism at the same time as they depended on it. But the political and social turmoil of the last century of the Republic, as well as the limited technology and communications of the time, brought into question Rome's indefinite expansion. Augustus is said to have advised in his will that Rome be kept within its boundaries. Borders are conceptual rather than real,

Figure 10.1 *"Sword of Tiberius." This silver relief—from a commemorative scabbard found in Germany, and now in the British Museum—depicts a young general in military costume presenting a small, winged statuette of Victory to an emperor, enthroned and represented as Jupiter. A shield inscribed* Felicitas Tiberi *("the Good Fortune of Tiberius") leans against the throne. The gods Mars Ultor and Victory flank the two mortals, and Victory carries a shield inscribed* Vic(toria) Aug(usti) *("the Victory of Augustus"). The scene has been interpreted as Tiberius offering to Augustus a victory that he gained in the Alps in 16–15 B.C., but it is perhaps better to see it as Germanicus offering to Tiberius his German victory of A.D. 14–16/17. In either case, the smaller stature of the general, his deferential gesture, and the iconography of the emperor as Jupiter, all emphasize the primacy of the Princeps as supreme commander-in-chief. The difficulties in identification highlight the similarities marking portrayals of Augustus and the Julio-Claudians.*

however, and the frontier was permeable everywhere, especially in the north and east. Moreover, borders were constantly renegotiated in Rome's vital yet shifting treaties with kings at its edges, most notably with the kingdom of Armenia that separated the Romans and their most organized enemy, the Parthians. The fifty-four years of Julio-Claudian power after Augustus' death witnessed different ways of dealing with the army and with the ideological and practical ramifications of militarism and its renunciation. Military revolts in 14 strikingly underscored the necessity of military support for imperial power. At the end of the Julio-Claudian dynasty, this truth was revealed again by the revolt of Julius Civilis and the wider military dissatisfaction of 68.

TIBERIUS (14–37)

Although at Augustus' death in 14 Tiberius hesitated to don the mantle of ruler, declaring his reluctance and inadequacy before the senate, he immediately assumed control of the Praetorian Guard; it was imperative that someone take this step. His authority as Augustus' heir also stemmed clearly from his tribunician power, his adoption by Augustus, and Augustus' bequest to him of most of his estate as well as the name Augustus. Yet Rome's armies in Pannonia and on the German border saw Augustus' death as an opportunity to mutiny. They clamored for higher pay, more humane treatment, fixed terms of enlistment, and no recalls to service. Tiberius sent his own son Drusus the Younger to Pannonia, and dispatched to Germany his nephew and adopted son Germanicus. The revolts were quelled primarily by capitulation to the soldiers' demands, which were reasonable enough. Among other concessions, legionary service was fixed at twenty years, although it was later restored to twenty-five—a saving to the state, since many fewer men would survive to receive their discharge bonus.

Tiberius had spent much of his adult life away from Rome before becoming Princeps, and he did not have many personal friends in the city. After an auspicious start in public life at Rome itself, he had then spent many years elsewhere on military service. His brilliant exploits during this period (see Map 9.2) have been obscured by the hatred he later aroused among senators, the authors of most Roman histories. In 20 B.C. he had advanced into Armenia in a show of force against the Parthians; in 15–14 he had campaigned in the Alps to secure Raetia and Noricum; from 12 to 9 he had fought insurgent tribes in Illyricum; and from 9 to 7 B.C., as well as again from A.D. 4 to 6, he had led strikes against Germanic tribes. From 6 to 9, he was again in Illyricum to take command during the bloody Dalmatian-Pannonian revolt, which was quelled only by the virtual extirpation of the tribes south of the Dravus River (modern Drava). From 6 B.C. to A.D. 2, however, he had withdrawn to the Aegean island of Rhodes. His eight-year stay there allowed him to deepen philosophical, astrological, and other intellectual interests, and to escape his failed marriage to Julia (see Chapter Nine).

Largely absent from Rome itself, therefore, for the thirty years between his twenties and his fifties, Tiberius had never developed the easy familiarity with his peers that Augustus enjoyed. His personality only aggravated the situation: From all accounts he seems to have been a secretive, even suspicious soul, reticent, introspective, and cautious. He did have some trusted senatorial and equestrian confidants and friends, such as Gaius Sallustius Crispus (related to the historian Sallust), to whom he turned for advice. But he was made uneasy by the blunders that individual senators committed when dealing with him. Unused to Tiberius, and unsure of how far he really wanted to be treated as an equal in his role as Princeps, at times they spoke too familiarly and apparently disrespectfully, while at other times they seemed sycophantic. Tiberius' interactions with senators only worsened as treason (*maiestas*) trials increased during his rule. By this date—although no formal enactment was ever issued—charges of treason could be made on the grounds of conspiracy against the Princeps' life, libel and slander against him, or adultery with a member of the imperial family; those laying successful charges received a portion of the convicted person's estate.

Tiberius' general distrust, combined with his military background, led him to rely on the Praetorian Guard. Between 19 and 23 he built them a huge barracks at the edge of Rome itself (see Map 11.3). This ensured that all future emperors would have a personal bodyguard there, and over the next two centuries these troops did often influence the choice of emperors. Gaius, Claudius, Otho, and Didius Julianus all came to power through their support; Septimius Severus, however, broke their grip in 193. The prominence of these special troops, underscoring the military basis of imperial power, subverted the value of civil consensus and contributed to the difficulties of Tiberius' Principate. By the early 20s, Lucius Aelius Sejanus was sole Praetorian Prefect, and he exploited Tiberius' trust and confidence to advance himself. Treason trials proliferated. In 23, Sejanus may even have masterminded the death of Tiberius' own son, Drusus the Younger. Sejanus' influence increased after Tiberius' move to Capri in 26, since thereafter it was he who controlled communications with the Princeps. Although Sejanus' unscrupulous intrigues finally brought about his own denunciation and execution in 31, Tiberius looked at the individual and not the weakness of the system. The equally dissembling Quintus Sutorius Macro then took over as Praetorian Prefect, restricting access to the Princeps just as closely as had Sejanus.

Despite his early military successes and the construction projects in Rome sponsored by him or in his honor—such as the Porticus of Livia which he and his mother Livia dedicated in 7 B.C.—Tiberius never developed a close relationship with Rome's populace. The popularity once enjoyed by Gaius and Lucius was replaced at the beginning of Tiberius' rule by even more fervent approval for Germanicus, the son of Tiberius' deceased younger brother Drusus. A vivid impression of the public outcry at Germanicus' premature death is offered by a recently discovered senatorial decree concerning the elder Gnaeus Piso (see Box 10.1). As Princeps, Tiberius proved generally apathetic about providing Rome with monuments and amenities; other than the Praetorian barracks, he sponsored only the Temple of the Deified Augustus (which has yet to be located) and a new stage for Pompey's theater. His restraint may have stemmed from fiscal concern, since maintaining the pace of building and other expenditure set by Augustus would have beggared the treasury; even so, the change marked an unwelcome break with Augustan precedent. Tiberius did respond quickly to public calamity, yet he chose not to highlight his generosity; for instance, he is the only Princeps not to assume the honorific title *Pater Patriae*. When twelve cities in Asia were devastated by an earthquake in 17, he remitted taxes and gave other aid, perhaps even sending architects to the province. In 33 he lent 100 million sesterces at low interest to defaulting debtors, and in 37 he spent another 100 million sesterces to rebuild the houses and apartment blocks destroyed by a fire on Rome's Aventine Hill. Yet none of this liberality improved his reputation.

Some of Tiberius' decisions must have seemed harsh, as when a scandal induced him to have priests of Isis crucified, or when he deported 4,000 Jews from Rome to Sardinia (both in 19). We have no way of knowing how Rome's citizens reacted to the transfer of consular and praetorian elections from the Centuriate assembly to the senate in 14. By this time, however, the Roman populace was accustomed to communicating its likes and dislikes at gladiatorial games and other public spectacles in the Forum Romanum and similar public spaces. Augustus had encouraged this behavior by his constant attendance at public gatherings, by the creation of new public spaces such as the Forum Augustum, and by the embellishment of traditional gathering spots like the Forum Romanum and the Saepta Julia (both formerly voting sites). In contrast, Tiberius rarely attended public games, and he had actors expelled from Italy in 23, and the number of gladiators limited. After twelve years as Princeps, in 26 he moved to the island of Capreae (modern Capri) in the Bay of Naples. He never returned to Rome, not even for the public funeral of his mother, Livia, in 29. His absence meant that he had no direct contact with anyone there, and his relationships with both the elite and the populace remained at a low ebb to his death in 37.

Most of Tiberius' energies went to military and administrative matters. In 14, after Germanicus had quelled the uprising of the troops stationed in Germany, Tiberius ordered him to go on the offensive along and beyond the Rhine. These strikes against the Germans from 14 to 16–17 were ostensibly to avenge the great disaster of 9, when the Germans had cut down Varus' three legions in the Teutoburg Forest; but they also suggest Rome's customary use of external war to encourage internal harmony. Germanicus did not succeed in establishing a new border north of the earlier one at the Rhine, and Tiberius recalled him in 16–17. After a great triumph in Rome, he next sent the young general east with maius imperium (but subordinate to his own), since the Parthian king had just expelled the Roman nominee from the throne of Armenia. Amid his dealings with Armenia, the newly organized province of Cappadocia, and the recently annexed territory of Commagene, Germanicus visited famous sights. Egypt was among them, although

Augustus had declared this province off-limits to senators without express imperial permission. Then, in 19, Germanicus sickened mysteriously and died, allegedly poisoned by Gnaeus Calpurnius Piso the Elder, the governor of Syria, who had quarreled repeatedly with him.

To display Rome's military might, Tiberius also turned to his own son Drusus, two years younger than Germanicus, as well as to other men of less renown. It was Drusus the Younger who was dispatched to the rebellious legions in Pannonia in 14. Upon returning to Rome he held a consulship in 15, then from 17 to 20 served in Illyricum, another area of Tiberius' own early successes. The progression of honors that Drusus continued to receive—a triumph when he returned to Rome in 20, a second consulship in 21, and the grant of tribunician power in 22—signify Tiberius' preference for the military in his conception of the Principate. But Drusus' premature death in 23, allegedly by poison at Sejanus' agency, ended his career. Tiberius also relied on men who were not his relatives. He entrusted to

---

BOX 10.1: Senatorial Decree Concerning the Elder Gnaeus Piso

In 20, the year after Germanicus' death, Piso and his associates were tried in the senate. Even though Piso committed suicide before his formal condemnation, the senate still published its final verdict and recommendations. As the inscribed copies of these measures state, it was decided that: "this decree of the senate, inscribed in bronze, be posted in the most frequented city of every province and in the most frequented place of that city; and likewise . . . it should be posted in the winter quarters of each legion near the standards" (lines 170–72). The document is fascinating in many particulars. The one passage reproduced here illuminates the dynamics between Princeps and senate:

Whereas Tiberius Caesar Augustus, son of the deified Augustus . . . referred to the senate for decision: how the case of the elder Gnaeus Piso had seemed, and whether he seemed to have taken his life with due cause, and . . . what the senate's judgment was concerning Visellius Karus and Sempronius Bassus, members of the elder Gnaeus Piso's staff, CONCERNING THESE MATTERS THEY DECREED AS FOLLOWS: THAT the senate and Roman people, before all else, expressed gratitude to the immortal gods because they did not allow the tranquility of the present state of the Republic—than which nothing better can be desired, and which it has fallen to our lot to enjoy by the favor of our Princeps—to be disturbed by the wicked plans of the elder Gnaeus Piso; then to Tiberius Caesar Augustus, their own Princeps, because he made available to the senate everything necessary for seeking out the truth; and THAT the senate admired his fairness and forbearance on this account also, because, although the crimes of the elder Gnaeus Piso are most manifest and Piso himself had exacted punishment from himself, nonetheless he wanted Piso's case to be tried, . . . (lines 4–20, excerpted from the translation by Cynthia Damon in *American Journal of Philology* 120.1 [1999], pp. 15–17).

Marcus Furius Camillus, governor of Africa in 17, the suppression of a chieftain's rising; in 22 renewed disturbances there were tackled by Quintus Junius Blaesus, the uncle of Sejanus. In 21 Gaius Silius and other generals suppressed a rebellion in Gaul. Problems in Thrace in the early 20s were finally resolved by Gaius Poppaeus Sabinus (grandfather of Poppaea, the later wife of Nero), who received triumphal ornaments for his success. Altogether, the number of commanders employed, as well as the readiness with which Tiberius authorized the use of force, demonstrated Rome's military preparedness and the emperor's willingness to associate others with himself in the empire's defense.

Tiberius also monitored the activities of provincial governors closely. Ironically, his habit of extending the tenure of good governors for more than the customary single year may have discredited him at Rome: Some men who had hoped for such a position possibly felt deprived of it by this practice. His death at the age of seventy-seven in 37 was generally welcomed in Rome itself. His standing in the provinces is harder to gauge. As Princeps he neither traveled through the empire nor, after the death of his son Drusus the Younger in 23, did he send family members out of Italy. Though this lack of mobility prudently spared communities the enormous costs of hosting an imperial visit, at the same time it significantly diminished opportunities for provincials to feel a personal link with the Princeps. Yet his rule did generally better the empire. How perceptible such benefits were, however, is hard for us to discern.

GAIUS (CALIGULA) (37–41)

Tiberius' grandnephew and successor Gaius is known by the nickname Caligula given him for the miniature military boots (*caliga*) that he wore as a toddler when he lived in military camps with his parents, Germanicus and Agrippina the Elder. He had a glorious lineage, directly descended from Augustus through his mother and from Livia through his father; he advertised this ancestry when, aged only seventeen, he gave a public funeral oration for his grandmother Livia. But he had a difficult childhood, and suffered severe bouts of epilepsy throughout his life. When he was seven, his father died amidst malicious rumors; as a teenager, he saw the exile and execution of his mother and brothers voted by the senate under apparent pressure from Tiberius. When eighteen he was summoned to Capri, where his companions were an ill-assorted group—his cousin, Tiberius' young grandson Tiberius Gemellus; royal hostages from Rome's bordering states; astrologers; and Tiberius himself, by then in his seventies. Gaius had no familiarity with his peers from the senatorial and equestrian orders, and although he was elected pontifex in 31 and quaestor in 33, he was not permitted to fulfill the duties of either position.

At Tiberius' death the Praetorians' favor for Gaius, rather than for Tiberius' grandson Tiberius Gemellus (made coheir by Tiberius), seemed suspicious to some. But Gaius' arrival in Rome from Capri was celebrated with high hopes, and the senate immediately conferred imperial power on him. After all, he was the son of the wildly popular Germanicus, a connection he paraded. Among his first acts was the rehabilitation of his mother's and brothers' memories and the public burning of their correspondence, with oaths that he had not read any of it. Further, he undertook both to restore senatorial prestige, by granting the senators full authority to make decisions, and to overturn the secrecy of Tiberius' later years, by publishing an imperial budget. Gaius attended races in Rome, and showed himself accessible to the people. He was interested in Italian roads and other utilitarian constructions, and in Rome he began two new aqueducts as well as the Vatican circus (later completed by Nero and famous as the site of St. Peter's martyrdom). The new Princeps' level of activity contrasted favorably with that of Tiberius.

Yet within a year Gaius fell seriously ill, perhaps with a brain fever, and, although he recovered, his erratic behavior escalated. By 38 he executed Tiberius Gemellus and the Praetorian Prefect Macro. By 39 he had quarrelled violently with the senate, and was ruling more and more autocratically. His insults ranged from the political, as when he allegedly planned a consulship for his favorite racehorse Incitatus, to the moral and religious, as when in 38 he had his sister Drusilla deified. He was rumored to have had incestuous relations with her before her death that year; she was the first Roman female to be deified (Livia was only deified later by Claudius). Gaius appeared in public in the dress of various gods, notably that of Castor and Pollux. He had a huge golden statue made of himself, and he evidently wanted a special temple of his own. In Rome he performed as charioteer, gladiator, and singer, pandering to the populace but shocking and insulting senators and *equites*. As part of this showy self-promotion, he even drove a chariot over a bridge of boats from Baiae to Puteoli, resplendent in the breastplate of Alexander the Great.

Yet Gaius also attended to the army and to foreign affairs, though in ways that often appear erratic. He launched small expeditions against Germany and Britain during the winter of 39–40. His other foreign and provincial activities cannot be dated with the same precision, mainly because Suetonius, our major source, shows little concern for matters of chronology. At any rate, in Mauretania Gaius had the king Ptolemy deposed and executed, thus prompting a revolt and Claudius' later annexation of the region as a province. Otherwise Gaius' attention was directed eastward. He dethroned the king of Armenia, triggering problems here that lasted through the rule of Nero. In 38 he restored the territory of Commagene to its king, Antiochus IV, only to depose him later (in 41 Antiochus was reinstated by Claudius and ruled until 72, when Vespasian incorporated Commagene into the province of Syria). Gaius appointed Agrippa I, the grandson of Herod the Great, to rule part of Judaea. For reasons that elude us, he also insisted that his own statue be installed in the Temple in Jerusalem and other synagogues. Although this order was countermanded following his death on January 24, 41, it contributed to the unrest which resulted in the First Jewish Revolt in 66.

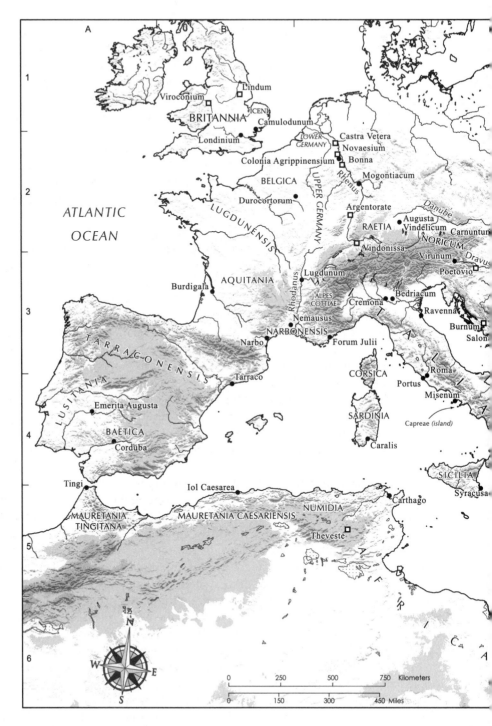

Map 10.1 *Roman Empire in* A.D. *69*

E   F   G

□ Legionary base (normally a single legion)
⊡ Principal settlement with legionary base adjacent

Not all legions' bases are known.

BLACK SEA

...inacium

Danube

Novae

Oescus

MOESIA

Odessus

THRACE

Amastris

BITHYNIA-PONTUS

...EDONIA

Perinthus

Nicomedia

Ancyra

CAPPADOCIA

...lonic...

GALATIA

Caesarea (Mazaca)

COMMAGENE

AEGEAN SEA

Pergamum

ASIA

Claros

Ephesus

CILICIA

Cyrrus

Corinth

LYCIA

Antioch

SYRIA

Euphrates

...ythium

RHODES

Myra

CYPRUS

Raphaneae

Paphos

CRETA

Gortyn

Caesarea

JUDAEA

...UM MARE

Jerusalem

Dead Sea

Cyrene

Alexandria

E   G   Y   P   T

RED SEA

Gaius' megalomania, unpredictability, and religious arrogance alienated many. He could harm even the masses in Rome, as when he shut down the public granaries and let the people go hungry. He traveled only to Gaul and the Rhine regions (in 39–40), in both instances at great cost to local communities. His isolated upbringing and illnesses added to his estrangement from his peers and from many of Rome's traditions. Unsuccessful though it was, the conspiracy in 39 of Gnaeus Cornelius Lentulus Gaetulicus, commander of the troops on the Upper Rhine, suggests the unease of generals and troops alike in the face of such instability. Gaius' deficient military leadership was the root cause of his assassination by members of the Praetorian Guard, whom he had relentlessly humiliated. Few mourned his passing.

CLAUDIUS (41–54)

Gaius' uncle, Claudius, had been born at Lugdunum (modern Lyon, France), as the youngest son of Drusus the Elder and Antonia; he was Livia's grandson and Tiberius' nephew. In his youth he had endured various illnesses, perhaps including cerebral palsy, and he was deaf in one ear as well as lame. Military and political preference had always gone to Germanicus, his older and more charismatic brother. On the other hand, Claudius had a scholar's mind and training, and the historian Livy was one of his tutors. Before becoming Princeps in 41, Claudius had held some high positions, serving as augur under Augustus and as consul with the new emperor Gaius for the latter part of 37. But he had exercised no real power. He had survived the lethal years of Tiberius and Gaius by playing the fool and keeping out of the public eye as much as possible. In a society that valued appearances so highly, Claudius' "deformities" or disabilities discredited him among the elite, and Suetonius (*Claudius* 3–4) preserves some particularly nasty words about him from Livia, Augustus, and even his own mother Antonia. The shame accorded his physical challenges consigned him to the inner rooms of the palace and the company of women and imperial freedmen, most untraditional companions for Roman leaders. This stigma was to disadvantage him throughout his life, as did his lack of ease in addressing his nominal equals.

Claudius' imperial power was due to the Praetorians. Suetonius comically narrates that after Gaius' assassination Claudius hid in the imperial palace, to be accidentally discovered there by a Guardsman who hailed him as Princeps. The senate had already convened in order to "restore the Republic," but as their deliberations dragged on, the people began to demand Claudius as Princeps. Claudius was thus emboldened to let the Guards acclaim him as emperor. Once in power, however, he reduced his reliance on the Praetorian Guard, and loosened its grip by appointing two Praetorian Prefects rather than one. But he had already alienated the senators, and he angered them further when he paid each Praetorian 150 gold pieces (*aurei*).

As princeps, Claudius took his imperial duties seriously, and treated the senate with respect. He consulted it frequently and involved himself actively in military and administrative affairs, even reviving the old Republican office of censor in 47–48. Yet his tone, as it emerges from surviving documents, often appears introverted and almost fussy. He considered it his task as Princeps to take part in

---

BOX 10.2: Claudius' Speech on the Admission of Gauls to the Senate

By a rare chance, we have two versions of a speech that Claudius made in the senate concerning the admission of prominent citizens from the Gallic provinces to that body. The version here is part of the actual speech as he delivered it in 48 during his censorship, which was copied and then "published" on a bronze inscription at Lugdunum (ILS 212). The other surviving version, not reproduced here, is a paraphrase by Tacitus (Annals 11.23.1–25.1). Comparison of the two offers instructive insight into Tacitus' aims and methods as a historian.

. . . Granted, my great-uncle, the deified Augustus, and my uncle, Tiberius Caesar, were following a new practice when they desired that all the flower of the colonies and municipalities everywhere—that is, good, wealthy men—should sit in this senate house. You ask me: Is not an Italian senator preferable to a provincial? I shall reveal to you in detail my views on this matter when I come to obtain approval for this part of my censorship. But I think that not even provincials ought to be excluded, provided they can add distinction to this body. . . .

The time has come, Tiberius Caesar Germanicus [here Claudius addresses himself], now that you have reached the furthest boundaries of Narbonese Gaul, for you to unveil to the members of the senate the direction of your speech.

All these distinguished youths whom I see here will no more give us cause for regret if they become senators than my friend Persicus, a man of most noble ancestry, has cause for regret when he reads on the portraits of his ancestors the name Allobrogicus [an honorific one derived from the Allobroges, a Gallic tribe presumably defeated in battle by an ancestor of Persicus]. But if you agree that this is so, what more do you want, when I point out to you this single fact, that the territory beyond the boundaries of Narbonese Gaul already sends you senators, since we have men in our ranks from Lugdunum and do not regret it ? It is indeed with hesitation, members of the senate, that I have gone beyond the borders of provinces with which you are routinely familiar, but I must now unreservedly plead the case of Gallia Comata [the part of Gaul conquered by Julius Caesar]. In this connection, if anyone observes that these people engaged the deified Julius in war for ten years, let him set against that the unshakable loyalty and obedience of the past hundred years, tested to the full in many of our crises. When my father Drusus was subduing Germany, it was these Gauls who by their passivity afforded him a safe and securely peaceful rear, even at a time when he had been summoned away to war from the task of organizing the census, which was still new and unfamiliar to the Gauls. How difficult such an operation is for us at this precise moment we are learning all too well from experience, even though the sole purpose of the census is to create an official record of our resources.

all sorts of trials. Senators, however, saw this judicial activity as meddling with their prerogatives and dignity, especially because his judgment was liable to prove erratic. When he began to recruit a few wealthy men from the western provinces into the senate, a process that ultimately contributed to imperial Rome's strength, he further estranged senators from Rome and Italy. Despite frequent consultation with the senate, for most advice Claudius relied on imperial freedmen rather equites or senators. His choice is understandable in view of his previous circumstances in the imperial household, but it antagonized Rome's elite, who felt that their power and prestige were being handed to social inferiors.

Claudius also seemed to be susceptible and credulous with women. In 41 he was married to his third wife, Valeria Messalina, a second cousin about thirty years his junior who bore him two children, Octavia and Britannicus. Claudius did not notice or care that she became unfaithful to him. When she conducted a mock marriage in 48 with Gaius Silius, however, her infidelity took on a political dimension: She was descended from Augustus' sister Octavia, and Silius was due to become consul the following year. Yet only with difficulty was Claudius persuaded to denounce her (leading to her suicide). His own niece Agrippina the Younger then schemed successfully to marry him in 49. Within a year she had greater public visibility than any other woman, and received the honorific title Augusta. By 53, she had secured the succession of her own son, Nero, who married Claudius' thirteen-year-old daughter Octavia and superseded the slightly younger Britannicus. Claudius' apparent inability to take charge in his own home only sharpened the resentment felt by many in Rome when he assumed the censorship and conducted public, but characteristically erratic, reviews of individuals' lives.

Claudius was much more active militarily than his two imperial predecessors; rather, he shared Augustus' concern to expand the empire. He temporarily overcame unrest in Judaea by granting local rule to the Jewish king Agrippa I, but he interfered more intrusively with other provinces and adjacent areas. In 43 he directed the invasion of Britain, emulating Julius Caesar's exploits there and going to the island personally for the climax of the campaign. This annexation of Britain was celebrated in various ways: In particular, the honorific name Britannicus was bestowed on the son born to Claudius and Messalina in 41, and a temple to Claudius was begun in the new provincial capital Camulodunum (modern Colchester) in the east of the island. In 43 he annexed Mauretania as a province, and in 46 Thrace. When Agrippa I died in 44, Judaea reverted to the status of an imperial province run by procurators. Claudius even launched exploratory expeditions into Germany in 47. The expansion of Roman power must have seemed inexorable. Claudius received as many as twenty-seven official salutations as *imperator*, underscoring the importance he attached to gaining and maintaining a military reputation.

Claudius unpretentiously enjoyed races, gaming, and dicing, pleasures that he shared with the majority of Rome's inhabitants (see Chapter Eleven). His many celebrations of military achievements brought in booty and created memorable

Figure 10.2 *Claudius subdues Britain. This marble relief was found at Aphrodisias in the province of Asia (modern Geyre, Turkey), a city that took pride in its special relationship with Rome in general and the family of Julius Caesar in particular. The relief is one of a series depicting the Julio-Claudian emperors and embellishing a centrally located sanctuary (sebasteion) of the imperial cult, which was begun in the rule of Tiberius and completed early in that of Nero. Here we see Claudius almost life-size, heroically costumed only in helmet, military cloak, and sword belt, about to strike down the female personification of Britain (his sword and most of his right arm are missing). He pins her down with his right knee, and with his left hand draws back her head, exposing her throat. The island's submission is emphasized by rendering Britannia as a woman, unarmed, and with her right breast exposed. The composition is based on earlier Greek models of the slaying of a female Amazon warrior ("Amazonomachy"), thus transcribing the Roman imperial theme into iconography familiar to a local audience in the province of Asia.*

festivities for the city. He was particularly alert to Rome's grain supply. When a grain shortage incited a mob in the Forum to pelt him with crusts and stale rolls, rather than punishing the rioters, Claudius devised special inducements for merchants to import grain during the winter. His public buildings and renovations tended to be utilitarian, such as the new port for Rome north of Ostia and the new aqueduct Aqua Claudia. Claudius seldom traveled far from Rome, but his constant military activity kept his name before the empire's inhabitants. Even so, his widespread popularity never overcame the resentment felt towards him by senators. His reputation in the literary record is mixed at best, despite his deification at death.

NERO (54–68)

Nero was not yet seventeen when he succeeded Claudius. At his accession in 54 he promised good relations with the senate, equites, and army, and one late source even reports praise of a golden five-year period until 59 (Aurelius Victor, *Caesars* 5). At first, without doubt, Nero did heed his two tutors—Lucius Annaeus Seneca, a brilliant philosopher, author, and senator hailing from Corduba (modern Córdoba, in southern Spain), and Sextus Afranius Burrus, a learned eques

Figure 10.3 *Nero and Agrippina in 54. This gold coin* (aureus) *was struck in the first year of Nero's rule. On the "obverse"—a coin's more important side, seen left—are depicted Nero and his mother Agrippina the Younger, face-to-face and of equal size. This is the first time that anyone had appeared on the obverse of a Roman coin with a current emperor. The surrounding text ("legend") translates: "Agrippina Augusta, wife of the deified Claudius, mother of Nero Caesar." Nero is referred to as the ruling Princeps only on the reverse of the coin, which depicts an oak wreath (symbolizing the protection of citizens), encircled by the words: "To Nero Caesar Augustus, son of the deified Claudius, Germanicus, Imperator, with tribunician power," and within the wreath: "In accordance with a decree of the senate." The image and texts evidently reflect Agrippina's dominant role in the transfer of imperial power to her son, and perhaps also the senate's hopes for a harmonious working relationship with the new Princeps.*

from Narbonese Gaul, who was one of the Praetorian Prefects. Agrippina also tried to exercise power through her young son, but her behavior was more scandalous than seriously detrimental to the empire. Meantime Nero's own interests were in the arts and showmanship rather than in government and the military, and he became more headstrong as he grew older.

In 59 Nero staged the Juvenalia festival marking the official shaving of his beard and whiskers for the first time, and in the same year he had his mother Agrippina killed in an elaborate ruse involving a staged shipwreck. In 62 his unlimited spending, together with protracted military actions in Britain and Armenia, caused him to devalue coinage and to revive the laws of treason. He forced Seneca first into retirement, and then to suicide three years later in 65. In 63 Burrus died, supposedly poisoned on Nero's orders; the Praetorian Prefect who succeeded him, Ofonius Tigellinus, seemed as venal and corrupt as Nero himself. Some senators, such as Publius Clodius Thrasea and Publius Helvidius Priscus, were suspect to Nero simply because they refused to adopt their fellow members' servility towards him, and adhered to Stoic philosophical principles. Other senators and equites actively colluded against him, however. The abortive Pisonian conspiracy of 65, which Tacitus (*Annals* 15.48–74) describes in some detail, united many at different levels of society in common hatred of Nero. By the end of his rule he was boasting openly that he would dispose of the entire senate. In 68, as reports streamed in about revolts in Gaul and Germany, and as Nero vacillated between terror and nonchalance, the senate finally disowned him, declaring him a public enemy or *hostis*. Terrified by the penalty—to be publicly stripped, tied to a stake, and scourged to death—Nero committed suicide.

Even so, his death was generally mourned by the people of Rome, for he was the most popular of the Julio-Claudians. Both as spectator and as performer he loved exhibitions and performances of all kinds. He considered himself a great actor, charioteer, and singer. He followed the Juvenalia of 59 with other extravagant games, including the Neronia of 60. He wrote poetry, and his literary circle at first included Lucan, who won a prize at the Neronia for a poem praising him. As time went on, and particularly after 59, Nero adapted his public image ever more to Rome's masses, and ever less to the senators and equites. His shows and productions often demeaned members of the upper classes by forcing them into ridiculous or humiliating situations in public. He was fickle in his friendships: For example, by 63 or thereabouts he had banned Lucan from reciting his poetry publicly and from speaking in the law courts, perhaps because of the poet's growing popularity.

Similarly, Nero's relationship with the populace in Rome was not always smooth. In 62, they reacted violently against his divorce and murder of Octavia, Claudius' daughter, and they were hostile to his subsequent marriage with Poppaea. He was rumored to have caused the great fire of 64, which damaged eleven of Rome's fourteen regions, because he then appropriated much of the devastated land for his immense Golden House. The scandal persisted even after he proposed

a rational plan for rebuilding the city and let the dispossessed camp in his imperial gardens. When he tried to provide a scapegoat by attacking a new sect, the
Christians, his plan backfired because the horrible tortures inflicted on the
accused provoked widespread sympathy. By 66, however, when he crowned
Tiridates as king of Armenia in Rome, he seems to have regained public favor in
the city.

Outside of Italy Nero's reputation was high in Greece, the sole part of the empire that he visited during his fourteen-year rule. During his tour of the Pan-
hellenic sanctuaries in 66–67, he declared the province of Achaia exempt from
taxes. But public favor in Rome and Achaia did not help him allay the problems
of Judaea, where the First Jewish Revolt broke out in 66. Nor did such popularity
secure Nero support against the generals and governors of the western provinces,
who began to rebel in 67.

There were many causes for the dissatisfaction. Nero was uninterested in military matters and never visited any Roman troops. Despite being served by some
capable commanders, he was unable to solve the provincial and foreign problems
created by Gaius' mismanagement and Claudius' expansionism. Upon accession
in 54 he sent Gnaeus Domitius Corbulo to the client kingdom of Armenia, where
the Parthian monarch had installed his own brother Tiridates as king in place of
Rome's nominee. Corbulo's military successes in the region eventually paved the
way for a diplomatic resolution whereby both sides moderated their stances, but
extensive campaigning by two or more legions had been required, often year-
round and under difficult conditions. Moreover the settlement itself in 66, a visit
to Rome by Tiridates, was an extravagantly expensive affair. The gala at which
Tiridates received his crown from Nero in an opulent public celebration dazzling
with gold was reported to have cost 8,000 *aurei* a day.

Some expansion of the empire occurred uneventfully under Nero when two
former client kingdoms were now annexed. Part of the mountainous area of
southeast Gaul became the small province of Alpes Cottiae around 58, and the
area of Pontus not yet annexed became a province in 64. But such gains were offset by difficulties beyond those in Armenia, not to mention Nero's general indifference to provincial and foreign affairs. Despite Claudius' conquest, Britain was
still far from secure, and Roman rapacity, embezzlement, and cruelty led to a
revolt there in 60. Headed by the queen of the Iceni, Boudicca, and supported by
other native leaders, this rising continued till 67. Much of its impetus came from
the Druids, dynamic female and male priestly leaders, and one of the war's first
casualties was the temple of the Deified Claudius in Camulodunum. The costs of
resecuring the province were high; each side is said to have suffered some 80,000
casualties. Just when this British uprising was ending, in 66 the First Jewish Revolt broke out as the combined result of Roman mismanagement and Judaea's
internal problems. In February 67 Nero sent Titus Flavius Vespasianus to take
command there, a solid military man who had risen from a successful command
in Britain under Claudius to a consulship in 51. Vespasian's unpretentious ances-

try and relative obscurity may have protected him from Nero's paranoia in the later 50s and 60s. No one suspected that such a first-generation senator would use initial victories against the Jews as a springboard to the Principate.

CIVIL WAR IN 68–69

While touring Greece in late 67, Nero summoned to him Corbulo and the two consular commanders of the armies in Upper and Lower Germany; on suspicion of conspiracy, he then compelled all three generals to take their own lives. The same year saw the revolt of Gaius Julius Vindex, governor of Gallia Lugdunensis. Vindex was a senator of Gallic descent, from a family granted Roman citizenship by Julius Caesar. Despite its lack of strength, it was this insurrection that precipitated Nero's downfall and a civil war. Vindex did at least gain the support of Servius Sulpicius Galba, the governor of Hispania Tarraconensis, who promised the single legion under his command. Nero, when recalled back to Rome from Greece, did nothing to address the growing crisis, and by the time Vindex's modest force was defeated in Gaul, the senate declared Nero a public enemy. In his place, it recognized as Princeps the seventy-one-year-old Galba, who came from a most distinguished patrician family and had been favored by Livia, Augustus, Gaius, and Claudius. Nero committed suicide on June 9, 68 in a villa on Rome's outskirts. The Julio-Claudian dynasty ended with him.

The civil war that filled the next eighteen months was particularly devastating both for northern Italy, through which various rival armies passed on their way to Rome, and for Rome itself, the traditional seat of power. Yet, as Tacitus remarked (*Histories* 1.4), the events of the period revealed "the secret of the empire . . . emperors could be made elsewhere than at Rome." In principle, Nero's maladministration and military indifference had opened the way for any commander with willing troops to bid for the imperial power. Two of the four contenders in 68–69 were originally declared emperor by forces outside of Rome—Vitellius, who was supported by eight legions on the Rhine, and Vespasian. Otho, a third contender, was declared emperor by Praetorian Guardsmen in Rome itself. Galba stressed that he had been acclaimed by the senate and people, but his quick downfall at Otho's hands emphasizes the predominance of the military. Yet even military support might not prove sufficient for a general to retain power once in Rome; at that point, maintaining authority depended upon securing the active goodwill of society as a whole.

Accompanied by Otho, Galba slowly made his way to Rome by October 68, but there he openly alienated a significant part of the army and failed to win the favor of the Praetorians or the populace. While still on the outskirts of the city he massacred as many as 7,000 men he thought loyal to Nero, unsettling all the troops in the city. He refused to pay a donative to the Praetorians, who had deserted Nero for him on their Prefect's promise of a lavish 30,000 sesterces to each man.

Perhaps also in misguided anxiety about money, Galba suspended public games. Worst of all, he did not placate the troops on the Rhine, who felt insufficiently rewarded for their suppression of Vindex's revolt. So on January 1, 69, the four legions of Upper Germany took the oath of allegiance in the name of the senate only, omitting Galba's name. The next day, at the urging of the legionary commanders Aulus Caecina and Fabius Valens, the four legions in Lower Germany declared their new general, Aulus Vitellius, as emperor, and were then seconded by the four legions in Upper Germany. Although Vitellius was inexperienced in military and civil positions, his father had acquired great fame and influence in faithful service to the Julio-Claudians.

Galba was by now attempting to strengthen support for himself by adopting a successor. He again misstepped, however, since his choice was the relatively unknown aristocrat Lucius Calpurnius Piso Frugi Licinianus, rather than the more popular Marcus Salvius Otho, who had already rendered him valuable service. Otho's reaction was to seek the Praetorians' backing for himself through bribes and promises. This he quickly achieved, so that on January 15, 69 both Galba and Piso were slaughtered in the Roman Forum in full sight of the populace. Cowed by the Praetorians, senate and people then declared Otho emperor.

As news of these developments at Rome spread, neither Vitellius nor the troops elsewhere were satisfied. Caecina and Valens had meanwhile been leading Vitellius' forces to Rome. Vitellius himself followed more slowly, indulging in banquets and games (he is said to have squandered nine hundred million sesterces on dinners alone during his brief rule). In April, the armies of Otho and Vitellius clashed decisively in northern Italy, first at Cremona, where casualties were reckoned to number 40,000 on each side, and then at Bedriacum, where Otho committed suicide. Vitellius was now the first Princeps since Tiberius to gain power without the immediate support of the Praetorian Guard. Once in Rome, however, he seemed incapable of making political or military decisions.

On July 1, 69 the troops in Judaea declared their general Vespasian emperor, seconded by the Syrian legions led by Gaius Licinius Mucianus. Vespasian also won the allegiance of Tiberius Julius Alexander, Prefect of Egypt. Since the latter controlled not only two legions but also the ample Egyptian grain supply destined for both the capital and Roman troops in the East, Vespasian's position was extremely strong. The threat of famine in Rome, outrage at the conduct of Vitellius' troops, revulsion at Vitellius' personal excesses and inability to rule, and news of Mucianus' approach, all bolstered support for Vespasian. The troops in Pannonia declared for him and, led by their commander Marcus Antonius Primus, marched to Italy. In October, they defeated Vitellius' forces in a second battle at Cremona; the unfortunate city was then sacked although it had taken neither side. By December Primus' men stormed Rome itself. Vitellius was killed in the fierce fighting that destroyed many sectors of the city, including the temple of Jupiter Optimus Maximus. Senate and people declared Vespasian emperor, and order was restored upon the arrival of Mucianus a few weeks later. Vespasian himself entered Rome only the following October (70). In the meantime, Mucianus took charge of the city, aided by Vespasian's younger son Domitian, who had survived by hiding and disguising himself as a follower of Isis.

In these eighteen terrible months of 68–69 Roman troops had repeatedly marched on Rome. The civil war destroyed everything in its path, was ruinously expensive, and diverted attention and manpower from more strategic points, particularly in the East. This catastrophe revealed the disunity of the empire in general, and the troops in particular. Much of Gaul had rebelled against Italy; the armies in Germany, and then those in the East, had threatened Rome; and each side had attacked the other. Who was at the center: the senate, Praetorians, or Roman people? The senate had some authority: When it had declared Nero a public enemy and named Galba emperor, Nero had killed himself in despair. On the other hand, Galba's failure to win support among Rome's populace and the Praetorians undermined the senate's decision. Otho's elevation once again underscores the power of the Praetorians in Rome. Yet this elite corps proved to be no match against more numerous troops from elsewhere. The eastern legions' declaration for Vespasian less than three months later, however, highlights the importance of the officers heading the various forces. Of the four contenders of 68–69, only Vespasian proved himself enduringly capable once in power, and his bid to gain it was the best prepared.

This turmoil made it clearer than ever that the dynastic principle instituted by Augustus was unable to guarantee the best ruler for the Roman world. His unique coordination of charismatic *auctoritas*, responsible vision, and military loyalty was simply not one that could be passed down by blood or adoption. Even so, Romans' ingrained respect for family, the slow pace of change, the widespread sense of obligation to the Julio-Claudians, and the benefits bestowed by Tiberius and Claudius, together enabled Augustus' extended family to continue his rule for just over half a century. Meantime the coincidence of minimal civil strife and no pressing external threats was a rare blessing for the empire.

ECONOMIC AND SOCIAL CHANGE

Archeological and documentary evidence confirms that the Julio-Claudians' continuation of Augustus' Principate is associated with profound changes for the empire. Augustus' dynastic principle precluded large-scale, destructive struggles for power on a ruler's death, and enabled peace to extend across the Mediterranean and over the areas under Roman control. This general peace had various components and effects. One could denounce Augustus as a military despot, but still the concentration of power into his hands had allowed him to demobilize the huge armies of the Triumviral period. After the loss of three legions in Germany in 9, the army was maintained more or less steadily at about 150,000 legionaries and an equal number of auxiliaries. These land-based forces were supplemented by marines in naval squadrons stationed at Misenum on the Bay of Naples, Ravenna, Forum Julii (modern Fréjus, France), and other ports to curb piracy and aid military communication.

ARMY

Although it was expensive to pay the armed forces and to offer the discharge bounties instituted by Augustus (see Chapter Nine), these expenses could be foreseen and budgeted for; in the first century legionary pay was 900 sesterces annually, and auxiliary pay no doubt less, although perhaps not by much. The general peace of the period possibly freed up some funds allocated for equipment and materials. Peace may also have allowed both legions and auxiliary units to be slightly undermanned, further cutting costs. In addition, the growing tendency to recruit soldiers, especially auxiliaries, from the areas in which they were stationed must have reduced movement costs. Most of the Julio-Claudian emperors' military activity took place along the frontiers, so that civilians elsewhere were now largely freed from armies marching through their territory and requisitioning supplies.

The simple fact of creating a standing, state-funded army, with its requirements of steady pay and supplies, encouraged the monetarization of the Roman state, the production of surplus goods, and trade. Imperial mints were established in Rome and Lugdunum, striking gold, silver, bronze, copper, and other alloy coins (*aurei, denarii, sestertii, dupondii*, etc.). Local coinage in nonprecious metals continued to be minted, in the West until Claudius' time, and in the East right up to that of Diocletian in the late third century. Important as this coinage is for the insight it provides into individual cities, it was only used for local, low-level exchanges, and not for larger, empire-wide transactions. The establishment of the imperial army helped break down barriers created by Rome's hitherto pervasive subsistence farming economy. To be sure, an agrarian economy still continued to characterize the Roman world; but a commodity economy also grew up. Towns, military camps, and other centers all needed and wanted finished products like shoes and boots, lamps and other pottery, glassware, cloaks, and other manufactured goods. This demand encouraged some economic mobility, and with it social and political change.

The "imperial peace," *pax Augusta*, was due not only to the cessation of internal strife, but also to the general absence of external conflict. Difficulties with Parthia over Armenia were mostly confined to a local level until Nero's Principate, although enduring Roman distrust is demonstrated by the permanent presence of four legions in Syria. Persistent stereotyping of the Germanic tribes and Trans-danubian groups as pitiless, lawless barbarians helped justify a buildup of troops along the Rhine and Danube rivers. Border skirmishes and Roman incursions across the Rhine continued even after the Teutoburg disaster in 9 (see Chapter

Nine). More concerted efforts came in 15–17 under Germanicus, fruitlessly in 39–40 under Gaius, and in 47 under Claudius. In the Julio-Claudian period, thirteen of Rome's twenty-five legions were stationed in the provinces along the Rhine and Danube. Gallia Belgica's two regions along the Rhine, Lower and Upper Germany (each with four legions), were under military legates of consular rank; Raetia, Noricum, Pannonia, and Moesia held the other troops. Three legions were in Spain, whose northwest region had been pacified only under Augustus; one was in Africa. The approximately 300,000 armed men along the empire's borders and elsewhere changed the economic, social, religious, cultural, and political lives of the areas they occupied, although Roman military groups could and often did also act as societies unto themselves.

ECONOMY

The general halt to expansion after the Teutoburg disaster in 9 altered Rome's economy by precluding new sources of income. Perhaps this limitation may account for the financial crisis of 33, an issue of liquidity that we hear about elliptically in Tacitus, Suetonius, and Cassius Dio. Possibly in an attempt to encourage cultivation in Italy, it was decreed that individual senators should invest two-thirds of their wealth in land there. But they were unable to comply, because when they called in the money owed them in order to purchase Italian land, their creditors did not have it. Banks, as we know them, did not exist; rather, wealth had been loaned by individuals to other individuals, and perhaps to associations, with no guarantees. To resolve the resulting panic and crisis, Tiberius made a loan of one hundred million sesterces free of interest for three years. Our understanding of the crisis is hampered because—like many other aspects of the Roman economy—the ancient authors present it to illuminate the moral qualities and political dynamics of individuals. For example, Cassius Dio (58.21.4–5) writes:

> About this time, however, a certain Vibullius Agrippa, an *eques*, swallowed poison from a ring and died in the senate-house itself. Nerva [not the later emperor], who could no longer endure any contact with the emperor, starved himself to death, chiefly because Tiberius had reaffirmed the laws on contracts enacted by Julius Caesar, which were sure to result in great loss of confidence and financial confusion; even though Tiberius repeatedly urged him to eat something, he declined to make any response. Tiberius then modified his decision regarding loans and gave one hundred million sesterces to the treasury, with instructions that senators should lend this money for three years without interest to those who needed it. He also ordered that the most disreputable of those who were bringing accusations against others should all be put to death on a single day.

Although the treasury had a surplus of thirty-seven million sesterces at Tiberius' death, almost all this sum was used up in the four years of Gaius' Principate. Some new resources were gained through Claudius' expansion of the empire, but not so

although never to a particularly high level. It is estimated that only between 150 and 350 elite officials oversaw the civilian government in the first century A.D., at most one for every three hundred and fifty to four hundred thousand subjects. Equestrian administrative positions were paid at fixed levels from Augustus' time. The equestrian and senatorial orders had great prestige, although more respect traditionally went to senators. Tacitus (*Annals* 16.17) recounts as a sign of Neronian "perversity" that Seneca's brother Lucius Annaeus Mela chose to remain an eques rather than enter the senate. Mela allegedly believed that he could enrich himself more easily as an eques in the emperor's service, and thereby match the authority of ex-consuls. The imperial freedmen who rose to prominence and extraordinary wealth under Claudius and Nero became the targets of far blunter snobbery. Ability and culture were the prerequisites to success, but even these talents could rarely overcome the stigma of a slave or freedman past. In any case, the political elite of Rome, whatever their origin, made up only a minuscule fraction of the empire's population.

CITIES AND PROVINCES

As established by Augustus, the empire relied not on bureaucracy imposed by the central government, but on communities' self-administration. Throughout Italy and the provinces, local magistrates and councilors were responsible for the collection of taxes, census registration, supply of men for the army when volunteers were lacking, provision of hospitality and transport animals for travelers on official business, and shelter, equipment, and supplies for any military units passing through. Such obligations to the central government coexisted with a high degree of local autonomy. As a general rule, individual cities were left to oversee their own public buildings and cults, the maintenance of their water supply and baths, local law and order, and embassies to Roman officials, including to the Princeps himself.

The empire, which encompassed perhaps fifty to sixty million inhabitants during the first and early second centuries, depended on cities. Achaia, Asia, Crete and Cyrenaica, southern Gaul, and eastern and southern Spain had long been urbanized along their coasts and waterways. Other provinces had different forms of social and political organization. In the interior of Gaul and the Iberian peninsula, for example, warrior elites commanded tribal groups, usually either nomadic or scattered in farmsteads and villages. Between them, Julius Caesar and Augustus established some seventy-five veteran settlements in the provinces, and over forty in Italy. They were located primarily in north Italy, southern Spain, north Africa, coastal Illyricum and Greece, and southern Turkey. In Italy they often supplanted communities that had been on the losing side during the Triumviral period; elsewhere, too, they could be just as disruptive to the local inhabitants. In addition, stationing troops on the borders of the empire encouraged the development of towns there, as well as along the roads leading there.

The new foundations and centers, like older cities in the Roman world, consisted of an urban nucleus and dependent agricultural land. The urban centers were quite small by modern standards. Most had a maximum of only five to fifteen thousand inhabitants, comprising local citizens (including freedmen and freedwomen) and their "families" (including slaves); nonlocal citizens, such as traders; and public slaves and other dependent labor. It was essential that cities govern themselves by some version of the tripartite system traditional to Rome: magistrates, advisory council, and citizen body. Even during the Republic (and sometimes with Rome's direct influence), municipal governments associated with Rome tended towards timocracy, in particular requiring magistrates to possess a certain level of wealth. This trend increased during the Principate. The common basis of landed wealth strengthened the bonds between municipal elite and Roman officials. Yet the urban conglomerations themselves offered various possibilities for financial gain and prestige. In cities, the imperial peace encouraged at least limited social mobility. Freedmen and freedwomen could engage in small businesses and gain some wealth and respectability for their children; as we saw in Chapter Nine, freedmen even could hold a priesthood as *Augustales* (note Figure 10.7 for one such individual). Descendants of former slaves often gained municipal offices and other priesthoods, sometimes even within a generation.

The growing number of cities in the Roman world was made possible not only by peace, but also by the Roman engineering responsible for urban amenities such as a forum, aqueducts, fountains, streets and sidewalks, temples, baths, spectacle buildings like theaters and amphitheaters, and multistoried dwellings. Some of these structures were built when new cities were founded; Agrippa, for example, sponsored the famous Pont du Gard and the entire long aqueduct carrying fresh water to Colonia Augusta Nemausus (modern Nîmes, France; see Figure 11.9). However, our vision of the "typical" Roman city took time to evolve in the provinces (see Chapter Eleven). The urban model was Rome itself, upon which Caesar, Augustus, and many subsequent emperors lavished attention. Although by the early third century the empire had attained a degree of urbanization not to be matched again in the West until the nineteenth century, the limitations of its preindustrial technology and science meant that many areas still remained scarcely urbanized. Cities were mostly found along coasts, rivers, and major inland routes. Inaccessible hinterlands were more desolate, and were normally left undisturbed so long as their few inhabitants did not cause problems.

One major type of imperial benefaction initiated by Augustus and resumed by Claudius was the building and maintenance of roads and harbors. Generally speaking, land transport cost at least five times more than water transport, and bulky commodities such as grain, timber, and fine stone were only conveyed long distances for the army or for the city of Rome itself. Yet archeology increasingly documents long-distance trade for luxury and semi-luxury goods too. The technologies essential to blown glass and to highly polished, molded ceramic bowls, lamps, and other pottery objects had been invented by the end of the Republic. In

Despite an increasing similarity of material culture, the empire still retained great diversity. Many different languages were spoken in the various provinces, even though Latin dominated in the army and official correspondence. In the Greek East—the region where already for centuries the common language of educated people had been Greek—Roman administrative correspondence was written in Greek. Instances of parallel texts in Greek and Latin, especially for records of important decisions, are numerous too. We also find bilingual texts apparently aimed at two different audiences.

Even so, indigenous languages and dialects persisted alongside these official languages for a variety of reasons—communities' autonomy in local affairs, the

Figure 10.6 *Bilingual funerary inscription. This modest marble inscription comes from Odessus in the province of Lower Moesia (modern Varna, Bulgaria). It probably dates to the second half of the second century A.D. The top four lines are in Latin, recording Malius Secundus' installation of the tomb for the departed shades and memory of his "most rare" wife, Antistia Firmina. Malius also specifies here that he is a special attendant on a man of consular standing. The bottom four lines, in Greek, state the financial penalties payable to the treasurer and people of Odessus by anyone who should have the temerity to place another body in the tomb. The use of Greek for this warning implies that the local population, on the west coast of the Black Sea, was more familiar with Greek than Latin. However, with his status as the holder of a desirable military position, Malius uses Latin to impress others like him with his control of resources and his assimilation of Roman ways.*

large number of static rural dwellers on their subsistence farms, the relatively low level of bureaucracy, the uneven spread of the military, and the absence of extensive mass communications. For similar reasons, local cultures remained dynamic, and still maintained a hold even when Roman material culture spread to a region. Our understanding of regional and cultural diversities within the empire has notably increased over the last generation, as archeological research and tools have become more sophisticated and sensitive. For instance, faunal bone analysis at excavations in Hungary has revealed the persistence of local diets even after Roman legionary camps were established in Pannonia.

RELIGIOUS PRACTICES AND PRINCIPLES

Rome's diversity, and its limits, are perhaps reflected most strikingly in the wide array of religious beliefs and practices of the polytheistic empire. Such an array reflects an empire gained by military conquest (primarily during the Republic), yet then consolidated and for the most part ruled by the cooption and collaboration of its indigenous peoples during the Principate. Thus the traditional Egyptian zoomorphic gods later decried by Christians as "dog-headed" could be, and were, worshipped with their traditional rites even after Egypt was annexed as a Roman province in 30 B.C. In Gaul, various powerful female deities, often called "mothers," were venerated alongside other gods less alien to the Romans, such as Jupiter sky gods. Silvanus, a god of the woodlands, was worshipped in the heavily forested areas of the northern empire. In Achaia and Asia the customary Olympian gods received dedications and temples, some even from Roman emperors. The famed oracle of Apollo at Claros (Asia) figured among the sites that Germanicus toured, and later in the first century oracles revived powerfully, continuing to thrive into the third century. Hero cults revived too, like that of Achilles on the shores of the Black Sea. The ancestral gods of the hearth were venerated in Italy, and deities without images received worship in the interior of Asia.

Since many monuments were erected to recognize the fulfillment of prayers, the formulaic nature of many of the religious sentiments preserved in literature, inscriptions, and other documents is liable to strike us as calculating. Also conspicuous are the apparent ease with which many individuals participated in disparate religious practices, and the wide range of religious dedications, even within a single town or sanctuary. This latter phenomenon was aided by what Romans termed *interpretatio*, the assertion of some form of equivalence between a foreign deity and a Roman one (as with Mars Belena). Romans and their subjects could believe as they pleased, so long as they did not actively reject religious rituals that had been made part of the state religion. In some instances syncretism occurred, as when a local deity or abstraction had "Augustan" added to its name.

In general, no belief was forced on citizens or subjects. Instead, Rome often accepted a foreign deity and rites even after recognizing its distinctive alien

on revelation (Christ was revealed as God, and the scriptures were revealed to the faithful); initiation at baptism and subsequent stages; and a belief in salvation and the afterlife. The Epistles of Paul and the Gospel of Mark were probably written between 50 and 70, and by 130 the other scriptures were completed. The roughly contemporary Dead Sea Scrolls and Book of Revelation similarly manifest the religious ferment of Judaea and the Greek East. Christianity spread in cities before the countryside, as indicated by the name "pagan" used for non-Christians (*paganus* denotes someone from the countryside). But we should always bear in mind that during the early Principate Christianity was merely one of what may now seem a bewildering number of religions.

IMPERIAL CULT

Christianity, Judaism, and a few other monotheistic religions aside, the imperial cult cut across all the varied beliefs and practices. This religious and societal phenomenon provided one of the strongest unifying forces for the diverse Roman empire. Imperial cult could be practiced on the personal level: Ovid in exile (*Letters from Pontus* 4.9) claims to have offered incense and prayers daily at a "shrine of Caesar" in his house. This shrine included images of Augustus, Livia (now priestess of the deified Augustus), Tiberius, and other imperial family members. Since the cult was principally public, however, there is much fuller evidence for it at the municipal and provincial levels and at Rome itself.

Roman imperial cult evolved from Hellenistic Greek and Republican Roman precedents and, like them, it was intrinsically tied to military and political power. Beginning with Alexander the Great, dominant kings (and later their queens) had commanded cults with temples or altars, priests, public sacrifices, and games—visible signs, in short, of their unmistakable power over their subjects. Rituals were enacted periodically at the cities where the shrines stood (see Chapter Four). As Rome became involved in the Greek East from the end of the third century B.C., certain Roman generals received extraordinary, quasi-divine honors there to mark their popularity or military success. In the West, too, leading figures could find it advantageous to exploit divine associations: Marius had sought guidance from a Syrian prophetess, Martha, and Sertorius gained inspiration from a white doe (see Chapter Seven). In Rome itself great charisma accrued to triumphing generals, who were dressed like the Capitoline statue of Jupiter Optimus Maximus as they paraded through Rome on a chariot pulled by four white horses. During the last century of the Republic, the senators responsible for minting increasingly featured heroic ancestors in the designs for their coins (see Figure 6.1). Julius Caesar advanced his claim to be descended from the goddess Venus both on coins and by building a temple to her in his new Forum in Rome. In what was to be the last year of his life, Caesar even had a temple for himself authorized by the senate, and Antony appointed as his priest (although these measures were never implemented). Later, the people of Rome spontaneously established a shrine where Caesar's body had been cremated in the Forum; the appearance of a meteor shortly thereafter reinforced the belief that he had ascended to heaven. The authority of the Triumvirs, and of Octavian in particular, was boosted when the senate eventually ratified Caesar's deification early in 42 B.C.

Designation as "son of a god" (*divi filius*) was only one of many divine associations that Octavian assumed over time, despite discouraging any cult that seemed too closely tied to his own person (see Chapter Nine). His position as *pontifex maximus* after 12 B.C. placed him as intermediary between the Roman people and the gods. Thereafter each Princeps until Gratian in the late fourth century took this leading priesthood on accession. The divinity that the senate ratified for Augustus after his death was only one of many such posthumous honors. These tributes, as well as an apparently more personalized cult, spread rapidly. In 15 the province of Tarraconensis successfully sought permission to establish a temple and *flamen* (priest devoted to a specific deity) to Divus Augustus in Tarraco (modern Tarragona, Spain). Although the senate had to give its permission, the emperor was also consulted—as demonstrated by a letter from Tiberius to Gythium in southern Greece concerning its measures honoring the deified Augustus, Tiberius himself, and his mother Livia. Even so, at this early date it was evidently the senate's permission that was essential before a city or provincial assembly could add imperial cult rituals to its public religious ceremonies. These rituals involved the apotheosis of dead emperors and veneration of the living one, specifically prayers for his preservation.

The imperial cult spread after Augustus. Although Tiberius steadfastly refused the organization of any cults to himself and was not deified after his death, Gaius assiduously pursued religious associations, as noted earlier in this chapter. Claudius promoted Livia's deification by the senate; he, too, was deified. Later the emperor Vespasian was to quip on his death bed, "Dear me! I must be turning into a god!" (Suetonius, *Vespasian* 23) Activities identified with the imperial cult will be discussed in the following chapter. Here, however, it is important to stress Rome's incipient imperial cult as an expression of the ambiguous relationship between the Princeps and his subjects. Individual cities and provincial assemblies voluntarily petitioned for permission to profess, through public rituals, their homage to the living emperor. Especially in its early stages, the cult often matched the emperor with Rome itself, whose personification as a female warrior underscores the military basis of the empire. As "good" emperors and members of their family were deified at their deaths, their veneration too was included in a community's rituals. Gold and silver images of them were added to the processions, for example, and animals were sacrificed on their behalf as *divi*. When the senate authorized a community's establishment of an imperial cult, it ostensibly claimed its customary role in power negotiations. At the same time, however, members of the senate were demonstrating their compliance with the extraordinary and superhuman domination of Augustus and his successors.

SUGGESTED READINGS:

Barrett, Anthony A. *Caligula: The Corruption of Power*. 1990. New Haven and London: Yale University Press.

Barrett, Anthony A. 1996. *Agrippina: Sex, Power, and Politics in the Early Empire*. New Haven and London: Yale University Press.

Beard, Mary, John North, and Simon Price. 1998. *Religions of Rome*. Vol. I, *A History*; Vol. II, *A Sourcebook*. Cambridge: Cambridge University Press.

Campbell, Brian. 1994. *The Roman Army, 31 B.C.–A.D. 337. A Sourcebook*. London and New York: Routledge.

Greene, Kevin. 1986. *The Archaeology of the Roman Economy*. Berkeley, Los Angeles, London: University of California Press.

Harl, Kenneth W. 1996. *Coinage in the Roman Economy, 300 B.C. to A.D. 700*. Baltimore: Johns Hopkins University Press.

Humphrey, John W., John P. Oleson, and Andrew N. Sherwood, *Greek and Roman Technology: A Sourcebook*. 1998. London and New York: Routledge.

Lefkowitz, Mary R., and Maureen B. Fant, (eds.). 1992 (second edition). *Women's Life in Greece and Rome*. Baltimore: Johns Hopkins University Press.

Levick, Barbara. *Tiberius the Politician*. 1999 (new edition). London and New York: Routledge.

Levick, Barbara. *Claudius*. 1990. New Haven and London: Yale University Press.

Price, Simon R.F. 1984. *Rituals and Power: the Roman Imperial Cult in Asia Minor*. Cambridge: Cambridge University Press. Despite its focus on Asia Minor, this book is of wider significance for understanding the imperial cult.

INSTITUTIONALIZATION
OF THE PRINCIPATE

*Military Expansion and Its Limits,
the Empire and the Provinces (69–138)*

SOURCES

Although we lack a continuous historical narrative for this period (Cassius Dio exists only in excerpts after 46), many authors provide extended analysis of individual aspects. Suetonius' imperial biographies continue through the death of Domitian. Pliny the Younger, Suetonius' contemporary and friend, offers many details about the lives of senators and *equites* in his ten books of letters. Moreover, his tenth book—correspondence he exchanged with Trajan while serving as a special imperial legate in the province of Bithynia-Pontus around 111—offers invaluable insights into provincial administration, relationships between emperor and official, and the province itself. Josephus' *Jewish War* has special significance because the author, a prominent Jew, was personally involved: He led his fellow countrymen against the Romans before defecting to the Roman side and ultimately receiving Roman citizenship from Vespasian. Pausanias, Plutarch, and lesser known writers reveal the concerns of Rome's intelligentsia in both Latin West and Greek East over such matters as ethics and philosophy, image and standing in one's own city, and the proper relationship with Roman power. Rome itself still dominates in literature, in contrast to the subsequent period when authors such as Apuleius and Tertullian focus more on local problems and politics.

The first part of the chapter weaves together military and civil topics, looking specifically at military expansion and its limits, and at the relationship of the central government to the provinces. Our understanding of social and cultural history, the subject of the second part of the chapter, is advanced by documentary and material evidence. The era's relatively abundant inscriptions give us a fuller picture of individuals' lives, careers, hopes, and aspirations. Public inscriptions illustrate the nature of imperial power and local governance. From the latter half of the first century and from the second come astonishing archeological finds, such as those at Pompeii and other Campanian sites buried by the eruption of the volcano Vesuvius in 79. The assembled data reveal growing urbanization through the early third century. This development seems tied to the "beneficial ideology" of the Principate, which held that the emperor both demonstrated his aptitude for the position and justified his *auctoritas* through his generosity (see Chapter Ten). In the later first and second century, such benefits often went to cities other than Rome itself. It is striking that the benefactions by Hadrian listed at a shrine in Athens are gifts of all types (temples especially) to non-Roman cities (Pausanias 1.5.5).

Other evidence for increased attention to Rome's provinces comes in ever more frequent imperial grants of the city status of *municipium* and *colonia*, and in military attention to peripheral regions such as the Danube lands. Both steps spurred the growth of cities. Yet they and more well-established ones could flourish only with surplus wealth dependent on Roman peace and the conquests of Trajan. Peace made possible the preoccupation with local priorities such as civic rivalry (often tied to the imperial cult), the exaltation of a glorious past in the Second Sophistic, and other cultural activities. These features were particularly notable in North Africa and the Greek East. But the picture should not be construed too positively, for as the Principate became more institutionalized it also took some steps towards autocracy. The delicate balance between beneficial paternalism and harmful interference surfaces in this chapter, and will emerge more clearly thereafter.

INSTITUTIONALIZATION OF THE PRINCIPATE

One of the earliest and starkest signs of the Principate's institutionalization is the law now called the *lex de imperio Vespasiani*, passed some time in 69–70. A substantial part of it—specifying various powers and rights of the emperor—survives on a bronze inscription now in Rome's Capitoline Museum. Ratified by the Roman people upon presentation by the senate, this law indicates the continuing significance both of popular support for the Princeps and of concern for Rome's governmental processes. Yet it also makes clear that the emperor's authority was no longer a nebulous auctoritas centered on the individual himself (as with Augustus) or on family loyalty (as with the Julio-Claudians). Rather, the document clearly defines various powers and prerogatives, justifying them by specific imperial precedent. Here we may note both Romans' respect for their past and their pragmatism: This law made custom binding. From now onwards, when the senate and people of Rome ratified the choice of a Princeps, not only was an individual being approved, but also the powers that he could legally wield. The lex de imperio Vespasiani seems to have been passed before Vespasian actually arrived in Rome in October 70. That sequence contrasts with the timing of earlier

Figure 11.1 *This relief, and a counterpart (not shown), once decorated an altar base and are known as the "Cancelleria reliefs" from their find spot in Rome; they are now in the Vatican Museum. Here we see Vespasian's arrival in Rome in 70; he is the first full figure on our right. With his right hand he touches his son, Domitian, who had been in Rome during the civil strife of the previous year. Behind and flanking Domitian stand two personifications, the "genius" of the senate (a mature, bearded man) and the "genius" of the Roman people (a youth with a cornucopia). Secular power is symbolized by the leftmost figure seen here, a lictor with fasces, the bundle of rods signifying the power of the magistrate he accompanies. Further to our left (but not shown here) stand the goddess Roma, personified as a female warrior with her right breast bared like an Amazon's, and a Vestal virgin. Domitian's central position in this scene, which commemorates Rome's unanimous welcome of the Flavians, is one reason why the reliefs are dated to the 80s (he became emperor in 81).*

constitutional innovations like Caesar's novel powers in 46–44, or the prerogatives granted to Augustus in 27 and again in 23 B.C., when extraordinary laws were passed in the presence of the new, indisputable leader.

Another sign of the institutionalization of the Principate is the adoption of *Imperator* by Vespasian and subsequent emperors as a first name (*praenomen*). As such, it now becomes a mark of the office held by the emperor. Imperator originally designated a man who legally held *imperium*, the right of life and death over Roman citizens first expressed in military contexts. It is hard for us to determine whether or not its use now as a personal name should be taken to mark a renewed consciousness of the military basis of imperial power.

The Principate's civil underpinnings were reestablished by a greater use of senators and equites, rather than freedmen, in the imperial service. This change, perhaps induced by loathing for Claudius' presumptuous freedmen and Nero's toadies, sent a clear signal that to rule the Roman world was not the exclusive prerogative of one individual or family. Added involvement of equites and senators in administration began with Vespasian and gained momentum in the second century. More subjects than ever actively participated in their own government, filling a quantity of prestigious positions hierarchically arranged. This social and political mobility seemed to confirm the Augustan ideal that equestrian and senatorial posts—from the prefecture of a cohort to administration of a great province like Asia—were open to any man of good birth, merit, and the requisite financial standing.

Such upward mobility was tied to the emperor's advancement of individuals to magistracies and special posts, one of the rights specified in the lex de imperio Vespasiani. Vespasian used this right most strikingly during the censorship that he held jointly with his elder son Titus in 73. Between them, they restored the senate to its former total of 600 from a low of about 200 caused by Nero's treason trials and the civil war of 68–69. As a further enhancement of prestige, the emperor could also bestow patrician status. To judge by inscriptions and other evidence, many of the "new men" in the Flavian senate came, as before, from north Italy and the nearer western provinces, especially Narbonese Gaul and Spain. By the end of the first century, Rome also saw senators whose hometowns were in North Africa, Greece, or Asia. The newcomers, like Pliny the Younger (from Comum), Tacitus (from Cisalpine or Narbonese Gaul), and Marcus Ulpius Trajanus (father of the later emperor Trajan, from Italica in southern Spain), were typically quick to embrace such traditional Roman values as service to the state (*virtus*) and thrift.

At the same time, imperial promotion of senators and equites, and increased use of both orders in administration, tightened the ties of imperial patronage even while sustaining the new political institutions. Pliny the Younger can exemplify the deference created by such a system. His *Panegyricus* is an expanded version of the customary speech of thanks that he delivered to Trajan in the senate in 100 on the occasion of taking up the consulship. Most modern readers, however, find it unbearably sycophantic. The many letters exchanged later between Pliny and Trajan about the affairs of Bithynia-Pontus betray similar insecurity concerning the boundaries between the powers of imperial functionaries and those of emperor (see further Chapter Twelve).

Another gauge of the Principate's institutionalization is the spread of the imperial cult, which is explored at the end of the chapter. The second half of the first century witnesses the appearance of more priests and priestesses of the cult in cities and in regional or provincial gatherings in Asia, Spain, and (more rarely) North Africa and elsewhere. Vespasian was ready enough to exploit others' superstitions in his rise to power, although he had few illusions about his own mortality and human failings.

Much of Vespasian's imperial imagery, especially on coins, marks him as the founder of a new Rome, and as a new Romulus. There is some truth to the latter identification: Vespasian was first and foremost a military man, like Romulus the son of Mars. Further, Vespasian struck a royal note in his commitment to dynastic succession, declaring to the senate: "Either my sons succeed me, or nobody" (Suetonius, *Vespasian* 25). His willingness to make this regal claim, which Augustus had studiously avoided, signals increasing acceptance of the Principate and its monarchical base. Although dynastic succession was resented by some—especially Stoics, Cynics, and traditionally minded senators—Vespasian's legacy of imperial power to his two sons, Titus and Domitian, ensured political continuity for twenty-seven years. Moreover, the underlying organization of the Principate was not to change for the next century. It allowed for much discretion on the part of the Princeps. When an emperor conformed to the role of first among equals, more or less as did Trajan and Vespasian, the government ran smoothly at all levels. But when rulers like the harsh Domitian and the aloof Hadrian were less concerned to mask their power, friction arose between the emperor and his notional peers, the senatorial and equestrian orders.

VESPASIAN (69–79)

Vespasian was an unpretentious man from Reate in north-central Italy. His family, the Flavii, had been respectable tax gatherers and custom agents of equestrian rank, with none of its members ever advancing to the senate before his elder brother and himself. Vespasian's special strength was his military acumen, demonstrated outstandingly in Germany, Britain, and Judaea. It was through the army that he came to power. His talents as a civilian leader, on the other hand, were unknown. Yet both aspects of the imperial position were demanded in 70: The Jewish and Germano-Gallic revolts had still to be suppressed, while Rome and Italy meantime needed to regain normalcy after all the destructive civil strife there.

The first problem that Vespasian had to face was the Jewish revolt, also known as the First Jewish War (66–73). The Jews conducted their desperate struggle against the Romans as a kind of guerilla war, and within the Jewish population there was much dissension, especially between Pharisees and Sadducees. The revolt had not yet been completely crushed when Vespasian, who had been sent to Judaea by Nero, was declared emperor by his troops with the support of Gaius Licinius Mucianus, the governor of Syria. Vespasian left Titus, his eldest son, as his legate in charge in Judaea; he and Mucianus departed for Rome, he via Alexandria and Egypt, Mucianus by the northern route. In 70 Titus stormed Jerusalem. To the Romans, the destruction of its great Temple signaled the end of the revolt, although pockets of resistance held out a few years longer. Of these, Masada is the most famous, thanks to Josephus' dramatic account, and the enduring symbolic importance of the site. Its Herodian palace-fortress fell only in 73, after the self-immolation of almost every one of the 390 men, women, and children besieged there for years by the Romans.

The revolt was extremely damaging for the Jews: It decimated Judaea's population, and in Jerusalem caused the deaths of the High Priests and the destruction of their Holy of Holies. Worship ceased at the site of the Temple. From now onwards, the tax previously paid to the Temple was earmarked for the temple of Jupiter Optimus Maximus in Rome. Jews were prohibited from proselytizing to gain new converts. A few concessions were made, however, in recognition of the antiquity of the Jewish religion: Those born in the faith could worship in it, and Jews were evidently not forced to participate in the imperial cult. The suppression of this Jewish revolt furthered the Jewish diaspora and began the distinction of Christians from Jews.

More immediately important for Vespasian, the fall of Jerusalem furnished the occasion for a huge triumph in Rome, lasting thirty days. This celebration advertised that Vespasian and his family had restored order in the Roman world; it simultaneously diverted attention from the bloodshed in Italy and Rome that had accompanied Vespasian's accession. To exhibit the booty seized from the Jews as well as the public statuary reclaimed from Nero's private appropriations, Vespasian built the Temple of Peace on land in central Rome previously appropriated by Nero's Golden House. Nearby he started the great amphitheater known today as the Colosseum, paying for it with booty taken from the sack of Jerusalem and using Jewish slaves as laborers (as newly found inscriptions indicate). He embarked on other huge building projects that emphasized peace, Jupiter Optimus Maximus, and his own role as re-founder of the city and state.

Facing page

Figure 11.2 *The triumphal procession of Vespasian and Titus in 71 (see Josephus,* Jewish Wars *7.121–158) was memorialized in various relief panels on the marble Arch of Titus. Since the main arch also contains a panel depicting the apotheosis of Titus (not shown), its completion must postdate his death in 81. Here we see part of the triumphal procession as it goes into Rome through an ornate city gate or arch. Soldiers wearing laurel wreaths (the symbol of victory) carry litters on which are displayed some of the booty seized in Jerusalem: (left to right) a menorah, the table of the Shewbread, and the silver trumpets. The placards carried by the soldiers may originally have offered painted identifications of the booty, or of the military units responsible for the victory. Such displays would precede the triumphing general himself, who was in a special chariot drawn by four white horses. The lower panel represents Titus as* triumphator, *but substitutes Roma (left) and allegorical figures for some of his escorts.*

and astrologers, and the resistance by Stoics and Cynics to his open dynastic intent led to at least one expulsion of Stoics from the senate. The year 75 even saw the execution of the Stoic senator Helvidius Priscus, who had survived a moral stand against Nero. The powers accruing to Vespasian help to account for the autocratic rule of his younger son, Domitian.

TITUS (79–81)

Before Domitian, however, his elder brother Titus was to serve as Princeps for no more than two years. Despite sporadic opposition to Vespasian, when he died in 79 the dynastic principle helped ensure Titus' succession. Titus was well groomed for the position: He had taken a leading role in the suppression of the Jewish revolt, and by 79 he had served as Praetorian Prefect, consul seven times, and censor. He held tribunican power and *maius imperium* every year after 70. He was popular and proven by experience when the senate and people ratified his position as Princeps after his father's death. Titus' unexpectedly brief tenure of power is marked by two disasters: the eruption of Mount Vesuvius in 79, and a devastating fire in Rome in 80. In good imperial fashion, he worked immediately to mitigate losses. Further, signaling a desire for a smooth relationship with Rome's upper orders, he banished informers from the city and refused to hear *maiestas* cases. What else he would have accomplished, however, will never be known, because he died prematurely and still unmarried in 81.

DOMITIAN (81–96)

Power passed smoothly to Vespasian's younger son, Domitian, with strong Praetorian backing that was encouraged by a distribution of 1,200 sesterces to each Guardsman. Domitian differed from his father and brother in many ways. He had no military experience, and he had held few positions in Rome other than six consulships that all seem to have been sinecures. Compared to Titus, he had been ignored; there had been no expectation that he would ever become emperor. Once he was, he somehow never gained the self-confidence or the patience to develop a satisfactory working relationship with the senate. In part, the alienation resulted from his tactless accumulation of offices: From 82 through 88 he held the consulship every year, and in 84–85 he became "perpetual censor." His neglect or contempt for the senate contrasts with his devotion to the army and his concern for the people of Rome and the provinces.

Many in Rome's highest circles were estranged by Domitian. Although he seduced his niece Julia and caused her death by a forced abortion, in his censorial role he had three Vestal virgins executed for immorality, and subsequently had another Vestal entombed alive. He was supposedly suspicious to the point of lining

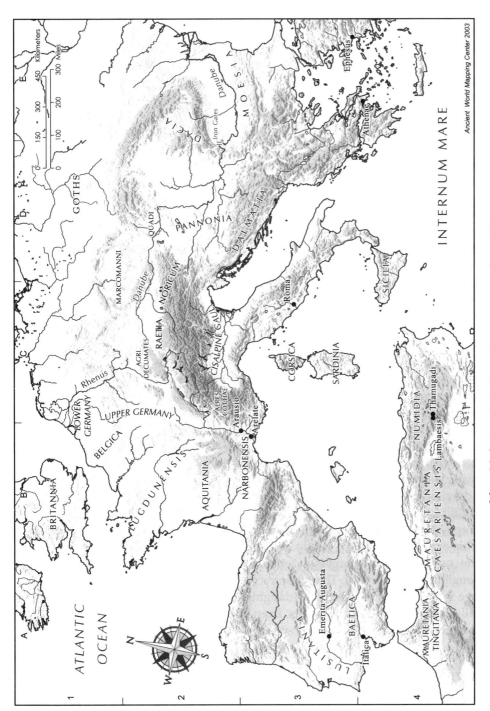

Map 11.1 *Rome's Northern Provinces Around* A.D. 100

Ancient World Mapping Center 2003

a senior ex-consul aged sixty-six. His seniority was what counted. Otherwise he lacked military distinction, and had passed through perilous times unscathed. He had been rewarded by Nero after the suppression of the Pisonian conspiracy in 65, and later served as consul with Vespasian in 71, and again with Domitian in 90, the year after Saturninus' revolt. Now, in 96, he was confirmed as emperor and given the honorary title Pater Patriae. He took an oath in the senate not to execute any senator. The first coins struck for him by the imperial mint emphasize virtues and worthy concepts: Equality, Liberty, Safety, and Justice.

Nerva devoted special attention to Italy during his two years as Princeps. He gave sixty million sesterces to buy land for distribution to citizens who had none, especially those living in Rome; the acquisition and assignment of this land was deputed to senators. Nerva also seems to have been the emperor who established the so-called *alimenta*. This complex child-support scheme—known almost exclusively from inscriptions—enabled emperors to furnish the principal for low-interest loans to Italian landowners. The interest paid by these borrowers funded monthly distributions to children. More boys are attested as recipients than girls, though this may simply be because only parents without eligible sons would put forward daughters for the scheme, since boys received higher payments. The scheme is often interpreted as an attempt to increase the birthrate in Italy and the amount of land under cultivation there. If so, however, we cannot gauge its effectiveness in either respect, nor can we be sure that these were its ultimate purposes.

Despite these benefactions, Nerva lacked the support of the Praetorians and of the army, who still remembered the favor shown to them by Domitian. By 97 the Praetorians were demanding the execution of Domitian's assassins. Dissatisfaction persisted even after Nerva gave his consent. Worse consequences were only precluded by an unexpected move on his part: In late October 97 he adopted Trajan, the newly appointed governor of Upper Germany (now with a garrison of three legions) and the son of a brilliant soldier-governor. Born and raised at Italica in southern Spain, and forty-four years of age at the time of his adoption, Trajan was to be the first emperor from the provinces. Nerva marked him out as successor by conferring the title "Caesar" on him, and by securing his election as consul for 98. Already in 97 the senate had conferred on him tribunicia potestas, maius imperium, and the title Imperator. When Nerva died a natural death on January 25, 98, Trajan's succession as Princeps was ratified despite his absence from Rome. He remained away until October 99, inspecting the frontiers along the Rhine and Danube. The maintenance of consensus of Rome at this time is a remarkable achievement, because it allowed the empire to survive Domitian's assassination without further civil war. The smooth transfers of power to Nerva, and then Trajan, offer a memorable contrast to the turmoil that erupted following the death of Nero and that was to resurface in the late second century.

TRAJAN (98–117)

In 99 Trajan entered Rome on foot and in a civilian toga rather than military uniform; he was welcomed by every segment of the population, according to Pliny's *Panegyricus*. Indeed, Trajan is one of the few Roman emperors who successfully combined the goodwill of the army and harmony with the senate. He was involved in many civilian initiatives, yet was decidedly eager to expand the empire. He has come down in the tradition as *Optimus Princeps*, "Best Princeps," a term appearing on coins and inscriptions beginning in 103.

From the start, Trajan acted independently despite conscientious consultation with others. He executed or discharged the mutinous Praetorians who had demanded the execution of Domitian's assassins. Moreover, contrary to the habit of new emperors to give ever bigger donatives to the Praetorians, Trajan actually halved the normal donative. He could do so because of his prestige among the regular rank and file of the army, whose size he was to increase by raising the total of legions to thirty. In Rome in 99 and 100 he was much praised, notably in 100 by Pliny's speech in the senate later revised as the *Panegyricus*. Trajan held his fourth consulship in 101. Thereafter, he never took the office again, no doubt conscious of the negative impression created by Domitian's continual tenure of it. Trajan aimed to strike the note that he was Princeps, not *dominus*, Rome's first among equals and not its monarch. Nevertheless, his accessibility was coupled with an iron will. His preeminence is underscored by Pliny's use of dominus ("lord") when writing letters to him.

Trajan expended much energy on civil matters. He remitted the "crown tax," a contribution that communities were expected to send to each emperor on his accession. In Rome itself he was responsible for distributions of cash to the populace on three occasions—in 99 (300 sesterces a head), in 102, and again in 107 (2,000 sesterces a head; a legionary's annual pay was now 1,200). Distributions of grain went to more recipients, too. Trajan gave lavish and frequent spectacles, celebrating the end of the Second Dacian War, for example, with 123 days of games spread over three years. With his support, the alimenta schemes begun by Nerva were extended in Italy. In addition, some of the last veteran colonies established by Rome are Trajan's initiatives. A prime example is North African Thamugadi (modern Timgad, Algeria), whose orthogonal planning, handsome public monuments, and evident prosperity seem to embody the effects of the "beneficial ideology" at the local level.

In response to local difficulties Trajan made special appointments to oversee cities and whole regions for limited periods. These troubleshooting caretaker officials (*curatores*)—including Pliny the Younger, dispatched to Bithynia-Pontus in 111–112—reported directly to the emperor; how their tasks meshed with those of the regular officials is far from clear. At least we can see how this innovation breaks with the traditional principle of cities' autonomy which all emperors from Augustus onwards had consistently upheld. Yet the work of such caretakers (who

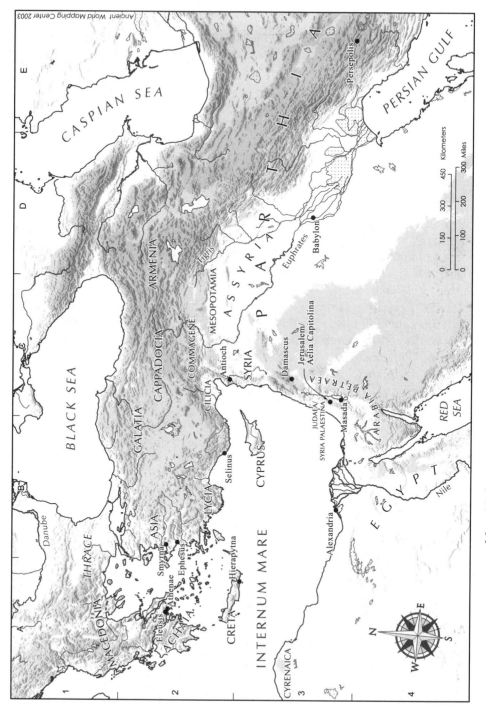

Map 11.2 *Eastern Expansion of the Empire in the Early Second Century*

Figure 11.3 *Thamugadi (modern Timgad, Algeria), a colony established by Trajan in 100. This view, from the interior of the city towards the west, shows in the foreground a well-paved street which forms part of the regular checkerboard grid. In the middle distance, dominating the smaller remains of houses and streetside porticoes, stands the triple arch that marks one of the principal entrances to the colony. Like most of the other large and imposing public monuments, this "Arch of Trajan," dating to c. 200, was only erected when the local economy allowed. Although they are not visible in this photograph, Timgad also came to boast a theater (begun c. 160) and, of course, a forum. A temple and city council building both opened onto the forum's central open space, which accommodated public meetings, processions, religious rituals, and other communal events.*

had seldom been appointed previously) seems to have been beneficial, and Pliny's letters to Trajan certainly document the concern with which both the emperor and his special representative approached the task of solving local problems (see Chapter Twelve). Finally in this connection, Trajan was responsible for numerous public works that featured opulent buildings of all types in Rome, as well as roads in Italy and the provinces.

Funds for these extensive benefactions came primarily from the Dacian Wars, which Trajan waged in 101–102 and 105–106. From the time of the Late Republic onwards, Rome had dealt intermittently with the Dacians of the Transylvanian plateau and the Carpathian Mountains—rich in gold, silver, and iron mines—above the loop of the lower Danube. Relations had intensified in the late first century, when the Dacian king Decebalus had consolidated power and fought against the Romans until his recognition as a "friendly king" by Domitian in 88. But Decebalus had then in fact renewed his bid for expansion, triggering further war with the Romans. Rome's victories are said to have yielded about 225 tons of gold, double that amount of silver, and 50,000 slaves. These spoils financed the great Forum of Trajan in the heart of Rome—its dimensions of 606×984 feet, or 185×300 meters, making it almost as large as all the other imperial fora combined. Dacian spoils also funded many other monuments in Rome, Italy, and elsewhere. After Decebalus' death and the destruction of much of Dacian culture, the Romans annexed the land. Dacia's mineral wealth prompted many immigrants to move there. Other newcomers were the soldiers from various parts of the empire who were stationed there. The more exposed location of the new province, beyond the well-defined Danube River boundary, shifted the weight of Rome's garrisons east from the Rhine to the lower Danube and to Dacia itself.

It was possibly the sheer success of the Dacian Wars that spurred Trajan to further expansion. In 105–106, during the second Dacian War, he annexed Arabia Petraea, "rocky Arabia," previously called Nabataea. The new province was wealthy because of its incense, spices, gold, and gems, as well as its active role in Roman trade with India. Almost immediately, Trajan marked the area as Roman by commissioning a great road from the Red Sea to Damascus in Syria. But the creation of the province destabilized an area already unsettled by the death of the king of Parthia to its east (probably in 105). In 110 problems surfaced in Armenia, when the new Parthian king replaced the Roman vassal king there with a noble of his own choosing. This action provoked the Parthian War, which was to occupy Trajan until his death in 117.

In October 113, Trajan set off to the East to command the war in person, and perhaps to explore the possibilities of advancing beyond Armenia. Mesopotamia, which was ruled by a land-owning military aristocracy under a king, was characteristically volatile. Its annexation would give Rome a very rich province as well as access to the Persian Gulf. Literary sources also cite Trajan's emulation of Alexander the Great, who had traversed this area on his famous eastern march. By 114, Trajan had captured Armenia and reduced it to a province. In 115 he made the lands between Armenia and the upper reaches of the Tigris into the province of Assyria; northern Mesopotamia was then reduced, and annexed as the province of Mesopotamia. Trajan was awarded the title "Parthicus" in 116, and the thirty legions now under his command must have seemed invincible. But they were also a heavy burden on Rome's economy and society, and the war itself was exacting. Long stretches of desert and semi-arid land obstructed communications. The Roman troops were unused to the harsh climate, and supplies were hard to obtain. Disasters, both natural and manmade, exacerbated the difficulties. In winter 114–115 a devastating earthquake hit Syrian Antioch (modern Antakya, Turkey). Although Trajan himself was spared, along with his distant relative Publius Aelius Hadrianus accompanying him, many other men of high rank died, as did soldiers assembling at Antioch for the following year's campaign against the Parthians. The city was wrecked, and it must have seemed to some as though the gods were trying to warn the Romans. In addition, later in 115 the second Jewish revolt broke out, diverting attention from the expansionist Parthian war to internal discontent.

In 115, Jewish communities in Cyrenaica, Egypt, Cyprus, and perhaps Judaea itself rebelled against the Romans. The outbreaks may have been coordinated. At the least, the exasperated Jews of the diaspora, exploited and scorned for years by gentile neighbors, took advantage of the authorities' preoccupation with the Parthian War. By 116, the unrest had spread to Mesopotamia, disturbing the new province. The crisis was not finally brought under control everywhere until late in 117. Repression of the Jews was especially brutal in Egypt, where a virtual pogrom extirpated all traces of them from the country outside of Alexandria. In every area of discontent, rebellious Jews attacked garrisons and destroyed towns. Trajan heard of the revolt in 116 while sacrificing to the spirit of Alexander at Babylon, and he had to dispatch forces immediately to the rebellious areas. But this Jewish revolt was not the only internal turmoil of the time. In 117, disturbances on the lower Danube required the transfer there of the outstanding general Gaius Julius Quadratus Bassus, who had been governor of Syria since the beginning of the Parthian War. Trajan now appointed Hadrian to replace him in Syria. He also concluded his Parthian campaigns, and embarked on his return journey to Rome.

However, in the course of this journey, Trajan died unexpectedly at the port of Selinus in Cilicia. Just before he died, he adopted Hadrian as his heir. The latter was aged forty-one at the time, and was still in Syria. In his youth, Trajan had been his guardian. Like Trajan, he came from Italica in southern Spain. In 100 he had married Trajan's grand-niece, Sabina, and later served him in different capacities—as speechwriter, for example. Despite these close links, however, Trajan did not clearly mark him out as his successor until the adoption. Cassius Dio and others insinuate that this was really arranged by Trajan's wife Plotina, who was close to Hadrian. Yet Hadrian was amply qualified to become Princeps. He had held many administrative and military positions, serving in Pannonia as well as Syria,

empire, visiting cities, natural wonders, and troops along the frontiers. His activity centered on bettering the empire internally in various ways: improving material and administrative infrastructure (including communications), boosting municipal elites as well as the senatorial and equestrian orders, invigorating religious practices, and encouraging cultural activities, especially those of a literary and ritual kind. An inward turn is detectable in other ways. Hadrian himself painted, designed buildings, and wrote poetry as well as speeches and an autobiography: He appreciated aesthetics deeply and actively. He had a mystical bent—expressed in his rising as high as the "second level" in the Mysteries at Eleusis, in his involvement in other types of mysteries and oracles, and in his heroization of his lover, Antinous, when the young man drowned in 130. None of these preoccupations would have been possible without widespread peace. Peace was further secured by the smooth transmission of power in this period, thanks to imperial adoptions and the fortuitous longevity of the emperors, from Trajan to Marcus Aurelius.

Hadrian ruled from 117 to 138. One of his many accomplishments was to settle the succession for the next two generations, although he had no children of his own (see Table 11.1). Towards the end of his life, in 136, he adopted Lucius Ceionius Commodus (renamed Lucius Aelius Caesar); but when he died within a year, Hadrian turned to others. At the beginning of 138 he adopted Titus Aurelius Fulvus Boionius Arrius Antoninus (later known as Antoninus Pius), and since Antoninus had no son, he had him adopt two younger men. One, the seventeen-year-old Marcus Annius Verus, was to become the Princeps Marcus Aurelius. The other, the seven-year old son of the deceased Lucius Aelius, would later rule as Lucius Verus jointly with Marcus Aurelius. All three of Hadrian's choices belonged to a circle of friends and relatives with ties to southern Gaul and Spain, typical of the senatorial and equestrian orders in early second-century Rome. Their family connections and the Roman custom of adoption may together have made the dynastic arrangement's political purpose more acceptable. In any event, Hadrian's foresight in this regard certainly preempted the suspicions surrounding his own deathbed adoption by Trajan, and contributed to the unusual stability of the second century.

Trajan's death in Cilicia in 117 led to countless rumors—as was only to be expected when a beloved ruler dies far from home—and Hadrian's choice of a circuitous route to Rome through Dalmatia and Pannonia only encouraged the spread of gossip. The principle of meritocracy—which had surely been the basis of Nerva's adoption of Trajan—may have influenced at least a few senators to think themselves more worthy than Hadrian to succeed Trajan. Before Hadrian returned to Rome in 118, four influential men had been condemned to death by the senate on charges of conspiracy. Although Hadrian swore that this had been done without his knowledge, the deaths tainted his first years. His own mercurial, sometimes difficult, personality increased senatorial animosity against him, as did the forced suicides of two distant relatives near the end of his life. Overall, the literary tradition

Table 11.1 The Antonine Family *The presentation follows the style of Table 9.1, explained there.*

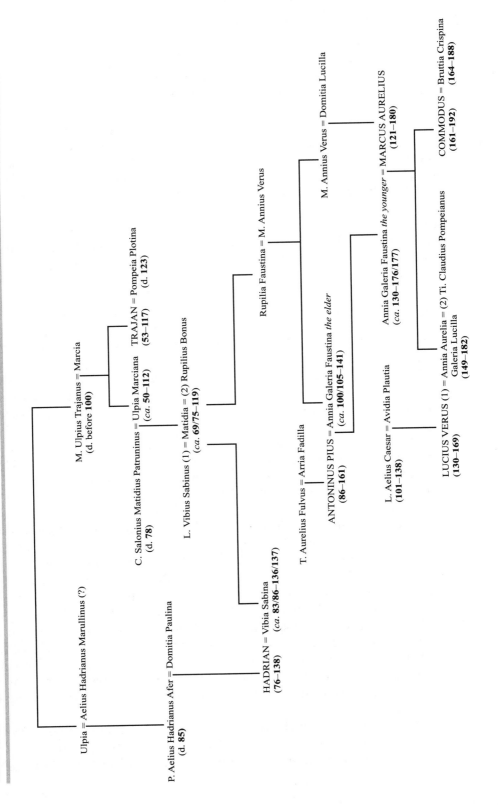

is hostile to Hadrian. Yet his earlier career, including his appointment as governor of Syria, suggests Trajan's confidence in his abilities, loyalty, and military acumen. This confidence was repaid over the twenty-one years of his Principate.

Some innovations can be credited to Hadrian; other changes are not due to him alone. One of his first acts was to complete Rome's decisive withdrawal from Trajan's farthest conquests, allowing Armenia, Mesopotamia, and Assyria to return to their previous forms of rule. The cessation of costly hostilities and the abandonment of military occupation in the East allowed Hadrian to cancel debts due to the treasury in 118, to make lavish donations in Rome and the provinces (especially from 118 to 121), and to excuse communities from the "crown tax." These benefactions, acclaimed on inscriptions and even in literature, may have resulted in greater public confidence in the economy, and an increase in public spending by affluent city elites and by the Princeps himself. Widespread confidence was also spurred by Hadrian's travels, during which local notables throughout the empire could meet him personally. In his first great journey, from 121 to 127, he visited Gaul, the Rhineland regions, Britain (where he began "his" Wall), Spain, Asia, Greece, and Sicily. He returned to Rome for less than a year, and then visited Africa briefly in 128. After returning to Rome again, at the end of 128 he embarked on his second great journey, which lasted until 131. In these years he visited Athens, and many regions of Asia, Syria, and Egypt. Sometime during this trip he may have visited Judaea, where his decision to settle a veteran colony at the site of Jerusalem (Colonia Aelia Capitolina), combined with his prohibition of circumcision, set off a major revolt.

The third Jewish revolt, also known as the Bar Kokhba War after the Jewish leader Shim'on bar-Cosiba (nicknamed Bar Kokhba, "Son of a Star," by a rabbi), lasted from 132 to 135. It devastated Judaea and exacted a heavy death toll from Jews and Romans alike. Cassius Dio summarizes the destruction: fifty Jewish outposts and 985 villages razed, 580,000 rebels slain; many more civilians perished by famine and fire, and numerous Romans fell (69.14). Afterwards, in what now seems an attempt to eradicate Judaism, Judaea was renamed Syria Palaestina, and Jews were forbidden entry into Jerusalem. The Jewish diaspora intensified, and Christians were more obviously differentiated from Jews and Jerusalem.

Hadrian plainly encouraged well qualified individuals to participate in administration, where his rule was less damaging. His Principate sees increased prominence of equites like the biographer and intellectual Suetonius, who was placed in charge of imperial correspondence. Hadrian accorded special respect to the emperor's traditional group of private advisers that dated back to Augustus' time (*consilium principis*), and he invited not only his friends (*comites*) to serve on it, but also legal experts ("jurists") approved by the senate. As a result, these senators and equites gained an influential role in decision-making and in adjudicating appeals referred to the emperor.

Another innovation by Hadrian—the appointment of four judges known as the *Quattuorviri consulares*, all of them ex-consuls—underscores the difficulties that now face us in determining emperors' motivations. These four judges heard cases and adjudicated disputes in Italy, which was divided administratively into four regions for the purpose. Previously, Roman citizens in Italy had to come to Rome itself to have appeals heard, or for cases of more than local significance; cases involving senators would be heard in the senate. Although Hadrian's innovation addresses the burdens and inequities caused by the earlier system, it was apparently thought to be treating Italy too much like a province. It has been interpreted as indicating a long-standing desire to streamline administration and legal proceedings, as well as an ecumenical vision of the Roman world as one in which all regions deserved equal respect. On the other hand, it was a step that apparently caused rancor in the senate, whose corporate prestige may have seemed diminished. The new office was to be dropped by Antoninus Pius, although later revived by Marcus Aurelius.

The blurring of legal and administrative functions for the Quattuorviri consulares is indicative of Hadrian's Principate, in which civil administration seems ever more concerned with judicial questions. The daily activities of the emperor centered on hearing cases and appeals. Hadrian's well-organized mind had a legal bent. Among his achievements is codification of the set of legal procedures and types of proceedings that praetors would allow in office. Previously, individual praetors, often advised by jurists, could choose or modify the rules and procedures they would follow, although already by the Augustan period the various praetorian edicts were more or less standardized and permanent. The same principle was followed by governors and other magistrates with judicial authority. Now, in the late 120s, Hadrian asked the jurist Salvius Julianus to compose a revised version of the Praetorian edict, which would be permanent. In 131 the senate ratified the document, and from the early third century the codification was to be known as the "Edictum Perpetuum." From now onwards, the procedures of civil law at Rome could be changed only by the Princeps or by decree of the senate. Although emperors tended to monopolize this prerogative, Hadrian also declared that in court cases the unanimous opinion of authorized jurists could count "as if it were law" (Gaius, *Institutes* 1.7). He thus signaled that others could make law as well as himself.

Hadrian worked hard to show that he was approachable and cordial, but with mixed success. At his accession he had forbidden treason trials; he visited senators and equites when they were sick; he consulted frequently with his comites. His concern went beyond Rome's highest ranks. He bettered the condition of slaves by requiring that an owner obtain the approval of a state magistrate before killing any slave who had committed crimes. The alimenta scheme was expanded; more curatores, and of several types, were appointed to oversee various communities. In addition, Hadrian engaged in an enormous program of building and other benefactions throughout the Roman world. He personally mingled with the people of Rome and the provinces. His constant travels proclaimed his accessibility and his care for all, and because he journeyed with the apparatus of the central government (still small in this period), important decisions were often made outside of Rome.

Hadrian's military background matches with his acute concern for the empire's security. Despite renouncing further expansion, he took a keen interest in the army and military matters. His rule sees greater attention to borders, especially fixed ones, than ever before. The great wall in northern England, "Hadrian's Wall," was established after 121. It cut through the lower of Britain's two narrow necks, from modern Bowness to Newcastle, a distance of 73 miles or 118 kilometers; Roman troops were also stationed both north and south of it. In all likelihood it was during Hadrian's rule, too, that the German-Raetian frontier came to be defined by a continuous high wooden barrier. Overall, he ensured that the army was well prepared and well disciplined. He frequently reviewed training exercises, and maintained the practice of employing troops on civil projects like aqueducts and roads during intervals between military activity.

Hadrian's most pressing military concerns were internal. The second and third Jewish Revolts mar the beginning and end of his rule, and further insurrections in

---

BOX 11.1: Hadrian Inspects Troops at Lambaesis, Numidia

When Hadrian visited North Africa in 128, he reviewed the troops of the province of Numidia at their Lambaesis headquarters (modern Lambèse, Algeria). The garrison later inscribed excerpts from his five addresses to the men (ILS 2487, 9133–35). The sections below give a flavor both of the troops' mundane tasks and of their military training; they also show Hadrian at work as commander-in-chief:

[To a cavalry cohort] . . . Defenses which others take several days to construct, you have completed in one. You have completed the lengthy task of building a strong wall—the type typically erected for permanent winter quarters—in not much more time than is needed to build a turf wall. For that type of wall, the turf is cut to a standard size and is easy to carry and to handle; its erection presents no problems because it is naturally pliable and level. But your wall was built of large, heavy, uneven stones which no one can carry or lift or position without them catching on each other because of their uneven surfaces. You cut a trench straight through hard coarse gravel, and made it smooth by leveling it. Once the job had been approved, you entered the camp speedily, and got your rations and your weapons....

[To the cavalry of the Sixth Cohort of Commagenians] It is difficult for cavalry attached to a cohort to make a good impression even on their own, and still harder for them not to incur criticism after a maneuver by auxiliary cavalry—they cover a greater area of the plain, there are more men throwing javelins; they wheel right in close formation, they perform the Cantabrian maneuver in close array; the beauty of their horses and the splendor of their weapons are in keeping with their level of pay. But, despite the heat, you avoided any boredom by doing energetically what had to be done; in addition you fired stones from slings and fought with javelins. On every occasion you mounted briskly. The remarkable care taken by my distinguished legate Catullinus is evident from the fact that he has men like you under his command. . . .

Figure 11.5 *Statue of Hadrian from Hierapytna, Crete. Hadrian wears full parade-dress military costume, including a large laurel crown. His magnificent breastplate includes a depiction of Romulus, his twin brother Remus, and the she-wolf (below its central figure) that is said to have rescued and nursed them. Hadrian triumphantly rests his left foot on the back of a captive barbarian boy. Some scholars have dated the image to between 120 and 125; others suggest that the boy is Jewish, which would date the statue to the third Jewish revolt (132–135) or (less likely) to the end of the second (117). The statue—originally set up in an imperial cult shrine on the island of Crete—embodies the merciless violence that the Romans inflicted on those who opposed them.*

Britain and Mauretania occurred around 117. Hadrian may have aimed his provincial benefactions at preventing discontent, but he apparently could not conceive that provincials might reject the Greco-Roman culture he so fervently promoted. As already noted, his blunders with the Jews in the 130s provoked one of the fiercest revolts that the Romans ever experienced. Hadrian thereafter slowed his activity and became more isolated. His suspicions caused the suicides of two of his distant relatives; his choice of Lucius Aelius as successor was unfortunate and unpopular; in 137 his wife, Sabina, from whom he had been distant ever since 122, died. In 138 Hadrian himself died, "hated by all" (*Historia Augusta, Hadrian* 25.7), and his deification earned its proposer, his successor Antoninus, the cognomen "pious" (Latin *pius*).

ROMAN CITIES AND THE EMPIRE'S PEOPLES

In size and population the Roman empire was at its peak between the reigns of Vespasian and Hadrian. Its vast expanse—from modern England, the Atlantic Ocean, and Germany,

Figure 11.6 *Theater at Emerita Augusta (modern Mérida, Spain), as restored in the early twentieth century. Originally commissioned by Agrippa in 16–15 B.C., this theater was remodeled in the early second century A.D. to include a shrine (sacrarium) for the imperial cult in the lowest part of the seating (the area now lacking seats in the rising semicircle). In the photograph can be seen reproductions of some of the statues originally placed between the columns of the stage's backdrop, commemorating local notables, members of the imperial family, and gods and goddesses. Also visible are traces of the marble that once covered the backdrop's structural elements, contributing to the public opulence and sense of urbanity.*

the details recounted by Suetonius (*Nero* 21) to demonstrate Nero's unsuitability as Princeps, is the point that when he appeared in operatic tragedies as a hero or god, or even a heroine or goddess, he wore masks modeled on his own face or on that of whichever woman happened to be his current mistress. Masks may have helped to amplify actors' voices, and amplification was also increased by technology. Comprehension of what was being staged was aided in addition by some standardization of the plays and performances; the stories would have been immediately obvious and familiar.

Religious and civic processions often began or ended at theaters. Such processions were an essential part of the public and official religion of Rome and its cities. A few are known in detail from inscriptions like that recording the foundation instituted by Gaius Vibius Salutaris at Ephesus early in the second century. On festal days the city's priests and priestesses would parade precious metal images of gods and goddesses, deified emperors and empresses, and personifications of civic groups through a city, stopping at various points for public prayer.

Figure 11.5 *Statue of Hadrian from Hierapytna, Crete. Hadrian wears full parade-dress military costume, including a large laurel crown. His magnificent breastplate includes a depiction of Romulus, his twin brother Remus, and the she-wolf (below its central figure) that is said to have rescued and nursed them. Hadrian triumphantly rests his left foot on the back of a captive barbarian boy. Some scholars have dated the image to between 120 and 125; others suggest that the boy is Jewish, which would date the statue to the third Jewish revolt (132–135) or (less likely) to the end of the second (117). The statue—originally set up in an imperial cult shrine on the island of Crete—embodies the merciless violence that the Romans inflicted on those who opposed them.*

Britain and Mauretania occurred around 117. Hadrian may have aimed his provincial benefactions at preventing discontent, but he apparently could not conceive that provincials might reject the Greco-Roman culture he so fervently promoted. As already noted, his blunders with the Jews in the 130s provoked one of the fiercest revolts that the Romans ever experienced. Hadrian thereafter slowed his activity and became more isolated. His suspicions caused the suicides of two of his distant relatives; his choice of Lucius Aelius as successor was unfortunate and unpopular; in 137 his wife, Sabina, from whom he had been distant ever since 122, died. In 138 Hadrian himself died, "hated by all" (*Historia Augusta*, *Hadrian* 25.7), and his deification earned its proposer, his successor Antoninus, the cognomen "pious" (Latin *pius*).

ROMAN CITIES AND THE EMPIRE'S PEOPLES

In size and population the Roman empire was at its peak between the reigns of Vespasian and Hadrian. Its vast expanse—from modern England, the Atlantic Ocean, and Germany, across to Syria, Armenia, and the Nile Valley—was studded with cities on the coasts and rivers. There were perhaps fifty to seventy million people living in Roman territory, with probably some 20 percent of these in cities (one million people in Rome itself). The percentage in cities is relatively large. At the end of the twentieth century, 47 percent of the world's people were living in cities, according to United Nations calculations. But this extraordinary proportion is possible only because of recent technological advances like refrigeration, heating and cooling, antibiotics and other advances of public health, gas-fueled transport, and the like. In the Roman world, there were probably as many as 2,000 cities, perhaps more.

After the great push by Caesar and Augustus, the numbers of veteran colonies settled by subsequent emperors dropped. Such colonies were extremely intrusive when imposed on earlier settlements, and the need for them was lessened by the establishment of a standing army. Some emperors reinforced towns by adding a group of discharged soldiers to its citizen rolls, as Nero did in 60 to Tarentum and Antium (modern Taranto and Anzio, Italy). But the period of Trajan and Hadrian marks the virtual end of veteran settlements. Trajan's colony at Thamugadi prospered; Hadrian's at Jerusalem caused a revolt.

Instead, emperors encouraged cities by other means both direct and indirect—through grants of colonial or municipal status, remissions of taxes, personal visits, and funding construction. Better communications and the necessity of supplying the Roman army assisted commerce, agriculture, and the creation of some surplus capital. Small-scale commerce and artisan work advanced, providing individuals with occupations other than simply agricultural ones. The provincial cities were above all where social and political mobility could take place. There, freedmen could gain some local prestige and wealth, opening doors for their descendants to rise still higher in the social and economic scale. Soldiers honorably discharged from the legions or auxiliary forces commanded great respect in the towns where they retired, and they often served as town patrons or in some other political capacity. Even working women are documented in Roman cities as greengrocers, midwives, and shopkeepers, besides the more traditional but disreputable professions of prostitute or barmaid.

Rome's cities were linked to one another and to Rome itself by roads and harbors, to which the Flavian emperors, Trajan, and Hadrian, paid much attention. Individuals might travel to nearby towns for games devoted to the imperial cult, local festivals, or visits from the provincial governor or some other Roman official. The relatively modest inns and taverns that have been found at Pompeii and elsewhere catered to such travelers. Long-distance travel was undertaken by ambassadors from cities to the emperor, and by troops on the move; both types of traveler would have been accommodated overnight by individuals either voluntarily or (for troops) under compulsion. Merchants and sailors also covered long distances. There is evidence—such as an inscription from Puteoli attesting a "station of the Tyrians"—to indicate that ethnic groups sometimes took care of their own travelers. But the Roman world's vast majority, whose horizons were limited to the land they tilled and to towns within a day's walk, can never have traveled far.

To this vast majority, did it really matter who ruled at Rome? In the early fifth century, a cultured bishop and philosopher from the coast of modern Libya suggested that even educated provincials were indifferent to, perhaps ignorant of, the ruling emperor (Synesius of Cyrene, *Letters* 148). Such must have been the case throughout Roman history for the mass of Rome's subjects, struggling to eke out a living from land prone to drought, flood, and other natural disasters. But during times of relative peace and prosperity, those inhabitants of the empire fortunate enough to live in or near a city probably had some inkling of the emperor, perhaps even of some benefaction from him. How did such people know of the emperor and other high-placed, almost untouchable individuals, and with what effects? These are obvious questions, but challenging ones when we take into account the absence of extensive mass communication.

THEATERS AND PROCESSIONS

One way that the imperial family affected Roman citizens and subjects was through the demonstration of their images at almost every event. As in the well-preserved theater of Emerita Augusta (modern Mérida, Spain), for example, care was taken to exhibit statues of the emperors and their relatives at public gathering places. Theatergoing was a favorite pastime of the Romans. A later, fourth-century calendar found in Rome designates 102 days a year as "theater days," and there is little reason to think that the total was much less during the three previous centuries. Behind their stages, Roman theaters characteristically exhibited an elaborate and unchanging architectural backdrop (*scaenae frons*), whose many niches were filled with statues of gods, heroes, and the imperial family. Theaters—dating predominantly after the mid-first century A.D.—are found throughout the Roman world: Some ninety are known from the area of modern France alone, for example. Typically seating some 5,000 spectators, but often much larger than seems warranted by just their city, they must also have accommodated countryfolk and visitors from neighboring towns alongside the local citizens. Spectators included men and women, slave, freed, and free. Although theatrical performances varied, invariably each "theater day" opened and closed with sacrifices and prayers on behalf of the Princeps, the imperial family, and Rome.

Theaters in the Greek East staged at least selected parts of the classic Greek plays like *Oedipus Rex*. The Latin West favored performances that could be described as mime or vaudeville, with stock characters in silly situations. "Atellan" farces, for example, featured a glutton, a fool, and a hunchback. Ironically, given the popularity of theatrical spectacles, professional actors and actresses were considered disreputable; in Roman law they were under certain restrictions, such as not being permitted to receive legacies. In both East and West actors usually wore masks. Among

Figure 11.6 *Theater at Emerita Augusta (modern Mérida, Spain), as restored in the early twentieth century. Originally commissioned by Agrippa in 16–15 B.C., this theater was remodeled in the early second century A.D. to include a shrine (sacrarium) for the imperial cult in the lowest part of the seating (the area now lacking seats in the rising semicircle). In the photograph can be seen reproductions of some of the statues originally placed between the columns of the stage's backdrop, commemorating local notables, members of the imperial family, and gods and goddesses. Also visible are traces of the marble that once covered the backdrop's structural elements, contributing to the public opulence and sense of urbanity.*

the details recounted by Suetonius (*Nero* 21) to demonstrate Nero's unsuitability as Princeps, is the point that when he appeared in operatic tragedies as a hero or god, or even a heroine or goddess, he wore masks modeled on his own face or on that of whichever woman happened to be his current mistress. Masks may have helped to amplify actors' voices, and amplification was also increased by technology. Comprehension of what was being staged was aided in addition by some standardization of the plays and performances; the stories would have been immediately obvious and familiar.

Religious and civic processions often began or ended at theaters. Such processions were an essential part of the public and official religion of Rome and its cities. A few are known in detail from inscriptions like that recording the foundation instituted by Gaius Vibius Salutaris at Ephesus early in the second century. On festal days the city's priests and priestesses would parade precious metal images of gods and goddesses, deified emperors and empresses, and personifications of civic groups through a city, stopping at various points for public prayer.

Often a local notable would pay for a public distribution, feast, or additional performance such as a singing contest, further enhancing the appeal of the day and simultaneously forging a personal link with the gods and emperors. Distributions were typically angled towards the privileged, and often given out hierarchically—for example, with the town magistrates and councilors receiving the most, then the Augustales, then the mothers of leading citizens, and finally free citizens in general. Seating in theaters was similarly arranged, with the seats closest to the orchestra reserved for those with the most prestige. On the other hand, at least the processions were open to all, and no business could be transacted on "theater days." Events staged in theaters clearly underscored the connections between leisure (*otium*), culture (*urbanitas*), official religion, the municipal elite, and the emperor and imperial house.

CIRCUSES AND CHARIOT RACING

Such connections were also obvious for circus races, another favorite diversion of the Romans. Again, the fourth-century calendar from Rome is illuminating: Then, at least, sixty-four days a year were designated for circus races at public expense. The most famous circus is Rome's Circus Maximus. It was supposed to date to the city's earliest times: According to tradition, at its site Romulus and the first Romans had abducted the Sabine women from their fathers and brothers. The site was then said to have been monumentalized by the king Tarquinius Priscus, with an Etruscan flair for civil engineering. It was rebuilt a few times during the Republic. Its popularity attracted Julius Caesar and Augustus, who both undertook renovations and additions. In Augustus' day it was claimed to hold between 150,000 and 180,000 spectators, men and women, slave and free; in *The Art of Love* (1.135–162), Ovid recommends the Circus as one of the best places for singles to meet. Every Princeps left some mark there, such as an embellishment of the central dividing island (*spina*), or improvements to the starting gates. After Trajan made repairs and additions at the beginning of his Principate, as many as 250,000 spectators could be accommodated.

Circus racing remained popular even into Late Roman times, when it became a Christianized event that provided an important venue for public demonstrations in Constantinople. But gatherings at Rome's Circus Maximus, just as those at theaters and amphitheaters, had always allowed the populace to express their opinions to emperors and other figures in authority. This function of the Circus Maximus was reinforced by the location of Augustus' house on the Palatine overlooking it, and by the later extension of Domitian's palace towards it. Biographies and histories often note interaction between emperor and subject at the races, so that Tiberius' infrequent attendance at the Circus only added to his unpopularity. Other features of circus spectacles also remained constant. In the standard arrangement, four-horse chariots lapped at least seven times, for a total distance of

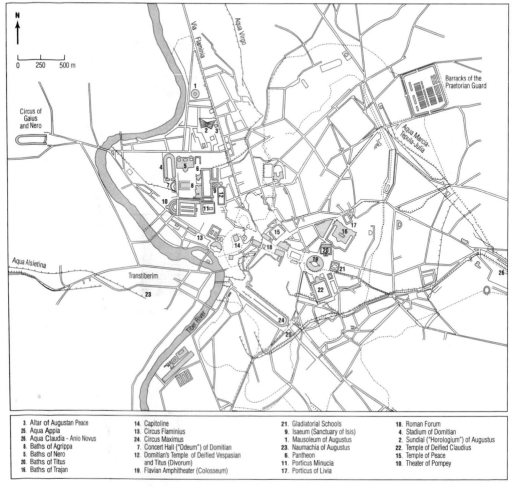

Map 11.3 *Rome Around* A.D. 100

3. Altar of Augustan Peace
25. Aqua Appia
26. Aqua Claudia - Anio Novus
8. Baths of Agrippa
5. Baths of Nero
20. Baths of Titus
16. Baths of Trajan

14. Capitoline
13. Circus Flaminius
24. Circus Maximus
7. Concert Hall ("Odeum") of Domitian
12. Domitian's Temple of Deified Vespasian and Titus (Divorum)
19. Flavian Amphitheater (Colosseum)

21. Gladiatorial Schools
9. Isaeum (Sanctuary of Isis)
1. Mausoleum of Augustus
23. Naumachia of Augustus
6. Pantheon
11. Porticus Minucia
17. Porticus of Livia

18. Roman Forum
4. Stadium of Domitian
2. Sundial ("Horologium") of Augustus
22. Temple of Deified Claudius
15. Temple of Peace
10. Theater of Pompey

Barracks of the Praetorian Guard

Circus of Gaius and Nero

Via Flaminia

Aqua Virgo

Aqua Marcia-Tepula-Julia

Aqua Alsietina

Transtiberim

Tiber River

5.25 miles (8.4 km). Each race took about fifteen minutes, and twenty-four different races were usually staged in a day. The contenders were traditionally divided into four teams—Reds, Whites, Blues, and Greens (Domitian's innovation of additional Gold and Purple teams did not outlive him). Competition was fierce, and successful charioteers were richly rewarded. Racing—not to mention betting—was extremely popular: Mosaics and terracotta lamps depicting the Circus Maximus have been found throughout the Roman world, and charioteers were much acclaimed in their communities.

The potential use of circuses elsewhere—other than at Rome and, later, Constantinople—to express political dissatisfaction was also recognized, to judge by

Figure 11.7 A Roman charioteer. This top of a four-sided marble funerary monument shows a Roman charioteer much as he would have been dressed in a race. Over his tunic—which would probably have been painted the color of his team (green, red, blue, or white)—are wrapped the reins of his chariot, both to help him steer during the race, and to provide support for his ribs in a crash. The palm trees at the four corners of the monument recall the palms of victory that were given to the winners. On the side can be seen a racehorse. The monument is dated to Hadrian's time by the beard and hairstyle of the charioteer, as well as by the general carving technique, including the excised pupils of his eyes; previously, pupils on marble statues would be painted.

surviving regulations on the status of impresarios and the annual number of races in Italy and the provinces. The senate heard complaints about communities that had not offered appropriately good seating to senators and others of high status. Even so, like other festivals, circus races staged outside of Rome opened and closed with rituals celebrating the emperor and imperial family, and the gods that formed part of the state religion.

THE AMPHITHEATER, AND GLADIATORIAL GAMES

Similar rituals were integral to spectacles at the amphitheaters. Although these are perhaps the most notorious feature of Roman civilization, they were not held as often as is commonly assumed. The fourth-century calendar from Rome lists only ten days a year devoted to games in the amphitheater. Gladiatorial and beast fights are documented there as early as the third century B.C., but the earliest known permanent amphitheater was only built around 70 B.C. (see Figure 7.1), and the first permanent amphitheater in Rome dates to the Augustan Age. Both Roman and modern amphitheaters are commonly called "Colosseum" after the great Flavian amphitheater that rose in place of the lake of Nero's Golden House. The name in fact derives from the adjacent colossal 120 foot-tall (36 m) statue of Nero, which the Flavians then modified to resemble Titus or the sun god, Sol. This Flavian amphitheater is a marvel of engineering, harmoniously proportioned, designed to maximize visibility and audibility, and structured so that it could be emptied of its 50,000 or so spectators in five minutes. Its design, which also rendered it fairly impervious to earthquakes, set the standard for all later amphitheaters throughout the Roman world. These structures were more prevalent in the West than in the East, although many remain in both halves of the empire.

Together with mosaics, gems, lamps, and inscriptions commemorating events in amphitheaters, these arenas attest to a Roman liking for "blood sports" that shocks many modern sensibilities. Spectators in the amphitheater watched men fighting against men, almost always in individual pairs except on extraordinary occasions funded by the emperor. Other events pitted men against wild beasts; beasts against men or even women, as when an individual found guilty of a capital crime was condemned to the beasts (*ad bestias*); and various types of beasts against each other. Gladiatorial costumes and weaponry were standardized, and gladiatorial training schools were usually maintained at public expense. Most gladiators began as slaves; men of good repute and high social standing were to be spectators, not actors, in the amphitheater. Many rich men financed games there in a display of public benefaction as well as a conspicuous sign of their wealth and power. The search for exotic beasts—whose display reflected the extent of Roman rule—contributed to emptying North Africa and other regions of indigenous fauna.

Figure 11.8 *Scenes from the amphitheater, as shown on a mosaic from Zliten, Tripolitania, now in the Archeological Museum of Tripoli, Libya. These two mosaic bands formed part of a larger floor, which depicted on its edges numerous scenes from gladiatorial and other shows exhibited in the amphitheater. From left to right, here we see (above) condemned criminals' public slaughter in the arena by wild beasts (damnatio ad bestias); various wild beast hunts (venationes); (below) a fight between a man on foot and a man on a horse (the unhorsed rider's left arm and leg can be seen on the left); a fight between a bear and a bull; and one man whipping another towards lions. The mosaic perhaps dates to around 200, and the room from which it came was probably used for banquets or receptions.*

Smaller and more intimate baths were built in almost every city, however, and many cities boasted more than one: Thamugadi had at least fourteen, Athens twenty. After undressing in a foyer, individual bathgoers would typically go first to the *tepidarium*, then to the *sudatorium* (sweat room), and then to the great cool pool of the *frigidarium*. Some open ground was also provided, where people could roll hoops, throw balls, sprint, or do other exercise. Peddlers hawked their wares in the baths, and teachers and poets often used the larger rooms and courtyards to teach or declaim.

Pompeii and a few other cities preserve evidence for separate baths catering to each sex. Elsewhere—to judge from a few inscribed bath regulations—the two sexes may have used the same facilities at different hours. We do not know if individuals bathed in the nude or with some modest covering, although Roman paintings and sculptures suggest a deep-seated aversion to total nudity. Baths were one of the most accessible places that the ordinary individual could go to be surrounded by opulent architecture and embellishment evoking Rome's majesty; statues of the imperial family were frequently displayed in them. Baths were extremely popular, therefore. They were good meeting spots. Often found near taverns, they had something of a racy reputation. As a famous epigram of the second century holds:

> Baths, wine, and lovemaking destroy our bodies,
> Yet lovemaking, wine, and baths make life worth living.
>   (*Palatine Anthology* 10.112)

EDUCATION

Integral to Roman culture was the Roman system of education. Schooling and literary culture were based on a thorough knowledge of the past, and the skill to re-shape the past for the present. There was little emphasis on innovation of a technological sort. Memorization was essential, and students had to learn by heart speeches of Cicero and long passages of Vergil, for example. Papyri found in the Roman camps at Masada record lines from Vergil's *Aeneid* scribbled by soldiers during the long siege. The most famous Roman libraries were those at Rome and Alexandria, but smaller ones were to be found in Athens, Ephesus, Comum, Thamugadi, and other cities. Vespasian and subsequent "good" emperors encouraged education by offering teachers immunity from public duties, and by funding professorships of rhetoric at Rome, Athens, and elsewhere. By the second century, girls could also participate in classes offered by publicly funded teachers in cities, at least through the basics of reading, writing, and grammar. Some elite women such as Balbilla, one of Sabina's companions, could even be as highly educated as their brothers and husbands.

The cultural and literary movement termed the Second Sophistic, which lasted from around Nero's time into the third century, reached its peak in the Antonine period. Public speakers like Dio Chrysostom, Polemo of Smyrna, Aelius Aristides, and Herodes Atticus thrived under the emperors from Trajan through Marcus Aurelius. Their speeches and essays—deeply imbued with nostalgia for the classical Greek past, yet keenly aware of present political realities—dazzle with rhetorical flourishes. Thanks to the *Lives of the Sophists*, written by Philostratus in the early third century, the best known participants in this movement are those from the Greek East or men like Favorinus of Arelate (modern Arles in France), who wrote in Greek. Orators and writers in Latin, however, also won great acclaim and public standing through rhetorical bravura. For all a reader's or translator's expertise, the surviving texts can scarcely convey the excitement of the mass gatherings that hung on these speakers' displays of learning and brilliant turns of phrase. Wealthy, ambitious young men flocked to study under the leading sophists, above all at Athens, Ephesus, or Smyrna. Such esteemed teachers were often active, arrogant public figures in their communities, as well as effective envoys to provincial governors or the emperor himself. Philostratus (*Lives* 535) admiringly comments that Polemo, for instance, "conversed with cities as his inferiors, emperors as not his superiors, and the gods as his equals."

STATE RELIGION AND IMPERIAL CULT

Religious practices show the empire at its most diverse, but even here there was a common thread, the acknowledgment of Roman state religion. As previously noted, apart from a few cults considered threatening to public order, individuals generally could do as they pleased in terms of religion. Many religious practices and beliefs initially considered "un-Roman" or alien were later acknowledged by the Roman state and made an official part of its religion. For example, despite Tiberius' expulsion of worshippers of Isis from Rome, Domitian disguised himself as an acolyte of Isis and evaded Rome's street fighting during the civil war of 69. Once Princeps, he magnificently rebuilt the Isaeum in Rome's Campus Martius, linking it to the imperial cult and featuring it on his coinage.

During the Principate the touchstone of Roman state religion was the imperial cult. So long as men and women participated in it by means of their community's rituals, the authorities generally paid little attention to their other religious acts and beliefs. Beginning with the Flavian period, we find ever more priests and priestesses of the cult in cities and provincial (or regional) gatherings in the Spanish provinces, North Africa, and Asia. Similarly, the first appearance of more than one imperial cult temple in a province of the Greek East dates to the 80s. The imperial cult spread elsewhere in the second century. Its prestigious priests and priestesses, titled *flamen, flaminica, archiereus* and the like, administered to their communities the annual oath of allegiance to the emperor and his family. They oversaw community-wide celebrations on the emperor's birthday, and on the birthdays of earlier deified emperors and empresses. They organized city festivals for military victories and the suppression of revolts, and for special events in the imperial family like the birth of a child. Today, the pervasiveness of television, the Internet, and other forms of electronic personal entertainment makes it hard to grasp the impact of a community's games, processions, sacrifices, and prayers. Such days of public festivity must have been particularly welcome to the working poor, like the Egyptian weaving apprentice whose contract allowed him only "twenty holidays a year on account of festivals without any deduction from his wages."

It is important to stress that the imperial cult was never imposed on a community by Rome. Individual cities and assemblies applied to the senate and emperor for permission to erect sanctuaries. If this were granted, the community usually chose its own priests and determined the statues to be paraded in processions, the order of the parades, and even the type of games to be performed. As a way to gain extra prestige, the patron or community might reapply to the emperor and senate for ratification of its decision. Although again the initiative had to be a local one, games organized in the emperor's honor likewise needed ratification by the emperor. Such procedures inevitably meant that the imperial cult took many different forms throughout the empire. In one city festivities might include contests of verse and prose panegyrics praising the emperor; in another, the celebration might be less highbrow, centered instead on animal sacrifices and offerings of incense and wine. The unifying thread was public awe and acknowledgment of imperial power. As we shall see in the following chapter, this is precisely why Christianity posed such a challenge to the Roman world.

SUGGESTED READINGS:

Bennett, Julian. 2001 (second edition). *Trajan: Optimus Princeps*. London and New York: Routledge.

Birley, Anthony R. 1997. *Hadrian. The Restless Emperor*. London and New York: Routledge.

Boatwright, Mary T. 2000. *Hadrian and the Cities of the Roman Empire*. Princeton: Princeton University Press.

Bowersock, Glen W. 1969. *Greek Sophists in the Roman Empire*. Oxford: Oxford University Press.

Evans, Harry B. 1994. *Water Distribution in Ancient Rome: The Evidence of Frontinus*. Ann Arbor: University of Michigan Press.

Jones, Brian W. 1992. *The Emperor Domitian*. London and New York: Routledge.

Macmullen, Ramsay. 1981. *Paganism in the Roman Empire*. New Haven and London: Yale University Press.

Potter, David S., and David J. Mattingly (eds.). 1999. *Life, Death, and Entertainment in the Roman Empire*. Ann Arbor: University of Michigan Press.

Smallwood, E. Mary. 1976. *The Jews Under Roman Rule from Pompey to Diocletian: A Study in Political Relations*. Leiden: Brill.

Wallace-Hadrill, Andrew. 1994. *Houses and Society in Pompeii and Herculaneum*. Princeton: Princeton University Press.

12

ITALY AND THE PROVINCES
Civil and Military Affairs (138–235)

SOURCES

For the period covered in this chapter—at least until about 220—inscriptions, papyri, archeology, coins, and legal treatises and opinions reflect general prosperity and marked attention to justice and law. Ulpian, Paulus, and other jurists flourished at the beginning of the third century, encouraged by the *constitutio Antoniniana* of 212 that granted Roman citizenship almost universally within the empire. Ulpian, for example, wrote 200 books to explain Roman law to the new citizens. Such initiatives must be kept in mind when reading the literary sources for this period, which tend to be critical of all the emperors except Antoninus Pius and Marcus Aurelius, and to paint a picture of general decadence.

Cassius Dio's record now draws upon personal experience and oral testimony. A senator from Bithynia, Dio rose to high civil and military positions under the Severan emperors, almost losing his life around 228 in a military insurrection while governor of Lower Pannonia. He usually portrays the Severans and their predecessor Commodus as hostile to individual senators and senatorial freedom, and he comments at the death of Commodus' father Marcus Aurelius, "Our history now descends from a kingdom of gold to one of iron and rust, as did the Romans' situation at that point" (71.36.4). Herodian, also writing in Greek in the early third century but serving in lower civil administration, describes events from 180 to 235 in eight books divided by individual rulers. He is a moralizer, and the rhetorical nature of his work can make it seem shallow, but he also furnishes vivid details that illuminate Rome's culture and society, like the funeral rites for Septimius Severus. Later and less reliable is the *Historia Augusta*, a set of imperial biographies beginning with

Hadrian, composed at the end of the fourth century. Its unknown author delights in salacious anecdotes about emperors' immorality and capriciousness, and shares a common perception of their growing neglect or mistreatment of the senate. Further, the apparent power of imperial women greatly increased with the Severans, creating another source of irritation for traditionalists. Overall, the historical texts for this era are fragmented, focused on the imperial court, and generally biased against individual emperors.

Further literature, less directly concerned with political and military events, sheds light on a wide variety of cultural and other aspects. Marcus Aurelius, a philosopher as well as Princeps, wrote *To Himself* (now called *Meditations*) in Greek, a startlingly personal exploration of his own conceptions of the Good and his place in human society. The *Metamorphoses* (now commonly called *The Golden Ass*), a picaresque Latin novel written by Apuleius (c. 125 to after 170, from North Africa), describes the adventures of a young man magically transformed into an ass, the lowliest of creatures, before Isis returns him to human form. Besides offering a fascinating tale, it is a good example of the recondite style of the Latin writing fashionable at that date. Numerous authors represent the Greek Second Sophistic: for example, Aelius Aristides (born in 118 in the province of Asia) wrote his *To Rome* around 144. A very different set of preoccupations is seen in the trenchant works of the first Christian apologists, including Tertullian (160s to 240s, from Carthage). Much can be learned from such sources: Tertullian's *On the Games*—a fierce denunciation of the shows in circus, theater, and amphitheater, and their ties with the Roman gods—incidentally preserves rich detail about these significant social occasions.

The first half of the chapter discusses the rulers of the period, and its volatile political and military events. The second half treats three broad topics that now come to assume increasing importance: Roman law, Roman citizenship, and religious practices and beliefs, including Christianity.

ANTONINUS PIUS (138–161)

Hadrian's successor Antoninus Pius never left Italy during the twenty-three years of his rule. He was much less involved with the military than were his predecessors and successors. Yet he maintained the appearance of military preparedness and encouraged good officers. A governor of Britain, Quintus Lollius Urbicus, reconquered southern Scotland. This advance was consolidated by the Wall of Antoninus, a turf wall on cobble foundations some hundred miles north of Hadrian's Wall; even so, for reasons no longer identifiable, Antoninus' Wall was abandoned not long after his death in 161, and Hadrian's Wall was then regarrisoned. Other military action, apparently overseen by Marcus Gavius Maximus (Praetorian Prefect from about 139 to 159), included a show of force against the Parthians at the beginning of Antoninus' rule, repulse of invading Moorish tribes in Mauretania and Numidia (145–150), minor skirmishes in Dacia, and a modest extension of Roman territory along the Rhine.

Figure 12.1 *The dynastic hopes of the Antonine family. The obverse of this bronze coin, a* ses-tertius *struck in the last year of Antoninus Pius' rule (160–161), depicts the emperor with a laurel crown of victory. The legend translates: "Antoninus Pius, Augustus, Father of the Fatherland, with tribunician power for the 24th time." The legend on the reverse reads: "To Augustan Piety. Consul for the fourth time," and also carries S C, denoting that the coin was issued with the senate's author-ity. The standing woman with four children on the reverse is to be identified with Faustina the Younger, Antoninus Pius' daughter, who by now had presented her husband Marcus Aurelius with four daughters (Lucilla, Cornificia, Fadilla, and Annia Faustina). Among other values, the coin highlights Rome's concern for population increase.*

Under Pius, no far-reaching legal changes were enacted, nor were there notable administrative changes other than the withdrawal of Hadrian's consular judges in Italy. This latter step, like many other actions by Antoninus, contributed to harmony between emperor and senate, one hallmark of his Principate. Another characteristic of the time is the firm stress on family and the imperial dynasty, which has meant that the era is often called the "Antonine" age. Although Antoninus may seem the most unmemorable of emperors, the sheer uneventfulness of his rule reflects both the accomplishments of the preceding half-century and his own capability. Antoninus' time seems to mark the empire's climax as an organized, benevolent, and self-assured form of rule. The diverse forces that would undermine its stability were already pre-sent—unrest along the borders, inequities at home—but the vast majority of the empire's inhabitants still accepted their present condition more or less willingly.

MARCUS AURELIUS (161–180) AND LUCIUS VERUS (161–169)

Antoninus Pius was deified immediately after his death. Power then passed smoothly to Marcus Aurelius and Lucius Verus, as Hadrian had arranged in 138

news of Antoninus' death. For much of the time, they divided their energies and attention, Verus commanding in the East against the Parthians from 162 to 166, and Marcus Aurelius ruling in Rome or, after 167, often on the northern frontiers. The double threat to East and North led to the creation of two new legions in the mid 160s.

Verus' Parthian war was prompted by the Parthians' seizure of Armenia and invasion of Syria in 161. In 162 he went to Antioch to organize the Roman counter-offensive, which was boosted by three legions and additional troops dispatched to the East from the Rhine and Danube. Much of the actual fighting was undertaken for Verus by others, however. In 165–166 Gaius Avidius Cassius, then governor of Syria, won conspicuous victories in Mesopotamia, destroyed Seleucia, and razed the Parthian king's palace at neighboring Ctesiphon (near modern Baghdad, Iraq). The Parthians sued for peace, relinquishing part of northern Mesopotamia to Roman control, and Verus celebrated a triumph in Rome jointly with Marcus Aurelius. This brief offensive against Parthia underscores the dead-locked, evenly matched strength of the two empires. Parthian forces were well organized and equipped, and Avidius Cassius' victories would turn out to be short-lived.

Roman troops returning from the East brought back with them a violent infectious disease, perhaps smallpox. After 166, it spread through the empire for some twenty-five years. More than a fifth of the inhabitants of Alexandria are said to have perished, other cities were decimated, and military camps were particularly hard hit. Heavy mobilization of troops for the campaigns against the Marcomanni in the North must have increased the death toll. Even rural areas were afflicted, so that suffering was then exacerbated by ensuing famines. Only the interior of North Africa may have escaped the epidemic. Given the rudimentary understanding of germs and disease, this plague must have been terrifying as well as devastating. It may have contributed to increasing tensions between Christians and the polytheistic majority, which had already led to mob violence against Christians at Smyrna (modern Izmir, Turkey) during the 150s. Another such outbreak, at Lugdunum in Gaul, occurred in 177. The decrease and demoralization of the military and urban populations—that is, the skilled individuals who undertook defense, commerce, and administration—undoubtedly weakened the empire. It is true that in the city of Rome itself, as well as in those provinces not directly affected by warfare, literature, monuments, art, and architecture all continue to convey the impression of a comfortable urban elite through the beginning of the third century. By then, however, we also begin to hear more frequent complaints about difficulties in filling municipal administrative positions.

Life-threatening epidemic disease was a regular feature of the ancient world. We cannot identify precisely the closest modern equivalent for each "pestilence" reported by our sources, but smallpox, malaria, tuberculosis, typhus, measles, and leprosy were almost certainly common. Ironically, epidemics were spread and made more devastating by the general peace that encouraged travel, long-

BOX 12.2: Morbidity and Mortality in the Roman Empire

Other contemporary authors note the effects of the Antonine plague, but the sophist Aelius Aristides gives a vivid description of its effects on him personally. Even the short excerpt below allows us to discern misunderstandings about communicable diseases and the lack of proper medicines:

I happened to be in the suburbs at the height of summer [165]. A plague infected nearly all my neighbors. First two or three of my servants grew sick, then one after another. Then all were in bed, both the younger and the older. I was the last to be attacked. . . . The livestock, too, became sick. And if anyone tried to move, he immediately lay dead before the front door. . . . Everything was filled with despair and wailing and groans, and every kind of difficulty. There was also terrible sickness in the city . . . I was attacked by the terrible burning of a bilious mixture and prevented from taking nourishment. . . . The doctors gave up, and announced that I would die immediately . . . [But after seeing visions of the divinities Asclepius and Athena,] I took goose liver and sausage, and little by little with trouble and difficulty I recovered. The fever did not leave me completely until the most valued of my foster children died. (*Orations* 48.38–44, excerpted from P. Aelius Aristides, *The Complete Works*, translated into English by Charles A. Behr, Leiden: Brill, 1981–)

distance transport, and concentration of populations in cities and military camps. To judge by the limited evidence available, the young were particularly susceptible to disease and ill health. Our understanding of Roman mortality patterns depends on 100,000 or more inscribed epitaphs (mostly dating between 50 B.C. and A.D. 235), human skeletal remains, and an excerpt from the *Digest* (35.2.68.pr) that concerns inheritance taxes. Despite many problems with this material, some facts emerge. Without question, there was very high infant and childhood mortality: Perhaps 33 percent of all children born in a given year died before reaching their first birthday, and 55 percent before reaching their fifth. Once a teenager passed the fifteen-year-old threshold, however, he or she might expect to live to be at least thirty-six; even so, in view of infant and child mortality, the median age of the population was only about twenty-five years. No more than about 8 percent of the Roman population lived to be more than fifty years old.

These general patterns are very broad, and ignore many distinctions. Military medicine was excellent in its provision of doctors, quarantine wards, fresh water, and medicinal herbs to the troops. But such advantages were certainly offset during warfare, since there were no antibiotics. Rural civilians living far from a port or a major Roman road would be less exposed to epidemics; on the other hand, they surely suffered from malnutrition, polluted water, and overwork, unless they were part of the small wealthy minority. Ample running water brought by aqueducts must have made the Roman cities supplied in this way least vulnerable to

Map 12.1 *Campaigns of Marcus Aurelius and the Severan Emperors*

E F G

SARMATIANS

incum

□ Potaissa
lum
● Sarmizegetusa
num
ninacium
● Novae □ Durostorum

MOESIA (LOWER)

Danube

BLACK SEA

● Amastris

ARMENIA

□ Satala

THRACE Byzantium

SIA
ER) BITHYNIA-PONTUS

ACEDONIA Perinthus

CAPPADOCIA

Nicomedia ● Ancyra Melitene
□

Cyzicus GALATIA MESOPOTAMIA Tigris

Caesarea (Mazaca) Samosata Resaina
□

essalonice Pergamum ● Faustinopolis Carrhae ● Singara
□

Smyrna CILICIA Issus OSROENE PARTHIA

Ephesus Tarsus Antioch

Corinth LYCIA SYRIA Euphrates Ctesiphon

AIA Myra CYPRUS Raphaneae COELE ● Palmyra Seleucia

Paphos Emesa

Gortyn Berytus SYRIA
Tyre PHOENICE

Caparcotna Bostra
Caesarea ⊡

ARE Aelia Capitolina

Petra

● Cyrene Alexandria ARABIA PETRAEA
□

E
G
Y Nile
P
T

water-borne disease. But at the same time the amenities and opportunities offered by cities must have led to the kind of crowding that admitted more air- and vector-borne disease. Even the rich, who could enjoy the indisputable advantages of roomy living space, a varied, plentiful diet, and clean water, were exposed to ills that have come to be recognized in modern times: lead poisoning both from the water pipes to their residences and from women's cosmetics, and inadvertent poisoning from abortifacients and other medicines.

The Romans' decision to end the Parthian war in 166 coincides with growing problems along the Danube, caused in part perhaps because one key legion and auxiliaries had been removed from the forces here. Beginning in 166, the German Lombards, Marcomanni, and Quadi, as well as the eastern Sarmatians and Iazyges, crossed the middle Danube into the Pannonian provinces and Dacia, and then pushed farther south. Both Marcus Aurelius and Verus went north to engage them in 168; when Verus died of a stroke in 169, Marcus Aurelius continued as sole Princeps. In fact he was to spend most of the rest of his life fighting in the north, and in his *Meditations* he steels himself to carry through his obligations even though he considers warfare contrary to philosophy and the Good (10.9). Before 170, the Marcomanni and Quadi reached Aquileia, an important port on the Adriatic Sea. Although they were then both turned back in hard fighting, other tribes joined the assault meantime. These persistent hostilities divide into the First and Second Marcomannic Wars (166–173, 176–180). At some stage during them, the Romans evidently felt sufficiently successful and confident to envision the creation of two further provinces north of the Danube that would be named Marcomannia and Sarmatia.

Roman success depended in part on Marcus Aurelius' acceptance of trans-Danubian migrants within the borders of the empire. Such *dediticii*—said to number 10,000 in all—are known to have been settled in the German provinces, Pannonia, Dacia, Moesia, and possibly even in Italy too. Their status is controversial, since the key document—a papyrus recording part of the *constitutio Antoniniana* (see Caracalla, below)—is damaged. It seems, however, that they were permanently debarred from full integration into the Roman state. Even so, their settlement within its borders satisfied their land hunger, and made them responsible for protecting Rome's assets and land, even though they were perceived as "barbarians." Archeological evidence—mostly grave goods and tombstones, but also domestic and religious structures—indicates that at least some dediticii did assimilate Roman culture. In practice, the distinction between Roman and non-Roman was not as sharp as literature and the visual arts represent it to be. Archeology also reveals the presence of Roman forts and outposts across the Danube within barbarian territory (*barbaricum*).

Marcus Aurelius' great fame rests not on his military victories but on his frank, and apparently genuine, commitment to Rome's "beneficial ideology." In line with his own philosophical interests, he endowed professorships of rhetoric and philosophy at Athens. Rather than increase taxes to fund the two new legions

Figure 12.3 *This white marble relief panel from a lost monument in Rome shows part of a religious ceremony. In the background, the temple of Jupiter Optimus Maximus is depicted frontally; to its right is shown one of the many covered walkways (or colonnades) on Rome's Capitoline hill. Marcus Aurelius, the large, individualized figure just left of center, offers a libation at a portable altar; he has pulled a fold of his toga over his head ritually. Next to him, a boy holds an incense box, and a bearded man (shown small because of his low social status) plays music to accompany the ritual and to mask any ill-omened sounds. The bare-chested man with the axe is a* victimarius, *a specialized religious attendant who slew a bull (as here) or other victims in blood sacrifices. Behind Marcus Aurelius stands a tall senator identified as Tiberius Claudius Pompeianus, his close friend and later son-in-law (see Table 11.1). The emperor appears as the intermediary between humans and gods, and as the preserver of Rome and its order.*

raised in the 160s, he auctioned off crown jewels and imperial finery. His council of advisers worked well, with its members in Rome handling routine administration while he was far away on campaign. When he reinstated four consular judges for Italy (Hadrian's initiative, dropped by Antoninus), there was no protest by leading figures in Italy or in Rome itself.

Only one significant civil disturbance marred the general atmosphere of harmony under Marcus Aurelius. It occurred in spring and summer 175, and reveals some fundamental tensions in the empire, although our disjointed source material leaves the background obscure. Avidius Cassius, the general largely responsible for the successful Parthian War of 162–166, was appointed governor of Egypt in 171, where he suppressed an uprising of desert peoples. Later, probably in early March 175, he announced to his troops that Marcus Aurelius was dead, but that he himself was willing to assume imperial power. Duly acclaimed emperor, he ruled in the East for almost four months. He was then killed by a subordinate, just as Marcus Aurelius was making his way to the East with his wife Faustina and the fourteen-year-old Commodus, their sole son to survive childhood.

According to some versions of these events, Avidius undertook his coup only after receiving a report that Marcus Aurelius had died. In other versions, however, he is said to have been encouraged to revolt by Faustina, either on sheer impulse or because she feared for her husband's health and wanted to ensure the succession of her son. The first variant highlights the empire's inadequate communications; the second, the deep-seated mistrust of women, especially those in power, and the perpetual problem of imperial succession. A final striking aspect of Avidius Cassius' rule over Egypt, Syria, and most of Asia Minor is that it reflects the underlying division of the empire. Without mass communication and rapid transport, it was inherently difficult to maintain political unity over Rome's wide expanse of territory and cultures.

After personally reestablishing his imperial authority in the East, Marcus Aurelius returned to Rome in 176. Faustina died in Cappadocia on the return journey; the senate deified her, and the city where she died was renamed Faustinopolis. Together with Commodus, Marcus Aurelius then celebrated a great triumph over the northern barbarians. Commodus received further honors, the consulship and acclamation as Augustus. But by the end of 176, father and son, now joint Augusti, were in Pannonia and Raetia to confront renewed threats from the North. When Marcus Aurelius died of natural causes in early March 180 at Vindobona (modern Vienna, Austria), nineteen-year-old Commodus was acclaimed sole emperor. It is not clear whether he had personally participated in any battles or major military decisions yet, but his father had always surrounded him with the best tutors and a loyal, capable group of advisers. In the ancient sources, Marcus Aurelius' designation of his son to succeed him as Princeps is the one blot on his reputation. Yet his choice was in line with Rome's traditional emphasis on kinship, and even most of the adopted emperors in fact had family links to their predecessors.

COMMODUS (176–192, SOLE AUGUSTUS AFTER 180)

During the first five months of his sole rule, Commodus concluded the Marcomannic wars, and abandoned the plans for the prospective new provinces of Marcomannia and Sarmatia. Although Herodian and the *Historia Augusta* maintain that his decision ran completely counter to his father's aims as well as the opinion of his advisers, some scholars today believe that by now Marcus Aurelius himself had decided to abandon these campaigns to extend Roman control across the Danube. Protracted difficulties in Pannonia had already highlighted the limits of Roman communications and manpower, and Commodus' peace treaty with the Marcomanni and Quadi may have included the one-time recruitment of a large number of their young men. Yet once again—just as in 117 after the abandonment of Trajan's eastern conquests—many observers regarded the preference for peace and the consolidation of borders as inglorious expedients, and they criticized Commodus accordingly.

Commodus returned to Rome and another triumph, and the Column of Marcus Aurelius (still a prominent monument today) was erected at Rome to mark the wars' end and Rome's invincibility. Although Commodus did take some initiatives in the provinces, he never came close to matching his father's exceptional concern for the empire. Rather, Commodus' council of advisers was entrusted with much of the administration, and successive Praetorian Prefects exercised great power. Commodus behaved erratically towards the senate, and conspiracies soon began. In 182, his sister Lucilla (once married to Lucius Verus) was implicated in a failed assassination plot involving one of the Praetorian Prefects and other highly placed men; many were executed. Disorder in Rome itself increased, with the Praetorians lynching their Prefect, Sextus Tigidius Perennis in 185. Commodus then fell under the influence of Marcus Aurelius Cleander, his freedman servant whom he promoted to be Praetorian Prefect.

Figure 12.4 *Commodus as Hercules. This bust, dated to around 190, was found in an underground walkway* (cryptoporticus) *of a luxury garden belonging to the imperial family. The face is that of the adult Commodus as it is known from other portraits, but he is portrayed as Hercules. He wears the lion skin over his head, and carries a club in his right hand. In his left he holds apples, recalling another of Hercules' legendary labors—taking the apples of the Hesperides. The bust is balanced on an Amazonian shield whose corners are fashioned as imperial eagles, and on the tops of two cornucopias. All these elements rest on a small globe that symbolizes the entire world. Two Amazons (one now entirely missing) flanked the support, looking upwards in homage to the hero. The bust corresponds to ancient writers' claims that Commodus "accepted statues in the costume of Hercules, and sacrifices were made to him as a god"* (Historia Augusta, Commodus 9.2). *Its remarkable preservation suggests that it was carefully hidden after Commodus' violent death.*

To judge by the accounts in our sources, Commodus' own major concerns were his personal gratification and that of Rome's masses. He made many distributions in the city, and restructured its grain imports. Like Nero before him, he frequently appeared in untraditional public roles. He fancied himself a great gladiator and wild beast hunter (*bestiarius*). With his own hands he supposedly killed many thousands of animals, including elephants and ostriches. He is also said to have fought as a gladiator 365 times during his father's rule, and so often during his own Principate that he won a thousand gladiatorial crowns just by defeating or killing "net-fighters," quite apart from other types of gladiator (*Historia Augusta, Commodus* 13.1).

From 185 to 192 the situation grew grimmer for everyone, the populace included. Cleander's fall from power in 190 was marked by rioting, and authority then passed to Commodus' mistress and one of his servants. In 192, he sponsored two full weeks of gladiatorial games in which he personally performed. He planned to take up the consulship on January 1, 193, dressed as a gladiator rather than in the traditional toga, and to rename Rome "Colonia Commodiana." His dangerous instability finally provoked his assassination on December 31, 192, and the senate then immediately condemned his memory (*damnatio memoriae*).

The chaos that followed stems from Rome's lack of constitutional means either to expel unworthy emperors or to ensure an orderly succession. This deficiency was to cause two more serious internal crises within the next half-century (in 193–197 and 217–221), and ever more frequent ones after 235. From the turmoil of 193 emerged the dynasty known as the Severans (Latin, Severi), and an apparent renaissance for the city of Rome, the northern provinces, North Africa, and the East. The Severans are named after Lucius Septimius Severus, who seized power in 193. All subsequent rulers until 235—even the eques Macrinus and his ten-year-old son Diadumenianus who ruled briefly in 217–218—either were, or claimed to be, related to Septimius Severus or to his wife, Julia Domna (see Table 12.1).

SEPTIMIUS SEVERUS (193–211)

Upon Commodus' assassination, various groups vied for power—the senate, the Praetorians, and the army, or rather three different divisions within the army that each promoted its own commander. Each group proved strong enough to bring a candidate to imperial power, but only one of these, Septimius Severus (promoted by the troops along the Danube), was then able to maintain and expand his control.

The first Princeps to be proclaimed in 193 was Lucius Helvius Pertinax. A sixty-six-year-old senator who had loyally served Marcus Aurelius in military and civil positions, Pertinax was the senate's choice. His position as City Prefect in 192 gave him command of the Urban Cohorts in Rome. The Praetorians, however, acclaimed him only reluctantly, despite being paid a donative of about 12,000 sesterces per man. Pertinax vowed to respect the senate, and to restore the

Table 12.1 The Severan Family *The presentation follows the style of Table 9.1, explained there.*

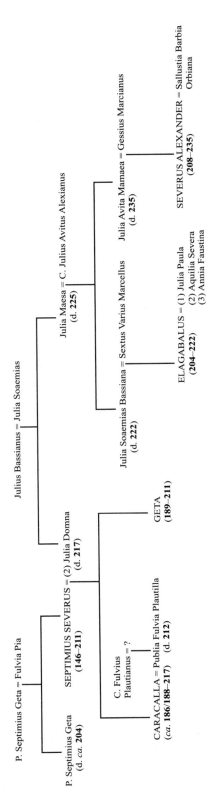

imperial finances ravaged by Commodus' extravagant games and luxuries. To raise money, he auctioned Commodus' property, cut back on expenditures, and announced other reforms. He promised full ownership and ten years free from taxes to those who would settle and farm abandoned land; this initiative would bring back into cultivation acreage no longer cultivated because of the plague and the losses in Rome's northern and eastern wars. But Pertinax failed to enlist the Praetorians' wholehearted support, and at the end of March 193 they murdered him in the palace. To judge by Cassius Dio's comment that Pertinax had "failed to comprehend that one cannot safely reform everything at once" (73.10.3), it was not just the Praetorians who were becoming dissatisfied with Pertinax. Nonetheless, it was they who determined Rome's next emperor.

The ensuing episode is reported with disgust by Herodian and others: After assassinating Pertinax, the Praetorians proceeded to auction off the Principate at the gates of their barracks in Rome. Two senators were in the bidding: Titus Flavius Sulpicianus, the City Prefect and father-in-law of Pertinax, and Marcus Didius Severus Julianus. The latter won with his promise of 25,000 sesterces per man, more than double what Pertinax had given three months earlier. Cowed by the Praetorians, the senate ratified their choice. The Roman populace rioted throughout the city and staged an all-night protest in the Circus Maximus.

But the armies outside of Rome, who vastly outnumbered the Praetorians, had already declared emperors of their own. The three legions in Syria declared for Gaius Pescennius Niger, and seven other legions in the East followed their lead. Britain's three legions and auxiliary troops declared for their own commander, Decimus Clodius Albinus. The legion at Carnuntum in Upper Pannonia (modern Petronell, Austria) acclaimed as emperor their commander and governor, Lucius Septimius Severus; his support then spread to the other legions on the Danube and the Rhine, sixteen in all. Severus was the shrewdest of the three claimants, according to Cassius Dio. He set off for Rome immediately, and reduced the threat from his rivals by appointing Albinus "Caesar" over Britain, Gaul, and Spain. As the Praetorians' loyalty to Didius Julianus began to waver, the senate sentenced him to death, and acclaimed Septimius Severus instead. Didius Julianus was killed at the beginning of June 193. A week later, Septimius Severus entered Rome as Princeps.

Septimius Severus was as politically astute as he was militarily brilliant. He entered the city as a civilian in a toga, as had Trajan, but he did not disband the cavalry and infantry forces accompanying him. He had the damnation of Commodus' memory cancelled, and Pertinax deified; the senate confirmed his own assumption of the name Pertinax. The purpose of these measures was to link himself to recent emperors, and to forge a tie with the senatorial favorite Pertinax. In order to break the excessive power that the Praetorians had been wielding in the city, he dismissed this fickle body of troops, and replaced them with legionaries selected for their valor and loyalty. He stationed a legion about thirteen miles (21 km) southeast of Rome at Castra Albana (modern Albano Laziale), and increased

BOX 12.3: Deification Ceremonies for Pertinax in Septimius Severus' Rome

Cassius Dio, as an eyewitness, describes Septimius Severus' honors for Pertinax in 193. The following excerpt shows the awesome elaboration of the ceremony, as well as some of the ways in which divine attributes and trappings were bestowed upon emperors.

Upon establishing himself in power, Septimius Severus erected a shrine to Pertinax, and commanded that his name should be mentioned at the close of all prayers and all oaths; he also ordered that a golden image of Pertinax should be carried into the Circus Maximus on a chariot drawn by elephants. . . . In the Roman Forum a wooden platform was constructed next to the marble rostra, upon which was set a shrine made of ivory and gold. In it there was placed a bier of the same materials adorned with coverings of purple and gold. Upon the bier rested an effigy of Pertinax in wax, laid out in triumphal costume; there was a handsome youth keeping the flies away from it with peacock feathers, as though it were really a person sleeping. . . . There moved past, first, images of all the famous Romans of old, then choruses of boys and men, singing a dirge-like hymn to Pertinax; next followed all the subject nations, represented by bronze figures attired in native costume, and then groups within Rome itself—lictors, scribes, heralds, and the like. . . . Behind these were the cavalry and infantry in armor, the racehorses, and all the funeral offerings sent by the emperor, by us [senators] and our wives and the more distinguished *equites*, as well as by communities and by associations in Rome. Following them came an altar gilded all over and decorated with ivory and Indian gems. [After a eulogy by Septimius Severus, the bier was taken in procession to a funeral pyre built like a tower in the Campus Martius. Then, after the offerings had been thrown onto the pyre, and soldiers had performed some further pageantry around it,] at last the consuls applied fire to the structure, and when that had been done, an eagle flew up out it. In this way Pertinax was made immortal. (75.4.1–5.5; translation excerpted and adapted from the Loeb edition)

the size of the city's "watchmen" units (*vigiles*) and the Urban Cohorts. These additional forces there offset the extraordinary power that the Praetorians had wielded. No legion had ever been stationed far from a war zone or disturbed area before, let alone in Italy.

With Rome secured and Albinus placated, Septimius Severus next marched east against Niger, who had moved north into the province of Asia. He proceeded to chase after Niger's army, clashing with it at Byzantium, Cyzicus, Nicaea, and finally Issus. At Issus alone, the casualties were said to have been so heavy that the nearby river ran red. In further pursuit, Septimius Severus seized Antioch, the leading city of Syria, and Niger was killed fleeing farther east. The cities that had supported him now had to pay enormous indemnities as well as suffer other punishments: Antioch and Byzantium, for example, were no longer permitted to administer their own affairs, and Byzantium's famous city walls were pulled down. Looking to the future, Septimius Severus then acted on the lesson that he had learned from Niger's strength. He divided the large province of Syria into two smaller ones, Syria Coele and Syria Phoenice, thus reducing the number of troops under the command of any single governor.

To boost his image and to deflect attention from civil war, Septimius Severus campaigned against the Parthians in 194–195 and again in 197–199, claiming first that they had offered to help Niger, and then that they had seized Roman territory. In these offensives, he annexed northern Mesopotamia as a Roman province (as had Trajan briefly), and also created the province of Osroene. Both campaigns were heralded as glorious triumphs, and were celebrated on the Arch of Septimius Severus that is still a prominent feature of the Roman Forum today. Cassius Dio (75.3.3), however, deplores the conquest of Mesopotamia as "a source of constant wars and great expense to us," seeing it as an overextension of Roman power. It is true that these new provinces did set off a chain of events which weakened the Parthian kingdom, ultimately causing it to fall by 226 to a new group, the Sasanids or Persians. The Sasanid kingdom proved notably more aggressive than its Parthian predecessor, and better able to coordinate the resources of the large area under its control. Moreover, the Sasanids combined their rule with a monotheistic religion, Mazdaism, encouraging fierce loyalty and unity throughout the kingdom. The Sasanids fell only in the seventh century (to Muslim Arabs), and in their long tenure of power they caused grave difficulty for Rome as well as for its successor in the East, the Byzantine Empire.

Between the two Parthian wars Septimius Severus eliminated his rival Albinus, and had himself and his family adopted posthumously into the family of Marcus Aurelius. This latter step, confirmed by the senate, was intended to claim for Septimius Severus a dynastic relationship with the quintessential "good" emperor. When Septimius Severus at the same time renamed his eleven-year-old son Septimius Bassianus as Marcus Aurelius Antoninus and elevated him to the rank of Augustus, he demonstrated yet again the primacy of family at Rome. This son is better known by his nickname "Caracalla," derived from the Latin word for the long overcoat used by Roman soldiers stationed in the north. Caracalla's designation as Caesar called into question his father's earlier grant of that title to Albinus, and in fact by 196 Severus had turned west to face his rival there. The two-year campaign against Albinus (196–197) was conducted primarily in Gaul, culminating in his defeat at Lugdunum. Casualties on both sides were high, and Albinus' defeat in this battle also led to the elimination of many senators who had supported him in Rome.

Despite such appalling loss of life, Septimius Severus enjoyed great popularity among the troops. Like Trajan, he fought alongside them and shared their hardships on campaign. He readily engaged in warfare. In addition to his Parthian wars and civil conflict, he fought in Britain from 208 until his death there in 211, trying to deter invasions from the north or perhaps attempting to conquer Caledonia (Scotland). He also enacted many far-reaching military reforms. He further increased the number of legions by three (making a total of thirty-three), stationing one of them

near Rome itself as noted above, and the other two in the new province of Mesopotamia. He improved the terms of military service. Around 200, he permitted
soldiers to be married while in service, removing the ban on such marriages imposed by Augustus (see Chapter Nine). Soldiers no doubt appreciated this official
recognition of the army as a way of life; documentary evidence shows that veterans' sons were already making up a large proportion of recruits. Septimius Severus increased the pay for legionaries from 1,200 to 2,000 sesterces a year, with
corresponding increases in the stipends of auxiliary units. Herodian and others
denounce these substantial pay increases and other military reforms as blatant
attempts to buy the army's favor, but on the other side it is important to recognize
that, despite inflation, there had been no increase in military pay since 84, over a
century earlier. The personal nature of Septimius Severus' ties to the military is
demonstrated by the spread of the title "Mother of the Camp(s)" (*mater castrorum*)
for his wife Julia Domna.

Our literary sources contrast Septimius Severus' generosity to the army with his
rough handling of the senate and individual senators. His violent rise to power
prompted numerous treason trials which he and his close advisers heard rather
than the senate as a whole. The sentences handed down were arbitrary and usually harsh: On one occasion, for example, Septimius Severus released thirty-five
senators charged with having supported Albinus, but killed twenty-nine others.
He reduced the number of administrative posts open to senators, and gave more
prestige and positions to equites. Equites now held almost all the great prefec-
tures as well as new salaried positions created specifically for them. Both the City
Prefect and Praetorian Prefects extended their administrative and military duties
to include judicial ones, and the former's jurisdiction was extended to a one hun-
dred-mile limit. All three of Septimius Severus' new legions were placed under
equestrian rather than senatorial commanders, and the army's command structure
was reformed, making it possible for equites to rise all the way through the ranks.
Within a generation, the equestrian officer Macrinus had done precisely this (see
Macrinus, below).

Our fragmentary, biased literary sources make it impossible to date most of
Septimius Severus' reforms at all precisely or, more important, to assess their aims
with confidence. Cassius Dio and others admit that he was a Princeps who had a
brilliant, wide-ranging mind, and that he diligently attended to all the business of
Roman government and law. He was closely associated with outstanding jurists
like Aemilius Papinianus, who wrote extensively as well as taking charge of petitions to the emperor (the post of *a libellis*) and later becoming Praetorian Prefect;
by the fourth century, Papinian was widely considered the greatest Roman jurist.
Despite his heavy spending, Septimius Severus left a surplus in the treasury. He
clearly had a talent for manipulating public opinion. He lavishly praised Cassius
Dio (73.23) for writing a "little book about the dreams and portents which had
given the emperor reason to hope for the imperial power"; marks of divine favor
towards him are frequently noted. He built and restored temples and other mon-

uments in Rome. Very notably, the "Septizodium," which he dedicated at the corner of the Palatine Hill in 203, was a multistoried, multicolored marble façade that displayed statues to visitors approaching Rome from the south; the figure of Septimius Severus himself dominated it. In 202, on the tenth anniversary of his accession, he gave the Praetorian Guard and the Roman populace *aurei* amounting to two hundred million sesterces—more than any other single donative had ever totaled. He frequently presented public displays, including the spectacular funeral

Figure 12.5 *This painting on wood depicted Septimius Severus, his wife Julia Domna, and their two sons Caracalla and Geta; Geta has been defaced, however. The painting dates to soon after 198, when Geta was awarded the title "most noble Caesar," and his older brother Caracalla was made Augustus with their father. Here, Septimius Severus and Caracalla wear gem-studded gold crowns, and Julia Domna wears a smaller, opulent diadem on her head; Geta, too, presumably wore some sort of crown. The three males also carry scepters. This image of a happy, united family is belied by a history of persistent discord between the two brothers. Although on his deathbed Septimius Severus is said to have advised his sons, "Stay partners, enrich the soldiers, and don't care about anyone else at all" (Cassius Dio 76.15.2), within a year Caracalla had ordered his brother's murder. Geta's name and image were then erased from all public records* (damnatio memoriae). *As in the present instance, however, such erasures themselves were often prominent, a striking reminder of the power of public opinion.*

arranged for Pertinax in the Roman Forum and Campus Martius. Meantime he by no means neglected the empire outside the city of Rome. In the course of his rise to power and his travels as emperor—to Syria and Egypt in 199–202, to North Africa in 202–203, and to Britain in 208-211—he visited most of the Roman world, and evidently did so with a genuine sense of duty.

Even when all this is said, the overall picture remains incoherent. Septimius Severus is undeniably one of Rome's great reforming emperors: Like Augustus and Hadrian, he profoundly changed many Roman institutions. Unlike the rule of these two predecessors, however, his was not followed by prosperity and general peace. Instead, his successors were so politically incompetent and militarily inept that their failures damage Severus himself and his reforms. Further, his years as Princeps—unlike those of Augustus, by contrast—were not long enough to efface his use of civil war to gain power. The senatorial bias of the literary sources, our relative ignorance of much of the wider context, and Rome's subsequent history all combine to leave Septimius Severus with less than his due.

CARACALLA (198–217, SOLE AUGUSTUS AFTER 211)

Caracalla (officially Marcus Aurelius Antoninus), a less charismatic and more brutal personality than Septimius Severus, followed his father's deathbed advice to show special concern for the military, and even raised legionary pay further from two to three thousand sesterces a year. It may have been the need to fund this substantial increase that caused him to issue the *constitutio Antoniniana* in 212, known from a fragmentary papyrus, Ulpian, and Cassius Dio. By this decree he granted Roman citizenship to virtually all the free inhabitants of the empire. Cassius Dio (77.9–10) says that he did this to gain revenue, and various other motives have been advanced too. Only Roman citizens had been liable to pay the 5 percent inheritance tax that had been earmarked for legionaries' discharge bonuses ever since the time of Augustus; Caracalla's decree made many more liable for the tax. But if the aim of the universal grant of citizenship was to raise money, it failed. Around the same time as he made the grant, Caracalla issued a new coin, the "Antoninianus," that was nominally worth twice the silver denarius and eight times the bronze sestertius (four sesterces = one denarius). Even at its issue, however, the Antoninianus contained only half as much silver as the denarius. It later became more debased and led to inflation.

Caracalla needed the goodwill of the soldiers, since the empire's borders were increasingly under attack and he spent most of his Principate on campaign. In 213–214, he campaigned against Alamanni and Goths in Germany, where he defeated some tribes and settled other difficulties by diplomacy. In 215 he moved to Armenia in order to tackle problems caused by his father's Parthian wars. He traveled there through the Danubian regions, and this was where he mobilized his army. By 216, he had successfully battled through Armenia to points farther east and south in Parthia. In 217, however, he was assassinated at Carrhae. His officers feared his erratic paranoia, and his troops were disgruntled at seemingly endless campaigns in desert conditions.

MACRINUS (217–218)

The leader of the coup, now saluted as Augustus by the troops, was Marcus Opellius Macrinus, an *eques* from Mauretania who had held the position of Praetorian Prefect under Caracalla since 212, but had never been made a senator. He thus becomes the first Roman emperor without senatorial rank. Although he had plotted Caracalla's assassination, he quickly saw the need to associate himself with the Severan family because of its widespread popularity among the military. He adopted the name Severus for himself, and added "Antoninus" to the name of his young son Marcus Opellius Diadumenianus, whom he also designated as Caesar. He was unsuccessful in continuing the campaign against the Parthians, and caused outrage among his troops when he negotiated a treaty, because this was seen as a cowardly attempt to buy off the enemy. Even more damaging were his decisions to make reductions in army pay, and to keep the Danubian troops in the East. In 218 the increasingly dissatisfied troops were approached by Julia Maesa, the sister of Septimius Severus' wife Julia Domna, who claimed that Caracalla was really the father of her fourteen-year-old grandson, Varius Avitus Bassianus (see Table 12.1). As a result, the army eagerly saluted him as Marcus Aurelius Antoninus. Macrinus and Diadumenianus were then hunted down and killed by the same troops who had supported their supplanting Caracalla as emperor only a year before.

ELAGABALUS (218–222)

The four-year rule of Marcus Aurelius Antoninus—or Elagabalus (alternatively Heliogabalus) as he preferred to be called—was one of the strangest that Rome ever experienced. Elagabalus differed from all previous emperors. His advancement resulted not from his own ambitions but from those of his grandmother, Julia Maesa, and his mother, Julia Soaemias Bassiana. His name derived from the god he worshiped as hereditary priest, Elah-Gabal, the sun god of Emesa (modern Homs, Syria). This god was represented not in human form but as a "betel," a sacred black stone. Although some other deities in Rome likewise lacked anthropomorphic representations—the Magna Mater, for example, brought to the city in the late third century B.C.—many Romans were antagonized by the conspicuous orgiastic rites for Elah-Gabal, as well as by Elagabalus' fervid promotion of his own religion. When he arrived in Rome a year after his acclamation in 218, it was religious rituals and spaces that preoccupied him, not government. He built two temples for his sun god, one of them in the imperial palace on the Palatine. When he "married" his sun god to the Carthaginian deity Juno Caelestis, he divorced his own wife to marry a Vestal Virgin, Aquilia Severa, in a parallel "sacred marriage" that appalled traditionalists. He then made "the Unconquerable God, the Sun Elagabalus" (*deus invictus Sol Elagabalus*) the main deity of Rome. Novel and shocking choice though this was for Romans, Elagabalus' promotion of monotheism does at least correspond to other sentiments of the time (see next section).

The senatorial authors, stung by Elagabalus' indifference to administration, depict him as a freakish tyrant, and maintain that everything was entrusted to his mother and grandmother. In 221 his grandmother, Julia Maesa, certainly forced him to adopt his cousin, Gessius Alexianus Bassianus, as Caesar. Thereafter the power play intensified. The following year, Julia Avita Mamaea, Elagabalus' aunt and the mother of his cousin, bribed the Praetorians to murder both Elagabalus and his mother, Julia Soaemias, Mamaea's own sister. His cousin Alexianus was then acclaimed emperor as Marcus Aurelius Severus Alexander.

SEVERUS ALEXANDER (222–235)

Although only fourteen years old at his accession, Severus Alexander ruled with some success for the relatively long period of thirteen years. Part of the credit must go to his mother, Julia Mamaea, whose title "Mother of Augustus, and of the Camps, and of the Senate, and of the Fatherland," indicates, however conventionally, that attention was directed to military and civil matters alike. But Severus Alexander also gained by his ostensible deference to the senate. He placed some senators in advisory positions, and entrusted the key post of Praetorian Prefect to senators rather than equites—fresh prestige for the former, which may have masked the continued equestrian control of most administrative positions. Severus Alexander's rule was a time of great legal advances, the heyday of the outstanding jurists Domitius Ulpianus and Julius Paulus. Severus Alexander was also alert to economic and social concerns, reducing taxes, aiding the grain supply of Rome, and subsidizing teachers and scholars.

His relationship with the military was more problematic. In 223 the Praetorians revolted, killing their Prefect the jurist Ulpian. In contrast to Trajan's execution of rebellious Praetorians in 98, Severus Alexander failed to punish this outrage. Nor could the young emperor identify with rank-and-file soldiers in the way that, say, Trajan and Septimius Severus had been able. Soldiers apparently despised him as a weak general, and this disgust only led to further military uprisings, in one of which Cassius Dio was nearly killed. In 231, generalship was demanded of Severus Alexander when the aggressive Sasanids under King Ardashir I—now dominant in the former Parthian empire—invaded Mesopotamia. Accompanied by his mother Julia Mamaea, Severus Alexander went on campaign from Antioch,

city" (see the senatorial decree concerning the elder Gnaeus Piso in Chapter Ten). An emperor's *maius imperium* gave him the right to interpret and execute the law, and his decisions were generally definitive. He heard appeals from citizens, non-citizens, and communities even outside the areas of the empire for which he was primarily responsible. Provincial magistrates also turned to him for legal advice, as Pliny did to Trajan from Bithynia-Pontus; time and again, imperial letters from the first to third centuries urge that matters be settled locally rather than referred to the emperor.

Emperors made law, too; their rulings were generally termed constitutions (*constitutiones*, singular, *constitutio*). These included *rescripta* and *epistulae*, responses to petitions (*libelli*) on points of law sent not only by prominent officials but also by private individuals, especially humbler folk, women, freedmen, and even alleged slaves. Some modern experts maintain that Roman private law can be detected as becoming gradually more liberal and humane: Slaves, for example, are increasingly recognized as having some rights, and women gain more legal independence. More sweeping were the measures that the emperor issued as either *decreta*, sayings or pronouncements with the force of law; or *mandata*, instructions to governors and other officials; or *leges*, laws enacted by means of the emperor's tribunician power.

Emperors thus made law and influenced it in numerous ways, so much so that contemporary writers tend to emphasize the sole agency of individual emperors as lawmakers. But an emperor could not respond single-handed to the crush of legal questions directed to him. We know that when Augustus, for example, had to determine questions relating to wills and inheritance, he often assembled a group of jurists, asked their opinion, and then added his authority to their response; even so, no Princeps was bound to accept the majority view of such a group. Later, however, Hadrian seems to have affirmed the ability of jurists to lay down the law if acting unanimously (Gaius, *Institutes* 1.7). One mark of a virtuous Princeps was his consultation with jurists, and his respect for them.

The variety of ways in which legislation could be enacted begs the question of where actual laws were kept, and who had access to them. Some collections were in Rome, in the Record Office (*tabularium*) constructed in the early first century B.C. at the western end of the Forum Romanum, as well as in various archives, including one in the emperor's palace; other collections were kept in provincial capitals, the main seats of governors. Individual cities, too, kept archives of their own. Yet people did not always trust the ability of the Roman state, or even of their own city, to store and retrieve laws and legal decisions. For example, papyri from the province of Arabia in the early second century A.D. document the personal collection of legal decisions pertaining to a woman named Babatha and her legal difficulties. In addition, as it happens, Babatha's archive underscores a growing tendency for Roman law to eclipse local law: although Babatha seems not to have been a Roman citizen, she turned for legal redress to the court of the Roman governor at Petra (in modern Jordan). Free persons within the Roman world who were not Roman citizens—that is, the majority of provincials until the *constitutio Antoniniana* of 212—could use the law of their indigenous community when the case did not involve a Roman citizen. Yet Babatha's documents and other evidence, like the incomplete Flavian municipal laws found at Irni and other Spanish communities, reveal the spread of Roman law in the provinces.

What we know of Roman private law is mostly due to the astonishing efforts of the emperor Justinian and his jurists in 528–534. In an attempt to reassert imperial control in the fragmenting empire of his day, Justinian decided to revive the judicial experience and wisdom in classical writings and imperial rescripts, and to make all this material more accessible. He commanded his minister of justice, Tribonianus, and legal committees in Berytus (modern Beirut, Lebanon) and Constantinople (modern Istanbul, Turkey) to collect the great legal writings in the empire, and to synthesize them into three different works. With a team of helpers, Tribonian reduced roughly three million lines of text to about 150,000, arranging them in three main parts. The resulting "Collection of Civil Law" (*Corpus Juris Civilis*) divides as follows: (1) law relating to individuals (either as persons, or corporations [*collegia*], which gained recognition as legal entities in mid-second century A.D. Rome), and focusing on the individual and his or her free will, subjective rights, and social obligations; (2) law relating to property, including wills, trusts, and estates; and (3) legal interactions: civil procedure, encompassing how, where, and why to file a lawsuit. Laws are often quoted in the original form that emperors issued them, sometimes with a jurist's interpretation added.

Roman criminal law has important distinctive aspects of its own. There was no public prosecutor. Instead, every case had to be instigated by a citizen who assumed the role of accuser by denouncing the wrongdoer and filing a charge against him with the head of the competent criminal court (the procedure is *delatio nominis*, and the accuser a *delator*). Beginning in the second century B.C. all citizens of good repute had the right to bring an indictment and to conduct a prosecution, but this opportunity was never open to women, slaves, or anyone disgraced as *infamis* (see next paragraph). If the accuser proved his case, he could receive some part of the accused's property in proportion to the type of crime. Frivolous prosecutions were discouraged: For example, if an accuser was found guilty of having made an accusation in bad faith, he was to be branded on the forehead with the letter K (for *kalumniator*, slanderer). If an accuser were not himself of high status, and not even connected in some way to someone who was, he was likely to experience difficulty in initiating his case, because the praetor or another magistrate with appropriate jurisdiction had first to be convinced that the case should be heard. Further, Roman criminal cases, like civil ones, often depended not so much on legal issues like the validity of the evidence, but on the reputation and status of the accused, the accuser, and even their advocates.

Status and prestige loomed large in Roman law, as indeed in our own. A common penalty was *infamia*, a political and social stigma that could remove, for example, a citizen's right to vote or to bring an accusation, or an individual's senatorial or eques-

BOX 12.4: Grant of Roman Citizenship (*Tabula Banasitana*)

Inscriptions, such as the following part of a bronze tablet dating to around 168 (AE 1971.534), proudly record imperial grants of citizenship, and allow us to see specific instances of the emperor conferring such benefits. This document comes from Banasa in southwest Mauretania (modern Sidi Ali bou Jenoun, Morocco), where Augustus had settled a veteran colony; the Zegrenses were a local tribe. The last phrase in the wording of the grant is an important warning that a beneficiary's new status as a Roman citizen does not supersede his former civic identity, nor exempt him from local obligations. Dual citizenship of this type can be seen as a strength of the empire, but both the imperial authorities and local ones were keen to ensure that such privileged individuals did not seek to stop supporting their community of origin on this account.

Copy of the letter of our Emperors Marcus Aurelius and Verus, Augusti, to Coiiedius Maximus [governor of Mauretania Tingitana, who had forwarded Julianus' request for citizenship]. We have read the petition of Julianus the Zegrensian attached to your letter, and although it is not usual to give Roman citizenship to men of that tribe except when very great services prompt the emperor to show this kindness, nevertheless since you assert that he is one of the leading men of his people and is very loyal in his readiness to be of help to our affairs, and since we think that there are not many families among the Zegrenses who can make equal boasts about their services—whereas we wish that very many be impelled to emulate Julianus because of the honor conferred by us upon his house—we do not hesitate to grant Roman citizenship, without impairment of the law of the tribe, to himself, his wife Ziddina, likewise to their children Julianus, Maximus, Maximinus, Diogenianus.

privileges, however. They alone could join a legion, or (at the top level) seek equestrian or senatorial status at Rome; altogether, without question, they had the greatest social and political mobility. They might also expect easier access to the emperor—by custom, if not always by law—when appealing a sentence, say, or requesting some exemption from civic obligations. In the early Principate, Roman citizenship seems to have been attractive to non-Romans; it was no doubt seen as the pathway to power and privilege.

However, inscriptions and other items of evidence suggest that by the end of the second century Roman citizenship was losing its allure. Among municipal elites we find increasing instances of men unable or unwilling to serve their community politically—participation that by tradition had been seen as an enviable privilege, not a burden. Local political service was essential to the functioning both of individual cities and of the empire as a whole, and by the second century the city councils (whose members are termed "decurions") were the most powerful local political figures. Men paid a sum of money, the so-called *summa honoraria* (usually 20,000 sesterces), upon being elected magistrate or coopted into the city council. Among other duties, a city's officials were responsible for local law and

Figure 12.6 *Tombstone of the mid-second century from Gorsium, Pannonia (near modern Székesfehérvár, Hungary). This monolithic tombstone combines decoration in the Greco-Roman style—such as the grape-vine spiraled columnettes—with local elements. The two women portrayed are wearing "native" dress, with heavy turbans, prominent pendant necklaces, and large pins on their shoulders. They are framed, however, by two elegant herm figures. At the foot of the stone, two servants are shown frontally under a curved border characteristic of art from the region, but these plain figures are flanked by sinuous Bacchanalian dancers. The beautifully cut Latin inscription translates, "To the spirits of the dead. Publius Aelius Respectus, city councilor of the municipality, while alive made this for himself and for Ulpia Amasia, his wife. Aelia Materio, their daughter aged ten, is placed here. The parents put up this monument for her memory." The names indicate that the family are all Roman citizens, and the father specifies that he is a city councilor in his community, although without naming it. The unusual "Amasia" and "Materio" apparently maintain the area's indigenous names, as does the women's dress. This tombstone represents the creative interaction of Roman and provincial cultures.*

order, public contracts, religious rituals, and entertainment; they also supervised the collection of the tax quota demanded from their community by Rome. Roman, as opposed to local, administration could accordingly be relatively lean (see Chapter Eleven). The obligations of a city's council and magistrates were offset by their relative autonomy, an underlying principle of the Principate. But this civic autonomy would function successfully only so long as the empire's cities were willing and able to regulate themselves. Various developments, such as the appointment of "caretakers" (*curatores*) from Rome, acted to alter the balance between Rome and its cities. In the long term, relations were to be ideologically changed, too, by some drastic imperial legislation: Thus, by the fourth century, decurions were made personally responsible for their cities' obligations, and by the fifth the position of decurion was made hereditary by law.

Even by the early second century, some of the distinctive privileges of Roman citizenship had begun to erode, as we saw with the enlistment of non-Romans in the legions and the two-tiered treatment of Roman citizens in the courts. At the lowest levels of Roman society, however, such legal disparities were always almost meaningless. Whether someone from the rural poor or urban homeless—who had few or no possessions, and no education—was freeborn, freed, or even slave, probably made little difference to the authorities in court or elsewhere, because the elite were so superior in every way to such powerless individuals. The latter themselves were hardly likely to be much preoccupied by the question of their legal status, when it was a constant struggle for such poverty-stricken people just to stay alive.

It is against this background that we must set Caracalla's grant of Roman citizenship to virtually all free inhabitants of the empire. What functional and ideological difference did it make? And what constituted being "Roman" at this date? Septimius Severus and his family may illuminate these difficult questions, at least at the top of the social scale. His *origo* was Lepcis Magna, an important city found-

Figure 12.7 *Lepcis Magna, Tripolitania (75 miles/120 km east of modern Tripoli, Libya). Lepcis Magna was developed as a Phoenician trading settlement from around 600 B.C., using a harbor at the end of a stream bed, from where a route led far inland to sub-Saharan Africa. Later, the settlement also derived prosperity from its rural territory, which produced olive oil in great quantities. By the late first century B.C., Lepcis Magna was shipping three million pounds of olive oil annually to Rome. By the end of the first century A.D. it had become a* municipium, *and then under Trajan its city status was raised to that of a colony. Later, Septimius Severus, who was from Lepcis himself, patronized it lavishly, although it could already boast handsome buildings. He sponsored an enormous forum—whose ruins are prominent here—flanked by a public hall or "basilica" (behind the high wall on the right); an adjoining, long colonnaded street (partly visible in the right foreground; compare Fig. 10.5); and a multistoried, elaborate fountain that marked the shift in the city's street grid. Altogether, the ruins of this magnificent city—preserved by the silting-up of its harbor and subsequent disuse—represent dramatic testimony to emperors' wealth, and to the potential power of imperial patronage.*

ed by the Carthaginians on the coast of what is now Libya. Although Latin sources call Septimius Severus "Italic"—descended from Italian emigrants—his Punic background was at least as strong. His grandfather served as chief magistrate of Lepcis Magna, an office which still retained its Punic title *sufes* even long after the city had become a Roman municipality. Septimius Severus himself allegedly never lost his provincial accent when speaking Latin, although his Greek was excellent. The origo of his wife, Julia Domna, was Emesa in Syria, and Greek and Syriac were her first languages. Thus what we might consider ethnicity apparently mattered little as a constituent of Roman identity.

On the other hand, those identifying themselves as Romans aspired to adopt Greco-Roman culture and its devotion to, among other tastes, Latin and Greek literature, rhetoric, art, and city life. Although as emperor, Septimius Severus never attempted to mask his reliance upon the military, he participated fully in the Greco-Roman cultural ideal: One of his most spectacular accomplishments was the magnificent rebuilding of Lepcis Magna. Julia Domna is said to have regularly met with members of the intelligentsia, including the orator and physician Galen, and Philostratus, author of the *Lives of the Sophists*. Thus at the beginning of the third century, the imperial family—despite its origins—conspicuously embraced traditional values of Greco-Roman culture, providing a model for the rest of the empire. Some have argued that a key factor in the emergence of changed forms of government and society in the empire from the third century onwards was a shift of individuals' attention from such traditional values to a new focus on individual salvation and personal belief. This prospect leads to the next section.

ROME AND CHRISTIANITY

Renewed cautions about our sources are essential when we discuss religion in the Roman world, and particularly the development of Christianity. Religion is notoriously difficult to investigate, because it combines practice, or ritual, with belief, or faith. Rituals, which are enacted periodically, are transient even with the best of documentation, such as a movie: Participants are caught up in the moment, and observers are disconnected from the experience. Roman rituals are known by various means—descriptions in literature, which are invariably incomplete; depictions on coins, reliefs, mosaics, pottery, wall paintings, and other artifacts, which present only a snapshot of the action; notices in calendars; and incidental references in other documents. As for beliefs, we cannot measure the sincerity of what we read in the stylized writings of the Romans, or even in the public proclamations of belief made in inscriptions, graffiti, or other documents. At the same time, however, we should not dismiss all such declarations as hollow just because they are not statements of Christian or other religious belief as understood today. We should bear in mind that the Roman authorities were to make repeated attempts to eradicate Christianity during the third and early fourth centuries, and that later Christian emperors would seek to obliterate polytheism likewise. It is no wonder that the relationship between Rome and Christians was an uneasy one, and that the literary sources for early Christianity are radically polarized.

The close connection between religion and politics in Roman society helps to account for the vehemence of the interchange. As we have seen, religious ceremonies preceded all Roman political activity. The same individuals frequently held political and religious positions at Rome, and minimal specialized training or knowledge was required for most of the latter. At the same time, the Roman state seldom sought to impose any particular religion, concerning itself mainly with the appropriate performance of public cult and the prohibition of any human sacrifice. This apparent laxity is clear even in the most salient instance of religious and political linkage, the imperial house. From 12 B.C. onwards, each Princeps assumed the position of *pontifex maximus* and also became a member of all the other major priestly colleges, making him the head of Roman religion. The institution of an imperial cult made various deified emperors and empresses— even the living emperor at times—the object of public religious rituals. Although individuals might not believe that an emperor was a god, this did not matter as much as the participation of all Roman citizens in state cult.

But Christian belief demanded absence from polytheistic state rituals. There was a fundamental difference between Christian and polytheistic religious sensibilities. The Christians' religious affiliation provided them, individually and collectively, with an identity distinct from that of city, tribe, or family. By contrast, for polytheistic Romans, religious rituals and practices were integral to all civic and familial activities, and religious roles overlapped with political ones. Romans and their subjects could "believe" as they pleased, so long as they did not actively reject rituals that had been made part of the state religion. Through revolts and legislation, the monotheistic Jews and Rome gradually worked out a compromise over the first two centuries of the Principate, which allowed Jews to be excused from participating in state cult rituals. Initially, the Romans regarded Christianity, too, as a sect of Judaism. But once it became clear that Christians did not accept this identity, they became more problematic for the Roman state.

Widespread incomprehension about Christians in the first century met with a range of reactions in the second. From about 120 to 220, Christians struggled to formulate their own hierarchy, and to explain themselves to non-Christians. In part, this attempt came in response to sporadic "persecutions" that were launched spontaneously by non-Christians. We are told of outbreaks of violence against Christians during the rule of Domitian in Rome, under Trajan in Bithynia-Pontus (see Box 12.5), in Smyrna during the 150s, in Lugdunum in 177, and in Carthage and Alexandria at the beginning of the third century. To defend Christianity, Clement of Alexandria, Tertullian, and other "apologists" wrote brilliant tracts that are strikingly sophisticated in their rhetoric and philosophical argument. These authors aimed not so much to convert non-Christians as to persuade them that they had no good cause to fear Christians or persecute them. It is important to note that brutal treatment suffered by Christians at this period was not initiated by the state.

BOX 12.5: Pliny, Trajan, and Christians

This celebrated exchange between Pliny and the emperor Trajan regarding Christians in Bithynia-Pontus around 112 (Pliny, Letters 10.96–97) provides valuable insight into the Roman state's reaction to Christians. It also sheds light on the rituals associated with imperial cult, and the economic and social ramifications of state religion.

[Pliny to Trajan] It is my practice, my lord, to refer to you all matters about which I have doubts. For who is better able to resolve my hesitation or to inform my ignorance? I have never been present at trials of Christians. So I do not know what offenses it is the practice to punish or investigate, and to what extent. And I have hesitated considerably over whether there should be any distinction on account of age, or no difference between the very young and the more mature; whether pardon is to be granted for a change of mind, or, if a man has once been a Christian, it does him no good to have ceased to be one; whether the name itself, even without offenses, is to be punished, or only the offenses associated with the name.

Meanwhile, in the case of those who were denounced to me as Christians, I have observed the following procedure: I asked them personally whether they were Christians; those who confessed, I asked a second and a third time, threatening them with punishment; those who persisted, I ordered to be executed. For I had no doubt that, whatever the nature of their admission, their stubbornness and inflexible obstinacy surely deserve to be punished. There were others gripped by the same folly; but because they were Roman citizens, I assigned them to be transferred to Rome.

Soon accusations spread, as usually happens, because of these proceedings, and several incidents occurred. An anonymous document was published containing the names of many persons. My view was that I should discharge those who denied that they were or had been Christians, when they called upon the gods in words dictated by me, offered prayer with incense and wine to your image (which I had ordered to be brought in for this purpose, together with statues of the gods), and in addition cursed Christ—none of which actions those who genuinely are Christians can be made to take, I am told. Others named by an informer declared that they were Christians, but then denied it, asserting that they had been but had ceased to be, some three years before, others many years, some as much as twenty years. All these individuals also worshipped your image and the statues of the gods, and cursed Christ.

They declared, however, that what their fault or error amounted to was that they were accustomed to meet on a fixed day before dawn and sing alternately among themselves a hymn to Christ as to a god, and to bind themselves by oath, not to some crime, but rather not to commit fraud, theft, or adultery, not to commit a breach of trust, nor to deny a deposit when called upon to restore it. After doing this, it was their custom to depart and to reassemble to consume food—but of an ordinary, harmless type. Even this, they said, they had stopped doing after my edict by which, in accordance with your instructions, I had banned associations. Accordingly, I believed it all the more essential to find out what the truth was by torturing two female slaves who were called "attendants." I discovered nothing further except depraved, excessive superstition.

I therefore postponed the trial and hastened to consult you, since I felt the matter warranted consulting you, especially because of the number of people at risk. For many persons of every age, every rank, and also of both sexes are and will be exposed to danger. The contagion of this superstition has spread not only to the cities, but also to the villages and farms. But it seems possible to check and cure it. It is certainly quite clear that the temples, which had been almost deserted, have begun to be thronged again, that religious rites are being resumed after a long interval, and that the flesh of sacrificial victims is on sale everywhere, even though up to this point almost nobody could be found to buy it. So it is easy to realize what a mass of people can be reformed if they are given a chance to change their minds.

[Trajan to Pliny] You have observed appropriate procedure, my dear Pliny, in sifting the cases of those denounced to you as Christians. For it is not possible to lay down some general rule to serve as a kind of fixed standard. They are not to be sought out; if they are denounced and proved to be guilty, they are to be punished, with this reservation, that whoever denies that he is a Christian and quite clearly proves it—that is, by worshipping our gods—he shall gain pardon because of his change of mind, despite having been under suspicion in the past. But anonymously posted accusations ought to have no place in any prosecution, since they set the worst precedent and are unworthy of our times.

Pliny's ignorance partly reflects the limited spread of Christianity by his time. Although he states that its adherents were "of every age, every rank, and also of both sexes," no contemporary of his own high rank is known to have been a Christian. Until the second half of the second century, most Christians lived in cities in Judaea and elsewhere in the Greek East, and in a few large cities such as Rome and Carthage in the West. The third Jewish revolt of 132–135 and its aftermath unequivocally differentiated Christians from Jews, and Christians began to be found among the municipal elite a generation or so thereafter. The increasing sophistication of the church is reflected in the formation of a church hierarchy in Rome, and in the growth of the concepts of heresy and orthodoxy in a debate apparently evolving in the third quarter of the second century. In the Severan period, Christianity evidently gained its first adherents in the equestrian and senatorial orders. These were women. But it remains difficult to say with any certainty who was Christian, and in what numbers, since few publicly professed their adherence. As Pliny's exchange with Trajan makes all too plain, anyone identifying with Christianity was liable to denunciation before Roman officials, as well as exposure to mob violence and fear.

From the mid-third century, into the early fourth, the Roman state actively persecuted Christians. They were labeled a menace to society, and officially sponsored efforts were made to extirpate their cult. In the first "Great" Persecution (249–251), an empire-wide requirement of sacrifice to the Roman gods allegedly resulted in thousands of deaths, many at the hands of mobs. All who duly offered sacrifices were issued certificates (*libelli*), which in the case of Christians served to record their renunciation of Christianity. The second Great Persecution (253–260) initially targeted clergy, but then widened to eliminate upper-class men and women who refused to renounce their faith; their property was to be seized, and they themselves were to suffer execution, exile, and other severe penalties. Finally, the third Great Persecution, initiated by the emperors Diocletian and Galerius in 303, targeted Christian meeting places for destruction, deprived Christian honestiores of their legal privileges, and finally required sacrifice to the Roman gods as a test of loyalty. Although Diocletian ended this persecution in the West as early as 305, in the East it continued until Galerius' Edict of Toleration in 311, and was even briefly reauthorized during the following decade or so. Christians were fairly easy to identify, because they refused to participate in state cult. As a result, they could not serve in the army, where religious ritual was an integral part of the routine. By the same token, they faced difficulty in taking up municipal or state positions. A major reason for the hostility shown to Christians may well have been their general refusal to assist the community in a civil or military capacity during a period when such help was urgently needed.

The persecutions created a category of persons known as "martyrs" from the Greek word for "witness," since these individuals were considered to have witnessed their faith through their public refusal to deny it. When ordered to sacrifice and to curse Christ, the martyrs refused, even though they were aware that this would lead to torture and death. Some Christians bewildered and irked the authorities by presenting themselves voluntarily for martyrdom. Altogether, the persecutions actually strengthened Christianity: They provided inspiring examples of brave Christians whose faith was unshakable, and they encouraged Christian self-perception as a beleaguered, suffering minority. "Martyrologies," stories of the martyrs, were widely circulated, often in an embedded form: Thus the early third-century *Martyrdom of Perpetua* contains a martyr's retelling of another martyr's tale as a way to strengthen conviction and faith.

Christianity was appealing in other ways, too. The martyrologies and scriptures promised victory over death. Even in this life Christianity could be powerful, as when Christian churches offered aid to widows, orphans, and other marginalized or dispossessed individuals. In the mid-third century, for example, 1,500 widows and needy people were said to be receiving aid from the bishop of Rome alone (Eusebius, *History of the Church* 6.43). This form of charity contrasts sharply with the distributions given by the Princeps or by wealthy individuals, which were sporadic and almost invariably directed more towards prestigious recipients. The egalitarian Christian "community" (*agape*) ignored differences of legal, social, or political status: This alternative approach attracted many individuals excluded from Rome's elites. Women were welcome in the Christian community, too, and they seem to have played important roles as organizers and proselytizers in the early church.

For these and other reasons, there developed the impression that Christians rejected Roman order and society. Their scriptures advocated peace. Many of their rites and customs were misunderstood: Their "eating the body and drinking the blood of their Savior" was called cannibalism, and their habit of addressing one another as "brother" and "sister" was taken to signify incestuous promiscuity.

The high proportion of lower-class Christians must have alienated elitist Romans, with their established hierarchical institutions and their concern for social and political standing. But Roman order and society had been changing from the beginning of the Principate. The age-old self-identification according to political and social distinction was shifting. From the second century onwards, it is possible to identify a growing phenomenon, which may be termed "conversion": deliberate and public acts of religious commitment that often acknowledged psychological change. These are mostly associated with what have been termed "mystery" or oriental religions, like those of Isis, *Magna Mater*, and Mithras. Christianity shares some characteristics with these cults insofar as it, too, is based on a revealed doctrine, and features initiation, a dedicated priesthood, the promise of an afterlife, and community on earth. Yet Christianity differs from mystery religions in its greater openness to converts (one of the most widespread mystery religions, Mithraism, excluded women altogether), its proselytizing, its monotheism, its emphasis on scripture, and its stress on belief and behavior.

These distinctions became more marked during the Great Persecutions, which were episodes that also made the numbers and whereabouts of Christians more obvious. Perhaps 5 to 10 percent of the Roman world was Christian in the early fourth century. This seemingly low number is offset by the fact that many of these individuals lived in cities, and were thus among the fortunate. By now, Christians really could be found among all sections of Roman society: At its pinnacle, the emperor Diocletian's own wife and daughter were at least Christian sympathizers, if not practicing Christians. Even so, before the rule of Constantine in the early fourth century, there was no good reason to predict that within less than another century Christianity would emerge as the most powerful religion in the Roman world. Constantine's favor towards Christianity greatly altered its development, but those changes fall outside the scope of this book.

SUGGESTED READINGS:

Birley, Anthony R. 1987 (revised edition). *Marcus Aurelius: A Biography*. New Haven and London: Yale University Press.

Birley, Anthony R. 1988 (revised edition). *Septimius Severus: The African Emperor*. New Haven and London: Yale University Press.

Bowman, Alan K. 1994. *Life and Letters on the Roman Frontier: Vindolanda and Its People*. London and New York: Routledge.

Crook, John A. 1970. *Law and Life of Rome*. Ithaca, New York: Cornell University Press.

Gardner, Jane. F. 1986. *Women in Roman Law and Society*. Bloomington: Indiana University Press.

Gardner, Jane F. 1993. *Being a Roman Citizen*. London and New York: Routledge.

Hekster, Olivier. 2002. *Commodus: An Emperor at the Crossroads*. Amsterdam: Gieben.

Lendon, Jon E. 1997. *Empire of Honour: The Art of Government in the Roman World*. Oxford: Oxford University Press.

Mattern, Susan P. 1999. *Rome and the Enemy: Imperial Grand Strategy in the Principate*. Berkeley, Los Angeles, London: University of California Press.

13

THE THIRD CENTURY, THE DOMINATE, AND CONSTANTINE

SOURCES

Difficulties with our sources contribute to the controversies and confusion attending most of the events covered in this final chapter. The lack of surviving contemporary literary accounts makes the third century appear chaotic; the relatively well-documented first and second centuries may appear "normal" by comparison, although we must realize that in fact their stability was unusually fortuitous. Fourth-century authors are quite selective about the information they include. Several, such as Aurelius Victor and Eutropius in the 370s, wrote nothing more than concise historical summaries. These focus on the emperors—especially their personal merits and faults—and they offer little insight into social, economic, or cultural history. The *Historia Augusta* (see Chapter Twelve) likewise prefers to moralize rather than to analyze, and its concluding *Lives* of third-century emperors are remarkably fallacious and sensationalist. The early fourth century is a relatively well documented period, but problems abound here too. Anonymous imperial panegyrics celebrate some events, although they are frustratingly vague on dates, and their fulsome praise glosses over details. Historical information in *On the Deaths of the Persecutors*, by the Christian Lactantius (written around 315), is colored by his determination to hammer home the horrible end of all who persecuted Christianity, especially the emperors of his own day. Thereafter the figure of Constantine dominates. For the most part, the ancient authors who write about him divide sharply over the key issue of his adherence to Christianity. His contemporary and biographer, Bishop Eusebius of Caesarea in Palestine, praises him extravagantly, but offers self-contradictory evidence in the long course of his writings. Almost unswervingly hostile is the polytheistic Zosimus, who wrote at the end of the fifth century and presents a narrative designed to discredit the first Christian emperor.

Coins and inscriptions provide insight into the chosen images of various rulers and usurpers. But the general decrease in the number of Roman inscriptions, especially ones commissioned by private individuals, reduces information for social history. Archeology reveals an overall impoverishment of material culture in many areas, though not all (Britain and parts of North Africa seem to have thrived). Many issues lie beyond the scope of archeology in any case. Further, the empire's political fragmentation makes it hard to determine how representative the evidence from any one region may now be: This problem diminishes the potential value of the relatively abundant papyri from third- and fourth-century Egypt, for example. Legal codes are instructive about imperial attitudes, but less so about social conditions and behavior. Given the scarcity of other information, there is often no knowing whether a law against a certain act indicates widespread behavior of that kind, or an emperor's idiosyncratic concern, or a reaction to a single, but untypical, petition. Beyond question, the tone of the laws from this period, and the penalties they prescribe, are notably harsh, suggesting deteriorating conditions for most of the population. Overall, it is frequently impossible to discern the various stages of important developments, or who initiated them and why. This chapter first discusses the mid-third century by topic, rather than by ruler, and then turns to the important emperors of the later third and early fourth centuries. The narrative ends with Constantine's consolidation of the entire empire under his sole rule in 324.

MID-THIRD CENTURY

The years from the assassination of Severus Alexander in 235 to the acclamation of Diocletian in 284 witnessed rapid, often violent political change. In less than fifty years, at least eighteen emperors took power with their legitimacy confirmed or ratified by the Roman senate. Even more men claimed to be Princeps without such sanction. The list of would-be emperors—most of whom were initially appointed by armies on the borders—includes sons appointed to hold office with their fathers, usurpers, and pretenders; most met a violent death. The senate had little power, no longer provided political stability, and must have seemed obsolete when Marcus Aurelius Carus was accepted as emperor in 282 without even applying to it for validation. The period is often called the Age of Crisis, or Age of the Soldier Emperors. At the time, however, there was a strong stress on continuity with the past and the promise of a bright future. The era emphasized the timelessness, imperturbability, and transcendence of the empire. For example, despite ongoing internal insurrections and invasions by trans-Danubian Carpi and Goths, Rome's thousandth anniversary in 248 was celebrated with great pomp by

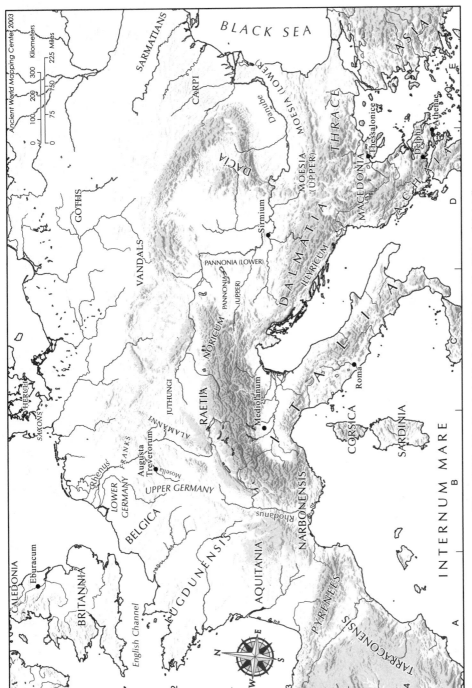

Map 13.1 *The Empire's North and West in the "Age of Crisis"*

the emperor Philip "the Arab" (who came from the region of Damascus). Imperial inscriptions and coins insistently cite *Roma Aeterna* ("Eternal Rome") and describe emperors as *Invictus* ("Unconquerable") and the like. There seems to have been a greater resistance to innovation, to judge from the empire-wide Christian persecutions of the emperors Decius (249–251) and Valerian (253–260), which were resumed in the early fourth century (see Chapter Twelve).

Just as shortsighted and futile were the efforts of various emperors to assert their supremacy over rivals, rather than to address systematically the problems that the empire faced on its northern and eastern borders. These were the areas of the greatest external dangers. The jagged northern boundaries—for the most part, the great rivers of the Rhine and Danube—divided the empire from various Germanic and other tribes. But the separation was never complete. Commercial, social, and cultural interaction regularly occurred during peaceful times. During hostilities, the rivers were by no means impenetrable barriers, since they could freeze over in winter, and become low enough in dry summers to be forded. Perhaps because of a gradual decline in annual temperatures, and a corresponding decrease in agricultural productivity in northern Europe, from about the middle of the second century A.D. northern tribes had attempted to enter Roman territory ever more frequently.

By the mid-third century, the Rhine and Danube were being crossed repeatedly by warlike groups, including Franks, Alamanni and Juthungi, and Vandals and Sarmatians. Franks and Saxons crossed the English Channel to harass Roman Britain, too, which also suffered attacks from the north by tribes in Scotland. The middle Danubian provinces—Noricum, Upper and Lower Pannonia, Dacia, and Upper Moesia—saw recurrent fighting and military threats. This general region, often termed Illyricum, was famous as the source of fearless soldiers. It provided many of the emperors of the mid-third century; these men, like all "Illyrians," were stereotyped as semi-barbarian but valiant protectors of Rome. The Roman provinces along the lower Danube were often attacked by Goths, a Germanic people who by this time had migrated and settled beside the Black Sea. In addition to Rome's Danubian territory—where they defeated and killed the emperor Decius in Lower Moesia in 251—the Goths also assaulted Roman provinces in northern Asia Minor, sacking Trapezus (modern Trabzon, Turkey) in 256. Goths and Heruli invaded the Balkans, and sacked Athens, Delphi, and other Greek centers in 267.

Further to the east was the Sasanid (or Persian) Empire. Here, after overpowering the Parthians in the 220s, the fiercely aggressive Sasanids strove to continue their westward expansion. Sasanid invasions reached Antioch in Syria, sacking it in 253 and again in 260; in the latter year, the Sasanids even captured alive the emperor Valerian at Edessa in Osroene (modern Urfa, Turkey). The centrally controlled government of the Sasanids, under its King of Kings, was strikingly different from the less cohesive, shifting groups encountered by the Romans on their borders elsewhere. The Sasanids' political sophistication, and the relative difficulty of maneuvers through the dry lands separating them and the Romans, led the Romans to use diplomacy as well as force to settle or prevent problems in the East. The two empires were often in conflict, however.

Foreign invasions and pressure were not the only causes of Rome's political instability. The Principate had never evolved a clear system for the succession. The hereditary monarchy instituted by the Julio-Claudians, and reasserted by the Flavians, faltered when first Nero and then Domitian had no heir. The practice of adoption taken up by Nerva, Trajan, and Hadrian was less a policy than a reaction to the coincidence that no second-century emperor until Marcus Aurelius had a son to succeed him. No recognized hierarchy was ever established among the positions below that of emperor: The governors of the major provinces, for example, were all notionally equal rather than ranked. So when a ruling emperor was assassinated or died on the battlefield—common enough occurrences in the mid-third century—anyone could be selected, and there was no impartial way to distinguish between claims. Under Gallienus, who ruled from 253 to 268 (jointly with his father Valerian from 253 until 260), senators may actually have been barred from military commands. Few senators are known to have held positions

Figure 13.1 *The Roman emperor Valerian submits to the Sasanid King Shapur I. This Sasanid rock carving (ca. 270), at Naqsh-i Rustam near Persepolis, is part of a trilingual textual and visual display commissioned by Shapur to commemorate his accomplishments. Here Valerian pays him homage after being captured in 260. The Roman emperor wears military costume, including the paludamentum (general's cloak; see Fig. 13.2), and a small diadem on his head. Shapur I, resplendent as the King of Kings with his large crown, jewelry, and silk clothing, imperiously gestures with his right hand towards the captive Valerian, while grasping his sword firmly with his left. Some Roman sources note that Valerian's later "ignominious servitude" to Shapur included acting as his footstool when the King mounted his horse (compare Fig. 11.5).*

struck coins, and Aurelian had secure command of the army. In the city of Rome, he imposed state control on the associations (*collegia*) that were responsible for such services as construction and baking bread. Finally, he tried to extend his religious authority by encouraging a monotheism centered on the cult of the "Unconquered Sun" (*Sol Invictus*). This Illyrian sun god was very popular in the army, and its similarity to solar deities worshipped in the East (like Elah-Gabal) encouraged its acceptance. In Rome, Aurelian built an enormous temple to Sol Invictus, which became famous for the gold and jewels he dedicated there. He also styled himself as the vice-regent of Sol Invictus, featuring on coins and inscriptions the title *Dominus et Deus natus* ("born Lord and God").

Two other steps taken by Aurelian are important. First, he abandoned the province of Dacia, regarding its exposed position north of the Danube as no longer tenable in the face of persistent onslaughts throughout the previous century. Removing all Roman forces stationed there to the south bank of the Danube, he carved out a new province with the name Dacia from parts of Upper and Lower Moesia, and Thrace. It is unclear how many civilians followed the army south, since no mass emigration is suggested by archeology, religious practices, or linguistics. Aurelian issued coins proclaiming *Dacia Felix* ("Fortunate Dacia"), but his withdrawal from north of the Danube was an acknowledgment that Rome could no longer maintain control of all its territory.

Second, in 271 Aurelian ordered a twelve-mile-long (20 km) brick wall to be built around the city of Rome. Beginning in the mid-third century, and notably in Gaul, Spain, and the East, an increasing number of cities had devoted resources to building or repairing walls. But Aurelian's wall around Rome was the largest, most uniform set of defenses erected there since as long ago as the fourth century B.C. The changed conditions to which they are a response seem a far cry from the confidence felt by Aelius Aristides only a century before Aurelian's time, when he boasted that Rome had city walls, not around the city itself—"as if you [Rome] were hiding or fleeing from your subjects"—but only at the edges of the empire, as far distant from Rome and other noble cities as possible (*To Rome* 80; see Chapter Twelve).

Like many of his predecessors, Aurelian was killed by another military officer. His assassination in 275 ushered in ten more years of political and military strife that ended only in 284 with the acclamation of Gaius Aurelius Valerius Diocletianus. He was to be the first emperor in half a century who would maintain power for more than a few years; he would also be the first to abdicate voluntarily (in 305).

DIOCLETIAN, THE TETRARCHY, AND THE DOMINATE (284–305)

Given his unprepossessing background, Diocletian's success is all the more remarkable. He came from modest circumstances in Dalmatia, without senatorial status, higher education, or extensive military training. But he more than compensated for these handicaps—which the traditional Roman elite would consider almost unsurmountable weaknesses—by his forceful, methodical mind and personality, and his willingness to make changes empirically and gradually. In the course of his twenty-one-year rule he introduced many reforms, and established the system now called the "Tetrarchy." It was much more than a simple "rule by four," the literal meaning of the word. It is true that the actual division of rule among four men—two senior "Augusti," each assisted by a "Caesar"—failed almost immediately after Diocletian's retirement in 305. However, other innovations devised by him to support the imperial power were to last for two centuries in the West, and in the East until the fall of the "Byzantine" empire in 1453. Diocletian established a complex bureaucracy, reorganized administration and finances, and revived the army's loyalty and effectiveness. It is his reforms that were responsible for the preservation of Rome's empire, and that in many instances formed the basis for further measures by Constantine and later rulers. However, Diocletian's changes transformed the style of regime established by Augustus as the Principate—with the ruler claiming to be no more than first among equals—into what is now termed the "Dominate," absolute rule by a remote *dominus* (master) elevated far above his subjects, and approachable only through innumerable layers of officials and functionaries.

After his acclamation as emperor by troops outside of Rome, Diocletian first eliminated the relatives of his predecessor (by 285). He then turned to more recalcitrant problems. Discontent within the empire was most obviously articulated by the Bacaudae (or Bagaudae), a group of rebellious peasants or simply bandits in Gaul, and by the Isaurians, a dissident native group in southern Asia Minor. External threats included incursions of Franks, Alamanni, and Goths along the lower Rhine and the Danube; the restless Sasanids; and raids by Berbers, nomadic tribesmen of the African desert, into Mauretania and Spain across the Straits of Gibraltar. Diocletian dispatched a fellow Illyrian, Marcus Aurelius Valerius Maximianus, against the Bacaudae in southern Gaul, and in recognition of his success raised him to be co-Augustus in 286. Between them, this pair of Augusti now headed the Roman world (as when Marcus Aurelius and Lucius Verus ruled jointly from 161 to 169), allowing Diocletian himself to tackle the threats along the Rhine and Danube. Yet further crises developed. Around 287, Britain rebelled under its governor Marcus Aurelius Mausaeus Carausius, and Maximian was unable to regain it for the empire. After a year of fruitless fighting, the two Augusti decided to abandon Britain for the time being, since new incursions by Franks and others called for Maximian to transfer to the upper Rhine and Raetia. Diocletian meantime moved further east to confront Sarmatians and Goths crossing the lower Danube. In 287 he negotiated a peace with the Sasanids, and in 290 he campaigned against the Saracens, Arabian nomads. It was clear that he and Maximian needed more support.

In 293, therefore, Diocletian organized the Tetrarchy, dividing the Roman world among four men. All four corulers were military men from Illyricum. They were united in intense loyalty to Diocletian, and connected also by the marriages

Map 13.2 *Roman Empire of Diocletian and Constantine*

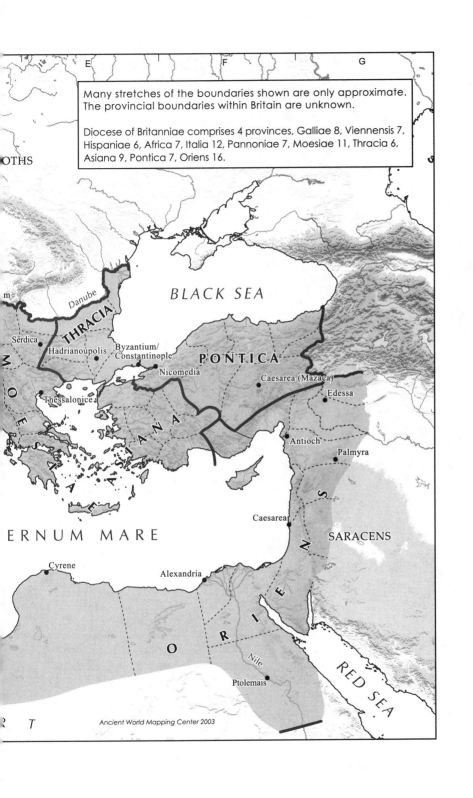

E   F   G

Many stretches of the boundaries shown are only approximate.
The provincial boundaries within Britain are unknown.

Diocese of Britanniae comprises 4 provinces, Galliae 8, Viennensis 7,
Hispaniae 6, Africa 7, Italia 12, Pannoniae 7, Moesiae 11, Thracia 6,
Asiana 9, Pontica 7, Oriens 16.

OTHS

m

Danube

BLACK SEA

THRACIA

Sérdica

Hadrianoúpolis

Byzantium/
Constantinople

PONTICA

Nicomedia

M O E S

Caesarea (Mazaca)

Edessa

Thessaloníce

A
S
I
A
N
A

Antioch

Palmyra

Caesarea

ERNUM MARE

SARACENS

Cyrene

Alexandria

O
R
I
E
N
S

O

Nile

Ptolemais

RED SEA

R   T

Ancient World Mapping Center 2003

Figure 13.2 *This group portrait of the four Tetrarchs (ca. 300) was originally mounted on a column in Constantinople. In the foreground, the senior Augustus is bearded, and grasps his Caesar with his right arm. Otherwise Augustus and Caesar are identical to one another and to their mirror images, the other two Tetrarchs. All four wear the identical military cloak (paludamentum) fastened at the right shoulder; abrasion suggests that a metal brooch or a stone of a different color was fixed here originally. Each man's breastplate is held in place by an elaborate military belt. Each also carries an eagle-headed sword in a rich scabbard, and wears a Pannonian cap, the front of which was originally ornamented with a jewel or stone in its center. In rendering all the Tetrarchs alike and positioning them so closely together, this group portrait embodies the unanimity that the four men were resolved to uphold. Their furrowed brows indicate their concern for the empire. But at the same time their elevation above their subjects is conveyed by the gems they wear, as well as by the use of porphyry —a rare, hard, reddish-purple stone reserved by this time exclusively for emperors and their families. During the Middle Ages, this statue was taken from Constantinople to Venice, where it now stands at the southwest corner of St Mark's Basilica.*

of the two Caesars to daughters of the Augusti they served. Religious sanctions and elaborate court ceremonial distinguished the four corulers from all others. Diocletian, whose epithet *Jovius* ("Jupiter-like") confirmed his preeminence, was the Augustus, chief ruler, in the East. His capital at Nicomedia (modern Izmit, Turkey) commanded the west-east land routes, as well as the sea routes through the Propontis. His Caesar or vice-ruler, the man marked to succeed him, was Gaius Galerius Valerius Maximianus, whose capitals at Sirmium (modern Sremska Mitrovica, Yugoslavia) and at Thessalonice (modern Thessaloniki, Greece) were closer to the insecure northeastern borders. Maximian, the western Augustus, ruled from Mediolanum, and his epithet, *Herculius* ("like Hercules," the hero who helped both men and gods), designated him as the second most powerful individual in the empire. Maximian's Caesar was Flavius Valerius Constantius (the father of Constantine), who may have previously served as Maximian's Praetorian Prefect; Constantius' capital at Augusta Treverorum (modern Trier, Germany) was strategically located on the lower Mosella River (modern Mosel) near the German border. All four Tetrarchs were constantly on the move, and it is a sign of the changing times that they seldom visited Rome either individually or together. Each of the two Augusti was called Imperator Caesar and pontifex maximus; other honorific titles, such as Sarmaticus Maximus ("greatest conqueror of the Sarmatians"), seem to have been assumed equally by all four Tetrarchs.

The Tetrarchs proved effective in tackling the widespread threats facing the empire. Troubles that had surfaced in Egypt in 292 were finally suppressed by Diocletian in 298. Galerius made a preemptive strike against the Sasanids in Mesopotamia, and with Diocletian's aid (also in 298), he not only regained previous Roman territory here, but was also able to secure more under the terms of a treaty that would become a long-standing cause of Persian resentment. Around the same time, Maximian regained control of Mauretania from the Berbers. Already, in 296, Constantius had retaken Britain from a successor of Carausius, who had been assassinated three years earlier. Constantius' continued presence in Britain and the upper Rhine region maintained stability there. In subsequent years the Tetrarchs undertook lesser but similarly successful campaigns, thus justifying the great celebration of Diocletian's and Maximian's *vicennalia* (twenty-year anniversary) in Rome in 303.

Even so, it was the reorganization of the Roman world achieved by Diocletian and his corulers—in which each Tetrarch headed his own administration and army—that gained more significance than their military victories. Once the Tetrarchy itself collapsed soon after Diocletian's abdication in 305, the sole ruler who ultimately emerged, Constantius' son Flavius Valerius Constantinus, gathered all the armies under his own command. Yet he and his successors adopted Diocletian's restructured provincial administration largely unchanged. Constantine also advanced many of Diocletian's far-reaching military reforms. Overall, changes made by Diocletian substantially increased the numbers and complexity of both the administration and the military.

The empire was now divided into 101 provinces (about twice the previous number, and including Italy itself for the first time) within twelve—ultimately fifteen—larger units called "dioceses" (*dioecesis*). Each diocese was supervised by a "vicar" (*vicarius*, literally "deputy"). These vicars in turn answered to the Praetorian Prefects, whose roles changed to become the chief administrators for the Tetrarchs. Provincial governors (*praesides*) had executive power for administering justice and collecting taxes. Almost all governors were now of equestrian status, although senators are occasionally known to have headed some of the less important provinces. In

themselves most closely with Jupiter, ruler of the gods and (as Jupiter Optimus Maximus) Rome's protector, and with Hercules, Jupiter's son and mankind's helper. Moreover, the Tetrarchs openly articulated the belief that the maintenance of Rome's rule rested on respect for religion and tradition, and on ritual worship of the state gods. At the same time, unlike Augustus, Trajan, and most other emperors, the Tetrarchs personally exploited religious conventions as a means to distance themselves from their subjects. They encouraged the practice of prostration (Latin, *adoratio*, Greek, *proskynesis*), whereby anyone coming into their presence had to fall to his knees in a gesture customary in prayer and supplication. They decorated their clothing and shoes with brilliant gems and gold; the diadems they wore also had religious significance. According to some later authors, Diocletian even allowed himself to be adored and greeted as a god. Although Constantine was ultimately to associate himself with a very different god, he still retained the quasi-religious court rituals instituted by Diocletian, and so did his successors for centuries.

In time, the Tetrarchs' fervent promotion of Jupiter, Hercules, and traditional polytheism led them to attempt the suppression of other cults. Diocletian issued a stern edict against Manichaeans, followers of the teaching of Mani, most probably in 302 (although a date five years earlier has been considered possible). Manichaeans were believed to come from Persia, or at the least to be Sasanid supporters, thus providing a political motive for Diocletian's action. But his edict also condemns their beliefs as un-Roman and depraved. It calls for the sect's founders and leaders to be burnt alive, together with their writings, and for their followers to suffer capital punishment and confiscation of their estates. What impact the edict made is unknown, since the historical record focuses on the Christian persecution instigated at almost the same time but with much wider repercussions.

Harassment of Christians began in Diocletian's own palace in 299–300, and was followed by a purge of army officers in the East. In 303 he began the third and last "Great Persecution" by issuing the first of what would eventually be three edicts aimed against Christians. Their specific concern for church leaders, Christian meeting places, and Christian *honestiores* who persisted in their faith, reinforces the likelihood that Christians could now be found among the highest levels of society. The persecution was to be implemented throughout the empire, reflecting the uniformity of the Tetrarchic system. In practice, however, its enforcement was uneven. For the most part, only minimal action was taken in the West, especially in Constantius' area of Britain and Gaul, where the Christian population was in any case small. North Africa, however, was seriously affected, as were Egypt, Palestine, and other areas in the East. Lactantius explains the unevenness of enforcement by reference to each Tetrarch's personal prejudices; for example, he alleges evasion on the part of Constantius, Constantine's father (*On the Deaths of the Persecutors* 15.7). But the political breakdown of the Tetrarchy after 305 also served to divert attention to other pressing concerns.

DISSOLUTION OF THE TETRARCHY (305–313), AND THE RISE OF CONSTANTINE (306–324)

Increasingly ill, Diocletian retired in 305 from his capital in Nicomedia to a palace he had begun earlier near Salona (modern Split, Croatia). During the twenty-one years of his rule, he had established what could have seemed a reliable new means of regulating the succession. His abdication in the East presumed that his own Caesar, Galerius, would move up to become Augustus. At the same time, he forced retirement upon Maximian, his fellow Augustus in the West, elevating Maximian's Caesar, Constantius, to be Augustus there. Galerius and Constantius were then to select as their own Caesars the two men whom Diocletian had groomed for these positions, Flavius Valerius Severus in the West and Gaius Galerius Valerius Daia in the East; the latter now took the further name Maximinus, and is usually referred to as Maximin Daia. Both he and Severus were military leaders with an Illyrian background, as well as associates of Galerius. In addition, Maximin Daia was Galerius' nephew, and shared his hatred of Christianity.

But this planned scheme for the succession disintegrated almost immediately. In the East, the relatively unknown Valerius Licinianus Licinius, who had also served under Galerius, was eager for power. Few knew Severus, and he had many rivals for his position as Caesar in the West. Meanwhile Maximian did not want to retire, and his ambitious son, Marcus Aurelius Valerius Maxentius, had ambitions of his own despite being ignored in the deliberations. Further, Constantius' son Constantine had been marked as an imperial favorite by being raised at Diocletian's court, and had subsequently proven himself a talented army officer. A further complication was soldiers' deep-seated preference for the new leaders to be related to ones they had already served.

This unstable political situation was worsened by internal and external pressures. Although in the West persecution of Christians was not continued after 305, in the East the new Augustus Galerius actually intensified it. The result was that he divided communities, threatened property rights, and provoked hatred and resentment; even so, he persisted until a serious illness finally caused him to revoke his orders in 311. Before his death the same year, he issued an Edict of Toleration that restored Christian places of worship and reinstated the clergy. But this prolonged period of persecution in the East left deep scars, which were soon reopened first by Maximin Daia, and later by Licinius.

In the West, incursions across the Rhine and renewed turmoil in Britain offered others ample opportunity to command armies on campaign. In 305, Constantius summoned his son, Constantine (then at Galerius' court), to help him in Britain. When Constantius died in battle in July 306, the Tetrarchy began to dissolve openly. The troops in Britain declared Constantine the new Augustus rather than Constantius' Caesar, Severus. Galerius in the East, as senior Augustus, rejected this radical change, but he did yield to the troops by making Constantine Severus' new Caesar. Thus Severus now duly became Augustus of the West in accordance

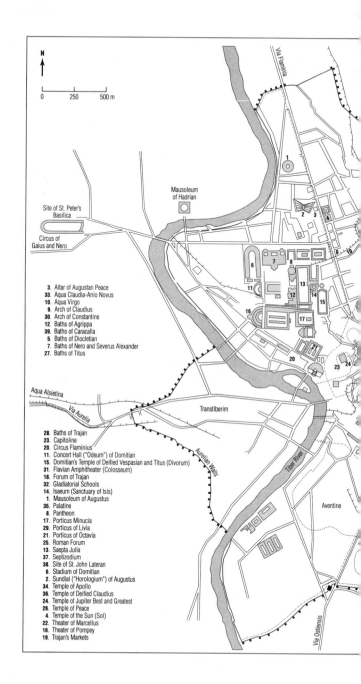

Map 13.3 *Rome in the Age of Constantine*

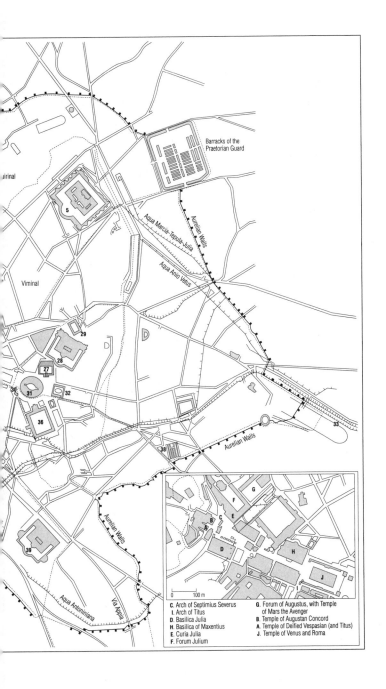

Barracks of the
Praetorian Guard

uirinal

5

Aqua Marcia-Tepula-Julia

Aurelian Walls

Aqua Anio Vetus

Viminal

29

28

27

30 31

32

36

38

Aurelian Walls

33

Aurelian Walls

39

Aqua Antoniniana

Via Appia

G

F

C
B E
A

D

H

J

I

0   100 m

C. Arch of Septimius Severus
I. Arch of Titus
D. Basilica Julia
H. Basilica of Maxentius
E. Curia Julia
F. Forum Julium

G. Forum of Augustus, with Temple
     of Mars the Avenger
B. Temple of Augustan Concord
A. Temple of Deified Vespasian (and Titus)
J. Temple of Venus and Roma

BOX 13.2: Galerius' Edict of Toleration (April 311)

In this record of the edict quoted by Lactantius, note that Galerius' change of attitude supposedly stems from a desire that Christians pray for the recovery of his health—a traditional Roman sentiment.

Among all the other arrangements which we are always making for the advantage and benefit of the state, we had earlier sought to set everything right in accordance with the ancient laws and public discipline of the Romans, and to ensure that the Christians, too, who had abandoned their ancestors' way of life, should return to a sound frame of mind. For in some way such willfulness had overcome these same Christians, such folly had taken hold of them, that they no longer followed those practices of the ancients which their own ancestors perhaps had first instituted; but simply following their own judgment and pleasure, they were making up for themselves the laws which they were to observe, and were gathering various groups of people together in different places. When finally our order was published that they should devote themselves to the practices of the ancients, many were subjected to danger, many too were struck down. Very many, however, persisted in their determination, and we saw that these same people were neither offering worship and due religious observance to the gods, nor practicing the worship of the god of the Christians. Bearing in mind, therefore, our own most gentle clemency and our perpetual habit of showing lenient pardon to all, we have taken the view that in the case of these people too we should extend our speediest leniency, so that once more they may be Christians and restore their meeting places, provided they do nothing to disturb good order. . . . Consequently, in accordance with this leniency of ours, it will be their duty to pray to their god for our safety and for that of the state and themselves, so that from every side the state may be kept unharmed, and they may be able to live free of worries in their own homes. (Lactantius, *On the Deaths of the Persecutors* 34; translation based on J. L. Creed, *Lactantius, De Mortibus Persecutorum*, Oxford, 1984, p. 53).

with Diocletian's scheme, and Constantine was content for the time being to be his Caesar. He kept command of his father's troops, however, and during the next few years used them successfully in the Rhine borderlands.

As early as October 306, however, this fragile compromise was threatened when the senate and people of Rome chose to acclaim Maxentius as the new Augustus of the West. Maxentius was energetic and effective, and he had the support of the Praetorians. In 307, he defeated Severus, who killed himself after being beaten in battle in northern Italy. Maxentius also repelled attempts by Galerius to take Italy and Rome itself. Meanwhile, Maxentius' father, Maximian, long resentful at being forced to retire at the same time as Diocletian in 305, was scheming to reclaim his earlier supreme position as Augustus in the West.

In November 308 Galerius tried to repair the Tetrarchy by holding a conference at Carnuntum in Upper Pannonia (modern Petronell, Austria); its results were short-lived. Diocletian was urged to resume power, but in vain because he was by now desperately ill; he probably died around 311. Galerius reaffirmed himself as Augustus in the East, with Maximin Daia as his Caesar. Galerius' friend and associate, Licinius, was now made Augustus in the West, with Constantine continuing as Caesar there. But these arrangements did not satisfy or eliminate either Maxentius or his father Maximian. Though declared a usurper, Maxentius kept control of Rome and Italy, effectively limiting Licinius to no more than Illyricum; by 312 Maxentius had even extended his rule to North Africa. In the meantime, Maximian unsuccessfully turned against his son, and fled to Constantine in Gaul, whom he also later tried to overthrow—an attempt that led to his death in 310. Maximin Daia, resentful that Galerius had chosen Licinius rather than himself as Augustus in the West, had induced his own troops to proclaim him Augustus; Galerius recognized the title in 309–310.

Throughout these events Constantine generally restricted his own movements to Gaul, campaigning against Franks, Alamanni, and Bructeri on the Rhine in 309 and 310. In accordance with his acclamation by the troops in Britain in 306, he continued to use the title Augustus, and in 309–310 Galerius recognized it too. Constantine's larger ambitions are indicated by an anonymous Latin panegyric of 310, which claims that in a vision he saw the gods Apollo and Victory, who each predicted great victories for him (*Latin Panegyrics* 6.21.4). At this time his coins begin to display Sol Invictus, suggesting a conscious shift away from the Tetrarchic system and its promotion of Jupiter and Hercules.

Galerius' death in 311 could only unsettle whatever stability had been achieved. Licinius now temporarily abandoned his claims to the West, turning instead against Maximin Daia, who duly moved up in rank to replace Galerius as Augustus in the East. Licinius' absence from the West allowed Constantine to concentrate his efforts on eliminating Maxentius, whom he denounced as a "tyrant." In 312 he first defeated Maxentius' forces in northern Italy, and then proceeded down the peninsula to Rome. The decisive battle occurred in October, just outside the city walls, at the Milvian Bridge. Maxentius and many of his troops drowned in the Tiber, and Constantine swept into the city. Our sources, clearly influenced by his success, emphasize his welcome in Rome and his restoration of rights that Maxentius had supposedly abolished. One of Constantine's first measures was to disband—forever, as it turned out—the Praetorian Guard, whose support had been so vital to Maxentius.

Constantine's victory at the Milvian Bridge has been glorified by Eusebius, Lactantius, and many others as the key episode for his acceptance of Christianity and his subsequent emergence as sole emperor. Before the battle, we are told, Constantine received an omen of his coming victory. Eusebius and Lactantius differ on the nature of the omen—either a dream or an apparition in the sky—but they agree that it was understood as coming from the Christian god. Christian sources further maintain that Constantine's victory persuaded him of the truth of their god. He allegedly saw a cross over the sun, and heard the militant encouraging words, "Conquer

CONSTANTINE AND THE EMPIRE

Constantine remained emperor for thirteen more years, and died a natural death in 337. The length of his rule, which he dated from his acclamation as Augustus by the troops in Britain in 306, was immensely beneficial for the empire. Individuals, communities, and resources had all been devastated by seemingly incessant internal and external warfare ever since the 230s. The relative internal stability offered by twelve years of Tetrarchic rule (and the previous seven years of Diocletian's joint rule with Maximian) had been shattered by eighteen more years of civil strife. Constantine's sole rule, with its promise of long-term stability, must have seemed welcome. Further, its length allowed his reforms—and those of Diocletian that he continued—to achieve their full effect. His rule thus became a decisive step forward in the empire's recovery.

Constantine was baptized just before his death: Like many Christians of his day, he wanted to die in a state of grace, and so postponed baptism as long as possible. Much discussion has centered on the question of his religious beliefs. Some scholars accept the claim that he was converted to Christianity by his vision before the battle at the Milvian Bridge. Others are more skeptical, stressing the utility of divine sanction in a civil war and his continued respect for non-Christian religions. Symbols of Sol Invictus, for example, continued on his coinage until 323, and even in the mid 330s he granted the Italian city of Hispellum (modern Spello) permission to build a traditional temple to the imperial family (his own *gens Flavia*) for biennial celebrations of theatrical and gladiatorial games—on the one condition that no sacrifices were performed there. We have no hope of being able to recover the exact nature of his beliefs, nor even to date with confidence the stages by which they evolved over time. More important is the assessment of his activity as emperor, since that is above all what influenced his own time and subsequent generations so strongly.

From 312, Constantine openly tolerated Christianity, urging first Maximin Daia and then Licinius to stop Christian persecutions, and issuing the Edict of Toleration with Licinius in 313. He even proved

Figure 13.4 *Colossal bronze head of Constantine. This portrait is about five times life-size. Constantine here is the first emperor in over two centuries to be portrayed without a beard. He is apparently modeled on Augustus, whose achievement of gaining sole control of the empire he matched. This likeness depicts Constantine at the end of his life, with the upward gaze that is characteristic of his portraits. It may variously suggest his piety towards the Christian god, his chosen role as intermediary between god and the Roman world, and even perhaps his aloofness from petty human concerns.*

willing to go further by involving himself in church affairs. In particular, as early as 312–313 he displayed concern for the so-called "Donatist" controversy. This had erupted not long before over the question of who was the appropriately consecrated bishop of Carthage; the nub of the dispute was the status of those clergy who had submitted to demands made by the authorities during the third "Great Persecution" rather than die as martyrs. Entire communities in North Africa— where Christianity had somehow gained an exceptionally strong hold, in both the cities and the countryside—were divided over the question, with Donatists insisting that "lapsed" persons should not be readmitted to the church, let alone continue as its leaders. Following earlier models of turning to the emperor to settle difficulties (see Chapter Twelve), the Donatists appealed to Constantine. He first referred the question to two successive church councils, one held in Rome in 313, the other at Arelate (modern Arles) in Gaul the following year. Both ruled against the Donatists, who then pressed Constantine to issue his personal ruling. When it too went against their position, their unapologetic reaction was to reject the authority they had sought from him in the first place: "what has the emperor to do with the church?" they asked scathingly (*quid imperatori cum ecclesia?*).

This bitter controversy had set some formative precedents, however. It had drawn the emperor into matters of Christian doctrine and other church affairs. It had also led him to be gripped by the conviction—characteristically Roman rather than Christian—that if he personally failed to ensure that all Christians worshipped their god in the same "catholic" way as he did, then that god might no longer continue to favor his rule. This latter prospect so disturbed Constantine that he was even prepared to authorize the persecution of Donatists for their refusal to conform, though in frustration he soon abandoned the attempt and thereafter ignored them. Even so, the Donatists' schism with "catholic" Christians was to cause wrenching divisions in North Africa for a further century and more.

As early as 313, Constantine also began to show favor to the church and its adherents on a larger scale. The Edict of Toleration offered not only freedom for all religious practices, but also the restoration of church property. Further, each Christian church could be recognized as a legal entity, enabling it to own property, make contracts, sue or be sued, and receive legacies. After defeating Licinius in 324, Constantine extended empire-wide the valuable privilege bestowed on Christian clergy in the West a decade or so earlier, of exemption from all obligations imposed on individuals by the state. Altogether, with extra confidence acquired from gaining sole control in 324, he became much less tolerant of all non-Christian religions, and within the Christian community much readier to press for "catholic" forms of worship to the exclusion of all others. As a result, therefore, a wholly new relationship began to evolve between the emperor and the church in all areas of its life and organization.

Other changes made by Constantine demand no less attention. The separation of military and civil commands was reinforced by the restriction of Praetorian Prefects to civil functions. Zosimus (*History* 2.34) laments that Constantine, unlike

Potter, David S. 1990. *Prophecy and History in the Crisis of the Roman Empire: A Historical Commentary on the* Thirteenth Sibylline Oracle. Oxford: Clarendon Press. The opening discussion of the empire's economic and political situation in the mid-third century is notably valuable.

Southern, Pat. 2001. *The Roman Empire from Severus to Constantine*. London and New York: Routledge.

TIMELINE

West	Rome & Italy	East	Cultural & Other Landmarks
	4000 B.C. Emergence of agriculture		
	2000 Appearance of copper tools and ornaments		
	1800–1200 Bronze Age	1400–1100 Mycenaean contacts with Italy and Sicily	
	c. 1000 First undoubted traces of settlement at the site of Rome		
c. 800 Phoenicians found Carthage	900–700 Iron Age; Villanovan and Latial cultures	c. 775 Greeks begin to settle in Italy and Sicily	
	c. 750 Formation of first city-states		700s Introduction of writing to Italy

West	Rome & Italy	East	Cultural & Other Landmarks
	186–183 Suppression of the cult of Bacchus	192–189 Rome defeats Antiochus III in the Syrian War	
		171–168 Third Macedonian War; end of its monarchy	168 Polybius comes to Rome as a hostage
mid-150s–130s Roman wars with Lusitanians and Celtiberians	149 "Extortion" court (*quaestio de repetundis*) is established	149–148 After the suppression of Andriscus' rising, Macedon becomes a Roman province	
149–146 Third Punic War, ending with the destruction of Carthage; its territory becomes the province of Africa		146 Destruction of Corinth	
133 Capture of Numantia	133 Tribunate of Tiberius Gracchus	136–132 First Slave War in Sicily	130s Secret ballot is introduced for voting in Roman assemblies
		133 Kingdom of Pergamum is bequeathed to Rome and (129) becomes the province of Asia	
122 Gaius Gracchus attempts to establish a colony (Junonia) on the site of Carthage	123, 122 Tribunates of Gaius Gracchus		
121 Province of Transalpine Gaul is formed	121 *Senatus Consultum Ultimum* authorizes the elimination of Gaius Gracchus		
113–101 Confrontation with Cimbri and Teutones	107, 104, 103, 102, 101 Consulships of Marius		c. 107–101 Major reform of the Roman army

West	Rome & Italy	East	Cultural & Other Landmarks
112–105 War with Jugurtha in Numidia			
104–100 Second Slave War in Sicily	100 Tribunate of Saturninus and (sixth) consulship of Marius		
	91 Tribunate of Livius Drusus		
	91–87 Social or Marsian War		90–89 Extension of Roman citizenship throughout Italy
	88 Tribunate of Sulpicius Rufus; Sulla's first march on Rome	90–85 War with Mithridates in Asia Minor and Greece; Sulla offers peace terms	
	87–84 Cinna works to restore stability; death of Marius (86), after he and Cinna had both marched on Rome (87)		86 Financial crisis: three-quarters of all debts are cancelled
	83–82 Sulla's second march on Rome; Pompey raises forces in support		
	82–81 Dictatorship of Sulla; proscriptions		
80–73 Sertorius in Spain resists Sullan commanders (Pompey among them) until murdered	78–77 Lepidus fails to overturn key features of Sulla's program by marching on Rome	75 Kingdom of Bithynia is bequeathed to Rome	

West	Rome & Italy	East	Cultural & Other Landmarks
	73–71 Slave revolt of Spartacus	74–63 Lucullus, then (from 66) Pompey, resume war against Mithridates	c. 70 Earliest known construction of an amphitheater in stone (at Pompeii)
	70 Consulship of Crassus and Pompey		70 Cicero secures the condemnation of Verres for misgovernment in Sicily
		67 Pompey suppresses piracy in the Mediterranean	
	65 Censorship of Crassus	64–63 Bithynia/Pontus, Cilicia, Syria are instituted or reshaped as provinces by Pompey	
	63–62 Cicero (consul in 63) exposes Catiline's conspiracy	63 Death of Mithridates	63 Julius Caesar is elected *pontifex maximus*
	60–59 Formation of "First Triumvirate" (Caesar, Crassus, Pompey)		61–55 Pompey builds a theater complex in the Campus Martius
	59 Consulship of Julius Caesar		
58–51 Caesar campaigns in Gaul and (55–54) England	58 Tribunate of Clodius	58–57 Cato makes Cyprus a Roman province; Cicero in exile	58–51 Caesar's "commentaries" on his Gallic campaigns
56 "Triumvirs" meet at Luca to strengthen and extend their partnership			

West	Rome & Italy	East	Cultural & Other Landmarks
	55 Consulship of Crassus and Pompey		50s or thereabouts Development of glassblowing technology
	54 Premature death of Julia		
		53 Crassus' army invades Parthia and is slaughtered at Carrhae	
	52 Death of Clodius; sole consulship of Pompey		
		51–50 Cicero governs Cilicia and Cyprus	
49 (March to fall) Caesar campaigns against Pompeians in Spain and besieges Massilia	49 (January) SCU is passed; Caesar crosses Rubicon River to invade Italy	49 (March) Pompey evacuates Italy	
	48 Caesar holds (second) consulship, together with one-year dictatorship	48 Pompey is defeated by Caesar at Pharsalus (August), and killed on arrival in Egypt as a fugitive (September)	48 Debtors' rising in Italy is suppressed by force
		October 48–mid-47 Caesar in Alexandria establishes Cleopatra as ruler of Egypt, and fathers a son by her	
Fall 47–mid-46 Campaign in Africa ends with Caesar's victory over Pompeians at Thapsus; Cato commits suicide	46 Caesar holds (third) consulship, and is appointed to ten-year dictatorship	47 (summer) Caesar defeats Pharnaces at Zela	46 New "Julian" calendar introduced; dedication of Forum Julium in Rome

West	Rome & Italy	East	Cultural & Other Landmarks
Fall 46–mid-45 Second campaign in Spain ends with Caesar's victory over Pompeians at Munda	45 Caesar holds (fourth) consulship, and continues dictator		
	44 Caesar holds (fifth) consulship, and (February) is made perpetual dictator; on March 15, he is assassinated		44 Caesar becomes the first living Roman whose head appears on coins; his worship as a god is authorized
	44 (May) Octavian arrives in Rome to claim his inheritance from Caesar		44 Lepidus becomes *pontifex maximus*
	43 (April) Antony is repulsed from Mutina by both consuls and Octavian; (August) Octavian becomes consul; (November) Formation of Second Triumvirate; Cicero is a victim of the ensuing proscriptions		
	42 (January) Deification of Julius Caesar	42 (fall) Antony and Octavian defeat Brutus and Cassius at Philippi	
	41–40 Perusine War	41–40 Antony meets Cleopatra, and fathers twins by her	
	40 Antony and Octavian redivide their control of the Roman world; Antony marries Octavia		

West	Rome & Italy	East	Cultural & Other Landmarks
	39 Agreement is reached between Antony, Octavian, and Sextus Pompey	39–38 Parthian invasions of Syria and Asia Minor are repulsed	38 Octavian marries Livia
	37 Second Triumvirate is renewed		
36 Sextus Pompey is defeated by Octavian and Lepidus; Lepidus' attempt to eliminate Octavian results in his own exile		36 Invasion of Parthia by Antony fails badly	
35–33 Octavian campaigns in Illyricum		35–34 Antony subdues Armenia; "Donations of Alexandria" (34)	
	32 Italy and the West swear loyalty to Octavian	32 Antony divorces Octavia	
		31 (September) Octavian defeats Antony and Cleopatra at Actium	
		30 Octavian captures Alexandria; Antony and Cleopatra commit suicide; Egypt becomes a Roman province	29 Curia Julia is dedicated
27–c. 1 B.C. Extension of Roman control in Spain, the Alps, and central Europe to the Danube River; Raetia, Noricum, Dalmatia, Pannonia, Moesia are formed as provinces	27 "First Settlement"; Octavian is renamed Augustus	25 Galatia becomes a Roman province	

West	Rome & Italy	East	Cultural & Other Landmarks
	23 (July) "Second Settlement"; (fall) Marcellus dies		late 20s According to tradition, Vergil reads his *Aeneid* to Augustus
	21 Marriage of Agrippa and Julia	20 Parthia returns legionary standards captured from Crassus and Antony	
	18–17 Augustus introduces legislation affecting marriage, childbearing, and adultery		
	17 Augustus adopts Gaius and Lucius		17 Secular Games
	13 New conditions for army service are introduced		
	12 Agrippa dies; Augustus becomes *pontifex maximus* following the death of Lepidus		
9 B.C. Drusus the Elder dies			9 B.C. Endpoint of Livy's *History*; Dedication of Ara Pacis
7 B.C. Monument at modern La Turbie commemorates Augustus' subjugation of "all the Alpine peoples"	2 B.C. Title of *Pater Patriae* is bestowed on Augustus	6 B.C.–A.D. 2 Tiberius retires to Rhodes	2 B.C. Dedication of Temple of Mars the Avenger in Augustus' new forum
A.D. 2 Lucius Caesar dies			
	A.D. 4 Augustus adopts Tiberius	A.D. 4 Gaius Caesar dies	

West	Rome & Italy	East	Cultural & Other Landmarks
6–9 Rebellions in Germany, Dalmatia, Pannonia; (A.D. 9) three Roman legions are massacred in Teutoburg Forest		6 Judaea becomes a Roman province	8 Augustus exiles Ovid to Tomis, where he remains until his death in 17
14 Legions stationed in Germany and Pannonia mutiny	14 Augustus dies, and is succeeded by Tiberius		14 Promulgation of Augustus' *Res Gestae*
14–16/17 Germanicus campaigns in Germany		17 Cappadocia becomes a Roman province	
		17–19 Germanicus is dispatched to the East, and dies in Syria	
	20 Trial of Piso for the death of Germanicus		
	23 Drusus the Younger dies		
	14–31 Sejanus serves as Praetorian Prefect, until (31) denounced and executed		23 Praetorian Guard is grouped together and based in Rome
	26 Tiberius takes up residence on Capri		
	33 Financial crisis, which Tiberius attempts to alleviate		
	37 Tiberius dies, and is succeeded by Gaius Caligula		

West	Rome & Italy	East	Cultural & Other Landmarks
	41 Assassination of Caligula, who is succeeded by Claudius		40s–50s Claudius constructs a new harbor (Portus) north of Ostia
43 Britain and Mauretania become Roman provinces		46 Thrace becomes a Roman province	
	47–48 Claudius conducts a census		
	54 Claudius dies, and is succeeded by Nero		
	59 Nero orders the murder of his mother Agrippina		
60–67 Boudicca leads a rebellion in Britain	64 Great Fire of Rome; Christians are persecuted as scapegoats; much of the devastated area is appropriated by Nero for his Golden House		
	66 Nero crowns Tiridates King of Armenia in Rome	66–67 Nero visits Greece	
		66–73 First Jewish Revolt, culminating in the destruction of the Temple in Jerusalem (70) and capture of Masada (73)	
67–68 Rising and defeat of Vindex	68 (June) Nero commits suicide, and is succeeded by Galba		

West	Rome & Italy	East	Cultural & Other Landmarks
69 (early January) Legions in Germany support Vitellius for emperor	69 (mid-January) With Praetorians' support, Otho murders Galba and succeeds him; (April) defeated in battle at Bedriacum, Otho commits suicide, and is succeeded by Vitellius; (October) Vitellius' army is defeated by Pannonian legions at Cremona; (December) Vitellius is killed, and is succeeded by Vespasian	69 (July) Legions in the East and Pannonia support Vespasian for emperor	69 (December) Temple of Jupiter Optimus Maximus on the Capitol is destroyed by fire
69–70 Germano-Gallic revolt	70 (October) Vespasian arrives in Rome as emperor		71 (June) Triumph of Vespasian and Titus to celebrate the fall of Jerusalem
70s–90s "Latin" status awarded to Spanish communities	73–74 Vespasian and Titus conduct a census		70s Vespasian builds the Temple of Peace in Rome, and begins the Colosseum
	79 Vespasian dies, and is succeeded by Titus		70s Completion of Pliny the Elder's *Natural History*
	80 Fire devastates city of Rome		79 Eruption of Mt. Vesuvius
	81 Titus dies, and is succeeded by Domitian		
85–92 Domitian campaigns north of the Danube, especially against the Dacians			89 A rising by the commander in Upper Germany is suppressed
	96 Domitian is assassinated and succeeded by Nerva		

West	Rome & Italy	East	Cultural & Other Landmarks
	97 Nerva adopts Trajan		96–98 Nerva establishes *alimenta*
	98 Nerva dies, and is succeeded by Trajan		98 Completion of Tacitus, *Agricola*; and of c. 98 Frontinus, *On the Aqueducts of Rome*
100 Trajan establishes colony at Thamugadi	100 (Sept.) Pliny the Younger delivers speech of thanks (*Panegyricus*) on becoming consul		
101–102, 105–106 Dacian Wars; Dacia then becomes a Roman province		105–106 Arabia Petraea (Nabataea) becomes a Roman province	
		c. 111/112 Pliny the Younger's special governorship of Bithynia-Pontus	112 Forum of Trajan is dedicated
		113–117 Trajan campaigns to seize Armenia and Mesopotamia from Parthian control, and creates new provinces there	113 Column of Trajan is dedicated
		115–117 Second Jewish Revolt	c. 115 Trajan adds an inner basin to Claudius' harbor at Portus
		117 Trajan dies, and is succeeded by Hadrian, who abandons Trajan's eastern conquests	

West	Rome & Italy	East	Cultural & Other Landmarks
120s Hadrian constructs "his" Wall across northern England, and defines the German-Raetian frontier by erecting a wooden barrier	121–127, 128–131 Hadrian makes extended journeys through the empire		130 Hadrian's favorite Antinous drowns in the Nile
	131 Permanent Praetorian Edict ("Edictum Perpetuum") is instituted	132–135 Third Jewish Revolt (Bar Kokhba War)	
	138 Hadrian dies, and is succeeded by Antoninus Pius		
139–142 Turf "Wall of Antoninus" is built across southern Scotland	c. 144 Aelius Aristides delivers his oration *To Rome*	150s Anti-Christian violence at Smyrna	
	161 Antoninus Pius dies, and is jointly succeeded by Marcus Aurelius and Lucius Verus		
		162–166 Lucius Verus campaigns against Parthia	mid 160s–190s Plague sweeps through the empire
166–173, 176–180 First and Second Marcomannic Wars	169 Lucius Verus dies		
177 Anti-Christian violence at Lugdunum	176 Marcus Aurelius makes his son Commodus co-emperor	175 Avidius Cassius proclaims himself emperor and briefly rules the East until assassinated	

West	Rome & Italy	East	Cultural & Other Landmarks
180 Marcus Aurelius dies, and is succeeded by Commodus, who abandons his father's attempts to secure territory north of the Danube			
	192 (Dec. 31) Commodus is assassinated		
193 Legions in Britain support Clodius Albinus for emperor, those on the Rhine and Danube support Septimius Severus; Septimius Severus appoints Clodius Albinus his "Caesar"	193 (Jan. 1) Pertinax becomes emperor, only to be murdered in March; after an auction by the Praetorian Guard, Didius Julianus becomes emperor; (June) Didius Julianus is killed, and Septimius Severus reaches Rome to replace him	193 Legions in the East support Pescennius Niger for emperor	193 Septimius Severus enlarges the forces in Rome, and stations others nearby
		193–194 Septimius Severus pursues, defeats, and kills Pescennius Niger	
196–197 Septimius Severus defeats and kills Clodius Albinus at Lugdunum		194–195, 197–199 Septimius Severus campaigns against the Parthians	
203 Martyrdom of Perpetua at Carthage	c. 200 Septimius Severus lifts the ban on marriage by soldiers	c. 200 Northern Mesopotamia and Osroene become Roman provinces	203 Arch of Septimius Severus and Septizodium are both dedicated at Rome

West	Rome & Italy	East	Cultural & Other Landmarks
208–211 Septimius Severus campaigns in northern Britain; he dies here, and is succeeded by Caracalla and Geta			
211 (December) Caracalla orders the murder of Geta	212 Caracalla extends Roman citizenship empire-wide (*Constitutio Antoniniana*)		
213–214 Caracalla campaigns in Germany		216–217 Campaigns of Caracalla into Armenia and Parthia, during which he is assassinated	
		217 Macrinus (first *eques* to be emperor) replaces Caracalla	
		218 Macrinus is assassinated, and replaced by Elagabalus	
	222 Elagabalus is murdered, and succeeded by Severus Alexander		
	223 Praetorian Guard's murder of their Prefect Ulpian goes unpunished		
		226 Sasanid dynasty takes control of Parthia/Persia	
	229 Cassius Dio is consul with the emperor and ends his *Roman History* at this point	231–232 Severus Alexander regains Mesopotamia from Sasanid invaders	

West	Rome & Italy	East	Cultural & Other Landmarks
235 On campaign in Raetia, Severus Alexander and Julia Mamaea are assassinated by mutinous soldiers; their leader Maximinus replaces him			
	238–284 Age of Crisis		
			248 Celebration of Rome's thousandth anniversary
	249–250, 257–259 Empire-wide persecution of Christians by Emperors Decius, and then Valerian		
		260 Sasanid King Shapur I captures and kills Valerian	
260–274 "Gallic Empire" of Postumus exerts broad control over the West	260–268 As sole emperor, Gallienus seeks to secure the core of the empire	mid 260s–272 Odenath, and then his widow Zenobia, control the East from Palmyra	
270 Emperor Aurelian abandons the province of Dacia	271 Aurelian fortifies Rome with an encircling wall	272 Aurelian regains the East from Zenobia	
273–274 Aurelian regains all areas once controlled by Postumus			
		284 Diocletian becomes emperor	

West	Rome & Italy	East	Cultural & Other Landmarks
c. 287 Carausius rules Britain in defiance of Maximian	286 Maximian becomes co-emperor (Augustus) with Diocletian		
293 "Tetrarchy" is instituted; Constantius becomes Maximian's Caesar	290s Provinces are redivided, and dioceses instituted; civil and military positions are separated	293 Galerius becomes Diocletian's Caesar	
296 Constantius regains Britain		298 Galerius defeats Sasanid forces and extends Roman territory in Mesopotamia	
	301–302 Coinage reform; Edict on Maximum Prices		
	303 "Great Persecution" of Christians (in the West to 305, in the East to 311)		
	305 Diocletian and Maximian relinquish their positions		
306 Constantine is acclaimed Augustus in Britain	306 Maxentius is acclaimed Augustus in Rome		
	312 In a battle at the Milvian Bridge, Constantine eliminates Maxentius and wins Rome		312 Constantine disbands the Praetorian Guard
	313 Constantine and Licinius issue the Edict of Milan, and unite to defeat Maximin Daia		315 Dedication of Rome's arch honoring Constantine

West	Rome & Italy	East	Cultural & Other Landmarks
313–316 Church councils at Rome (313) and Arles (314) adjudicate the Donatist controversy, and Constantine issues his own ruling (316)	313–324 Constantine rules the West of the empire, Licinius the East		c. 315 Completion of Lactantius, *On the Deaths of the Persecutors*
		320 Licinius resumes persecution of Christians	
	323–324 Constantine defeats Licinius, and becomes sole emperor	324 Constantine chooses Byzantium as his capital, and renames it Constantinople	324 Endpoint of Eusebius, *History of the Church*; 324 onwards Constantine promotes Christianity with growing confidence
			528–534 Emperor Justinian's "Collection of Civil Law"

GLOSSARY

[Most terms mentioned only once in the text are omitted here]

aedile—Four annual magistrates in the city of Rome, two of whom had to be plebeian. The office was originally a plebeian one, charged with oversight of the temple (*aedes*) established by the *plebs*. Later, duties came to include general oversight of trade, markets, weights and measures, public games (*ludi*), public grain supply, public buildings, and law and order in the city.

aerarium—Roman treasury and depository of state documents overseen by *quaestors*, situated in the Temple of Saturn in the Forum (*Forum Romanum*). In A.D. 6 Augustus established in addition the "military treasury" (*aerarium militare*) to pay the lump sums promised to legionaries on their discharge.

ager (*publicus, Gallicus*, etc.)—("land") *Ager publicus* ("public land") is property owned by the Roman state (as opposed to a private individual) that it could assign or lease (for rent), normally through the *censors*.

agger—("mound") A military rampart.

Agri Decumates—Territory that forms a re-entrant angle between the upper Rhine and Danube rivers.

Alexander the Great (356–323)—King of Macedon, whose astonishing conquest of the Persian Empire, and accompanying honors (worship among them), became the envy and inspiration of many Romans and others.

alimenta—Community-based child support schemes devised in the first century A.D. and funded both by emperors (especially Trajan in Italy) and by private benefactors.

ambitio, ambitus—("circuit" or "going round") The quest for public office by promising favors, paying voters, or giving them gifts. Unlike *ambitio* (legal canvassing), *ambitus* is illegal bribery of voters.

cohors—("cohort") denotes a group of one kind or another, frequently a tactical unit within a legion, but also a governor's entourage, for example.

collegium—("group," "association") denotes an organized group of many different kinds (religious, social, commercial, professional), including the groups (or "colleges") of priests such as augurs and pontiffs.

colonia (pl. *coloniae*)—"colony" or settlement (in Italy, or elsewhere in the Roman world) founded to settle discharged veterans or civilians eager to improve their prospects; each participant received a plot of land assigned by *triumviri coloniae deducendae*. After the early second century A.D., new foundations of this type were rare. However, the privileged civic status of *colonia* might still be awarded by an emperor to an existing community.

colonus (pl. *coloni*)—1) farmer (especially a tenant) or country dweller; 2) inhabitant of a Roman *colonia*.

Colosseum—see amphitheater above.

comes (pl. *comites*)—"companion," "adviser" (especially of the emperor), and (from the time of the Tetrarchy) a high-ranking military commander ("count").

comitium (pl. *comitia*)—In all Roman communities, a designated place for citizens to meet when summoned by officials; at Rome, this was situated north of the Forum at the foot of the Capitoline hill. The plural *comitia* denotes such a citizen assembly itself.

commercium—1) "business," "commerce"; also 2) the right of a Latin to own Roman land and to make a contract with a Roman that would be enforceable in a Roman law-court; the same right was sometimes granted to other non-Romans too.

concilium (pl. *concilia*)—"assembly," especially that of Rome's plebeian citizens (*concilium plebis*). In addition, during the Principate, the term was used for the assemblies of delegates from cities within one or more provinces that met to discuss issues of common concern, and in particular to organize celebrations of the imperial cult. In Greek-speaking provinces the term used for such assemblies was the Greek *koinon* (pl. *koina*).

consilium—"advice," and by extension the group that provided it, in particular to the emperor (hence *consilium principis*).

constitutio Antoniniana—the legal enactment (*constitutio*) of A.D. 212 by which Caracalla (whose official name was Marcus Aurelius Antoninus) extended Roman citizenship to almost all the free inhabitants of the empire.

consul—Chief annual magistrate of the Roman Republic (always one of a pair).

contio (pl. *contiones*)—Public meeting convened by an officeholder to address a matter of current concern (legislative, judicial in particular). There could be discussion, but no binding vote of any kind.

conubium—Marriage, and the right to enter into a marriage recognized by Roman law. Both partners to such a marriage had to have either Roman citizenship or this right, which was given to Latins and sometimes to other non-Romans.

"crown tax"—Contributions that communities were required to send to the emperor on certain special occasions, especially his accession.

curator (pl. *curatores*)—General descriptive term for anyone who shoulders a special responsibility, above all in public life (thus to oversee food supply, or construction of an aqueduct, for example). Most notably, from the second century A.D., the term was used for high officials dispatched by emperors to intervene in the affairs of cities, or even a whole province, at a time of difficulty.

curia (pl. *curiae*)—1) the earliest group into which Roman citizens were divided; 2) the meeting place of a citizen unit or other group, in particular a senate or town council. The principal meeting place for Rome's own senate was the building called the Curia in the Forum.

cursus honorum—literally "succession of offices," the prescribed series of magistracies which Roman senators sought to hold (subject to various regulations and restrictions) in order to become leading public figures.

Cynics—philosophers who advocated living "according to nature," and hence were (in varying degrees) hostile to the established order, especially the Roman Principate.

damnatio memoriae—("damning of the memory") After the deaths of individuals declared by the senate to be enemies of the state (certain emperors especially), measures taken to blot out their memory: These could include destruction of images, erasure of names from public records, annulment of decisions.

decurion—city councilor, the equivalent at a local level to a senator at Rome. To serve thus, as at Rome, was a lifelong responsibility only open to wealthy, respectable citizens of the community.

dediticii—literally, individuals who have made a formal surrender (*deditio*) to Rome; in particular, from the second century A.D. onwards, the many peoples from outside the empire's borders who were admitted into it to settle. For whatever reason, Caracalla seems to have made a point of excluding *dediticii* from his grant of universal citizenship (*constitutio Antoniniana*).

demos—the citizen body of a community (Greek).

denarius (pl. *denarii*; see also *aureus, sestertius*)—Roman coin made of silver. Initially, during the Second Punic War (218–201), it was valued at 10 bronze *asses*. After this war, however, it was revalued at 16 bronze *asses* or 4 sesterces (4 *asses* = 1 *sestertius*).

dea, deus—goddess, god.

dictator—Magistrate appointed to take sole control of the state temporarily in order to overcome a crisis. He appointed a second-in-command (*magister equitum*) himself.

dignitas—"high rank," and hence the "esteem" due to the holder of it, a sense of respect about which ambitious Romans were prone to be very sensitive.

dilectus—levy for choosing men to draft into the army.

diploma (pl. *diplomata*)—Document comprising a pair of folded bronze tablets that certified the holder's privileges on discharge from military or naval service.

divus (pl. *divi*)—"deified," used only of deceased humans who had been declared deified by the senate (thus members of the imperial family in particular).

Dominate (compare *dominus* below)—Period of more openly authoritarian rule instituted by Diocletian (284–305) after the Principate.

dominus—"lord," "master".

donative—Originally, money or loot distributed by a commander to his soldiers after a successful campaign. Later, a supplementary cash payment offered to soldiers to induce or cement their loyalty, especially by emperors on special occasions.

Druids—Priests (male and female) of the Celtic religion.

Edictum Perpetuum ("Perpetual Edict")—Revised, permanent (from A.D. 129) version of the edicts issued by successive praetors.

legion—the standard large Roman military formation, comprising around 5,000 heavily armed infantry.

lex (pl. *leges*) ("law")—Statute passed by a citizen assembly or issued by the emperor, and then generally known by the name(s) of its proposer(s): thus, for example, *lex Licinia-Sextia*.

lictor (pl. *lictores*)—Official attendant who escorted and assisted a Roman magistrate, in particular by carrying the *fasces* (see above) before him. The number of lictors to which magistrates were entitled varied according to their office.

lituus—Curved stick used by an *augur* (see *auspicium* above).

ludi—Public "games" such as beast hunts (*venationes*), gladiatorial shows, chariot races (*ludi circenses*), theatrical events (*ludi scaenici*), and mock naval battles. Such entertainments might be offered (usually free) by officials or private individuals, either on a regular basis (e.g. an annual religious festival) or as a special occasion (e.g. a funeral).

magister equitum—("master of cavalry") See *dictator*. In addition, as part of his military reforms, Constantine instituted a high-ranking commander of cavalry with this title.

Magna Graecia—("Great Greece") Broad descriptive term for the whole region of southern Italy and Sicily colonized by Greeks from the eighth century B.C.

Magna Mater ("Great Mother," Cybele)—goddess whose cult was officially introduced to Rome from Asia Minor in 204 B.C.

maiestas—"treason".

maius imperium—See *imperium* above.

manus ("hand") marriage—an increasingly rare form of Roman marriage. It came to be regarded as unduly restrictive for the wife, because it placed both her person and property under her husband's absolute control.

municipium (pl. *municipia*)—Descriptive term for the legal status of an autonomous city located in Roman territory, but governed by its own laws and city council, while obligated to assist Rome as an ally. Increasingly, these cities adopted institutions on the Roman model.

necropolis (pl. *necropoleis*)—(Greek "city of the dead") Area of a town where the dead were buried—traditionally outside the walls in order to protect the inhabitants from disease and the religious defilement of death.

negotiator (pl. *negotiatores*)—"businessman".

new man—see *novus homo* below.

nobilis (pl. *nobiles*) ("nobles")—Rome's governing elite. More specifically, the members of those families with an ancestor who had attained the consulship.

nomen (pl. *nomina*)—("name")—Middle component of the typical Roman "three names," representing an individual's clan (*gens*); see also *cognomen* and *praenomen*.

novus homo (pl. *novi homines*) ("new man")—First member of a family to become a Roman senator. The higher he rose in the *cursus honorum*, the more remarkable his achievement was; for a *novus homo* to attain the consulship was especially difficult.

optimates, populares—Names used to describe the holders of contrasting political attitudes from the late second century B.C. *Optimates* ("the best people") continued to uphold traditional methods of competition among senators. *Populares* ("people's men"), on the other hand, sought wider popularity among the citizen body as a means of advancement.

origo—("origin") Line of descent, in particular a Roman citizen's community of origin, to which he owed political obligations (in addition to the ones he owed Rome); hence part of a citizen's political identity.

ovatio—Victory celebration in Rome awarded to a successful general, but on a distinctly lesser scale than a "triumph" (see below).

panegyric—see *laudatio* above.

papyrus—In Greek and Roman civilization, the equivalent of modern paper; sheets of it were made from strips of the pith of a plant which grew in the marshlands of Egypt's Nile delta.

pater patriae, also *parens patriae*—("father" or "parent of the fatherland") In origin, a special title awarded to an individual for extraordinary service to the state. It was bestowed on Augustus in 2 B.C., and almost all subsequent emperors took it, with the notable exception of Tiberius. It suggests the holder's role as *paterfamilias* ("father") of the state, and his *patria potestas* ("fatherly power") over Roman citizens.

patria potestas ("fatherly power")—Legal authority of the male head of a family (*paterfamilias*) over his family and descendants, including other adult males, women, freedmen, slaves, and children. Terminated for children when a daughter was transferred to the power of her husband's family by marriage, or when a male descendant became independent (*sui iuris*) by legal procedure.

paterfamilias—Male head of a family, usually a father or grandfather, if his marriage was valid in Roman law. In principle, he had complete legal authority (*patria potestas*) over the life, death, and freedom of his family.

patrician—Member of the more privileged group of Roman citizens (in contrast to the *plebs*, or plebeian group, see below). Patrician status could only be gained by birth (at least, until emperors bestowed it).

patronus ("patron")—see "client". Note that once a slave is freed by his owner, he becomes a freedman and the former owner becomes his patron.

pax Augusta—("Augustan peace") Descriptive term for the long period of relative peace and stability following Augustus' expansion and consolidation of the empire.

Penates—Roman spirits connected with the inner part of a private house.

peregrinus ("foreigner")—Any free individual who is not a member of a Roman community.

"Perpetual Edict"—see Edictum Perpetuum.

plebs—Strictly speaking, the "plebeians," the less privileged group of Roman citizens (in contrast to patricians, see above). More generally, the term is also used of the common people anywhere, often dismissively.

podium—1) Supporting platform of a building or temple, from which public speeches were often delivered; 2) balcony of a theater or arena from which the emperor viewed the event; imperial dais.

polis (pl. *poleis*)—"city," "city state" (Greek).

pomerium—Sacred boundary of a city ritually marked by a priest. At Rome, a vital marker of the limit either side of which political and military authority could, or could not, be exercised.

pontifex (pl. *pontifices*)—("bridge builder," "pontiff") Member of one of the major groups or "colleges" of Roman priests, headed by the *pontifex maximus*; from the time of Augustus onwards, this headship was always taken by the emperor.

populares—see *optimates*.

populus (*Romanus*) ("people," "Roman people")—Broad collective term for the citizen body of the Roman state, as in the standard formulation "Senate and People of Rome" (*Senatus Populusque Romanus*, SPQR).

porticus—1) Long (usually roofed) colonnade; 2) large, roofed market building with multiple rows of columns (such as the Porticus Aemilia in Rome's warehouse district); 3) courtyard enclosed on all four sides by rows of columns with colonnades (such as the Porticus of Octavia in the Campus Martius).

praenomen (pl. *praenomina*)—First component of the typical Roman "three names" (see also *nomen* and *cognomen*). The *praenomen* represents an individual's given or "first" name, and distinguishes members of the same family (e.g., **Marcus** Tullius Cicero, and his brother **Quintus** Tullius Cicero).

praetor—Annual magistracy with *imperium*, an important step in the *cursus honorum*. Its holders were placed in a variety of assignments, in particular to preside over lawcourts in Rome.

Praetorian Guard—Elite military force formed to serve as the emperor's bodyguard; it was instituted by Augustus, and disbanded by Constantine in 312.

princeps (pl. *principes*)—("leading figure") During the Republic, an informal general term for those senators who carried the greatest weight in matters of state. *Princeps* therefore appealed to Augustus as the unassuming term that best fitted the position which he developed for himself. From this usage by Augustus stems "Principate," the descriptive term for the two and a half centuries during which the ideal of his nonauthoritarian style of rule was maintained (superseded by the "Dominate," see above).

princeps senatus ("leader of the senate")—Informal title used for the senator whose name was placed first in the roll of senators when this was reviewed by the censors; to be distinguished from the broader usage of simply *princeps* (see above).

proconsul—ex-consul who, at the end of his term in office, accepts an assignment (governorship of a province, for example) that continues, or "prorogues," his magistrate's authority for a set period.

procurator ("agent")—In particular, an individual (often an *eques*) appointed by the emperor to manage property or to represent him in court.

proletarii—Roman citizens whose declaration of property at a census was too low to qualify them for military service; notionally, therefore, all they could contribute to the state was their children (*proles*).

propraetor—ex-praetor who, at the end of his term in office, accepts an assignment (governorship of a province, for example) that continues, or "prorogues," his magistrate's authority for a set period.

proscription—Publication of a list of individuals who can be killed with impunity, and whose property is confiscated.

provincia ("province")—The sphere of activity which a magistrate is assigned to exercise his authority; and hence, in particular, a foreign territory which he is required to oversee for Rome.

publicanus (pl. *publicani*)—Private individual who performs work for the Roman state under contract (construction, supply, tax collection, for example). The fulfilment of larger contracts might require a group of such individuals to work together as a "syndicate" (*societas*).

Punic—In Latin usage, Phoenician, hence Carthaginian.

quaestio (pl. *quaestiones*)—Tribunal or court for criminal matters, which could always be established as required in individual instances. In addition, between 149 and the late 80s B.C., a succession of permanent such courts (*quaestiones perpetuae*) with juries was established, each empowered to adjudicate a specific crime. The first was the *quaestio de repetundis* ("concerning items to be recovered"), which heard charges of extortion, embezzlement, and related crimes, brought against senators who had served in the provinces.

quaestor—Annual magistracy (without *imperium*), the first step in the *cursus honorum*. Holders could be placed in a variety of assignments in Rome or abroad, usually relating to the state's financial interests.

Regia—Sacred building in the Roman Forum between the Via Sacra and the Temple of Vesta, believed to have been built by king Numa. Residence of the king during the regal period, thereafter headquarters of the *pontifex maximus*.

repetundae—see *quaestio* above.

rex—"king".

rostra—Raised platform in the Forum from which speeches were made; named after the prows (*rostra*) of captured enemy ships used for its decoration.

sacrosanctity—Attribute which made it a crime (subject to instant death) on the part of anyone who used violence towards its holder (a tribune of the *plebs*, for example).

Second Sophistic—Greek cultural and literary movement that spanned the mid-first to the third centuries A.D.; it drew its inspiration from the teachers and researchers termed "sophists" in the Greek world of the fifth century B.C.

senatus ("senate")—Advisory council first of Rome's kings, thereafter of the state's senior magistrates. Its role in affairs, and hence its *auctoritas*, came to be increasingly important, until it suffered challenges from powerful individuals during the last century of the Republic, and was eventually overshadowed by the emperors.

senatus consultum (SC)—"resolution" or "decree of the senate".

sestertius (English pl. "sesterces;" see also *denarius*)—Roman coin originally of silver, but from Augustus' time minted in bronze. Often abbreviated "HS," because 1 *sestertius* was originally valued at 2.5 bronze *asses*; in Roman numerals, IIS or "HS" = 2.5.

Severans—Line of emperors ruling from the accession of Septimius Severus (193) through the death of Severus Alexander (235). See Table 12.1.

socius (pl. *socii*)—"ally" (of the Roman state).

Stoicism—Greek philosophical and ethical movement, some of whose adherents among Rome's upper classes objected to the autocratic style of certain emperors.

Struggle of the Orders—Prolonged struggle (early fifth to early third centuries B.C.) by Rome's plebeian citizens to overcome domination of the state's affairs by patricians.

suffect consul (or other officeholder)—Replacement elected to fill the remaining term of office when its original or "ordinary" holder died or resigned.

tabularium ("record-office")—Rome's tabularium at the western end of the Forum was constructed in the early first century B.C.

Tetrarchy—("rule of four") Short-lived system of joint rule established by Diocletian (284–305), with an emperor (*Augustus*) in the West and another in the East, each with a deputy (*Caesar*).

toga—The undyed woolen robe that was the distinctive garment of adult Roman civilians; it could not be worn by non-Roman citizens. Holders of certain ranks and distinctions were entitled to wear togas that were decorated in various ways: Consuls, for example, wore a *toga praetexta* that was bordered in purple.

tribune (*tribunus*, pl. *tribuni*)—From the early fifth century B.C., annually elected "tribunes of the plebs" (*tribuni plebis*) with their own authority (*tribunicia potestas*) were recognized as the leaders of the plebeian citizen body (*plebs*). In addition, and quite separately, "military tribunes" (*tribuni militum*) were army officers of sufficient importance for some of them even to be chosen as joint heads of state in certain years during the late fifth and early fourth centuries B.C. (*tribuni militum consulari potestate*). Thereafter, there continued to be army officerships with the title *tribunus militum*, but typically these were no longer of high rank.

tributum—a tax on property.

triumph—Voted by the senate to honor a general who had won an outstanding victory against a non-Roman enemy (no victory in a civil war could be recognized in this way); celebrated by a procession through Rome from the Campus Martius to the Capitoline hill. In these exceptional circumstances, the triumphant general (*triumphator*), dressed like the god Jupiter, rode in a chariot, and was permitted to march his army inside the *pomerium*.

triumvir (pl. *triumviri*)—member of a group, or commission, of three men.

Twelve Tables—Rome's first set of written laws (around 450 B.C.).

Vestal virgins—Prestigious priestesses who performed the rites of Vesta (goddess of the hearth) from her shrine near the Regia in the Forum; maintenance of the sacred flame here was considered vital to Rome's survival.

via—"road".

vigiles ("watchmen")—Paramilitary patrols of freedmen, instituted by Augustus to reduce the danger from outbreaks of fire in the city of Rome.

virtus—"manly courage," more broadly "excellence" or "distinction" as demonstrated in service to the Roman state.

PRINCIPAL ANCIENT AUTHORS

This list aims to be no more than a concise identification of the principal authors mentioned in the book, together with a few anonymous writings (under their commonly used titles). The list omits three categories, however: nonhistorical authors whose writings are of lesser significance for modern readers new to Roman history; historical authors (such as Herodotus and Thucydides) whose subject is not related to Rome; and historical authors whose work is entirely, or almost entirely, lost.

An English translation is cited only in those instances where none is readily available in any of the standard series, such as the Loeb Classical Library (Harvard University Press), Oxford World's Classics, Penguin Classics, or (for the third century A.D. onwards) Translated Texts for Historians (Liverpool University Press).

For further information in every case, consult, for example, the appropriate entry in *OCD*. A wide range of translated extracts from authors (including fragments), along with inscriptions, papyri, and coin legends, is assembled in sourcebooks such as Lewis, Naphtali, and Meyer Reinhold. 1990 (third edition). *Roman Civilization*, vol. 1 *The Republic and the Augustan Age*, vol. 2 *The Empire*. New York: Columbia University Press.

*Acts of the Apostles: Fifth book of the New Testament, written by Luke, author of the third gospel, outlining the mission of the Church from Christ's ascension to Paul's visit to Rome around 62. This work—most likely to date to the 80s—was evidently not known to contemporary Roman authors.

---

*Authors who write in Greek (rather than Latin) are asterisked.

491

become increasingly unreliable and sensationalist. The work's own claim to be by six different writers is surely false, and no more than a reflection of the (single) author's teasing wit.

*Flavius **Josephus**: Jewish aristocrat, priest, and leader in the First Jewish Revolt (66–73), until he defected to the Romans and was rewarded with citizenship by Vespasian (hence his Roman name Flavius). His extensive writings include a history of the revolt in which he took part (*Jewish War*), and a larger treatment of the Jews' entire history to that date (*Jewish Antiquities*).

Decimus Junius **Juvenal**is: Early second century A.D. satirist of Roman society and its morals. His true identity is beyond recovery, and autobiographical statements that he makes should not be taken at face value.

Lactantius: Teacher of rhetoric at the imperial court, who (among other works) wrote *On the Deaths of the Persecutors* around 315. Its purpose—in a presentation that is far from objective—is to celebrate Christians' deliverance by Constantine, and to demonstrate that all the earlier emperors who persecuted them met a terrible fate. Translation: Creed, John L. 1984. *Lactantius, De Mortibus Persecutorum*. Oxford: Clarendon Press.

Titus Livius (**Livy**): Native of Patavium in Cisalpine Gaul, probably born in 59 B.C. and died in A.D. 17, although it is possible that each of these dates should be five years earlier. Since he came to know both Augustus and Claudius personally, he must have spent time in Rome, but the circumstances are not recorded; there is no sign that he played a role in public life. His immense history, "Books from the Foundation of the City" (*Ab Urbe Condita Libri*), spanned Rome's origins to 9 B.C., but only two substantial portions of it survive—the opening books to 290, and coverage of the Second Punic War to the end of the Third Macedonian War (218–167).

Panegyrics: A collection of twelve panegyric speeches (some anonymous) is a chance survival discovered in the fifteenth century. The collection preserves the speech of thanks that Pliny the Younger (see below) made on his entry to the consulship in A.D. 100. Otherwise, two of the speeches date to the late fourth century A.D., but the remaining nine all belong to the late third and early fourth centuries, and thus make an important contribution to our knowledge of the period of Diocletian and Constantine. Translation: Nixon, Charles E.V. and Barbara S. Rodgers. 1994. *In Praise of Later Roman Emperors: the* Panegyrici Latini. Berkeley, Los Angeles, London: University of California Press.

Aemilius **Papinian**us: Leading jurist of the early third century A.D. and close associate of the emperor Septimius Severus. Writings by him form a notable part of the *Digest* (see above).

Julius **Paulus**: Leading jurist of the early third century A.D., who worked closely with emperors from Septimius Severus to Severus Alexander. Writings by him form a notable part of the *Digest* (see above).

Martyrdom of Perpetua: Anonymous account of the martyrdom—at Carthage in 203—of Perpetua, a Roman woman (young, respectable, married), and her female slave, Felicitas. The account incorporates impressions said to have been recorded by Perpetua herself. Translation: Ehrman, Bart D. (ed.). 1999. *After the New Testament: A Reader in Early Christianity*. New York and Oxford: Oxford University Press, Chapter 3.8.

*Pausanias: From Asia Minor; his *Description of Greece*—of mid-second century A.D. date—offers an extensive treatment of many monuments and sanctuaries in the province of Achaia, together with their historical background. He had visited these sites personally, and proves to be an accurate observer.

*Philo: A leader in the Jewish community at Alexandria (Egypt), and an expert philosopher in both the Jewish and Greek traditions. Among his voluminous surviving writings, two works—*Against Flaccus* [Prefect of Egypt, 32–38], and *Embassy to Gaius*—offer insight into the increasing ill-treatment of the Jewish community at Alexandria from the time of Augustus onwards. The latter work is Philo's vivid account of a Jewish embassy which he led to Gaius (Caligula) in Rome to plead with the emperor (in 39–40).

*Lucius Flavius **Philostratus**: Intellectual from the Aegean island of Lemnos, who studied at Athens and later lived in Rome, where he enjoyed the patronage of Julia Domna, wife of the emperor Septimius Severus. His admiring *Lives of the Sophists* illuminates the "Second Sophistic" movement.

Gaius Plinius Caecilius Secundus (**Pliny the Younger**): Senator (*novus homo*) from Comum (modern Como) in Cisalpine Gaul, born around 60, nephew of Pliny the Elder (see below), who raised him. He was promoted by Domitian, Nerva, and Trajan, and also had marked success as a trial advocate. A revised version of the traditional speech of thanks he made in the senate on taking up the consulship in September 100 survives (see under *Panegyrics* above). So do ten books of *Letters*. The last of these preserves official correspondence between Trajan and himself while serving in Bithynia-Pontus as a governor specially appointed by the emperor (around 111). The other nine books gather earlier private letters—rich, varied material, but all of it revised, if not composed, for publication.

Gaius Plinius Secundus (**Pliny the Elder**): *Eques*, uncle of Pliny the Younger (see above), who rose through the imperial service to become naval commander at Misenum on the Bay of Naples, and lost his life in 79 during a personal inspection of the eruption of Mt. Vesuvius. He was a polymath and an astonishingly productive author, but only his *Natural History* survives. An encyclopedia with even broader scope than its title might indicate, this work distils and preserves a staggering range of ancient learning.

*Plutarch: Born at Chaeronea in the province of Achaia, he chose to remain there as an active local figure, but also visited Rome and was well connected to leading Romans; his lifespan is at least A.D. 50–120. Many of his rhetorical and philosophical works survive, but for historians his *Lives* of outstanding statesmen and generals (written as pairs, a Greek figure matched and compared with a Roman) are of greater significance. There survive *Lives* of twenty-three such Romans—as far apart as Romulus and Antony—together with two (Otho, Vitellius) which are all that remain of an earlier set of imperial biographies.

*Polybius: Greek, born around 200, who as a young man took a leading role in the Achaean League, but after the Third Macedonian War (171–168) was deported to Rome as a hostage, where he forged close contacts with members of the elite; he supposedly lived to the age of eighty-two (around 118). The main purpose of Polybius' *History* is to explain what he views as Rome's meteoric rise to "world" dominion in the half-century between the onset of the Second Punic War (around 220) and the end of the Macedonian monarchy in 167. As background, however,

ART CREDITS

Cover and frontispiece photograph: Zandra Talbert. Italica bust: Museo Arquelógico de Sevilla. Fig 1.1: The Metropolitan Museum of Art, Rogers Fund, 1903. Fig 1.2: after Small, Jocelyn P. 1971. "The banquet frieze from Poggio Civitate (Murlo)," *Studi Etruschi* 39, p. 28, fig. 1. Fig 1.3: after Nielsen, Erik and Kyle M. Phillips, Jr. 1976. "Poggio Civitate (Siena). Gli scavi del Bryn Mawr College dal 1966 al 1974," *Notizie degli Scavi di Antichità* 30, p. 115, fig. 1. Fig 1.4: Deutsches Archäologisches Institut, Rome. Fig 1.5: Ashmolean Museum, Oxford, UK/The Bridgeman Art Library. Fig 1.6: after Östenberg, Carl E. 1975. *Case etrusche di Acquarossa*. Rome: Multigrafica Editrice, p. 182. Fig 2.1: Museo Archeologico di Villa Giulia, Rome, Italy/The Bridgeman Art Library. Fig 2.2: Scala/Art Resource, NY. Fig 2.3: Deutsches Archäologisches Institut, Rome. Fig 3.1: Deutsches Archäologisches Institut, Rome. Fig 3.2: Alinari/Art Resource, NY. Fig 3.3: Alinari/Art Resource, NY. Fig 3.4: after Brown, Frank E. 1980. *Cosa: The Making of a Roman Town*. Ann Arbor: University of Michigan Press, fig. 9. Fig 4.1: British Museum. Fig 4.2: British Museum. Fig 4.3: after Keay, Simon J. 1988. *Roman Spain*. London: British Museum Publications, p. 41. Fig 5.1: American Academy in Rome/Fototeca Unione. Fig 5.2: after Zanker, Paul. 1998. *Pompeii: Public and Private Life*. Cambridge, MA: Harvard University Press, p. 36, fig. 5. Fig 5.3: Alinari/Art Resource, NY. Fig 6.1a&b: British Museum. Fig 6.2: after Coarelli, Filippo. 1987. *I Santuari del Lazio in Età Repubblicana*. Rome: La Nuova Italia Scientifica, p. 39, fig. 10. Fig 7.1a: Alinari/Art Resource, NY. Fig 7.1b: Vince Streano/Corbis. Fig 7.2: Ny Carlsberg Glyptotek, Denmark. Fig 7.3: British Museum. Fig 7.4: Alinari/Art Resource, NY. Fig 8.1: Ancient Art and Architecture Collection Ltd. Fig 8.2: after Potter, Timothy W. 1987. *Roman Italy*. London: British Museum Publications, p. 105. Fig 8.3a&b: after Higginbotham, James. 1997. *Piscinae: Artificial Fishponds in Roman Italy*. Chapel Hill: UNC Press, p. 153-154, fig. 62 & 63. Fig 8.3c: James Higginbotham. Fig 8.4: Hulton/Archive by Getty Images. Fig 8.5: British Museum. Fig 8.6: after Favro, Diane. 1996. *The Urban Image of Augustan Rome*. Cambridge: Cambridge University Press, p. 197, fig. 84. Fig 8.7a: Alinari/Art Resource, NY. Fig. 8.7b: Deutsches Archäologisches Institut, Rome. Fig 8.7c: American Academy in Rome/Fototeca Unione. Fig 9.1: British Museum. Fig 9.2: The National Trust Photo Library. Fig 9.3a: ALEA (Archive of Late Egyptian Art—Robert Steven Bianchi). Fig 9.3b Hunterian

Antinous, 374
Antioch, 132, 371, 409, 434
Antiochus III (king of Syria), 130
Antiochus IV (king of Syria), 131–132
Antonia minor, *311*, 328
Antonine emperors, 480
  family tree, 375
Antoninianus (coin), 413
Antoninus Pius, 374, 379, 394–395
Antonius, Lucius (brother of Mark
    Antony), 277
Antonius, Marcus (praetor, 74 B.C.), 212
Antonius Hybrida, Gaius, 219–220
Antonius Primus, Marcus, 336
Antonius Saturninus, Lucius, 364
Antony (Marcus Antonius)
  battle of Philippi, 273, 276
  clash with Octavian, 284–285, 288
  and Cleopatra, 279–288
  in the East, 279–288, 305
  hostility of sources, 267
  images, *276, 285, 290*
  marriage to Octavia, 277, 284–285
  meets Octavian at Brundisium, 277
  offers Caesar diadem, 264–265
  ousted from Mutina, 271
  and Perusine War, 277, 281
  priest of Caesar cult, 264, 350
  reaction to Caesar's assassination,
    270–271
  suicide, 288
  tribune, 246
  triumvir, 272, 273, 278
Apennine Mountains, 1–2
Aphrodisias, *331*
Apollo, *37, 286*, 347, 451
Appeals, 376–377, 418, 420, 422
Appian, 154, 158–159, 163, 166, 193,
    195–197, 267, 276, 492
Appian Way. *See* Via Appia
Appuleius Saturninus, Lucius. *See*
    Saturninus
Apuleius, 353, 394
Apulia, 2, 142, 152
Aquae Sextiae, 170
Aqueducts, 84, 86, 93, 312, 325, 332,
    388–*389*
Aquileia, 402
Aquilonia, 86
Ara, 480
Ara Maxima, 34
Ara Pacis Augustae, *311*
Ara Ubiorum, 313
Arabia, 305
Arabia Petraea, 370, 418
Arausio, 170, 361
Arch of Constantine, *452*–453
Arch of Septimius Severus, 410
Arch of Titus, *358–359*
Arch of Trajan (Thamugadi), *369*
Archeology, 4–6
Archelaus, 215
Architecture, monumental, 16–20,
    102–103, 191, 227
Archives, 418
Arelate, 391, 455
Aristocracy. *See* Elite, Nobles

Armenia, 214, 217–218, 285, 320, 322,
    325, 334, 340, 360, 370, 376, 398,
    413–414
Arminius, 309
Army. *See* Military
Arnus (river), 2
Arpinum, 143, 171, 220
Arx, 83, 481
As (pl. asses), 69, 480
Asculum, 183
Asia (province), 162, 214, *289*, 322,
    331, 396
  punished by Sulla, 216
Asia Minor, *129*
Asian Vespers, 215
Assemblies
  composition, 44
  operation, 67–71, 417
  scope of authority, 137–138
  unrepresentative, 192
  voting process, 50, 68–70
Associations (collegia), 220, 237, 419,
    427, 438, 482
Assyria, 371, 374
Athens, 216, 285, 390–391, 402, 434
Atilius Regulus, Marcus, 108
Atrium (pl. atria), 103, 147, 480
Attalus I (king of Pergamum), 128
Attalus III (king of Pergamum), 159
Atticus, 225
Auctoritas, 99, 292, 314, 337, 354, 396,
    480, 489
Augur, 55, 74, 137, 480
August (month), 291
Augusta Treverorum, 443
Augustales, 313, 343, *348*, 383, 480
Augustus (Gaius Octavius, Gaius
    Julius Caesar Octavianus)
  and army, 301–304
  assessment of, 315–316
  battle of Philippi, 273, 276
  Caesar's heir, 270–271, 273, 351
  and city of Rome, 309–312
  clash with Antony, 284–288
  and contemporary writers, 295
  eliminates Sextus Pompey, 277–279
  and equites, 300–301
  expansion of empire, 304–305, 309,
    314–315, 319
  family tree, 296
  First Settlement, 288–292
  images, *282–283, 289, 308*
  march on Rome, 271
  marriage legislation, 211
  marriages, 277
  meets Antony at Brundisium, 277
  ousts Lepidus, 279
  and Parthia, *283*, 305, 309
  Perusine War, 277–278
  pontifex maximus, 293, 351
  provincials' attitudes to, 312–313
  public works, *260*, 309, 312
  record of achievements. *See* Res
    Gestae
  relieves Mutina, 271
  succession, 295, 297–298
  renamed Augustus, 291, 480

restores "Turia"'s husband, 275
Second Settlement, 292–293
and senate, 291–292, 299–300, 318
settlement of veterans, 276, 422
succession, 295–298, 304
style of rule, 291–292, 295, 297,
    315–316
triumvir, 271–273, 278, 289
underrated by Cicero, 272–273
victory monuments, 286–287
worship of, 313, 322, 345, 351
Augustus (title), 439, *442*, 480
Aurelian, 373, 437–438
Aurelius Antoninus, Marcus. *See*
    Caracalla
Aurelius Antoninus, Marcus
    (Elagabalus), 414–415
Aurelius Cleander, Marcus, 405–406
Aurelius Fulvus Boionius Arrius
    Antoninus, Titus. *See*
    Antoninus Pius
Aurelius Mausaeus Carausius,
    Marcus, 439
Aurelius Valerius Diocletianus, Gaius.
    See Diocletian
Aurelius Valerius Maxentius, Marcus.
    See Maxentius
Aurelius Valerius Maximianus,
    Marcus. *See* Maximian
Aurelius Victor, Sextus, 332, 431, 492
Aureus (pl. aurei), 328, *332*, 334, 412,
    480
Ausculum, 93
Auspices/auspicium, 54–*55*, 61, 74,
    480
Auxilia, 421, 480
Auxilium, 56, 480
Aventine (hill), 45–47, 322
Avidius Cassius, Gaius, 398, 404

B

Babatha, 418
Bacchus cult, *142*–143
Baetis (river), 115, 124
Balbilla, 390
Banasa, 422
Bar Kokhba War, 376
Baths, Roman, 388–390
Bedriacum, 336
Beneficial ideology, 341–342, 354, 367,
    402
Beneficium (pl. beneficia), 421, 480
Berytus, 419
Bibulus, 234
Bithynia, 214, 216–217, 393, 426–428
Bocchus (king of Mauretania), 167
Bona Dea, 229
Bondage, through debt, 51
Bononia, 272
Book of Revelation, 350, 492
Boudicca, 334
Bread and circuses, 341
Britain. *See also* England
    305, 325, 408, 410, 434, 454

advances under Domitian, 360
costly to administer, 340
invasion by Claudius, 330–*331*
rebellion, 439
secured by Nero, 334
Britannicus, 330
Bronze Age, 6–7
Brundisium, 277
Bruttium, 2, 115
Brutus. *See* Junius
Burials. *See also* Tombs
5, 9, 15, 21–22, 34
Byzantium (subsequently
Constantinople), 409

C

Caecilius Metellus, Quintus, 100
Caecilius Metellus, Quintus (cos. 109,
Numidicus), 167, 172, 174–175
Caecilius Metellus Pius, Quintus (son
of Numidicus), 205
Caecina, Aulus, 336
Caelius, Marcus, *303*
Caelius Rufus, Marcus, 249–251, 256
Caere (Etruria), 8, 13, 30, 82, 87
Caesar (title), 366, 408, *412*, 439, *442*,
480
Caesar. *See* Julius Caesar, Gaius
Caesarea (Palestine), 431
Caesarion (son of Caesar and
Cleopatra), 253, 265, *281*, 288
Caledonia. *See* Scotland
Calendar. *See also* Months
Julian, 256
priests' supervision, 72, 102
in Rome, 381, 383
Caligula. *See* Gaius
Calpurnius Bibulus, Marcus, 233–235
Calpurnius Piso, Gnaeus, 321, 323, 418
Calpurnius Piso, Lucius, 140
Camillus, 59–60
Campania, 2, 8, *78*–79, 180
Campus Martius, 64, 227, 261, 297,
312, 389, 391, 409, 480
Camulodunum, 330, 334
Cancelleria reliefs, *355*
Cannae, 114
Capitol (Mons Capitolinus), 32, 35, 64,
403, 481
Cappadocia, 213–214, 218, 322, 361, 404
Capreae, 321–322, 324
Capua, 79, 81, 115
Caracalla, 410, *412*, 413–414
Carbo, 189–190
Carnuntum, 450
Carrhae, 239, 414
Carteia, 125
Carthage. *See also* Punic Wars
destruction of, 134
empire, 104
foundation, 10
rebellion by allies, 109
in Spain, 115–119
resettled by Gaius Gracchus
(Junonia), 164
resettled by Caesar, 256

treaties with Rome, 48, 104
violence against Christians, 426
Carthago Nova, 116, 118, 146
Cassianus Latinius Postumus, Marcus,
436–437
Cassius Dio, 193, 267, 317, 353, 393,
415, 492
on adoption of Hadrian, 371
on conquest of Mesopotamia, 410
on Constitutio Antoniniana, 413
on financial crisis under Tiberius,
339
on Pertinax, 408–409
and Septimius Severus, 408,
411–*412*
on Third Jewish revolt, 376
on Trajan's spectacles, 388
Cassius Longinus, Gaius
battle of Philippi, 273
Caesar's assassination, 265
reaction to Caesar's assassination,
270–271
Cassius Longinus, Quintus, 246
Castel di Decima tombs, 13
Castra Albana, 408
Catiline, 183, 219–223
Cato the Elder (the Censor)
on agriculture, 151
on Carthage, 134
command in Spain, 124, 127
concern for frugality, 145, 149
historian, 38
Cato ("Young," great-grandson of
Cato the Elder)
and Marcus Calpurnius Bibulus, 233
annexes Cyprus, 237
obstructive opposition, 232–235
suicide, 253
urges execution of Catiline's asso-
ciates, 223
Catullus, 294
Caudine Forks, 84
Cavalry, 163, 378, 436, 456
Celtiberians, 124–125
Cemeteries. *See* Burials, Tombs
Censor, 63–64, 68, 299, 329, 362, 481
Census, 63, 163, 312, 361, 444, 481, 484
assignment process, 67–68
Livy's account, 69
social organization, 43
Centuria (pl. centuriae), 43–44, 50, 68,
481
Centuriate assembly. *See* Comitia cen-
turiata
Centurion, 302, *303*, 481
Chariot, *14*, 101, 350, *358–359*
Chariot racing, 364, 383, 385–386
Cherusci, 309
Children. *See also* Alimenta, Infant
mortality
52, 210–211, *348*, 399
Christ, Jesus, 349–350, 427, 481
Christianity, 425–430, 481
appeal of, 429
Constantine's support, 451,
453–457
Galerius' toleration, 450

Christians, 349–350
persecution of, 334, 428–429,
436–437, 446–447, 453, 455
Pliny and Trajan on, 427–428
violence against, 398, 426–428
Chyretiai, 131
Chrysogonus, 201
Cicero, Marcus Tullius
attitude to civil war, 247
on Cato, 234
on civil war strategies, 252
gains consulship, 219–220
death, 272–273
defense of Sextus Roscius, 201
exile, 237–238
and First Triumvirate, 233–235,
238, 248
on fishponders (piscinarii), *231*
governor of Cilicia, 178, 248–251
hailed by Caesar's assassins, 267
image, *222*, *290*
letters, 225, 234, 492
opposition to Catiline, 222–223
poet, 294
recall from exile, 238–239
rejection of land proposal, 220–221
on Social War, 182–183
speeches, 193, 220, 223, 248, 267,
390
testifies against Clodius, 229
transmitter of history, 38
urges elimination of Antony, 271
Cilicia, 212–213, 216, 248–251
Cimbri, 170
Cincinnatus, 53
Cinna, 187–189
Circeii, *231*, 279
Circus, 325, 383, 385–386, 481
Circus Flaminius, 102
Circus Maximus, 73, 102, 383, 385,
408–409
Cirta, 167
Cities
charters, 416, 419
development of, 10–12
emperors' support, 380
founding ritual, 39
population, 380
service to Rome, 342–344, 367, 380,
421–423, 456
Citizenship, Roman
Aelius Aristides on, 396
duties, 42, 76, 422–423
extension by Caesar, 258
extension by Flavian emperors, 361
extension by Marius, 174
extension in second century B.C.,
143
granted by Caracalla, 413
grants, 421–422
mark of, 44
Crassus' proposal, 219
Gaius Gracchus' proposal, 163–164
Livius Drusus' proposal, 179–180
rights, 421–422
after Social War, 183–189, 192
cause of Social War, 180–183

Civilis, Julius, 360
Civilitas, 318
Claros, 347
Classis, 43
Claudius, Appius, 51
Claudius Caecus, Appius, 63, 84, 86, 93
Claudius Marcellus, Marcus, 297
Claudius Nero, Tiberius, 297
Claudius
    author, 341
    image, *331*
    legislation, 341
    rule, 328–330, 332, 351, *397*
    urges admission of Gauls to senate, 329
Cleander, 405–406
Clementia, 256, 481
Cleopatra
    and Antony, 279–288
    and Caesar, 253, 265, 270
    hairstyle, *290*
    images, *280–281, 285*
    suicide, 288
Client (cliens, pl. clientes), 23, 481
Client kingdom, 305, 481
Clodius Albinus, Decimus, 408, 410
Clodius Pulcher, Publius
    death, 242–243
    gang leader, 238
    trial for trespass on sacred rites, 229–231
    tribune, 235–238
Clodius Thrasea, Publius, 333
Clusium, 74
Cluvius, Gaius, 274–275
Cocceius Nerva, Marcus. *See* Nerva
Cognomen, 103, 264, 481
Cohors (of governor), 176, 482
Cohort (military), 171, 176, 482
Coinage, 338, 350, 437
    of Antoninus, *395*
    of Augustus, *289*
    of Brutus, *273*
    of Caesar, *255*, 264
    of Cleopatra, *281, 285*
    debasement, 413, 437
    of Diocletian and Constantine, 444–445, 451
    denarii, *118*
    first appearance, *111*
    of Italians in Social War, 182
    of Mithridates, *214*
    of Nero, *332*
    of Octavian/Augustus, *282*
    of Philip, 434
Collection of Civil Law, 419
Collegia. *See* Associations
Collegium, 482
Colline Gate (Rome), 190
Colonia (pl. coloniae), 482
Colonies. *See also* Veterans
    in early Latium, 53
    founded by Augustus, 313
    founded by Caesar, 256
    founding process, 82
    land assignment, 156–157
    after Second Punic War, 141

Colonus (pl. coloni), 482
Colosseum, 358, 386, 388, 480
Columella, 341
Column of Marcus Aurelius, 405
Column of Trajan, *372*
Comes (pl. comites), 376, 444, 482
Comitas, 318
Comitia centuriata, 68–71, 222, 238, 322, 420, 481
Comitia curiata, 50
Comitium (pl. comitia), 35, 39, 482
Commagene, 322, 325, 361
Commercium, 47, 482
Commodus, 393, 404–406
Comparatio, 121
Comum, 341, 356, 390
Concilium (pl. concilia), 313, 482
Concilium plebis, 70–71
Conobaria, 304
Consilium, 176, 482
Consilium principis, 376, 404, 482
Conspicuous consumption
    banquet implements, 15
    evidence of glory, 100
    fishponds, *230–231*
    funerary urn, *148*
    houses, *146–147*
    tombs as, 13–14
Constantine
    image, *454*
    as sole ruler, 454–457
    and Tetrarchy, 443, 447, 450–453
Constantinople (previously Byzantium), 419, *442*, 456–457
Constantius, 443, 446–447
Constitutio Antoniniana, 393, 402, 413, 423, 482–483
Constitutions (imperial), 418
Consul/Consulship, 60–61, 356, 482
    assignment of province, 162
    in early Republic, 49–50, 66
    election, 54, 172
    relative rank, 99
    use by Augustus, 292–293, 298–299
    use by Domitian, 362, 367
Contio (pl. contiones), 67, 482
Contractor. *See* Publicanus
Conubium, 47, 482
Corbulo. *See* Domitius
Corduba, 125, 332
Corfinium, 180, 183, 251
Corinth, 133–134, 256
Coriolanus, 53
Cornelia (mother of the Gracchi), 156
Cornelia (daughter of Cinna), 221, 236
Cornelius Cinna, Lucius, 187–189
Cornelius Lentulus Gaetulicus, Gnaeus, 328
Cornelius Scipio, Gnaeus (uncle of Scipio Africanus), 112, 116, 118
Cornelius Scipio, Lucius (brother of Scipio Africanus), 130
Cornelius Scipio, Publius (father of Scipio Africanus), 112, 116, 118
Cornelius Scipio, Publius. *See* Scipio Africanus
Cornelius Scipio Aemilianus, Publius. *See* Scipio Aemilianus

Cornelius Sulla, Lucius. *See* Sulla
Corona civica, *303*
Corpus Juris Civilis, 419
Corruption, 162–163, 177
Corsica, 109
Cosa, *82–83, 229*
Courts. *See also* Quaestio
    establishment, 139–140, 489
    influence on governors, 178–179
    jury membership, 162–163, 179–180, 197, 208
    in Twelve Tables, 51
Crassus, Marcus Licinius. *See also* Triumvirate, First
    consul with Pompey, 208, 239
    death, 239
    defeats Spartacus, 207
    First Triumvirate, 233–234
    joins Sulla, 189–190
    obstructed by Cato, 232
    seeks to rival Pompey, 219
Cremona, 114, 336
Crete, 212, 271, *379*
Crimea, 214, 218–219, 253
Crixus, 207
"Crown tax," 367, 376, 482
Ctesiphon, 398
Cult, 18–19, 45–47, 313. *See also* Bacchus cult; Imperial cult
Curator (pl. curatores), 367, 370, 377, 423, 482
Curia (pl. curiae), 42–44, 50, 483
Curia (senate house), 195, *262*, 483
Curia Hostilia, 35, 42, 64
Curia Julia, *260, 262–263,* 309
Curio, 245–246
Curius Dentatus, Marcus, 86–87, 93
Cursus honorum, 139, 195, 299, 483
Cynics, 357, 362, 483
Cynoscephalae, 128
Cyprus, 237, 248–249, 371
Cyrene/Cyrenaica, 253, 271, 371, 381
Cyzicus, 217, 409

D

Dacia/Dacians, 340, 360, 364, 370–373, 394, 402, 434
    abandonment, 438
Dalmatia, 305, 309, 438
Damascus, 370, 434
Damnatio memoriae, 365, 406, 408, *412,* 483
Danube (river), 305, 309, 360, 370, 373, 402, 434
Dardanus, 216
Dea/deus, 483
Dead Sea Scrolls, 349–350, 492
Debasement of coinage, 413, 437
Debt
    Caesar's measures, 255–256
    Catiline's proposals, 222
    enslavement prohibition, 95
    relief, 188, 322, 339
    social ties, 24
    in Twelve Tables, 51
Decebalus (king of Dacia), 364, 370

Decemvirs, 50–51
Decimus Brutus, 271
Decius, 434
Decreta, 418
Decurion, 422–423, 483
Dediticii, 402, 436, 483
Deditio, 77
Deification of Caesar, 273, 350–351
Deification ceremonies for Pertinax, 409
Delator, 419
Delos, 133
Demos, 26–28, 483
Denarius (pl. denarii), 413, 437, 483
Depopulation, 436
Diana, 45–47
Dictator, 50, 194, 483, 254–255, 483
Didius Severus Julianus, Marcus, 408
Diet, 347
Digest, 399, 416, 493
Dignitas, 99, 246, 265, 483
Dilectus, 76, 483
Dio Chrysostom, 391
Diocese, 443
Diocletian
    Dominate and Tetrarchy, 438–446
    persecutes Christians, 429,
        446–447, 455
    succession plans, 447, 450–451
Diodorus Siculus, 26, 127, 161, 493
Dionysius of Halicarnassus, 73, 493
Dionysus, 142
Diploma (pl. diplomata), 360, 421, 483
Diplomacy, 121, 131
Disease, 398–399, 402
Divination, 71–72. *See also* Augur,
    Auspices
Divorce, 210, 274–275
Divus (pl. divi), 351, 483
Dominate, 439–446, 483
Dominus, 367, 439, 483
Dominus et deus, 364, 438
Domitian, 337, *355*, 360, 362, 364–365,
    383, 391
Domitius Ahenobarbus, Lucius, 238,
    251
Domitius Aurelianus, Lucius. *See*
    Aurelian
Domitius Corbulo, Gnaeus, 334–335,
    364
Domus publica, 41
Donations of Alexandria, 285
Donatists, 455
Donative, 124, 227, 302, 412, 483
Dowry, 209–210
Dravus (river), 320
Druids, 334, 349, 483
Drusilla (sister of Gaius), 325
Drusus (son of Livia Drusilla),
    297–298, 328–329
Drusus (the Younger, son of Tiberius),
    298, 320–321, 323
Duilius, Gaius, 108
Dux (pl. duces), 444
Dyrrhachium, 252, 288

E
Ebro (river), 112, 118
Economy
    under Diocletian, 444–445
    elite structure, 23–24
    under Julio–Claudians, 339–340
    rural, in Italy, *229, 231*
Edict of Milan, 453
Edict of Toleration, 429, 447, 450, 455
Edict on Maximum Prices, 445
Edictum Perpetuum, 377, 417, 483
Education, 209, 390–391
Egypt, 132, 219, 253, 305, 340
    annexed by Octavian, 288, 301,
        322–323
    Jewish revolt, 371
    religions, 347
    supplies grain, 312
Elagabalus, 414–415
Elah–Gabal, 414, 438
Elbe (river), 305
Elections, 50, 68, 70
Eleusis, 374
Elite. *See also* Nobles
    accumulation of wealth, 144–145
    in city–states, 11
    competition, 66–67, 138–139
    displays of wealth, 35–37
    emergence in Italy, 12–13
    Etruscan, 30
    intermarriage, 81
    migrations, 42
    patrician, 54
    in provincial cities, 342–344
    residences, 17–18
    social organization, 23–24
    tombs in early Italy, 13–14
Emerita Augusta, 381–382
Emesa, 414, 425
Empire, Roman
    expansion by Claudius, 330
    expansion under Augustus,
        304–305, 309, 314–315
    expansion under Nero, 334
    population, 342
    revenue increased by Pompey, 227
    unfolding, 119–120, 338–339, 360
Emporiae, 116, 118, 124
Engineering, Roman, 343, 388
England. *See also* Britain
    242
Enna, 152
Ennius, 295
Ephesus, 382, 390–391, 396
Epidemics, 398–399
Equites, 68–70, 484
    under Augustus, 300–301
    imperial service, 341–342, 356,
        443–444, 456
    jury membership, 179, 197, 208
    roles in Rome, 163
    and Septimius Severus, 411
    treatment by Sulla, 195, 197
Esquiline (hill), 34
Etruria/Etruscans, 1–2, 26, 180
    cities in, 28, 30–31

Iron Age culture, 8
Roman conquest, 87–88
Eulogies. *See* Laudatio
Eumachia, *345*
Eumenes (king of Pergamum),
    130–131
Eunus, 152
Eusebius, 429, 431, 451, 493
Euphrates (river), 217, 309, 361
Eutropius, 431, 493
Evocatio, 349

F
Fabius Maximus, Quintus, 114
Fabius Pictor, Quintus, 38, 73
Falerii, 87
Fasces, 60, *355*, 484
Fasti, 93, 102, 484
Faustina the Younger (daughter of
    Antoninus Pius, wife of Marcus
    Aurelius), *395–396*, 404
Favorinus, 391
Feriae, 484
Feridius, Marcus, 249
Festus. 64, 77, 493
Ficoroni Cista, *65*
Fides, 77, 108, 484
Fimbria. *See* Flavius
Final Decree (SCU). *See* Ultimate
    Decree
First Settlement (of Augustus),
    288–292
Fishponds, *231*
Flaccus (Fulvius), 161, 163–164
Flaccus (Valerius), 188, 215
Flamen/flaminica, 351, 391, 484
Flamen Dialis, 75
Flamininus. *See* Quinctius
Flaminius, Gaius, 114
Flavian emperors. *See also* Domitian,
    Titus, Vespasian
    484
Flavius Fimbria, Gaius, 188, 215
Flavius Philostratus, Lucius. *See*
    Philostratus
Flavius Vespasianus, Titus. *See*
    Vespasian
Florus, 124–125, 183, 493
Fortuna Muliebris, 75
Fortuna Primigenia, 71, *191*
Forum (pl. fora), 369, 484
Forum Augustum, 322
Forum Boarium, 34–35
Forum Julii, 338
Forum Julium (Rome), 258, *260*
Forum of Trajan, 370
Forum Romanum
    formation, 32, 35
    new construction by Caesar and
        Augustus, *260, 262–263*, 322
    site of Pertinax's funeral, 409
Fossa, 20, 484
Franks, 434
Freedman, *303*, 313, 343–344, 421, 484
    imperial, 330, 342, 356

Freedom of the Greeks proclaimed, 130
Fregellae, 84
Friendly kingdom. *See* Client king-
    dom
Frontinus, 388–389, 493
Fucine Lake, 180
Fulvia (Mark Antony's wife), 277
Fulvius Flaccus, Marcus (cos. 264 B.C.),
    88
Fulvius Flaccus, Marcus, 161–164
Funerals. *See also* Laudatio
    103–104, 409
Funerary urn, *148*
Furius Camillus, Marcus, 59–60

G

Gabii, 9, 13, 41
Gabinius, Aulus, 212–213, 236, 238
Gaius (Caligula), 324–325, 328, 351
Gaius (teacher of law), 417–418, 493
Gaius Caesar, 298, 304, *311*
Gaius Gracchus, 160–165
Galatia, 130–131, 305, 314
Galba, 335–337
Galen, 425
Galerius Valerius Daia, Gaius. *See*
    Maximin Daia
Galerius Valerius Maximianus, Gaius,
    429, 442–443, 447, 450–453
Gallienus, 435–436
Games. *See also* Amphitheater,
    Gladiator, Ludi, Theater
    animals for, 249, 386–*387*
    demonstrations at, 322, 385–386,
        408
    denounced by Tertullian, 394
    at funerals, 104
    public celebrations, 102, 367
Gaul/Gauls, 59, 87, 114, 141, 324
    Caesar's campaigns, 236, 239, 242
    religions, 347, 349
    revolt, 360
Gaul, Cisalpine, 183
Gaul, Transalpine, 170
Gellius, Aulus, 82, 493
Genius, 313, *355*
Gens (pl. gentes), 24, 42, 54, 484
Genucius, Lucius, 61, 66
Germanicus, *311*, *319*–324, 341, 347
Germano–Gallic revolt, 360
Germans/Germany, 170, *319*–320, 322,
    325, 330, 434
    provinces, 360
Geta, *412*
Gibbon, Edward, 364–365, 457
Gladiator/gladiatorial games, 104,
    199, 312, 386–388, 406, 484
Glaucia, Gaius Servilius, 173–174
Glassblowing, 343
Gloria, 99, 484
Golden House (of Nero), 333, 340, 358,
    386
Gorsium, *423*
Goths, 413, 432, 434, 439
Governors (of provinces), 122, 145,
    176–178, 199–200, 235, 243,

248–251, 291, 324, 340, 443–444
    Jurists on the duties of, 416–417
Gracchurris, 124
Grain supply (at Rome)
    under Augustus, 301, 312
    Caesar's reforms, 258
    Clodius' subsidy, 236–237
    disrupted by pirates, 212
    distribution halted by Sulla, 197
    provision, 162, 173, 205, 328, 332,
        406, 415
Graviscae, 30
Greece, *129*, 131, 215
Greek (language), use of, 346
Greeks
    cities, 26, 88, 90–91
    cultural imitations of, 101, 132,
        147–149, 191, 294–295
    elite lifestyle, 15
    history–writing, 25, 38
    hoplites, 21
    kingship, 90
    settlements in Italy, 10, 26
Gythium, 351

H

Hadrian
    adoption by Trajan, 371, 373
    image, *379*
    inspects military, 378
    rule, 373–374, 376–379
Hadrian's wall. *See* Wall
Hadrianoupolis, 453
Hamilcar Barca, 105, 109, 111
Hannibal Barca
    campaigns in Italy, 112–115
    negotiates with Macedon, 128
    recall to Carthage, 119
    rise to commander, 111
Harbors. *See also* Ostia/Portus
    343, 380
Hasdrubal, 118–119
Hellenistic culture, 91–92, 484
Helvetii, 239
Helvidius Priscus, Publius, 333, 362
Helvius Pertinax, Lucius. *See* Pertinax
Heraclea, 92
Hercules, 446
    Commodus as, *405*
Herdonius, Appius, 42
Herennius Modestinus, 416
Herodes Atticus, 391
Herodian, 393, *405*, 408, 411, 493
Heruli, 434
Hierapytna, *379*
Hiero, 105
Hirtius, Aulus, 239, 271, 492
Historia Augusta, 393–394, *405*–406,
    431, 493–494
Honestiores, 420, 446, 484
Hoplite, 21–23, *80*, 484
Horace, 295
Hortensius, Quintus, 62–63
Hostis, 187, 333, 485
House of the Faun (Pompeii), *147*
Humiliores, 420, 484

I

Iberia. *See* Spain
Ides of March, 265
Illyria/Illyricum, 128, 246, 284, 320,
    323, 434, 439
Imago (pl. imagines). *See* Masks
Imperator, 250, 291, 330, 356, 485
Imperial cult
    development, *331*, 351, 357, *379*,
        381–383, 391–392, 426
    evolution, 313, 350–351
Imperium, 61–62, 122, 271, 292, 356, 485
Inauguration, 74
Incitatus, 324–325, 328
India, 305, 340, 370
Infamia, 419
Infant mortality, *348*, 399
Inflation, 437
Instauratio, 72
Intercessio, 63, 485
Interpretatio, 347
Interrex, 54, 239, 485
Iron Age, 6–10
Iron Gates (rapids), 373
Irni, 416, 419
Isis, 322, 337, 391, 430, 485
Issus, 409
Italica (Spain), 123, 356, 366, 371
Italy
    changes in second century B.C.,
        140–144
    equated with provinces by
        Diocletian, 444
    judicial divisions by Hadrian, 377
    pre–Roman characteristics, 6–7
Iteration, 66
Iugerum (pl. iugera), 485
Ius (pl. iura), 485
Ius Latii. *See* Latin status
Ius migrationis, 47
Iustitium, 185, 485

J

Janus, 314–315
Jerusalem, 218, 325, 358, 374, 376
Jesus. *See* Christ
Jewish Revolts/Wars
    First, 325, 334, 357–358
    Second, 371
    Third, 376, *379*, 428
Jews/Judaism, 318, 349, 358, 426, 485
Josephus, Flavius, 318, 353, 358, 494
Judaea, 305, 325, 330, 340, 358, 371
    renamed, 376
Judaism. *See* Jews
Jugurtha, 166–167
Julia (aunt of Julius Caesar), 172
Julia (daughter of Julius Caesar), 236,
    243
Julia (daughter of Augustus), 297–298,
    304, 320
Julia Avita Mamaea, 415
Julia Domna, 406, 411–*412*, 414, 425
Julia Maesa, 414–415
Julia Soaemias Bassiana, 414–415

Julianus (Zegrensian), 422
Julio–Claudian emperors, 485
   army, 338–339
   beneficial ideology, 341–342
   cities and provinces, 342–344
   civil government, 318
   economy, 339–340
   family tree, 296
   imperial cult, 350–351
   intellectual life, 340–341
   military concerns, 318–320
   religious practices and principles,
      347, 349–350
Julius (month), 273
Julius Agricola, Gnaeus, 360
Julius Caesar, Gaius. *See also*
   Triumvirate, First
   activity as dictator, 254–264, 289, 339
   assassination, 265
   attitudes to provincials, 178
   campaigns in Gaul, 239, 242, 329
   civil war campaigns, 251–254
   clemency, 251, 253, 256, 265
   and Cleopatra, 253, 265
   cognomen, 480
   deification, 264, 273, *331*, 350–351
   divorces Pompeia, 229
   early career, 221
   election as pontifex maximus, 221
   first consulship, 234–236
   First Triumvirate, 233–234
   governor in Spain, 232
   historian, 225, 294, 492
   images, *254–255, 290*
   impact on city of Rome, 258–261
   and kingship, 264–265
   mocks Sulla, 264
   motives for civil war, 246–248
   opposes execution of Catiline's
      associates, 223
   plans for return to Rome from
      Gaul, 243
   Pompey's support wanes, 244–245
   reactions to assassination of, 267,
      270–271
   relations with senate as dictator,
      261–265, 291
   seeks first consulship, 232–233
Julius Caesar Octavianus, Gaius. *See*
   Augustus
Julius Civilis, Gaius, 360
Julius Frontinus, Sextus. *See* Frontinus
Julius Quadratus Bassus, Gaius, 371
Julius Vindex, Gaius, 335–336, 356
Junius Brutus, Lucius, 49, 265
Junius Brutus, Marcus, 249, 265
   battle of Philippi, 273
   coin, *273*
   reaction to Caesar's assassination,
      270–271
Junius Brutus Albinus, Decimus, 271
Junius Juvenalis, Decimus. *See* Juvenal
Juno, 349
Junonia, 162
Jupiter, 35, 37, 74, 101, 119, 264, *319*,
   350, 358, *403*, 445, 481
Juries
   restoration of equites to, 208

membership disputed, 179–180
   senators on, 161–163
   Sulla's reforms, 197
Jurist, 376–377, 417, 485
Justinian, 419, 493
Juvenal, 341, 494
Juvenalia, 333

K

Kalkriese, 308
Kalumniator, 419
Kings. *See* Monarchy
Koinon. *See* Concilium

L

La Turbie, 286–*287*
Lactantius, 431, 446, 450–451, 494
Laelius, Gaius, 156–157, 234
Lambaesis, 378
Land
   assignment, 81–82, 95, 156–157, 173
   consolidation of holdings, 152
   labor requirements, 150–151
   respectability, 144–145
Land reforms
   Appian on, 158–159
   under Caesar, 235
   Gaius Gracchus, 162
   Livius Drusus (the Younger), 179
   opposition of Optimates, 232, 234
   Rullus' proposal, 220–221
   Tiberius Gracchus, 156–157
Lar (pl. Lares), 71, 485
Latin festival, 45
Latin (language),
   refinement of, 295
   spread of, 144, 346, 373
Latin Name, 80
Latin status (ius Latii), 361, 421, 482,
   485
Latin War, 79–80
Latium/Latins, 2, 47, 143, 180, 183
   common culture, 34, 45
   conquest by highlanders, 52–53
   consolidation under Rome, 80–81
   Iron Age culture, 9
   organization, 47–48
   Roman expansion, 77–79
Laudatio, 100, 103, 274–275, 313–315,
   485
Laus (praise, fame), 99, 485
Lavinium, 45–47
Law. *See also* Appeals
   criminal, 419–420
   enactment, 417–418
   importance of status and prestige,
      419–420
   repositories of, 418
   respect for, 194
   Roman, 416–420
   Ulpian's explanations, 393
   Value as evidence, 432
Legate (legatus, pl. legati), 121, 137,
   176, 239, 291, 485

Legion, 43–44, 171, 338–339, 486
Lepcis Magna, *424–425*
Lepidus
   abuses "Turia", 275
   death, 293
   ousted by Octavian, 279
   reaction to Caesar's assassination,
      270
   triumvir, 272, 278
Lex (pl. leges), 62, 418, 486
Lex de imperio Vespasiani, 354, 356
Lex Hortensia, 62–63
Lex provinciae, 176
Libelli, 418, 428
Libraries, 294–295, 390
Licinian–Sextian Laws, 60–61
Licinianus Licinius, Valerius. *See*
   Licinius
Licinius, 447, 451, 453–454
Licinius Crassus, Marcus. *See* Crassus
Licinius Lucullus, Lucius. *See*
   Lucullus
Licinius Mucianus, Gaius. *See*
   Mucianus
Licinius Murena, Lucius, 216
Lictor, 60, 62, *355*, 486
Life expectancy, 210, 399
Ligures, 141
Liris (river), 2
Literacy, 12
Literature, Latin, 293–295, 340–341
Lituus, 18, 55, 74, 486
Livia Drusilla (wife of Augustus), *283*,
   290, 297, 321–322, 324–325, 345,
   350–351
Livius Drusus, Marcus (the Elder), 164
Livius Drusus, Marcus (tribune 91
   B.C.), 179–180
Livy, 38, 69, 97, 103, 116, 146, 494
Lots, casting of, 121, 191, 221
Luca, 238
Lucan, 333, 340
Lucceius, Lucius, 294
Lucilla, *395*, 405
Lucius Caesar, 298, 304
Lucius Verus, *395*–404
Lucretia, 48
Lucretius (poet), 294
Lucretius Afella, Quintus, 195–197
Lucullus
   jealous of Pompey, 218
   and Mithridates, 188, 216–217
   obstruction of Pompey's arrange-
      ments, 235
   piscinarius, *231*
   trial of Clodius, 229
Ludi (public entertainments), 72–74,
   101–102, 312, 381–388, 486
Lugdunum, 313, 328–329, 338, 398,
   410, 426
Lusitanians, 124–125, 205

M

Macedon, 90–91, 127–129, 131–133
Macrinus, 406, 411, 414
Macro. *See* Sutorius
Maecenas, 295

murders Pertinax, 408
and Nerva, 366–367
and Septimius Severus, 408–409
and Severus Alexander, 415
and Tiberius, 321
Praetorian Prefect, 411, 443, 455
Priests (male and female), 72, 137, 209, 343, 345, 356, 382, 391
Princeps (pl. principes), 137, 291, 488
Princeps Juventutis, 304
Princeps senatus, 64, 299, 488
Principate, 291, 354, 356–357, 488
Processions, 382–383
Proconsul, 121, 488
Procurator, 301, 488
Proletarii, 68, 70, 488
Propraetor, 121, 488
Prorogation, 120–121
Proscription, 193–194, 200–201, 247, 272, 275, 488
Prostration, 446
Province (provincia, pl. provinciae). *See also* Governors
    administration, 175–179, 235, 248–251
    assignment to consuls, 162
    concept, 122, 489
    difficulty in governing, 124
    divided, 410, 443–444
    initial purpose, 109–110
Ptolemies, 127
Ptolemy Caesar. *See* Caesarion
Publicanus (pl. publicani), 110, 488
    dissatisfaction with Lucullus, 217
    military supply, 118, 123
    senators debarred, 145
    tax collection, 162, 177–178, 232, 258
    wealth accumulation, 146
Publicola, 49
Pudicitia, 75
Punic, 104, 489
Punic Wars
    First, 105
    Second, 111–119
    Third, 134
Pydna, 131
Pyrrhus (king of the Molossians), 90, 92–93, *111*

Q

Quadi, 364, 402, 405
Quaestio (pl. quaestiones). *See also* Courts
    489
Quaestio de repetundis, 178–179
Quaestor, 62, 139, 176, 251, 489
    increases in number, 195, 264
    relative rank, 99
Quattuorviri consulares, 376–377, 395, 404
Quinctilius Varus, Publius, *303*
Quinctius, Titius, 77
Quinctius Cincinnatus, Lucius, 53
Quinctius Flamininus, Titus, 128, 130–131
Quindecimviri sacris faciundis, 349

R

Rabirius, Gaius, 221
Raetia, 305, 320, 404, 416
Ravenna, 338
Reate, 357
Recruitment. *See* Military
Red Sea, 340, 370
Regia, 17–18, 35, 41–42, 489
Regolini–Galassi tomb, 13
Religion. *See also* Cult, Temples
    adoption of foreign cults, 115, 391
    under Diocletian, 445–446
    Elah–Gabal, 414
    growing diversity, 347–350
    mystery religions, 430
    pervasiveness, 71–72, *397*
    and politics, 426
    and public office, 61
    reciprocity in, 116
    restrictions on officials, 137
    role of patricians, 54
    in Roman culture, 425–430
    state, 391–392
Remus, *379*, *397*
Res Gestae (of Augustus), 267, 298, 304, 311, 313–316
Residences, 17–18, 37, 147
Resorts, *191*
Revolts
    Germano–Gallic, 360
    under Hadrian, 378–379
    Lepidus, 204
    Sertorius, 205–207
    Spartacus, 207
Rex, 264, 489
Rex sacrorum, 41
Rhetoric, 149
Rhine (Latin, Rhenus) river, 242, 305, 309, 360, 394, 434
Rhodes, 133, 298, 320
Roads, 86, 343, 370, 380, 490
Roman Forum. *See* Forum Romanum
Romanization, 344, *346*, 373, 402, *423*, 425
Rome
    assault by Cinna, 187
    assaults by Sulla, 185–186, 189–192, 246
    under Augustus, 301, 309, 312
    Aurelian's wall, 438
    baths, 388–390
    Caesar's construction plans, 258, 260–261
    cult of, 313–314, *355*, *358–359*
    early expansion, 41
    early settlements, 34
    Etruscan influence, 30–31, 101
    expansion in Campania, 79
    expansion in Latium, 48, 77
    foundation legend, 39, *379*
    in Late Republic, *259*
    location, 2, 32–34
    millennium celebration, 432
    population in second century B.C., 149
    Praetorian barracks, 321–322

relationship with allies, 82–84, 114–115, 143–144
    sack by Gauls, 59
    conquest of southern Italy, 93–94
    treaties with Carthage, 48, 104
Romulus, 37–39, 265, 357, *379*, 383, 397
Roscius, Sextus, 201
Rostra, *260*, 489
Rubicon (river), 246

S

Sabina, 371, 379, 390
Sabinum/Sabines, 53, 87, 143, 383
Sacra Via, 35
"Sacred spring," 52, 116
Sacrifices, 116
Sacrosanctity, 56, 293, 489
Saepta Julia, 261, 322
Saguntum, 112
Salamis (Cyprus), 249
Sallustius Crispus, Gaius (Sallust), 99, 166, 172, 175, 206, 223, 321, 496
Salona, 447
Salvius Otho, Marcus, 335–337
Samnite Wars
    First, 79
    Second, 84–86
    Third, 86
Samnium/Samnites, 52, 79, 182, 189–190, 199
Sardinia, 104, 109, 145, 161, 322
Sarmatia/Sarmatians, 402, 405, 434
Sasanids, 410, 415, 434–435, 439, 446
Satricum, 19, 49
Saturn, temple of, 35, 62, 479
Saturninus, Lucius Appuleius,173–175, 221, 235
Scaevola, 187
Scipio, Lucius, 100
Scipio Aemilianus (son of Lucius Aemilius Paullus, grandson through adoption of Scipio Africanus)
    destroys Carthage, 134
    military successes, 155
    political career, 154–156
    reaction to Tiberius Gracchus' legislation, 160
    in Spain, 125–126
Scipio Africanus
    as commander, 118–119, 146
    triumph, 101
    withdraws from public life, 140
Scotland, 410, 434
Scribonia (wife of Octavian), 277–278, 297
Scribonius Curio, Gaius, 245–246
SCU. *See* Ultimate Decree
Secession of the plebs, 55–56
Second Settlement (of Augustus), 292–293
Second Sophistic, 390–391, 394, 396, 489
Secret ballot, 153
Sejanus. *See* Aelius

Seleucia, 398
Seleucids, 127
Seleucus IV (king of Syria), 131
Selinus (Cilicia), 371
Selinus (Sicily), 26
Sella curulis (chair), 60, *289*
Sempronius Gracchus, Gaius, 160–165
    Tiberius Sempronius Gracchus
        (governor in Spain, father of
        the Gracchi), 124, 127
Sempronius Gracchus, Tiberius,
    156–160
Sempronius Longus, Tiberius, 112
Senate (senatus), 35, 489
    advisory role, 63–64
    after Sulla, 201
    approval of legislation, 63
    attitude toward provinces, 178–179
    and Augustus, 291–292, 299–300
    authority, 99, 137–138, 154–155, 432
    and Claudius, 329–330
    confrontations with Julius Caesar,
        233–236, 245–246
    curbed by Gaius Gracchus,
        162–163, 233
    diplomatic role, 121, 131
    and Domitian, 362, 364–365
    functioning, 136–139
    image, *355*
    and imperial cult, 351, 392
    leadership in war, 121
    membership, 64–66, 179–180, 341
    oath–taking, 174
    quest for popular support, 154–155
    reaction to Caesar's assassination,
        270
    reformed by Sulla, 194–197, 200
    regulation of officials, 121
    relations with Julius Caesar as dic-
        tator, 261–265
    rise of personalities, 153–154
    and Septimius Severus, 411
    and Severus Alexander, 415
    trials in, 323
    awards triumphs, 102
    and Vespasian, 356
Senators, 211, 339, 341–342, 356, 456
Senatus consultum, 136, *395*, 417, 489
Senatus consultum ultimum. *See*
    Ultimate Decree
Seneca, 332–333
Sentinum, 86
Septimius Odenaethus, 436
Septimius Severus, Lucius, 406–413,
    424–425
Septimius Vaballathus, 436–437
Septizodium, 412
Sergius Catilina, Lucius. *See* Catiline
Sertorius, Quintus, 205–207, 350
Servilius Glaucia, Gaius, 173–174
Servilius Rullus, Publius, 220–221
Sestertius, 413, 489
Settefinestre, *228–229*
Settlements (of Augustus). *See*
    Augustus
Severan emperors, *400–401*, 407, 489
Severus (Tetrarch), 447, 450

Severus Alexander, 415–416
Sextilis, 291
Sextus Pompey
    condemnation, 272
    elimination, 278–279
    naval blockade of Rome, 276
    survives defeat at Munda, 253
    threat to Second Triumvirate, 277
Sextus Roscius, 201
Shapur I (Sasanid king), 436
Sicily, 2–4
    in First Punic War, 104–105,
        108–109
    Latin status, 258
    slave revolts, 152–153
    Verres as governor, 248–249
Sidon, 10
Silvanus, 347
Sirmium, 442
Skywatching, 234–235, 237
Slave Wars, 152–153, 207
Slaves/slavery
    conditions of, 95, 151, *344*, 377,
        418, 420, 456
    Delos market, 133
    freedom from conscription, 150
    freedom grants, 149–150, 421
    owners' rights, 456
    Spartacus' revolt, 207
    in Twelve Tables, 51
Smallpox, 398
Smyrna, 391, 398, 428
Social War, 180–183, 417
Societas (pl. societates), 177–178, 488
Socius, 489
Sol (Invictus), 386, 415, 438, 451, 454
Soudales, 49
Spain
    after Punic Wars, 123–127
    campaigns in, 111–112, 115–119,
        253, 305
    grants of Latin status, 361
    held by Sertorius, 205
Spartacus, 207
Stoics, 333, 357, 362, 364, 489
Strabo, 133, 199, 340, 496
Struggle of the Orders, 53–56, 489
Suetonius Tranquillus, Gaius, 225, 252,
    264, 267, *312*, 317, 325, 328, 340,
    353, 357, 361, 376, 496
Suffect consul (or other officeholder),
    299, 489
Sulla
    assaults on Rome, 185–186,
        189–192, 246
    autobiography, 294
    and Cinna, 187–188
    possible image, *200*, *290*
    and Mithridates, 188, 215–216
    mocked by Caesar, 264
    model for Pompey, 252
    in Numidia, 167
    program as dictator, 193–204
    restraint, 200
    and Sulpicius Rufus, 184–185
Sulpicius Galba, Servius (commander
    in Spain, 150 B.C.), 125

Sulpicius Galba, Servius, 335–337
Sulpicius Rufus, Publius, 184–186
Surrender (to Romans), 77
Surveying, Roman, 82
Sutorius Macro, Quintus, 321, 325
Sword of Tiberius, *319*
Sybaris, 28
Symposia, 15
Synesius (bishop of Cyrene), 381
Syracuse, 26, 28, 93, 115
Syria, 130, 218, 323, 360, 398, 408–410,
    434
Syria Palaestina, 376

T

Tabularium, 418, 489
Tacitus, Cornelius, 317, 329, 333, 335,
    342, 356, 360, 364–365, 496
Tarentum, 88, 90, 92, 94, 115, 278
Tarquinii, 8, 42, *55*
Tarquinius Priscus, Lucius, 48, 383
Tarquinius Superbus, 37, 265
Tarracina, 258
Tarraco, 118, 351
Tax collection, 162, 177, 232, 258, 302,
    413, 445, 456
Technology, 343–344
Telamon, 114
Temples
    early forms, 18–19, 35
    Greek influence, *191*
    model, *19*
    as monuments, 103
    origin of sites, 47
Tenant farmers, 456
Terentius Varro, Marcus, 37–38
Tertullian, 353, 394, 426, 496
Tetrarchy, 439–447, 489
Teutoburg Forest, *303*, *308*, 322
Teutones, 170
Thamugadi, 367, *369*, 390
Thapsus, 253
Theater, 147, 227, 381–383
Theophanes of Mytilene, 294
Thessalonice, 442
Thrace, 324, 330, 340, 438
Thucydides, 25–26
Thurii, 88
Tiber (Latin, Tiberis) river, 2
Tiberius
    expansion of the empire discour-
        aged by Augustus, 309, 319
    heir to Augustus, 298
    image, *319*
    imperial cult, 351
    liberality, 322, 339, 341
    on provincial taxes, 340
    rule, 320–324, 383
    son of Livia Drusilla, 297
Tiberius Gracchus, 156–160
Tibur, 53, 77, 80
Tigranes I (king of Armenia), 214,
    217–218
Tigris (river), 371
Tiridates (king of Armenia), 334, 340

Titus Livius. *See* Livy
Titus, 356, *358–359,* 361–362, 389, *395*
Toga, 60, 101, *403,* 408, 490
Toleration, religious, 447, 450, 453–455
"Tomb of the Augurs" (Tarquinii), *55*
Tombs. *See also* Burials
    13–14, 35–37
Tomis, 295
Torture, 420, 427
Trade
    early routes, 4
    in luxury goods, 24–25, 340, 370
    metallurgy, 6–7
    through Ostia, *397*
    by senators, 145
Trajan
    adoption by Nerva, 366
    under Domitian, 364
    image, *372*
    and Pliny on Christians, 427–428
    rule, 367, 370–371, 373–374, 383,
        388, 390, *397*
Transhumance, 151
Transpadana, 219, 258
Transport
    relative costs, 343
Trasimene (lake), 114
Treason trials, 321
Trebia (river), 112
Tribes (Roman), 43–44, 70–72, 184, 221
Tribune, military, 49, 60–61, 490
Tribune of the plebs, 56, 62–63, 99, 490
    restricted by Sulla, 197, 205, 208
    scope of authority in principle and
        practice, 137–138
    veto power, 154, 157–159
Tribunicia potestas, 293, 298, 320, 323,
    490
Tributum, 68, 76, 110, 144, 490
Triumph, 93, 100–102, 108, 208, 232,
    318, 350, *358,* 490
Triumvir (pl. triumviri), 82, 490
Triumvirate, First
    benefits to partners, 236
    Caesar's consulship, 235
    as cause of civil war, 247–248
    formation, 233–234
    renewal, 238–239
Triumvirate, Second, 272–273
Tullius, Servius, 37, 44–45, 69
Tullius Cicero, Marcus. *See* Cicero
Tullius Cicero, Quintus, 251
Turia, 274–275
Twelve Tables, 50, 490
Tyre/Tyrians, 10, 380
Tyrrhenian Sea, 2–4

U

Ulpianus, Domitius (Ulpian), 393, 413,
    415–417, 496
Ulpius Trajanus, Marcus (father of
    Trajan), 356
Ulpius Trajanus, Marcus. *See* Trajan
Ultimate decree of the senate (SCU)
    against Caesar, 246

after Clodius' death, 243
criticism of, 221
against Marius, 174
rigin, 164–165
against rebellious debtors, 256
Umbria, 87, 180
Univira, 210
Urban cohorts (Rome), 312, 409
Urbanitas, 383

V

Vaballath, 436–437
Vadimon (lake), 87
Valens, Fabius, 336
Valeria Messalina, 330
Valerian, 434–436
Valerius Constantius, Flavius. *See*
    Constantius
Valerius Constantinus, Flavius. *See*
    Constantine
Valerius Flaccus, Lucius, 188, 215
Valerius Maximus, 187, 496
Valerius Publicola, Publius, 49
Valerius Severus, Flavius. *See* Severus
Vandals, 434
Varro, 37–38
Vatican circus, 325
Vatinius, Publius, 236
Veii, 8, 19, 37, 49, 58, 77, 349
Velia (hill), 32
Velleius Paterculus, 197, 496
Veneficium, 142
Ventidius, Publius, 284
Venus, *260,* 350
Vercellae, 170
Vercingetorix, 242
Vergil, 295, 390
Verginia, 51
Verres, Gaius, 220, 248–249
Verus, Lucius, 374, 393–398, 402, 405
Vespasian
    authority as emperor, 354
    command in Britain, 334
    declared emperor, 335, 336
    desire for revenue, 361
    First Jewish revolt, 357–358
    Germano–Gallic revolt, 360
    image, *355, 358*
    imperial cult, 351, 357
    rule, 357–362, 364–365, 390
    on succession, 357
Vesta, temple of, 35, 41, 74
Vestal virgins, 74–75, *355,* 362, 415,
    420, 490
Vesuvius (Mt.), 361–362
Veterans
    Caesar's settlements, 256, 342
    conspicuous presence, *199*
    discharge certificates, 360
    Hadrian's settlement at Jerusalem,
        376
    land awards, 173
    Octavian/Augustus' settlements,
        276–277, 301–302, 313, 342, 422
    Pompey's rewards, 227

respect for, 380
Sulla's settlements, 196–*199*
Trajan's settlements, 367, 380
use of in politics, 174–175
Via Appia, 86, 207
Vibius Pansa Caetronianus, Gaius, 271
Vicar, 443–444
Victory (cult), 103, 451
Vigiles, 301, 312, 409, 490
Villa, *228*
Villages, 6, 52
Villanovan culture, 8
Villius, Lucius, 139
Vindex. *See* Julius
Vindobona, 404
Vine cultivation, 23
Vipsanius Agrippa, Marcus
    care for aqueducts, 312, 343
    commissions theater, 382
    consul with Octavian, 289
    defeats Sextus Pompey, 278
    friend of Octavian, 270
    possible image, *311*
    possible successor to Augustus,
        297–298
Viriathus, 125
Viritane land assignment, 81
Virtus, 99, 356, 490
Vitellius, Aulus, 335–336
Vitis, *303*
Volsinii, 16, 86, 88, 142
Volturnus (river), 2, 79
Voting
    in assemblies, 67–70
    in early Rome, 42–43
    secret ballot, 153
Votives, 5–6, 19, *397*
Vulci, 42, 142

W

Wall of Antoninus, 394
Wall of Hadrian, 376, 378
Walls, 34, 39, 438
Warfare
    changing nature of, 110, 150
    as civic institution, 75–77, 94–95
    evolution, 20–23
    impact on Rome's allies, 144
    source of wealth, 146
Women, Roman, 74–75, 209–211,
    274–275, 345, 380, 418, 420,
    428–429
    rulers of Rome, 414–415
Writing, 12

Z

Zama, 119
Zegrenses, 422
Zela, 217, 253
Zenobia (ruler of Palmyra), 436–437
Zosimus, 431, 455–456, 496

GAZETTEER

Unless otherwise stated, numbers refer to pages. Where a feature or place appears often, not all its appearances may be listed; these omissions are indicated by "etc". BP = Back endpaper map, FP = Front endpaper map.

A

Achaea, 129
Achaia, 307, 327, 368, 401, 433
Acquarossa, 3, 29, 33
Acragas/Agrigentum, 27, 106, 107, BP
Actium, FP, 268
Adriatic Sea, FP, 3, BP, etc
Aegean Sea, 129, 169, etc
Aegyptus, 169, 203, 241
Aelia Capitolina, 401
Aequi, 46, 78
Aesernia, 89, BP
Aetolia, 129
Africa, 106, 168, 202, 226, 240, etc
Agri Decumates, FP, 363
Agrigentum. See Acragas
Alamanni, 433
Alba Fucens, 78, 107, BP
Alban Mount, 33, 46
Aleria, FP, 196, BP
Alesia, 240
Alexandria, 169, 203, 241, 269, etc
Allobroges, 202
Alpes Cottiae, 326, 363, 400
Alpes Montes, 3, 29, 113, 168, etc
Amanus Mons, 241
Amaseia, FP, 307
Amastris, FP, 327, 401
Ameria, BP
Amphipolis, 129

Anas, R., FP, 117
Ancona, 168, 257
Ancyra, 307, 327, 401
Anio, R., 29, BP
Antioch, 169, 203, 269, 307, etc
Antium, 33, 46, BP
Apennine Mountains, 3, 27, 29, 46, etc
Aphrodisias, FP
Apollonia, 129, 268
Apulia, 3, 27, 85, 89, BP, etc
Apulum, 401
Aquae Sextiae, 168
Aquileia, FP, 400, BP
Aquilonia, 85, BP
Aquincum, FP, 400, BP
Aquinum, 257, BP
Aquitania, 306, 326, 363, 400, 433
Ara Ubiorum, 306
Arabia, FP, 307
Arabia Petraea, 368, 401
Arausio, 168, 363
Ardea, 33
Arelate, FP, 363, 440
Argentorate, FP, 326, 400
Aricia, 46
Ariminum, 46, 113, 240, 257, BP
Armenia, FP, 203, 269, 307, etc
Arnus, R., 3, 29, 46, 257, BP
Arpinum, 107, BP
Arretium, 46, 196, BP
Arverni, 240
Asculum, 181, 257, BP

Asia (province), FP, 169, 203, 226, 241, etc
Asia Minor, 129
Asiana, 441
Assyria, 368
Ateste, 257, BP
Athenae (Athens), FP, 129, 169, 203, etc
Atlantic Ocean, FP, 106, 117, 306, etc
Augusta Praetoria, 257, BP
Augusta Taurinorum, 257, BP
Augusta Treverorum, FP, 326, 433, 440
Augusta Vindelicum, 326
Ausculum, 89, BP

B

Babylon, 368
Baetica, 306, 326, 363, 400
Baetis, R., FP, 117, 226
Balearic Islands, FP, 106, 117
Balkan Region, 3, 129
Banasa, 400
Bay of Naples, 3
Bedriacum, 326, BP
Belgae, 240
Belgica, 306, 326, 363, 400, 433
Beneventum, 89, 257, BP
Berytus, 401
Bithynia, FP, 169, 203
Bithynia-Pontus, 226, 307, 327, 401

Black Sea, FP, 129, 169, etc
Boii, 113
Bon, Cape, 3, BP
Bonna, 326, 400
Bononia, 257, 268, BP
Bosporus, FP, 203
Bostra, FP, 401
Bovianum, 257, BP
Bovillae, BP
Brigetio, 400
Britannia, FP, 240, 306, 326, etc
Britanniae, 440
Brixellum, 257, BP
Brixia, 257, BP
Bructeri, 440
Brundisium, FP, 107, 129, 168, BP, etc
Bruttium, 89, 107, 196, 202, BP
Burdigala, FP, 326, 400, 440
Burnum, 326
Byzantium, 129, 169, 307, 401
Byzantium/Constantinople, FP, 441

C

Caere, 3, 29, 33, 46, 78, BP
Caesarea (in Palestine), FP, 327, 401, 441
Caesarea (Mazaca), FP, 327, 401, 441
Caesariensis, Mauretania, 326, 363, 400
Caieta, 268
Calatia, 257
Caledonia, FP, 400, 433
Cales, 85, BP
Camarina, 27, BP
Campania, 3, 27, 29, etc
Camulodunum, 326
Cannae, 107, BP
Canopus, FP
Caparcotna, 401
Cappadocia, FP, 169, 203, 226, etc
Capreae (island), 326, BP
Capua, 3, 27, 29, BP, etc
Caralis, FP, 326, 400, BP
Carecini, 78
Caria, 241
Carnuntum, FP, 326, 400, 440
Carpi, 433
Carrhae, FP, 241, 401
Carteia, 117
Carthago, FP, 3, 106, 107, 268, BP, etc
Carthago Nova, FP, 117
Casilinum, 257
Caspian Sea, FP, 269, 307, 368
Castel Di Decima, 33
Castra Albana, 400
Castra Regina, 400
Castra Vetera, FP, 326, 400
Caudine Forks, 85
Caudini, 78
Celtiberians, 117
Chaeronea, 169
Charybdis, 3, BP
Cherusci, 306
Chyretiai, 129
Cilicia, FP, 169, 203, 226, 241, etc
Circeii, 33, 46, 268, BP

Cirta, FP, 168
Cisalpine Gaul, 168, 202, 226, BP, etc
Claros, 327
Clusium, 33, 196, BP
Coele Syria, 401
Colonia Agrippinensium, 326
Commagene, 327, 368
Comum, BP
Conobaria, 306
Constantinople. See Byzantium
Coptos, FP
Corcyra, 129
Corduba, FP, 117, 326, 400, 440
Corfinium, 240, BP
Corfinium/Italica, 181
Corinth, FP, 129, 327, 401
Corsica, FP, 3, 29, 106, BP, etc
Cortona, 46, BP
Cosa, 78, BP
Cremona, 113, 257, 326, BP
Creta, FP, 129, 203, 226, 268, etc
Crimea, FP, 203, 241
Croton, 27, 89, BP
Ctesiphon, FP, 269, 401
Cumae, 3, 27, 46, 268, BP
Cynoscephalae, 129
Cyprus, FP, 241, 269, 307, etc
Cyrenaica, 368
Cyrene, FP, 169, 203, 226, 241, etc
Cyrrus, 327
Cyzicus, 203, 401

D

Dacia, FP, 363, 401, 433
Dalmatia, 306, 326, 363, 400, 433
Damascus, FP, 368
Danube, FP, 168-169, 202-203, 268-269, BP, etc
Dardanus, 169
Dead Sea, FP, 327
Delos, 129
Delphi, 129, 433
Dendera, FP
Dertona, 257
Deva, 400
Dravus, R., FP, 326, BP
Durius, R., FP, 117
Durocortorum, FP, 326, 400
Durostorum, 401
Dyrrhachium, 129, 241

E

Ebro, R., FP, 117
Eburacum, FP, 400, 433
Eburones, 240
Edessa, FP, 441
Egypt, 269, 307, 327, 368, 401
Elbe, R., FP, 306
Eleusis, 368
Emerita Augusta, FP, 326, 363, 400, 440
Emesa, FP, 401
Emporiae, 117
English Channel, FP, 240, 433

Enna, 107, BP
Ephesus, FP, 129, 169, 269, etc
Epidamnus, 129, 241
Epirus, FP, 129
Etna M., 27, BP
Etruria, 3, 29, 33, BP, etc
Euphrates, R., FP, 203, 226, 241, etc

F

Faesulae, 196, BP
Falerii, 78, BP
Fanum Fortunae, 257, BP
Faustinopolis, 401
Felsina, 3, 29, BP
Firmum, 46, 257, BP
Florentia, 257, BP
Formiae, 107, BP
Forum Julii, 326
Franks, 433, 440
Fregellae, 78, BP
Frentani, 78, 85
Fucine Lake, 78, 181, 257, BP
Fundi, 107, BP

G

Gabii, 3, 33, BP
Gades, FP, 117, 306
Galatia, FP, 307, 327, 368, 401
Galatians, 129
Gallia, FP, 106, 240
Galliae, 440
Garumna, R., FP, 240
Gauls, 113
Gela, 27, BP
Germania, FP, 306
Germany, Lower, 326, 363, 400, 433
Germany, Upper, 326, 363, 400, 433
Gibraltar, Straits of, FP
Gorsium, 400
Gortyn, FP, 327, 401
Goths, 363, 433, 441
Gracchurris, 117
Graecia (Greece), 3, 27
Graviscae, 29, BP
Gythium, 327

H

Hadrianoupolis, 441
Hadrian's Wall, FP, 400
Halicarnassus, FP
Hatria (in Padus delta), 29, BP
Hatria, 46, 257, BP
Hellespont, 129, 269
Helvetii, 240
Heraclea, 89
Hernici, 78
Heruli, 433
Hibernia, FP
Hierapytna, FP, 368
Hirpini, 78
Hispania, FP
Hispaniae, 440
Hispellum, 257, 440, BP

I

Iapyges, 107
Iazyges, 400-401
Iberian Peninsula, 106, 117
Iceni, 326
Illyria, 129, 202
Illyricum, FP, 226, 240, 268, 433, BP
Insubres, 113
Internum Mare, FP, 3, 117, 129, etc
Iol Caesarea, FP, 326, 400, 440
Ionian Sea, 3, 27, 129
Irni, 400
Iron Gates, 363
Isca Silurum, 400
Issus, 401
Isthmus, 129
Italia, FP, 3, 106, 226, etc
Italica, FP, 117, 363

J

Jerusalem, FP, 203, 327
Jerusalem/Aelia Capitolina, 368
Judaea, 203, 241, 307, 327
Judaea/Syria Palaestina, 368
Julia Concordia, 257, BP
Juthungi, 433
Jutland, FP

K

Kalkriese, FP, 306
Kush, 307

L

La Turbie, FP, 306
Lambaesis, 363, 400
Lanuvium, 3
Latium, 3, 27, 29, 33, etc
Lauriacum, 400
Laus, 27, BP
Lavinium, 33, BP
Legio VII Gemina, FP, 400
Lemnos, FP
Lepcis Magna, FP, 401, 441
Lesbos, FP
Libya, 268
Liger, R., FP, 240
Lindum, 326
Lipari Islands, 3, BP
Liris, R., 3, 27, 46, 78, BP
Locri, 27, 89, BP
Lombards, 400
Londinium, FP, 326, 400, 440
Luca, 240, 257, BP
Lucania, 27, 85, 89, 107, BP, etc
Luceria, 85, 257, BP
Lucus Feroniae, 257
Lugdunensis, 306, 326, 363, 400, 433
Lugdunum, FP, 326, 400, 440
Lusitania, 117, 202, 306, 326, etc
Lycia, 327, 368, 401

M

Macedon, 129
Macedonia, FP, 169, 203, 226, etc
Magna Graecia, 3, 27
Magnesia, 129
Marcomanni, 306, 363, 400
Marrucini, 78
Marsi, 78, 181
Masada, 368
Massilia, FP, 106, 117, 240
Mauretania, FP, 106, 168, 202, etc
Media, 269
Mediolanum, FP, 433, 440, BP
Melitene, 401
Meroe, 307
Mesopotamia, FP, 307, 368, 401
Messana, 27, 89, 106, 107, BP
Messapii, 27, 107
Messina, Straits of, FP, 3, 268, BP
Metaurus, R., 113, BP
Miletus, 129
Minturnae, 257, BP
Misenum, 268, 326, BP
Moesia, FP, 307, 327, 363
Moesia, Lower, 401, 433
Moesia, Upper, 401, 433
Moesiae, 441
Mogontiacum, FP, 326, 400
Mosella, R., 433
Munda, 240
Murlo, 3, 29, BP
Mutina, 257, 268, BP
Myra, 327, 401
Mytilene, FP

N

Naqsh-i Rustam, FP
Narbo, FP, 326, 400
Narbonensis, 268, 306, 326, 363, etc
Narnia, 78
Naulochus, 268, BP
Neapolis, 27, 46, 78, 85, 89, BP
Nemausus, 326
Nicomedia, FP, 327, 401, 441
Nicopolis, 241
Nile, R., FP, 169, 203, 241, 269, etc
Nola, 29, 181, 196, 257, BP
Noricum, FP, 306, 326, 363, 400, 433
Novae, 327, 401
Novaesium, 326
Nuceria, 257, BP
Numantia, FP, 117
Numidia, FP, 106, 168, 326, 363, 400

O

Odessus, FP, 327
Oescus, 327
Orchomenus, 169
Oriens, 441
Osroene, FP, 401
Ostia, BP

P

Padus, R. (Po), FP, 3, 29, 106, BP, etc
Paeligni, 78
Paestum (Poseidonia), 27, 85, 89, 107, BP
Palmyra, FP, 401, 441
Pannonia, FP, 306, 326, 363, 400
Pannonia, Lower, 433
Pannonia, Upper, 433
Pannoniae, 440
Panormus, 106, 107, BP
Paphlagonia, 169, 203
Paphos, FP, 327, 401
Parma, 257, BP
Parthia, FP, 203, 241, 269, 307, etc
Patavium, BP
Pella, 129
Peloponnese, 129, 268
Pentri, 78
Pergamum, FP, 129, 169, 203, etc
Perinthus, 327, 401
Persepolis, FP, 368
Persian Gulf, FP, 368
Perusia, 46, 113, 268, BP
Petra, FP, 401
Pharsalus, 241
Philippi, 268
Phoenice, 129
Phoenice Syria, 401
Picenum, 46, 113, 168, 240, BP
Pietrabbondante, 78, BP
Pisae, 257, BP
Pisaurum, 257, BP
Pithecusa, 3, 27, BP
Placentia, 113, 257, BP
Poetovio, 326
Pola, 257, BP
Pompeii, 196, BP
Pomptine Marshes, 257
Pont du Gard, FP
Pontica, 441
Pontus, FP, 169, 203, 241
Populonia, 29, BP
Portus, 326, BP
Poseidonia/Paestum, 27, 85, 89, 107, BP
Potaissa, 401
Praeneste, 33, 46, 78, 113, BP, etc
Propontis, 129, 203
Ptolemais, 441
Puteoli, 257, BP
Pydna, 129
Pyrenees, Mts., FP, 117, 168, 202, 433
Pyrgi, 29

Q

Quadi, 363, 400
Qumran, FP

R

Raetia, FP, 306, 326, 363, etc
Raphaneae, FP, 327, 401

Ravenna, FP, 326, BP
Reate, BP
Red Sea, FP, 269, 307, 327, etc
Resaina, 401
Rhegium, 27, 89, 107, BP
Rhenus, R., FP, 168, 202, 240, BP, etc
Rhodanus, R., FP, 106, 117, 168, BP, etc
Rhodes, FP, 129, 203, 307, 327
Roma (Rome), FP, 3, 27, 29, 33, BP, etc;
    see also Maps 2.2, 8.4, 9.3, 11.3,
    13.3
Rubicon, R., 240, BP
Rusellae, 3, 29, 46, 257, BP

S

Sabinum, 33, 78, 113
Saena, 257, BP
Saguntum, 117
Sahara Desert, FP, 268, 306, 440
Salamis, 241
Salinae (salt pans), 33
Salona, FP, 326, 400, 440, BP
Samnium, 46, 78, 85, 89, etc
Samosata, 401
Saracens, 441
Sardinia, FP, 3, 106, 107, 226, BP, etc
Sarmatians, 400, 433
Sarmizegetusa, FP, 401
Satala, 401
Satricum, 3, 46, BP
Savus, R., BP
Saxons, 433
Scidrus, 27
Seleucia, FP, 401
Selinus (Cilicia), 368
Selinus (Sicily), 27
Sena Gallica, 46, BP
Senones, 46
Sentinum, 46, BP
Sequana, R., FP, 240
Serdica, 441
Sicels, 27
Sicilia, FP, 3, 27, 89, 106, BP
Sicilian Sea, 3, BP
Singara, 401
Singidunum, 401
Sirmium, FP, 433, 441
Smyrna, FP, 368, 401
Sora, 257

Spain, Further, 117, 168, 202, 226, etc
Spain, Nearer, 117, 202, 226, 240, etc
Sparta, FP, 129
Spina, 29, BP
Suessa, 257
Sutrium, 257
Sybaris, 27, BP
Syracusae, FP, 27, 89, 106, BP, etc
Syria, FP, 169, 203, 226, 241, etc
Syria Coele, 401
Syria Phoenice, 401

T

Tagus, R., FP, 117
Tarentum, 27, 85, 89, 107, 268, BP
Tarquinii, 3, 29, 33, 46, 78, BP
Tarracina, 33, 46, BP
Tarraco, FP, 117, 168, 202, 268, etc
Tarraconensis, 306, 326, 400, 433
Tarsus, FP, 269, 401
Teanum, 257, BP
Telamon, 113
Tergeste, 257, BP
Teutoburg Forest, 306
Thamugadi, FP, 363
Thapsus, 240
Thermopylae, 129
Thessalia, 129
Thessalonice, FP, 327, 401, 433, 441
Theveste, 326
Thrace, FP, 129, 327, 368, 401, 433
Thracia, 441
Thurii, 27, 89, 202, BP
Tiber, R., 3, 27, 29, 33, BP, etc
Tibur, 33, 46, 78, BP
Tigranocerta, 203
Tigris, R., FP, 269, 368, 401
Tingi, FP, 326, 400, 440
Tingitana, Mauretania, 326, 363, 400
Tomis, FP, 307
Transalpine Gaul, 168, 202, 226, 240,
    268
Transpadana, 181, 202
Trapezus, FP
Trasimene, Lake, 33, 113, BP
Trebia, R., 113, BP
Tuder, 257, BP
Tunis, 106
Turbie, La, FP, 306

Tusculum, 46, BP
Tyre, FP, 401
Tyrrhenian Sea, 3, 27, 29, BP, etc

U

Umbria, 29, 46, 78, 113, BP
Urbana, 196
Urso, FP
Utica, 107, 240, BP

V

Vadimon, Lake, 78
Vandals, 433
Veii, 3, 29, 33, 46, 78, BP
Velia, 27, BP
Velitrae, 3, BP
Venafrum, 257, BP
Venusia, 85, 257, BP
Vercellae, 168, BP
Verona, 440, BP
Vestini, 78
Vesuvius Mt., 202
Vetulonia, 46, BP
Via Appia, 78
Viennensis, 440
Viminacium, FP, 327, 401
Vindobona, FP, 400
Vindonissa, 326
Viroconium, 326
Virunum, 326
Volaterrae, 29, 46, 113, 196, BP
Volsci, 46, 78
Volsinii, 3, 29, 33, 46, 78, 113, BP
Volturnus, R., 3, 46, 78, 85, BP
Vulci, 3, 29, 33, 46, 113, BP

W

Wall of Antoninus, 400

Z

Zama, 106
Zegrenses, 400
Zela, 203, 241
Zliten, FP

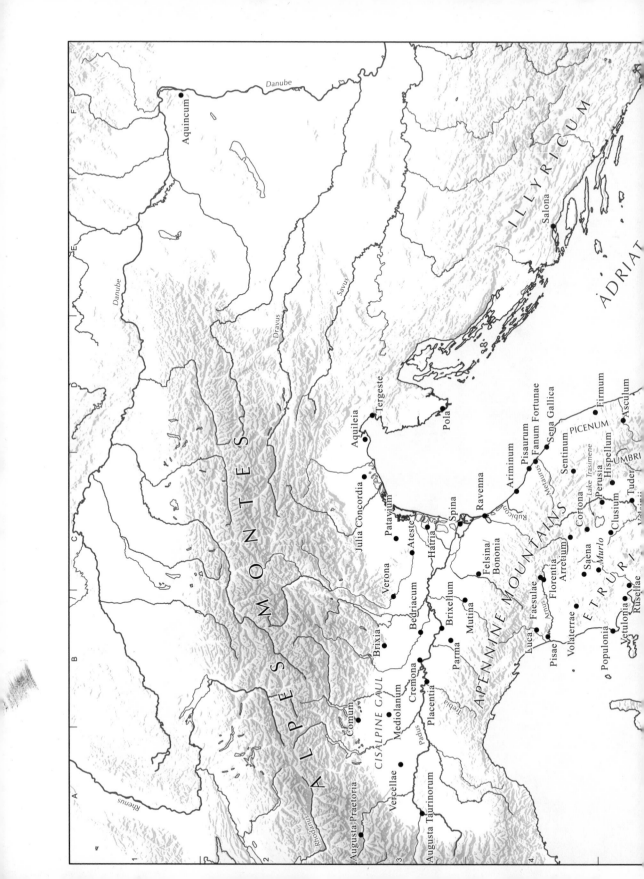